100% Renewable Energy Transition: Pathways and Implementation

100% Renewable Energy Transition: Pathways and Implementation

Special Issue Editors

Claudia Kemfert
Christian Breyer
Pao-Yu Oei

MDPI • Basel • Beijing • Wuhan • Barcelona • Belgrade

Special Issue Editors
Claudia Kemfert
German Economic Research Institute (DIW Berlin)
Germany

Christian Breyer
School of Energy Systems
Finland

Pao-Yu Oei
CoalExit Research Group
Germany

Editorial Office
MDPI
St. Alban-Anlage 66
4052 Basel, Switzerland

This is a reprint of articles from the Special Issue published online in the open access journal *Energies* (ISSN 1996-1073) from 2018 to 2019 (available at: https://www.mdpi.com/journal/energies/special_issues/Renewable_Energy_Transition).

For citation purposes, cite each article independently as indicated on the article page online and as indicated below:

LastName, A.A.; LastName, B.B.; LastName, C.C. Article Title. *Journal Name* **Year**, *Article Number*, Page Range.

ISBN 978-3-03928-034-6 (Pbk)
ISBN 978-3-03928-035-3 (PDF)

© 2019 by the authors. Articles in this book are Open Access and distributed under the Creative Commons Attribution (CC BY) license, which allows users to download, copy and build upon published articles, as long as the author and publisher are properly credited, which ensures maximum dissemination and a wider impact of our publications.

The book as a whole is distributed by MDPI under the terms and conditions of the Creative Commons license CC BY-NC-ND.

Contents

About the Special Issue Editors vii

Preface to "100% Renewable Energy Transition: Pathways and Implementation" ix

Tom Brown, Mirko Schäfer and Martin Greiner
Sectoral Interactions as Carbon Dioxide Emissions Approach Zero in a Highly-Renewable European Energy System
Reprinted from: *Energies* 2019, *12*, 1032, doi:10.3390/en12061032 1

Felix Wejda, Hans-Karl Bartholdsen, Anna Eidens, Frederik Seehaus, Thorsten Burandt, Konstantin Löffler, Pao-Yu Oei, Claudia Kemfert, Christian von Hirschhausen
Pathways for Germany's Low-Carbon Energy Transformation Towards 2050
Reprinted from: *Energies* 2019, *12*, 2988, doi:10.3390/en12152988 17

Hannah Mareike Marczinkowski, Poul Alberg Østergaard and Søren Roth Djørup
Transitioning Island Energy Systems—Local Conditions, Development Phases, and Renewable Energy Integration
Reprinted from: *Energies* 2019, *12*, 3484, doi:10.3390/en12183484 50

Linus Lawrenz, Bobby Xiong, Luise Lorenz, Alexandra Krumm, Hans Hosenfeld, Thorsten Burandt, Konstantin Löffler, Pao-Yu Oei and Christian von Hirschhausen
Exploring Energy Pathways for the Low-Carbon Transformation in India—A Model-Based Analysis
Reprinted from: *Energies* 2018, *11*, 3001, doi:10.3390/en11113001 70

Luis Sarmiento, Thorsten Burandt, Konstantin Löffler, and Pao-Yu Oei
Analyzing Scenarios for the Integration of Renewable Energy Sources in the Mexican Energy System—An Application of the Global Energy System Model (GENeSYS-MOD)
Reprinted from: *Energies* 2019, , 3270, doi:10.3390/en12173270 93

David Ritter, Roland Meyer, Matthias Koch, Markus Haller, Dierk Bauknecht and Christoph Heinemann
Effects of a Delayed Expansion of Interconnector Capacities in a High RES-E European Electricity System
Reprinted from: *Energies* 2019, *12*, 3098, doi:10.3390/en12163098 117

Philip Tafarte, Marcus Eichhorn and Daniela Thrän
Capacity Expansion Pathways for a Wind and Solar Based Power Supply and the Impact of Advanced Technology—A Case Study for Germany
Reprinted from: *Energies* 2019, *12*, 324, doi:10.3390/en12020324 149

Mihai Sanduleac, João F. Martins, Irina Ciornei, Mihaela Albu, Lucian Toma, Vitor Fernão Pires, Lenos Hadjidemetriou and Rooktabir Sauba
Resilient and Immune by Design Microgrids Using Solid State Transformers
Reprinted from: *Energies* 2018, *11*, 3377, doi:10.3390/en11123377 172

Siavash Khalili, Eetu Rantanen, Dmitrii Bogdanov and Christian Breyer
Global Transportation Demand Development with Impacts on the Energy Demand and Greenhouse Gas Emissions in a Climate-Constrained World
Reprinted from: *Energies* 2019, *12*, 3870, doi:10.3390/en12203870 191

Michael Child, Alexander Nordling and Christian Breyer
The Impacts of High V2G Participation in a 100% Renewable Åland Energy System
Reprinted from: *Energies* **2018**, *11*, 2206, doi:10.3390/en11092206 245

Amtul Samie Maqbool, Jens Baetens, Sara Lotfi, Lieven Vandevelde and Greet Van Eetvelde
Assessing Financial and Flexibility Incentives for Integrating Wind Energy in the Grid Via Agent-Based Modeling
Reprinted from: *Energies* **2019**, *12*, 4314, doi:10.3390/en12224314 264

Aleksandar Cuculić, Dubravko Vučetić, Rene Prenc and Jasmin Ćelić
Analysis of Energy Storage Implementation on Dynamically Positioned Vessels
Reprinted from: *Energies* **2019**, *12*, 444, doi:10.3390/en12030444 296

Joao C. Ferreira and Ana Lucia Martins
Building a Community of Users for Open Market Energy
Reprinted from: *Energies* **2018**, *11*, 2330, doi:10.3390/en11092330 315

About the Special Issue Editors

Claudia Kemfert has been Professor of Energy Economics and Sustainability at the private university, Hertie School of Governance, in Berlin since 2009 and Head of the department Energy, Transportation, and Environment at the German Institute of Economic Research (DIW Berlin) since April 2004. Her research activities concentrate on the evaluation of climate and energy policy strategies. From 2004 until 2009, she was Professor for Environmental Economics at Humboldt University Berlin. In 2016, Claudia Kemfert was appointed by the Federal Ministry for the Environment, Nature Conservation, Building, and Nuclear Safety as a member of the German Advisory Council on the Environment. Claudia Kemfert studied economics at Oldenburg, Bielefeld (Germany) and Stanford University (USA). Claudia Kemfert worked for the Fondazione Eni Enrico Mattei (FEEM) (Italy) and Stuttgart University (Institute for Rational Energy Use).

Christian Breyer, Ph.D. (Tech). Christian Breyer is Professor for Solar Economy at LUT University, Finland. His major expertise is the integrated research of technological and economic characteristics of renewable energy systems specialising in energy system modeling for 100% renewable energy, on a local but also global scale. His team published the most studies on 100% renewable energy for countries or major regions globally. Energy system transition studies are carried out in full hourly and high geo-spatial resolution. Publications cover integrated sector analyses with power, heat, transport, desalination, industry and negative CO_2 emission options. Carbon capture and utilisation as part of comprehensive Power-to-X investigations is a core research field for his team. He worked previously for Reiner Lemoine Institut, Berlin, and Q-Cells (now: Hanwha Q Cells). He is member of ETIP PV, IEA-PVPS, the scientific committee of the EU PVSEC and IRES, chairman for renewable energy at the Energy Watch Group, reviewer for the IPCC and a co-founder of Desertec Foundation. His academic background is general business, physics and energy systems engineering and has a Ph.D. in electrical engineering. He can be contacted on Twitter at @ChristianOnRE.

Pao-Yu Oei works at the Technische Universität Berlin and is head of the 20-member research group CoalExit and the corresponding www.CoalTransitions.org Research Hub examining the transition from fossil fuels towards renewable energy sources. He has been involved in numerous projects on the German and Global coal phase-out, worked for the German Advisory Council on the Environment (SRU) and as managing editor of the Journal Economics of Energy & Environmental Policy (EEEP). He holds a Dipl. Ing. as industrial engineer and a Ph.D. in Economics from TU Berlin and spent research visits at the University of Maryland and the International Institute of Applied System Analysis (IIASA). He is also a guest researcher at the German Economic Research Institute (DIW Berlin) and has been part of several International Energy Policy partnership delegations. His work with the open source Global Energy System Model GENeSYS-MOD examines various 100% renewable energy pathways for different countries within this book as well as in other peer-reviewed publications.

Preface to "Renewable Energy Transition: Pathways and Implementation"

1. Introduction to this Special Issue

Energy markets are already undergoing considerable transitions to accommodate new (renewable) energy forms, new (decentral) energy players, and new system requirements, e.g., flexibility and resilience [1]. Traditional energy markets for fossil fuels are therefore under pressure [2], while not yet fully mature (renewable) energy markets are emerging [3]. As a consequence, investments in large-scale and capital intensive (traditional) energy production projects are surrounded by high uncertainty, and are difficult to hedge by private entities as they might result in stranded assets [4]. Traditional energy production companies are transforming into energy service suppliers and companies aggregating numerous potential market players are emerging, while regulation and system management are playing an increasing role. To address these increasing uncertainties and complexities, economic analysis, forecasting, modeling, and investment assessment require fresh approaches and views. Novel research is thus required to simulate multiple actor interplays and idiosyncratic behavior [5]. The required approaches cannot deal with energy supply only, but need to include active demand and cover systemic aspects. Energy market transitions challenge policy-making. Market coordination failure, the removal of barriers hindering restructuring, and the combination of market signals with command-and-control policy measures are some of the new aims of policies [6].

The aim of this Special Issue is therefore to collect research papers that address the above issues using novel methods from any adequate perspective, including economic analysis, modeling of systems, behavioral forecasting, and policy assessment. The issue will include, but is not be limited to

- Local control schemes and algorithms for distributed generation systems;
- Centralized and decentralized sustainable energy management strategies;
- Communication architectures, protocols, and properties of practical applications;
- Topologies of distributed generation systems improving flexibility, efficiency, and power quality;
- Practical issues in the control design and implementation of distributed generation systems;
- Energy transition studies for optimized pathway options aiming for high levels of sustainability.

2. Individual Articles

2.1. Analysis of Case Studies

The Special Issue includes various case studies examining the implementation of 100% renewable scenarios. Brown et al. [7] investigate different decarbonization pathways for the European energy system considering the interactions of the electricity, heating, transport, and industry sector to avoid inefficient investments due to false sectoral prioritization caused by separate consideration. Germany's energy sector, including power, heat, and transportation, is modelled on a Federal State resolution by Bartholdsen et al. [8] in order to derive cost-efficient pathways and technology mixes for different levels of decarbonization until 2050. The paper of Marczinkowski et al. [9] compares the pathways of three European islands in order to identify features, namely, e.g., smart grid, sector integration, local conditions, and balancing technologies, that play a major role in achieving the goal of a 100% renewable energy system for these islands and comparable regions.

Leaving Europe, Lawrenz et al. [10] analyze three different pathways for the Indian energy system until 2050 using a linear, and cost-minimizing, global energy system model. The scenarios range from a conservative New Policies scenario by the IEA to a 100% renewable energy source pathway. Sarmiento et al. [11] examine the effect of current national renewable targets and climate goals on the Mexican energy system and examines the cost optimal share of renewables.

2.1.1. Sectoral Interactions as Carbon Dioxide Emissions Approach Zero in a Highly-Renewable European Energy System—Brown et al. [7]

In this paper, interactions between the electricity, heating, transport, and industry sector are examined for the period after 2030 in an existing openly available, hourly-resolved, per-country, and highly-renewable model of the European energy system, PyPSA-Eur-Sec-30, that includes electricity, land transport, and space and water heating. A parameter sweep of different reduction targets for direct carbon dioxide emissions is performed, ranging from no target down to zero direct emissions. The composition of system investments, the interactions between the energy sectors, shadow prices, and the market values of the system components are analyzed as the carbon dioxide limit changes. Electricity and land transport are defossilized first, while the reduction of emissions in space and water heating is delayed by the expense of new components and the difficulty of supplying heat during cold spells with low wind and solar power generation. For deep carbon dioxide reduction, power-to-gas changes the system dynamics by reducing curtailment and increasing the market values of wind and solar power. Using this model setup, cost projections for 2030, and optimal cross-border transmission, the costs of a zero-direct-emission system in these sectors are marginally cheaper than today's system, even before the health and environmental benefits are taken into account.

2.1.2. Pathways for Germany's Low-Carbon Energy Transformation Towards 2050—Bartholdsen et al. [8]

Like many other countries, Germany has defined goals to reduce its CO_2-emissions following the Paris Agreement of the 21st Conference of the Parties (COP). The first successes in decarbonizing the electricity sector were already achieved under the German Energiewende. However, further steps in this direction, also concerning the heat and transport sectors, have stalled. This paper describes three possible pathways for the transformation of the German energy system until 2050. The scenarios take into account current climate politics on a global, European, and German level and also include different demand projections, technological trends, and resource prices. The model includes the sectors power, heat, and transportation and works on a Federal State level. For the analysis, the linear cost-optimizing Global Energy System Model (GENeSYS-MOD) is used to calculate the cost-efficient paths and technology mixes. They find that a reduction of CO_2 of more than 80% in the less ambitious scenario can be welfare enhancing compared to a scenario without any climate mitigating policies. Even higher decarbonization rates of 95% are feasible and needed to comply with international climate targets yet related to high effort in transforming the subsector of process heat. The different pathways depicted in this paper render chances and risks of transforming the German energy system under various external influences.

2.1.3. Transitioning Island Energy Systems: Local Conditions, Development Phases, and Renewable Energy Integration—Marczinkowski et al. [9]

Islands typically have sensitive energy systems depending on natural surroundings, but innovative technologies and the exploitation of renewable energy (RE) sources present opportunities like self-sufficiency, but also challenges, such as grid instability. Samsø, Orkney, and Madeira are in the transition to increase the RE share towards 100%; however, this is addressed in different ways depending on the local conditions and current development phases in the transition. Scenarios focusing on the short-term introduction of new technologies in the energy systems are presented, where the electricity sector is coupled with the other energy sectors. Here, both smart grid and sector-integrating solutions form an important part in the next 5–15 years. The scenarios are analyzed using the modeling tool EnergyPLAN, enabling a comparison of today's reference scenarios with 2030 scenarios of higher RE share. By including three islands across Europe, different locations, development stages, and interconnection levels are analyzed. The analyses suggest that the various smart grid solutions play an important part in the transition; however, local conditions, sector integration, and balancing technologies even more so. Overall, the suggestions complement each other and pave the way to reach 100% RE integration for both islands and, potentially, other similar regions.

2.1.4. Exploring Energy Pathways for the Low-Carbon Transformation in India—A Model-Based Analysis—Lawrenz et al. [10]

With an increasing expected energy demand and current dominance of coal electrification, India plays a major role in global carbon policies and the future low-carbon transformation. This paper explores three energy pathways for India until 2050 by applying the linear, cost-minimizing, global energy system model (GENeSYS-MOD). The benchmark scenario "limited emissions only" (LEO) is based on ambitious targets set out by the Paris Agreement. A more conservative "business as usual" (BAU) scenario is sketched out along the lines of the New Policies scenario from the International Energy Agency (IEA). On the more ambitious side, they explore the potential implications of supplying the Indian economy entirely with renewable energies with the "100% renewable energy sources" (100% RES) scenario. Overall, the results suggest that a transformation process towards a low-carbon energy system in the power, heat, and transportation sectors until 2050 is technically feasible. Solar power is likely to establish itself as the key energy source by 2050 in all scenarios, given the model's underlying emission limits and technical parameters. The paper concludes with an analysis of potential social, economic and political barriers to be overcome for the needed Indian low-carbon transformation.

2.1.5. Analyzing Scenarios for the Integration of Renewable Energy Sources in the Mexican Energy System—An Application of the Global Energy System Model (GENeSYS-MOD)—Sarmiento et al. [11]

This paper uses numerical techno-economic modelling to analyze the effect of current national renewable targets and climate goals on the cost and structural composition of the Mexican energy system. For this, the authors construct a scenario base analysis to compare current policies with two alternative states of the world—one without climate policies and one attaining full decarbonization. Furthermore, an additional iterative routine allows them to estimate the cost-optimal share of renewable technologies in the energy sector and the effect that deviating from this share has on total discounted system costs, emissions, and the structure of the energy mix. In general, model results exhibit three key insights: (1) a marked dependence of the energy system on photovoltaics and natural gas; (2) the 2050 cost-optimal share of renewables for the production of electricity, transportation and industrial heating is respectively 75%, 90%, and 5%, and (3) as national renewable targets for the power sector are lower than the cost-optimal share of renewables, equivalent to the shares in a scenario without climate policies and completely disconnected from national climate goals, these should be modified.

2.2. Analysis of Technical Aspects: Focus on Electricity Grids

Within the Special Issue, several papers examine the importance of electricity grid infrastructure within the energy system transition. Ritter et al. [12] therefore examine the effects on the cost of electricity generation and CO2 emissions resulting from a delayed expansion of interconnector capacities in a European high renewables electricity system by comparing different scenarios for the years 2030, 2040, and 2050. In a similar manner, Tafarte et al. [13] model the most efficient and fastest capacity expansion pathways of wind and solar photovoltaics in Germany considering aspects of electric energy storage and power grid expansions. Sanduleac et al. [14] simulate the effect of Solid State Transformers in a future energy system which play a crucial role to safely connect clusters of prosumers or low voltage networks with the bulk power system.

2.2.1. Effects of a Delayed Expansion of Interconnector Capacities in a High RES-E European Electricity System—Ritter et al. [12]

In order to achieve a high renewable share in the electricity system, a significant expansion of cross-border exchange capacities is planned. Historically, the actual expansion of interconnector capacities has significantly lagged behind the planned expansion. This study examines the impact that such continued delays would have when compared to a strong interconnector expansion in an ambitious energy transition scenario. For this purpose, scenarios for the years 2030, 2040, and 2050 are examined using the electricity market model PowerFlex EU. The analysis reveals that both CO2 emissions and variable costs of electricity generation increase if interconnector expansion is delayed. This effect is most significant in the scenario year 2050, where lower connectivity leads roughly to a doubling of both CO2 emissions and variable costs of electricity generation. This increase results from a lower level of European electricity trading, a curtailment of electricity from a renewable energy source (RES-E), and a corresponding higher level of conventional electricity generation. Most notably, in Southern and Central Europe, less interconnection leads to higher use of natural gas power plants since less renewable electricity from Northern Europe can be integrated into the European grid.

2.2.2. Capacity Expansion Pathways for a Wind and Solar Based Power Supply and the Impact of Advanced Technology: A Case Study for Germany—Tafarte et al. [13]

Wind and solar photovoltaics (solar PV) have become the lowest-cost renewable alternatives and are expected to dominate the power supply matrix in many countries worldwide. However, wind and solar are inherently variable renewable energy sources (vRES) and their characteristics pose new challenges for power systems and for the transition to a renewable energy-based power supply. Using new options for the integration of high shares of vRES is therefore crucial. In order to assess these options, the authors model the expansion pathways of wind power and solar PV capacities and their impact on the renewable share in a case study for Germany. Therefore, a numerical optimization approach is applied on temporally resolved generation and consumption time series data to identify the most efficient and fastest capacity expansion pathways. In addition to conventional layouts of wind and solar PV, the model includes advanced, system-friendly technology layouts in combination with electric energy storage from existing pumped hydro storage as promising integration options. The results provide policy makers with useful insights for technology-specific capacity expansion as the authors identified potentials to reduce costs and infrastructural requirements in the form of power grids and electric energy storage, and to accelerate the transition to a fully renewable power sector.

2.2.3. Resilient and Immune by Design Microgrids Using Solid State Transformers—Sanduleac et al. [14]

Solid State Transformers (SST) may soon become key technological enablers for decentralized energy systems. This work proposes a paradigm change in the hierarchically and distributed operated power systems where SSTs are used to asynchronously connect small low voltage (LV) distribution networks, such as clusters of prosumers or LV microgrids, to the bulk power system. The need for asynchronously coupled microgrids requires a design that allows the LV system to operate independently from the bulk grid and to rely on its own control systems. The aim is to achieve immune and resilient by design configurations that allow maximizing the integration of Local Renewable Energy Resources (L-RES). The paper simulates the way in which SST-interconnected microgrids can become immune to disturbances occurring in the bulk power system and how sudden changes in the microgrid can damp out at the Point of Common Coupling (PCC), thus achieving better reliability and predictability and enabling strong and healthy distributed energy storage systems (DESSs). Moreover, it is shown that in a fully inverter-based microgrid there is no need for mechanical or synthetic inertia to stabilize the microgrid during power unbalances. This happens because the electrostatic energy stored in the capacitors connected behind the SST inverter can be used for a brief time interval, until automation is activated to address the power unbalance for a longer term.

2.3. Analysis of Transport Sector

Two papers within this Special Issue take a closer look at the evolvement of the transport sector. Khalili et al. [15] examine the expected transportation demand and impact of alternative transportation technologies along with new sustainable energy sources on energy demand and emissions in the transport sector until 2050. Another paper by Child et al. [16] analyses the impact of high participation in vehicle-to-grid (V2G) in a 100% renewable Energy system on the island Åland in 2030 and the roles of various energy storage solutions

2.3.1. Global Transportation Demand Development with Impacts on the Energy Demand and Greenhouse Gas Emissions in a Climate-Constrained World—Khalili et al. [15]

This paper examines the expected transportation demand and impact of alternative transportation technologies along with new sustainable energy sources on energy demand and emissions in the transport sector until 2050. Battery-electric and fuel-cell electric vehicles are the most promising technologies. Electric ships and airplanes for shorter distances and hydrogen-based synthetic fuels for longer distances may appear around 2030 to reduce emissions from marine and aviation transport modes. The railway remains the least energy-demanding among the transport modes. An ambitious scenario for achieving zero greenhouse gas emissions by 2050 is applied, demonstrating the high relevance of direct and indirect electrification of the transport sector. Fossil-fuel demand can be reduced to zero by 2050; however, the electricity demand will to rise from 125 TWhel in 2015 to about 51,610 TWhel in 2050, substantially driven by indirect electricity demand of synthetic fuels. While the transportation demand roughly triples from 2015 to 2050, substantial efficiency gains enable an almost stable final energy demand for the transport sector, as a consequence of broad electrification. The overall well-to-wheel efficiency in the transport sector increases from 26% in 2015 to 39% in 2050. Power-to-fuels needed mainly for marine and aviation transport is not a significant burden for overall transport sector efficiency.

2.3.2. The Impacts of High V2G Participation in a 100% Renewable Åland Energy System—Child et al. [16]

A 100% renewable energy (RE) scenario featuring high participation in vehicle-to-grid (V2G) services was developed for the Åland islands for 2030 using the EnergyPLAN modelling tool. Hourly data was analyzed to determine the roles of various energy storage solutions, notably V2G connections that extended into electric boat batteries. Two weeks of interest (max/min RE) generation were studied in detail to determine the roles of energy storage solutions. Participation in V2G connections facilitated high shares of variable RE on a daily and weekly basis. In a Sustainable Mobility scenario, high participation in V2G (2,750 MWhel) resulted in less gas storage (1,200 MWhth), electrolyzer capacity (6.1 MWel), methanation capacity (3.9 MWhgas), and offshore wind power capacity (55 MWel) than other scenarios that featured lower V2G participation. Consequently, total annualized costs were lower (225 M/a). The influence of V2G connections on seasonal storage is an interesting result for a relatively cold, northern geographic area. A key point is that stored electricity need not only be considered as storage for future use by the grid, but V2G batteries can provide a buffer between generation of intermittent RE and its end-use. Direct consumption of intermittent RE further reduces the need for storage and generation capacities.

2.4. Analysis of Pricing, Storage, and Digitalization

Additional aspects of pricing, storage and digitalization are examined in the remaining three papers of the Special Issue. Maqbool et al. [17] provide an agent-based model of a hypothetical standalone electricity network to identify how the feed-in tariffs and the installed capacity of wind power, calculated in percentage of total system demand, affect the electricity consumption from renewables. In a paper by Cuculic et al. [18], a dynamic simulation model of a ship electrical power system is used to explore the suitability of large-scale energy storage for blackout prevention and to assess the possibility of an implementation of existing storage technologies in the maritime transportation sector. Ferreira and Martins [19] examine the integration of the "Internet of Things" (for the accounting of energy flows) and blockchain approach (to overcome the need for a central control entity) on energy markets and how these can create new open markets and revenues for stakeholders.

2.4.1. Assessing Financial and Flexibility Incentives for Integrating Wind Energy in the Grid Via Agent-Based Modeling—Maqbool et al. [17]

This article provides an agent-based model of a hypothetical standalone electricity network to identify how the feed-in tariffs and the installed capacity of wind power, calculated in percentage of total system demand, affect the electricity consumption from renewables. It includes the mechanism of electricity pricing on the Day Ahead Market (DAM) and the Imbalance Market (IM). The extra production volumes of Electricity from Renewable Energy Sources (RES-E) and the flexibility of electrical consumption of industries is provided as reserves on the IM. Five thousand simulations were run by using the agent-based model to gather data that were then fit in linear regression models. This helped to quantify the effect of feed-in tariffs and installed capacity of wind power on the consumption from renewable energy and market prices. The study concludes that the effect of increasing installed capacity of wind power is more significant on increasing consumption of renewable energy and decreasing the DAM and IM prices than the effect of feed-in tariffs. However, the effect of increasing values of both factors on the profit of RES-E producers with storage facilities is not positive, pointing to the need for customized rules and incentives to encourage their market participation and investment in storage facilities.

2.4.2. Analysis of Energy Storage Implementation on Dynamically Positioned Vessels—Cuculić et al. [18]

Blackout prevention on dynamically positioned vessels during closed bus bar operation, which allows more efficient and eco-friendly operation of main diesel generators, is the subject of numerous studies. Developed solutions rely mostly on the ability of propulsion frequency converters to limit the power flow from the grid to propulsion motors almost instantly, which reduces available torque until the power system is fully restored after failure. In this paper, a different approach is presented where large-scale energy storage is used to take part of the load during the time interval from failure of one of the generators until the synchronization and loading of a stand-by generator. In order to analyze power system behavior during the worst-case fault scenario and peak power situations, and to determine the required parameters of the energy storage system, a dynamic simulation model of a ship electrical power system is used. It is concluded that implementation of large-scale energy storage can increase the stability and reliability of a vessel's electrical power system without the need for the reduction of propulsion power during a fault. Based on parameters obtained from simulations, existing energy storage systems were evaluated, and the possibility of their implementation in the maritime transportation sector was considered. Finally, an evaluation model of energy storage implementation cost-effectiveness was presented.

2.4.3. Building a Community of Users for Open Market Energy—Ferreira et al. [19]

Energy markets are based on energy transactions with a central control entity, where the players are companies. In this research work, the authors propose an IoT (Internet of Things) system for the accounting of energy flows, as well as a blockchain approach to overcome the need for a central control entity. This allows for the creation of local energy markets to handle distributed energy transactions without needing central control. In parallel, the system aggregates users into communities with target goals and creates new markets for players. These two approaches (blockchain and IoT) are brought together using a gamification approach, allowing for the creation and maintenance of a community for electricity market participation based on pre-defined goals. This community approach increases the number of market players and creates the possibility of traditional end users earning money through small coordinated efforts. They apply this approach to the aggregation of batteries from electrical vehicles so that they become a player in the spinning reserve market. It is also possible to apply this approach to local demand flexibility, associated with the demand response (DR) concept. DR is aggregated to allow greater flexibility in the regulation market based on an OpenADR approach that allows the turning on and off of predefined equipment to handle local microgeneration.

3. Need for Further Research

The body of 100% renewable energy research is growing fastly for the various aspects, in particular for specific technical solutions, sector coupling insights and regions not yet researched much. Due continued demand for respective research a new Special Issue for 100% renewable energy insights is initiated. The scope is widened and also would like to attract papers covering

- Macroeconomic analyses of 100% renewable pathways;
- (Positive) side effects of 100% renewable pathways on other emissions and therefore health or, water-related aspects and other SDGs;
- Interdisciplinary approaches;
- Linkages of various models;
- Case studies for under researched areas around the world.

Claudia Kemfert, Christian Breyer and Pao-Yu Oei
Guest Editors

References

1. *IEA World Energy Outlook 2018*; International Energy Agency: Paris, France, 2018;
2. Oei, P.-Y.; Mendelevitch, R. Prospects for steam coal exporters in the era of climate policies: A case study of Colombia. *Clim. Policy* **2019**, *19*, 73–91.
3. *IRENA Stranded Assets and Renewables: How the Energy Transition Affects the Value of Energy Reserves, Buildings and Capital Stock*; International Renewable Energy Agency (IRENA): Abu Dhabi, 2017.
4. Löffler, K.; Burandt, T.; Hainsch, K.; Oei, P.-Y. Modeling the Low-Carbon Transition of the European Energy System - A Quantitative Assessment of the Stranded Assets Problem. *Energy Strategy Rev.* **2019**, *26*.
5. Hansen, K.; Breyer, C.; Lund, H. Status and perspectives on 100% renewable energy systems. *Energy* **2019**, *175*, 471–480.

6. *Energiewende "Made in Germany": Low Carbon Electricity Sector Reform in the European Context*; Hirschhausen, C. von, Gerbaulet, C., Kemfert, C., Lorenz, C., Oei, P.-Y., Eds.; Springer International Publishing: New York, NY, USA, 2018; ISBN 978-3-319-95125-6.
7. Brown, T.; Schäfer, M.; Greiner, M. Sectoral Interactions as Carbon Dioxide Emissions Approach Zero in a Highly-Renewable European Energy System. *Energies* **2019**, *12*, 1032.
8. Bartholdsen; Eidens; Löffler; Seehaus; Wejda; Burandt; Oei; Kemfert; von Hirschhausen Pathways for Germany's Low-Carbon Energy Transformation Towards 2050. *Energies* **2019**, *12*, 2988.
9. Marczinkowski, H.M.; Alberg Østergaard, P.; Roth Djørup, S. Transitioning Island Energy Systems—Local Conditions, Development Phases, and Renewable Energy Integration. *Energies* **2019**, *12*, 3484.
10. Lawrenz, L.; Xiong, B.; Lorenz, L.; Krumm, A.; Hosenfeld, H.; Burandt, T.; Löffler, K.; Oei, P.-Y.; Von Hirschhausen, C. Exploring Energy Pathways for the Low-Carbon Transformation in India—A Model-Based Analysis. *Energies* **2018**, *11*, 3001.
11. Sarmiento, L.; Burandt, T.; Löffler, K.; Oei, P.-Y. Analyzing Scenarios for the Integration of Renewable Energy Sources in the Mexican Energy System—An Application of the Global Energy System Model (GENeSYS-MOD). *Energies* **2019**, *12*, 3270.
12. Ritter; Meyer; Koch; Haller; Bauknecht; Heinemann Effects of a Delayed Expansion of Interconnector Capacities in a High RES-E European Electricity System. *Energies* **2019**, *12*, 3098.
13. Tafarte, P.; Eichhorn, M.; Thrän, D. Capacity Expansion Pathways for a Wind and Solar Based Power Supply and the Impact of Advanced Technology—A Case Study for Germany. *Energies* **2019**, *12*, 324.
14. Sanduleac, M.; Martins, J.; Ciornei, I.; Albu, M.; Toma, L.; Pires, V.; Hadjidemetriou, L.; Sauba, R. Resilient and Immune by Design Microgrids Using Solid State Transformers. *Energies* **2018**, *11*, 3377.
15. Khalili; Rantanen; Bogdanov; Breyer Global Transportation Demand Development with Impacts on the Energy Demand and Greenhouse Gas Emissions in a Climate-Constrained World. *Energies* **2019**, *12*, 3870.
16. Child, M.; Nordling, A.; Breyer, C. The Impacts of High V2G Participation in a 100% Renewable Åland Energy System. *Energies* **2018**, *11*, 2206.
17. Maqbool; Baetens; Lotfi; Vandevelde; Eetvelde Assessing Financial and Flexibility Incentives for Integrating Wind Energy in the Grid Via Agent-Based Modeling. *Energies* **2019**, *12*, 4314.
18. Cuculić, A.; Vučetić, D.; Prenc, R.; Ćelić, J. Analysis of Energy Storage Implementation on Dynamically Positioned Vessels. *Energies* **2019**, *12*, 444.
19. Ferreira, J.; Martins, A. Building a Community of Users for Open Market Energy. *Energies* **2018**, *11*, 2330.

Article

Sectoral Interactions as Carbon Dioxide Emissions Approach Zero in a Highly-Renewable European Energy System

Tom Brown [1,*], **Mirko Schäfer** [2,3] **and Martin Greiner** [3]

[1] Institute for Automation and Applied Informatics, Karlsruhe Institute of Technology, 76344 Eggenstein-Leopoldshafen, Germany
[2] Department of Sustainable Systems Engineering (INATECH), University of Freiburg, Emmy-Noether-Strasse 2, 79110 Freiburg, Germany; mirko.schaefer@inatech.uni-freiburg.de
[3] Department of Engineering and Interdisciplinary Centre for Climate Change (iClimate), Inge Lehmanns Gade 10, 8000 Aarhus C, Denmark; greiner@eng.au.dk
* Correspondence: tom.brown@kit.edu

Received: 22 January 2019; Accepted: 12 March 2019; Published: 16 March 2019

Abstract: Measures to reduce carbon dioxide emissions are often considered separately, in terms of electricity, heating, transport, and industry. This can lead to the measures being prioritised in the wrong sectors, and neglects interactions between the sectors. In addition, studies often focus on specific greenhouse gas reduction targets, despite the uncertainty regarding what targets are desirable and when. In this paper, these issues are examined for the period after 2030 in an existing openly-available, hourly-resolved, per-country, and highly-renewable model of the European energy system, PyPSA-Eur-Sec-30, that includes electricity, land transport, and space and water heating. A parameter sweep of different reduction targets for direct carbon dioxide emissions is performed, ranging from no target down to zero direct emissions. The composition of system investments, the interactions between the energy sectors, shadow prices, and the market values of the system components are analysed as the carbon dioxide limit changes. Electricity and land transport are defossilised first, while the reduction of emissions in space and water heating is delayed by the expense of new components and the difficulty of supplying heat during cold spells with low wind and solar power generation. For deep carbon dioxide reduction, power-to-gas changes the system dynamics by reducing curtailment and increasing the market values of wind and solar power. Using this model setup, cost projections for 2030, and optimal cross-border transmission, the costs of a zero-direct-emission system in these sectors are marginally cheaper than today's system, even before the health and environmental benefits are taken into account.

Keywords: energy system optimisation; carbon dioxide reduction; renewable energy; sector-coupling; open energy modelling; market value

1. Introduction

Many studies have focused on the reduction of carbon dioxide emissions in the electricity sector. Typically, the studies that restrict to renewable energy sources examine the flexibility requirements for high levels of variable renewable energy (VRE) generation, with flexibility options that include dispatchable renewables, storage, demand-side management, and grid expansion [1–6] (see [7] for a survey of studies with very high penetrations of VRE). The integration of VRE can be analysed using proxy metrics, such as the levels of curtailment, the market value of individual generation technologies [8], and other price statistics. However, focusing on electricity also means neglecting greenhouse gas emissions from other demand sectors, such as heating, transport, and industry, as well as ignoring sources of flexibility from, for example, delayed charging of electric vehicles, power-to-gas, or thermal energy storage. Such flexibility options could help to integrate renewables and mitigate the decline in market value of VRE as their penetration increases, which has been observed in several studies [9].

Many other studies have included other energy demand sectors, such as heating, transport, and non-electric industrial demand, but typically only consider a single region, thus neglecting cross-border energy trading, or do not consider the effects of sector coupling on market dynamics. Examples of single-region studies include studies for Germany [10–13], Denmark [14–16], Ireland [17,18], and the whole of Europe [19]. Other studies include multiple regions in Europe and the transmission networks between them [20–26], but then reduce the time resolution below the level required to assess the variability and flexibility requirements for high shares of wind and solar power [27,28]. Furthermore, the usual approach of reducing time resolution using typical representative days makes it impossible to represent multi-day extreme events and long-term energy storage properly. In [29], a multi-region, multi-sector European energy model was studied, on an hourly basis, for a full year. It was found that transmission helps to reduce the system costs in all scenarios, but the tighter the energy sectors are coupled, the smaller the benefit. Multi-day winter wind lulls with high heat demand were shown to be critical to driving up costs, but high costs could also be mitigated by power-to-gas and long-term thermal energy storage technologies.

Many studies have focused on specific carbon dioxide reduction targets for given periods, or have studied investment dynamically over multiple decades. Given the path uncertainty about exactly which target is necessary for a given period to reach a given temperature target [30], or about what is politically possible, very few studies have considered a broad range of possible targets for a given period. Other studies look at varying VRE penetration [5,9], where a carbon dioxide reduction target would better represent the desired end-goal of global warming mitigation.

From a policy perspective, the European Union (EU) has a variety of reduction targets for the time span 2030– 2050. By 2030, the EU aims to reduce domestic greenhouse gas (GHG) emissions by 40%, compared to 1990 [31], which is the same target as submitted as its Intended Nationally Determined Contribution (INDC) for the Paris Agreement [32]. For 2050, there is a wider span: A target of GHG reduction by between 80% and 95%, compared to 1990, was called for by the European Council in 2009 [33] and endorsed by the Commission [31], while the European Commission's 2018 'Long-Term Strategy for a Clean Planet' calculated additional scenarios for net-zero emissions in 2050 [34]. The fact that these targets encompass all sectors of the economy reinforces the necessity to model all energy sectors in low-emission scenarios. Of the 4.3 gigatonnes of CO_2-equivalent GHG emissions in the EU in 2016 (excluding land use, land-use change, and forestry), public electricity and heat production made up only 24%, while land transport comprised 21%, residential and services heating amounted to 13%, with the rest coming from process heat and process emissions in industry (21%), agriculture (10%), shipping (4%), aviation (4%), and waste management (3%) [35].

In this study, we address the deficiencies in the literature identified above by considering an existing European energy model, PyPSA-Eur-Sec-30 [29], that includes current electricity demand, land transport, and space and water heating at an hourly time resolution and with one node per European country, connected by cross-border transmission. We go beyond the standard approach in the literature and beyond the single target studied in [29] (95% CO_2 reduction), by examining the effects of a broad range of possible targets for direct carbon dioxide emissions for the period after 2030, which represents the period by which emissions in these sectors should reach zero, in order to keep warming below 1.5 °C above industrial levels [30,36]. By focusing on a specific period, our approach allows us to include every hour of a representative weather year and focus on the interactions between the sectors, variability, market prices, curtailment, and market values for different levels of carbon dioxide reduction. Previous works have often focused either on the electricity sector only, or have used typical days for their analysis, which hides the impact of extreme events and the full cost-benefit of long-term storage. As will be shown here, long-term storage has a strong effect on system costs and market metrics, so it is crucial to model it in sufficient temporal detail.

2. Methods

For this study we use the open model PyPSA-Eur-Sec-30, which covers the electricity, low-temperature heating, and land transport demand in Europe, with one node per country and an hourly time resolution for a historical year of demand and weather data. A full description of PyPSA-Eur-Sec-30 can be found in [29]; here, we restrict ourselves to describing the details necessary for the present study.

PyPSA-Eur-Sec-30 is a linear optimisation model which minimises the total investment and operational costs subject to technical constraints, the most important of which are: Meeting energy demand, respecting the weather dependence of a renewable energy supply, respecting the constraints on plant and grid capacity, and meeting carbon dioxide emission reduction targets. The objective function

$$\min_{\substack{G_{n,s}, F_\ell, \\ g_{n,s,t}, f_{\ell,t}}} \left[\sum_{n,s} c_{n,s} G_{n,s} + \sum_{n,s,t} o_{n,s,t} g_{n,s,t} + \sum_{\ell} c_\ell F_\ell \right]$$

runs over all nodes n, times t, and technologies s; summing generation and storage capacities $G_{n,s}$ and investment costs $c_{n,s}$, generation and storage dispatch $g_{n,s,t}$ and variable costs $o_{n,s,t}$, and, finally, the capacities F_ℓ of transmission lines and energy converters ℓ between buses, their flows at each hour $f_{\ell,t}$ and their capital costs c_ℓ.

The most important technology investments available to the model are listed in Table 1, along with cost projections for 2030; a full list of technologies, costs, and other technical parameters (such as efficiencies), along with references, can be found in [29]. All costs are in 2010 euros €$_{2010}$. Finally, 2030 was chosen for the cost projections, to remain on the conservative side of the time period under consideration (after 2030).

Table 1. Technology assumptions projected for 2030 (FOM is Fixed Operation and Maintenance costs, given as a percentage of the overnight cost).

Quantity	Overnight Cost [€$_{2010}$]	Unit	FOM [%/a]	Lifetime [a]
Wind onshore	1182	kW$_{el}$	3	25
Wind offshore	2506	kW$_{el}$	3	25
Solar PV rooftop	725	kW$_{el}$	3	25
Solar PV utility	425	kW$_{el}$	3	25
Battery power	310	kW$_{el}$	3	20
Battery energy	144.6	kWh	0	15
H$_2$ electrolysis	350	kW$_{el}$	4	18
H$_2$ fuel cell	339	kW$_{el}$	3	20
H$_2$ steel tank storage	8.4	kWh$_{H_2}$	0	20
Methanation	1000	kW$_{H_2}$	2.5	25
Ground-sourced HP	1400	kW$_{th}$	3.5	20
Air-sourced HP	1050	kW$_{th}$	3.5	20
Large CHP	600	kW$_{th}$	3	25
Large hot water tank	30	m^3	1	40
Transmission line	400	MWkm	2	40
HVDC converter pair	150	kW	2	40

Each country is linked to the others by expandable cross-border electricity grid capacity (see Figure 1 for the topology), and can also convert energy between sectors, as shown in Figure 2. The available electricity generation technologies are: Solar photovoltaic (PV), onshore and offshore wind, hydroelectricity, and open-cycle gas turbines (OCGT). Heat supply is split into high-heat-density areas with district heating (60% of urban areas, following [37]) and the remaining low-heat-density areas with decentralised individual heating units. In both areas, heat can be provided by gas boilers, heat pumps (HP), resistive heaters, and solar thermal collectors; in urban areas, large combined heat and power (CHP) plants are also available. Electricity can be stored in batteries, or water can be electrolysed to hydrogen, and/or then converted to methane. Heat can be stored in small short-term water tanks in rural areas, or large long-term water tanks in district heating networks. All road and rail transport is assumed to be electrified, since both the running costs and projected vehicle costs are assumed to be lower than fossil-fuelled vehicles with combustion engines by 2030 [38]. The capital costs of the vehicles are not included in the model. Passenger vehicles are represented by battery electric vehicles (BEV), 50% of which participate in demand-side management and can feed back into the grid, depending on market prices. Each participating vehicle makes 50 kWh available to the grid; the state of charge must return to at least 75% capacity each morning, for consumer convenience. The model can build new capacities of all energy infrastructure assets, with the exception of hydroelectric generators, for which existing capacities are assumed.

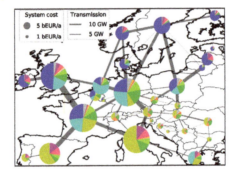

Figure 1. Costs by country with zero CO_2 emissions and optimal transmission. The colour assignments follow Figure 3.

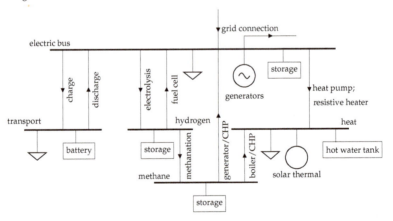

Figure 2. Energy flow at a single node. In this model, a node represents a whole European country. Within each node, there is a bus (thick horizontal line) for each energy carrier (electric, transport, heat, hydrogen, and methane), to which different loads (triangles), energy sources (circles), storage units (rectangles), and converters (lines connecting buses) are attached. The lines with arrows show the direction of energy transfer (Source: [29]).

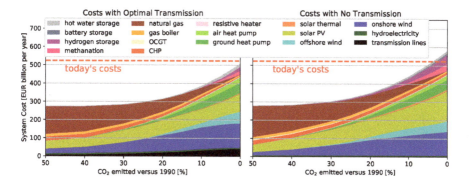

Figure 3. System costs for electricity, land transport, and space and water heating in Europe with a changing CO$_2$ limit, assuming the 2030 cost projections from Table 1. Left is the case with cost-optimal transmission, right is with no transmission. Estimated costs for today's system are marked with a red dashed line.

The inelastic energy demand $d_{n,t}$ at each bus n must be met at each time t by either local generators and storage $g_{n,s,t}$ or by the flow $f_{\ell,t}$ from a connector ℓ

$$\sum_s g_{n,s,t} + \sum_\ell \alpha_{\ell,n,t} \cdot f_{\ell,t} = d_{n,t} \quad \leftrightarrow \quad \lambda_{n,t} \ \forall n, t, \tag{1}$$

where $\alpha_{\ell,n,t} = -1$ if ℓ starts at n, and $\alpha_{\ell,n,t} = \eta_{\ell,t}$ if ℓ ends at n, and $\eta_{\ell,t}$ is a factor for the efficiency of the energy conversion in ℓ; it can be time-dependent—for example, depending on the outside temperature, like for a heat pump. The Karush-Kuhn-Tucker (KKT) multiplier $\lambda_{n,t}$ represents the market price of the energy carrier.

Direct CO$_2$ emissions are limited by a cap, CAP$_{CO_2}$, which is set relative to the total emissions from electricity, heating, and land transport in 1990 (3016 megatonnes of CO$_2$ [39]). Only CO$_2$ emissions are considered, because other greenhouse gas emissions in these sectors comprised less than 2% of the CO$_2$-equivalent emissions in these sectors in 1990. The cap is implemented using the specific emissions ε_s, in CO$_2$-tonne-per-MWh$_{th}$, of the fuel s, the efficiency $\eta_{n,s}$, and the dispatch $g_{n,s,t}$ for generators, as well as the difference in energy level $e_{n,s,t}$ for non-cyclic storage (relevant for methane, which is depleted during the year):

$$\sum_{n,s,t} \varepsilon_s \frac{g_{n,s,t}}{\eta_{n,s}} + \sum_{n,s} \varepsilon_s \left(e_{n,s,t=0} - e_{n,s,t=T} \right) \leq \text{CAP}_{CO_2} \quad \leftrightarrow \quad \mu_{CO_2}. \tag{2}$$

The KKT multiplier μ_{CO_2} indicates the CO$_2$ price necessary to obtain this reduction in the model without the constraint.

In this study, the CO$_2$ limit is varied to represent different possible reduction targets. This could also be interpreted as different CO$_2$ targets on the path down to zero emissions, over time, but note that, here, the cost assumptions remain fixed for the different targets, and previous investment decisions are not considered (except for existing hydroelectric generators).

To focus on low-emission technologies and avoid additional computational complexity, the only fossil fuel available in the model is natural gas, whose cost and emissions factors are 21.6 €/MWh$_{th}$ and 0.19 tCO$_2$/MWh$_{th}$ respectively.

The model was implemented in the open energy modelling framework 'Python for Power System Analysis' (PyPSA) [40]. The code and data for the model is freely available online [41,42].

3. Results

3.1. Total System Costs

In Figure 3, the composition of the total system costs, including transmission, generation, and storage, is shown as the CO_2 limit is made successively stricter, with cost-optimal cross-border transmission (left) and no cross-border transmission (right). The case of no cross-border transmission is provided as a reference point for the many single-country studies in the literature [10–18] that do not consider cross-border transfers, and to quantify the full benefit of interconnection. Interconnection was shown, in many studies, to help to balance variable renewable energy sources, particularly wind, and to reduce the costs of carbon dioxide mitigation [2,4,6,43–51].

In both systems, the CO_2 constraint is non-binding, down to 50% of the 1990 emissions. In other words, the greenfield cost optima with no CO_2 constraint or pricing already result in a large CO_2 reduction, largely due to new installations of CHPs fired by natural gas and around a 50% share of renewables in the electricity supply. If there were other cheaper, but more CO_2 intensive, generators in the model, such as coal, this minimum would be at a higher level of CO_2 emissions. For comparison, the 2016 emissions in the energy sectors considered here were 14.2% below their 1990 level.

The cost of today's system is estimated to be 524 billion euros per year, making the greenfield, unconstrained cost-optimum 48% cheaper than the current system. Today's costs are hard to gauge precisely, because of legacy investments over decades, but for this estimate we have assumed an average cost of electricity generation (including investment) of 70 €/MWh$_{el}$, 8 €/MWh$_{th}$ for solid fuels, 47 €/MWh$_{th}$ for oil, and 22 €/MWh$_{th}$ for gas, and assume that the entire non-electric heat load is met by fossil fuel boilers priced like gas boilers, which are dimensioned to meet the peak thermal load in each country. With these assumptions and energy consumption figures from the Eurostat energy balances for 2011 [52], the costs are 221 billion €/a for electricity generation (this agrees with the estimate based on price tariff statistics in [7], which excludes network costs and taxes), 3 billion €/a for cross-border transmission, 167 billion €/a for land transport fuels, 98 billion €/a for heating fuels, and 35 billion €/a for the boilers; resulting in a grand total of 524 billion €/a.

As the CO_2 limit is reduced below 50% and down to zero, costs rise by 108% with no transmission, and by 85% with optimal transmission. With zero direct CO_2 emissions and optimal transmission, system costs are 3% below today's costs, for the 2030 cost projections used here. Higher costs at lower emissions are driven by the need to defossilise heating, which is supplied by a combination of heat pumps and synthetic methane to bridge multi-day periods with low wind and solar energy. Bioenergy could also be used to bridge these periods and, thus, lower costs. However, as we discuss in Section 4, there is uncertainty regarding the sustainability of its widespread use and also strong competition from aviation, shipping, production of plastics, and other non-electric industrial demand for limited sustainable bioenergy resources.

The cost rise is more pronounced with no transmission, since variable renewables cannot be balanced between countries, but must be balanced for each country, in a self-sufficient manner, by using storage. In the case of optimal transmission, despite the extra costs of the transmission infrastructure, the costs of the total zero-CO_2 system are 13% lower than the no-transmission case. The optimal amount of transmission grows by a factor of 5 as the CO_2 limit is reduced, reflecting how the benefit of transmission increases as more variable renewables enter the electricity system. Transmission helps to balance the variability of renewables over space, particularly for wind, because wind has a synoptic-scale correlation length of 400–600 km [53], which is smaller than the size of the continent. At zero direct carbon dioxide emissions, the total volume of cross-border transmission (the sum of length times capacity for each line, where the length is the distance between the country centres) is 382 TWkm, which is over 12 times today's volume of 31 TWkm. Given the current public acceptance issues for overhead transmission, some of these transmission projects would have to be traded against the slightly higher costs of scenarios with less cross-border transmission.

For the rest of this article, we focus on the results from the case with optimal transmission.

From the map of investments, in Figure 1, it can be seen that the optimal transmission network is particularly strong between northern countries, where it can balance their plentiful wind resources. Power-to-gas investment is strongest in the peripheral countries, where it is not cost-optimal to build cross-border grid capacity to absorb all excess renewable generation. In central countries, such as Germany, there is so much grid capacity that power-to-gas is not cost effective, at least for the 2030 cost projections used here.

In Figure 4, the total cost behaviour is reflected in the shadow price μ_{CO_2} of the CO_2 constraint (Equation (2)) as the CO_2 limit is tightened. The CO_2 price rises from zero at the non-binding 50% CO_2 reduction, to around 500 €/tCO_2 once all CO_2 is eliminated from the model. As pointed out in [29], this high price is a direct reflection of the difference between the cost of natural gas (21.6 €/MWh$_{th}$) and the high price of synthetic methane in the model (113.7 €/MWh$_{th}$), which is needed for low-fossil heating. It is significantly higher than the January 2019 price of 20–25 €/tCO_2 in the European Emissions Trading System (ETS), which covers power generation, some industrial sectors, and aviation, amounting to around half of all European CO_2 emissions. The price is so high that it may be more cost-effective to eliminate CO_2 in the other sectors not covered in the model, such as aviation, shipping, industry, or, indeed, by capture directly from the air.

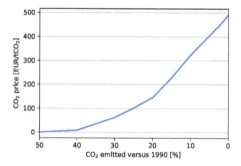

Figure 4. CO_2 shadow price in the model as CO_2 emissions are restricted in the case of cost-optimal cross-border transmission.

3.2. Defossilisation of Sectors

Next, we examine how the different sectors are defossilised. Because the model includes only the transport fuel costs and not the capital costs of vehicles, transport is electrified immediately as the electricity consumed for each kilometre travelled is less costly than petrol or diesel. The fossil-share for transport, then, reflects the fossil-share in electricity. The projected capital costs for electric vehicles in 2030 are comparable or lower than those for internal combustion engine vehicles [38], so the inclusion of these costs would not alter the early electrification of transport. Turning to electricity and heating, the picture is more complicated, as can be seen from the fossil fuel shares in Figure 5, the electricity supply in Figure 6, and the water and space heating supply in Figure 7. Electricity and electrified transport are defossilised swiftly, whereas heating only begins to be defossilised in earnest below 30% total CO_2 emissions, with the majority of the reduction coming at the end below 20%. This can also be seen in the total investments in Figure 3.

The electricity supply in Figure 6 sees a rapid increase in wind and solar installations, with the remaining electricity demand being supplied by existing hydroelectric plants and combined heat and power (CHP) stations. The renewable energy share increases (Figure 5) at the same time as total electricity demand increases (Figure 6). With zero net emissions, the total electricity demand is more than double the 2011 total of 3153 TWh$_{el}$/a. This increase is due to the electrification of transport and heating, as well as conversion losses in the power-to-gas and other storage units.

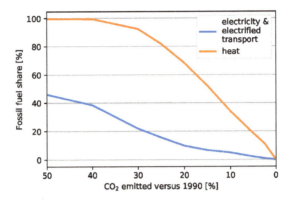

Figure 5. Share of fossil fuel energy provision in electricity, electrified transport, and heat.

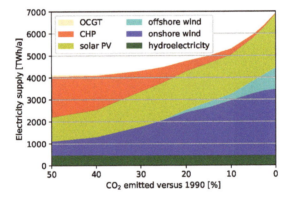

Figure 6. Breakdown of electricity supply by technology.

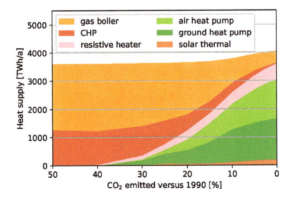

Figure 7. Breakdown of space and water heating supply by technology.

In the heating sector (Figure 7), when the CO_2 constraint is non-binding, heating is provided cheaply by natural gas in either gas boilers or CHPs. Heating is defossilised mostly by heat pumps, which drive up costs because, as well as the units themselves, they also require additional electricity generation capacity. Smaller contributions are made from resistive heaters and solar thermal collectors, while some gas boilers remain at the end to provide backup heat with synthetic methane. The overall heat demand rises slightly towards zero emissions, because of conversion losses in long-term thermal storage facilities in district heating networks.

It was identified, in [29], that one of the hardest aspects of the defossilisation of heating is the long winter cold spells with low generation from wind and solar, high heating demand, and lower heat pump coefficients of performance. Heating in these periods can be achieved by producing synthetic methane or by using long-term thermal energy storage, but particularly the former drives up system costs significantly. This effect can be seen in the rise of system costs, in Figure 3, as the last CO_2 is removed from the system using the power-to-gas facilities.

The expense of fully defossilising space and water heating was also confirmed in [54], which showed that cheap and abundant renewable energy is not sufficient to incentivise the full defossilisation of heating. CO_2 prices are also required to narrow the cost differential between gas and low-carbon options.

3.3. Metrics for VRE Integration

In this section, the curtailment, market prices, and market values of the different technologies are considered.

Power-to-gas is forced into the system primarily by the need for synthetic fuels in the heating sector during cold spells. However, its introduction has big effects on the operation of other system components and market behaviour. In Figure 8, the effect on curtailment is plotted. As CO_2 is reduced below 20%, curtailment initially rises, reaching a peak of 26% of offshore wind, 7% of onshore wind, and 3% of solar available energy, at a level of 10% CO_2. This reflects the strong seasonal peaking of the heating demand, which is hard to match with the output of solar and even with wind, which also peaks in the winter. Below 10% CO_2, it becomes cost-optimal to invest in power-to-gas. This means that any excess renewable energy can can be converted into synthetic fuels, removing almost all the curtailment when direct carbon dioxide emissions reach zero. Curtailment is worse for offshore wind than onshore or solar as, during times of excess, the dispatch rules were chosen so that offshore wind is curtailed first, then onshore wind, then solar. Offshore wind is not plotted above 25% carbon dioxide reduction, because its feed-in was negligible for these values.

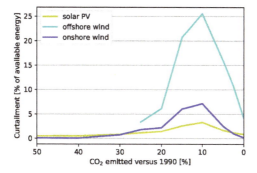

Figure 8. Curtailed variable renewable energy, as a percentage of the available energy.

A similar turning point can be seen in the electricity price statistics, plotted in Figure 9. For these statistics, all averages are weighted by the electric load, which includes electric vehicles, heat pumps, resistive heaters, and storage units in charging mode. The percentage of hours with zero marginal prices in the model drops from a peak of 31% of hours at 10% CO_2, to just 6.9% of hours at 0% CO_2. With power-to-gas, it becomes worthwhile to put renewables to economic use in almost every hour, and only in a small fraction of hours is there an excess of renewable energy. Figure 9 also shows rising market prices until 10% CO$_2$, reflecting the increase in total system costs, at which point the introduction of large flexible demand from electrolysers allows low-price hours to be better used. This drives down average prices since, here, the prices are weighted by the volume of the electrical load in each hour. The simple time-weighted average electricity price increases monotonically to 78 €/MWh$_{el}$ as emissions tend to zero. Prices for heating, hydrogen, and methane also increase monotonically. The rising standard deviation in the electricity prices reflects rising volatility from the increasing shares of variable wind and solar generation.

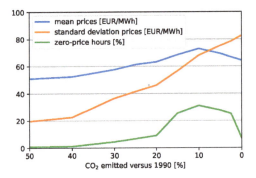

Figure 9. Load-weighted statistics of electricity prices.

The turning point is, again, reflected in the market values of the different technologies connected to the electricity system, as shown in Figure 10. Here, we define the market value as the average price of each unit of electricity consumed or produced by each technology, relative to the average load-weighted price; that is,

$$MV_s = \frac{\sum_{n,t} \lambda_{n,t} g_{n,s,t}}{\sum_{n,t} g_{n,s,t}} \left(\frac{\sum_{n,t} \lambda_{n,t} d_{n,t}}{\sum_{n,t} d_{n,t}} \right)^{-1}, \qquad (3)$$

where $\lambda_{n,t}$ is the locational marginal price from Equation (1), $g_{n,s,t}$ is the generator dispatch, and the demand $d_{n,t}$ includes electric vehicles, heat pumps, resistive heaters, and storage units in charging mode. In the language of [9], MV_s is the long-term value factor. The market value gives a useful indication of the value of each technology to the system.

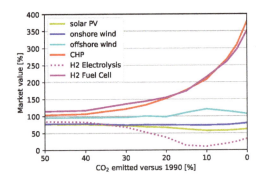

Figure 10. Market values relative to the average load-weighted price.

In general, it is expected, from other studies [8,9], that the market value of variable renewable generators, such as wind and solar, should reduce with higher penetration, as they decrease the market prices in exactly the hours when they produce at high volume, thanks to the merit order effect. Down to 10% CO_2, the relative market values do indeed diverge, with onshore wind and solar receiving low market values, while less-variable offshore wind reaches 121% market value and storage units achieve ever-stronger price arbitrage. However, below 10% CO_2, the market values of the variable generation technologies begin to converge to 100% again, as increased flexibility, in particular from power-to-gas, creates a market for wind and solar power. Below 10%, electrolysers pay increasingly higher prices for electricity as the demand for hydrogen increases, reaching an average price of 22 €/MWh$_{el}$ paid for electricity by electrolysers at zero CO_2 emissions (this price is obtained by multiplying the value factor 34% from Figure 10 with the average price 64 €/MWh$_{el}$ from Figure 9). This results in an average marginal price of hydrogen of 49 €/MWh$_{th}$ (27.5 €/MWh$_{th}$ for the electricity and the rest for investments in electrolysers and hydrogen storage).

It can be concluded that in a highly-integrated sector-coupled low-carbon system, the market values of wind and solar do not decline as precipitously as has been observed at lower renewable penetrations in electricity-only models [9]. Theoretically, this is inevitable: Given that all actors make back their costs from market prices in a long-term equilibrium (like this model), and that VRE make up the majority of the total system costs, VRE cost recovery constitutes a large share of the market prices.

The increasing interaction between electricity market prices and the production and consumption of synthetic gas is also strongly reflected in the time series; see Figure 11. The gas dispatch and electricity price are strongly correlated, with a Pearson correlation coefficient of 0.82 with zero CO_2 emissions. This correlation is stronger than the correlation of the prices with the residual load (-0.30) or variable renewable generation (-0.33). When renewables are abundant and other demand is low (particularly, in the summer), prices are low, and so a lot of synthetic gas is produced; the methanation units achieve an average of 4953 full load hours, thus enabling them to recover their high capital costs. When renewables are scarce and demand is high, particularly in the winter, gas is consumed in electricity and heating as a backup.

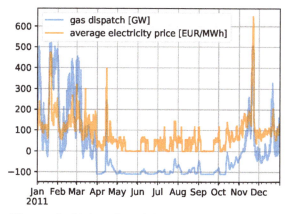

Figure 11. Zero CO_2 scenario: Methane dispatch (positive when synthetic methane is consumed, negative when produced by methanation) versus average electricity prices.

4. Limitations of this Study

An extensive discussion of the limitations of the model PyPSA-Eur-Sec-30 can be found in the paper that introduced the model [29], while a sensitivity analysis on many of the costs and other assumptions in the electricity sector was carried out in [55]. Here, aspects are highlighted that particularly impact the results discussed in this paper.

One of the primary limitations of this study is the exclusion of biomass as a technology option. Biomass was excluded, partly because of the large uncertainties surrounding the sustainability of its widespread use [56], and partly because there is likely to be intense competition for limited sustainable biomass potentials from the other hard-to-defossilise sectors that are not included in this model: Plastics production, other non-electric industrial demand, shipping, and aviation. Biomass could help to alleviate the cost peak in Figure 3, by reducing the need for synthetic gas. Biofuels could act as a bridge for existing internal combustion engine vehicles before electric vehicles become prevalent, although, in the long-term, their use should probably be restricted to hard-to-electrify sectors, such as aviation [57]. Bioenergy with carbon capture and sequestration (BECCS) may also play an important role in long-term mitigation scenarios by providing negative emissions, although there is some scepticism about the widespread use of this technology in integrated assessment models [58–61]. Given that sustainable biomass resources are limited [62], once the other sectors are included, the demand for synthetic fuels will remain high, so that the effects seen in this paper are likely to remain. This has been confirmed in an upcoming study by some of the authors.

Including the full industrial sector would also allow the model to consider the indirect emissions during production of energy infrastructure assets (only direct emissions have been included here).

Given the focus in this paper on a high share of renewables, which is also the policy goal of many EU member states, nuclear and fossil generation with carbon capture and sequestration (CCS) were not considered. The time-weighted mean electricity price with zero emission was 78 €/MWh$_{el}$, which is the price with which nuclear or fossil with CCS would have to compete. Recent nuclear projects in Europe have not been able to attain this price level. CCS may still be necessary in the future for the net negative emissions that are required in many scenarios that meet the Paris Agreement targets [32].

Other uncertainties concern the availability and costs of relatively new technologies, such as battery electric vehicles with vehicle-to-grid functionality and power-to-gas infrastructure; the sensitivity of the results to these assumptions was examined in [29,55] and found to be below 10%. As can be seen from their shares in the cost structure in Figure 3, the primary sensitivities are, in fact, to the costs of wind, solar, and heat pumps and, of course, to the discount rate. Even doubling the costs of power-to-gas infrastructure has only a limited effect on the total costs. The solar cost reductions for 2030 assumed here are ambitious, but are in line with recent cost declines. A full range of PV costs, going all the way down to zero, were examined in [55], and, although more PV investment is seen with lower costs, in Europe the PV penetration is limited by a generation pattern that is anti-correlated with the seasonal variations in demand. If the cost projections for electric vehicles used here prove to be too ambitious, this may delay the electrification of land transport.

Further modelling limitations include the restriction to a single representative historical year and the assumption of perfect foresight and of perfect markets; these limitations are driven by computational restrictions. Distribution grid reinforcement was not considered, since it does not represent a public acceptance problem, and because the costs of reinforcement are likely to be low compared to total system costs [7].

5. Conclusions

In this paper, we have studied the changes in energy system properties as the constraint on allowed direct CO_2 emissions is varied, in a sector-coupled model covering European electricity, heating, and land transport demand. A reduction in CO_2 emissions of 50%, compared to 1990 levels, for the considered low-carbon technologies is cost-effective, regardless of the level of transmission expansion, thanks to increasing shares of cheap wind and solar electricity and the electrification of land transport. Below this level, costs rise as carbon dioxide is initially pushed out of the system by heat pumps and, finally, by the synthetic fuels that are necessary to bridge long cold spells with low wind and sun. However, even with zero direct CO_2 emissions, the total system costs are comparable to the costs of today's energy system, when using cost projections for 2030.

The introduction of power-to-gas, driven by these cold spells when cheap low-emission electricity is scarce, alters market dynamics because of the ease of the long-term storage of gas. This results in fewer hours of zero prices, substantially less curtailment, and a re-convergence of the market values of variable renewable generators towards the average market price.

While some synthetic gas could be replaced by bioenergy in the model, either in the form of solid biomass or biogas upgraded to biomethane, it should also be borne in mind that scarce sustainable bioenergy resources will also be required in other sectors which are harder to electrify, such as aviation, shipping, plastics production, and other non-electric industrial demand. Exploring these trade-offs in a high resolution model is an interesting topic for future research.

While model limitations should be borne in mind, several relevant policy measures can be deduced from the results: Increasing low-emission technologies in electricity generation is a priority, particularly given that defossilisation strategies in other sectors rely on electrification; reducing emissions in space and water heating is more expensive and sees investment accelerate towards the end of the energy transition; CO_2 prices (or equivalent second-best measures, like mandates for district heating or heat pumps) will be required across all sectors and at levels much higher than seen today in the European Emissions Trading System; power-to-gas is an important part of guaranteeing system security during cold winter wind lulls, and so investment in research, development, and deployment should be increased to guarantee that power-to-gas can scale up in time; zero-emission systems can be cost-effective, even before accounting for the health and environmental benefits, so expense is not a limitation for the energy transition; it may be cost-effective to go further than the EU's current 40% greenhouse gas reduction target for 2030 and aim for zero net-emissions in 2050, pending further investigations of the integration of industrial, shipping, and aviation demand.

Author Contributions: All authors contributed to the design of the research. T.B. performed the numerical simulations and took the lead in the analysis of the results and in writing the manuscript. All authors provided critical feedback and helped shape the research, analysis and manuscript

Funding: T.B. acknowledges funding from the Helmholtz Association under grant no. VH-NG-1352. M.G. is partially funded by the Innovation Fund Denmark under grant number 6154-00022B.

Conflicts of Interest: The authors declare no conflicts of interest.

Abbreviations

The following abbreviations are used in this manuscript:

a	annum (year)
BEV	Battery Electric Vehicle
CCS	Carbon Capture and Sequestration
CHP	Combined Heat and Power plant
CO_2	Carbon dioxide
ETS	Emissions Trading System
EU	European Union
FOM	Fixed Operation and Maintenance
GHG	Greenhouse Gas
H2	Hydrogen gas
HP	Heat Pump
HVDC	High Voltage Direct Current
INDC	Intended Nationally Determined Contribution for the Paris Agreement [32]
KKT	Karush-Kuhn-Tucker
MV	Market Value
OCGT	Open Cycle Gas Turbine
PV	Photovoltaic
PyPSA	Python for Power System Analysis
PyPSA-Eur-Sec-30	30-node sector-coupled PyPSA model for Europe
VRE	Variable Renewable Energy

References

1. Czisch, G. Szenarien Zur Zukünftigen Stromversorgung. Ph.D. Thesis, Universität Kassel, Kassel, Germany, 2005.
2. Scholz, Y. Renewable Energy Based Electricity Supply at Low Costs—Development of the REMix Model and Application for Europe. Ph.D. Thesis, Universität Stuttgart, Stuttgart, Germany, 2012.
3. Gils, H.C.; Scholz, Y.; Pregger, T.; de Tena, D.L.; Heide, D. Integrated modelling of variable renewable energy-based power supply in Europe. *Energy* **2017**, *123*, 173–188. [CrossRef]
4. Schlachtberger, D.; Brown, T.; Schramm, S.; Greiner, M. The benefits of cooperation in a highly renewable European electricity network. *Energy* **2017**, *134*, 469–481. [CrossRef]
5. Reichenberg, L.; Hedenus, F.; Odenberger, M.; Johnsson, F. The marginal system LCOE of variable renewables—Evaluating high penetration levels of wind and solar in Europe. *Energy* **2018**, *152*, 914–924. [CrossRef]
6. Child, M.; Kemfert, C.; Bogdanov, D.; Breyer, C. Flexible electricity generation, grid exchange and storage for the transition to a 100% renewable energy system in Europe. *Renew. Energy* **2019**, *139*, 80–101. [CrossRef]
7. Brown, T.; Bischof-Niemz, T.; Blok, K.; Breyer, C.; Lund, H.; Mathiesen, B. Response to 'Burden of proof: A comprehensive review of the feasibility of 100% renewable-electricity systems'. *Renew. Sustain. Energy Rev.* **2018**, *92*, 834–847. [CrossRef]
8. Joskow, P.L. Comparing the costs of intermittent and dispatchable electricity generating technologies. *Am. Econ. Rev.* **2011**, *101*, 238–241. [CrossRef]
9. Hirth, L. The market value of variable renewables: The effect of solar wind power variability on their relative price. *Energy Econ.* **2013**, *38*, 218–236. [CrossRef]
10. Henning, H.M.; Palzer, A. A comprehensive model for the German electricity and heat sector in a future energy system with a dominant contribution from renewable energy technologies—Part I: Methodology. *Renew. Sustain. Energy Rev.* **2014**, *30*, 1003–1018. [CrossRef]
11. Palzer, A.; Henning, H.M. A comprehensive model for the German electricity and heat sector in a future energy system with a dominant contribution from renewable energy technologies—Part II: Results. *Renew. Sustain. Energy Rev.* **2014**, *30*, 1019–1034. [CrossRef]
12. Gerhardt, N.; Scholz, A.; Sandau, F.; Hahn, H. *Interaktion EE-Strom, Wärme und Verkehr*; Technical Report; Fraunhofer IWES: Kassel, Germany, 2015.
13. Quaschning, V. *Sektorkopplung Durch die Energiewende*; Technical Report; HTW Berlin: Berlin, Germany, 2016.
14. Lund, H.; Mathiesen, B. Energy system analysis of 100% renewable energy systems—The case of Denmark in years 2030 and 2050. *Energy* **2009**, *34*, 524–531. [CrossRef]
15. Mathiesen, B.V.; Lund, H.; Conolly, D.; Wenzel, H.; Østergaard, P.; Möller, B.; Nielsen, S.; Ridjan, I.; Karnøe, P.; Sperling, K.; et al. Smart Energy Systems for coherent 100% renewable energy and transport solutions. *Appl. Energy* **2015**, *145*, 139–154. [CrossRef]
16. Lund, H.; Andersen, A.N.; Østergaard, P.A.; Mathiesen, B.V.; Connolly, D. From electricity smart grids to smart energy systems—A market operation based approach and understanding. *Energy* **2012**, *42*, 96–102. [CrossRef]
17. Connolly, D.; Lund, H.; Mathiesen, B.; Leahy, M. The first step towards a 100% renewable energy-system for Ireland. *Appl. Energy* **2011**, *88*, 502–507. [CrossRef]
18. Deane, J.; Chiodi, A.; Gargiulo, M.; Gallachoir, B.P.O. Soft-linking of a power systems model to an energy systems model. *Energy* **2012**, *42*, 303–312. [CrossRef]
19. Connolly, D.; Lund, H.; Mathiesen, B. Smart Energy Europe: The technical and economic impact of one potential 100% renewable energy scenario for the European Union. *Renew. Sustain. Energy Rev.* **2016**, *60*, 1634–1653. [CrossRef]
20. *The PRIMES Model*; Technical Report; NTUA: Athens, Greece, 2009.
21. Leimbach, M.; Bauer, N.; Baumstark, L.; Luken, M.; Edenhofer, O. Technological change and international trade—Insights from REMIND-R. *Energy J.* **2010**, *31*. [CrossRef]
22. Capros, P.; Paroussos, L.; Fragkos, P.; Tsani, S.; Boitier, B.; Wagner, F.; Busch, S.; Resch, G.; Blesl, M.; Bollen, J. European decarbonisation pathways under alternative technological and policy choices: A multi-model analysis. *Energy Strategy Rev.* **2014**, *2*, 231–245. [CrossRef]
23. Hagspiel, S.; Jägemann, C.; Lindenburger, D.; Brown, T.; Cherevatskiy, S.; Tröster, E. Cost-optimal power system extension under flow-based market coupling. *Energy* **2014**, *66*, 654–666. [CrossRef]

24. Simoes, S.; Nijs, W.; Ruiz, P.; Sgobbi, A.; Thiel, C. Comparing policy routes for low-carbon power technology deployment in EU—An energy system analysis. *Energy Policy* **2017**, *101*, 353–365. [CrossRef]
25. Löffler, K.; Hainsch, K.; Burandt, T.; Oei, P.Y.; Kemfert, C.; von Hirschhausen, C. Designing a model for the global energy system—GENeSYS-MOD: An application of the open-source energy modeling system (OSeMOSYS). *Energies* **2017**, *10*, 1468. [CrossRef]
26. Blanco, H.; Nijs, W.; Ruf, J.; Faaij, A. Potential for hydrogen and power-to-liquid in a low-carbon EU energy system using cost optimization. *Appl. Energy* **2018**, *232*, 617–639. [CrossRef]
27. Ludig, S.; Haller, M.; Schmid, E.; Bauer, N. Fluctuating renewables in a long-term climate change mitigation strategy. *Energy* **2011**, *36*, 6674–6685. [CrossRef]
28. Kotzur, L.; Markewitz, P.; Robinius, M.; Stolten, D. Impact of different time series aggregation methods on optimal energy system design. *Renew. Energy* **2018**, *117*, 474–487. [CrossRef]
29. Brown, T.; Schlachtberger, D.; Kies, A.; Greiner, M. Synergies of sector coupling and transmission extension in a cost-optimised, highly renewable European energy system. *Energy* **2018**, *160*, 720–730. [CrossRef]
30. Millar, R.J.; Fuglestvedt, J.S.; Friedlingstein, P.; Rogelj, J.; Grubb, M.J.; Matthews, H.D.; Skeie, R.B.; Forster, P.M.; Frame, D.J.; Allen, M.R. Emission budgets and pathways consistent with limiting warming to 1.5 °C. *Nat. Geosci.* **2017**, *10*, 741. [CrossRef]
31. European Commission. *Energy Roadmap 2050—COM(2011) 885/2*; European Commission: Brussel, Belgium, 2011.
32. UNFCCC. Adoption of the Paris Agreement. Report No. FCCC/CP/2015/L.9/Rev.1. 2015. Available online: http://unfccc.int/resource/docs/2015/cop21/eng/l09r01.png (accessed on 21 January 2019).
33. European Council. *Presidency Conclusions—Brussels, 29/30 October 2009*; Council of thr European Union: Brussels, Belgium, 2009.
34. European Commission. *A Clean Planet for All—COM(2018) 773*; European Commission: Brussel, Belgium, 2018.
35. *National Emissions Reported to the UNFCCC and to the EU Greenhouse Gas Monitoring Mechanism*; Technical report; European Environmental Agency: Copenhagen, Denmark, 2018.
36. Rogelj, J.; Popp, A.; Calvin, K.V.; Luderer, G.; Emmerling, J.; Gernaat, D.; Fujimori, S.; Strefler, J.; Hasegawa, T.; Marangoni, G.; et al. Scenarios towards limiting global mean temperature increase below 1.5 °C. *Nat. Clim. Chang.* **2018**, *8*, 325–332. [CrossRef]
37. Persson, U.; Werner, S. Heat distribution and the future competitiveness of district heating. *Appl. Energy* **2011**, *88*, 568–576. [CrossRef]
38. *Electric Vehicle Outlook 2017*; Technical report; Bloomberg New Energy Finance: New York City, NY, USA, 2017.
39. *ODYSSEE Database on Energy Efficiency Data & Indicators*; Technical report; Enerdata: Grenoble, France, 2016.
40. Brown, T.; Hörsch, J.; Schlachtberger, D. PyPSA: Python for power system analysis. *J. Open Res. Softw.* **2018**, *6*. [CrossRef]
41. Brown, T.; Schlachtberger, D. Supplementary Data: Code, Input Data and Result Summaries: Synergies of sector coupling and transmission extension in a cost-optimised, highly renewable European energy system (Version v0.1.0) [Data set]. *Zenodo* **2018**. [CrossRef]
42. Brown, T.; Schlachtberger, D. Supplementary Data: Full Results: Synergies of sector coupling and transmission extension in a cost-optimised, highly renewable European energy system (Version v0.1.0) [Data set]. *Zenodo* **2018**. [CrossRef]
43. Bahn, O.; Haurie, A.; Kypreos, S.; Vial, J. Advanced mathematical programming modeling to assess the benefits from international CO_2 abatement cooperation. *Environ. Model. Assess.* **1998**, *3*, 107–115. [CrossRef]
44. Unger, T.; Ekvall, T. Benefits from increased cooperation and energy trade under CO_2 commitments—The Nordic case. *Clim. Policy* **2003**, *3*, 279–294. [CrossRef]
45. Czisch, G. Szenarien zur Zukünftigen Stromversorgung: Kostenoptimierte Variationen zur Versorgung Europas und Seiner Nachbarn mit Strom aus Erneuerbaren Energien. Ph.D. Thesis, Universität Kassel, Kassel, Germany, 2005.
46. Schaber, K.; Steinke, F.; Hamacher, T. Transmission grid extensions for the integration of variable renewable energies in Europe: Who benefits where? *Energy Policy* **2012**, *43*, 123–135. [CrossRef]
47. Schaber, K.; Steinke, F.; Mühlich, P.; Hamacher, T. Parametric study of variable renewable energy integration in Europe: Advantages and costs of transmission grid extensions. *Energy Policy* **2012**, *42*, 498–508. [CrossRef]
48. Rodriguez, R.; Becker, S.; Andresen, G.; Heide, D.; Greiner, M. Transmission needs across a fully renewable European power system. *Renew. Energy* **2014**, *63*, 467–476. [CrossRef]

49. MacDonald, A.E.; Clack, C.T.M.; Alexander, A.; Dunbar, A.; Wilczak, J.; Xie, Y. Future cost-competitive electricity systems and their impact on US CO_2 emissions. *Nat. Clim. Chang.* **2017**, *6*, 526–531. [CrossRef]
50. Eriksen, E.H.; Schwenk-Nebbe, L.J.; Tranberg, B.; Brown, T.; Greiner, M. Optimal heterogeneity in a simplified highly renewable European electricity system. *Energy* **2017**, *133*, 913–928. [CrossRef]
51. Galán-Martín, A.; Pozo, C.; Azapagic, A.; Grossmann, I.E.; Mac Dowell, N.; Guillén-Gosálbez, G. Time for global action: An optimised cooperative approach towards effective climate change mitigation. *Energy Environ. Sci.* **2018**, *11*, 572–581. [CrossRef]
52. *Energy Balances 1900–2014*; Technical Report; Eurostat: Luxembourg, 2016.
53. Kiss, P.; Jánosi, I.M. Limitations of wind power availability over Europe: A conceptual study. *Nonlinear Process. Geophys.* **2008**, *15*, 803–813. [CrossRef]
54. Zhu, K.; Victoria, M.; Brown, T.; Andresen, G.; Greiner, M. Impact of CO_2 prices on the design of a highly decarbonised coupled electricity and heating system in Europe. *Appl. Energy* **2019**, *236*, 622–634. [CrossRef]
55. Schlachtberger, D.; Brown, T.; Schäfer, M.; Schramm, S.; Greiner, M. Cost optimal scenarios of a future highly renewable European electricity system: Exploring the influence of weather data, cost parameters and policy constraints. *Energy* **2018**, *163*, 100–114. [CrossRef]
56. Creutzig, F.; Ravindranath, N.H.; Berndes, G.; Bolwig, S.; Bright, R.; Cherubini, F.; Chum, H.; Corbera, E.; Delucchi, M.; Faaij, A.; et al. Bioenergy and climate change mitigation: An assessment. *GCB Bioenergy* **2015**, *7*, 916–944. [CrossRef]
57. Connolly, D.; Mathiesen, B.; Ridjan, I. A comparison between renewable transport fuels that can supplement or replace biofuels in a 100% renewable energy system. *Energy* **2014**, *73*, 110–125. [CrossRef]
58. Fuss, S.; Canadell, J.G.; Peters, G.P.; Tavoni, M.; Andrew, R.M.; Ciais, P.; Jackson, R.B.; Jones, C.D.; Kraxner, F.; Nakicenovic, N.; et al. Betting on negative emissions. *Nat. Clim. Chang.* **2014**, *4*, 850–853. [CrossRef]
59. Smith, P.; Davis, S.J.; Creutzig, F.; Fuss, S.; Minx, J.; Gabrielle, B.; Kato, E.; Jackson, R.B.; Cowie, A.; Kriegler, E.; et al. Biophysical and economic limits to negative CO_2 emissions. *Nat. Clim. Chang.* **2015**, *6*. [CrossRef]
60. Anderson, K.; Peters, G. The trouble with negative emissions. *Science* **2016**, *354*, 182–183. [CrossRef]
61. Vaughan, N.E.; Gough, C. Expert assessment concludes negative emissions scenarios may not deliver. *Environ. Res. Lett.* **2016**, *11*, 095003. [CrossRef]
62. Ruiz, P.; Sgobbi, A.; Nijs, W.; Thiel, C.; Longa, F.; Kober, T. *The JRC-EU-TIMES Model: Bioenergy Potentials*; Technical Report; JRC: Petten, The Netherlands, 2015. [CrossRef]

© 2019 by the authors. Licensee MDPI, Basel, Switzerland. This article is an open access article distributed under the terms and conditions of the Creative Commons Attribution (CC BY) license (http://creativecommons.org/licenses/by/4.0/).

Article

Pathways for Germany's Low-Carbon Energy Transformation Towards 2050

Hans-Karl Bartholdsen [1,†], Anna Eidens [1,†], Konstantin Löffler [1,2,†], Frederik Seehaus [1,*,†], Felix Wejda [1,†], Thorsten Burandt [1,2,3], Pao-Yu Oei [1,2], Claudia Kemfert [2,4,5] and Christian von Hirschhausen [1,2]

1. Workgroup for Infrastructure Policy, Technische Universität Berlin, Straße des 17. Juni 135, 10623 Berlin, Germany
2. Deutsches Institut für Wirtschaftsforschung (DIW Berlin), Mohrenstraße 58, 10117 Berlin, Germany
3. Department of Industrial Economics and Technology Management (IØT), Norwegian University of Science and Technology (NTNU), Høgskoleringen 1, 7491 Trondheim, Norway
4. Hertie School of Governance, Friedrichstraße 180, 10117 Berlin, Germany
5. German Advisory Council on Environment (SRU), Luisenstraße 46, 10117 Berlin, Germany
* Correspondence: frs@wip.tu-berlin.de
† These authors contributed equally to this work.

Received: 2 July 2019; Accepted: 23 July 2019; Published: 2 August 2019

Abstract: Like many other countries, Germany has defined goals to reduce its CO_2-emissions following the Paris Agreement of the 21st Conference of the Parties (COP). The first successes in decarbonizing the electricity sector were already achieved under the German Energiewende. However, further steps in this direction, also concerning the heat and transport sectors, have stalled. This paper describes three possible pathways for the transformation of the German energy system until 2050. The scenarios take into account current climate politics on a global, European, and German level and also include different demand projections, technological trends and resource prices. The model includes the sectors power, heat, and transportation and works on a Federal State level. For the analysis, the linear cost-optimizing Global Energy System Model (GENeSYS-MOD) is used to calculate the cost-efficient paths and technology mixes. We find that a reduction of CO_2 of more than 80% in the less ambitious scenario can be welfare enhancing compared to a scenario without any climate mitigating policies. Even higher decarbonization rates of 95% are feasible and needed to comply with international climate targets, yet related to high effort in transforming the subsector of process heat. The different pathways depicted in this paper render chances and risks of transforming the German energy system under various external influences.

Keywords: decarbonization; energy system modeling; GENeSYS-MOD; renewables; energy policy; energy transformation; Energiewende

1. Introduction

Human activities have already caused approximately 1.0 degree Celsius of global warming above pre-industrial levels by 2017 [1]. Based on the analysis conducted by the Intergovernmental Panel on Climate Change (IPCC) [1–4], the global carbon budget to limit the temperature rise to 1.5 °C will soon be exhausted. With an increasing global mean temperature, the risk of abrupt and major irreversible changes will grow and impact human life in many ways [1,5]. Therefore, the global community must undertake measures to find a collective climate policy towards decarbonization.

To get the world mobilized, all (then) 197 United Nations (UN) member countries agreed to the 2015 UN Climate Change Conference held in Paris [6,7]. Thereby, policymakers ratified their Nationally Determined Contributions (NDCs) in the so-called Paris Agreement. The are the nations self-defined emission reduction goals, aiming to keep the global mean temperature increase well below 2 °C and limit the share of carbon dioxide equivalents to less than 450 parts per million (ppm) within the atmosphere [7]. They are, however, not sufficient to reach the climate target.

Induced by the German Energiewende, there is a remarkable uptrend in using renewable energy sources in Germany: Since 2010, in the framework of the Energiewende a series of decisions where made to decarbonize and decentralize the German energy system and more general, find a concept of a future energy system [8]. Nevertheless, there are still doubts if an energy system based on 100% renewable energy is viable and achievable, both in technical, as well as economic terms, illustrated in the debate of Heard et al. [9] and Brown et al. [10]. A correlating attribute for realizing a renewable energy integration is the consideration of technology-specific storage aspects. However, there are still conflicting opinions on the necessity and size of electric storages in the power grid, as exemplified in the dispute between Sinn [11] and Schill et al. [12] (See also Section 1.3).

Thus, it is crucial to elaborate scenarios, driven by different storylines that target a rather holistic perception than solely absolute numbers [13]. To do so, this paper examines three different scenarios for Germany's low-carbon transformation concerning the ratified NDCs. To establish a differentiated impact assessment, those are implemented into the Global Energy System Model (GENeSYS-MOD) v2.0 [14,15]. This multi-sectoral energy system model is used to analyze national trajectories for the sectors electricity, heat, and transportation until 2050 by applying a cost-optimization algorithm. Based on its federal system, Germany is divided into 16 sub-regions to indicate bottlenecks and potentials for a sophisticated recommendation for action. Despite a limited transferability to other countries, a close consideration of the German case bears insights on its past and future development and might offer some lessons and best practices for other nations, because of Germany's fruitful start and the *Energiewende's* success in laying down a base for an decarbonized energy system [8], its close interdependence with other European nations and a certain maturity of the idea of renewable energy supply [8]. Section 1.1 gives a brief overview on the status quo of Germany's climate policy and energy system within its national and international context. Sections 2.1 and 2.2 introduce three different scenarios and their implementation in GENeSYS-MOD. The model results of the scenarios are displayed and discussed in the following Section 3 to provide holistic recommendations for political action. Section 4 concludes the paper.

1.1. German Climate Policy

Germany takes part in the United Nations Framework Convention on Climate Change (UNFCCC) since its foundation. The first Conference of the Parties (COP) took place in 1992 in Berlin, the capital of Germany. Since then, Germany took part in various multilateral agreements and programs for global climate protection, like the Montreal Protocol to protect the ozone layer [16] and the Kyoto Protocol [17]. As part of the European Union (EU), Germany commits itself to a number of further climate protection measures and targets. Since 2005, for example, emissions from the domestic energy industry and heavy industry have been covered by an Emissions Trading System (ETS). This accounts for 45% of European emissions [18]. A second approach to reducing greenhouse gas (GHG) emissions on a European level is pan-European reduction targets, which should include emissions outside the ETS. These targets are also included in the Paris Agreement and state that by 2020, greenhouse gas (GHG) emissions should be reduced by 10 percent compared to 2020 [19] and by 30 percent compared to 2030 [20]. In order to balance the burden between the countries according to their economic performance, the Effort Sharing scheme is implemented. Hence, relatively underdeveloped countries can even increase their emissions by a certain amount, while other countries have to reduce beyond the European target. Germany is to reduce its emissions by 14 percent by 2020 compared to 2005 [19] but will miss this European target [21]. Aside the European targets, Germany has set itself own targets for 2030 and 2050, based on the reference year of 1990. These targets are also subject to the Paris Agreement ratified by Germany. The main goal is to provide a reduction of GHG emissions of at least 55% until 2030 and 80–95% in 2050 compared to 1990-levels. Additionally, renewable energy sources are prescribed to account for at least 60% of the energy consumption in 2050, while efficiency rates should increase by 50% [22]. The final decision to phase out nuclear power by 2022 has already been cushioned by the addition of renewable energy plants. The annual nuclear power production fell from 170 Terawatt Hours (TWh) in 2000 to 76 TWh in 2018 while at the same time renewables rose from 38 TWh to 229 TWh. However, power production with coal decreased only from 291 TWh to 229 TWh in the respective timespan [23]. Hence, there is a large gap between the own decarbonization targets and the actual implementation so far. In 2018, the German government convened a commission "Growth, Structural Change, and Employment" ("Coal-Commission") for the purpose of implementing practical measures to concretize the goals set out in the climate protection plan. In January 2019, their final report on the gradual reduction and cessation of coal-fired power generation was published [24]. This report suggests that by 2022, coal-fired power plant capacities have to be reduced gradually to around 15 Gigawatt (GW) of lignite and 15 GW of hard coal. Phasing out coal is recommended at the latest by 2038 [24]. In the second half of 2018, a new global movement gained medial presence: Every Friday, schoolchildren, supporters from universities, and the scientific community protest for a more decisive approach of politics in climate questions. The German branch of the "Fridays for Future" movement demands Germany shall have no net emissions of carbon dioxide (CO_2) by 2035 and complete phase-out of coal by 2030. Also, they demand an electricity supply that is entirely renewable by 2035. By the end of 2019, the movement further demands to shut down one-quarter of capacity of coal-fired power plants an end to all subsidies on fossil fuels and a pricing scheme for CO_2 that internalizes all external effects and thus they refer to the German Environment Agency which estimates a price of 180 € per ton of CO_2 [25].

Further insights on the regional differences, stakeholders in Germany, and the division of competences among the ministries can be found in the Appendix A.

1.2. Energy System

The German energy system is undergoing fundamental restructuring intending to achieve a renunciation of fossil fuels, a switch to renewable energies, and more efficient use of energy. The driving force behind this transformation is the man-made global climate change through the emission of GHG and the climate protection targets developed in response [26].

The current supply structure of the power, heating, and transport sectors, as well as the transmission grid and the final energy demand, serve as a starting point for modeling the future energy system of Germany.

Even though electricity generated by renewable technologies reached a share of approximately 37.8% in 2018, the four conventional sources coal (hard coal and lignite), oil, fossil gas, and nuclear are still dominating [23]. This translates to 313 million tons of CO_2 equivalents released in the atmosphere in the year 2017 [27]. Lignite and hard coal account for the highest share (35.4%) of electricity produced in Germany in 2018. Gas fired power plants are held as a flexible reserve to cushion the renewables' volatility and grid compensatory measures. Most of the renewable power generation comes from wind and solar with wind energy already providing 17.2% of the total electricity production [23]. With the further development of offshore capacities in the Baltic- and North Sea, as well as onshore wind turbines focused in northern Germany, this share will increase. Among more cost-intensive technical requirements [28], the maximum potential for offshore installations of 85 GW [29] is lower compared to the potential of onshore installations, which is set at 200 GW [30]. Photovoltaics (PV) are another important pillar of Germany's future electricity supply, contributing about 7% of the electricity supply today [23]. Braun et al. [31] calculated a potential for open-field PV of 297 GW following the target set in German Renewable Green Energy Act (EEG) 2017 of locating open-field PV plants along traffic routes [32]. Storing the generated electrical energy will become a challenge concerning the volatility of the feed-in of power into the grid by solar and wind plants. Storage technologies, such as batteries, pumped hydro power plants, or gas- and heat storages can be used to effectively reduce the fluctuating power feed in by renewables. CCS technology will not play a role in the German nor

European power sector in the future. It has turned out that the implementation is technologically too demanding, very expensive and not needed [33–35].

Compared to the power sector, the heating sector faces more difficulties to become renewable. In fact, the transition of the heating sector towards less carbon dioxide emissions requires a renewable electricity sector, as electric heating alternatives are only renewable if the electricity used is renewable. The heating sector consists of space and water heating but also implies process heating in the industry. Fossil fuels still play a major role in heat generation, particularly fossil gas. In 2018, 49% of German households were supplied with heat by direct gas heating and 13% by district heating [36]. In the industry, coal and gas are mainly used for the supply of process heat [37]. The use of renewable energy sources for heat generation is not yet as established as in the electricity sector, although their share in heating and cooling in Germany rose from 4.4% to 13.9% between 2000 and 2018 [38]. Also, the application of renewables is mainly used for generating low-temperature heat, lesser for process heat in the industry. The share of renewables is at only 5.3%, while coal and gas remain the dominating energy sources [39]. Further deployment of renewables could be implemented through electric furnaces and renewable gas, produced via renewable energy inputs. In the low-temperature heating sector, heat pumps, as an electric alternative to fossil boilers, can contribute to the decarbonization. The efficiency of heat pumps is higher for small differences in temperature. Therefore, they are primary only used in the low-temperature heating sector. Contrary, process heat also demands temperatures above 1000 °C. Therefore, renewable gas is the only option to decarbonize specific processes, according to Naegler et al. [40]. As a result, Biogas and Biomass are getting more relevant but are limited by the existing arable lands and grasslands [41]. Also, a renewable heating sector will rely on direct electric heat generation (e.g., heat pumps or electric (arc) furnaces) and thereby coupling the sectors electricity and heat. Furthermore, synthetic hydrogen has substantial potential in the heating sector, as well as in the transportation sector. Still, this would lead to a higher total electricity demand because of increased need for hydrogen produced by electrolysis. Consequently, the higher demand for electricity will also possibly generate the need for an expansion of the electricity grid.

Currently, the German electricity distribution networks have a line length of 1.7 million kilometres (km) in total and are operated by approximately 880 Distibution System Operators (DSOs) [42]. The existing transmission grid has a length of 35,000 km and is operated by four privately organized Transmission System Operators (TSOs) [43]. The transformation of the energy supply to renewable energies involves a profound change in the German electricity supply structure [44], which leads to new challenges for the grid infrastructure.

The final energy demand in Germany amounted to 9329 petajoules (PJ) in 2017, in which power and heat applications accounted for 70.5%. The remaining energy demand was caused by the transportation sector [45]. Even with efficiency improvements and climate goals, the final energy demand in the household sector increased slightly from 2383 to around 2430 PJ in the past 27 years [45]. Finally, the energy demand in the mobility sector increased by almost 376 PJ from 1990 to 2017 [45].

1.3. Literature Review

Since Conference of the Parties (COP) 21 in 2015 at the latest, limiting the effects of climate change and decarbonizing and decentralizing the existing energy systems has become a topic and a task not only for scientists but also for states and subnational state institutions. As the Renewable Energy Policy Network for the 21st Century (Ren21) stated in its annual report of 2018 [46], 169 countries have already set their own targets for renewable energies. The transformation of energy systems is underway around the world with varying degrees of ambition, as shown, among other things, by the large volumes of investment in renewable energy plants. Nevertheless, the Ren21 report also shows a slightly reduced effort globally: Compared to 2017, global investment has fallen, CO_2 emissions increased by 1.7% last year, some countries have retired from their own climate targets, and overall efforts are insufficient to meet the climate targets of the Paris Agreement [46]. That is why it is important that research continues on a global, supranational, national, and regional level in this area and that studies are being published that demonstrate the relevance of the issue and can put pressure on decision-makers.

There is a variety of studies available that analyze possible pathways for decarbonized energy systems. While some studies are focusing on a global context [47,48] or on a European level [49–53]. Connolly et al. [53] used the 2013 version of the EU reference scenario [54] to calculate a European energy system in 2050 with integrated transportation, heating and cooling and industry sectors, which relies on renewables by 100%. They conclude, that it is possible without using unsustainable amounts of biomass and by additional system costs of 12%. Following the question of technical feasibility and the burden that lies on the power sector and the European transmission grid, Zappa et al. [52] used various reference scenarios determining future power demands and data from entso-e, to conclude that the installed power generation capacity has to increase from 1 Terawatt (TW) to 1.9 TW in 2050. Around 8.5 Exajoule (EJ) from Biomass will be used in the power sector, compared to Connolly et al. [53] 13.5 EJ in the whole European energy system. Also using GENeSYS-MOD, Hainsch et al. [49] model a low carbon energy system for Europe. They conclude that achieving a target where global warming is limited to 1.5 is only feasible under certain conditions while staying below 2.0 will only generate 1.5% additional costs compared to the business as usual case. Using the Dynamic Investment and Dispatch Model for the Future European Electricity Market (dynELMOD), Gerbaulet et al. [50] calculate that PV throughout Europe, as in Germany, is only used half as much as wind power in 2050. Also, they figure out that by 2050, a 98% decarbonization can be achieved, which goes hand in hand with levelized costs for electricity of around 27–32 € per MWh.

Considering a global level with some regional detail, Ram et al. [48] conclude that 100% renewable energies are feasible, as well as levelized costs in electricity are falling, but are rising in heat supply. In contrast to Gerbaulet et al. [50], their calculations suggest that Germany's renewable energy system will be based primarily on solar energy generation.

Considering the issue of imports and exports, the role of individual countries plays a decisive role. A breakdown for European countries is provided by Child et al. [51] who use the LUT Energy System Transition model also used by Ram et al. [48]. They come to the conclusion: power trade within Europe is increasing massively from 63 GW to 262 GW. They calculate that the United Kingdom, Ireland, Norway, Denmark, and the Baltic states will be exporters of electricity, while Germany will import 1% of its requirements.

The same questions arise also in the national context of Germany: numerous studies consider pathways towards a possible decarbonization of the German energy system [11,12,55–59]. However, the German studies are usually done on a national level and only seldomly in a federal context.

Pregger, Nitsch, and Naegler's [55] study compares necessary developments for achieving the aims of the German federal government's "Energy Concept" under different costs for technologies and resources. To accomplish the lower boundary of 80% emission reductions until 2050, they find that an increase of renewable power generation is needed, accompanied by the need for substantial efficiency gains across the sectors. In their base case scenario, they compute a rather moderate amount of installed renewable capacity of 179 GW in 2050.

Palzer and Henning [56] take a look at the electricity and heating system and conclude that given significant efficiency gains in the heating sector (40% to 50% of heat demand compared to 2010), both sectors can be decarbonized by 2050– with an installed renewable energy generation capacity of 465 GW. In another study, Henning and Palzer [57] also include the sectors transportation and industry and conclude that a transformation towards 80% GHG emission reduction is theoretically feasible, although additional costs would be around EUR 30 billion annually, compared to the reference case. Regarding the nearer future, Oei et al. [60] conclude in their study that Germany will not meet its intermediate targets for 2020 and 2030 if it keeps the current trends (and limited efforts). One main message is the fact that an extensive phase-out of coal-generated electricity until 2030 to meet the targets could be feasible without endangering the security of electricity supply.

While these studies do not put much weight on electricity import and export, Samadi et al. [58] point out that usual scenarios are relying on high values of net imports of electricity, thus needing fewer storage capacities but increasing technological, financial, and political complexity [58]. However, Pleßmann et al. [47] conclude that after modeling the demand for energy storage for a 100% renewable and thus fluctuating electricity supply, the integration of electricity storages will not increase the levelized costs of electricity (LCOE) in comparison to conventional energy sources. The question as to how important energy storage is for a 100% renewable energy system is also extensively discussed in a German context: In a comparing study, Cebulla et al. [61] found a large variance between the estimated requirements for electric energy storage in an energy system relying heavily on renewables: One cited study estimates a storage capacity of up to 83 TWh in a system that is 100% renewable (or 6.3 TWh in the case of 80% market penetration) [62]. By 2050, Child et al. [51] estimate that up to 147 TWh of storage capacity have to be built in Germany to compensate for grid fluctuations which is far higher than Hartmann's estimate which is even more astonishing, when having in mind, that this study calculated a fully integrated European power sector. Concentranting on Germany, Sinn [11] calculated a need for electric storages of around 16.3 TWh Schill et al. [12] however, argue that with the regulation of generation peaks from renewable energy plants, as well as sector coupling, there would be no need for large electricity storage additions. Today, there exist multiple storage technologies and solutions that can play a role in compensating the strong fluctuations in the feed-in of renewable energies. In this context, Zsiborács et al. [63] argue that European energy storage market developments and regulations which motivate the increased use of stationary energy storage systems are of importance for a successful renewable energy integration. Decentralized power storage systems, for example, can contribute to increasing local self-consumption and thus to relieving the pressure on distribution networks, as decentralized systems become more widespread [64].

With focus on the power sector and technical feasibilty within the transmission grids [65,66] also modeled the German energy system including demands for the transportation, heating and industry sectors. Different from other approaches, they chose to model in different steps which allowed them not only to have a simple cost optimization but also include some market and grid simulations. In both papers they conclude, that with a sufficient electrification of the non-power sectors an energy system largely decarbonized is feasible and that power to gas will pose as a main driver [65]. Furthermore, Müller et al. [65] also looked at cross-border power trade and conclude, that Germany will become a net importer on at the norther borders and a net exporter on all borders, making Germany a net exporterin 2050.

Regarding the electrification of the mobility sector, and the possible effects on the German power sector and grids, some studies have been published in recent years. Hanemann et al. [67] found out that vehicle-to-grid (V2G) charging mechanisms would be supportive for the stability of German power grids, would help to decrease electricity costs from renewables by increasing rates of utility and that a high CO_2-price would support the two aforementioned points. Furthermore, transnational powertrade could be reduced and the electrification of the transportation sector could go in hand with the decarbonization of the power sector [67]. More general, Schill and Gerbaulet [68] point out that not scarcity of energy should be of the policymakers' concerns but demand peaks. This means that a user-driven charging scheme will endanger the grid stability and support coal fired power plants, as they are used as a back up reserve. Further, price-driven or market-driven charging schemes will only work if an adequate CO_2-price is deployed. Just like V2G, a controlled charging would increase grid stabilities and support higher rates of utilisation of renewables thus, decrease the overall costs for electricity. In contrast to that, Loisel et al. [69], who examined different grid-to-vehicle and V2G-schemes, point out, that, as of today, battery technology is not mature enough to support such schemes and that in current pricing regimes of the power and mobility sector, electricity simply is worthier in the latter. Hence, a full integration of both sectors, as projected is still a far- away goal.

Considering the issue of imports and exports, the role of individual countries plays a decisive role.A breakdown for European countries is provided by Child et al. [51] who use the LUT Energy System Transition model also used by Ram et al. [48]. They come to the conclusion: power trade within Europe is increasing massively from 63 GW to 262 GW. They calculate thatthe United Kingdom, Ireland, Norway, Denmark, and the Baltic states will be exporters of electricity, while Germany will import 1% of its requirements.By 2050, they estimate up to 147 TWh of storage capacity will be built in Germany to compensate for grid fluctuations. Similar considerations are also carried out with the heating sector in connection with the electricity sector. Thus, Bloess [70] in her investigation of possible electrification mechanisms of space heating has determined that, similar to the mobility sector, flexibility options arise. Flexibilities in turn help the market penetration of renewables. On the other hand, there is great pressure on the electricity sector, with an additional demand for about 200 TWh of electricity by 2030 [70].

The high number of studies focusing on different sectors and regions and their interactions in the next decades presents how important this field of research is. Nevertheless, only a few studies try to have a holistic look and to model an energy system as a whole. One of the most recent studies that did that is published by Hansen et al. [59]. They conclude that even full decarbonization is possible by 2050 utilizing only domestic energy sources. This is achievable by strong sector coupling but at high costs of more than EUR 400 billion per year. Interestingly, decarbonizing the transport sector would make up 55–65% of the total costs. Touching on overall costs of the energy transformation, it becomes apparent that any non-implementation of measures would lead to even higher expenses in the long run. According to Stern [5], not acting would intensify climate change and lead to severe consequences for human life on this planet such as access to water, food production, health, and the environment. In sum, the costs and risks for not acting will be equivalent to losing at least 5% of global Gross Domestic Product (GDP) per year, respectively 20% if a wider range of risks is taken into account. However, reducing GHG emissions, in contrast, would limit the cost burden substantially to 1% [5].

Although a large number of different studies examine the German energy system and its future developments, a quantitative approach at the federal level is not yet comprehensively covered. In particular, data on the heating sector accurate to the federal state, as well as a desirable high level of detail for the location potentials of renewable energies are capable of extension and improvement is missing in these studies.

1.4. Research Question

This work aims to give further insight into the development of the German energy system by computing the sectors of power, heat, and transportation endogenously and coupled. The developed scenarios, which are described in the next chapter, shall stretch out a space of possible pathways. Results shall represent the techno-economical optimum and provide information on future technology mixes and pathways towards a 100% renewable energy system. Furthermore, this work intends to offer new insights to policymakers and the modeling community by contributing to existing literature gaps.

2. Methodology

2.1. Description of the Model

The next paragraphs provide some insights into the applied model. However, a detailed description of the mathematical formulation is not provided; at relevant passages, a reference to the respective literature is given.

2.1.1. Summary of GENeSYS-MOD

This study uses the Global Energy System Model (GENeSYS-MOD) v2.0 described by Löffler et al. [14] and Burandt et al. [15]. It is an open-source tool for the modeling of energy systems based on the Open Source Energy Modelling System (OSeMOSYS) by Howells et al. [71]. The model uses a system of linear equations to minimize total system costs while meeting energy demands and respecting externally defined constraints (see Appendix B for a more detailed description of the model structure and workings). GENeSYS-MOD allows to model multiple regions, time periods, and sectors.

Therefore, it enables to show the development of an energy system, encompassing the sectors power, heat, and transport for Germany on a federal level until 2050.

2.1.2. Basic Structure of the Model

Essentially, GENeSYS-MOD can be defined as a flow-based optimization model. Its structure is made up of a network of nodes which are connected with each other, as illustrated in Figure 1. The nodes, called technologies, represent all entities producing, using, or transforming energy, for instance, power plants, vehicles, storages, and heat pumps. The different technologies are connected by fuels, which represent all energy carriers, electricity or fossil fuels, or their proxies, such as transport.

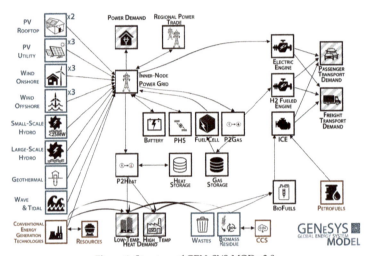

Figure 1. Structure of GENeSYS-MOD v2.0.

Energy demands are endogenously defined for every year and region and can be classified into heating, electricity, and transportation. Using a mixture of technologies and trade between different regions, GENeSYS-MOD aims to meet the given demands. The model seeks the minimization of total system costs, which are defined as the discounted costs of all regions over the model period. This includes investment costs, operating costs of technologies, trading costs of fuels, expansion costs of trade capacities, and penalties for the emission of CO_2. This objective is restricted by several constraints, which aim to depict real-life restrictions of an energy system, including maximum capacities and operational life spans. Furthermore, phase-out plans of several fossil fuels, as well as emission limits, are included under the given scenario.

For a more elaborate description of GENeSYS-MOD see the Appendix B, as well as Löffler et al. [14] and Burandt et al. [15].

2.1.3. Node Split

To analyze the development of the German energy system on a regional level, Germany was divided into a network of 16 nodes, each representing one federal state. Every node has its own energy demand, renewable potential, and existing capacities. Furthermore, there exist power transmission capacity limits between these notes according to the existing power transmission grid. In addition to the 16 nodes in Germany, neighbouring countries that are connected to Germany via a transition line are also represented by 9 nodes, to model the interlinking between Germany and its surrounding countries (following Hainsch et al. [49]). These nodes represent Denmark, Poland, the Czech Republic, Austria, Switzerland, France, and the Netherlands. Belgium and Luxembourg are gathered into one node—the BeLux node. The Scandinavian node combines Sweden, Norway, and Finland. Even though most constraints apply for each node individually, there are some constraints that apply to Germany as a whole. for example the emission targets are defined on national level not on state level.

2.2. Elaboration of the Scenarios

In the following paragraphs, three different scenarios for the energy system of Germany until the year 2050 are developed—namely European Island (EI), Green Democracy (GD), and Survival of the Fittest (SOTF). Each scenario draws up a different storyline regarding the global, European, and German trends in climate politics and the economy. The storylines were developed in a workshop with experts from governmental consultants, researchers and the business world, based on Europe's NDCs. Detailed information about the definition and elaboration of the narratives can also be found in [13]. Each scenario gives certain implications on the German energy system and thus, for the model. Developments for the global fuel prices, a price for CO_2—emissions, phase-out dates for certain technologies, and different energy demands in the sectors are derived from the storylines and implemented into the model. Relevant input data can be found in Appendix C.

It is important to say, that the narratives were designed on a global scale without specific implications for regions or nations. The derived scenarios then were designed after the model's aim and features were recognized. Therefore, forecasts or predictions of subjects that are not directly entangled with the model are not included. In this way, assumptions regarding the economic development and job markets are left untouched as well as possible policy measures that could not be integrated into the model's structure. Nevertheless, a brief examination of the stakeholders in politics, industry, and society was carried out to validate the legitimacy of the scenarios' assumptions (see Appendix A). Further, the aforementioned points are mapped via the different developments of energy demands in the various sectors. In light of these aspects, a comparison with European reference scenarios is generally difficult. Nevertheless, all scenarios are based on data and forecasts available and usually published by the countries' ministries or statistic authorities. Therefore, the baseline of this model is consistent in some aspects with, for example, the Reference Scenario of 2016 by the European Commission (*EC Ref16*) [54] or the EUCO scenarios (*EUCO323232.5*, *EUCO30*, and *EUCO27*) [72–74]: The efficiency gains in the individual scenarios are fairly consistent with the EUCO scenarios, with EI roughly correlating with *EUCO30* and GD with *EUCO323232.5*. Commodity prices here are based on world market prices and therefore differ somewhat from *EC Ref16*, especially in the gas sector, which has implications on resource prices paid in Europe. Technology costs and costs developments are largely identical to *EC Ref2016* (and not further modulated between scenarios). The assumptions on the development of the CO_2 price in the *EC Ref2016* scenario are fairly identical to the EI scenario, with neither scenario reflecting recent developments. However, the Weighted Average Cost of Capital (WACC) in our scenarios is assumed to be 5% compared to 7.5% in *EC Ref2016* [54]. In general, this study shows an increased sector coupling compared to the European average, with an accompanying increase in electricity consumption. Since SOTF and GD are not alternations of the baseline scenario but explorations of alternatives or extremes, commonalities to the European reference scenarios are fewer.

2.2.1. European Island Scenario

The EI scenario serves as the baseline scenario of this paper and is characterized by a strong European alliance, while global conflicts continue. Due to a strengthening of European institutions and greater influence of green parties, mutual politics focus on previously set climate goals. Countries within the EU are committed to enabling the EU to push for the fulfillment of the lower bounds of their climate goals, which is in the German case, an emission reduction of 40% in 2030, and 80% in 2050 compared to 1990. To realize these goals, phase-out dates for fossil fuels are set. The planned nuclear phase-out is enforced and carried out in 2022. Besides, the phase-out of hard coal and lignite for power production is set to 2035, and fossil gas and oil for power production to 2045. The heating sector and the transport sector continue to use fossil fuels. However, in terms of decarbonization, it is hoped for a spillover effect (E.g.: The heating sector is retrieving energy from a decarbonized power sector. Hence, the decarbonization in this sector is advancing, even without changing technology mix.) with increasing sector coupling.

As part of the mutual climate politics, an EU-wide CO_2 price is set (see Table 1) which rises rather slowly until 2035 but increases momentum afterward, until it reaches 85 € per t CO_2 in 2050 (With an increase of 1.50 € per year, a ton of CO_2 would cost 12.50 € in 2019. However, the European Energy Exchange (EEX) lists European Emission Allowances varying between 18–26 € per t CO_2 in 2019. www.eex.com/en/market-data/environmental-markets/spot-market/european-emission-allowances#! Last accessed: 25 May 2019). World market prices for fossil fuels hard coal, oil, and fossil gas are influenced by two opposing trends: Due to increasing worldwide demand, decreasing availability, and political instability outside the EU, prices for fossil fuels increase. However, a decrease in demand in the EU and the effect of governmentally set phase-outs reduces the price increases slightly (see Table A2). These assumptions are based on the "450 ppm scenario" from the World Energy Outlook 2016 [75] and are adapted to the following scenarios as well.

Table 1. Overview of policy measures implemented in the model for the three different scenarios.

	European Island [EI]	Green Democracy [GD]	Survival of the Fittest [SOTF]
linear increase of the CO_2 tax from €5 per t in 2015	to €35 in 2030 and to €85 in 2050	to €130 in 2050	to €15 in 2035 to €50 in 2050
limit the CO_2 emissions compared to 1990 by	40% in 2030 80% in 2050	55% in 2030 95% in 2050	no limit
phase-out in the electricity sector	Lignite in 2035 hard coal in 2035 gas/oil in 2045	Lignite in 2025 hard coal in 2030 gas/oil in 2035	no phase-outs

2.2.2. Green Democracy Scenario

Characterized by a reduction of international tensions, increased communication between stakeholders, and a holistic approach, the GD scenario visualizes the effects of fast action towards a sustainable energy system.

Within this scenario, the public opinion plays a vital role, as they put pressure on policymakers to advance climate protection, comparable to what the "Fridays for Future" movement achieves currently. Therefore, Germany sets itself a CO_2 reduction goal based on the NDCs. With 55% (2030) and 95% (2050), less CO_2 emissions compared to 1990 levels, Germany focuses on the more ambitious targets. This includes the sector-specific goals of an emission reduction by 2030 in the transport sector by 40% and in the space heating sector by 67%, both compared to 1990 [22].

Derived from those developments, Germany carries out its nuclear phase-out until 2022. In comparison to the EI scenario, fossil fuels phase-out are earlier due to prior interventions and increasingly cost-effective renewable energies. The phase-out of fossil fuels for power generation is set in 2025 for lignite, in 2030 for hard coal, and in 2035 for fossil gas and oil.

The growing efforts for climate protection, and therefore, a related decrease in demand for fossil fuels leads to a slightly falling price for conventional energy sources (likewise to EI). At the same time, the CO_2 price increases from €5 in 2015 to €130 in 2050 in a linear manner. This increase is due to the strong focus on climate action, which includes that all sectors are covered with emission prices. Especially in previously excluded sectors, effects will become noticeable, such as the transportation sector. Due to increasing urbanization and population, metropolitan areas will drastically change, which makes a holistic planning process for sustainable energy supply and infrastructure necessary.

2.2.3. Survival of the Fittest

In the SOTF scenario, the world is presented as one that has regressed from current climate policies to go back towards a more protectionist and nationalist environment. The scenario does not represent a world that is in complete refusal of climate problems, but rather one that prioritizes other issues, like national conflicts, conservative movements, and breakdowns of partnerships, until the effects of abrupt climate change are immediate and drastic.

Until 2035, the main driver is the need for energy security and independence, while the NDCs are mostly ignored. Interruptions in global trade as a result of protectionism lead to high prices for fossil fuels as well as imported technologies. Governments may choose to use renewables to gain energy independence but have no preference over conventional energy carriers.

In Germany, this scenario is marked by increasingly high prices for gas and other fossil fuel imports (see Table A2), as well as a slower rate of technological innovation. Consequently, already existing resources and infrastructures is used more than in the other scenarios, including reviving Germany's lignite reserves. Government-based emission initiatives are non-existent in the first half of the modeled period, while the carbon price is kept low at only €5 per t CO_2 in 2015, increasing to €15 per t CO_2 by 2035. (This increase is smaller than the actual increase of the CO_2 price from 2015 to 2019 reaching €25 per t CO_2).

From 2035 on, when the negative effects of climate change are even more visible, the focus starts to shift towards climate policy to mitigate further damages. From then on, the carbon price is increased linearly up to €50 per t CO_2 in 2050. Renewables are supported, leading to falling prices, however, no phase-outs for fossil fuels are set. This can be traced back to a growing focus on more acute global conflicts. Hence, the development of the energy system and eventual fossil fuel phase-outs are fully market-driven, given the cost assumptions.

3. Results

In the following chapter, the model results of the scenarios are discussed. In doing so, respective figures specifying the power, heat, and transport sector are presented and elaborated on. The graphs are resolved in five-year time steps and show the trend of the investigated sector in the period from 2015 to 2050, in accordance with the model calculations.

3.1. Final Energy

As Figure 2 illustrates, Germany's final energy consumption decreases along the scenarios' development paths by 2050. The decrease in final energy demand is due to decreasing demands in the different sectors: better insulation of the housing structure (see Figure 6), market penetration of electric vehicles, more efficient electric applications and a slow reshaping of the industry landscape (see Figure 7) have a significant impact on the amount of energy needed. On the other hand the electrification of different sectors plays a key role, which is reflected in increasing electricity production (see Figure 3). The paths displayed have significant points and trends for the various scenarios that represent the cornerstones of the transformation of the energy system. All scenarios are affected by the phase-out of nuclear power production set for each scenario. However, the gradual trend towards the decommissioning of coal-fired and fossil-fired energy generation and its use in different sectors is reflected in individual phase-out dates for the scenarios. Common in all scenarios is the nearly constant use of biomass and hydropower until 2050, as its potential is almost at its maximum at the beginning of the model period. A more detailed overview of the sector transformations is presented in the following model results.

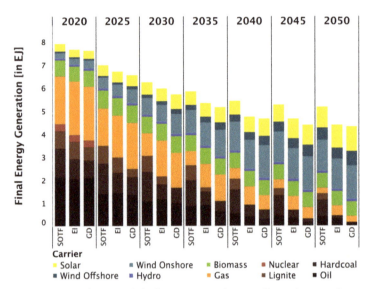

Figure 2. Development of Germany's final energy generation according to the respective scenario.

Survival of the Fittest The SOTF scenario has the most carbon-intensive transformation path and, at 5180 PJ, has the comparatively highest final energy demand in 2050, which is attributed to assumed low efficiency gains. Also, in this scenario, there are hardly any policy-driven restrictions such as phase-outs, so that model decisions, in this case, are primarily price-driven. Although the consumption of lignite (−70%), oil (−85%), and gas (−88%) are significantly reduced by 2050 compared to 2015, the use of hard coal decreases only slightly (−34%). The primary purpose of hard coal in the energy system of 2050 is to provide industrial high-temperature heat. Even though there is no phase-out date set for hard coal, it does no longer play a role in the electricity sector from 2040 on (see Figure 3). Compared to the other scenarios, renewable technologies are the last and least to expand in this scenario. Until 2050, the production of solar energy increases by 724 PJ (+370%) and wind energy by 1663 PJ (+780%).

European Island The EI scenario, as a reference case, accounts for only about half of final energy consumption in 2050, with 4388 PJ, compared to the base year 2015. Lignite is being phased-out in 2035. From 2035, hard coal no longer plays a role in the electricity sector, but is then only used for the medium- and high-temperature industrial heat generation, with decreasing volumes. The consumption of hard coal is reduced by 717 PJ (−87%) by the end of 2050. Oil as an energy carrier is drastically reduced by 2365 PJ (−86%) until 2050, in particular in the transport sector and residential low-temperature heat generation. However, it is still used for transportation to a limited extent in 2050. The use of gas (particularly fossil gas) also falls by 1962 PJ (−82%). Accordingly, the consumption of fossil gas in the industrial sector is steadily decreasing, but is being replaced to a low extent by synthetic gas. On the renewable technology side, the expansion of wind power generation is the most important. Power production from offshore wind will increase by 453 PJ (+1562%), for onshore wind even by 1120 PJ (+602%) until 2050. Solar energy generation is used for power generation through open field PV and rooftop PV systems. Furthermore, solar thermal systems are applied in residential low-temperature heat generation. With an increase of 797 PJ (+387%), solar energy likewise plays a major role in the renewable transformation path.

Green Democracy The GD scenario, which reflects the most ambitious transformation path, shows a reduction of the final energy demand by 48% (4317 PJ). The reduction rates of conventional technologies, over the entire model period, are only slightly lower than in the reference scenario (EI). However, due to strict guidelines regarding the reduction path, these reductions are achieved earlier, which goes hand in hand with the expansion of renewable technologies. As early as 2030, lignite is completely substituted by renewable sources and coal technologies are no longer used for power production (see Figure 3). By 2050, hard coal, which previously played an important role in high-temperature industrial heating, is phased out in this sector. Even stronger than in the other scenarios, oil experiences a significant drop of 2634 PJ (−96%), primarily through reductions in the transport sector. Further, it loses its role in the area of low-temperature heat generation in 2030 and from then on is only used in the transport sector. Concerning gas, it is noticeable that the utilization of fossil gas in the individual sectors is strongly declining while small quantities are substituted by the use of synthetic gas. In total, however, gas consumption declines by 2166 PJ (−89%) by 2050.

On the contrary, the technologies of wind power and solar energy have significantly higher growth rates. Led by onshore wind power with growth of 1292 PJ (+783%), and followed by solar power 860 PJ (+395%) and offshore wind power 591 PJ (+1555%), the renewable expansion in total lies slightly higher than in the other scenarios considered.

3.2. Power Sector

In all three scenarios, the energy system of Germany experiences a strong coupling of the power sector with the heat and transportation sector. This can be observed in the increasing generation of power see Figure 3. Among the scenarios, there are some variations in the power sector which are depicted more detailed in the following paragraphs. Again, biomass and hydropower contribute to the system in all scenarios but stay rather constant in generation due to almost exhausted hydro potentials in Germany and no added capacity for biomass in the power sector.

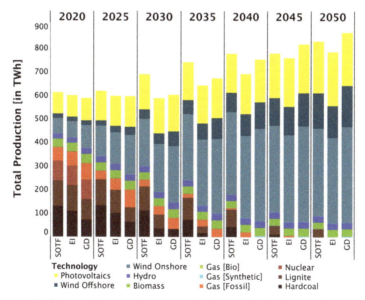

Figure 3. Development of Germany's power production according to the respective scenario.

When looking at electricity exports and imports of the federal states, it is noticeable that not only the electricity transported across federal state borders increases per year but also the inter-temporal fluctuations of the values between individual time slices. The model has two options available for absorbing strong volatilities in electricity production with high shares of variable renewable energy sources and for keeping the electricity grid stable even in dark lull periods. On the one hand, the model is allowed to expand the power grid to a certain percentage. To count in local resistance and lengthy approval procedures, the grid expansion was limited to 20% existing capacity per 5-year period. The second option is the use of intermediate storage facilities. Since the potential of pumped storage power plants in Germany is low and completely exhausted early on, lithium-ion battery storage systems are being introduced into the power grid. Depending on the scenario, large quantities of electricity will be temporarily stored in 2050. In GD this is 50.7 TWh in 2050, in EI 30 TWh, and in SOTF 20 TWh. Power-to-Gas technologies are another measure, as discussed in more detail in Section 3.3.

Survival of the Fittest The transformation of the power sector is slower than in the other two scenarios. The generation from hard coal and lignite stays rather constant in the first ten years. Nevertheless, in 2025 more than 50% of the electricity generation comes from renewable sources. The total electricity demand of SOTF is the highest among the three scenarios, due to fewer incentives to save energy, mainly in the heating sector, but also in general. Therefore, the added capacity of renewables in SOTF and EI is comparable. Overall, the generation by conventional sources declines. Lignite stays the prevalent conventional source, due to the comparably lower costs to hard coal, and fossil gas. In 2050 hard coal is phased out due to rising global prices for coal. In 2050, the electricity generation is 95% renewable even in this scenario without CO_2—targets, due to cost advantages.

European Island The development in the first 20 years is characterized by the phase-out of one energy carrier each timestep of five years: nuclear in 2025, hard coal in 2030, lignite in 2035, and fossil gas in 2040. The renewable sources wind and PV replace this conventional power generation. Already in 2035, the energy system in EI is 95% supplied with electricity from renewable sources; only fossil gas remains as a conventional source. From 2030 onwards, the total power generation increases by around 10 TWh each year, due to the increasing sector coupling, resulting in a generation of 875 TWh in 2050. In 2050 for Germany the generation from wind turbines is twice as high as the generation from PV.

Green Democracy Until 2025, the nuclear phase-out and the reduction of power generation from hard coal and lignite by 50% is replaced by power generation via wind and sun. Therefore, additional capacities of 85 GW are installed. The abandonment of lignite for electricity production is connected with a decrease in hard coal or fossil gas generation, with a reduction of fossil gas and hard coal of nearly 50% by 2030. In 2035 hard coal is phased out without resulting in a temporary increase of fossil gas. Instead, the more volatile electricity generation from wind turbines and PV is balanced via power trade, hydropower, and battery storage. In 2040, the electricity generation in Germany is 100% renewable and decarbonized. Electricity production via wind turbines contributes two thirds to the generation, PV a quarter. Synthetic gas is mainly used in the industry heavy region of North Rhine-Westphalia. After 2040, only onshore wind turbines and PV utilities are built, increasing the power production by additional 100 TWh. The expansion of renewable energy sources adds up to 180 GW onshore wind, 39 GW offshore wind, and 99 GW capacity connected to the grid in 2050. In the same time, the demand for electricity in the heat and transport sector increases by 130 TWh. In general, since low-carbon electricity generation technologies are available at low costs, the electricity sector is the first to be decarbonized.

Figure 4 shows the regional breakdown of the power production for 2020, 2030, and 2050. It can be seen, that, over the years, each federal state will have increased power production. However, the change in the coastal states might be the biggest: Yielding the potential from offshore windpower, Lower Saxony, Schleswig Holstein, and Mecklenburg-Vorpommern will become net exporters of energy. Especially the exchange of power between Lower Saxony and North Rhine-Westphalia is very important, as North Rhine-Westphalia is depending on large amounts of electricity produced by wind turbines from the north. Furthermore, in 2030, North Rhine-Westphalia will be one of the last states with significant shares of conventionally produced power. Another state with conventional generation is the city-state of Bremen, which is close to the global coal markets with its harbor. Furthermore, states like Hesse, Thuringia, and Saxony-Anhalt, which have low production rates in 2015 will increase their production by the factor three or higher. This change in production rates is a consequence of the different technologies used for electricity generation. In 2015 with a high share of fossil generation, the power plants are located near demand centers or mining areas. Contrary, in 2050, with mainly electricity generation from wind and PV, the place of the generation is determined by renewable potentials and available space. Consequently, city states like Berlin or Hamburg, Hamburg or Bremen will be more dependent on importing electricity from neighboring states, as they will shut down own production capacities (The 2019-elected local government of Bremen note in their coalition agreement of July to phase out of coal already in 2023. This would affect three powerplants in Bremen [76].). These developments go along with an increase in electricity transmission and storage.

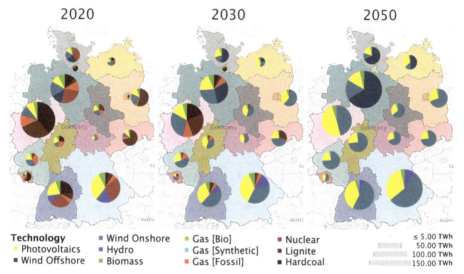

Figure 4. Regional development of Germany's power production for the Green Democracy scenario.

3.3. Sector Coupling

With increasing decarbonization of the sectors of heat and transportation, they also demand more electricity. As Figure 5 demonstrates, in 2015, the power demand from sector-coupling is well below 100 TWh per year, consisting mainly of demand in the industry sector. Over the next 15 years, the power use in sector coupling increases due to the electrification of space heating in the residential area and to a smaller extent by the market penetration of Battery Electric Vehicles (BEVs) and an increase of electric trains. By 2030, SOTF has the highest amount of electricity used in other sectors, due to less energy efficient buildings and overall energy savings. This electrification is also linked to an increase in fossil fuel prices on the world market. However, in 2050, the lead of SOTF is overtaken by EI and GD, where stricter mitigation goals have to be achieved. While the power demand in residential applications stays rather constant over the latter 20 years, the industry sector becomes decarbonized to a high extent, with a five fold power demand in the GD scenario. Passenger transport is already relying on electricity in the 2030s, with an increasing power demand until 2050. Freight transport has the same, but delayed development. At the end of the modeled period, hydrogen produced by electrolysis plays a significant role. The produced hydrogen is either used directly in the transportation sector or reformed into synthetic gas. In the GD scenario, hydrogen and synthetic gas are used primarily in low-temperature heating. Furthermore, small parts of high temperature heat are generated by synthetic gas in the EI and GD scenarios. In general, the energy that is transferred from the power sector to the transport and heating sector exceeds the 50%-mark of total power production in 2045 in GD, in 2050 in EI and reaches 46.3% in the SOTF scenario at the end of the model period.

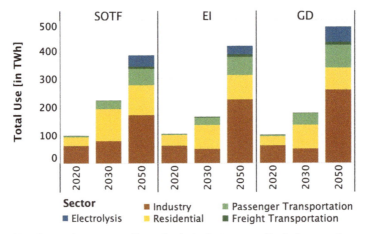

Figure 5. Use of power for sector coupling technologies by type according to the respective scenario.

3.4. Heat Production

The model results concerning heat production are displayed using the GD scenario as it provides the most drastic changes. The heating sector is divided into residential heating (warm water and space heating) and industrial heating, which is broken up into demands for low temperature heat (process heating and space heating below 100 °C), medium temperature heat, and high temperature heat (above 1000 °C).

Residential heat demand The demand for residential space heat, warm water, and energy for food preparation is with 750 TWh higher than the total heat demand in the industrial sector. However, due to the expected improved insulation of the German building structure, the demand will decrease until the end of the model period by one third, as Figure 6 shows. In 2015, the vast majority of demand is met using oil and fossil gas. Only small fractions are supplied by heat pumps or biomass. Until 2030, oil will be phased out, while the share of fossil gas stays rather constant. Air-based heat pumps are constantly gaining in importance but will soon reach their potential limit. Ground-based heat pumps will have their first appearance in 2030, but will also not reach higher market penetration rates. Close to the end of the model period, solar thermal technologies will also be helpful to decrease the share of fossil gas in this sector. However, solar thermal has to compete against PV modules on a limited space on roofs, which makes them interesting solutions only in regions, where electricity is rather abundant. To decarbonize this sector further in 2050, with decreasing costs for electrolysis and methanization, synthetic gas might also be a possible substitute for fossil gas.

Industrial heat demand In 2015, the total demand for industry heat was about 570 TWh per year, of which, low and medium temperature heat demand was at 220 TWh each. This number declines to 370 TWh per year in 2050, supported by efficiency gains from the use of power to heat technologies, as Figure 7 presents. In the first years, a slight overproduction of low temperature heat is measurable as the model can produce heat as a byproduct of the power generation of industrial power plants. Overcapacities will soon be eliminated as the expensive oil firing and emission-heavy lignite firing heating applications are dismantled. Interestingly, the share of the more expensive fossil gas is decreasing earlier than hard coal. This is partly due to the fact that hard coal is extensively used in high temperature applications (e.g., blast furnaces for steel melting), where alternatives are rather expensive and thus, decarbonization is more difficult. In the low and medium temperature range, biomass poses as a good substitute to conventional energy carriers, but availability is limited and this sector is in competition with the other sectors as well. From 2030 on, solar thermal modules are installed on roofs, but also here, the heating sector is in direct competition with the power sector due to limited roof space. In the medium temperature range, direct electric applications become very important in the second half of the model period. In the high temperature range, molten (steel/aluminium) electrolysis substitutes the remaining coal fractions in the later years. Synthetic gas is only used in small shares, mostly in low temperature heat applications.

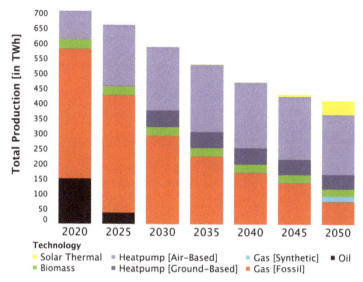

Figure 6. Development of residential low temperature heat production by carrier for the Green Democracy scenario.

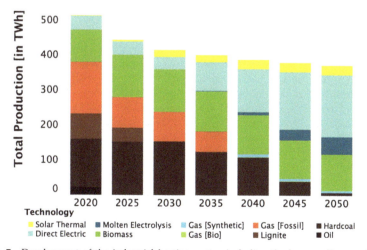

Figure 7. Development of the industrial heating sector, including the low, medium, and high temperature heat range for GD.

Energies **2019**, *12*, 2988

3.5. Transportation

The transportation sector is split up in passenger and freight transport, each of which has three different modal types: Road, rail, and air for passenger or ship for freight transport. To present the results, only the GD scenario is depicted. However, the other two scenarios have resembling results. For a visualization of the result refer to the Appendix D Figures A2 and A3.

Freight Transport The total volume of tons of freight transported in Germany will be steadily increasing by 50% until 2050. To cope with the rising traffic, an increasing share of freight will be transported via train. However, the preferred fuel for rail transport will be petrofuels until the '30s. After that, the share of electrified rail transport will increase sharply in relative as well as in total numbers. In 2050, 32% of freight kilometers are by rail with electric trains, only 3.5% by conventional trains. The road-based freight transport is also growing in total numbers in the first half of the model period. Internal combustion engines are the predominant technology used. Only in some years, petrofuels are being utilized. Beginning in 2030, a network of streets with overhead power supply is being set up. This rather expensive way to decarbonize the freight transport becomes an important factor in 2040 with increasing shares of up to 30% in 2050. Heavy-duty freight vehicles with only batteries will not penetrate the market extensively but have a small but constant share. Internal combustion engines and petrofuels will be dominant over the whole model period.

Passenger Transport Unlike freight transport, passenger transport will have a stagnating volume over the years, with an increasing share of traffic handled by rail. In absolute numbers, the volume of passenger kilometers handled by rail increases from 87.2 billion person-kilometers (GPkm) per year to 291.5 GPkm. Road based traffic will be handled mainly by BEVs. The market penetration will increase from 15% in 2025 to 62% in 2050. Plug-In Hybrid Electric Vehicles (PHEVs) will stay in a niche with a share of only 0.11 % until 2040. Even after that, this technology is only used as an intermediate solution or bridging technology. Biofuels are not an alternative in the long term but being used in the years 2020 and 2050, as an intermediate solution to achieve the reduction targets.

3.6. Emissions

Figure 8 compares the various developments in annual emissions and total CO_2 emissions and puts them into relation with carbon budgets. The left *y*-axis and the clomumns represent the annual CO_2 emissions. Here, the main differences in the scenarios are visible: GD shows a drastic decline in annual emissions on account of drastic policy measures, namely the phase out of coal in the power sector early on. Together with a quick electrification of the other sectors and steeply increasing costs of CO_2, the emissions can be more than halved in between 2020 and 2035. These measures also lead to very high rates of emission reduction in 2050, even though a net zero, as German chancellor Angela Merkel announced in May 2019, to be an objective for 2050 is not feasible under the model's and scenario's assumptions (www.tagesschau.de/inland/merkel-klima-111.html Last accessed: 25 June 2019). EI follows the same pattern, however, less strict reduction targets and policy measures, as well as later coal phase outs will result in higher annual emissions for the entire modeling period. This throws a rather negative picture on the current climate efforts of the Federal Government, considering that this scenario is largely in line with the decisions of the Coal Commission, as far as the phase out of coal from the electricity sector is concerned (see also Section 1.2). SOTF resembles future developments of annual emission when all mitigation action is mainly driven by the market powers of resource prices, demands and technology development and costs. As Figure 8 clearly shows, the emission reduction is not sufficient enough and is more than twice as high as the emission from EI. Unlike both other scenarios the pathway is not characterized by a period of high reduction rates, instead it constantly declines by decreasing demand and assumed increasing fuel costs.

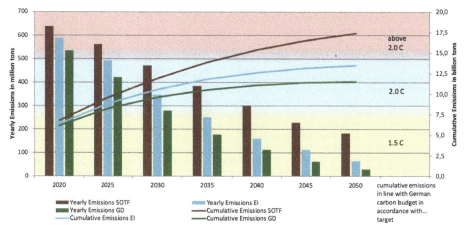

Figure 8. Development of yearly and cumulative CO$_2$ emissions per scenario. CO$_2$ emissions from material conversions in industry processes, meat production, and land use, land use change and forestry (LULUCF) land use, land use change and forestry (LULUCF) are not taken into account. The green area marks being calculated in the model and thus excluded from the German carbon budget for 1.5 °C if the global carbon budget was shared according to the countries' population. The blue marks the same share for the 2.0 °C target, the red area marks the the remaining German carbon budget for 1.5 °C target if it was shared according to the countries' GDP. Calculations is L based on 2015. The global carbon budget according to Rogelj et al. [1] was taken and counted back to 2015. Share the share of Germany's population in the world in 2015: 1.12%.

The right y-axis of Figure 8 represents the over the model period accumulated emissions of all three scenarios in comparison to certain carbon budgets. The global carbon budget according to climateactiontracker.org (climateactiontracker.org is a cumulative project by the NGOs Climate Analysis, NewClimate Institute, Ecofys and the Potsdam Institute for Climate Impact Research and is funded by the ClimateWorks Foundateion and the German BMU via the International Climate Initiative.) was taken, split up by the German share of the global population and calculated for 2015. All carbon budgets are calculated until the year 2100, while this study's time horizon ends in 2050. Especially the SOTF and EI scenarios, therefore, have to undergoo further decarbonization action after 2050 to stay within budget limits. Most strikingly, this figure shows, that not even GD will stay within the Paris Agreement's target to limit the global warming below 2 °C and aiming at 1.5 °C (see also Section 1 and 1.1. Nevertheless, by comparing the development of the three scenarios' cumulative emissions, one can see that early, drastic measures are helping a lot to decrease overall emissions: The final cumulative emissions will differ by 33% between GD and SOTF.

3.7. Model Limitation and Further Research

The model was set up using available data for technology costs and potentials as well as demands for power, heat, as well as personal and freight transport. The model was calibrated with data for the base year of 2015. Installed power plant capacity, as well as demands for power and heat, kilometers travelled, and freight moved can be found in different governmental statistics agencies.

However, GENeSYS-MOD lacks some features macro-economical models might provide, thus exogeneously defined demand projections had to be included. This also includes assumptions concerning efficiency gains and progress of technological progress. This forces the model into a corridor of boundaries which are set up under somewhat different assumptions than the scenarios' narratives. Nevertheless, under- or overestimations of technologies and their impact on developments are inevitable. Hence, the approach to use three different story lines is an attempt to mitigate this bias.

Another characterization of the model is its linearity: As soon as one technology is marginally cheaper than an alternative, the model will choose this one until there is a constraint. This usually leads to jumps in the utilization of technologies and drastic technology swaps. To circumvent this, smoothing factors where included, which, on the one hand pose as restrictions on the model's freedom, while on the other hand also pose as a tool to calibrate the model to fit into realistic predictions.

Furthermore, GENeSYS-MOD uses relatively large time steps of five years with 16 annual time slices. Each year is separated into four seasons and four time slices of different length, each to represent a typical demand curve over the day (night, morning, midday, afternoon) of each season (for the length of each time-slice refer to Burandt et al. [15]). Compared to load curves in energy economics with a resolution of 15 min time steps, the possible loss of information seems quite high. Still, the deviation is small, as [77] found out comparing an enhanced OSeMOSYS implementation with 16 time slices to a full hourly dispatch model. Nevertheless, a more granular model would be optimal and might be subject to further research.

The lack of integration and calculation of other GHG emissions apart from CO_2 is another limiting point of the model and its results. Primarily methane, although it has a shorter residence time in the atmosphere, has a strong GHG effect and is therefore not irrelevant for Germany's climate balance. The same also applies to the conversion of substances in industry, which sometimes emit large quantities. All of this is not further illustrated in this model, but represent about 10 to 20 percent of total German emissions [78]. An integration of emissions outside of the energy market and emissions of other GHG are also subject to further research.

4. Conclusions

This study analyzes three possible scenarios for the German energy transformation in the light of climate change and global resource scarcity. The scenarios, namely European Island (EI), Green Democracy (GD), and Survival of the Fittest (SOTF), outline possible pathways in the period between 2015 and 2050, including different phase-out policies, carbon- and resource price developments, and efficiency improvements. Therefore, the sector coupling model Global Energy System Model was applied. Irrespective of a scenario-specific consideration, the expansion of wind energy and PV play a major role in the cost-optimized development of the German energy system, especially in the electricity sector (see Section 3.2). The expansion of renewable energies for power generation is a key element on the development path to combine low costs with low emissions. A discernible trend towards increasing electricity demand corresponds to the gradual electrification of the individual sectors and the utilization of electrolysis to provide hydrogen and methane as alternative fuels (see Section 3.3). Nuclear energy thereby is neither required in the long term nor as a bridging technology. The use of power-operated heatpumps plays an important role in the provision of residential space heating and is gradually replacing fossil fuels such as oil and fossil gas. In the industrial sector, emission reductions in high-temperature heat generation exclusively require electrification, whereas for medium- and especially low-industrial heat generation, biomass can be a vital part of possible decarbonization pathways (see Section 3.4). In the transport sector, battery-powered passenger vehicles and electric overhead freight trucks are gradually replacing conventional combustion engines. The transport sector electrification is also reflected in the expansion of electric rail transport (see Section 3.5).

In EI and GD, the model calculated the cost optimal energy system given the desired emission reduction pathway based on Germany's climate protection targets [22]. As a result of the ambitious restrictions of the GD scenario already in the 2020's, the associated early emission reductions demonstrate that the time is a decisive determinant for achieving the lowest possible cumulative emissions. However, in the SOTF scenario, neither emissions constraints nor fossil phase-outs were applied. Even without any given emissions reduction pathway, Germany still reduces its yearly emissions by 85% based on 1990 level. This represents the lower boundary of the targets Germany has defined for 2050. However, the measures are not sufficient to reach the 1.5- nor 2-degree limit and therefore not in line with the climate targets of the Paris agreement. The decisive factor for the remaining emissions in SOTF is the high-temperature heat sector powered by hard coal. This underlines that the phase-out from coal as an energy carrier is a major key for a successful renewable energy transition. This transformation is highly needed to start taking action to face the real threats of climate change. A net decarbonization in Germany by 2050 is needed to comply with internationally agreed on-climate targets.

More general, these results show, that a country with a relatively high energy consumption per inhabitant or per ground area is able to decarbonize its energy system by large fractions within a given timeframe. Being an early adopter, Germany was able to push first decarbonization methods early on and also gain experience in the deployment and application of renewable technologies. Nevertheless, the current system and industries surrounding it are reluctant to undergo big changes, as hesitancies among industry association, local politics and even the society shows. On the other hand, decarbonization and deep intergration of all sectors also offer chances in flexibilization of energy supplies and demands, offer jobs even in rather underdeveloped areas and help decrease accumulation of power and influence on few stakeholders or regions in Europe as wind and solar irradiance are rather omnipresent sources of energy. Even though, the cross boarder trade of electricity decreases with a decentralization of the power generation landscape, there is a demand for grid expansions in between regions of supply and demand. While the regions of demand remain unchanged, the regions of supply may differ in future decades. Other countries, that are also trying to decarbonize their energy system can take some valuable insights: (A) Many countries have a lower power demand by ground area while even having a higher energy supply, due to better wind or solar exposition. This means, the endeavours Germany has to take to decarbonize its system might not be as high for another country. (B) Deployment of solar farms and wind farms is necessary, even in regions where the relative power demand is quite low. This might not be accepted by the people affected by it, therefore it is important to start a discussion early on and find concepts of participation to counteract movements lead by the "not in my backyard" (NIMBY)-principle. The same NIMBY-thinking applies for needed grid expansions measures and thus needs to be addressed early on. (C) Conflicts of distribution will rather increase than decrease, since technologies from all sectors will have to compete for resources. This can be examplified in the case of biomass: Being the cheapest way to decarbonize several processes and applications, each sector would like to use as much of it as possible. Nevertheless, in some applications biomass might be worthier than in others. Therefore, in the planning of future generation technologies and demands, it is indispensable to always look at the energy system as a whole and then to decide on means of distribution.

The results presented in this paper pose as a first successful elaboration and implementation on the complete decarbonized German energy system on a federal level. Further next steps include a more detailed representation of the largest branches of industry in Germany and their decarbonization options. This could more accurately resolve and endogenously calculate the requirements for process heat, which have so far only been considered superficially, instead of prescribing exogenously.

Author Contributions: Conceptualization, H.-K.B., A.E., F.S., F.W., K.L. and P.-Y.O.; methodology, H.-K.B., A.E., F.S., F.W. and K.L.; software, H.-K.B., A.E., T.B. and K.L.; validation, K.L., T.B., P.-Y.O. and C.v.H.; formal analysis, H.-K.B., F.S. and F.W.; investigation, H.-K.B., F.S., F.W. and K.L.; resources, T.B., K.L., and P.-Y.O.; data curation, H.-K.B., T.B. and K.L.; writing—original draft preparation, H.-K.B., A.E., F.S. and F.W.; writing—review and editing, T.B., P.-Y.O., C.v.H.; visualization, H.-K.B., F.S., F.W.; supervision, K.L., P.-Y.O.; project administration, P.-Y.O.; funding acquisition, P.-Y.O., C.v.H. and C.K.

Funding: This work was supported by the German Ministry for Education and Research (BMBF) under grant number 01LN1704A for the research group CoalExit and under grant number 01LA1810A for the research project "Future of Fossil Fuels in the wake of greenhouse gas neutrality".

Acknowledgments: Previous works of this research have been presented at various workshops and conferences in Germany and across Europe. We therefore thank the conference and workshop audiences as well as three anonymous reviewers for useful discussions and suggestions, the usual disclaimer applies. We would also like to thank Simon Bauer and Raphaela Sing for contributing in this paper in earlier stages.

Conflicts of Interest: The authors declare no conflict of interest.

Abbreviations

The following abbreviations are used in this manuscript:

BDEW	German Association of Energy and Water Industries
BDI	Federation of German Industries
BEE	German Renewable Energy Federation
BEV	Battery-Electric Vehicle
BMBF	German Ministry for Education and Research
BMU	German Ministry of the Environment, Nature Conservation, and Nuclear Safety
BMWi	Germany Ministry for Economic Affairs and Energy
CHP	combined heat and power
COP	Conference of the Parties
CSU	Christian Social Union in Bavaria
DSO	Distribution System Operator
DUH	Deutsche Umwelthilfe e.V.
dynELMOD	Dynamic, Investment and Dispatch, Model, for the Future European Electricity Market
EEG	German Renewable Green Energy Act
EI	European Island
EJ	Exajoule
EnWG	Energy Industry Act
ETS	Emission Trading System
EU	European Union
GD	Green Democracy
GDP	Gross Domestic Product
GENeSYS-MOD	Global Energy System Model
GHG	Greenhouse Gas
GPkm	billion person-kilometers
GW	Gigawatt
IGBCE	Labour Union of the Mining, Chemical and Energy Industries
IPCC	Intergovernmental Panel on Climate Change
km	kilometer
LCOE	Levelized Costs of Electricty
LULUCF	Land Use, Land Use Change and Forestry
NDC	Nationally Determined Contribution
NIMBY	"Not in my Backyard"
OSeMOSYS	Open Source Energy Modelling System
PHEV	Plug-In Hybrid Electric Vehicle
PJ	Petajoule
ppm	parts per million
PV	Photovoltaics
SOTF	Survival of the Fittest
TSO	Transmission Grid Operator
TW	Terawatt
TWh	Terawatt Hour
UN	United Nations
UNFCCC	United Nations Framework Convention on Climate Change
V2G	Vehicle to Grid
VDA	German Association of the Automotive Industry
VDMA	Mechanical Engineering Industry Association
WACC	Weighted Average Cost of Capital

Appendix A. Stakeholder of the German Energiewende

Germany has a federal system with the fundamental principle of subsidiary. Therefore, decisions should only be made on a higher level if the lower level is not able to, or the consequences would impact the higher level [79]. Due to the decentralized character of the low-carbon transformation, the federal states have a great opportunity to influence the implementation. In general, all states have adopted own climate targets, which differ greatly in their ambitions. Geographical circumstances, the structure of the local economy, and the respective state governments are important factors influencing this. While on the one side, a state-driven approach can lead to more fitting and localized solutions (Biomass is mostly promoted in rural areas, observable in the CSU-governed state Bavaria [80]), on the other side however, state governments tend to concentrate more on their own voters which might lead to decisions made by the "not in my backyard" (NIMBY)-principle [81]. A prime example is the so-called H10 regulation in Bavaria, which requires that the distance between wind power plants and settlements must be ten times higher than the total height of the windmills [82]. This halves the effective area for wind power plants [83]. The phenomenon of federal governments being tempted to support local interests rather than the "greater" plan of nationwide goals is also visible in the different resorts of the government (See also Section 1.1): In §1 of the Energy Industry Act (EnWG), the objective to provide a safe, low-cost, consumer-friendly, efficient, and environmentally compatible energy system was announced [32]. This set of objectives illustrates the basic conflict potential between the Ministry of the Environment, Nature Conservation, and Nuclear Safety (BMU) and the Ministry for Economic Affairs and Energy (BMWi) [84]—a confrontation of environment against economy [85]. The focus of the BMWi concerning decarbonization is set on using the energy transformation as a "success story for Germany" [86]. For this purpose, the ministry created a ten point agenda to merge loose initiatives into a structured energy roadmap in 2014 [87]. Furthermore, the BMWi integrated the energy department so that it has the overall control over most of the energy reforms within Germany's policy, such as the EEG or the EnWG [88]. This ensemble should combine the economic and environmental responsibility into one ministry to ensure a more efficient problem-solving [89]. The BMU, on the other hand, operates in the field of frugal handling with resources and the preservation of habitat, for instance in the Emission Control Act. Thus, this remit positions the BMU on the side of advocates for environment and climate protection and initiatives [90]. In general, the German government is influenced by a range of different entities and serves as a hub for different interest groups. While there are top-down targets given by international agreements or EU-wide guidelines, there are also influences through established industry and demands by the public that need to be brought in line. Within the political system of Germany, the separation of power and the federal system leads to a discourse between many different departments which are entangled in multi-level governance. The discrepancy between pro-environment interests and pro-economic interests of the ministries can be transferred onto the economy itself: most of the economic spectrum can be divided into two camps. Those industries that tend to appear as "polluters" or "emitters" are more in favor of a slow transformation and no regulations, and those industries that benefit from the energy transformation are clear proponents of stronger incentives and clear government targets [90].

Influencing policy is usually done through lobbying by industry associations. Here, it can be clearly observed that associations tied to large and heavy industry, such as the Federation of German Industries (BDI) (The so-called Federation of German Industries (BDI) has 100,000 members with a total of 8 million employees: https://english.bdi.eu/bdi/about-us/#/article/news/the-federation-of-german-industries-bdi/), have an influence on draft laws. For instance, the BDI was working on an exemption from the EEG levy for energy-intensive companies in the amount of 5 billion Euros in 2014, designed in a way that does not violate European state aid law [89]. However, due to heterogeneity of its members, the BDI also supports a low carbon transformation. In contrast, branch associations with more homogenous members tend to have stricter positions: among others, the German Association of Energy and Water Industriess (BDEW) and the German Association of the Automotive Industry (VDA), argue that a fast decarbonization would harm the industry due to higher energy prices and lower reliability, risk jobs due to changing production lines (Süddeutsche Zeitung. 2018. "Elektromobilität gefährdet 75,000 Jobs in der deutschen Autoindustrie." https://www.sueddeutsche.de/wirtschaft/studie-zu-e-autos-elektromobilitaet-gefaehrdet-jobs-in-der-deutschen-autoindustrie-1.4002449), and decrease attractiveness of Germany as an industrial standpoint. The argument that the transformation is endangering a multitude of jobs, especially in so-called structurally weak regions, is also supported by trade unions: the Labour Union for the Mining Chemical and Energy Industries (IGBCE) in particular is working side by side with the major energy suppliers for the continuation of lignite power generation, arguing that with a phase-put of coal, 20,000 directly and numerous indirectly affected jobs could be lost (Most of them in structurally weak (former industrially shaped) regions like the Lusatia (8500 workers) in former East Germany or the Rhineland (9903 workers). This number is repeatedly confirmed, it originates from DEBRIV (federal German association of all lignite producing companies and their affiliated organizations) (Statistik der Kohlenwirtschaft e.V. 2018) but could be a little lower in reality.).

On the other side, associations supporting the benefitting sectors like the German Renewable Energy Federation (BEE) argue that the transformation would provide numerous jobs and the renewable energies sector itself is already an important factor on public wealth and development. Among others, the Mechanical Engineering Industry Association (VDMA) is one of the largest associations in the engineering sector, and, unlike the BDI, represents the German medium-sized companies (VDMA. Maschinenbau in Zahl und Bild. 2018. https://www.vdma.org/documents/105628/20243678/MbauinZuB2018_1524470187749.pdf/14e4650e-bb39-37de-92f1-cf43902e05e5 Last accessed: 18 June 2018). Aligned with the general arguments of the benefitting sectors, the VDMA focuses on export possibilities and global competitiveness. According to the association, a policy regime of incentives (e.g., the expansion of the ETS) and clear regulations lead to innovation and investments in the areas of energy infrastructure and production, sector coupling, and transformation technologies [91]. Furthermore, there are several state-funded or private research institutes and think tanks, as well as environmental organizations which are rather supportive of the energy transformation and also have an influence on the public opinion. With the instrument of the so-called "right of collective action", environmental associations recognized by the Federal Environmental Agency [92] are able to make sure environmental directives are enforced. Most prominently, this tool is used by the Deutsche Umwelthilfe e.V. (DUH) to force cities to comply with emission values and driving bans.

At last, the public opinion plays a major role of the success of energy transformation: Unlike the industrial sector, the vast majority of people are supporting the transformation: Representative polls reveal a positive public agreement of up to 95% (AEE. 2017. "Repräsentative Umfrage: 95 Prozent der Deutschen wollen mehr Erneuerbare Energien." https://www.unendlich-viel-energie.de/akzeptanzumfrage2017.). However, some surveys record a negative tendency in the past years [93]. Especially on a municipal level—in areas where onshore wind turbines are installed—projects are confronted with criticism and skepticism that might lead to heavy protests and the foundation of a countermovement which could significantly hamper the energy transformation [94–97]. The motivation of energy transformation opponents goes beyond the NIMBY pattern which is often used to hastily explain countermovement [93,98]. NIMBY arguments (e.g., potential negative consequences for health or any decreasing value of the own property) are among the motives, but are accompanied by other concerns such as protection of the environment, aesthetic reasons concerning the landscape, or a general critique of the present energy policy.

Appendix B. Model Description

GENeSYS-MOD is a cost-optimizing linear program, focusing on long-term pathways for the different sectors of the energy system, specifically targeting emission constraints, the integration of renewables, and sector-coupling. The model minizes the objective function, which comprises total system costs (encompassing all costs occuring over the modeled time period) [14,71].

(Final) Energy demands are given exogenously for each modeled time slice, with the model computing the optimal flows of energy, and resulting needs for capacity additions and storages. Additional demands through sector-coupling are derived endogenously. Constraints, including energy balances (ensuring all demand is met), maximum capacity additions (e.g., to limit the usable potential of renewables), RES feed-in (e.g., to ensure grid stability), and emission budgets (given either yearly or as a total budget over the modeled horizon) are given to ensure proper functionality of the model and yield realistic results. Figure A1 shows a graphical representation of the functional units of GENeSYS-MOD, as well as additions and changes between model versions.

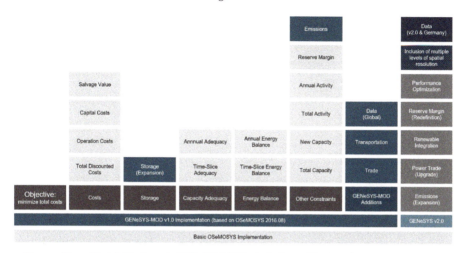

Figure A1. Model blocks of GENeSYS-MOD, including objective function, constraints, and version changes.

The model allows for investment into all technologies (Except when given fixed, predetermined phase-out dates, such as for nuclear power in Germany.) and acts purely economical when computing the resulting pathways (while staying true to the given constraints). It assumes the role of a social planner with perfect foresight, optimizing the total welfare through cost minimization. All fiscal units are handled in 2015 terms (with amounts in other years being discounted towards the base year). The effects of myopic/limited foresight, as well as the analysis of different discount rate models are planned for further reasearch and might yield even more insight in the possible developments of the energy system.

Fore more information on the mathematical side of the model, as well as all changes between model versions, please consult Howells et al. [71], Löffler et al. [14], and Burandt et al. [15].

Appendix C. Relevant Input Data

Appendix C.1. Technology Costs

Table A1. Capital Costs of main electricity generating technologies in M€/GW.

	2015	2020	2025	2030	2035	2040	2045	2050
Utility PV	1000	580	466	390	337	300	270	246
Onshore Wind	1250	1150	1060	1000	965	940	915	900
Offshore Wind Deep								
Offshore Wind Shallow								
Offshore Wind Transitional	3500	2637	2200	1936	1800	1710	1642	1592
Geothermal	5250	4970	4720	4470	4245	4020	3815	3610
Coal-Fired Thermal Plant	1600	1600	1600	1600	1600	1600	1600	1600
Gas-Fired Thermal Plant	650	636	621	607	593	579	564	550
Oil-Fired Thermal Plant	650	627	604	581	559	536	513	490
Coal-Fired CHP	2030	2030	2030	2030	2030	2030	2030	2030
Gas-Fired CHP	977	977	977	977	977	977	977	977

Appendix C.2. Fuel Costs

Table A2. Fossil Fuel Cost Assumptions in M€/PJ.

		2015	2020	2025	2030	2035	2040	2045	2050
Oil [Import]	EI/GD	7.12	10.18	11.02	11.86	11.37	10.88	10.39	9.91
	SOTF	7.12	10.91	12.60	14.40	14.62	14.77	14.85	14.86
Coal [Import]	EI/GD	1.52	1.54	1.53	1.52	1.44	1.36	1.28	1.20
	SOTF	1.52	1.65	1.75	1.84	1.85	1.84	1.82	1.80
Fossil Gas [Import]	EI/GD	6.63	6.54	7.72	8.91	9.15	9.38	9.62	9.86
	SOTF	6.63	7.01	8.83	10.82	11.76	12.73	13.74	14.79
Lignite [Domestic]	EI/GD	1.09	1.11	1.14	1.17	1.13	0.99	0.72	0.42
	SOTF	1.09	1.19	1.39	1.73	2.17	2.56	2.68	2.33

Appendix C.3. Renewable Potentials

Table A3. Renewable Potentials in GW installed capacity per region.

	Onshore Wind	Offshore Wind	Utility PV
DE_BB [Brandenburg]	13	0	19.2
DE_BE [Berlin]	0.3	0	0.6
DE_BW [Baden-Württemberg]	23	0	23.1
DE_BY [Bavaria]	41	0	45.6
DE_HB [Bremen]	0.2	0	0.3
DE_HE [Hesse]	14	0	13.6
DE_HH [Hamburg]	0.3	0	0.5
DE_MV [Mecklenburg-Western Pomerania]	11	6.6	15
DE_NI [Lower Saxony]	26	49.8	30.8
DE_NRW [North Rhine-Westphalia]	20	0	22
DE_RP [Rhineland-Palatinate]	12	0	12.8
DE_SH [Schleswig-Holstein]	9	28.6	10.2
DE_SL [Saarland]	2.4	0	1.7
DE_SN [Saxony]	10	0	11.9
DE_ST [Saxony-Anhalt]	7.4	0	13.2
DE_TH [Thuringia]	7.5	0	10.5

Appendix D. Additional Result Graphs

Appendix D.1. Transport

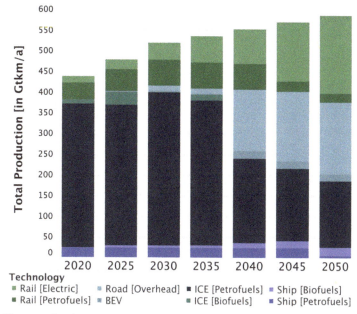

Figure A2. Development of freight transportation for the Green Democracy scenario.

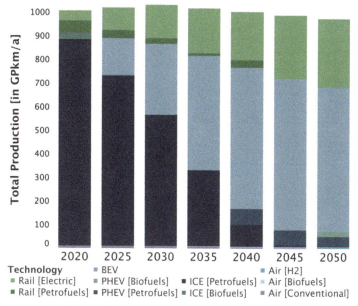

Figure A3. Development of passenger transportation for the Green Democracy scenario.

Appendix D.2. Regional Power Development for the EI and SOTF Scenarios

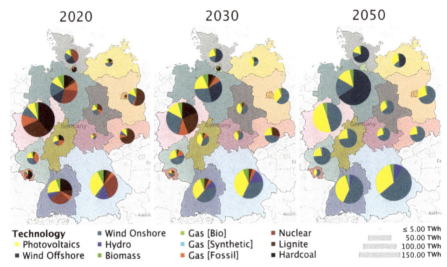

Figure A4. Regional development of Germany's power production for the scenario.

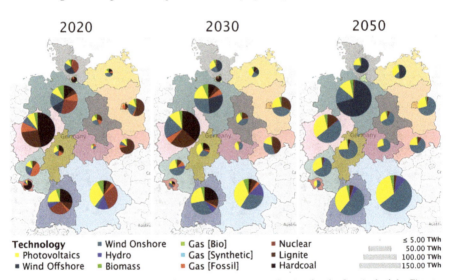

Figure A5. Regional development of Germany's power production for the Survival of the Fittest scenario.

References

1. Rogelj, J.; Shindell, D.; Jiang, K.; Fifita, S.; Forster, P.; Ginzburg, V.; Handa, C.; Kheshgi, H.; Kobayashi, S.; Kriegler, E.; et al. Mitigation pathways compatible with 1.5 C in the context of sustainable development. In *Global Warming of 1.5 C. An IPCC Special Report on the Impacts of Global Warming of 1.5 C Above Pre-Industrial Levels and Related Global Greenhouse Gas Emission Pathways, in the Context of Strengthening the Global Response to the Threat of Climate Change, Sustainable Development, and Efforts to Eradicate Poverty*; Masson-Delmotte, V., Zhai, P., Pörtner, H.-O., Roberts, D., Skea, J., Shukla, P., Pirani, A., Moufouma-Okia, W., Péan, C., Pidcock, R., et al., Eds.; IPCC: Geneva, Switzerland, 2018; Chapter 2.

2. IPCC. *Climate Change 2014: Mitigation of Climate Change: Working Group III Contribution to the Fifth Assessment Report of the Intergovernmental Panel on Climate Change*; Cambridge University Press: New York, NY, USA, 2014.
3. IPCC. *Climate Change 2013: The Physical Science Basis: Working Group I Contribution to the Fifth Assessment report of the Intergovernmental Panel on Climate Change*; Cambridge University Press: New York, NY, USA, 2014.
4. IPCC. *Climate Change 2014: Synthesis Report. Contribution of Working Groups I, II and III to the Fifth Assessment Report of the Intergovernmental Panel on Climate Change*; Intergovernmental Panel on Climate Change: Geneva, Switzerland, 2015.
5. Stern, N. *The Economics of Climate Change: The Stern Review*; Cambridge University Press: Cambridge, UK; New York, NY, USA, 2007.
6. UNFCCC. *Paris Agreement*; Technical Report; United Nations Framework Convention on Climate Change: Paris, France, 2015.
7. UNFCCC. *Adoption of the Paris Agreement*; Technical Report; United Nations Framework Convention on Climate Change: Paris, France, 2015.
8. Von Hirschhausen, C.; Gerbaulet, C.; Kemfert, C.; Lorenz, C.; Oei, P.Y. *Energiewende "Made in Germany": Low Carbon Electricity Sector Reform in the European Context*; Springer Nature Switzerland AG: Cham, Switzerland, 2018.
9. Heard, B.; Brook, B.; Wigley, T.; Bradshaw, C. Burden of proof: A comprehensive review of the feasibility of 100% renewable-electricity systems. *Renew. Sustain. Energy Rev.* **2017**, *76*, 1122–1133. [CrossRef]
10. Brown, T.; Bischof-Niemz, T.; Blok, K.; Breyer, C.; Lund, H.; Mathiesen, B. Response to 'Burden of proof: A comprehensive review of the feasibility of 100% renewable-electricity systems'. *Renew. Sustain. Energy Rev.* **2018**, *92*, 834–847. [CrossRef]
11. Sinn, H.W. Buffering volatility: A study on the limits of Germany's energy revolution. *Eur. Econ. Rev.* **2017**, *99*, 130–150. [CrossRef]
12. Schill, W.P.; Zerrahn, A.; Kemfert, C.; von Hirschhausen, C. Die Energiewende wird nicht an Stromspeichern scheitern. *DIW Aktuell* **2018**, *2018*, 1–10.
13. Ansari, D.; Holz, F.; Tosun, H.B. Global futures of energy, climate, and policy: Qualitative and quantitative foresight towards 2055. *DIW Berl. Discuss. Paper* **2019**, *1782*, 1–33. [CrossRef]
14. Löffler, K.; Hainsch, K.; Burandt, T.; Oei, P.Y.; Kemfert, C.; von Hirschhausen, C. Designing a model for the global energy system—GENeSYS-MOD: An application of the open-source energy modeling system (OSeMOSYS). *Energies* **2017**, *10*, 1468. [CrossRef]
15. Burandt, T.; Löffler, K.; Hainsch, K. *GENeSYS-MOD v2.0—Enhancing the Global Energy System Model: Model Improvements, Framework Changes, and European Data Set*; DIW Data Documentation 94; Deutsches Institut für Wirtschaftsforschung (DIW): Berlin, Germany, 2018.
16. Montreal Protocol. *Montreal Protocol on Substances that Deplete the Ozone Layer*; US Government Printing Office: Washington, DC, USA, 1987; Volume 26, pp. 128–136.
17. United Nations. *Kyoto Protocol to the United Nations Framework Convention on Climate Change*; Technical Report; United Nations: New York, NY, USA, 1998.
18. Ellerman, A.D.; Buchner, B.K. The European Union emissions trading scheme: Origins, allocation, and early results. *Rev. Environ. Econ. Policy* **2007**, *1*, 66–87. [CrossRef]
19. European Commission. Decision 406/2009/EC of the European Parliament and of the Council of 23 April 2009 on the effort of Member States to reduce their greenhouse gas emissions to meet the Community's greenhouse gas emission reduction commitments up to 2020. *Off. J. Eur. Union* **2009**, *140*, 136–148.
20. European Commission. Regulation (EU) 2018/842 of the European Parliament and of the Council of 30 May 2018 on binding annual greenhouse gas emission reductions by Member States from 2021 to 2030 contributing to climate action to meet commitments under the Paris Agreement and amending Regulation (EU) No 525/2013 (Text with EEA relevance). *Off. J. Eur. Union* **2018**, *61*, 26–42.
21. Deutsch, M.; Buck, M.; Patrick Graichen, P.; Vorholz, F. *Die Kosten von unterlassenem Klimaschutz für den Bundeshaushalt*; Agora Energiewende; Agora Verkehrswende: Berlin, Germany, 2018.
22. BMUB. *Klimaschutzplan 2050—Klimaschutzpolitische Grundsätze und Ziele der Bundesregierung*; Bundesministerium für Umwelt, Naturschutz und nukleare Sicherheit: Berlin, Germany, 2016.

23. AG Energiebilanzen e.V. *Bruttostromerzeugung in Deutschland ab 1990 nach Energieträgern*; Deutsches Institut für Wirtschaftsforschung (DIW) and DEBRIV: Berlin/Bergheim, Germany, 2019.
24. BMWi. *Abschlussbericht Kommission "Wachstum, Strukturwandel und Beschäftigung"*; Technical Report; Bundesministerium für Wirtschaft und Energie: Berlin, Germany, 2019.
25. Matthey, D.A.; Bünger, D.B. *Methodenkonvention 3.0 zur Ermittlung von Umweltkosten—Kostensätze*; Technical Report; Umweltbundesamt: Dessau-Roßlau, Germany, 2018.
26. Prahl, A.; Umpfenbach, K.; Oei, P.Y.; Brauers, H.; Herpich, P.; von Hirschhausen, C.; Lorenz, C.; Teichmann, I.; Kemfert, C.; Wehnert, T.; et al. *Die Beendigung der energetischen Nutzung von Kohle in Deutschland—Ein Überblick über Zusammenhänge, Herausforderungen und Lösungsoptionen*; Technical Report; DIW: Berlin, Germany; Wuppertal Institut für Klima, Umwelt, Energie and Ecologic Institut gemeinnützige GmbH: Wuppertal, Germany, 2018.
27. UBA. *National Trend Tables for the German Atmospheric Emission Reporting*; Technical Report; Umweltbundesamt: Dessau, Germany, 2018.
28. Lüers, S.; Wallasch, A.K.; Vogelsang, K. *Status des Offshore-Windenergieausbaus in Deutschland*; Technical Report; Deutsche WindGuard GmbH: Varel, Germany, 2017.
29. Henning, H.M.; Palzer, A. *100% Erneuerbare Energien für Strom und Wärme in Deutschland*; Technical Report; Fraunhofer-Institut für Solare Energiesysteme ISE: Freiburg im Breisgau, Germany, 2012.
30. Bofinger, S.; Callies, D.; Scheibe, M.; Saint-Drenan, Y.M.; Rohrig, K. *Potenzial der Windenergienutzung an Land*; Technical Report; Bundesverband WindEergie e.V.: Berlin, Germany, 2011.
31. Braun, M.; van Oehsen, A.; Saint-Drenan, Y.M.; Stetz, T. Vorstudie zur Integration großer Anteile Photovoltaik in die elektrische Energieversorgung. In *Studie im Auftrag des BSW-Bundesverband Solarwirtschaft eV Ergänzte Fassung vom 29.05.2012*; Fraunhofer Institut für Windenergie und Energiesystemtechnik (IWES): Kassel, Germany, 2012.
32. BMJV. Erneuerbare-Energien-Gesetz-EEG 2017. 2014. Available online: https://www.bmwi.de/Redaktion/DE/Gesetze/Energie/EEG.html (accessed on 2 August 2019).
33. Von Hirschhausen, C.; Herold, J.; Oei, P.Y.; Haftendorn, C. CCTS-Technologie ein Fehlschlag—Umdenken in der Energiewende notwendig. *DIW Wochenbericht* **2012**, *79*, 3–10.
34. Hirschhausen, C.V.; Herold, J.; Oei, P.Y. How a "Low Carbon" Innovation Can Fail—Tales from a "Lost Decade" for Carbon Capture, Transport, and Sequestration (CCTS). *Econ. Energy Environ. Policy* **2012**, *1*, 115–124. [CrossRef]
35. Oei, P.Y.; Mendelevitch, R. European scenarios of CO_2 infrastructure investment until 2050. *Energy J.* **2016**, *37*, 171–194. [CrossRef]
36. BDEW. *Beheizungsstruktur des Wohnungsbestandes in Deutschland 2018*; Technical Report; Bundesverband der Energie- und Wasserwirtschaft: Berlin, Germany, 2019.
37. Prognos; EWI-Köln; GWS. *Entwicklung der Energiemärkte—Energiereferenzprognose*; Studie im Auftrag des Bundesministeriums für Wirtschaft und Technik; BMWi: Berlin, Germany, 2014.
38. Arbeitsgruppe Erneuerbare Energien-Statistik. *Zeitreihen zur Entwicklung der erneuerbaren Energien in Deutschland*; Technical Report; UBA: Dessau, Germany, 2019.
39. Agentur für Erneuerbare Energien. *Erneuerbare Energien für die Industrie: Prozesswärme aus Bioenergie sorgt für Unabhängigkeit und Klimaschutz*; Agentur für Erneuerbare Energien (AEE): Berlin, Germany, 2018.
40. Naegler, T.; Simon, S.; Klein, M.; Gils, H.C. Quantification of the European industrial heat demand by branch and temperature level. *Int. J. Energy Res.* **2015**, *39*, 2019–2030. [CrossRef]
41. Fachagentur Nachwachsende Rochstoffe e.V. (FNR); Landwirtschaft und Verbraucherschutz (BMELV). *Nachhaltige Nutzung von Biomassepotenzialen—Projektförderung des Bundesministeriums für Ernährung, Landwirtschaft und Verbraucherschutz*; BMELV: Berlin, Germany, 2013.
42. E-Bridge; IAEW; OFFIS. *Moderne Verteilernetze für Deutschland*; Abschlussbericht Forschungsprojekt Nr. 44/12; BMWi: Bonn/Aachen/Oldenburg, Germany, 2014.
43. Agricola, A.C.; Seidl, H.; Mischinger, S.; Rehtanz, C.; Greve, M.; Häger, U.; Hilbrich, D.; Kippelt, S.; Kubis, A.; Liebenau, V.; et al. *Dena Studie—Systemdienstleistungen 2030. Voraussetzung für eine sichere und zuverlässige Stromversorgung mit hohem Anteil erneuerbarer Energien*; Endbericht, Dena: Berlin, Germany, 2014.
44. Ecofys; Fraunhofer IWES. *SmartMarket-Design in deutschen Verteilnetzen. Studie im Auftrag von Agora Energiewende*; Technical Report; Agora Energiewende: Berlin, Germany, 2017.

45. AG Energiebilanzen e.V. *Auswertungstabellen zur Energiebilanz Deutschland 1990–2017*; Technical Report; AG Energiebilanzen e.V.: Berlin, Germany, 2018.
46. REN21. *Global Status Report—Renewables 2019*; Technical Report; REN21 Secretariat: Paris, France, 2019; ISBN 978-3-9818911-7-1.
47. Pleßmann, G.; Erdmann, M.; Hlusiak, M.; Breyer, C. Global energy storage demand for a 100% renewable electricity supply. *Energy Procedia* **2014**, *46*, 22–31. [CrossRef]
48. Ram, M.; Bogdanov, D.; Aghahosseini, A.; Gulagi, A.; Oyewo, A.; Child, M.; Caldera, U.; Sadovskaia, K.; Farfan, J.; Barbosa, L.; et al. *Global Energy System based on 100% Renewable Energy—Power, Heat, Transport and Desalination Sectors*; Technical Report; Lappeenranta University of Technology, Lappeenranta: Berlin, Germany, 2019; ISBN 978-952-335-339-8.
49. Hainsch, K.; Burandt, T.; Kemfert, C.; Löffler, K.; Oei, P.Y.; von Hirschhausen, C. Emission pathways towards a low-carbon energy system for Europe—A model-based analysis of decarbonization scenarios. *DIW Berlin Discussion Paper* **2018**, *1745*, 1–34.
50. Gerbaulet, C.; von Hirschhausen, C.; Kemfert, C.; Lorenz, C.; Oei, P.Y. European electricity sector decarbonization under different levels of foresight. *Renew. Energy* **2019**, *141*, 973–987. [CrossRef]
51. Child, M.; Kemfert, C.; Bogdanov, D.; Breyer, C. Flexible electricity generation, grid exchange and storage for the transition to a 100% renewable energy system in Europe. *Rene. Energy* **2019**, *139*, 80–101. [CrossRef]
52. Zappa, W.; Junginger, M.; van den Broek, M. Is a 100% renewable European power system feasible by 2050? *Appl. Energy* **2019**, *233–234*, 1027–1050. [CrossRef]
53. Connolly, D.; Lund, H.; Mathiesen, B. Smart Energy Europe: The technical and economic impact of one potential 100% renewable energy scenario for the European Union. *Renew. Sustain. Energy Rev.* **2016**, *60*, 1634–1653. [CrossRef]
54. European Commission. *EU Reference Scenario 2016: Energy, Transport and GHG emissions—Trends to 2050*; Technical Report; European Commission: Brussels, Belgium, 2016.
55. Pregger, T.; Nitsch, J.; Naegler, T. Long-term scenarios and strategies for the deployment of renewable energies in Germany. *Energy Policy* **2013**, *59*, 350–360. [CrossRef]
56. Palzer, A.; Henning, H.M. A comprehensive model for the German electricity and heat sector in a future energy system with a dominant contribution from renewable energy technologies—Part II: Results. *Renew. Sustain. Energy Rev.* **2014**, *30*, 1019–1034. [CrossRef]
57. Henning, H.M.; Palzer, A. *What will the Energy Transformation Sost?* Technical Report; Fraunhofer ISE: Freiburg, Deutschland, 2015.
58. Samadi, S.; Lechtenböhmer, S.; Prantner, M.; Nebel, A. *Vollständig auf erneuerbaren Energien basierende Stromversorgung Deutschlands im Jahr 2050 auf Basis in Europa großtechnisch leicht erschließbarer Potentiale—Analyse und Bewertung anhand von Studien*; Technical Report 27/2014; Wuppertal Institut for Climate, Environment and Energy: Dessau, Germany, 2014.
59. Hansen, K.; Mathiesen, B.V.; Skov, I.R. Full energy system transition towards 100% renewable energy in Germany in 2050. *Renew. Sustain. Energy Rev.* **2019**, *102*, 1–13. [CrossRef]
60. Oei, P.Y.; Brauers, H.; Kemfert, C.; Kittel, M.; Göke, L.; von Hirschhausen, C.; Walk, P. *Kohleausstieg in NRW im deutschen und europäischen Kontext—Energiewirtschaft, Klimaziele und wirtschaftliche Entwicklung*; Deutsches Institut für Wirtschaftsforschung (DIW), Politikberatung Kompakt: Berlin, Germany, 2018; Volume 129, pp. 1–80.
61. Cebulla, F.; Haas, J.; Eichman, J.; Nowak, W.; Mancarella, P. How much electrical energy storage do we need? A synthesis for the U.S., Europe, and Germany. *J. Clean. Prod.* **2018**, *181*, 449–459. [CrossRef]
62. Hartmann, N. *Rolle und Bedeutung der Stromspeicher bei hohen Anteilen erneuerbarer Energien in Deutschland: Speichersimulation und Betriebsoptimierung*; Technical Report; University of Stuttgart: Stuttgart, Germany, 2013. [CrossRef]
63. Zsiborács, H.; Baranyai, N.H.; Vincze, A.; Zentkó, L.; Birkner, Z.; Máté, K.; Pintér, G. Intermittent renewable energy sources: The role of energy storage in the european power system of 2040. *Electronics* **2019**, *8*, 729. [CrossRef]
64. Figgener, J.; Haberschusz, D.; Kairies, K.P.; Wessels, O.; Tepe, B.; Sauer, D.U. *Wissenschaftliches Mess- und Evaluierungsprogramm Solarstromspeicher 2.0—Jahresbericht 2018*; Jahresbericht, Institut für Stromrichtertechnik und Elektrische Antriebe RWTH Aachen: Aachen, Germany, 2018.

65. Müller, C.; Hoffrichter, A.; Wyrwoll, L.; Schmitt, C.; Trageser, M.; Kulms, T.; Beulertz, D.; Metzger, M.; Duckheim, M.; Huber, M.; et al. Modeling framework for planning and operation of multi-modal energy systems in the case of Germany. *Appl. Energy* **2019**, *250*, 1132–1146. [CrossRef]
66. Müller, C.; Falke, T.; Hoffrichter, A.; Wyrwoll, L.; Schmitt, C.; Trageser, M.; Schnettler, A.; Metzger, M.; Huber, M.; Küppers, M.; et al. Integrated planning and evaluation of multi-modal energy Systems for Decarbonization of Germany. *Energy Procedia* **2019**, *158*, 3482–3487. [CrossRef]
67. Hanemann, P.; Behnert, M.; Bruckner, T. Effects of electric vehicle charging strategies on the German power system. *Appl. Energy* **2017**, *203*, 608–622. [CrossRef]
68. Schill, W.P.; Gerbaulet, C. Power system impacts of electric vehicles in Germany: Charging with coal or renewables? *Appl. Energy* **2015**, *156*, 185–196. [CrossRef]
69. Loisel, R.; Pasaoglu, G.; Thiel, C. Large-scale deployment of electric vehicles in Germany by 2030: An analysis of grid-to-vehicle and vehicle-to-grid concepts. *Energy Policy* **2014**, *65*, 432–443. [CrossRef]
70. Bloess, A. Impacts of heat sector transformation on Germany's power system through increased use of power-to-heat. *Appl. Energy* **2019**, *239*, 560–580. [CrossRef]
71. Howells, M.; Rogner, H.; Strachan, N.; Heaps, C.; Huntington, H.; Kypreos, S.; Hughes, A.; Silveira, S.; DeCarolis, J.; Bazillian, M.; et al. OSeMOSYS: The open source energy modeling system: An introduction to its ethos, structure and development. *Energy Policy* **2011**, *39*, 5850–5870. [CrossRef]
72. European Commission. *Technical Note Results of the EUCO3232.5 Scenario on Member States*; Technical Report; European Commission: Brussels, Belgium, 2019.
73. E3Mlab; IIASA. *Technical Report on Member State Results of the EUCO Policy Scenarios*; Technical Report; European Commission: Brussels, Belgium, 2016.
74. E3Mlab. *Technical Report on Macroeconomic Member State Results of the EUCO Policy Scenarios*; Technical Report; European Commisssion: Brussels, Belgium, 2016.
75. IEA. *World Energy Outlook 2016*; International Energy Agency: Paris, France, 2016.
76. SPD; Die Linke; Bündnis90/Die Grünen. *Vereinbarung zur Zusammenarbeit in einer Regierungskoalition für die 20. Wahlperiode der Bremischen Bürgerschaft 2019–2023*; SPD Land Bremen: Bremen, Germany, 2019 .
77. Welsch, M.; Deane, P.; Howells, M.; O Gallachoir, B.; Rogan, F.; Bazilian, M.; Rogner, H. Incorporating flexibility requirements into long-term energy system models—A case study on high levels of renewable electricity penetration in Ireland. *Appl. Energy* **2014**, *135*, 600–615. [CrossRef]
78. UBA. *Submission under the United Nations Framework Convention on Climate Change and the Kyoto Protocol 2019*; Technical Report 24; Umweltbundesamt: Dessau, Germany, 2019.
79. Agentur für Erneuerbare Energien. *Bundesländer mit neuer Energie*; Technical Report 5; Agentur für Erneuerbare Energien: Berlin, Germany, 2018.
80. Hildebrandt, A.; Wolf, F. *Die Politik der Bundesländer: zwischen Föderalismusreform und Schuldenbremse*, 2nd ed.; Springer VS: Wiesbaden, Germany, 2016.
81. Wolsink, M. Undesired reinforcement of harmful 'self-evident truths' concerning the implementation of wind power. *Energy Policy* **2012**, *48*, 83–87. [CrossRef]
82. Bayerische Staatskanzlei. *Bayerische Bauordnung*; Bayerisches Staatsministerium für Wirtschaft, Landesentwicklung und Verkehr: Munich, Germany, 2017.
83. Agentur für Erneuerbare Energien. Politik und Gesetze zur Energiewende in den Bundesländern. 2018. Available online: https://www.foederal-erneuerbar.de/auf-einen-blick-detailseite/items/politik-und-gesetze-zur-energiewende-in-den-bundeslaendern (accessed on 2 August 2019).
84. Maubach, K.D. *Energiewende: Wege zu Einer Bezahlbaren Energieversorgung*, 2nd ed.; Springer VS: Wiesbaden, Germany, 2014.
85. Gründinger, W. *Lobbyismus im Klimaschutz: Die Nationale Ausgestaltung des Europäischen Emmissionshandelssystems*; Springer VS: Wiesbaden, Germany, 2012.
86. BMWi. *Die Energiewende: Unsere Erfolgsgeschichte*; Bundesministerium für Wirtschaft und Energie: Berlin, Germany, 2017.
87. BMWi. *Zentrale Vorhaben Energiewende für die 18. Legislaturperiode*; Bundesministerium für Wirtschaft und Energie: Berlin, Germany, 2018.
88. BMWi. *Sechster Monitoringbericht zur Energiewende*; Bundesministerium für Wirtschaft und Energie: Berlin, Germany, 2018.

89. Haas, T. *Die politische Ökonomie der Energiewende*; Springer Fachmedien Wiesbaden: Wiesbaden, Germany, 2017. doi:10.1007/978-3-658-17319-7.
90. Seibt, A. *Lobbying für erneuerbare Energien*; Springer Fachmedien Wiesbaden: Wiesbaden, Germany, 2015. doi:10.1007/978-3-658-09259-7.
91. VDMA. Die Energiepolitischen Kernforderungen des VDMA. 2017. Available online: https://www.vdma.org/v2viewer/-/v2article/render/16246640 (accessed on 2 August 2019).
92. Töller, A.E.; Böcher, M. Wirtschaftsverbände in der Umweltpolitik. In *Handbuch Arbeitgeber- und Wirtschaftsverbände in Deutschland*; Springer VS Handbuch; Springer VS: Wiesbaden, Germany, 2017; pp. 531–564.
93. Eichenauer, E.; Reusswig, F.; Meyer-Ohlendorf, L.; Lass, W. Bürgerinitiativen gegen Windkraftanlagen und der Aufschwung rechtspopulistischer Bewegungen. In *Bausteine der Energiewende*; Kühne, O., Weber, F., Eds.; Springer Fachmedien Wiesbaden: Wiesbaden, Germany, 2018; pp. 633–651. doi:10.1007/978-3-658-19509-0.
94. Reusswig, F.; Braun, F.; Heger, I.; Ludewig, T.; Eichenauer, E.; Lass, W. Against the wind: Local opposition to the German Energiewende. *Util. Policy* **2016**, *41*, 214–227. [CrossRef]
95. Weber, F.; Kühne, O. Räume unter Strom: Eine diskurstheoretische Analyse zu Aushandlungsprozessen im Zuge des Stromnetzausbaus. *Raumforschung und Raumordnung* **2016**, *74*, 323–338. [CrossRef]
96. Hübner, G. Die Akzeptanz von erneuerbaren Energien. Einstellungen und Wirkungen. In *Erneuerbare Energien: Ambivalenzen, Governance, Rechtsfragen*; Ekardt, F., Hennig, B., Unnerstall, H., Eds.; Number Bd. 1 in Beiträge zur sozialwissenschaftlichen Nachhaltigkeitsforschung; Metropolis-Verlag: Marburg, Germany, 2012.
97. Wolsink, M. Planning of renewables schemes: Deliberative and fair decision-making on landscape issues instead of reproachful accusations of non-cooperation. *Energy Policy* **2007**, *35*, 2692–2704. [CrossRef]
98. Wolsink, M. Wind power implementation: The nature of public attitudes: Equity and fairness instead of 'backyard motives'. *Renew. Sustain. Energy Rev.* **2007**, *11*, 1188–1207. [CrossRef]

© 2019 by the authors. Licensee MDPI, Basel, Switzerland. This article is an open access article distributed under the terms and conditions of the Creative Commons Attribution (CC BY) license (http://creativecommons.org/licenses/by/4.0/).

Article

Transitioning Island Energy Systems—Local Conditions, Development Phases, and Renewable Energy Integration

Hannah Mareike Marczinkowski, Poul Alberg Østergaard * and Søren Roth Djørup

Department of Planning, Aalborg University, Rendsburggade 14, 9000 Aalborg, Denmark
* Correspondence: poul@plan.aau.dk; Tel.: +45-9940-9940

Received: 7 August 2019; Accepted: 5 September 2019; Published: 10 September 2019

Abstract: Islands typically have sensitive energy systems depending on natural surroundings, but innovative technologies and the exploitation of renewable energy (RE) sources present opportunities like self-sufficiency, but also challenges, such as grid instability. Samsø, Orkney, and Madeira are in the transition to increase the RE share towards 100%—however, this is addressed in different ways depending on the local conditions and current development phases in the transition. Scenarios focusing on the short-term introduction of new technologies in the energy systems are presented, where the electricity sector is coupled with the other energy sectors. Here, both smart grid and sector-integrating solutions form an important part in the next 5–15 years. The scenarios are analyzed using the modeling tool EnergyPLAN, enabling a comparison of today's reference scenarios with 2030 scenarios of higher RE share. By including three islands across Europe, different locations, development stages, and interconnection levels are analyzed. The analyses suggest that the various smart grid solutions play an important part in the transition; however, local conditions, sector integration, and balancing technologies even more so. Overall, the suggestions complement each other and pave the way to reach 100% RE integration for both islands and, potentially, other similar regions.

Keywords: island energy system transition; 100% RE pathways; RE integration; smart grid technologies; energy sector integration; smart energy system; Samsø; Orkney; Madeira

1. Introduction on RE Integration on Islands

Islands' energy systems are like most other energy systems aiming to utilize renewable energy (RE) to supply their demands. However, they are under more pressure due to their inherent isolation and higher dependence on their natural surroundings, including conditions affecting possible RE utilization. The European Union (EU) has the general ambition to increase the use of RE in the near future [1], and various studies suggest how to increase the use up to 100% through sector integration [2,3].

The EU specifically targets "clean energy for EU islands" to support this transition [4]. Islands are to follow the same trend despite their limitations, but they can also benefit much more from local utilization of local resources to increase self-sufficiency. Research has already touched on the present and potential future, but also the limits of RE on islands as it can be difficult to increase the RE share without proper step-by-step integration and balancing.

A review of RE utilization on islands by Kuang et al. [5] presented various cases of current developments, as well as suggested strategies to improve the utilization further. While solar, wind, hydro, and other technologies have been implemented to various extents, the sole exploitation of these potentials does not seem enough to reach high levels of self-sufficiency. Instead, further exploration of storages, demand side management, and micro and smart grids are mentioned to increase the RE shares further.

Praene et al. [6] presented the example of Reunion, where the self-sufficiency rate with RE has been decreasing over a period of years due to increasing energy demands. While hydropower has been a technology early and substantially explored on Reunion, by 1982, the limited potentials were almost fully exploited and unable to match the growing demands, resulting in a decreasing RE share.

While some islands in the Pacific are still struggling with small-scale RE projects hitting barriers of financial, institutional, environmental, and skill basis, the willingness for these was shown by Weir [7], but the information on how best to approach this on islands is yet to be evaluated. Thushara et al. [8] presented an example of an island (Sri Lanka) without grid connection or fuel reserves on the verge of finding the right future power generation, showing limits and conflicts to a full renewable supply.

Ioannidis et al. argued that islands are forced to invest in RE to avoid dependence on fossil fuel imports, energy scarcity, and other uncertainties [9]. These investments might happen uncontrolled, resulting in imbalanced energy systems. Meschede et al. [10] applied the EnergyPLAN model to the island of La Gomera and, based on analyses of different supply time series, the authors' results show advantages of diversified energy supply for this case study.

New technological solutions are currently being tested and studied on islands in this regard. Dorotić et al. presented a novel approach of relying on vehicle-to-grid (V2G) in combination with wind and photovoltaic (PV) power for the Croatian island of Korčula [11]. Meschede et al. discussed the necessary determination of appropriate smart energy system design for various-sized Philippine islands, including solutions around hybrid and storage technologies, besides connection to larger grids [12].

Rakopoulos et al. [13] mentioned the trend towards smart grids in the development of island energy systems. Colmenar-Santos et al. [14] discussed the development of RE for islands from a grid regulation perspective. Besides the requirement to align regulatory plans between islands and the rest of the country, the continental part of the country can benefit from using islands as testbeds, as they often present the same energy system aspects. To test large RE shares, the consideration of smart grid, storage, and electric vehicle (EV) implementation is suggested. For this, the specific locations and characteristics, as well as the involvement of the people of the islands, should be included. With the advance of information and communication technologies, grids can transition to smart grids that allow the use of monitoring, analysis, and control within its supply chain with the aim to improve the energy system. Rakopoulos et al. [13] further defined the framework for the development of island smart grids under the prospect of this technology becoming a priority for the European Commission. They are to help decrease carbon footprint and costs of energy by improved automation, distribution, and reduction of peaks in the grid.

Demonstration and evaluation of selected smart grid and sector integration technologies is addressed in the 2017–2021 project SMILE (Smart Island Energy systems) [15]. This focuses on the new phase in the RE transition with smart technologies to reach 100% RE shares on three demonstration islands: Samsø, Orkney, and Madeira. These islands are all investigating ways of increasing the RE share in their energy system, though local conditions and potentials differ widely, as well as their level of progress in this transition. While Samsø has been undergoing a decade-long transition from nearly zero to a high RE share after winning a competition of being Denmark's officially designated RE island [16], it has, however, not solved the full energy system integration. The Orkney Isles are characterized by a large number of wind turbines and offshore energy production testing facilities, but suffer from fuel poverty and curtailment [17]. Madeira lies far off the European continent and stands out in European terms with great solar potential, while having to balance their energy system and grid stability autonomously [18]. These islands are therefore good case studies with challenges, as well as potentials, for the evaluation of RE integration in the transition to 100% RE.

Scope and Structure

While some islands still largely depend on fossil fuels and struggle to introduce RE, other islands already exploit most of their RE potential, but also face problems related to this. The literature study shows that growing energy demands, various barriers, and imbalances require more research and exploration of solutions. While new technologies, such as V2G, hybrid and storage options, and other smart grid solutions, have been introduced or studied, they have mainly been considered individually and in limited contexts. In addition, they have not been studied as part of a holistic island energy system transition process considering and comparing local conditions' impacts.

With trends and plans aiming at full self-sufficiency in the near future, further transition is suggested with various new technologies, yet it is not clear how the smartening of the grid and wider energy systems with these could be addressed, realized, and aligned on islands. Hence, it can be said that a new phase in the transition towards 100% RE is emerging. In contrast to previous publications, this paper presents an alternative approach to explore the transition towards higher shares of RE by presenting a three-phase characterization and important criteria to help the transition within. The study and presentation of the case studies' complex energy systems and the alignment, as well as distinction of the transition of three similar yet individual islands, further address the research gap.

The work presented here should be seen as the first technical explorative step in a required energy system transition, where the explorative step unveils the technical possibilities. This is not limited by local economic, social, or political aspects. Subsequent steps assess what is required to implement the technical solutions, focusing on social acceptance and business and socio-economic costs—and finally, possibly the adaption of policies, regulations and business economic framework conditions to advance technically and socio-economically favorable solutions. These later steps, however, are beyond the scope of the work presented in this article.

Section 2 presents the scenario simulation tool EnergyPLAN, along with scenario data acquisition and scenario design methods. They are used to evaluate the case study islands as presented in Section 3, specifically addressing the steps from today's to 2030 energy systems. This is adopted from the framework of the EU-founded research project SMILE, resulting in Samsø, Orkney, and Madeira as cases [15]. A final overview of the case studies is added and discussed in relation to the general ongoing transition progress in Section 4, before the conclusions are presented.

2. Materials and Methods

This section presents the EnergyPLAN model applied in the scenario simulations, as well as the data gathering and verification methodology applied. Finally, the scenario design approach is detailed.

2.1. EnergyPLAN

The EnergyPLAN model can simulate the electricity, heating, cooling, industry, and transport sectors of an energy system on an hourly basis over a one-year time horizon, and can be used on various geographic levels and sizes of energy systems. Hence, it can be adjusted to specific locations and years by applying the respective data, such as projections to 2030. It simulates the mix of technologies in the whole system by identifying and exploiting synergies across the sectors. It is able to model fluctuating energy sources, and simulates their effects on the rest of the energy system. Depending on the inputs, such as technology capacities, efficiencies, and costs, as well as the demand and supply of the investigated case, various simulations become possible [19,20].

EnergyPLAN's simulation strategy is either technical or economic. While the economic strategy focuses on the most economically feasible operation of the energy production units based on exogenously given market data, the technical strategy focuses on primary energy supply (PES) and hourly system balance. For this article, the technical strategy is chosen as the basis for comparisons of technical possibilities in the transitions. As Sorknæs et al. [21] and Djørup et al. [22] point out, RE influences market prices, thus for 100% RE systems, existing market data (as used in EnergyPLAN) cannot be used for simulations, whereas technical simulations show the technical possibilities. Nonetheless, the socio-economic assessment includes technology costs without taxes or subsidies and CO_2 costs, assuming to bring socio-economic perspective to the otherwise technical simulation. Any variation between the business economic and socio-economic cost will be comparable between different technologies.

The reference models are adjusted to fit to a reference year for which sufficient data is available. These are compared to future scenarios that include other technologies or changes in demand and supply profiles, according to the suggestions for the case studies of the transition towards 100% RE. Especially relevant for this study, EnergyPLAN may simulate island mode, allowing for an analysis irrespective of interconnections. Any export or import is therefore not evaluated further in terms of fuel consumption or related emissions avoided through export and caused by import.

The resulting relevant effects in this study include RE shares of PES and electricity production, import/export balance, CO_2 emissions, and annual socio-economic costs for each scenario investigated. The scenarios presented include the reference scenarios, which are created through research and in cooperation with the SMILE partners, as well as the future scenarios, which focus on high RE shares in relation to local conditions.

EnergyPLAN has been used in a high number of articles [23,24], including island studies on Korčula [11], Samsø [25–27], Gran Canaria [28], La Gomera [10], Flores [29], and Bornholm [30], to name a few.

2.2. Data Gathering and Verification

The modeling of island energy systems entails the study of energy supply, conversion, and consumption. The unique characteristics of each of the studied island systems in this article are established in cooperation with SMILE partners of the respective islands. This includes the consideration of data from annual energy accounts and reports, as well as applicable literature for a reference year to build a reference model upon [31,32].

References are based on data of existing technologies with capacities, efficiencies, and costs. Furthermore, hourly distribution profiles are gathered and added to the models for the simulation of production of renewable electricity and heat, as well as for the consumption of electricity, heat, and transport. The hourly production of electricity is based on local inputs [33] or numerical models [34], [35]. The one for hot water with solar collectors is simulated with the help of energyPRO [36], with the temperature and radiation data of the selected reference year and an inclination angle typical for each region [37]. energyPRO is a simulation model created to make detailed business–economic simulations of particularly district heating plants (see [38] for a more thorough description); however, here, it is only applied due to its facility to model solar collectors. Consumption data results from local measurements or studies of households [39] and weather data.

The hourly distributions are applied in the model according to the annual values for each of the production and consumption units to represent the energy systems as close to reality as possible. For verification, EnergyPLAN is run and the annual modeled values compared to the actual ones—for example, the remaining required production from conventional power plants. If needed, alignments and corrections are made in the models, in coordination with the partners, to improve their representation of the reference energy systems [31].

2.3. Transition Scenario Design

After establishing and verifying the reference scenarios, a classification of the respective energy systems is made, categorizing them into the specific RE integration phase, as illustrated in Table 1. These phases are typical for systems going from fossil reliance to RE integration and finally complete independence from fossils as defined by Lund [40]. Energy systems with up to 20% of RE are thereby grouped in the RE Introduction phase, characterized by no to little RE integration problems, where RE would be able to directly reduce fossil fuel consumption. The next phase is large-scale RE integration, with RE influencing and interfering with the existing system(s), requiring hourly analyses due to the time-dependence intermittency of RE. This second phase might already require balancing technologies as the influence from RE on the system becomes complex. The final phase of the transition to 100%

RE systems requires the integration and comparison of various technologies supporting stability depending on the local conditions.

Table 1. The phases of renewable energy (RE) integration in the transition to 100% RE to classify energy systems and respective technical requirements, based on [40].

Phases	RE Introduction	Large-Scale RE Integration	Towards 100% RE
Example energy system	Small share of RE, no problem integrating, direct fuel reduction	Existing large share of RE, system influence and interference time-dependent due to large share of intermittent RE	Transformation into 100% RE-based system, complex comparison of various technologies requiring balance, sector integration, optimized biomass utilization

The next step in a transition depends on already existing RE utilization, local demands, and further potentials, but also on the availability of technologies. These might include various RE technologies, power-to-heat, power-to-gas, power-to-transport, thermal energy storage (TES), battery electricity energy storage (BESS), and fuel storages, as well as demand side management and algorithmic approaches—including various smart grid solutions. With EnergyPLAN, it is possible to define and model the respective technologies depending on the local data gathered. For example, the potential addition of electric transport can be included and defined with various charging and V2G options that are most suitable for the individual case.

In this paper, a short-term analysis of the transition of three island energy systems is made. Therefore, the resulting scenarios are created under consideration of the current energy system, as well as the planned actions in the upcoming 5–15 years. With this approach, certain possible changes are neglected, such as potential changes in weather conditions, demography, and unforeseeable changes in production or consumption. Related rebound effects are thereby also not studied, and neglected in the simulation. In relation to this, the temporal distribution profiles for heating and electricity are kept the same, unless specifically studied and changed due to a certain technical modification.

The scenarios consider the following: Case-specific savings potentials, case-specific RE availability, and case-specific potential energy conversion shifts. Furthermore, as an integrated part, they consider the extent to which the systems should or could rely on interconnection to the mainland or be self-sufficient. Reducing or limiting the amount of import and export is therefore aimed not to rely on the balancing capability of surrounding energy systems. Instead, local products should be used for the local systems to the largest sustainable extent possible, including using otherwise exported or curtailed electricity. For this, the integration and balancing of energy sectors becomes important.

As introduced, sector integration—partly through smart grid solutions—is key to the transition towards high RE shares in the total PES [40], and is therefore included in the scenario design, which goes beyond the idea of SMILE. In line with the RE aspect, fossil fuels, but also biomass, should be limited to a sustainable level, respectively. This goes hand in hand with the target of reducing CO_2 emissions, and aligns with the EU climate targets [1]. While costs play a secondary role in the scenario making, its reduction should nonetheless also be aimed to ease implementation. Finally, the aim should be to minimize losses in the various sectors and throughout the entire energy system. This illustrates the detailed requirements for the transition of these islands towards large-scale and eventually 100% RE integration.

The scenarios are made in parallel and involve similar tasks for the different geographical areas—though different starting points and RE options result in scenarios of varying complexity and composition. Adopting this methodology for the demonstration islands of the SMILE project somewhat predefines the scenarios, yet they are further dependent on the local conditions and demands. Finally, this presents a variety of suggestions on smart grid solutions and, though being tested for three specific island cases, it can give insight into further planning approaches for most energy systems. The SMILE islands and their approaches to transit towards higher RE shares are presented in the following.

3. Case Study and Island Scenarios

To evaluate RE potentials on Samsø, Orkney, and Madera, scenarios are developed which include (1) the SMILE smart grid demonstrations, (2) a potentially larger deployment of them if suitable, and (3) in general a shift from energy systems relying on fossil fuels to energy systems relying highly on RE by 2030. The focus of the scenarios is the approach of the ongoing transition to ensure a balanced energy system with increased RE share, which may look very different for each island.

With the definition of the three phases in Table 1, the islands are classified in different stages as seen in Table 2. Samsø is furthest ahead in terms of self-sufficiency and supply through RE. With a reference RE share of almost 60% in 2015, Samsø is classified as being in the second phase of RE integration, aiming for the third phase: 100% RE. It can be said that Samsø achieved the first phase of RE introduction already in 2007. This shapes the evaluation of technologies and creation of the future scenario.

Table 2. The SMILE islands and respective required technologies for the varying phases in the transition to 100% RE (shares are current references and projected targets with respective year).

Phases	RE Introduction	Large-Scale RE Integration	Towards 100% RE
Samsø (Large-scale to 100% RE)	Wind turbines, PV, biomass and solar district heating, individual heating with biomass and electricity >25% RE share (2007)	More PV, wind turbines, and individual heating with biomass, electric, and solar thermal, savings 60% RE share (2015)	SMILE: BESS, PV, heat pump Short-term: Update district heating, Biogas plant, EV, further RE capacity, heat pumps ~100% RE share (2030)
Orkney (Introduction to large-scale RE)	Wind turbines, electric heating 18% RE share (2014)	SMILE: BESS, TES, heat pumps, EV Short-term: More PV, wind turbines, wave and tidal capacity, savings, more heat pumps and TES, hydrogen, electrolyzer ~50% RE share (2030)	Discussion to include in longer term: District heating (biomass or electric), TES, heat pumps, savings, synthetic fuels, EV ~100% RE share (?)
Madeira (Introduction to large-scale RE)	Hydro, wind, PV, autonomy 11% RE share (2014)	SMILE: PV, BESS, EV Short-term: More PV, wind turbines, hydro and pump storages, geothermal ~50% RE share (2030)	Discussion to include in longer term: District cooling, solar thermal and TES, BESS, EV, savings ~100% RE share (?)
Short-term (2014/2015–2030)		2030 scenarios Large-scale—100% RE	Longer-term (2030–?)

Orkney and Madeira have RE shares in the reference year 2014 of 18% and 11%, respectively, classifying them as still being in the RE introduction phase. Consequently, the next step is to reach large-scale RE integration, before aiming at the 100% target. This is characterized by the expansion of RE, such as wind and PV capacity, instead of a focus on integration and balancing, as would be the case afterwards. However, due to the long-term goal of reaching higher RE shares, some technologies, mostly defined through SMILE, already include sector-integrating and balancing options. The technologies considered for these steps are presented in the overview in Table 2, showing that different phases are reached in the addressed 2030 scenarios.

Based on the methodology, the EnergyPLAN models of Samsø, Orkney, and Madeira are introduced in the following, including the 2014/2015 references and the 2030 scenarios with the incorporation of transition suggestions. The corresponding data of all scenarios are shown in the overview Section 4.

3.1. Samsø, Denmark

Samsø is located off the east coast of the Danish mainland. It presents typical characteristics of Danish municipalities regarding energy supply, but also specifics related to being an exemplary RE island [41]. Being part of Denmark and its ambitious targets for sustainability, district heating has become an important cornerstone to supply clusters of heat demands. The employment of wind power is another important aspect, which makes up a major characteristic of Samsø's reference and future energy system. With most data available for 2015, this year is used in the reference scenario.

3.1.1. Samsø Today

Today, Samsø's population is at around 3700 inhabitants, and their electricity supply is mainly covered by both onshore and offshore wind power, as well as some PV capacity. With fixed capacities and temporal distributions, yearly productions are fixed in the model. These are aligned with known yearly reference productions in EnergyPLAN. Next to solar and wind resources producing mainly electricity, but also some hot water from solar panels, Samsø relies on the electricity imported through a 40 MW connection to the mainland of Denmark. This connection is mainly used for the export of surplus wind power, as well as for a limited amount of hours for import of electricity. There is no fuel-based power generation on Samsø [42–45].

Heat is supplied from four district heating plants running on woodchips, straw, and solar heat, or by individual heating devices using further biomass, oil, solar collectors, or electricity [44]. The transport sector is 99% fossil fuel-dependent, with only a small number of EVs. The main consumers—ferries connecting Samsø to Danish mainland—run mostly on oil and some natural gas.

With a high share of wind power, as well as an extensive exploration of biomass, the RE share of the PES reached 60% in the reference year 2014. Especially the transport sector, and some of the individually-heated buildings, still require fossil fuels. When it comes to electricity needed on Samsø, 94% is produced by wind and PV and the remaining 6% is imported.

Samsø is the smallest of the three case study islands, with the highest RE share and the comparably lowest CO_2 emissions (28.5 kt). The biomass heating share is 69% in the reference system with 35% of the heat supplied through district heating, but still 18% from oil boilers. The electric and solar heating shares are at 11% and 2%, respectively, and the electric transport share at 1%—hence having room for improvement, especially with 78% of the local RE electricity being exported.

3.1.2. Transition of Samsø

In SMILE, Samsø therefore addresses the possibility of employing more local electricity on the island. For this, some further PV capacity is installed, but also unused existing capacity can be better integrated with smart controls and a BESS. This is tested in the scope of Ballen Marina, which is used by both locals and tourists, hence an integrated part of the energy system. Here, PV power is planned to be smartly used and stored to decrease the dependency on imports, which in combination with heat pumps further contributes to this local test scope. If successful, this idea could be replicated in the other marinas on Samsø and elsewhere [46].

The impact of the Ballen demonstration can be integrated in the EnergyPLAN reference model by adapting the total remaining electricity demand and by adding the excess PV production as supply available for other uses. The expected outcome is a reduction of imports by shaving the marina's peaks, increasing the usage of fluctuating renewable electricity locally, and thereby decreasing the island's dependency on others. Looking further ahead, the improved utilization of local RE becomes important when more electric heating and EVs are introduced.

The smart controlling of heat production via heat pumps further opens up the possibility to reduce the use of biomass boilers. While biomass heating is renewable, it is not an optimal use of a storage fuel, and the biomass could alternatively enable the production of biofuel for other uses—e.g., for running one of the ferries such as the natural gas-run Prinsesse Isabella. The overall goal of Samsø is therefore the reduction of imports by using more otherwise exported electricity, reducing further biomass consumption in the heating sector and freeing it for the transport sector. Thereby, Samsø is currently in transition phase two, with an already large RE share and aiming for 100% RE.

Further steps besides the SMILE ideas for the further transition to 100% RE include local biogas production and electricity for transport, improving the district heating plants, as well as an increase in RE capacity. By 2030, a biogas plant is to be realized, contributing to reducing the fossil fuel demand of the ferries and potentially also to the road transport. In addition, the road transport is considered to be further electrified, with focus on passenger vehicles, as recommended by Mathiesen et al. [2] and Connolly et al. [47]. With the implementation of EVs, some of the excess electricity is utilized, while it also increases the island's electricity demand. Overall, the higher efficiency of electric compared to internal combustion vehicles decreases the total energy demand [48].

District heating plants are considered retrofitted with heat pumps due to the availability of excess electricity and the scarcity of biomass resources. By keeping the existing boilers for peaks, heat pump support, and backup, the heat pumps can be operated to run entirely on excess electricity from RE. This is furthermore supported by additional TES next to the existing ones. Depending on the available excess RE electricity on Samsø, the amount of heat produced from heat pumps depends on the increase of electricity consumption in the other sectors. Hence, if the number of EVs increases, the heat pump production might be reduced to avoid increasing electricity imports.

Furthermore, additional wind and PV capacity under the condition of limiting the critical excess electricity production is evaluated. Large RE capacities of one technology can result in large amounts of excess electricity in certain (e.g., windy) hours, so an increase of PV capacity with a total of 10 MW is suggested. Electricity from PV is shown to be better integrable in the energy system and potentially easier realized regarding space demand and potential opposition in the population [49].

To reduce the remaining fossil fuel use, heat pumps should replace the individual oil boilers, after which any remaining fossil fuel consumption is found in the transport sector. One option to lower this and to integrate the still high RE export further is through electrolyzers and hydrogen production as fuel replacement. In total, with the short-term steps in the transition of Samsø, the RE share reaches 85% and the CO_2 emissions are below 10 kt per year compared to the reference model with 59.5% and 28.5 kt.

3.1.3. Samsø's Future

The concluding Figure 1 presents data for demand and supply before and after the transition steps (see tables in Section 4). Most notably, the connections between sectors increase as sector integration and balance options are pointed out as important parts of the transition. However, a small share of the now increased electricity demand needs to be imported due to the inflexibility of the modeled demand. Despite an overall electricity demand increase of 64%, the RE share of the electricity consumption is increased by 2% point to 96% from the 2015 to the 2030 model (cf., Table 6).

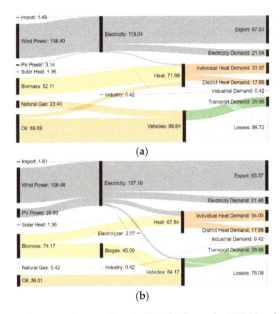

Figure 1. Sankey diagrams of energy flows in GWh for Samsø for 2015 (a) and 2030 (b) [32].

To replace the remaining fossil fuels, alternative fuels are needed, which can also further reduce system losses. An extension of the biogas plant or a replacement of remaining fuels with electro- or biofuels could be considered. Next to the further increase of the RE capacity, more efficient heating and transport options are still required for a full transition to a 100% RE island. Additionally, smart controlling and management of various demands could support the transition, so further exploration and integration of solutions such as those presented in SMILE is recommended.

3.2. Orkney, United Kingdom

The 70 islands in the Orkney archipelago, out of which 20 are inhabited, lie to the north of the Scottish mainland. The Orkney Isles are characterized by a mild climate with open waters on three sides, which offers good opportunities for wind and ocean energy exploitation. Within the United Kingdom and over the last 30 years, Orkney has been a frontrunner in the development of RE technologies [50]. With an Energy Audit made for 2014, this is chosen as the reference year.

3.2.1. Orkney Today

Orkney represents the medium size case study island, with around 22,000 inhabitants, and lies between Samsø and Madeira in terms of RE share and CO_2 emissions (186 kt). Wind and some PV power supply the majority of the islands' electricity demand in the reference year: Only 7% of the demand is imported and 27% is supplied by the local power plant. A large part of the heat is still relying on oil, as is the industry and transport sector, despite the relatively high amount of EVs compared to other regions in the UK or Europe; its share is estimated at only around 0.1% of the total transportation demand (0.2% of the road transport).

Utility-scale turbines and around 500 domestic-scale turbines [51] almost reach the annual electricity demand of Orkney in the reference year, but due to the fluctuation of its production, other electricity needs to be provided [52]. Next to the fluctuation, intra-island grid bottlenecks are a problem, causing high degrees of curtailment and a limit of firm connections from turbines to the grid. For the remaining electricity demand [53], a small share of PV systems and two subsea cables supply some of the additionally required electricity [50,52]. Since the wave and tidal power facilities are still considered test facilities and not in commercial operation, they are not considered in the reference system.

Additionally, fuels are used for electricity production through a local thermal power plant. The total amount of fuel for electricity production results from the EnergyPLAN model, which simulates the production of electricity from fossil fuels when not enough wind and PV power is produced. Therefore, the amount of gas to supply the energy system of Orkney is made up of a large share for power production, as well as gas-fueled heating systems [54,55]. Solar radiation is also used to produce heat through around 20 solar thermal collectors [56,57].

While the electricity sector is mainly supplied by locally produced electricity, the heating sector still relies a lot on fossil fuels, even though Orkney has an electric heating share above the average [54,58]. Together with the fuels needed in the transport and industrial sector, this results in the overall RE share of 18%. All data of the reference as well as the future model are presented in Section 4.

3.2.2. Transition of Orkney

In the reference model of Orkney, the CO_2 emissions are at a similar amount per capita as on Samsø. The biomass share, however, is much smaller, with 1% of the modeled heat sector for 2014, while the electric heating share is at 44%, resulting in a high share of fuel poverty in the area [58]. With a current export share of 32% of the local RE production and no district heating grid, there is room for improvement.

To address the option of more efficient heating, in combination with otherwise curtailed or exported electricity, the SMILE demonstration project on Orkney focuses on new domestic electric heaters with storage, as well as on including electric transport through more EV charging stations. Both options include smart planning and operation, meaning taking into account the temporality of excess RE production and the potential demands.

By integrating RE in a smarter way, the local energy can be used locally and benefit both the heating and the transport sector. Furthermore, it can reduce imports and production at the power plant if demands can be shifted to hours of excess production. This reduces the islands' fuel use and CO_2 emissions, as well as reduced electricity exchange and curtailment. An increase in self-sufficiency is the overall goal and is presented in the following through a technical approach, including the SMILE demonstration.

The resulting impact on CO_2 emissions can be connected to the reduction in heating oils, while the heat pumps increase the total electricity demand, causing a reduction in exported electricity. Adding more EVs, even though smart-charged, adds to this reduction of export and CO_2 because of the shift from transport oils to electricity. Furthermore, an increase of import happens due to inevitable temporal mismatches between RE production and charging.

Besides the SMILE approaches of heat and transport sector, some other changes that are taking place on Orkney need to be incorporated and matched with the transition to achieve higher RE shares. One such change is the addition of marine energy exploitation, including wave and tidal power, as well as hydrogen and electrolyzers, which have shown promising test results for future exploration [50,59,60]. Not all included technologies have an appropriate technology readiness level today, but there is an ongoing technology development in the field. Thus, for future scenarios, particularly in islands setting, the technologies must be considered.

Additionally, with a focus on banning the sale of diesel and petrol cars by 2032 in Scotland [61], Orkney is on the way to increasing the use of EVs to a suggested maximum around the year 2030 [2,47]. Therefore, 80% of the road transport (all passenger vehicles) is modeled to be reliant on EVs with V2G balancing the electricity import and export to the highest extent possible. This is modeled by allowing the EVs to supply the grid via a standard 10 kW capacity per car of battery to grid connection [48].

As part of the further transition and to improve the heating sector of the island, district heating is proposed to be implemented in the largest town on Orkney, namely Kirkwall, as previous studies [62,63] suggest large heat densities there. With the selection of this central heat demand, 33% of the current heat demand on Orkney could be covered with district heating. Due to the still large amounts of excess electricity, a heat pump is to supply this district heating grid, as well as a biomass boiler as a supplement and back-up to avoid increased electricity imports. In addition, the individual heating sector is to develop further towards renewable heat: The remaining boilers are to change to biomass or heat pumps. While this, on the one hand, increases the RE share beyond 30%, it also increases both electricity demand and biomass consumption.

3.2.3. Orkney's Future

All the suggested transition steps, together, result in an RE share of 38% (cf., before 18%) for the PES of Orkney next to a 33% reduction in CO_2 emission, while the other key parameters can be found in Section 4. Figure 2 shows all input and output specifications of the reference and transition scenario for Orkney. This illustrates that one of the focus areas in the transition, namely fossil fuel consumption, is changing the most. Instead of using these, electricity replaces some of the corresponding demands, while biomass supplies others.

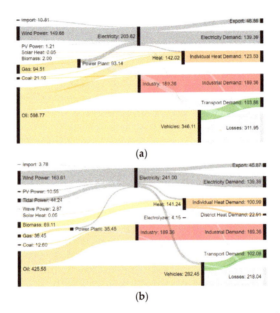

Figure 2. Sankey diagrams of energy flows in GWh for Orkney for 2014 (**a**) and 2030 (**b**) [32].

To address the remaining fossil fuels in transport, a replacement with electro- or biofuels could be considered, similar to Samsø, with either local biogas production or additional hydrogen. However, if electricity-based fuels are considered, the amount of excess electricity can be taken into account, which still makes up a large share. Alternatively, additional RE capacity might be required to allow these further electrification measures.

As further illustrated in Figure 2, the industrial demands have not been addressed with these improvements of heating and transport sector. Due to insufficient data and the unusually complex conditions in the industrial sector, an optimization of it requires an in-depth study. Another recommendation is therefore the investigation of this sector, besides the transport sector, which still relies largely on fossil fuels. The second Sankey diagram in Figure 2 presents Orkney in the second RE integration phase, after which further balancing and interconnections are needed to approach the next phase towards the 100% RE target.

3.3. Madeira, Portugal

Madeira lies isolated both from the lands and from the electricity grids of Europe and Africa. In comparison to Samsø and Orkney, it therefore presents the only true island system, supplying itself almost independently and even incinerating its produced waste to the best extent possible. Further differentiating it from most other European areas, Madeira has the typical characteristics of a southern climate, with high solar radiation and cooling demands rather than a heating demand. For the reference model, 2014 is selected to represent a normal weather year, especially in regards to precipitation and the impact on hydropower.

3.3.1. Madeira Today

With a population of around 250,000, Madeira represents the largest population and island of the three. However, the production of RE and some of the energy demands are not necessarily as big as to be expected in comparison to Samsø and Orkney. The demands are, to a large extent, covered by fossil fuels, but also a variety of RE [64–66].

Thermal power plants are still used for grid stabilization, run mostly on fuel oil or gas, and produce most of the electricity needed on Madeira [65]. Hydropower plants form the second largest production group with dammed and river hydro plants with small reservoirs suitable for hourly flexibility [65]. The wind farms have a total capacity similar to the reference models of Samsø and Orkney, but a much larger PV capacity relating to the comparably higher potential. This, however, is limited due to difficulties with the grid frequency. Finally, the annual waste of more than 100,000 t produces electricity through incineration [66].

Next to the RE for electricity production, solar radiation is further used for heat production. Other heating fuels are electricity, biomass, gas, and a minor share of oils—50% of the oil is otherwise needed in the transport sector [67]. In total, the reference model shows that 11% of the PES is based on RE, including waste incineration. The electricity production, however, is made up by 29% RE, despite limits in the RE exploitation.

3.3.2. Transition of Madeira

Without an interconnection, Madeira is the only SMILE island with an autonomous electricity grid. Therefore, the dependency on fuel imports and need for better utilization of local resources are even greater than for most other islands. With a current RE share of 11% and CO_2 emissions of 895 kt, Madeira presents a contrast to the other islands with a much lower CO_2 per capita, but a similar transition process towards 100% RE system is required nonetheless.

The Madeira reference energy system has 115 MW RE capacity, which is far from sufficient for the comparably large electricity demands, resulting in major fossil power production. However, there are limits to an RE expansion due to grid and stabilization issues. The transition of Madeira towards higher RE shares therefore looks a bit different from Samsø and Orkney, with the RE introduction phase reached and large steps required to reach the second phase.

The existing circumstances are considered in the definition of the SMILE demonstration projects for Madeira, as well as the further transition steps. SMILE addresses the existing PV installations and the sensitive grid with BESS for both residential and commercial buildings, as well as the optimization of the transport sector through touristic and private EVs. This is tested in a comparable small scale considering the size of the island, but is further explored as can be projected by 2030. The overall target on Madeira lies in the optimization of local resources and the reduction of fossil fuels in the power production and transport sector through smart grid solutions [18]. For this, power plant stabilization is reduced and the new SMILE technologies added to the EnergyPLAN model.

Next in line in the transition is the incorporation of the plans for additional PV, hydro, and wind capacity [68]. Thereafter, the transport sector is addressed closer: After the introduction of EV for commercial, touristic, and private purposes, with the addition of smart chargers, a further exploration is expected. Similar to Orkney, an exponential increase of EV by the year 2030 is modeled with the inclusion of a V2G option, reducing the production at the power plant by enabling EVs to be used as temporary electrical storages. The same approach as on Orkney is assumed and modeled [48].

Eventually, also the heating sector must be addressed to reach higher RE shares. A first logical step is the replacement of oil and natural gas for heating with heat pumps. In the same step, more solar thermal is explored, while reducing the electricity requirement to hours with insufficient solar resources.

3.3.3. Madeira's Future

The result of the additional capacities, as well as of the other assumed improvements by 2030, is an RE share of the PES of 31%, while the share for the electricity demand is at 71%. Additional RE capacity would increase both even further, but would at the same time result in critical excess electricity production, so the benefits would be limited. Therefore, a more balanced approach towards the 100% RE share is required in the longer term, especially for an autonomous energy system like Madeira.

Figure 3 shows the resulting energy flows of the reference and transition scenario, while the detailed data are found in Section 4. The major change that can be noted is the reduction in fossil fuels, mainly oil from 2014 to 2030. Instead, electricity is produced more from RE, but further optimization should be found for the remaining oil and gas consumption. Generally, the transition could be more successful with the RE integration on all levels and in combination with balancing and storing technologies.

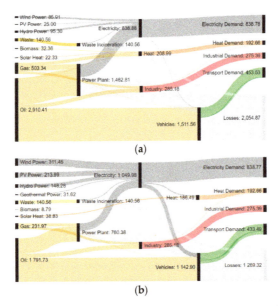

Figure 3. Sankey diagrams of energy flows in GWh for Madeira for 2014 (a) and 2030 (b) [32].

As it could be tested for Samsø and expanded on Orkney, hydrogen production through electrolyzer could become relevant for the replacement of fossil fuels in the transport sector. Alternatively, biogas production could be pursued. For the second technology, the local biomass potential—both dry and wet—should be evaluated before it can be included in the model.

The final point of discussion relates to the heating sector transition, since—also here—changes are required for the overall development of the Madeira energy system towards 100% RE. The uncertain heating demands currently covered by electricity can provide relevant information for possible improvements. If inefficient boilers and heaters are used, a replacement with efficient heat pumps or even the establishment of district heating could improve the energy system. Besides the uncertainties in the heating sector, the cooling supply could be evaluated and improved. With the possibility of district cooling, the service sector of Madeira could achieve benefits through more suitable supply technologies, ultimately benefitting large-scale RE integration.

4. Overview and Discussion

This section presents an overview of the different scenarios and resulting island energy systems' characteristics after implementation of various smart grid and balancing technologies in the transition towards 100% RE. It shows the short-term changes with their potentials and challenges on three cases and suggests options for other islands. Even though the three islands are of different sizes and populations, some similarities in regard to their energy systems can be identified. By presenting the different RE capacities and their impacts, possible gaps or potentials in the plans and models of other islands can be found and help shape the future creation of sustainable island energy systems.

The energy demands are presented by sectors with the reference and short-term scenarios in Table 3. Here, the main changes are due to more electricity being used in the heating or the transport sector, while the total demands generally stay the same.

Table 3. Comparison of energy demands.

Annual Data	Samsø		Orkney		Madeira	
	2015	2030	2014	2030	2014	2030
Electricity Demand (GWh)	25.5	41.8	154.7	195.0	838.8	1042.7
Heat Demand (excl. electric) (GWh)	46.3	21.3	69.4	38.7	192.7	76.0
Transport Demand (GWh)	30.0	28.9	103.9	99.7	453.5	433.8
Industry Demand (GWh)	0.4	0.4	189.4	189.4	275.4	275.4

The different approaches for the islands in regard of added RE capacity and resulting RE production are shown in Table 4. Despite the plans of decommissioning the power plants on Madeira, as well as reducing the dependence on the power plant on Orkney, the energy system analyses show some still required power production from these.

Table 4. Comparison of electricity production.

Annual Data	Samsø		Orkney		Madeira	
	2015	2030	2014	2030	2014	2030
Wind power capacity (MW)	34.4	34.4	48.3	52.8	45.1	133.1
PV capacity (MW)	1.3	11.5	1.2	11.5	19.1	121.7
Tidal and wave capacity (MW)	-	-	-	19.0	-	-
Geothermal capacity (MW)	-	-	-	-	-	30.0
Hydro power capacity (MW)	-	-	-	-	50.7	111.6
Waste incineration (GWh)	-	-	-	-	32.9	32.9
Transmission capacity (MW)	40	40	40	40	-	-
Power plant power supply (GWh)	-	-	41.9	16.0	599.7	311.8

Since the fossil fuel reduction was paid special attention to in order to increase the RE share in the energy systems, they are included in Table 5. It shows that the fossil fuel consumption on Samsø is reduced by 68% between 2015 and 2030 with the presented scenarios. Similarly, on Orkney, this number is reduced by 34% and on Madeira by 40%.

Table 5. Comparison of fuel consumption.

Annual Data	Samsø		Orkney		Madeira	
	2015	2030	2014	2030	2014	2030
Biomass consumption (GWh)	52.2	74.2	2.0	69.1	172.9	149.4
Oil consumption (GWh)	89.0	36.0	598.8	425.6	2910.4	1791.7
Gas consumption (GWh)	23.4	0.4	94.5	35.5	503.3	232.0
Coal consumption (GWh)	-	-	21.1	12.6	-	-
Total fossil fuels (GWh)	112.4	36.4	714.4	473.7	3413.8	2023.7
Total consumption (GWh)	164.6	110.6	716.4	542.8	3586.7	2173.1

In Table 6, the comparison of the RE share generally shows great improvements, with increases of 20% points and more. However, for Orkney and Madeira, it is still a long way to the large-scale and 100% RE share targeted, despite the ambitious scenarios to improve the energy systems presented in this report. This can partly be explained by the more balanced approached taken in the scenario creation, rather than a simple increase in RE capacities. The latter would increase the RE share, but also the export and potential curtailment/critical excess production. Instead, more moderate capacity additions are introduced, together with balancing options, such as smart charging and storage options, presenting one approach for the smooth transition to 100% RE.

Table 6. Comparison of energy system indicators.

Annual Data	Samsø		Orkney		Madeira	
	2015	2030	2014	2030	2014	2030
RE share of PES	60%	85%	18%	38%	11%	31%
RE share of electricity demand	94%	96%	66%	85%	29%	71%
Imported electricity (GWh)	1.5	1.8	10.8	3.8	0.0	0.0
Exported/Excess electricity (GWh)	87.5	93.4	48.9	46.0	0.0	0.2
CO_2 emissions on island (kt)	28.5	9.7	186.0	124.9	894.5	541.1
CO_2 emissions per capita (t)	7.7	2.6	8.5	5.7	3.5	2.2
Total socio-economic costs (M€)	16.5	15.6	57.7	59.6	315.7	337.2

Further indicators included in Table 6 are electricity import and export/excess production to show the share of local energy consumption and self-sufficiency. Samsø's share of RE electricity is close to 100% and, despite the suggested RE capacity increase, the share of the local electricity that is exported is reduced, as more can be used on Samsø now. The same applies to Orkney, which furthermore reduces the import share from 7 to 2% of the electricity demand. Finally, with different framework conditions on Madeira without import/export option, it is possible to keep the critical excess production at 0.02%. This shows the strength of including the full energy system in the transition, instead of focusing on the electricity sector only. While RE capacity could be further increased, improving the RE share in the electricity sector, it would lead to increased excess production, if not integrating the energy sectors. A step-by-step transition approach is therefore proven and recommended, despite being more complex and requiring a more integrated energy system.

Similarly, the CO_2 emissions are reduced with the increase of RE and decrease of fossil fuel combustion. On Samsø, the reduction is 66%, 33% on Orkney, and 40% on Madeira. The final CO_2 emissions are equal to annually 2.6, 5.7, and 2.2 t per capita for Samsø, Orkney, and Madeira, respectively. The high amount for Orkney might relate to the big industrial sector and limited biomass potential.

Finally, the last row of Table 6 shows the tendencies for annual total socio-economic system costs with current data on technologies, fuels, operation, and CO_2 costs. For each of the islands, the annual costs are similar or even decreased in the short term—compared to the references—by −5, +3, and +7%. Considering the large investments in new technologies and infrastructure, these values are acceptable and come with possible long-term benefits. While fuel and CO_2 costs drastically decrease, the annual investments increase by 34, 61, and 120%, respectively, showing how the money is being spent on local infrastructure instead of imported goods now.

The three islands are all presenting cases of reduced or stabilized electricity import and export, with strongly improved CO_2 values at acceptable socio-economic costs, in the transition to 100% RE systems. Taking into consideration the different phases of the transition, as well as the sensitive and specific circumstances for each island, an increase in RE share can be achieved.

5. Conclusions

Investigating the transition towards 100% RE supply for islands, this paper presents transition scenarios for Samsø, Orkney, and Madeira with their potentials and challenges. Built upon reference energy systems of 2014/2015, scenarios are created incorporating smart grid demonstration projects, as well as further possibilities in the energy system, to present energy system scenarios of 2030. Local conditions influence the possibilities, as do local plans and strategies. These are incorporated into suggested steps for a transition to higher RE shares as a three-phase approach, of which Samsø is the farthest ahead, while Orkney and Madeira are in the second phase from low towards high RE share. The resulting short-term scenarios of 2030 generally show that local conditions and opportunities vary, which leads to the conclusion that every transition, island, and energy system is unique and must be evaluated separately, while some similarities exist.

This article presents Samsø's energy system moving from the reference system, with already large-scale RE integration, towards a system with 100%, resulting in the incorporation of technologies focusing at balancing the energy system instead of further increasing RE capacity. As part of this transition, the local abundance of wind energy and biomass, as well as transmission capabilities, influence the technical choices leading to the next phase. While some technologies are specific for Samsø, they can generally be replicated and thereby improve island energy systems in various ways.

Orkney's reference energy system is characterized in the RE introduction phase, hence the increase of this to large-scale RE integration is currently in focus, instead of balancing the energy production and demands. With local limits in their transmission grid, but otherwise good RE conditions, the smart grid solutions and integration technologies are chosen accordingly. As this paper shows, more potential RE capacity would still be required, as well as the further exploration of sector integration, to support fragile energy systems such as this.

Madeira is in the process of introducing more RE to their energy system and aiming at an increase of its share, hence being in the beginning of the RE integration phase. Therefore, Madeira's short-term development focuses on the expansion of various RE capacities, as well as the potentials in the transport and heating sector. Without a transmission line, the autonomous energy island already requires balancing options through sector integration and making use of local hydropower production and storage. The combination with smart grid applications plays another major part in autonomous energy systems, such as Madeira.

This case study demonstrates possible transitions to 100% RE systems, which is taking place all over the world. With new problems coming into view with an increased RE share, new solutions are presented and tested for three islands. With islands being potential representatives of bigger energy systems, the results can be transferred to other systems as well. However, individual variations are also to be expected, as is shown from the demonstration islands in this report depending on their current development phase. While an interconnection can ease the transition, balancing and integrating technologies are even more important, as well as the local conditions. Further smart grid technology employment could support this further. This case study shows a variety of energy systems and solutions and therefore gives examples of the required transition of islands towards 100% RE share. The general tendency points to smart and balanced planning of the next steps to ensure this.

Author Contributions: Conceptualization and validation, H.M.M., P.A.Ø., and S.R.D.; methodology and software, H.M.M. and P.A.Ø.; formal analysis, investigation, data curation, visualization, and writing—original draft preparation, H.M.M.; writing—review and editing, H.M.M., P.A.Ø., and S.R.D.; supervision, P.A.Ø. and S.R.D.; project administration and funding acquisition, P.A.Ø.

Funding: This research was funded by the Horizon2020 research programme under the grant agreement no. 731249.

Acknowledgments: This work is supported by the SMILE partners on Samsø, Orkney, and Madeira for helping in the data gathering and optimization process of the full reports that this paper is based on [31,32] and which are available on www.h2020smile.eu.

Conflicts of Interest: The authors declare no conflicts of interest.

References

1. European Commission. 2030 Climate & Energy Framework. Climate Action. 2014. Available online: https://ec.europa.eu/clima/policies/strategies/2030_en (accessed on 2 April 2019).
2. Mathiesen, B.V.; Lund, H.; Connolly, D.; Wenzel, H.; Østergaard, P.A.; Möller, B.; Nielsen, S.; Ridjan, I.; Karnøe, P.; Sperling, K.; et al. Smart Energy Systems for coherent 100% renewable energy and transport solutions. *Appl. Energy* **2015**, *145*, 139–154. [CrossRef]
3. Connolly, D.; Lund, H.; Mathiesen, B.V. Smart Energy Europe: The technical and economic impact of one potential 100% renewable energy scenario for the European Union. *Renew. Sustain. Energy Rev.* **2016**, *60*, 1634–1653. [CrossRef]
4. European Commission. Clean Energy for EU Islands Launch. European Commission Energy News. 2017. Available online: https://ec.europa.eu/energy/en/news/clean-energy-eu-islands-launched-malta (accessed on 20 April 2019).
5. Kuang, Y.; Zhang, Y.; Zhou, B.; Li, C.; Cao, Y.; Li, L.; Zeng, L. A review of renewable energy utilization in islands. *Renew. Sustain. Energy Rev.* **2016**, *59*, 504–513. [CrossRef]
6. Praene, J.P.; David, M.; Sinama, F.; Morau, D.; Marc, O. Renewable energy: Progressing towards a net zero energy island, the case of Reunion Island. *Renew. Sustain. Energy Rev.* **2012**, *16*, 426–442. [CrossRef]
7. Weir, T. Renewable energy in the Pacific Islands: Its role and status. *Renew. Sustain. Energy Rev.* **2018**, *94*, 762–771. [CrossRef]
8. Thushara, D.S.M.; Hornberger, G.M.; Baroud, H. Decision analysis to support the choice of a future power generation pathway for Sri Lanka. *Appl. Energy* **2019**, *240*, 680–697. [CrossRef]
9. Ioannidis, A.; Chalvatzis, K.J.; Li, X.; Notton, G.; Stephanides, P. The case for islands' energy vulnerability: Electricity supply diversity in 44 global islands. *Renew. Energy* **2019**, *143*, 440–452. [CrossRef]
10. Meschede, H.; Hesselbach, J.; Child, M.; Breyer, C. On the impact of probabilistic weather data on the economically optimal design of renewable energy systems—A case study on La Gomera island. In Proceedings of the 13th International Renewable Energy Storage Conference (IRES 2019), 12–14 March 2019, Messe Düsseldorf, Germany. [CrossRef]
11. Dorotić, H.; Doračić, B.; Dobravec, V.; Pukšec, T.; Krajačić, G.; Duić, N. Integration of transport and energy sectors in island communities with 100% intermittent renewable energy sources. *Renew. Sustain. Energy Rev.* **2019**, *99*, 109–124. [CrossRef]
12. Meschede, H.; Esparcia, E.A., Jr.; Holzapfel, P.; Bertheau, P.; Ang, R.C.; Blanco, A.C.; Ocon, J.D. On the transferability of smart energy systems on off-grid islands using cluster analysis–A case study for the Philippine archipelago. *Appl. Energy* **2019**, *251*, 113290. [CrossRef]
13. Pramangioulis, D.; Atsonios, K.; Nikolopoulos, N.; Rakopoulos, D.; Grammelis, P.; Kakaras, E. A Methodology for Determination and Definition of Key Performance Indicators for Smart Grids Development in Island Energy Systems. *Energies* **2019**, *12*, 242. [CrossRef]
14. Colmenar-Santos, A.; Monzón-Alejandro, O.; Borge-Diez, D.; Castro-Gil, M. The impact of different grid regulatory scenarios on the development of renewable energy on islands: A comparative study and improvement proposals. *Renew. Energy* **2013**, *60*, 302–312. [CrossRef]
15. Rina Consulting S.p.A. SMart IsLand Energy Systems Project. 2017. Available online: http://www.h2020smile.eu/ (accessed on 20 September 2017).
16. Hermansen, S.; Johnsen, A.; Nielsen, S.P.; Jantzen, J.; Lundén, M.; Jørgensen, P.J. *Samsø—A renewable energy island—10 years of Development and Evaluation*, 2nd ed.; Chronografisk: Ballen, Denmark, 2007.
17. Community Energy Scotland. *Smart Island Energy Systems Deliverable D2.1*; Community Energy Scotland: Kirkwall, Scotland, 2017.

18. ACIF-CCIM. *Smart Island Energy Systems Deliverable D4.1*; ACIF-CCIM: Funchal, Portugal, 2017.
19. Aalborg University. *EnergyPLAN—Department of Development and Planning*; Aalborg University: Aalborg, Denmark, 2017.
20. Østergaard, P.A. Reviewing optimisation criteria for energy systems analyses of renewable energy integration. *Energy* **2009**, *34*, 1236–1245. [CrossRef]
21. Sorknæs, P.; Djørup, S.R.; Lund, H.; Thellufsen, J.Z. Quantifying the influence of wind power and photovoltaic on future electricity market prices. *Energy Convers. Manag.* **2019**, *180*, 312–324. [CrossRef]
22. Djørup, S.; Thellufsen, J.Z.; Sorknæs, P. The electricity market in a renewable energy system. *Energy* **2018**, *162*, 148–157. [CrossRef]
23. Cantarero, M.M.V. Reviewing the Nicaraguan transition to a renewable energy system: Why is "business-as-usual" no longer an option? *Energy policy* **2018**, *120*, 580–592. [CrossRef]
24. Østergaard, P.A. Reviewing EnergyPLAN simulations and performance indicator applications in EnergyPLAN simulations. *Appl. Energy* **2015**, *154*, 921–933. [CrossRef]
25. Marczinkowski, H.M.; Østergaard, P.A. Residential versus communal combination of photovoltaic and battery in smart energy systems. *Energy* **2018**, *152*, 466–475. [CrossRef]
26. Marczinkowski, H.M.; Østergaard, P.A. Evaluation of electricity storage versus thermal storage as part of two different energy planning approaches for the islands Samsø and Orkney. *Energy* **2019**, *175*, 505–514. [CrossRef]
27. Østergaard, P.A.; Jantzen, J.; Marczinkowski, H.M.; Kristensen, M. Business and socioeconomic assessment of introducing heat pumps with heat storage in small-scale district heating systems. *Renew. Energy* **2019**, *139*, 904–914. [CrossRef]
28. Cabrera, P.; Lund, H.; Carta, J.A. Smart renewable energy penetration strategies on islands: The case of Gran Canaria. *Energy* **2018**, *162*, 421–443. [CrossRef]
29. Haydt, G.; Leal, V.; Pina, A.; Silva, C.A. The relevance of the energy resource dynamics in the mid/long-term energy planning models. *Renew. Energy* **2011**, *36*, 3068–3074. [CrossRef]
30. Pillai, J.R.; Heussen, K.; Østergaard, P.A. Comparative analysis of hourly and dynamic power balancing models for validating future energy scenarios. *Energy* **2011**, *36*, 3233–3243. [CrossRef]
31. Marczinkowski, H.M. *Smart Island Energy Systems Deliverable D8.1*; Aalborg University: Aalborg, Denmark, 2017.
32. Marczinkowski, H.M. *Smart Island Energy Systems Deliverable D8.2*; Aalborg University: Aalborg, Denmark, 2018.
33. Henriques, A.; Vasconcelos, D. *EEM Dispatch Center Production 2014*; Empresa de Eletricidade da Madeira: Funchal, Portugal, 2015.
34. Staffell, I.; Pfenninger, S. Using bias-corrected reanalysis to simulate current and future wind power output. *Energy* **2016**, *114*, 1224–1239. [CrossRef]
35. Pfenninger, S.; Staffell, I. Long-term patterns of European PV output using 30 years of validated hourly reanalysis and satellite data. *Energy* **2016**, *114*, 1251–1265. [CrossRef]
36. EMD International A/S. *Energypro—EMD International A/S*; EMD International A/S: Aalborg, Denmark, 2018.
37. Saha, S.; Moorthi, S.; Wu, X.; Wang, J.; Nadiga, S.; Tripp, P.; Behringer, D.; Hou, Y.-T.; Chuang, H.-Y.; Iredell, M.; et al. The NCEP Climate Forecast System Version 2. *J. Clim.* **2014**, *27*, 2185–2208. [CrossRef]
38. Østergaard, P.A.; Andersen, A.N. Booster heat pumps and central heat pumps in district heating. *Appl. Energy* **2016**, *184*, 1374–1388. [CrossRef]
39. Andersen, F.M. Electricity Profiles. 2012. Available online: http://www.elforbrugspanel.dk/Pages/Rapportering.aspx (accessed on 12 April 2018).
40. Lund, H. *Renewable Energy Systems—A Smart Energy Systems Approach to the Choice and Modeling of 100% Renewable Solutions*, 2nd ed.; Academic Press: Cambridge, MA, USA; Elsevier: Cambridge, MA, USA, 2014.
41. Samso Energy Academy. Samsø Energy Academy. *Vedvarende Energi-Ø*. Available online: https://energiakademiet.dk/vedvarende-energi-o/ (accessed on 20 October 2017).
42. Danish Energy Agency. Data for Energy Sector (Wind Turbines), Version 2017. 2017. Available online: https://ens.dk/service/statistik-data-noegletal-og-kort/data-oversigt-over-energisektoren (accessed on 5 August 2019).
43. Energinet.dk. PV in Denmark. 2017. Available online: https://www.energinet.dk/-/media/Energinet/El-CSI/Dokumenter/Data/Graf-for-solceller-i-Danmark.xlsx (accessed on 12 April 2018).

44. Region Midtjylland. Energy Account Samsø. 2017. Available online: http://www.rm.dk/regional-udvikling/klima-og-miljo/strategisk-energiplanlagning/ (accessed on 5 August 2019).
45. Christensen, B.G. *Personal Communication with NRGi on SAMSØ Connections*; Aalborg University: Aalborg, Denmark, 2017.
46. Jantzen, J.; Bak-Jensen, B. *Smart Island Energy Systems Deliverable D3.1*; Samsø Energy Academy: Ballen, Denmark, 2018.
47. Connolly, D.; Mathiesen, B.V.; Ridjan, I. A comparison between renewable transport fuels that can supplement or replace biofuels in a 100% renewable energy system. *Energy* **2014**, *73*, 110–125. [CrossRef]
48. Lund, H.; Kempton, W. Integration of renewable energy into the transport and electricity sectors through V2G. *Energy Policy* **2008**, *36*, 3578–3587. [CrossRef]
49. Kaldellis, J.K.; Kapsali, M.; Kaldelli, E.; Katsanou, E. Comparing recent views of public attitude on wind energy, photovoltaic and small hydro applications. *Renew. Energy* **2013**, *52*, 197–208. [CrossRef]
50. Orkney Renewable Energy Forum (OREF) and Community Energy Scotlant. *Orkney-Wide Energy Audit 2014: Energy Sources and Uses*; Orkney Renewable Energy Forum (OREF) and Community Energy Scotland: Stromness, Scotland, 2015.
51. Orkney Renewable Energy Forum (OREF). OREF Homepage. 2017. Available online: http://www.oref.co.uk/ (accessed on 27 November 2017).
52. Department for Business Energy & Industrial Strategy. UK Statistics on Renewable Electricity. 2018. Available online: https://www.gov.uk/government/statistics/regional-renewable-statistics (accessed on 23 November 2017).
53. Department for Business Energy & Industrial Strategy. UK Statistics on Electricity Consumption. 2017. Available online: https://www.gov.uk/government/statistical-data-sets/regional-and-local-authority-electricity-consumption-statistics-2005-to-2011 (accessed on 23 November 2017).
54. Department for Business Energy & Industrial Strategy. UK Statistics on Residual Fuel Consumption. 2016. Available online: https://www.gov.uk/government/statistical-data-sets/estimates-of-non-gas-non-electricity-and-non-road-transport-fuels-at-regional-and-local-authority-level (accessed on 23 November 2017).
55. Department of Energy & Climate Change. UK Statistics on Road Transport. Sub-National Road Transport Fuel Consumption 2014–2016. Available online: https://www.gov.uk/government/statistical-data-sets/road-transport-energy-consumption-at-regional-and-local-authority-level (accessed on 23 November 2017).
56. Department for Business Energy & Industrial Strategy. RHI statistics. Collective Renewable Heat Incentive Statistics; 2015. Available online: https://www.gov.uk/government/collections/renewable-heat-incentive-statistics (accessed on 28 November 2017).
57. Danish Energy Agency. *Technology Data for Energy Plants—Individual Heating Plants and Energy Transport*; Danish Energy Agency: København, Denmark, 2013.
58. National Records of Scotland. Scotland's Census. Area Profiles; 2017. Available online: http://www.scotlandscensus.gov.uk/ods-web/area.html#! (accessed on 29 November 2017).
59. Allan, G.; Gilmartin, M.; McGregor, P.; Swales, K. Levelised costs of Wave and Tidal energy in the UK: Cost competitiveness and the importance of 'banded' Renewables Obligation Certificates. *Energy Policy* **2011**, *39*, 23–39. [CrossRef]
60. Astariz, S.; Iglesias, G. The economics of wave energy: A review. *Renew. Sustain. Energy Rev.* **2015**, *45*, 397–408. [CrossRef]
61. Orkney Renewable Energy Forum (OREF). *Orkney Electric Vehicle Strategy 2018–2023*; OREF: Stromness, Scotland, 2018.
62. The Scottish Government. Scotland Heat Map. 2017. Available online: http://heatmap.scotland.gov.uk/ (accessed on 29 November 2017).
63. Mathiesen, B.V. Heat Roadmap Europe: A Low-Carbon Heating and Cooling Strategy for Europe. 2018. Available online: http://heatroadmap.eu/ (accessed on 5 August 2019).
64. Miguel, M.; Nogueira, T.; Martins, F. Energy storage for renewable energy integration: The case of Madeira Island, Portugal. *Energy Procedia* **2017**, *136*, 251–257. [CrossRef]
65. Empresa de Eletricidade da Madeira. *Annual Report EEM 2014*; Empresa de Eletricidade da Madeira: Funchal, Portugal, 2015.
66. DREM—Direção Regional de Estatística da Madeira. Statistics Madeira. Available online: https://estatistica.madeira.gov.pt/ (accessed on 20 June 2017).

67. Miguel Martins. Energy balance of RAM. In *Autonomous Region of Madeira*; Governo Regional da Madeira: Funchal, Portugal, 2017.
68. Vasconcelos, D.; Correia, H.; Barros, L. *Personal communication with EEM and M-ITI*; mpresa de Eletricidade da Madeira: Funchal, Portugal, 2018.

© 2019 by the authors. Licensee MDPI, Basel, Switzerland. This article is an open access article distributed under the terms and conditions of the Creative Commons Attribution (CC BY) license (http://creativecommons.org/licenses/by/4.0/).

Article

Exploring Energy Pathways for the Low-Carbon Transformation in India—A Model-Based Analysis

Linus Lawrenz [1], Bobby Xiong [1], Luise Lorenz [1], Alexandra Krumm [1], Hans Hosenfeld [1], Thorsten Burandt [1,2], Konstantin Löffler [1,2], Pao-Yu Oei [1,2,*] and Christian von Hirschhausen [1,2]

1. TU Berlin, Workgroup for Infrastructure and Policy, Straße des 17. Juni 135, 10623 Berlin, Germany; l.lawrenz@campus.tu-berlin.de (L.L.); bx@wip.tu-berlin.de (B.X.); ll@wip.tu-berlin.de (L.L.); alexandra.krumm@campus.tu-berlin.de (A.K.); hosenfeld@hotmail.de (H.H.); thb@wip.tu-berlin.de(T.B.); kl@wip.tu-berlin.de (K.L.); cvh@wip.tu-berlin.de (C.v.H)
2. DIW Berlin, Energy, Transport, and Environment, Mohrenstraße 58, 10117 Berlin, Germany
* Correspondence: pyo@wip.tu-berlin.de; Tel.: +49-(0)-30-3147-5846

Received: 29 September 2018; Accepted: 25 October 2018; Published: 1 November 2018

Abstract: With an increasing expected energy demand and current dominance of coal electrification, India plays a major role in global carbon policies and the future low-carbon transformation. This paper explores three energy pathways for India until 2050 by applying the linear, cost-minimizing, global energy system model (GENeSYS-MOD). The benchmark scenario "limited emissions only" (LEO) is based on ambitious targets set out by the Paris Agreement. A more conservative "business as usual" (BAU) scenario is sketched out along the lines of the New Policies scenario from the International Energy Agency (IEA). On the more ambitious side, we explore the potential implications of supplying the Indian economy entirely with renewable energies with the "100% renewable energy sources" (100% RES) scenario. Overall, our results suggest that a transformation process towards a low-carbon energy system in the power, heat, and transportation sectors until 2050 is technically feasible. Solar power is likely to establish itself as the key energy source by 2050 in all scenarios, given the model's underlying emission limits and technical parameters. The paper concludes with an analysis of potential social, economic and political barriers to be overcome for the needed Indian low-carbon transformation.

Keywords: energy system modeling; decarbonization; global energy system model (GENeSYS-MOD); renewables; India; energy transformation; energy transition; sector coupling

---

1. Introduction

India is one of the crucial actors when international climate mitigation goals are to be met. Today, the country already contributes almost 18% to the world's population and is set to account for around one-quarter of the projected rise in global energy demand by 2040 [1].

In 2015, India emitted 1869 Mt CO_2 in total, of which 51% came from power and heat generation. At present, the Central Electricity Authority of India (CEA) projects total estimated CO_2 emissions of 983 million tons for the year 2021–2022 and 1165 million tons in 2026–2027 [2]. The main driver of this absolute increase is expected growth of total energy demand. The projected peak demand is 235 GW, with an overall energy requirement of 1611 TWh at the end of the year 2022 [2]. Energy consumption is expected to rise further by 32% from 2022 to 2027 [2].

India submitted its Intended Nationally Determined Contribution (INDC) on 1 October 2015. On the national level for India, it implies three key goals to achieve this agreement:

(i) to reduce the emissions per gross domestic product (GDP) output by 33% to 35% by 2030 from 2005 levels;

(ii) to increase the cumulative electric power installed capacity from non-fossil fuel-based energy resources up to 40% by 2030;
(iii) to create an additional carbon sink of 2.5–3 billion tons of CO_2 equivalent through additional forest and tree cover by 2030 [3].

The Draft National Electricity Plan by the CEA [2] includes the INDCs, targeting a path of electricity generation and reduction of greenhouse gas (GHG) emissions in line with the Paris pledges.

By contributing to global climate efforts, India pursues international but also domestic objectives. The adverse consequences of climate change have a significant impact on the Indian population and economy, as weather extremes influence the important agriculture sector and the security of food supply [4]. Furthermore, the rise of the world temperature affects India through climate migration, water scarcity, and famine. In addition, the energy sector is an important element of India's future development strategy, seeking to reduce poverty, reduce local pollutants, and assure access to electricity for all [5]. Along with the aim to achieve the sustainable development goals (SDG), especially SDG7 "Ensure access to affordable, reliable, sustainable and modern energy for all" and SDG13 "Take urgent action to combat climate change and its impacts" established by the United Nations (UN), India seeks to make its energy system sustainable, and thereby enhance the population's living conditions.

According to the 2015 Paris climate agreement, India will revise and resubmit its INDCs by 2020. In this context, the potential contributions of sustainable energy supply have received particular interest, e.g., the future of coal as the baseload power, the potential role of natural gas as a "transformation fuel", and the potential of renewable energy to contribute to sustainable energy development. Given the global acceleration of renewable deployment, in particular solar energy, the INDCs currently developed for 2020 may be more ambitions than those back in 2015, and perhaps not even more expensive.

In addition to meeting targeted climate goals, India may benefit from a fast energy transition from both a sustainable energy and a geopolitical perspective, due to its current dependency on fossil fuels and energy imports [6].

There is a broad and growing literature base on the perspectives of the Indian energy system, to which our paper seeks to contribute. Bhushan [7,8] laid out the principle challenges to governance of energy resources for India that are still valid today, e.g., the energy–poverty challenge, central and regional coordination, the role of coal, nuclear, and renewables, and the insertion of India into global resource markets and innovation systems. Bhushan [8] stressed that India is expected to fulfill its INDC targets for 2030 easily and the focus now lies on the long-term planning. Identifying challenges, such as the need for improvements in the transmission infrastructure and facilitating access to low cost finance, is important for successful development. Currently, there is a market shift towards renewable energy sources (RES) through decreasing prices for renewable power generation, including a rapid innovation in technology [9,10].

The role of coal, and the competition with other fuels for financial resources and policy considerations, is also addressed by the Boston Consulting Group (BCG) [11] and Tripathi et al. [12].

The Indian energy sector has also been subject to model-based analysis in the context of recent policy and technology developments. In the context of the global sustainability initiative launched by Sachs [13] and Transport Scenarios by Dhar et al. [14], both studies identify possible challenges and opportunities of a low-carbon transformation of the energy and economic systems.

Löffler et al. [15] developed a cost-minimal path for the global energy system up to 2050, including India as part of ten global regions. The paper focuses on the interdependencies between traditionally segregated sectors, including electricity, transportation, and heating. Due to the scale of the referenced model, detail within the model node India is lost, which this paper will address.

A comparably different model-based approach is chosen by the Integrated Research and Action for Development (IRADe) [16]. The IRADe's low-carbon sustainable development (LCSD) model is a dynamic, multi-sectoral and intertemporal linear programming activity analysis model based on an input–output framework. In addition to scenarios which target the compliance with CO_2 budgets of

155 Gt (LC1 scenario) and 133 Gt (LC2 scenario) for India by 2050 and a baseline scenario "dynamics as usual (DAU)", the IRADe also includes human development thresholds and well-being indicators within the "visionary development (VD)". The results of the LC1 and LC2 scenarios conclude that the CO_2 budgets can be met by 2050, but cause a decrease in the overall GDP growth throughout the years.

The Massachusetts Institute of Technology (MIT) has developed a multi-sector applied general equilibrium model of the Indian economy that uses CO_2 emissions from burning fossil fuels to generate a 2030 reference case [17]. Sectoral imports and exports capture transactions with the rest of the world. The MIT developed various scenarios, such as the "emission intensity" scenario, which imposes India's NDCs, and the "non-fossil scenario", corresponding to India's non-fossil electricity capacity target of 40% installed non-fossil electricity capacity by 2030. The "combined" scenario simulates the jointly pursued targets of both "emission intensity" and non-fossil electricity. While both "emission intensity" and "combined scenario" lead to the same emission intensity in 2030, the combined scenario includes the additional constraints of non-fossil electricity targets.

Shukla et al. propose an integrated modeling framework [18,19] for analyzing alternative development pathways with equal cumulative CO_2 emissions within the first half of the 21st century. They provide a comparison of alternative development strategies on multiple indicators, including energy security, air quality, and technology stocks. Short and long-term drivers of decarbonization pathways for several regions, including Europe, the United States, China, and India are explored in a multi-model decomposition analysis by Marcucci and Fragkos [20]. Their research finds that in the short term, energy efficiency improvements are the key strategy to achieving current climate targets. In a joint project between the Indian planning office National Institution for Transforming India (NITI Aayog) and MIT, Singh et al. [17] employed a numerical economy-wide model of India with energy sector detail to simulate the impact of India's commitments to the Paris Climate Agreement.

Focusing on India's important renewable potentials, Gulagi et al. [21] explored the conditions under which India could be supplied by 100% RES by 2050. Similar exercises, with a lower level of detail, for a 100% renewables-based energy supply for India were prepared by Teske et al. [22], Jacobsen et al. [23] and Löffler et al. [24]. International organizations, too, have put a focus on India and its energy challenges, such as the International Energy Agency (IEA) [25] World Energy Outlook ("India Focus"). Shortcomings of the above-mentioned research, however, include a limited focus on electric power (no sector coupling), which will be addressed in this paper.

This paper adds to the existing literature by exploring alternative pathways to sustainable energy system development in India that respect both the specifics of the current energy system, but also stringent climate targets and global technological trends favoring non-fossil, low-cost solutions. We deploy an open-source linear cost-optimizing global energy system model (GENeSYS-MOD) to analyze different scenarios to meet increasing demand in India until 2050. A particular feature of the model is the regionalization of India into 10 regions. Thus, the model is able to illustrate regional idiosyncrasies, as well as potential imbalances, in the future energy system. The model not only focusses on the electricity sector, but also provides an in-depth analysis of the heat and transportation sectors. The implementation of different scenarios enables a qualitative comparison of the total cost for the specific optimized energy pathways until 2050. Thus, the results provide a comparability of the total cost of the different scenarios.

Projecting future energy scenarios for India also needs to account for other aspects besides the technical potential of renewables. An assessment of present literature and expert interviews is therefore used to set the modeled low-carbon energy transformation in context with the social, political and economic environment. The low-carbon transformation of the energy sector is not solely driven by climate consideration, but is inserted into a complex process of sustainable development that includes (amongst others) reducing health risk, affordable energy and a circular economy. In order to make an evaluation about whether the country is truly able to become mostly RES based in 2050, further implications on India's energy transformation have to be considered. The main sources for the literature review regarding the contextualization of the model results were, in particular "The Political Economy of Clean Energy Transitions" by Arent et al. [26], which is a distilled compendium of cross-cutting academic projects on clean energy transitions, "India's low carbon transition" by Pandey [27], "India: Meeting Energy Needs for Development While Addressing Climate Change" by Joshi et al. [28], and "Coal Transition in India-Assessing India's energy transition options" by Vishwanathan et al. [29].

After this introduction, Section 2 sketches out the status quo of the energy system in India with respect to existing technologies and recent trends on policies and technological developments. Section 3 provides a non-technical description of the model, and develops the three scenarios, the results of which are reported and discussed in Section 4. Section 5 identifies potential barriers to a low carbon transition and is followed by the concluding Section 6.

2. Status Quo of the Indian Energy Sector

2.1. Energy Mix

The current energy mix of India is dominated by coal, with a share of 58% of electricity generation in 2017, and 193 GW installed capacity. India is the third largest producer of coal and still holds the fifth biggest reserves [30]. Most of India's coal resources can be found in the eastern regions of Jharkand, Chhattisgarh, and Odisha [31]; they are also the basis for the heavy industry, like steel and metallurgy, benefitting from close-by coking coal and convenient supply chains. The coal sector is currently one of the strongest lobbying groups in Indian energy politics. The public mining company Coal India Limited (CIL) alone employs over 310,000 people [32]. Power production relies mostly on coal and the biggest share of installed coal capacities has been added in the last 15 years [31]. Around 45% of all Indian thermal power plant capacities are coal based and younger than 10 years. This implies that the remaining power plants will potentially not be in line with medium and long-term climate targets.

Natural gas contributes about 7.2% to electric power generation [33]. A large share of the natural gas has to be imported and—given the relatively high cost—natural gas has not yet obtained a significant share of the electricity mix. Nuclear energy plays an important political role, in particular in regional and international conflicts (e.g., with Pakistan), but its contribution to electricity generation is small (2.7% of generation and capacity) [34].

Small-scale and large-scale hydropower have a share of 20% and 16% in installed capacity and electricity generation, respectively. There is a controversial discussion about the future development potential of hydropower, which has a high theoretical potential, but significant practical and political challenges to its realization [8].

Renewable energy in India has several applications, the most important being biomass fuels for cooking and heating. Non-commercial energies, mainly biofuels and waste, made up about 23.1% of India's primary energy supply in 2015 [1]. With respect to electricity, the installation of grid-connected renewable generation capacities (excluding large-scale hydropower) is small, but rapidly rising at a rate of 20–25% annually over the last 15 years [7,8]. Wind energy dominates this trend, accounting for 32.8 GW of installed capacity, followed by solar photovoltaics (PV) (17.1 GW), and small hydropower (4.4 GW) as of January 2018 [35]. India's renewable energy sector has already reached a size of economic relevance for the whole country. India has a total renewable capacity share, including large hydro power, of around 32% of its installed capacity as of January 2018 [36]. In 2016, it directly and indirectly employed around 385,000 people (large hydropower plants add additional 200,000 jobs) in the renewable energy sector [37]. From April 2014 to December 2016, the equity flow into India from foreign investors surpassed US$ 2 billion [38], which was established under the Paris Agreement and is to be fully implemented in the next couple of years. As these types of investments will continue to grow [39], specific plans for an expansion of investments into renewables in developing countries have been designed. India's Prime Minister Modi, along with former French President Hollande, initialized the International Solar Alliance to mobilize US$ 1 trillion of investment worldwide into solar energy programs [40]. In addition to fiscal incentives such as accelerated depreciation, India's government has also eased the path for renewable projects [38]. Some examples are the setup of big solar parks with over 500 MW over the coming years, and mandatory ratios for rooftop solar to involve cities in renewable investments.

Just like coal, the installed capacities for renewables vary significantly between different states and regions [26]. The western regions have invested much more into renewables compared to the rest of the country. These states are almost all governed by the Bharatiya Janata Party (BJP), the national ruling party. Furthermore, these states are also the ones with very little coal and steel industry.

2.2. Government Plans

2.2.1. Official Plans by the Indian Government

The CEA government regularly establishes longer-term development plans, the most recent one ranging from 2017 to 2022 [2]. This plan includes a capacity increase of about 50 GW of coal-based power projects currently under way, as well as an increase in RES share (Table 1). However, the plan also states that no additional coal power plants are required after 2022. The CEA also predicts additions of 4.3 GW of natural gas, and 2.8 GW of nuclear power until 2022.

Table 1. India's renewable energy sources (RES) addition in GW predicted by the Central Electricity Authority of India (CEA) based on GOI—Ministry of Power [2].

RES Category	Installed Capacity as on 31 March 2016	Expected Capacity Addition from 2017 to 2022	Target RES Installed Capacity as on 31 March 2022	Expected Capacity Addition from 2022 to 2027
Solar	18.7	81.3	100	50
Wind	31	29	60	40
Biomass	5.4	4.6	10	7
Small Hydro	4.5	0.5	5	3
Total	59.7	115.3	175	100

Simultaneously, the CEA has set ambitious plans to expand renewable capacities by 2022 (Table 2). Thereby, the summarized total capacity addition until 2022 is targeted at 137.8 GW [2]. Consequently, the expected share of "non-fossil" based installed capacity, which is defined as nuclear power, hydropower, and RES by the CEA, is likely to increase to 46.8% by the year 2022 and will further increase up to 56.5% by the year 2027. Total renewable energy generation of about 20.3% will contribute to the total energy generation requirement in 2022 [2].

Table 2. India's RES addition predicted by the CEA based on GOI—Ministry of Power [2].

Year	Energy Requirement (TWh) [1]	Peak Demand (GW) [2]
2015	1114	153.4
2022	1611	235.3
2027	2132	317.7

[1] After considering reduction in demand due to demand side management (DSM). [2] After reducing solar and wind generation (i.e., variable renewable energy (VRE) generation).

3. Model and Scenarios

3.1. Global Energy System Model: A Linear Energy System Model

This paper uses a modified version of the GENeSYS-MOD, an open source tool for the linear optimization of energy systems. It is based on the open-source energy modeling system (OSeMOSYS) by Howells et al. [41] and minimizes a cost function to find the lowest discounted cost solution for an energy system to meet a given energy demand. It also allows for temporal and regional disaggregation and is thereby able to model pathways of development of diverse energy systems. In particular, our implementation is based on the version of GENeSYS-MOD by Löffler et al. [15], whereby calculations were done using their general algebraic modeling system (GAMS) code adaption based on the initial OSeMOSYS GAMS translation by Noble [42]. GENeSYS-MOD is a powerful tool to help to identify the lowest-cost solutions and pathways for the energy transformation necessary to keep global warming below 2 °C.

One of the strengths of GENeSYS-MOD is its adaptable and flexible structure. As shown in Figure 1, it is organized into multiple blocks. The basic OSeMOSYS implementation contains seven blocks, including the *objective function*, *costs*, *storage*, *capacity adequacy*, *energy balance*, *constraints*, and *emissions*. GENeSYS-MOD includes three additional blocks *renewable target*, *trade*, and *transportation*, as well as a reworked implementation of the *storage* block. All these blocks serve different functionalities within the energy system model, as all costs, energy production, consumption values, and constraints, such as on investments or capacity additions, need to be accounted for. The block *capacity adequacy* ensures that necessary capacities are met at all times, while the *energy balance* levels energy use and production, taking into account efficiencies of technologies. A more detailed discussion of the blocks composing the model can be found in Löffler et al. [15] and Howells et al. [41]. This research paper includes an endogenous transmission network upgrade as part of the *trade* block, which allows the model to extend existing transmission capacities, focusing on the trade of electricity. For this extent, capacities of grid infrastructure, as well as capacity expansion costs based on line length, have been added to the model equations.

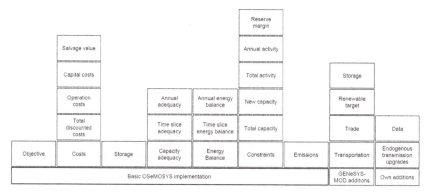

Figure 1. Layout of the Global Energy System Model (GENeSYS-MOD) with new additions based on Löffler et al. [15]. OSeMOSYS: open-source energy modeling system.

The original, global model application was adjusted for the analysis of India's energy system on a detailed level. Amongst other things, we have introduced a constraint on renewable capacity extensions (50% on previous figure every five years), which reflects institutional and political constraints of expanding renewables. Also, grid connections between the ten regions can now be calculated endogenously, improving the interpretation of the spatial aspects of energy system development.

3.2. Data and Limits of Our Model

Our model requires strong assumptions for input; hence, reliable data on, i.e., demand or RES potentials is essential (see Appendix A for key representative data). The power, heat (Table A1), and transport (Table A2) demand in our model is significantly determined by projected population growth and to a smaller extent due to a rise in urbanization [43]. Due to the integrated modeling approach for the entire modeling period from 2015 until 2050, only a limited number of time slices per year can be included (six time slices, including three distinct seasons, winter, summer and intermediate (autumn, spring), each consisting of day and night to model seasonal fluctuations, respectively, see Table A3). Furthermore, cost developments of implemented technologies are given exogenously.

The results allow for a both qualitative and quantitative assessment for: (1) whether India can achieve an energy system consisting of 100% RES; (2) where the current trend is going; and (3) where we see further steps are necessary.

3.3. Regional Disaggregation of the Indian Energy System

India has an enormous potential for renewable energies. Due to geographical circumstances, regional disparities in potentials for renewable energy technologies occur and are considered within the model according to Table 3. In total, India has a total solar power potential of 11,195 GW as of 2015 [44]. Estimates of India's wind power potential vary greatly, depending on assumptions on efficiency, hub heights, turbine-size and land-use considerations. The model is based on data which is retrieved from a report of India's wind power potential by Hosain et al. [34]. The total onshore wind power potential for India is estimated to range between 2733 GW and 6439 GW. The highest potentials are observed in the western and southern regions, where most of the installed onshore wind capacities already exist. Data regarding India's offshore wind energy potentials are retrieved from Löffler et al. [15] and are proportionally assigned to the coastal regions (see Section 3.1) according to the coastal kilometers of the relevant regions.

Table 3. RES potentials in GW based on GOI – Ministry of Power [45] and Hosain et al. [44]. N = north. NW = north-west. W = west. CW = central-west. CS = central-south. S = south. E = east. CE = central-east. NE = north-east. UP = Uttar Pradesh. PV: photovoltaics.

RES Technology	N	NW	W	CW	CS	S	E	CE	NE	UP
Solar PV	724	3096	1705	2069	1135	391	276	500	1000	300
Onshore wind	0	394	359	555	955	309	154	0	5	2
Offshore wind	0	0	61	41	14	74	0	0	0	0
Hydro	51	4	3	7	11	5	10	1	59	1

Hydro energy can be divided into large and small hydropower. In India, large hydropower is defined to have a capacity of more than 25 MW, whereas small hydropower has a capacity of less than 25 MW [45]. According to this definition, the country has a total installed capacity of more than 35 GW in large and small hydropower cumulated in 2015 [46]. These capacities are mostly located in the northern regions, as well as in the central–south areas. India has a potential of more than 151 GW of large hydropower, especially in the northern region, due to the Himalaya Mountains and other important river systems such as the Indus. The north, north-west (NW), and north-east (NE) account for more than 75% of the total large hydropower potential in India. In addition, small hydropower has a potential of 19.7 GW.

In order to represent its geographical, industrial, and political diversity, India is split into different zones. We follow the approach by Gulagi et al. [47] and split India into ten zones, along respective federal state borders (Figure 2). Thus, the following regions are obtained:

- the north (N) consists of Jammu and Kashmir, Himachal Pradesh, and Uttarakhand, and Is characterized by a decent potential of solar power and very large hydropower potential (51 GW);
- the NW consists of Punjab and Rajasthan, quite rural regions with a significant potential of solar power;
- Gujarat and Madhya Pradesh form the west (W) region, with a broad portfolio of renewables potential (solar, onshore and offshore wind);
- central-west (CW) is comprised of Maharashtra, Goa, and Chhattisgarh, likewise large solar and wind resources, but, particular in Chhattisgarh, a higher level of heavy industrialization and coal;
- India's central-south (CS) is comprised of Karnataka and Andhra Pradesh, with the highest onshore wind potential of the country (955 GW);
- the south (S) comprises Tamil Nadu and Kerala, also featuring solar and wind potential, but very little fossil fuels (except for the liquefied natural gas (LNG) import terminal in Chennai);
- the east (E), consisting mainly of Orissa and West Bengal, appended by Sikkim, has quite heavy industrial roots, and is continuously struggling for electricity supply;

- somewhat similar, the central-east (CE), consisting of Bihar and Jharkhand, has high energy demand, but also a significant potential, in particular of solar energy (1000 GW);
- the NE consists of the somewhat isolated states of Assam Arumachal Pradesh, Nagaland, Manipur, Mizoram, Tripura, and Meghalaya, with some solar and significant potential hydro resources (59 GW);
- Uttar Pradesh (UP), bordering the national capital territory of Delhi, is one of the largest and most heavily industrialized states, with a particular dynamic energy demand.

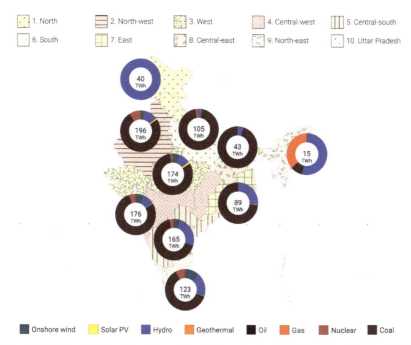

Figure 2. India's regional configuration and electricity production (2015) based on Gulagi et al. [47].

3.4. Scenarios

Current discussions about the future energy direction of the Indian energy sector are quite diverse, varying between the continuations of the traditional coal-based pattern, to the possibility of a 100% supply by renewable energies. In order to cover some of this research gap, while still respecting India's INDC targets, we have developed three distinct scenarios.

3.4.1. Limited Emissions Only Scenario

The limited emissions only (LEO) scenario describes a development where the goal of limiting global warming to 2 °C is respected, and the globally available CO_2 budget is distributed according to current population size. Generally, this corresponds to the 450 ppm scenario of the IEA [48] (now renamed "Sustainable Development Scenario"). The derived emission budget for India is about 118 gigatons from 2015 until 2050 in order to meet the 2 °C target. This budget would be considerably lower if the distribution was based on other characteristics, e.g., GDP or current emissions. The LEO scenario informs decision makers about the potential cost for the Indian economy, especially compared to the rather deviant scenarios and the respective role of fossil fuels and renewables therein.

3.4.2. Business as Usual Scenario

In the business as usual (BAU) scenario, the Indian government (and all other governments) stick to given commitments and signed treaties, but nothing more. In international terms, this corresponds to the new policy scenario (NPS) of the IEA. The BAU scenario uses the projected capacities for renewable energy capacities until 2040 of the new policies scenario by the IEA [31]. These projected capacities are included as upper limits and thus restrict the construction of renewable generation capacities in the model. No specific emission limits for CO_2 or other GHGs are included. The goal of the BAU scenario is to compare the resulting CO_2 emissions with the other two scenarios, where the national CO_2 emissions are fixed by using a national budget. Moreover, the point of interest lies on the pathways after 2040, when the usage of renewable energies is not limited by the projected IEA capacities anymore.

3.4.3. 100% Renewable Energy Sources Scenario

The Indian government has regularly updated its commitment towards using more RES in the future. In contrast to the LEO scenario, the aim of the 100% RES scenario therefore examines if it would be possible to fulfill the total energy demand with 100% renewable energy in 2050. Therefore, the model is restricted such that no non-renewable energies, including nuclear energy, can be used by 2050. The included CO_2 budget of 60 gigatons corresponds with the goal to restrict the amount of global warming to only 1.5 °C.

3.4.4. Further Assumptions

We adopt the assumptions on energy and electricity demand taken from the IEA 2017 World Energy Outlook. A sensitivity analysis is added for all scenarios that reduces demand growth by 50%. This accounts for the uncertainty on increasing energy efficiency, new demand patterns, and a slower adaptation of very energy- and electricity-intensive demand behavior. The assumptions on the cost of conventional and renewable energies (Table 4) are based on a variety of sources. [49–51].

Table 4. Assumptions on the cost of conventional and renewable energies in India based on Schröder et al. [49], Ram et al. [50] and the Energy Technology Reference Indicator (ETRI) [51].

	Technology	2015	2020	2025	2030	2035	2040	2045	2050
Cost in M€/GW	Onshore wind	1280	1152	1050	972	940	900	860	823
	Offshore wind	2560	2304	2100	1944	1880	1800	1720	1664
	Large-scale hydropower	826	826	826	826	826	826	826	826
	Utility-scale solar PV	1000	580	466	390	337	300	270	246
	Biomass	656	656	656	656	656	656	656	656
Cost in M€/PJ	Hard coal	1.06	1.11	1.17	1.23	1.29	1.35	1.42	1.49
	Natural gas	3.30	3.30	3.30	3.30	3.30	3.30	3.30	3.30

4. Results and Interpretation

4.1. Scenario Results and Comparisons

Model results suggest that in all three scenarios, the total energy demand can be met, and that a major change in the fuel mix, away from fossil (mainly coal-based production), to renewables is likely to occur. This change is not only imposed by environmental constraints, but also pushed by the increasing competitiveness of renewables, mainly solar energy.

4.1.1. Limited Emissions Only Scenario Results

In the LEO scenario, the share of fossil fuels is gradually reduced over time, though some fossil capacities are still available in 2050. In the electricity sector, upon which we focus on in this paper, solar takes over a leading role in power generation, resulting in an accumulated share of 69% for all regions in 2050 (Figure 3). Apart from solar, wind and hydropower are the main sources for power generation in 2050 with 17% and 9%, respectively. While wind power is continuously increasing in its capacity after the year 2035, hydropower stays almost constant over all periods. While coal is the main component in the power generation energy mix in 2015 with a share of 82%, it continuously reduced until 2050. A slight increase in coal usage can be observed in 2050. This is due to the huge increase in power generation (induced by sector-coupling effects in the other sectors) between 2045 and 2050, which is compensated for by the already installed coal capacity. Despite the growing energy demand, the power generated by coal is reduced by more than half by the year 2025. In 2050, coal still has a share of about 5% in power generation. Nuclear power is hardly used during the entire period, nor does natural gas play any significant role. Figure 3 illustrates the pathway within the LEO scenario.

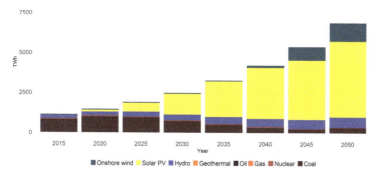

Figure 3. India's power pathway in the limited emissions only (LEO) scenario.

In the rest of the energy system, heat generation is dominated by biomass (60%) and coal-based heating (38%) in 2050. Natural gas, electric heating, and solar heating play only a minor role (Figure 4). The transportation sector has the chance to become emission free by 2050 as well.

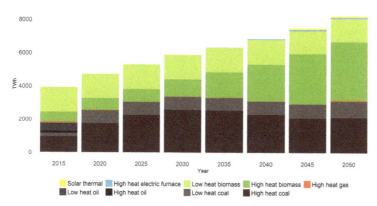

Figure 4. India's heat pathway in the LEO scenario.

Demands for passenger transportation will be fully supplied by electric fueled rail services and battery electric vehicles (BEV) in 2050 (Figure 5). As demand is assumed to increase by up to 3000 million freight km per year in 2050 (+273% compared to 2015), an increase in H_2 powered road trucks and electrical rail traffic can be observed from 2025 on. In addition, the shipping sector will completely become independent of conventional sources (conv.) by using biomass-powered means by 2050. Air traffic is assumed to convert from conventional fuels to hydrogen-based technologies (predicted breakthrough between 2030 and 2035).

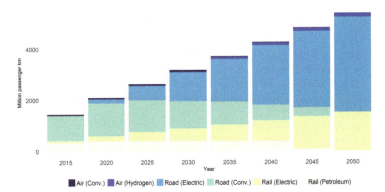

Figure 5. India's freight transportation pathway in the LEO scenario.

In the freight sector, conventional ships in 2015 will shift towards biomass (biom.) powered means. On the road, internal combustion engines will be replaced by hydrogen and biomass run vehicles. For freight transportation by rail, petroleum powered trains will fade out in favor of electric trains by 2050 (Figure 6).

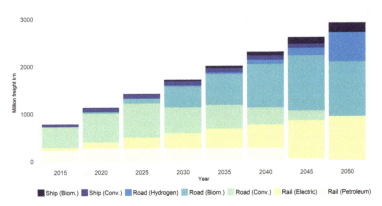

Figure 6. India's passenger transportation pathway in the LEO scenario.

The total emissions within the model amount to 96 gigatons of CO_2 from 2015 until 2050.

4.1.2. Comparison with Other Scenarios

A comparison between the LEO scenario and the BAU scenario confirms that with less stringent climate targets, more fossil energy (mainly coal) is used for electrification. Figure 7 shows the difference between the generation mixes of the LEO scenario, compared with the BAU scenario. In both scenarios, complete decarbonization of the Indian energy system is not accomplished. Differences mainly occur in the more dominant usage of natural gas and coal-based energy throughout the years. Overall, coal as an energy carrier is still declining in the years leading to 2050, having its peak in 2040. Coal still has a share of about 7.4%, whilst natural gas accounts for nearly 1% of the energy production in 2050. Compared to the LEO scenario, solar power (66%) develops on a smaller basis. Wind (17%) and hydro power (9%) remain rather constant over the years. The total emissions are about 9% higher compared to the LEO scenario, but still achieving the 2 °C goal.

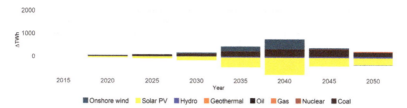

Figure 7. Comparison between the LEO and the business as usual (BAU) scenarios.

Figure 8 shows a similar comparison between the LEO scenario and the 100% RES scenario. The small share of coal (and the marginal share of natural gas) disappears by 2050, and more solar and onshore wind are generated. The contribution of offshore wind is marginal, and hydroelectricity observes a smaller share in the 100% scenario.

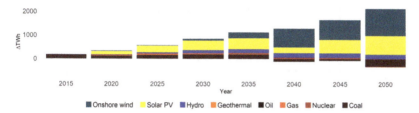

Figure 8. Comparison between the LEO and the 100% RES scenarios.

As stated in the scenario description, the model is forced to only use renewable energies in 2050 in the 100% RES scenario. This leads to a much higher power demand over the years, which is due to the increased usage of power-to-x technologies in the heat and transportation sector. Compared to the other scenarios, power trading between the nodes is even more relevant because of the regional differences in the potentials for renewable energy generation. Natural gas does not play a role in the energy mix within this scenario. Solar and wind power replace the then phased-out coal-based energy, leading to a 15% decrease in CO_2 emissions until 2050. The research shows that with the given potentials, a 100% renewable energy system, meeting the 1.5 °C climate target, would be feasible in the year 2050. Regarding heat and mobility, no significant differences were found.

Similar results and transformation pathways were found by Gulagi et al. [21,47]. Comparing the country-wide scenario by Gulagi et al. [47] to our 100% RES scenario, a moderate phase out of coal and fast expansion of solar PV and onshore wind can be observed. While India's power generation is dominated by coal in 2015, solar PV establishes itself as the key technology by 2050, followed by onshore wind and biomass [47]. Differences in absolute values can be traced back to the ability of GENeSYS-MOD to also include the heat and transport sector.

4.2. Regionalization of Scenario Results

The analysis of the regional supply mixes reveals significant differences (see Appendix B). In the LEO scenario in 2050, solar is the dominant source of supply in all regions, except for two: the north and the NE, both mountainous regions with a lot of hydropower. Onshore wind is most prominent in the west and the south, whereas offshore wind occurs hardly anywhere.

Starting from 2020, solar capacities heavily increase in all regions, whereby CE and UP are relying nearly solely on solar power in the final year. The north and NE regions exhibit the highest hydro potentials and account for about 64% of India's total hydropower generation.

In the LEO scenario, coal electrification is mainly concentrated in UP in 2050 (26%). The nodes CW (2%), NW (5%), south (3%), and west (6%) play a minor role. With relatively modest wind resources, UP is the only state that uses natural gas electrification.

All scenarios have a similar regionalization of energy sources. However, more conventional fuels are used in the BAU scenario, especially in the NW region (21%). In the 100% RES scenario, all regions are relying on RES with a similar distribution as the LEO scenario, substituting the conventional energy sources in the south-west, south-east, and UP with RES and electricity imports.

4.3. Energy System Cost and Long-Term Electricity Prices

Given that the energy mix between the three scenarios is not very different, it is not surprising that the energy system costs are quite similar as well. With the BAU scenario having the lowest discounted costs over the whole model period, it shows that feeding demand in the high-temperature heat and freight transportation sectors based on power-based technologies is more cost-intensive than using fossil fuels, especially in the case of high shares of RES. Although it might be the cheapest, external cost and effects on the environment that are difficult to be quantified need to be kept in mind. In comparison, the LEO scenario comes to a result with slightly higher costs (about 2%), while the 100% RES scenario results in 9% higher total discounted costs than the BAU scenario.

The average costs of electricity generation within the model will decline from 7.5 €cents/kWh in 2015 to less than 3 €cents/kWh in 2050 in the LEO scenario. However, infrastructure and transportation costs are not included. Nevertheless, variations in the power generating costs between the technologies can be observed and depend on the different operational lifetimes, operational and maintenance costs, as well as capital and fuel costs. Within the model, coal-based electricity ranges from 3.3 to 3.7 €cents/kWh. These costs are currently lower than the daily updated data of the Ministry of Power [52], as they do not include the costs for infrastructure. Apart from that, renewable technologies will become increasingly competitive, with solar and wind power observing the biggest reduction of power generating costs over time, which drive coal-based generation out of the market. Utility-scale solar power lies in the range of 1.3–2.8 €cents/kWh for power generation, with wind power ranging from 3 to 5 €cents/kWh. At the same time, hydro power shows up with 2–3 €cents/kWh for electricity generation within the model. Regarding the projections of Bloomberg New Energy Finance [53], similarities can be observed as there will be a tipping point where coal will be replaced by cheap renewable options. In between the regions of India, prices can vary up to 50%, which can be traced back to different capacity factors and full load hours of generation facilities. While different climate targets do play a role in the energy mix, their overall economic effects seem to be modest.

5. Barriers to the Low-Carbon Energy Transformation in India

As seen in the previous sections, renewable energy technologies have an enormous potential in India and a 100% RES based energy system in 2050 can be achieved. However, experience shows that economic theory and reality do not always match. An assessment of present literature and expert interviews aims to contextualize the low-carbon energy transformation and the model results within the social, political and economic contexts. The low-carbon transformation of the energy sector is not solely driven by climate consideration, but is inserted into a complex process of sustainable development that includes (amongst others) reducing health risk, affordable energy and a circular economy. In order to make an evaluation about whether the country is truly able to become 100% RES-based in 2050, further implications on India's energy transformation have to be considered. Based on this literature review, those factors can be divided into social, political, and economic barriers.

5.1. Social Barriers

In acknowledgement of the complexities associated with the low-carbon transformation in India, it is important to contextualize the transition against the overall economic situation of the broader population. India, having a GDP per capita of 1974.76 USD [54], a high share of its population living in extreme poverty, and a rapid urbanization, economic growth is often perceived as more pressuring than investment into green development projects [27].

Currently, there are still more than 300 million people with no access to electricity [8]. Consequently, environmental standards for power plants are perceived as barriers to economic growth. A prime example for this is the protest against higher environmental standards in 2014 by the population of Vapi, one of the most polluted cities in India [55]. This can mainly be explained by the cities' dependence on its large and highly-polluting pharmaceutical and chemical industries and the public fear of losing much-needed jobs and capital [26].

A low-carbon transition as planned by governmental motivations, however, holds various opportunities for further economic growth in green industries—despite the rate of employment in the coal industry decreasing constantly since 2002 [37]. Especially in regard to the enormous solar potential and the ambitions to extend the national capacities in wind and solar (see Section 2.2.1), it could generate up to 330,000 jobs over the next five years, i.e., in manufacturing, project design, construction, business development, and operations and maintenance [56]. Changing the perception of the low-carbon transition as a barrier for economic growth by educational work and improving social circumstances is thus crucial for a successful energy transformation.

5.2. Political Barriers

A significant barrier to the increase in RES are lobbies of the conventional energy sector. The coal industry still meets most of India's energy demand and employs over 400,000 people. Their businesses include rail, port, and road transport, loading and unloading, as well as the power plants (see Section 2.1). In addition, a substantial portion of the coal-mining sector is dominated by the state-owned company CIL. A possible depletion of coal mining would therefore have a negative influence on the government's budget. Consequently, past and current Indian governments have been pushing the expansion of the coal mining sector and plan to increase the annual production from a current level of 600 million tons to 1.5 billion tons in 2020 [26].

Not only external factors are of importance for the implementation of policies in a country. Internal factors, such as the lack of coordination and cooperation within and between various Indian institutions and other stakeholders, slow down and restrict the transformation to RES. Currently, multiple agencies (i.e., the Federal Ministry for New and Renewable Energy, Ministry of Power, Department of Environment and Forests, Department of Rural Development, as well as corresponding agencies in each state) have overlapping areas of responsibilities regarding renewable energy. A good example of this lack of coordination is the implementation of the generation based incentive (GBI) for solar power, a scheme provided to, among other things, "support small grid solar power projects connected to the distribution grid (below 33 KV) to the state utilities" [57]. Soon after its announcement by the Ministry of New and Renewable Energy (MNRE), the Indian Renewable Energy Development Agency (IREDA) started accepting applications for solar projects under the GBI scheme. Later, however, the Indian government rejected all applications that were made before the official announcement of the scheme through the federal gazette [58]. While this reaction is justified and the IREDA should not have accepted applications in advance, it is this lack of coordination between institutions that complicates the implementation of policies and discourages investors.

Furthermore, there are currently two policy narratives for the development of the Indian energy system: the centralized approach, in which the Indian government mainly pushes for the integration of renewables through a unified power grid, and the former being decentralized, providing basic energy access using off-grid solutions [59].

5.3. Economic Barriers

The fact that India's energy demand is predicted to increase heavily until 2050 forms one of the biggest challenges in its low-carbon transformation. The growth can be traced back to the increasing electricity access, especially in rural areas, and to urbanization. Lifestyle and dietary changes, i.e., increasing demand for meat, dairy products, and luxury goods are all factors which contribute to India's growing energy consumption [60]. Growing electrification in the agricultural sector, and more reliable energy supply for industry and highly populated areas, are coupled with India's economic growth. Merging those interactions represents a challenge for the energy system. Within the model results, India's electricity generation is estimated to increase by a factor of ten from 2015 to 2050, whereby the analysis shows that renewable energy potentials are sufficient. Correspondingly, Bhushan [8] points out that the organization of the distribution systems needs to be tackled. Thus, an ambitious increase in power-generating capacity and change towards renewable technologies on a large scale is necessary to ensure a sustainable power supply.

In general, renewable energy projects tend to have little or no fuel, operating, or maintenance cost, but their relative initial investment costs tend to be much higher than for those of conventional energy systems [58]. Renewables in India are often around 24–32% more expensive compared to similar projects financed in the US or Europe. Indian financial market conditions are the main cause of high interest rates for renewable energy. Growth, high inflation, and country risks all contribute [61]. Therefore, by requiring these large-scale upfront investments, renewable energy projects are reliant on long-term investors [27].

It has been difficult, however, to attract those long-term investors for a multitude of reasons. First and foremost, India's legal and regulatory system is often viewed as uncertain and risky, as manifested in various forms like changes in tax codes, a lack of protection for policy changes and enforcement of contracts [27]. Furthermore, there is a deficiency in information about renewable energy projects, as well as the value of different companies. That information, however, is crucial for the analysis and decision-making of investors.

India's losses in the transmission and distribution (T&D) power grid are one of the highest worldwide, with a total share of 19.4% [62]. Those high T&D losses are an additional consequence of the widespread power theft, illegal hook-ups, and a low payment morale [63]. Agriculture users in particular pay for less energy than they consume [63]. Regarding the model results, a 100% RES-based power supply is only feasible if regions can compensate imbalances in RES potentials through an efficient power exchange. A sensitivity analysis showed that a decrease down to 5% of losses ensures a feasible power supply for all regions in the 100% RES scenario. Overcoming this technical challenge through promoting investments forms one of the biggest hurdles in the low-carbon transformation for India.

To finance large-scale investments, private investors could impact the velocity of the transformation within the energy system. Considering the current share of 6.7% private players in the transmission network, it stands out that the regulatory framework is still not exhausting the full financing potential through private contributions. The "Doing Business" ranking by The World Bank underlines those circumstances, whereas India is on rank 185 in "Dealing with Construction Permits" and on rank 172 in 'Enforcing Contracts' out of 190 economies by comparison [64]. For that reason, the government is encouraging private investments. Financial mechanisms and policy frameworks for a faster commercialization of renewable energy technologies are analyzed by Balachandra et al. [65].

Currently, increasing attention is given to off-grid technologies, such as solar rooftops with battery back-ups to achieve energy access to all regions. This also concerns households in highly populated areas to become independent from local network operators [8]. Despite the high willingness to invest in off-grid technologies, low-income households still need to be addressed [66]. Within the National Electricity Plan, 40 GW of solar rooftops are planned to be installed by March 2022 to relieve the local power grids [2].

Regarding the model, the results of all three scenarios visualize that the most economically viable energy path leads to an energy mix dominated by solar. With a total share of 68% of solar energy in power generation, India will become a solar reliant country in 2050, which consequently takes risks within. Especially in times when solar power generation is very low, security of energy supplies is difficult to ensure. Considering the concentrated energy demand in conurbations (like UP), on the other hand, makes clear that a sufficient power supply can only be reached if the power system gets optimized. Therefore, storage technologies play a significant role to compensate for fluctuating energy generation.

6. Conclusions

With 6% of global GHG emissions and a predicted future increase, India plays a determining role in future climate policies. In this paper, we explore energy pathways for India from 2015 to 2050 by applying the GENeSYS-MOD to different scenarios. The model results of the LEO scenario visualize the future importance of solar energy within the low-carbon transformation. Even without setting a strict restriction for using conventional energy sources in 2050, renewables (especially solar) will satisfy almost the whole energy demand in 2050, whereas conventional sources will have a negligible share of 2.8% (mainly located in densely populated regions, e.g., UP). In 2050, the share of solar takes over 67% of the whole power production, followed by wind (23%) and hydropower (6%) in the LEO scenario.

For progressive planning, crucial circumstances have to be kept in mind. First of all, India as a developing economy is facing an increasing demand in power, and energy access is an ongoing issue, especially in rural areas [2]. Furthermore, within the conventional energy sources, the future of coal electrification depends on market design, the implementation of existing environmental norms, and regional development perspectives in affected areas. Apart from that, the recent growth of utility-scale solar needs to be accompanied by distributed solar (and batteries), both at the urban and the rural level, to become sustainable and extend the rural electrification progress. As current plans are perceived to be achieved before 2025, set goals submitted in the INDCs and the current Five-Year Plan are assessed as not ambitious enough. Moreover, it is illustrated within the BAU scenario that current electricity plans of the Indian government diverge from needed requirements to contribute to the global rising limit of 2 °C to pre-industrial levels. Tightening the government's goals until 2030 would consequently both counterbalance and reduce the total cost of the path from there on to 2050, which is projected to be a largely renewable energy-based system. Consequently, fulfilling the Paris Agreement will require stronger efforts in India's current policies, especially in the last two decades leading up to 2050 in comparison to a smoother and more cost-efficient increase of RES over time. While the model incorporates a high level of detail on a multitude of technologies, inter-sectoral-connections, and the resulting energy mix, its rather rough time disaggregation has to be noted. Variable renewable energy (VRE) technologies and their inherent unstableness, creating a need for flexibility options such as storage, might require a more detailed distinction between time slices. Future research should focus on how to implement such an assessment for even more detailed data on the different sectors and the effects of variable RES on the electricity system.

A reduction of the losses and tackling power theft within the power trade would ensure an efficient overcoming of imbalances in between the regions of different renewable energy potentials. Making up leeway in the transmission grid sector is one of the important actions. The results for the 100% RES scenario illustrate the cost-optimized pathway towards 2050 for a technically feasible energy system based on 100% RES, a finding which has been shown by Gulagi et al. [21,47] independently. Additionally, the difference between the LEO and 100% RES scenario in the use of conventional sources indicates that a 100% renewable energy supply is an ambitious goal for 2050. Noticing the negligibly higher total cost of an energy system based on 100% RES to the LEO benchmark or the BAU scenario, this goal may be ambitious but not impossible to achieve.

Author Contributions: L.L. (Linus Lawrenz), B.X., L.L. (Luise Lorenz), A.K., H.H. led the coding and modeling efforts, as well as data research and writing the paper. T.B., K.L., P.-Y.O., and C.v.H. initiated the research, supervised the model implementation, supported the data input and policy backgrounds, and contributed to writing the text. Additionally, T.B., L.L. (Linus Lawrenz), K.L., P.-Y.O., and B.X. (in alphabetical order) managed the reviewing and editing process.

Funding: This work was supported by the German Ministry for Education and Research (BMBF) under grant number 01LN1704A for the research group CoalExit.

Acknowledgments: Previous works of this research have been presented at various workshops and conferences in India and across Europe. We therefore thank the conference and workshop audiences, and in particular Christian Hauenstein, Claudia Kemfert and Roman Mendelevitch for useful discussions and suggestions, the usual disclaimer applies. We also thank the reviewers and editors of Energies for their helpful advice and constructive criticism during the submission process.

Conflicts of Interest: The authors declare no conflict of interest.

Appendix A. Model Parameters

Table A1. Regional electricity, high and low heat demand in PJ.

Region		2015	2020	2025	2030	2035	2040	2045	2050
Annual electricity demand (PJ)	North	136.51	173.39	220.25	279.76	355.36	451.38	573.35	728.28
	NW	700.57	889.87	1130.33	1435.77	1823.73	2316.53	2942.50	3737.60
	West	620.66	788.38	1001.41	1272.01	1615.72	2052.31	2606.88	3311.30
	CW	627.82	797.46	1012.95	1286.67	1634.35	2075.97	2636.93	3349.47
	CS	590.04	749.47	951.99	1209.24	1535.99	1951.04	2478.24	3147.90
	South	440.51	559.55	710.74	902.80	1146.75	1456.62	1850.22	2350.17
	East	319.53	405.87	515.54	654.85	831.80	1056.57	1342.07	1704.72
	CE	153.64	195.15	247.89	314.87	399.95	508.03	645.31	819.68
	NE	53.42	67.86	86.19	109.48	139.07	176.65	224.38	285.01
	UP	373.60	474.55	602.78	765.66	972.55	1235.35	1569.16	1993.18
Σ		4016	5102	6480	8231	10,455	13,280	16,869	21,427
Annual high heat demand (PJ)	North	217.00	302.10	373.46	444.83	503.68	562.53	635.46	708.39
	NW	1113.65	1550.38	1916.63	2282.88	2584.92	2886.96	3261.23	3635.50
	West	986.63	1373.55	1698.02	2022.50	2290.09	2557.68	2889.26	3220.84
	CW	998.00	1389.38	1717.60	2045.81	2316.49	2587.16	2922.57	3257.97
	CS	937.95	1305.77	1614.23	1922.70	2177.09	2431.47	2746.69	3061.91
	South	700.26	974.87	1205.16	1435.46	1625.38	1815.30	2050.63	2285.97
	East	507.94	707.13	874.17	1041.22	1178.98	1316.74	1487.44	1658.15
	CE	244.23	340.01	420.33	500.65	566.89	633.13	715.21	797.28
	NE	84.92	118.22	146.15	174.08	197.11	220.14	248.68	277.22
	UP	593.88	826.78	1022.09	1217.41	1378.48	1539.55	1739.14	1938.73
Σ		6384	8888	10,987	13,087	14,819	16,550	18,696	20,841
Annual low heat demand (PJ)	North	262.70	274.70	265.05	255.40	233.99	212.58	206.48	200.37
	NW	1348.19	1409.77	1360.26	1310.74	1200.86	1090.99	1059.65	1028.31
	West	1194.42	1248.97	1205.11	1161.24	1063.90	966.55	938.79	911.03
	CW	1208.19	1263.37	1219.00	1174.63	1076.16	977.69	949.61	921.53
	CS	1135.48	1187.34	1145.64	1103.94	1011.40	918.86	892.46	866.07
	South	847.73	886.45	855.32	824.18	755.09	686.00	666.30	646.59
	East	614.91	642.99	620.41	597.83	547.71	497.60	483.31	469.01
	CE	295.67	309.17	298.31	287.45	263.36	239.26	232.39	225.51
	NE	102.81	107.50	103.73	99.95	91.57	83.19	80.80	78.41
	UP	718.96	751.80	725.39	698.99	640.39	581.80	565.09	548.38
Σ		7729	8082	7798	7514	6884	6254	6074	5895

Table A2. Regional demand for transportation in Gpkm (passenger) and Gtkm (freight).

Region		2015	2020	2025	2030	2035	2040	2045	2050
Annual demand for passenger transportation (Gpkm)	North	49	71	89	107	126	145	164	183
	NW	252	364	458	552	647	743	841	940
	West	223	323	406	489	573	658	745	832
	CW	226	326	410	494	580	666	754	842
	CS	212	307	386	465	545	625	708	791
	South	158	229	288	347	407	467	529	591
	East	115	166	209	252	295	339	384	429
	CE	55	80	100	121	142	163	184	206
	NE	19	28	35	42	49	57	64	72
	UP	134	194	244	294	345	396	449	501
Σ		1443	2087	2625	3162	3710	4258	4822	5386
Annual demand for freight transportation (Gtkm)	North	26	38	48	58	68	78	88	99
	NW	136	196	247	297	349	400	453	506
	West	120	174	219	263	309	355	402	449
	CW	122	176	221	266	313	359	406	454
	CS	114	165	208	250	294	337	382	427
	South	85	123	155	187	219	252	285	318
	East	62	90	113	136	159	183	207	231
	CE	30	43	54	65	76	88	99	111
	NE	10	15	19	23	27	31	35	39
	UP	72	105	132	159	186	213	242	270
Σ		778	1125	1415	1704	2000	2295	2599	2903

Table A3. Regional capacity factors for solar PV, onshore and offshore wind. WN = winter night, WD = winter day, SN = summer night, SD = summer day, IN = intermediate night, ID = intermediate day.

Region		WN	WD	SN	SD	IN	ID
Solar PV	North	0.00	0.25	0.00	0.30	0.00	0.28
	NW	0.00	0.27	0.00	0.29	0.00	0.30
	West	0.00	0.30	0.00	0.24	0.00	0.30
	CW	0.00	0.32	0.00	0.23	0.00	0.29
	CS	0.00	0.35	0.00	0.22	0.00	0.28
	South	0.00	0.49	0.00	0.29	0.00	0.39
	East	0.00	0.32	0.00	0.21	0.00	0.31
	CE	0.00	0.28	0.00	0.26	0.00	0.30
	NE	0.00	0.32	0.00	0.21	0.00	0.31
	UP	0.00	0.32	0.00	0.21	0.00	0.31
Onshore wind	North	0.32	0.19	0.37	0.20	0.35	0.24
	NW	0.32	0.12	0.48	0.30	0.26	0.12
	West	0.28	0.17	0.36	0.42	0.22	0.13
	CW	0.25	0.14	0.43	0.57	0.20	0.14
	CS	0.27	0.13	0.44	0.52	0.20	0.13
	South	0.17	0.14	0.29	0.46	0.12	0.13
	East	0.23	0.09	0.33	0.29	0.20	0.14
	CE	0.24	0.16	0.19	0.17	0.24	0.21
	NE	0.33	0.17	0.24	0.20	0.36	0.24
	UP	0.27	0.15	0.20	0.17	0.31	0.19
Offshore wind	NW	0.19	0.34	0.49	0.52	0.19	0.27
	CW	0.14	0.22	0.47	0.42	0.15	0.13
	CS	0.08	0.17	0.39	0.37	0.10	0.10
	South	0.36	0.39	0.61	0.58	0.23	0.29

Appendix B. India's Regional Electricity Production

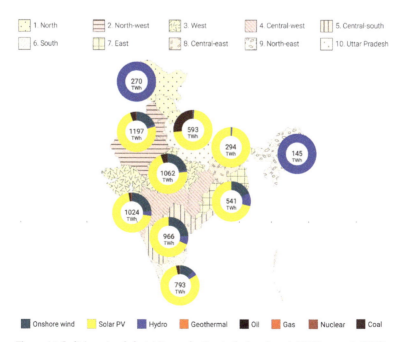

Figure A1. India's regional electricity production in the benchmark (LEO) scenario (2050).

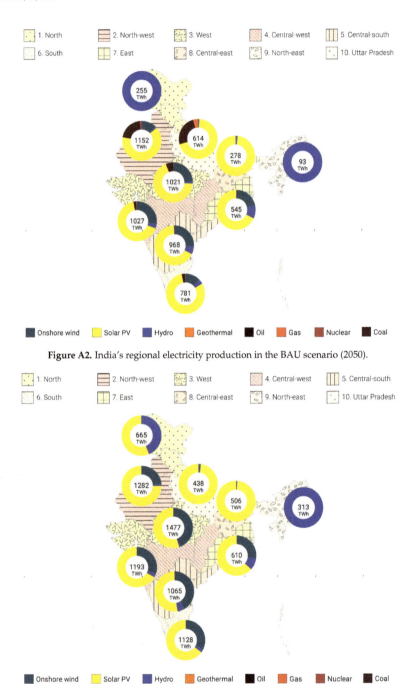

Figure A2. India's regional electricity production in the BAU scenario (2050).

Figure A3. India's regional electricity production in the 100% RES scenario (2050).

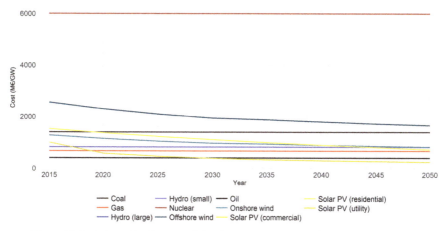

Figure A4. Capital cost development of electricity-generating technologies in million €/GW.

References

1. International Energy Agency (IEA). *India Energy Outlook—World Energy Outlook Special Report*; IEA Publications: Paris, France, 2015; ISBN 978 92 64 24365 1.
2. Government of India, Ministry of Power. GOI—Draft National Electricity Plan (Volume 1): Generation. Available online: http://www.cea.nic.in/reports/committee/nep/nep_dec.pdf (accessed on 10 July 2017).
3. Natural Resources Defense Council (NDRC). The Road from Paris: India's Progress toward its Climate Pledge. Available online: https://www.nrdc.org/sites/default/files/paris-climate-conference-India-IB.pdf (accessed on 2 April 2018).
4. Chakrabarty, M. *Climate Change and Food Security in India*; Observer Research Foundation (ORF): New Delhi, India, 2016; Available online: https://www.orfonline.org/research/climate-change-and-food-security-in-india/ (accessed on 16 September 2017).
5. GOI—Ministry of Power Press Release: Village Electrification. Available online: http://pib.nic.in/newsite/erelcontent.aspx?relid=161968 (accessed on 16 August 2017).
6. Sen, S.; Ganguly, S.; Das, A.; Sen, J.; Dey, S. Renewable energy scenario in India: Opportunities and challenges. *J. Afr. Earth Sci.* **2016**, *122*, 25–31. [CrossRef]
7. Bhushan, C. *The Indian Energy Sector-A Survey by Fuel and Institutional Framework*; Technical Report or Bulletin Number; Heinrich Boell Foundation-India: Delhi, India, 2014.
8. Bhushan, C. *India's Energy Transition-Potential and Prospects*; Heinrich Boell Foundation-India: New Delhi, India, 2017; Available online: https://in.boell.org/sites/default/files/india_renewable_energy_report_2017_final_1.pdf (accessed on 27 April 2018).
9. Greenpeace India Greenpeace India-Home. Available online: http://www.greenpeace.org/india/en/ (accessed on 12 June 2017).
10. Prakash Jena, L.; Meattle, C.; Shrimali, G. Getting to India's Renewable Energy Targets: A Business Case for Institutional Investment. Available online: https://climatepolicyinitiative.org/publication/getting-to-indias-renewable-energy-targets-a-business-case-for-institutional-investment/ (accessed on 2 May 2018).
11. Boston Consulting Group (BCG). *Future of Coal-Based Power Generation in India*; The Boston Consulting Group, Inc.: Mumbai, India, 2017; Available online: http://www.ciienergyconclave.com/download/BCGCII_Report_2017.pdf (accessed on 17 November 2017).
12. Tripathi, L.; Mishra, A.K.; Dubey, A.K.; Tripathi, C.B.; Baredar, P. Renewable energy: An overview on its contribution in current energy scenario of India. *Renew. Sustain. Energy Rev.* **2016**, *60*, 226–233. [CrossRef]
13. Sachs, J. *The Age of Sustainable Development*; Columbia University Press: New York, NY, USA, 2015; ISBN 978-0-231-17314-8.
14. Dhar, S.; Pathak, M.; Shukla, P.R. *Transport Scenarios for India: Harmonising Development and Climate Benefits*; United Nations Environment Programme (UNEP): Copenhagen, Denmark, 2015; ISBN 978-87-93130-67-8.

15. Löffler, K.; Hainsch, K.; Burandt, T.; Oei, P.-Y.; Kemfert, C.; von Hirschhausen, C. Designing a Model for the Global Energy System—GENeSYS-MOD: An Application of the Open-Source Energy Modeling System (OSeMOSYS). *Energies* **2017**, *10*, 1468. [CrossRef]
16. Parikh, J.; Parikh, K.; Ghosh, P.P.; Khedkar, G. *Low Carbon Development Pathways for a Sustainable India*; IRADe: New Dehli, India, 2014; Available online: https://www.researchgate.net/publication/274515855_Low_Carbon_Development_Pathways_for_a_sustainable_India (accessed on 23 September 2017).
17. Singh, A.; Karplus, V.J.; Winchester, N. *Evaluating India's Climate Targets: The Implications of Economy-Wide and Sector Specific Policies*; Report 327; MIT Joint Program: Cambridge, MA, USA, 2018.
18. Shukla, P.R.; Dhar, S.; Mahapatra, D. Low-carbon society scenarios for India. *Clim. Policy* **2008**, *8*, S156–S176. [CrossRef]
19. Shukla, P.R.; Dhar, S.; Fujino, J. Renewable energy and low carbon economy transition in India. *J. Renew. Sustain. Energy* **2010**, *2*, 031005. [CrossRef]
20. Marcucci, A.; Fragkos, P. Drivers of regional decarbonization through 2100: A multi-model decomposition analysis. *Energy Econ.* **2015**, *51*, 111–124. [CrossRef]
21. Gulagi, A.; Choudhary, P.; Bogdanov, D.; Breyer, C. Electricity system based on 100% renewable energy for India and SAARC. *PLoS ONE* **2017**, *12*, e0180611. [CrossRef] [PubMed]
22. Teske, S.; Sawyer, S.; Schäfer, O. *Energy [R]evolution—A Sustainable World Energy Outlook 2015—100% Renewable Energy for All*; Greenpeace, Global Wind Energy Council, SolarPower Europe: Brussels, Belgium, 2015; Available online: https://www.researchgate.net/publication/310018861_Energy_Revolution_-_A_sustainable_world_energy_outlook_2015 (accessed on 27 August 2017).
23. Jacobsen, M. Roadmaps to Transition Countries to 100% Clean, Renewable Energy for All Purposes to Curtail Global Warming, Air Pollution, and Energy Risk. *Earth's Futur.* **2017**, *5*, 948–952. [CrossRef]
24. Löffler, K.; Hainsch, K.; Burandt, T.; Oei, P.-Y.; von Hirschhausen, C. Decarbonizing the Indian Energy System until 2050: An Application of the Open Source Energy Modeling System OSeMOSYS. Available online: https://www.researchgate.net/publication/318966842_Decarbonizing_the_Indian_Energy_System_until_2050_-_An_Application_of_the_Open_Source_Energy_Modeling_System_OSeMOSYS (accessed on 1 November 2017).
25. International Energy Agency (IEA). *World Energy Outlook 2016*; IEA Publications: Paris, France, 2016; ISBN 978-92-64-26494-6.
26. Arent, D.; Arndt, C.; Miller, M.; Finn, T.; Zinaman, O. *The Political Economy of Clean Energy Transitions*; World Institute for Development Economics Research, Oxford University Press: New York, NY, USA, 2017; ISBN 978-0-19-880224-2.
27. Pandey, A. *India's Low Carbon Transition*; Observer Research Foundation: New Delhi, India, 2017; Available online: https://www.oecd.org/environment/cc/g20-climate/collapsecontents/ORF-India-low-carbon-transition.pdf (accessed on 18 April 2018).
28. Joshi, M.; Khosla, R. India: Meeting Energy Needs for Development While Addressing Climate Change. In *Sustainable Energy in G20: Prospects for a Global Energy Transition*; Institute for Advanced Sustainability Studies e.V.: Potsdam, Germany, 2016. [CrossRef]
29. Vishwanathan, S.S.; Garg, A.; Tiwari, V. Coal Transition in India. Assessing India's Energy Transition Options. Available online: https://www.iddri.org/en/publications-and-events/report/coal-transition-india (accessed on 22 September 2018).
30. India Brand Equity Foundation. Metals and Mining. Available online: https://www.ibef.org/industry/metals-and-mining-presentation (accessed on 5 November 2017).
31. International Energy Agency (IEA). *World Energy Outlook 2015*; IEA Publications: Paris, France, 2015; ISBN 978-92-64-24366-8.
32. The Hindu Business Line CIL Plans to Shut Down 65 Loss-Making Mines. Available online: http://www.thehindubusinessline.com/companies/cil-plans-to-shut-down-65-lossmaking-mines/article9717877.ece (accessed on 27 June 2017).
33. GOI—Ministry of Power Power Sector at a Glance. Available online: https://powermin.nic.in/en/content/power-sector-glance-all-india (accessed on 15 October 2018).
34. World Nuclear Association Nuclear Power in India. Available online: http://www.world-nuclear.org/information-library/country-profiles/countries-g-n/india.aspx (accessed on 12 February 2018).

35. GOI—Ministry of Power. *Power Sector: Executive Summary for the Month of March 2018*; Government of India, Ministry of Power, Central Electricity Authority: New Dehli, India, 2018; Available online: http://www.cea.nic.in/reports/monthly/executivesummary/2018/exe_summary-03.pdf (accessed on 7 April 2018).
36. GOI—Ministry of Power. *Power Sector: Executive Summary for the Month of Feb 2018*; Government of India, Ministry of Power, Central Electricity Authority: New Dehli, India, 2018; Available online: http://www.cea.nic.in/reports/monthly/executivesummary/2018/exe_summary-02.pdf (accessed on 7 April 2018).
37. International Renewable Energy Agency (IRENA). *Renewable Energy and Jobs—Annual Review 2017*; International Renewable Energy Agency: Abu Dhabi, UAE, 2017; ISBN 978-92-9260-027-3.
38. Department of Industrial Policy and Promotion (DIPP). *New & Renewable Energy Sector—Make in India Achievement*; Department of Industrial Policy and Promotion, Ministry of New and Renewable Energy: New Delhi, India, 2017; Available online: http://www.makeinindia.com/article/-/v/renewable-energy-sector-achievement-report (accessed on 12 April 2017).
39. Green Climate Fund (GCF). *Readiness and Preparatory Support—Proposal (India)*; GCF: New Delhi, India, 2015; Available online: https://www.greenclimate.fund/documents/20182/466992/Readiness_proposals_-_India___UNDP___NDA_Strengthening_and_Country_Programming.pdf/8dbb05a8-93b6-4a07-b7c2-8e74c68cc043 (accessed on 18 June 2017).
40. UNFCCC International Solar Alliance Mobilizing USD 1 Trillion for Solar Energy by 2030. Available online: https://unfccc.int/news/international-solar-alliance (accessed on 15 October 2018).
41. Howells, M.; Rogner, H.; Strachan, N.; Heaps, C.; Huntington, H.; Kypreos, S.; Hughes, A.; Silveira, S.; DeCarolis, J.; Bazillian, M.; et al. OSeMOSYS: The Open Source Energy Modeling System: An introduction to its ethos, structure and development. *Energy Policy* **2011**, *39*, 5850–5870. [CrossRef]
42. Noble, K. *OSeMOSYS: The Open Source Energy Modeling System-A translation into the General Algebraic Modeling System (GAMS)*; KTH: Stockholm, Sweden, 2017; Available online: https://www.kth.se/en/itm/inst/energiteknik/forskning/desa/publicationsdesa/osemosys-the-open-source-energy-modeling-system-a-translation-into-the-general-algebraic-modeling-system-gams-1.573937 (accessed on 24 October 2017).
43. O'Neill, B.C.; Ren, X.; Jiang, L.; Dalton, M. The effect of urbanization on energy use in India and China in the iPETS model. *Energy Econ.* **2012**, *34*, S339–S345. [CrossRef]
44. Hosain, J.; Mishra, N.; Ansari, M.Z.A.; Deepshikha, S. *Report on India's Wind Power Potential*; WinDForce/MNRE/Shakti Foundation/C-STEP: Delhi, India, 2015. [CrossRef]
45. GOI—Ministry of Power FAQs on Hydropower | Government of India | Ministry of Power. Available online: http://powermin.nic.in/en/content/faqs-hydropower (accessed on 21 July 2017).
46. Farfan, J.; Breyer, C. Structural changes of global power generation capacity towards sustainability and the risk of stranded investments supported by a sustainability indicator. *J. Clean. Prod.* **2017**, *141*, 370–384. [CrossRef]
47. Gulagi, A.; Bogdanov, D.; Breyer, C. The Demand for Storage Technologies in Energy Transition Pathways Towards 100% Renewable Energy for India. *Energy Procedia* **2017**, *135*, 37–50. [CrossRef]
48. IEA Scenarios and Projections. Available online: https://www.iea.org/publications/scenariosandprojections/ (accessed on 17 July 2017).
49. Schröder, A.; Bracke, M.; Gerbaulet, C.; Mendelevitch, R.; Islam, M.; von Hirschhausen, C. *Current and Prospective Costs of Electricity Generation until 2050*; Data Documentation 68; DIW Berlin, TU Berlin: Berlin, Germany, 2013.
50. Ram, M.; Bogdanov, D.; Aghahosseini, A.; Breyer, C. *Global Energy System Based on 100% Renewable Energy—Power Sector*; University of Technology Lappeenranta: Lappeenranta, Finland, 2017; ISBN 978-952-335-171-4.
51. Energy Technology Reference Indicator (ETRI). *Energy Technology Reference Indicator (ETRI) Projections for 2010–2050*; European Commission: Petten, The Netherlands, 2014. [CrossRef]
52. GOI—Ministry of Power. *Power Procurement*. Available online: http://meritindia.in/ (accessed on 14 September 2017).
53. Landberg, R. Clean Energy Is Approaching a Tipping Point. Bloomberg New Energy Finance. Available online: https://www.bloomberg.com/news/articles/2017-09-19/tipping-point-seen-for-clean-energy-as-monster-turbines-arrive (accessed on 29 October 2017).

54. CEIC India GDP per Capita. Available online: https://www.ceicdata.com/en/indicator/india/gdp-per-capita (accessed on 6 May 2018).
55. Barry, E.; Bagri, N.T. Narendra Modi, Favoring Growth in India, Pares Back Environmental Rules. The New York Times. Available online: https://www.nytimes.com/2014/12/05/world/indian-leader-favoring-growth-sweeps-away-environmental-rules.html (accessed on 3 August 2017).
56. World Resources Institute (WRI). *Can Renewable Energy Jobs Help Reduce Poverty in India*; World Resources Institute: Washington, DC, USA, 2017; ISBN 978-1-56973-924-2.
57. Farooq, A. *Generation Based Incentive Scheme; Ministry of New and Renewable Energy*; New Delhi, India, 2011. Available online: http://pib.nic.in/newsite/PrintRelease.aspx?relid=78829 (accessed on 14 July 2017).
58. Infrastructure Development Finance Company Ltd. (IDFC). *Barriers to Development of Renewable Energy in India & Proposed Recommendations*; IDFC: Chennai, India, 2010; Available online: http://www.idfc.com/pdf/publications/Discussion-paper-on-Renewable-Energy.pdf (accessed on 12 August 2017).
59. Mohan, A.; Topp, K. India's energy future: Contested narratives of change. *Energy Res. Soc. Sci.* **2018**, *44*, 75–82. [CrossRef]
60. Lebel, L.; Garden, P.; Banaticla, M.R.N.; Lasco, R.D.; Contreras, A.; Mitra, A.P.; Sharma, C.; Nguyen, H.T.; Ooi, G.L.; Sari, A. Integrating Carbon Management into the Development Strategies of Urbanizing Regions in Asia. *J. Ind. Ecol.* **2007**, *11*, 61–81. [CrossRef]
61. Shrimali, G.; Shobbit, G.; Srinivasan, S.; Nelson, D. *Solving India's Renewable Energy Financing Challenge: Which Federal Policies Can Be Most Effective?* Climate Policy Initiative (CPI): New Delhi, India, 2014. Available online: https://climatepolicyinitiative.org/publication/solving-indias-renewable-energy-financing-challenge-which-federal-policies-can-be-most-effective/ (accessed on 8 September 2017).
62. World Bank Group Electric Power Transmission and Distribution Losses (% of Output): India. Available online: http://data.worldbank.org/indicator/EG.ELC.LOSS.ZS?locations=IN (accessed on 24 July 2017).
63. Golden, M.; Min, B. Theft and Loss of Electricity in an Indian State. Available online: https://leitner.yale.edu/sites/default/files/files/resources/papers/GM_PowerTheft_20120409.pdf (accessed on 17 July 2017).
64. World Bank Ease of Doing Business in India. Available online: http://www.doingbusiness.org/data/exploreeconomies/india (accessed on 5 November 2017).
65. Balachandra, P.; Kristle Nathan, H.S.; Reddy, B.S. Commercialization of sustainable energy technologies. *Renew. Energy* **2010**, *35*, 1842–1851. [CrossRef]
66. Jolly, S.; Raven, R.; Romijn, H. Upscaling of business model experiments in off-grid PV solar energy in India. *Sustain. Sci.* **2012**, *7*, 199–212. [CrossRef]

© 2018 by the authors. Licensee MDPI, Basel, Switzerland. This article is an open access article distributed under the terms and conditions of the Creative Commons Attribution (CC BY) license (http://creativecommons.org/licenses/by/4.0/).

Article

Analyzing Scenarios for the Integration of Renewable Energy Sources in the Mexican Energy System—An Application of the Global Energy System Model (GENeSYS-MOD)

Luis Sarmiento [1,2,*,†], Thorsten Burandt [1,3,4,†], Konstantin Löffler [1,3,†] and Pao-Yu Oei [1,3,†]

1. DIW Berlin, Mohrenstraße 58, 10117 Berlin, Germany
2. CIDE Mexico, Carr. México-Toluca 3655, Santa Fe, Altavista, Ciudad de México 01210, CDMX, Mexico
3. Workgroup for Infrastructure Policy, Technische Universität Berlin, Straße des 17 Juni 135, 10629 Berlin, Germany
4. Department of Industrial Economics and Technology Management (IØT), NTNU Trondheim, Høgskoleringen 1, 7491 Trondheim, Norway
* Correspondence: asarmiento@diw.de; Tel.: +49-30-8978-9309
† These authors contributed equally to this work.

Received: 28 June 2019; Accepted: 18 August 2019; Published: 25 August 2019

Abstract: This paper uses numerical techno-economic modelling to analyse the effect of current national renewable targets and climate goals on the cost and structural composition of the Mexican energy system. For this, we construct a scenario base analysis to compare current policies with two alternative states of the world—one without climate policies and one attaining full decarbonization. Furthermore, an additional iterative routine allows us to estimate the cost-optimal share of renewable technologies in the energy sector and the effect that deviating from this share has on total discounted system costs, emissions and the structure of the energy mix. In general, model results exhibit three key insights—(1) A marked dependence of the energy system on photovoltaics and natural gas; (2) The 2050 cost-optimal share of renewables for the production of electricity, transportation and industrial heating is respectively 75%, 90% and 5%; and (3) As national renewable targets for the power sector are lower than the cost-optimal share of renewables, equivalent to the shares in an scenario without climate policies and completely disconnected from national climate goals, these should be modified.

Keywords: renewable transition; numeric modelling; Mexico; climate policies; energy transition; energy policy; GENeSYS-MOD

1. Introduction

Examining the cost and structure of energy systems under different decarbonization policies is an essential scientific exercise to understand the consequences of current renewable targets and climate goals on future energy outcomes. Policies seeking to decarbonize the energy sector are a response to the adverse effects of human emissions of environmental contaminants and greenhouse gases (GHGs) imposed on the planet, society and individuals, such as climate change [1–3], loss of biodiversity [4,5], adverse health outcomes [6–8] and productivity shocks to labour supply [9–12]. The National Aeronautics and Space Administration (NASA) states that climate change is likely to continue throughout this century, with changes in harvesting seasonality, variation in precipitation rates, an increasing number of droughts, stronger heatwaves, bigger hurricanes and higher water levels [2].

In the first United Nations Framework Convention on Climate Change (UNFCCC), the majority of national governments acknowledged the substantial evidence in favour of human-made climate change and, at the first conference of the parties (COP1), the Kyoto protocol was signed [13]. The Kyoto protocol was the first collective agreement to recommend a decrease in GHG emissions and, since then, serves as the cornerstone for all intergovernmental negotiations regarding climate change and mitigation of anthropogenic emissions. In 2015, during the 21st conference of the parties of the UNFCCC (COP21), 195 national governments, including Mexico, signed the Paris Agreement, a collective arrangement to hold global warming below two degrees Celsius. However, even though there is a common understanding to reduce anthropogenic emissions, each nation is independently developing its own mitigation strategies. Among these strategies are the introduction of national renewable targets for increasing the percentage of renewables in the energy sector and climate goals for decreasing national anthropogenic emissions. In Mexico, there is a general climate objective that goes hand in hand with the Paris Agreement. The law sets the aspirational goal to reduce emissions by 50% in 2050 (base year 2000). Furthermore, the country also has renewable targets aiming to generate 50% of its power through renewable production in 2050. This study aims to analyze not just the effect of current renewable targets and climate goals in the Mexican energy sector but also how these policy instruments deviate from two alternative scenarios: one without climate policies and another with full decarbonization. For this, we optimize the energy sector using the Global Energy System Model (GENeSYS-MOD), a bottom-up techno-economic model developed by Löffler et al. [14]. Techno-economic energy system models, like GENeSYS-MOD, can assist policymakers by providing unbiased assessments on the effects of different policies on future energy outcomes. Specifically, these models allow modelers to infer the consequences of different climate policies in the cost, structure and composition of the energy mix. Although the name of the model suggests a global approach, the application to specific regional energy sectors is possible. In this case, we apply the model to Mexico, using a regional extension of the global data set and warn the reader about the potentially misleading nature of the name.

The primary objective of this optimization study is to answer four questions: first, how do costs and power mixes change in response to variations in energy and climate policies? Specifically, what are the effects of current renewable targets and climate goals *vis-a-vis* a scenario without the implementation of climate policies and another attaining full decarbonization. Second, what is the 2050 cost-optimal share of renewables in the Mexican energy mix for the power, heating and transportation sectors? Third, what is the marginal cost increase in each sector resulting from deviating from cost-optimal renewable targets? And fourth, are the climate goals and renewable targets aligned and how much do these deviate from the full decarbonization and policy free scenarios? To answer these questions we use four different scenarios —BAU, National Targets, Climate Goals and 100 percent Renewables—plus a iterative optimization routine of the Mexican energy system. We answer the first question by comparing all four scenarios, allowing us to contrast current public policies for the introduction of renewables or the reduction of emissions with the two additional scenarios (BAU, and 100 percent Renewables). To answer the second and third questions, we use an iterative optimization routine consisting of 20 different scenarios under increasing and binding renewable targets. In each optimization, the share of renewables in the system increases from 0% to 100% in 5% intervals. After each optimization, we calculate total discounted system costs and, with this information, determine the cost-optimal share of renewables in the energy system and the marginal cost of deviating from this optimal share. Finally, to answer the last question, we compare the effect of current National Targets and Climate Goals between them and with BAU in order to infer the alignment between both goals and their specific effect in the system. This article is, to the best of our knowledge, the first techno-economic model looking at the optimal cost-share of renewable technologies and the associated costs of deviating from this optimal in the transportation, heating and power sectors while accounting for sector coupling.

The following list presents a detailed explanation of the four main scenarios and the iterative routine:

- *BAU*: the model has no requirements regarding renewable targets or climate goals.
- *National Targets*: the model has to comply with current renewable targets in the power sector: 25% by 2018, 35% by 2024 and 50% by 2050 (Mexico defines these targets for clean energies (including nuclear as well as carbon capture and storage facilities). However, to stay in line with international comparisons, this paper defines clean energies as only those related to traditional renewable technologies.) [15]. Additionally, Renewable targets are only set for the power sector and all Mexican states should jointly achieve them. This cooperation means that renewable-rich regions can export their renewably produced surplus to other parts of Mexico.
- *Climate Goals*: the model has to comply with current climate goals for the reduction of GHG emissions: 30% by 2020 and 50% by 2050 [16]. The climate objectives are defined on the national level across all sectors and regions of the economy. The model minimizes costs across all sectors with the underlying goal of achieving the necessary reductions in greenhouse gas emissions.
- *100 percent Renewables*: the model has to reach full decarbonization of the energy system by 2050.
- *Iterative routine*: The model runs 20 different optimization routines by assuming 20 different renewable shares. The share of renewables in the system starts at 0% and linearly increases in 5% intervals until it reaches 100%. At each iteration, the model is required to comply with the renewable share without exceeding it.

Analyzing the Mexican energy system is interesting for several reasons. First, Mexico is one of the largest greenhouse gas emitters (13th) [17], oil producers (11th), electricity producers (13th), electricity consumers (15th), natural gas consumers (9th) and oil consumers (10th) in the world [18]. Second, the country has a high potential for the deployment of renewable technologies, like solar and wind, with respective potential capacities of 1172 and 583 gigawatts [19]. Third, the geographical location of the country opens the possibility of further integrating its electricity system with the United States and Canada, forming an integrated North American energy market, which would be one of the largest in the world.

Currently, the Mexican energy mix is heavily reliant on fossil fuels. Figure 1 (left) plots the input share of each energy carrier in the mix. As can be seen, the system heavily relies on oil to satisfy its energy demands. Regarding the sectoral composition of the energy system, Figure 1 (right) illustrates that the transportation sector is responsible for the highest share of demand for energy in the country.

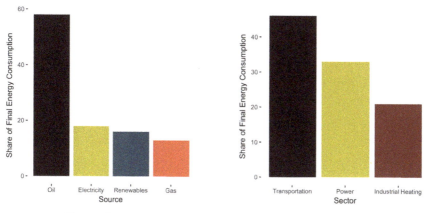

Figure 1. Percent Share of Final Energy Demand for Sources and Sectors.

Figure 2 plots the fuel and technology mix of the demand for energy in each sector. Industrial heating heavily relies on natural gas, transportation on oil and the generation of electricity on thermometric, carboelectric and hydroelectric power plants. Specifically, natural gas has increased its share in the energy mix because of steady increments in the national demand for electric power and drops in the price of natural gas due to fracking activities in the United States (see Wang et al. [20]) that push oil away from the energy demand in the power and heating sectors. In 2002, natural gas was responsible for 37% of national capacity and 46% of electricity generation. By 2015 these shares had grown to 49% and 53% respectively. In general, 81% of all required new capacity between 2002 and 2015 came from natural gas power plants.

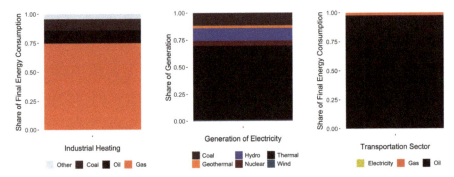

Figure 2. Fuel and Technology Composition of the Heating, Power and Transport Sectors.

In 2015, the country consumed 288,232 GWh of electric power. It reached minimum demand on 1 January, at 18,341 MWh/h and maximum on 14 August, at 39,840 MWh/h. Higher demand for electric power comes in the summer months and afternoons due to the use of air conditioning and cooling technologies. This peak demand coincides with periods of high solar radiation when photovoltaic facilities can produce more power but is counter-cyclical to the production of wind and hydroelectric technologies. Figure 3 plots the intraday behaviour (load curve) of the national electric system for an average winter and summer day.

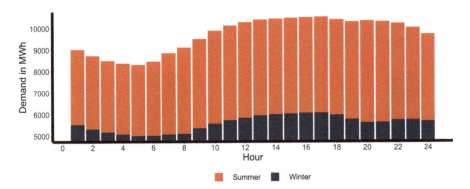

Figure 3. Load profile of the Mexican electric system.

The industrial heating sector (the heating sector consists of residential and industrial heating. However, due to its geographical location, Mexico has no relevant demand for house heating) has no available public information on its energy demand. However, data on total energy and electricity demand at the industry level is publicly available [21]. Using this information, under the assumption that industrial demand for energy comprises electricity and heating and then combining it with the gross domestic product estimates of each industry at the state level [22], allows us to create an approximated value for the demand for heat in each control region. Imputed values show an aggregated heating demand in 2015 of 1060 Petajoules (PJ). The industries contributing most to this share are steel, cement and chemical at 18%, 12% and 13%, respectively.

The national center for energy control (CENACE) divides the country into nine different regions. The model uses these regions to optimize the Mexican energy system. However, the regions of the model are slightly different than the regions of CENACE as the datasets with energy information come at the state level and the regions of CENACE are defined at the municipality level. Figure 4 maps each region into the map of Mexico and plots their respective installed capacity (for more information about the regional disaggregation, see Appendix A).

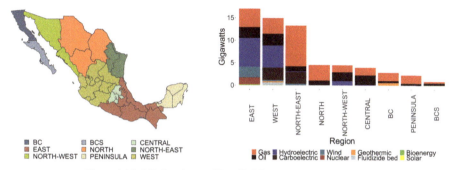

Figure 4. Modelled regions and Installed Capacity per Region.

The rest of this article is structured as follows: Section 2 describes the data sources. Section 3 provides a historical review of numerical models in energy markets, explains the structure and characteristics of GENeSYS-MOD and outlines some related literature. Section 4 presents the results of the model and Section 5 concludes, summarizing the main findings.

2. Data

Numerical models of energy systems require large quantities of information on the electric, transportation and heating sectors to provide accurate estimates on the behaviour of the whole energy sector. For the Mexican power sector, capacity and generation data come from the Energy Information System of the energy ministry [21] and the North American Cooperation on Energy Information System [23]. Data on the potential for renewable sources is taken from the National Atlas for the Assessment of Areas with High Renewable Potential [19] and the National Inventory of Clean Energies of the Energy Ministry [24]. Load profiles per state, nodal structure and transmission capacities come from citizen requests to the National Center for Energy Control. Finally, planned mid-term improvements to the transmission grid originate from the National Electric System Development Program 2017 [25].

Transportation data on the number of cars, buses, trains, passengers and cargo, as well as the length of highways, railways and motorways and total energy consumption was obtained from the Ministry of Transportation and Communications statistics portal [26].

For industrial heating, unfortunately, there is no publicly available data on the exact demand in each region. However, we impute the regional demand with the following method. We assume that national consumed energy by the industrial sector (δ_{st}) is the sum of electricity (ϕ_{st}) and heat consumption (γ_{st}): $\delta_{st} = \phi_{st} + \gamma_{st}$. (The data on energy and electricity consumption may disregard production or transportation losses. Unfortunately, there is no available information on the accountability process with which the government reached these figures. To determine the demand of industrial heat in each state we thus assume the following. All three: total consumed energy, power and heat are subject to a losses of the form $\delta_{st} - \hat{\delta}_{st} = (\phi_{st} - \hat{\phi}_{st}) + (\gamma_{st} - \hat{\gamma}_{st})$, where the hat above the variable indicates the aggregate of transmission, production and efficiency losses. By a simple exercise, we can see that $\delta_{st} = \phi_{st} + \gamma_{st} - (\hat{\phi}_{st} + \hat{\gamma}_{st} - \hat{\delta}_{st})$ which can be simplified to $\delta_{st} = \phi_{st} + \gamma_{st} + \epsilon_{st}$. The main assumption of this estimation is that $\epsilon_{st} \sim 0$ or equivalently $\hat{\phi}_{st} + \hat{\gamma}_{st} = \hat{\delta}_{st}$.) The national system of energy information provides national data on the first two elements: industrial consumed energy and electricity. This information allows us to determine the national demand for industrial heat. Once we obtain the national demand for industrial heat, we use additional segregated national data on national energy and power demand per industry to determine the share of the national heating demand that accrues to each industrial sector. Then we use data from the 2015 economic census of the national institute of geography and statistics (INEGI) to calculate the share of each industry in each state and, thus, the demand for heat that accrues to each state. For example, if the national heating demand of the cement industry is 6.816 PJ and if 50% of the national gross domestic product of the cement industry belongs to a specific state, this state will also have 50% of the total demand (3.408 PJ). Concerning additional inputs, Table 1 summarizes the main sources and assumptions. Fore additional input data, please refer to Appendix B.

Table 1. Key sources for demand and technology data.

Variable	Source
Energy and power demand	PRODESEN [25]
Demand for energy in transport	SCT [26]
Demand for energy in high temperature heating	Own calculations based on data from SENER [21]
Forecast for energy demand	PRODESEN [25] and linear growth based on GDP and population forecasts.
Power plant capacities in 2015	Global Power Plant Database and PRODESEN [25]
Capacity factors of RES	renewables.ninja, see Pfenninger and Staffell [27]
Potential of RES	Solar: own assessment based on capacity factors, available, usable, area and conversion efficiencies. Hydropower and Wind: SENER [19] Geothermal: Gerardo Hiriart Le Bert [28]
Fuel prices	SENER [21] and International Energy Agency [29]
Remaining technology data	Carlsson et al. [30], Basis [31], Gerbaulet and Lorenz [32], Ram et al. [33] and Burandt et al. [34]

Notes: The following table summarises the main data sources of the model. **Acronyms:** PRODESEN: National Program for the development of the electric system—SCT: Ministry of Transport and Communications—GDP: Gross domestic product—SENER: Energy Ministry.

3. Model

Numerical models of energy systems use a system of equations to simulate the consequences that exogenous shocks and different states of the world have on the overall structure of the energy sector. The necessity for this kind of model originated in the acute effects experienced by oil-dependent industrialized countries during the 1970s oil crisis. The oil crisis increased the necessity to simulate the behaviour and reliability of energy markets under exogenous supply and demand shocks [35]. After the development of these oil models, there was a steady change in scope to incorporate climate change, pollution and other relevant externalities from the energy sector. Traditionally, these new energy models analyze the interdependencies and optimal shares between the three main sources of primary energy: fossil fuels, nuclear and renewables. However, recent debates regarding the possibility of fully decarbonized energy systems (Clack et al. [36], Jacobson et al. [37], Hansen et al. [38], Geels et al. [39]) and the availability of low-cost storage technologies shifted interest to the analysis of decarbonization paths and the future development of green energy operations.

Overall, numerical models can be broadly divided into techno-economic and macroeconomic models [35]. Techno-economic models permit separating the energy system into different technologies, processes and interdependencies across energy carriers. This ability to divide the energy system into smaller technology blocks allows the model to internalize the impact of specific policies in each subdivision and to play with the relationships between sectors, technologies and regions.

Macroeconomic models, on the other hand, account for the economic determinants behind energy systems. They experience a trade-off between technical detail and economic insights while attempting to capture links between the energy sector, the economy and society. The separation between techno-economic and macroeconomic models resulted in the need to develop a new set of models that internalize the advantage of both approaches. For example, computable general equilibrium (CGE) models simulate energy systems up to a certain level of technical detail within a particular market structure. Prominent examples of *CGE* models are the MIT-EPPA model used to simulate the world economy and the GEM-E3 model used by the European Commission [40]. Concerning other prominent techno-economic models. One well known model is the MARKAL model, developed by the International Energy Agency [41]. While MARKAL belongs to the group of optimization models, recent modules try to bridge the gap between the techno-economic and macroeconomic models [42], one of them being TIMES (The Integrated MARKAL-EFOM System). TIMES combines a technical engineering with an economic approach, thus merging the characteristics of both [43]. Further, recent techno-economic models try to incorporate aspects of system dynamics into energy system models, for example, POLES [35,44]. System Dynamics models are used to analyze the behaviour of different actors and, thus, are able to provide new insights to energy system modelling.

GENeSYS-MOD is based on the Open-Source Energy Modelling System (OSeMOSYS) framework, developed by the Royal Institute of Technology in Stockholm, Sweden [45]. OSeMOSYS was used by Moura et al. [46] in a game-theoretical framework to understand the bargaining power of South American countries concerning energy policies, by Rogan et al. [47] to analyze the impact of different energy efficiency measures in the Irish energy market and by Lyseng et al. [48] to model the Alberta, Canada, energy system and to study the ability of the region to comply with the 2 degrees commitment of the COP 21. Löffler et al. [14] extended OSeMOSYS to GENeSYS-MOD by including new functionalities, such as a modal split for transportation, an improved trade system and an enhanced focus on environmental budgets. Lawrenz et al. [49] further enhanced GENeSYS-MOD in their case study on transition pathways of the Indian energy system, while Burandt et al. [34] introduced the second model version, with improvements to storages, time slices and performance optimization (for a detailed description of GENeSYS-MOD and its blocks of functionality, see Appendix C).

Specifically, GENeSYS-MOD is different from CGE models because of its capacity to split the energy market into different sectors, technologies and processes; from traditional electricity market models because of its capacity to endogenously optimize the power, transportation and heating sectors, while accounting for sector coupling (Sector coupling refers to the interdependency and substitutability of energy carriers across sectors, for example, electric vehicles and electrolysis.); and from macroeconomic models because of its high level of technical detail. Overall, GENeSYS-MOD is similar to the TIMES model regarding its modular structure and general modelling paradigm. The key advantage of GENeSYS-MOD is the open-source approach of code and data and that the model is freely available. The capacity of GENeSYS-MOD to subdivide the energy system into sectors, technologies and regions; its ability to account for sector coupling; and its high degree of technological features are necessary characteristics of a model attempting to understand the consequences of exogenous variations in energy and climate policies on each supply option, energy sector and modeled region. Overall, numerical models allow analyzing a great variety of problems across several sectors and sciences. Techno-economic models have shown the ability to analyze costs and effects of a transition toward low-carbon technologies in national energy and power mixes. The power sector is the one sector that historically and recently, has received the most attention. With European [50,51], American [52] and global models [14,53] analyzing different transition pathways and their effect on the aggregated cost of the system. Additionally, the scope of these models have expanded to other regions, like China [54] and India [49,55], as well as to other sectors of the energy system in multi-sectoral models [33]. The latter is of high importance, as most previous studies only target the power sector, omitting significant effects due to sector-coupling. Still, a detailed analysis of the Mexican energy system using an integrated, multi-sectoral, approach is missing.

GENeSYS-MOD optimizes the energy system by using a system of linear equations as constraints and inputs to minimize the aggregated cost of the energy system, while securing the supply of energy in a specific region. Equations (1) and (2) show the objective function, as well as the decomposition of technology costs in the model. Equation (1) minimizes the total discounted costs of the energy system (z). Furthermore, Equation (2) defines the costs of each technology as the discounted sum of operating costs, capital investment, emission penalties and salvage values. These equations serve as the core of the model, with additional constraints (see Appendix C) determining the proper functionality of elements, such as energy balances, emission limits or renewable integration.

$$\text{Min } z = \sum_{y,r} \left(\sum_t \left(TotalDiscountedCostByTechnology_{(y,t,r)} \right) + \sum_s \left(TotalDiscountedStorageCost_{(y,s,r)} \right) \right. \\ \left. + DiscountedAnnualTotalTradeCosts_{(y,r)} + \sum_{f,rr} \left(DiscountedNewTradeCapacityCosts_{(y,f,r,rr)} \right) \right) \quad (1)$$

$$TotalDiscountedCostByTechnology_{(y,t,r)} = \\ DiscountedOperatingCost_{(y,t,r)} + DiscountedCapitalInvestment_{(y,t,r)} \\ + DiscountedTechnologyEmissionsPenalty_{(y,t,r)} - DiscountedSalvageValue_{(y,t,r)} \quad \forall y,t,r \quad (2)$$

Figure 5 portrays a stylized version of the general structure of the model. From left to right, we have power generation technologies. These technologies provide electricity to the grid and extract resources from raw energy carriers that also provide energy for industrial and residential heating. The electricity provided to the power grid can be used to satisfy power demand in the region, regional power trade, electric engines, batteries and generation of gas or heat through power-to-heat and power-to-gas technologies. Other critical energy carriers are waste and biomass, which can be used for biofuels or direct use for heat. Finally, the transportation sector is divided into passenger and freight transport with respective technology options. The model then uses the range of technology options to fulfil the (exogenously) defined demands for electricity, heat and transportation, while staying true to constraints, such as renewable targets or emission reduction goals. To achieve this, the model optimizes the construction of new capacities of generation facilities, sector-coupling options, and energy storage. (Since the model can choose freely how to fulfil the final demands, it can use technologies that link the different sectors, usually by electrification. This means that heat or transportation can be provided by electric options, thus coupling the traditionally segregated sectors). As a result, the cost-optimal pathway toward the achievement of these long-term scenarios is obtained for all sectors. For more information on the technical side of the model, please refer to Appendix C, Löffler et al. [14], Howells et al. [45] and Burandt et al. [34].

As a techno-economic numerical model, GENeSYS-MOD is subject to the relevant limitations of these kind of models. It requires exogenous inputs on forecasted demands, costs and technological paths. Regarding the demand for transportation, power and heating, these come from third-party sources, such as the national program for the development of the energy system (PRODESEN) or are imputed with the use of GDP and population estimates. Furthermore, because of the integrated modelling approach for the entire period between 2015 and 2050, it is only possible to include a given number of time slices per year, sixteen-time slices, including four different seasons (spring, summer, autumn, winter) and four intraday cuts (morning, peak, evening, night). These time slices intend to account for peak demand periods in summer and afternoons. Welsch et al. [56] compare an enhanced OSeMOSYS implementation with 16 time slices to a full hourly dispatch model and find the differences to be relatively small (roughly 5% deviation). However, it is true that more granular time windows would be optimal, given the difficulties to push the system toward a full decarbonization path. Linking the more broadly-based energy system development done in this paper to more detailed electricity sector models might be a good point for further research. Further, assessing the cost-optimal transition on a smaller regional level (e.g., municipalities) can lead to additional insight into the development of the Mexican energy system. This also holds true for the assessment of optimal renewable shares, where a regional approach (instead of a sectoral approach) might provide further insights, especially since policies are often determined at a regional level (e.g., using decision making processes, instead of pure optimization) [57–59]. Finally, capital, variable and O&M costs come from exogenous sources and, therefore, influence the model results.

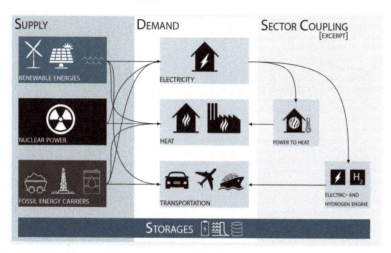

Figure 5. Stylized graph of the stucture of the Global Energy System Model (GENeSYS-MOD).

For this exercise, the model looks at the Mexican energy system by dividing it into three sectors (power, (low-and high-temperature) heat and (passenger and freight) transportation), 9 regions (BCN, BCS, North, Northeast, Northwest, West, Central, East and Peninsula), a multitude of generation technologies (e.g., utility PV, onshore wind, hydropower, biomass, gas (biogas), geothermal, nuclear, oil, gas (natural gas), hard coal, ...) and 16 time-slices. The modeled period runs from 2015 to 2050, computed in 5-year steps, with 2015 serving as the baseline (calibrated based on the data outlined in Section 2).

4. Results

Before addressing the results of each scenario run, it is essential to point out that there were no noteworthy differences between BAU and National Targets, as shown in Figure 6. The objectives of renewables penetration in the power sector of National Targets are attained even without the intervention of climate policies. This outcome means that current national targets in the power sector are insufficient and do not shape the behaviour of the market. Because the results from both scenarios are so similar, the remaining section presents them as a unified scenario: BAU/National Targets. To verify the proper workings of the model, a model validation has been conducted and can be found in Appendix D.

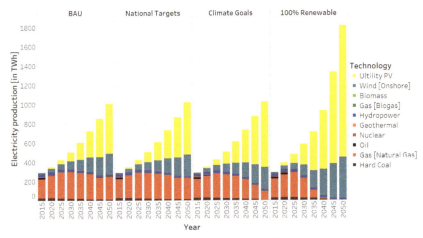

Figure 6. Electricity generation per year for all four scenarios.

4.1. Electricity Sector

The electricity sector sees a significant increase in generation from of renewable technologies. This general trend is independent of the scenario (see Figures 6 and 7). However, the Climate Goals and 100 percent Renewables scenarios result in overall higher renewable shares. Solar power reveals itself as the dominant technology in all scenarios. Even in the BAU/National Targets scenario, it reaches 52.3% of electricity generation, while for 100 percent Renewables, it provides as much as 75.4% by 2050. Electricity generation due to sector-coupling drastically reacts to more ambitious climate targets, with the 100 percent Renewables scenario clearly surpassing BAU/National Targets, as well as Climate Goals (see Figures 6 and 7). In the BAU/National Targets scenario, generation from natural gas increases in the early years of the modelling horizon, peaking in 2030 and then remaining steady with just a small decline toward the end of the modeled period. For the other two scenarios, it peaks in 2025, after which generation from gas-fueled technologies immediately starts to decline. In 100 percent Renewables, the production from natural gas facilities almost disappears by 2040.

Figure 7. Electricity generation from nat. gas, solar photovoltaic (PV) and onshore wind energy per scenario.

Each regional power mix heavily depends on its environmental endowments and demand structure. Figure 8 exhibits the regional development of electricity generation for each scenario. While the system is strongly reliant on natural gas across all scenarios for the year 2030, renewable generation also starts ramping up. Solar technologies are ubiquitous to Mexico and appear with varying intensities across all regions. Hydroelectric power generation remains relatively constant (in absolute terms), although its share diminishes due to the general increase in electricity generation. By 2050, all scenarios show large amounts of solar PV, especially in the Northern regions. Especially in the 100 percent Renewables scenario, the North region supplies large amounts of solar-based electricity to the surrounding regions. Finally, biofuels only appear competitive in the electricity sector for the Central region in the scenarios Climate Goals and, to a lesser extent, in 100 percent Renewables. This is due to the region's small size and comparatively small endowments of RES potentials, yet high energy demands.

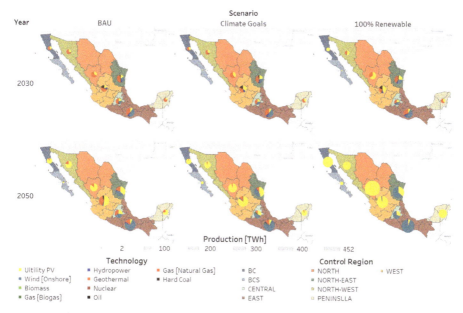

Figure 8. Regional generation of electricity in the years 2030 and 2050 per scenario.

Table 2 presents the installed capacity for natural gas, onshore wind, solar PV and storage technologies across years and scenarios. Intense solar radiation across the nation drives the steady increase in solar PV deployment, with 2050 values ranging from 320.73 GW (BAU/National Targets) to 842.89 GW (100 percent Renewables). Wind also experiences a steady expansion of generation capacities (especially in the East region) but to a much smaller degree than solar. Onshore wind capacities increase from 3.4 GW in 2015 to 56.9 GW in BAU/National Targets, 67.8 GW in Climate Goals and 121.5 GW in 100 percent Renewables by 2050. Strong sector-coupling effects between the electricity and other sectors (see Section 4.2 for more cross-sectoral information) drive the exponential growth behind wind and solar power in the 100 percent Renewables and Climate Goals scenarios. Furthermore, going hand-in-hand with generation from intermittent renewables, the need for electricity storage also increases. While BAU/National Targets utilizes about 110.1 GW of electric storage options, (electricity storage in GENeSYS-MOD v2.0 include Lithium-Ion Batteries, Redox-Flow Batteries, Pumped Hydro Storages and Compressed Air Electric Storages) the 100 percent Renewables scenario requires about 366.7 GW. This difference in storage capacities implies that the storage requirements of 100 percent Renewables are more than three times higher than in BAU/National Targets.

Table 2. Installed capacities for major electricity-generating and storage technologies across scenarios in GW.

		2020	2030	2040	2050
Gas	BAU / National Targets	33.20	36.54	36.22	46.19
	Climate Goals	32.87	32.87	34.02	40.44
	Green Future	32.97	32.84	28.18	26.89
Wind [Onshore]	BAU / National Targets	8.75	21.24	39.26	56.86
	Climate Goals	8.75	21.27	39.34	67.77
	Green Future	8.76	28.26	76.05	121.45
Solar	BAU / National Targets	11.88	56.63	164.81	320.73
	Climate Goals	13.05	78.63	209.22	430.19
	Green Future	21.60	129.81	372.08	842.89
Storages [Electricity]	BAU / National Targets	5.53	18.70	48.18	110.07
	Climate Goals	5.09	25.74	71.42	173.97
	Green Future	6.68	153.99	309.85	366.74

4.2. Energy System Development

Looking at the entire energy system, RES play a vastly different role for each scenario (see Figure 9). While the most ambitious 100 percent Renewables scenario sets the target of 100% renewables use in 2050 (and thus is required to achieve it), the more conservative BAU/National Targets does not enforce climate targets and, thus, remains significantly fueled by conventional energy sources, namely natural gas and oil, even as late as 2050. The Climate Goals scenario takes the middle ground, with about 50% RES-based energy generation by 2050. The total final energy generation only shifts marginally between the scenarios but with Climate Goals and 100 percent Renewables consistently lower than BAU/National Targets. This is due to efficiency gains made possible by sector-coupling, with electrification options being used far more extensively.

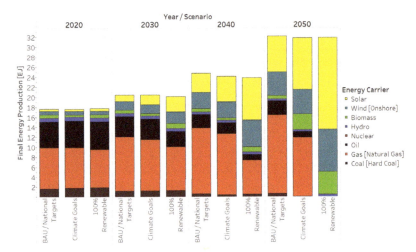

Figure 9. Final energy mix across all sectors per scenario in Exajoule (EJ).

4.2.1. Sectoral Analysis

Figure 10 plots the sectoral share of RES across scenarios. The figure also portrays (sector-coupling) electricity usage in the sectors mobility (aggregating passenger and freight transport) and industrial heating.

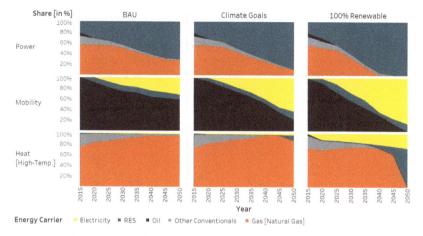

Figure 10. Share of Renewable Energy Sources per sector and scenario.

For the power sector, the entrance of solar and wind technologies to the power matrix replaces natural gas across scenarios. The only difference between them is the steepness of the decarbonization path. The electricity sector of 100 percent Renewables is fully decarbonized by 2045, while Climate Goals still has a marginal share of natural gas facilities in 2050 and under the BAU/National Targets, natural gas production remains at almost 30%. After the power sector, the transportation sector is the next to decarbonize. The sector remains oil-powered in the BAU/National Targets scenario, although a significant share of electricity and RES appears after 2025. For Climate Goals, the transportation sector is about 80% decarbonized by 2050, mostly with the use of electric vehicles and biofuels. 100 percent Renewables achieves 100% renewables in the transportation sector with a higher share of electric-powered vehicles. On the other hand, a particular issue in the path toward full decarbonization is high-temperature heating. In high-temperature heating, both BAU/National Targets and Climate Goals show almost no decarbonization, only 100 percent Renewables enforces a renewable target that obliges the total decarbonization of industrial heating. When the model decarbonizes industrial heating, it opts for a mixture of electricity, hydrogen and biomass (mostly in the form of biogas). The reason behind difficulties in the decarbonization of industrial heating is the sharp cost difference between low-carbon and (regular) carbon-intensive processes in the sector.

In general, a strong trend of sector-coupling can be seen when climate goals are prioritized. This holds mostly true for the mobility sector, where even the BAU/National Targets scenario achieves about 30% electricity share, reaching almost 90% in the 100 percent Renewables scenario. This behaviour also explains the heavy increase in electricity generation across scenarios, as observed in Section 4.1.

4.2.2. Costs

In this section, we analyze the effect of the iterative routine. This routine consists of optimizing the power, transportation and industrial heating sectors under 20 different and binding shares of renewables. The binding shares start at 0% and grow in 5% intervals until reaching full decarbonization. Figure 11 presents the sectoral percentage change in total-discounted-system-costs between a fully decarbonized system and a partially decarbonized one. This graph does not portray any specific scenario assumption but instead takes the technology learning curves and forces the model to use a fixed percentage of renewables in each respective sector(s). Electricity used in the heat or transportation sectors is being distributed to renewable/non-renewable energy via the annual share of RES in the power mix (e.g., RES produced 70% of electricity in 2035, then 70% of electricity in transport would count as renewable and 30% as non-renewable). In the figure, values above zero represent higher total costs than the 100 percent Renewables scenario, while values below zero mean that this level of RES integration would be more cost-competitive than 100 percent Renewables. Naturally, the minimum of the curves represents the cost-optimum share in each of the sectors. To the best of our knowledge, this is the first time a techno-economic optimization model looks at cost variations of the entire energy system across different shares of renewables while accounting for sector coupling.

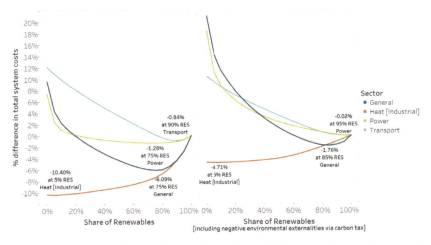

Figure 11. Relative cost difference of different levels of renewable integration (Baseline: 100% RES).

For the power sector and the energy system as a whole, the model portrays two U-shape convex curves. Industrial heating resembles a curve of positive slope, with the percentage increase in total system costs steadily increasing with the share of renewables. On the other hand, the transportation sector display the opposite behaviour, with a negative slope indicating that sector costs decrease with renewable integration. Two insights come from this figure. First, the energy-system cost-curve reaches its cost-optimal share at 75%. High-temperature heat reaches it at 5%, power at 75% and transportation at 90%. Another result is the low-cost difference between the cost-optimal point of 75% RES in the electricity sector and its marginal cost of increasing its share of renewables. Between 75% and 100%, the cost difference is merely 1.28%. For the entire energy system, this difference increases to 6.09% of total system costs due to the high costs of decarbonizing industrial heating. It is worth mentioning that uncertain technology learning curves, fossil fuel prices or energy demands drive these results. However, these results provide an estimate of the cost difference between different penetration scenarios of renewable sources in the energy sector.

A sensitivity exercise, introducing an exogenous CO_2 price, representing an internalization of adverse external effects of carbon dioxide emissions [60], is shown on the right-hand side of Figure 11. The introduction of such an environmental carbon tax (of 180€/tCO_2 in 2015) shifts results quite significantly, although the overall picture remains the same. Industrial heat still sees a low share of RES in its cost-optimal version, while the electricity sector moves up to 95%, pushing the cost-optimal share of RES in the energy system to 85%. In addition, the steepness of the curves is shifted, with a vastly higher increase in total system costs for low amounts of renewables. This exercise demonstrates that a CO_2 tax that internalizes these negative environmental effects can have a significant effect on the outcome of such cost-driven studies and move the cost-optimality even further in favour of RES.

4.2.3. Emissions

Figure 12 plots the relative annual emissions for each of the three scenarios compared to 2015. While the Climate Goals scenario reduces its emissions by 36%, the BAU/National Targets scenarios remain rather constant in their emissions and result in a net increase of about 4% in 2050. What is important to keep in mind, however, is that this 4% increase in emissions in BAU/National Targets goes against a major increase in energy demand across all sectors that comes along with the expected growth of population and wealth. Finally, 100 percent Renewables reaches its target of 100% decarbonization in 2050.

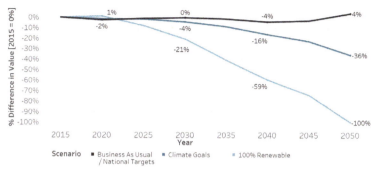

Figure 12. Annual CO_2 emissions per scenario (relative to 2015).

Summing up the yearly emissions, 100 percent Renewables, with its 100% renewable target in 2050, reaches total emissions of about 7.16 Gt CO_2, while Climate Goals emits about 9.63 Gt CO_2 and BAU/National Targets just above 12.0 Gt CO_2, thus more than 60% more than the 100 percent Renewables scenario.

5. Conclusions

In this article, we use the Global Energy System Model (GENeSYS-MOD) to optimize pathways for the Mexican energy system under different energy and climate policies. GENeSYS-MOD is a techno-economic cost-minimizing energy model that differentiates from traditional bottom-up models by the integration of traditionally segregated energy sectors (power, transport and heat). The goal of the study is to analyze the consequences of current renewable targets and climate goals in the future cost composition and structure of the energy sector, to do this we use four different scenarios: BAU, National Targets, Climate Goals and 100 percent Renewables. BAU optimizes the energy system without any constraints regarding renewable targets or climate goals. National Targets forces the model to attain current renewable targets. Climate Goals does the analogous with Mexico's climate goals, and, finally, 100 percent Renewables forces the optimization routine to decarbonize the energy system by 2050. Additionally, we also run an iterative optimization routine by increasing the share of renewables in each sector between 0% and 100% in 5% steps. In each iteration, the model attains, without exceeding, the imposed share of renewable sources. Our modelling approach allows us to investigate the cost consequences and changes in energy mix of national renewable targets and climate goals between the scenarios. Moreover, comparing BAU with Climate Goals and National Targets permits us to infer the suitability of these policies by understanding how much they deviate from the two extreme scenarios (BAU and 100 percent Renewables). Finally, the optimization routine allows us to determine the cost-optimal share of renewables in the energy system and the marginal cost of deviating from this optimal share. To the best of our knowledge, this paper is the first optimization approach analyzing how the total discounted costs of the energy system vary under different sectoral renewable targets. Additional contributions relate to the analysis of the Mexican energy sector while accounting for sector coupling and the insights gained from the comparison of various scenarios.

Results from the study show that Mexican renewable targets are insufficient and sub-optimal: the model shows that the optimal share of renewables for the generation of electricity is 80%, that is, 30% higher than current commitments in the national strategy for the promotion of clean fuels and technologies [15]. Even more, the share of renewables in the power mix between BAU and National Targets is very similar. This indicates that current renewable targets do not even deviate from a scenario without climate policies, meaning that there is a misalignment between climate goals and renewable targets. In principle, both policies should aim for the same goal. For example, if the power sector renewable target of 50% is significantly lower than the penetration of renewables under the fulfillment of climate goals, it is redundant and inefficient to implement both policies. At the minimum, renewable targets should mimic the sectoral decarbonization paths of climate goals. Regarding the energy mix, natural gas and photovoltaics shape the future of the Mexican energy system, across all regions, except for the wind-rich East region, strongly relying on onshore wind turbnies for the generation of electric power. In the intermediate term, however, an ongoing dependence on natural gas can be observed across all scenarios. When aiming for full decarbonization (100 percent Renewables), the energy mix relies on solar, wind and biomass to satisfy the energy needs of the country, using the grid, as well as energy storages, as load balancing options.

Concerning sectoral decarbonization paths, it is evident that the power, transport and heating sectors present different patterns. For electric power, the cost competitiveness of photovoltaics and wind turbines push the sector toward decarbonization across all scenarios and regions. Moreover, due to sector coupling, the introduction of these cost-competitive technologies in the power mix is a crucial factor for the decarbonization of the transportation sector. The higher the share of renewables in the power sector, the greater the introduction of electric vehicles in the transportation sector. The heating sector is the last sector to decarbonize because of substantial cost differences between conventional and renewable heat.

Furthermore, the computation of sectoral cost minima exhibits interesting results. As previously noted, the cost-optimal share of renewable targets in the power sector is 75%, 25% points higher than current renewable targets. For the transportation sector, the share is as high as 90%, suggesting significant economic advantages of increasing the share of electric vehicles in this sector. For the heat sector, its share reflects the high cost of renewable heat and present an optimal renewable target of only 5%. Finally, for the energy system as a whole, the 2050 optimal renewable share is 75%. As an additional exercise, we analyze how costly it is to increase the share of renewables in both the power and energy sectors. Increasing the power sector to full decarbonization only increases total costs by 1.28%; for the whole energy system, total costs would increase by 6.09% (mostly driven by industrial heating). Finally, the difference in total cumulative emissions between BAU/National Targets and 100% Renewable is 4.85 gigatonnes of CO_2 (more than 10 times the current yearly emissions of Mexico [61–63]).

The results of this study air several exciting conclusions: public policies for the introduction of renewables in the power sector need to change. They are equivalent to a scenario without climate policies, disconnected from the climate goals of the country and significantly lower than the estimated cost-optimal share of renewables in the power sector. Furthermore, aiming for more stringent shares of renewables in the power sector or stricter climate goals for the mitigation of greenhouse gases only marginally increases the total cost of the energy and power systems. Other relevant insights are the reliance of the power system on photovoltaic and natural gas, the high cost-optimal share of renewables in the transportation sector and its low counterpart in industrial heating. Moreover, this article can help policymakers in the design and implementation of specific targets and policies for the decarbonization of the heating and transportation sectors by providing the cost-optimal share of renewables in each sub-sector.

Author Contributions: Conceptualization, L.S., T.B., K.L. and P.-Y.O.; methodology, L.S., T.B. and K.L.; software, T.B. and K.L.; validation, L.S., T.B. and K.L; formal analysis, L.S. and P.-Y.O.; data curation, L.S., T.B. and K.L.; writing—original draft preparation, L.S., T.B., K.L. and P.-Y.O.; writing—review and editing, P.-Y.O. and K.L.; visualization, L.S. and K.L.; supervision, P.-Y.O.

Funding: This work was supported by the German Ministry for Education and Research (BMBF) under grant number 01LN1704A for the research group CoalExit.

Acknowledgments: Previous works of this research have been presented at various workshops and conferences in Mexico and across Europe. We therefore thank the conference and workshop audiences and in particular

Christian von Hirschhausen, Claudia Kemfert, Juan Rosellon and Elmar Zozmann for useful discussions and suggestions, the usual disclaimer applies.

Conflicts of Interest: The authors declare no conflict of interest.

Appendix A. Regional Disaggregation

East, located in the eastern-southernmost part of the country has the largest installed capacity and penetration of renewables across regions. Wind-parks and hydroelectric-dams cover up to 50% of the region's installed capacity. West, located in the center west of the country is the second largest region regarding installed capacity. Its energy mix has combined-cycle, hydroelectric, carboelectric and oil-indexed facilities as driving technologies. Northeast is located in the north-east of the country, next to the Gulf of Mexico and south of Texas. An extensive network of gas pipes connects it with the shale reserves of the United States making its power mix heavily dependant on natural gas. This region is also experiencing a surge of wind parks in the north part of the Gulf of Mexico. Northwest and North are industrial and scarcely populated regions that use combined natural gas, oil and dams to satisfy their energy demands. Central includes Mexico City and its metropolitan area plus additional center states. The region is poor in natural endowments and it is a net importer of electric power. Its power matrix consists of natural gas and oil. BC locates south of California, in the northwest of Mexico. It has natural gas and geothermal energy as the main sources of power. Finally, Peninsula, located in the Yucatan peninsula and BCS in the southern part of the California peninsula depend on natural gas and oil plants.

Table A1. States and their corresponding Regions.

Baja California (BC)	
Baja California	
Southern Baja California (BCS)	
Baja California Sur	
Central	
Hidalgo	Mexico City
Mexico	Morelos
East	
Chiapas	Guerrero
Oaxaca	Puebla
Tabasco	Tlaxcala
Veracruz	
North	
Chihuahua	Durango
North-East	
Coahuila	Nuevo Leon
Tamaulipas	
North-West	
Sonora	Sinaloa
Peninsula	
Campeche	Quintana Roo
Yucatan	

Table A1. Cont.

West	
Aguascalientes	Colima
Guanajuato	Jalisco
Michoacan	Nayarit
Queretaro	San Luis Potosi
Zacatecas	

Appendix B. Input Data

Appendix B.1. Technology Costs

Table A2. Capital Costs of main electricity generating technologies in M€/GW. Data based on Carlsson et al. [30], Basis [31], Gerbaulet and Lorenz [32], Ram et al. [33] and Burandt et al. [34].

	2015	2020	2025	2030	2035	2040	2045	2050
Utility PV	1000	580	466	390	337	300	270	246
Onshore Wind	1250	1150	1060	1000	965	940	915	900
Offshore Wind	3500	2637	2200	1936	1800	1710	1642	1592
Geothermal	3988	3775	3584	3392	3221	3049	2895	2740
Coal-Fired Thermal Plant	1600	1600	1600	1600	1600	1600	1600	1600
Gas-Fired Thermal Plant	650	636	621	607	593	579	564	550
Oil-Fired Thermal Plant	650	627	604	581	559	536	513	490
Coal-Fired CHP	2030	2030	2030	2030	2030	2030	2030	2030
Gas-Fired CHP	977	955	934	912	891	869	848	826
Oil-Fired CHP	819	790	761	733	704	675	646	617

Appendix B.2. Fuel Costs

Table A3. Fossil Fuel Cost in M€/PJ, based on SENER [21], International Energy Agency [29].

	2015	2020	2025	2030	2035	2040	2045	2050
Oil [Import]	7.12	10.18	11.02	11.86	11.37	10.88	10.39	9.91
Coal [Import]	1.52	1.54	1.53	1.52	1.44	1.36	1.28	1.20
Nat. Gas [Import]	6.63	6.54	7.72	8.91	9.15	9.38	9.62	9.86
Oil [Domestic]	6.76	9.68	10.47	11.27	10.80	10.34	9.87	9.41
Coal [Domestic]	1.44	1.47	1.45	1.44	1.36	1.29	1.21	1.14
Nat. Gas [Domestic]	6.30	6.21	7.34	8.46	8.69	8.91	9.14	9.36

Appendix B.3. Renewable Potentials

Table A4. Renewable Potentials in Gigawatts (GW) installed capacity per region. Data (wind and hydro) based on SENER [19]. The data used for the computation of solar capacity potentials can be found in Table A5.

	Utility PV	Onshore Wind	Hydro
BC	147.0	159.0	0.6
BCS	152.8	67.5	0.6
CENTRAL	25.4	33.0	0.4
EAST	369.9	188.9	8.3
NORTH-EAST	318.9	339.5	2.3
NORTH-WEST	841.7	85.7	1.0
NORTH	1815.1	418.6	1.2
PENINSULA	113.7	175.9	0.0
WEST	429.4	110.1	4.1

Table A5. Data and assumptions used for the computation of solar PV potentials.

Control Region	Irradiation [kWh/m²/d]	Surface Area [km²]	Total Population	Population per km²	Available Area [%]	Conversion Efficiency	Resulting Potential in GW
BC	7155.1	71,450	3,155,070	44.2	0.03	0.23	147.0
BCS	7190.0	73,909	637,026	8.6	0.03	0.23	152.8
CENTRAL	5354.0	49,538	28,469,187	574.7	0.01	0.23	25.4
EAST	5279.4	365,524	27,943,184	76.4	0.02	0.23	369.9
NORTH-EAST	5761.1	144,405	7,406,680	51.3	0.04	0.23	318.9
NORTH-WEST	7394.6	237,555	5,629,180	23.7	0.05	0.23	841.7
NORTH	7251.7	522,372	7,787,790	15.0	0.05	0.23	1815.1
PENINSULA	5578.8	141,736	4,103,596	29.0	0.015	0.23	113.7
WEST	6310.8	355,014	26,012,744	73.3	0.02	0.23	429.4

Appendix C. Model Structure

The GENeSYS-MOD framework consists of multiple blocks of functionality, that ultimately originate from the OSeMOSYS framework. GENeSYS-MOD is a cost-optimizing linear program, focusing on long-term pathways for the different sectors of the energy system, specifically targeting emission constraints, the integration of renewables and sector-coupling. The model minizes the objective function, which comprises total system costs (encompassing all costs occurring over the modeled time period).

(Final) Energy demands are given exogenously for each modeled time slice, with the model computing the optimal flows of energy and the resulting needs for capacity additions and storages. Additional demands through sector-coupling are derived endogenously. Constraints, including energy balances (ensuring all demand is met), maximum capacity additions (e.g., to limit the usable potential of renewables), RES feed-in (e.g., to ensure grid stability) and emission budgets (given either yearly or as a total budget over the modeled horizon) are given to ensure proper functionality of the model and yield realistic results.

All fiscal units are discounted towards the base year of 2015, using a discount rate of 5%. Also, the model assumes a sinking fund depreciation, with assets that are within their operating lifetime at the end of the modelling period (here: 2050) being given a *salvage value* that is added back to the objective function. This ensures that investment in the later periods of the model does not come to a halt.

In its basic configuration, GENeSYS-MOD operates from the perspective of an omniscient social planner, including perfect foresight and perfect competition within markets. Figure A1 present the underlying block structure of GENeSYS-MOD v2.0, with the additions made in this study (namely a more detailed regional data set and a new block that adds the option for finding the cost-optimal level of RES in the energy system).

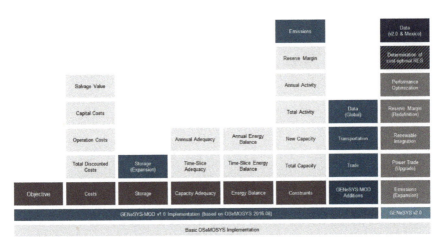

Figure A1. Model structure of the GENeSYS-MOD implementation used in this study.

This determination of the cost-optimal level of RES, as well as the resulting changes in total system costs are obtained via an iterative loop of model runs, each with a predefined and fixed level of RES penetration for the chosen sectors (ranging from 0% to 100% RES). This yields a cost level for each iteration of the process, thus yielding both the lowest (and thus cost-optimal) point, as well as the relative increase that occurs when deviating from the optimum.

Appendix D. Model Validation

To demonstrate the robustness of the model results, a comparison of computed model results of the (base) year 2015 with actual data from official international reports [61–65] has been conducted. Figure A2 shows the results for emissions, electricity and final energy generation, each with the respective counterpart.

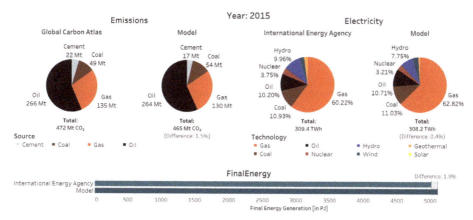

Figure A2. Comparison of model results with actual historical data for the year 2015. Data for emissions from Boden et al. [61], UNFCCC [62] and BP [63]; data for electricity from International Energy Agency [64]; and final energy from International Energy Agency [65].

It can be shown that reasonably close results are obtained within the model computation, with differences between total numbers ranging from 0.4% to close to 2%. As all model data stems from official sources or peer-reviewed academic articles (and is thus assumed to be correct), the model therefore demonstrates that it is working properly.

References

1. Houghton, J.T.; Jenkins, G.J.; Ephraums, J.J. *Climate Change*; Cambridge University Press: Cambridge, MA, USA, 1991.
2. NASA. *Global Climate Change—Vital Signs of the Planet*; NASA: Washington, DC, USA, 2019.
3. Nordhaus, W.D. A review of the Stern review on the economics of climate change. *J. Econ. Lit.* **2007**, *45*, 686–702. [CrossRef]
4. Bellard, C.; Bertelsmeier, C.; Leadley, P.; Thuiller, W.; Courchamp, F. Impacts of climate change on the future of biodiversity. *Ecol. Lett.* **2012**, *15*, 365–377. [CrossRef] [PubMed]
5. Thomas, C.D.; Cameron, A.; Green, R.E.; Bakkenes, M.; Beaumont, L.J.; Collingham, Y.C.; Erasmus, B.F.; De Siqueira, M.F.; Grainger, A.; Hannah, L.; et al.. Extinction risk from climate change. *Nature* **2004**, *427*, 145. [CrossRef] [PubMed]
6. Brunekreef, B.; Dockery, D.W.; Krzyzanowski, M. Epidemiologic studies on short-term effects of low levels of major ambient air pollution components. *Environ. Health Perspect.* **1995**, *103*, 3–13. [PubMed]
7. Brunekreef, B.; Holgate, S.T. Air pollution and health. *Lancet* **2002**, *360*, 1233–1242. [CrossRef]
8. Kampa, M.; Castanas, E. Human health effects of air pollution. *Environ. Pollut.* **2008**, *151*, 362–367. [CrossRef] [PubMed]
9. Graff Zivin, J.; Neidell, M. The impact of pollution on worker productivity. *Am. Econ. Rev.* **2012**, *102*, 3652–73. [CrossRef]
10. Hanna, R.; Oliva, P. The effect of pollution on labour supply: Evidence from a natural experiment in Mexico City. *J. Public Econ.* **2015**, *122*, 68–79. [CrossRef]
11. Meyer, S.; Pagel, M. *Fresh Air Eases Work–The Effect of Air Quality on Individual Investor Activity*; Technical report; National Bureau of Economic Research: Cambridge, MA, USA, 2017.

12. Chang, T.Y.; Graff Zivin, J.; Gross, T.; Neidell, M. The effect of pollution on worker productivity: Evidence from call center workers in China. *Am. Econ. J. Appl. Econ.* **2019**, *11*, 151–72. [CrossRef]
13. UNFCCC. *United Nations Framework Convention on Climate Change*; UNFCCC: Bonn, Germany, 1992.
14. Löffler, K.; Hainsch, K.; Burandt, T.; Oei, P.Y.; Kemfert, C.; von Hirschhausen, C. Designing a model for the glogbal energy system GENeSYS-MOD: An application of the open-source energy modelling system (OSeMOSYS). *Energies* **2017**, *10*, 1468. [CrossRef]
15. SENER. *Estrategia de Tansicion Para Promover el Uso de Tecnologias y Combustibles mas Limpios*; Government publication; SENER 2016: Mexico City, Mexico, 2016.
16. LGCC. *Ley General de Cambio Climatico*; Law, DOF 13-07-2018; LGCC: Mexico City, Mexico, 2018.
17. Boden, T.; Marland, G.; Andres, R. *National CO_2 Emissions from Fossil-Fuel Burning, Cement Manufacture, and Gas Flaring: 1751–2014*; Carbon Dioxide Information Analysis Center, Oak Ridge National labouratory, US Department of Energy: Washington, DC, USA, 2017.
18. EIA. International Energy Statistics. US Energy and Information Administration, Washington, DC, USA. 2011. Available online: http://www.eia.gov/countries/data.cfm (accessed on 10 June 2019).
19. SENER. Atlas Nacional De Energias Renovables. Atlas Nacional de Energias Renovables, Mexico City. 2017. Available online: https://dgel.energia.gob.mx/azel/ (accessed on 10 June 2019).
20. Wang, Q.; Chen, X.; Jha, A.N.; Rogers, H. Natural gas from shale formation–the evolution, evidences and challenges of shale gas revolution in United States. *Renew. Sustain. Energy Rev.* **2014**, *30*, 1–28. [CrossRef]
21. SENER, M. Sistema de Informacin Energetica. Secretaria de Energia, Ciudad de Mexico, Mexico. 2018. Available online: http://sie.energia.gob.mx/ (accessed on 12 April 2019).
22. inegi, M. Senso Economico 2014. Instituto Nacional De Estadistica y Geografia, Ciudad de Mexico, Mexico. 2014. Available online: http://www.beta.inegi.org.mx/app/saic/; https://www.youtube.com/watch?v=uUwpFeVgCJE (accessed on 12 April 2019).
23. nacei. North American Cooperation on Energy Information. USA, CAN, MEX. 2014. Available online: https://www.nacei.org/ (accessed on 8 May 2019).
24. SENER. Inventario Nacional de Energias Limpias. Inventario Nacional de Energias Limpias, Mexico City. 2017. Available online: https://dgel.energia.gob.mx/qa/INEL/INELV5/ (accessed on 8 May 2019).
25. PRODESEN. *Programa de Desarrollo del Sistema Electrico Nacional*; Government publication; SENER 2018: Mexico City, Mexico, 2018.
26. SCT. *Principales Estadisticas del Sector Comunicaciones y Transporte*; Government publication; SCT 2017: Mexico City, Mexico, 2016.
27. Pfenninger, S.; Staffell, I. Long-term Patterns of European PV Output using 30 Years of Validated Hourly Reanalysis and Satellite Data. *Energy* **2016**, *114*, 1251–1265. [CrossRef]
28. Le Bert, G.H.; Gutiérrez-Negrín, L.C.; Quijano León, H.L.; Ornelas Celis, A.; Espíndola, S.; Hernandez Carrillo, I. *Evaluación de la Energía Geotérmica en México*; Technical report; CRE: Ciudad de México, Mexico, 2011.
29. International Energy Agency. *World Energy Outlook 2016*; Technical report; OECD Publishing: Paris, France, 2016.
30. Carlsson, J.; Fortes, M.; de Marco, G.; Giuntoli, J.; Jakubcionis, M.; Jäger-Waldau, A.; Lacal-Arantegui, R.; Lazarou, S.; Magagna, D.; Moles, C.; et al. *ETRI 2014-Energy technology Reference Indicator Projections for 2010–2050*; European Commission, Joint Research Centre, Institute for Energy and Transport, Publications Office of the European Union: Luxembourg, 2014.
31. Basis, B. Report on conversion efficiency of biomass BASIS—Biomass Availability and Sustainability Information System. 2015. Available online: http://basisbioenergy.eu/ (accessed on 9 April 2019).
32. Gerbaulet, C.; Lorenz, C. DynELMOD: A Dynamic Investment and Dispatch Model for the Future European Electricity Market. Available online: https://www.econstor.eu/bitstream/10419/161634/1/888201575.pdf (accessed on 12 April 2019).
33. Ram, M.; Bogdanov, D.; Aghahosseini, A.; Gulagi, A.; Oyewo, A.; Child, M.; Caldera, U.; Sadovskaia, K.; Farfan, J.; Barbosa, L.; et al. *Global Energy System Based on 100% Renewable Energy*; Technical report; Lappeenranta University of Technology (LUT): Lappeenranta, Finland; Energy Watch Group: Berlin, Germany, 2019.

34. Burandt, T.; Löffler, K.; Hainsch, K. GENeSYS-MOD v2.0 - Enhancing the Global Energy System Model. Available online: https://www.econstor.eu/bitstream/10419/180395/1/1026898889.pdf (accessed on 12 April 2019).
35. Herbst, A.; Toro, F.; Reitze, F.; Jochem, E. Introduction to energy systems modelling. *Swiss J. Econ. Stat.* **2012**, *148*, 111–135. [CrossRef]
36. Clack, C.T.; Qvist, S.A.; Apt, J.; Bazilian, M.; Brandt, A.R.; Caldeira, K.; Davis, S.J.; Diakov, V.; Handschy, M.A.; Hines, P.D.; et al. Evaluation of a proposal for reliable low-cost grid power with 100% wind, water, and solar. *Proc. Natl. Acad. Sci. USA* **2017**, *114*, 6722–6727. [CrossRef] [PubMed]
37. Jacobson, M.Z.; Delucchi, M.A.; Cameron, M.A.; Frew, B.A. The United States can keep the grid stable at low cost with 100 clean, renewable energy in all sectors despite inaccurate claims. *Proc. Natl. Acad. Sci. USA* **2017**, *114*, E5021–E5023. [CrossRef] [PubMed]
38. Hansen, K.; Breyer, C.; Lund, H. Status and perspectives on 100% renewable energy systems. *Energy* **2019**, *175*, 471–480. [CrossRef]
39. Geels, F.W.; Sovacool, B.K.; Schwanen, T.; Sorrell, S. The socio-technical dynamics of low-carbon transitions. *Joule* **2017**, *1*, 463–479. [CrossRef]
40. Helgesen, P.I. *Top-down and Bottom-up: Combining Energy System Models and Macroeconomic General Equilibrium Models*; CenSES Working Paper, 1/2013; Center for Systainable Energy Systems (CenSES): Trondheim, Norway, 2013.
41. Fishbone, L.G.; Abilock, H. Markal, a linear-programming model for energy systems analysis: Technical description of the bnl version. *Int. J. Energy Res.* **1981**, *5*, 353–375. [CrossRef]
42. Seebregts, A.J.; Goldstein, G.A.; Smekens, K. Energy/environmental modelling with the MARKAL family of models. In *Operations Research Proceedings 2001*; Chamoni, P., Leisten, R., Martin, A., Minnemann, J., Stadtler, H., Eds.; Springer: Berlin/Heidelberg, Germany, 2001; pp. 75–82.
43. ETSAP. *Overview of TIMES Modelling Tool*; Energy Technology Systems Analysis Program (ETSAP): Lyngby, Denmark, 2005.
44. Russ, P.; Criqui, P. Post-Kyoto CO_2 emission reduction: The soft landing scenario analysed with POLES and other world models. *Energy Policy* **2007**, *35*, 786–796. [CrossRef]
45. Howells, M.; Rogner, H.; Strachan, N.; Heaps, C.; Huntington, H.; Kypreos, S.; Hughes, A.; Silveira, S.; DeCarolis, J.; Bazillian, M.; et al. OSeMOSYS: The open source energy modelling system: An introduction to its ethos, structure and development. *Energy Policy* **2011**, *39*, 5850–5870. [CrossRef]
46. Moura, G.; Howells, M.; Legey, L. Samba the open source south american model base: A brazilian perspective on long term power. KTH-dESA Working Paper Series, 2015. [CrossRef]
47. Rogan, F.; Cahill, C.J.; Daly, H.E.; Dineen, D.; Deane, J.; Heaps, C.; Welsch, M.; Howells, M.; Bazilian, M.; Gallacher, B.P. LEAPs and bounds; An energy demand and constraint optimised model of the Irish energy system. *Energy Effic.* **2014**, *7*, 441–466. [CrossRef]
48. Lyseng, B.; Rowe, A.; Wild, P.; English, J.; Niet, T.; Pitt, L. Decarbonising the Alberta power system with carbon pricing. *Energy Strategy Rev.* **2016**, *10*, 40–52. [CrossRef]
49. Lawrenz, L.; Xiong, B.; Lorenz, L.; Krumm, A.; Hosenfeld, H.; Burandt, T.; Löffler, K.; Oei, P.Y.; von Hirschhausen, C. Exploring energy pathways for the low-carbon transformation in India—A model-based analysis. *Energies* **2018**, *11*, 3001. [CrossRef]
50. Child, M.; Kemfert, C.; Bogdanov, D.; Breyer, C. Flexible electricity generation, grid exchange and storage for the transition to a 100% renewable energy system in Europe. *Renew. Energy* **2019**, *139*, 80–101. [CrossRef]
51. Gerbaulet, C.; von Hirschhausen, C.; Kemfert, C.; Lorenz, C.; Oei, P.Y. European electricity sector decarbonization under different levels of foresight. *Renew. Energy* **2019**. [CrossRef]
52. Jacobson, M.Z.; Delucchi, M.A.; Bazouin, G.; Bauer, Z.A.F.; Heavey, C.C.; Fisher, E.; Morris, S.B.; Piekutowski, D.J.Y.; Vencill, T.A.; Yeskoo, T.W. 100% clean and renewable wind, water, and sunlight (WWS) all-sector energy roadmaps for the 50 United States. *Energy Environ. Sci.* **2015**, *8*, 2093–2117. [CrossRef]
53. Bogdanov, D.; Farfan, J.; Sadovskaia, K.; Aghahosseini, A.; Child, M.; Gulagi, A.; Oyewo, A.S.; de Souza Noel Simas Barbosa, L.; Breyer, C. Radical transformation pathway towards sustainable electricity via evolutionary steps. *Nat. Commun.* **2019**, *10*, 1077. [CrossRef]
54. He, G.; Avrin, A.P.; Nelson, J.H.; Johnston, J.; Mileva, A.; Tian, J.; Kammen, D.M. SWITCH-China: A systems approach to decarbonizing China's power system. *Environ. Sci. Technol.* **2016**, *50*, 5467–5473. [CrossRef]

55. Gulagi, A.; Choudhary, P.; Bogdanov, D.; Breyer, C. Electricity system based on 100% renewable energy for India and SAARC. *PLoS ONE* **2017**, *12*, e0180611. [CrossRef]
56. Welsch, M.; Howells, M.; Bazilian, M.; DeCarolis, J.F.; Hermann, S.; Rogner, H.H. Modelling elements of smart grids—Enhancing the OSeMOSYS (open source energy modelling system) code. *Energy* **2012**, *46*, 337–350. [CrossRef]
57. Mirakyan, A.; De Guio, R. Integrated energy planning in cities and territories: A review of methods and tools. *Renew. Sustain. Energy Rev.* **2013**, *22*, 289–297. [CrossRef]
58. Pohekar, S.; Ramachandran, M. Application of multi-criteria decision making to sustainable energy planning—A review. *Renew. Sustain. Energy Rev.* **2004**, *8*, 365–381. [CrossRef]
59. Carli, R.; Dotoli, M.; Pellegrino, R. A hierarchical decision-making strategy for the energy management of smart cities. *IEEE Trans. Autom. Sci. Eng.* **2017**, *14*, 505–523. [CrossRef]
60. Matthey, A.; Bünger, B. *Methodological Convention 3.0 for the Assessment of Enviromental Costs—Cost Rates, Version 02/2019*; Technical Report; Umweltbundesamt: Dessau-Roßlau, Germany, 2019.
61. Boden, T.; Andres, R.; Marland, G. *Global, Regional, and National Fossil-Fuel CO_2 Emissions (1751–2014) (V. 2017)*; Carbon Dioxide Information Analysis Center, Oak Ridge National labouratory: Oak Ridge, TN, USA, 2017.
62. UNFCCC. *National Inventory Submissions 2018*; Technical Report; United Nations Framework Convention on Climate Change: Bonn, Germany, 2018.
63. BP. *BP Statistical Review of World Energy—June 2018*; Technical Report 67th Edition; BP: London, UK, 2018.
64. International Energy Agency. *Electricity Information 2018*; International Energy Agency: Paris, France, 2018.
65. International Energy Agency. *World Energy Balances 2018*; International Energy Agency: Paris, France, 2018.

© 2019 by the authors. Licensee MDPI, Basel, Switzerland. This article is an open access article distributed under the terms and conditions of the Creative Commons Attribution (CC BY) license (http://creativecommons.org/licenses/by/4.0/).

Article

Effects of a Delayed Expansion of Interconnector Capacities in a High RES-E European Electricity System

David Ritter [1,*], Roland Meyer [2], Matthias Koch [1], Markus Haller [1], Dierk Bauknecht [1] and Christoph Heinemann [1]

1. Öko-Institut e.V., Merzhauser Straße 173, 79100 Freiburg, Germany
2. Bremen Energy Research, Jacobs University Bremen, Campus Ring 1, 28759 Bremen, Germany
* Correspondence: d.ritter@oeko.de

Received: 28 June 2019; Accepted: 7 August 2019; Published: 12 August 2019

Abstract: In order to achieve a high renewable share in the electricity system, a significant expansion of cross-border exchange capacities is planned. Historically, the actual expansion of interconnector capacities has significantly lagged behind the planned expansion. This study examines the impact that such continued delays would have when compared to a strong interconnector expansion in an ambitious energy transition scenario. For this purpose, scenarios for the years 2030, 2040, and 2050 are examined using the electricity market model PowerFlex EU. The analysis reveals that both CO_2 emissions and variable costs of electricity generation increase if interconnector expansion is delayed. This effect is most significant in the scenario year 2050, where lower connectivity leads roughly to a doubling of both CO_2 emissions and variable costs of electricity generation. This increase results from a lower level of European electricity trading, a curtailment of electricity from a renewable energy source (RES-E), and a corresponding higher level of conventional electricity generation. Most notably, in Southern and Central Europe, less interconnection leads to higher use of natural gas power plants since less renewable electricity from Northern Europe can be integrated into the European grid.

Keywords: European electricity system; interconnector capacities; delayed grid expansion; electricity market modeling; decarbonization; renewable integration

---

1. Introduction

With the signing of the United Nations Paris Agreement on 12 December 2015, 195 states or associations of states [1] committed themselves to limiting global warming to well below 2° C when compared to the pre-industrial level [2]. To implement this goal, the European Commission (EC) presented its 2050 long-term strategy on 28 November 2018 [3]. In this document, the goal of a climate-neutral European economy for the year 2050 is outlined. In order to achieve this goal, a significant expansion of renewable energies especially in the electricity sector must be achieved [4]. For the electricity sector, most scenarios assume that a focus will be on the expansion of technologies providing electricity from renewable energy sources (RES-E) such as solar and wind [5–7]. Several studies have shown that an improved spatial distribution of RES-E capacities within Europe is helpful to balance the fluctuations of wind flow and solar radiation [8–10].

In 2017, the European Commission agreed to implement the European Energy Union [11]. This strategy consists of five dimensions: energy security, a fully-integrated internal energy market, energy efficiency, decarbonization, and research. An important component for achieving the Energy Union is the expansion of European electricity transmission capacities [12]. In Reference [13], the European Commission already reported in detail on the state of the internal energy market and pointed out that sufficient cross-border transmission capacities are a necessary requirement for achieving the energy policy goals. The advantages resulting from the expansion of the European transmission grid are also described in a large number of studies. Expansion of the transmission grid is being described as a "no regret" strategy [14], an efficient flexibility option [15], a requirement for a cost-efficient RES-E extension and integration [16,17], and as "needed to achieve the European targets cost-efficiently" [18].

However, the EU Commission has also pointed out the stalling of the expansion of interconnector capacities. This hampers the continued development of the internal energy market. On behalf of the EU Commission, Roland Berger Strategy Consultants [19] identified the regulatory framework as a major obstacle to the expansion of cross-border transmission capacity. In addition to regulatory issues, Battaglini et al. [20] also indicate a lack of public acceptance as a cause for the delay in grid expansion. In 2014, the EU Commission launched a package of measures called "Connecting Europe Facility" to improve investment conditions. These measures notably aim at improving and harmonizing approval procedures and adapting regulatory regimes with particular emphasis on dealing with risks in network expansion. The Agency for the Cooperation of Energy Regulators (ACER) has identified significant delays in the projects of common interest (PCI). ACER [21] has shown that 75% of PCIs in the phase of "permitting" are delayed or have been rescheduled.

Many studies compare different levels of grid expansion while maintaining CO_2 reduction [8,14] or RES-E targets [17,22,23], to determine the cost-optimal mix through a variation in the expansion of RES-E technologies, back-up capacities, or storage units. As part of the Ten-Year Network Development Plan (TYNDP) 2018, a "no grid" scenario was conducted for the year 2040, in which no further grid expansion is assumed after 2020. All other input data, such as power plant fleet or electricity demand, were kept corresponding to the reference scenario. The authors conclude that "No Grid is incompatible with the achievements of European emission targets" [24]. An additional 156 TWh of RES-E is curtailed per year on average across the scenarios considered and "the grid built between 2020 and 2040 allows a further 10% decrease in power sector CO_2 emissions as compared to the 1990 levels" [24].

The present paper focuses on the delay of interconnector expansion and analyzes what impact a persistence of current delays in the expansion of interconnector capacities would have in a high RES-E scenario. The focus is on quantifying the effects of delay of interconnector expansion on the indicators' CO_2 emissions, generation mix, electricity exchange, and variable costs of electricity generation. Scenario years 2030, 2040, and 2050 are being considered with RES-E shares in electricity demand of 62% to 99%. Results show that both CO_2 emissions and variable costs of electricity generation increase in case of delayed interconnector expansion. This effect is most significant in scenario year 2050, where lower connectivity roughly leads to a doubling of both CO_2 emissions and variable costs of electricity generation. Those effects arise from lower levels of European electricity trading, higher RES curtailment, and corresponding higher conventional electricity generation. With regard to the latter, the analysis indicates a more extensive use of natural gas power plants, especially in Southern and Central Europe, since less renewable electricity from Northern Europe can be integrated.

Section 2 describes methodology and data, including the electricity market model PowerFlex EU, which was used for this analysis. This also includes a review of existing scenarios regarding electricity demand, generation capacities, and net transfer capacities (NTC). The section also explains how the delays in NTC expansion have been derived. The modeling results can be found in Section 3. In Section 4, the results are being discussed and compared with other studies. Lastly, Section 5 concludes.

2. Methodology and Data

This paper examines in a what-if analysis what impact the persistence of current delays in the expansion of interconnector capacities would have in a high RES-E scenario. Electricity market scenarios from various literature sources were evaluated to determine future generation capacities and electricity demand. An ambitious energy transition scenario was derived from these data (cf. Section 2.2). To determine the effects of delayed interconnector expansion, the electricity market scenario was modelled with two different interconnector capacity expansion levels. The high connectivity (HiCon) scenario, with strong interconnector expansion, is based on literature values. The lower connectivity (LowCon) scenario was derived by extrapolating the current interconnector expansion delay (cf. Section 2.3).

For this study, scenario years 2030, 2040, and 2050 were considered. The data described was used as input for the electricity market model PowerFlex EU (see Section 2.1). The effect of a delayed expansion was determined with a delta analysis in which the scenarios high connectivity and lower connectivity were compared.

The following indicators were analyzed:

- CO_2 emissions.
- Electricity generation mix.
- Import, export, and transit flows.
- Variable costs of electricity generation.

2.1. General Model Description-PowerFlex EU

PowerFlex EU is a bottom-up partial model of the European power sector that has been applied in a range of consultancy and research projects on a German and European level, such as analysis on flexibility options [25,26] or scenario development [27,28]. It calculates the dispatch of thermal power plants, feed-in from renewable energy sources, and utilization of flexibility and storage options at minimal costs to meet electricity demand and reserve capacity requirements.

The model covers all ENTSO-E member states except Iceland and Cyprus. A transport model approach is used to represent electricity exchange between countries. For each individual country, a homogeneous market area without grid constraints is assumed. Exchange between countries is limited by net transfer capacities (see Section 2.3).

For Germany, thermal power plants with capacities exceeding 100 MW are represented as individual units. For other countries, the thermal power plant fleet is represented as aggregated vintage classes concerning age, fuel type, and technology of the individual plants.

The available electricity produced from run-of-river, offshore wind, onshore wind, and photovoltaic systems is represented by generic feed-in patterns in hourly resolution. The actual quantity of feed-in is determined endogenously, with the result that the available yield of fluctuating electricity can also be curtailed (e.g., in the case of negative residual load and insufficient storage capacity).

The model considers reservoir hydro plants, pumped hydro storage, battery storage, and power-to-gas (PtG) as flexibility options. The flexibility of reservoir hydro plants is modeled with an inflow profile of hydro in hourly resolution, a storage capacity of the reservoir, a given level of the reservoir for the first and the last time step, and an electrical capacity of the turbine. All other flexibility options mentioned are modeled with the following parameter's set: pumping or charging capacity, storage capacity, electrical capacity of the turbine or discharging, and the overall efficiency rate. Power–to-gas is modeled as an electricity to electricity storage option to keep the system boundary closed to the electricity system.

The available battery capacities scale with the installed photovoltaic (PV) capacities, and the available capacities of the electrolysers for Power-to-Gas (PtG) generation scale with variable RES-E capacities installed (for details, see Appendix B).

Heat sector coupling is modelled as a further flexibility option only for Germany and not for other ENTSO-E countries. It is represented by combined heat and power plants (CHP) that can shift their power-to-heat ratio within certain technological limitations. Additional generation and flexibility options in the heat sector include heat storage, electrical heating rods, and gas fired boilers.

Electricity demand is assumed to be inelastic. To derive demand profiles in hourly resolution, a standardized demand profile of the base year 2016 is scaled up using scenario-specific annual demand data (see Section 2.2.1). It is assumed that the load profile shape does not change over time (e.g., by increasing demand of new consumers and sector coupling).

Generation, transmission, and storage capacities are determined exogenously, i.e., the model does not endogenously calculate cost efficient investment or divestment pathways. The model assumes perfect foresight and calculates the cost-minimizing dispatch of given capacities in hourly resolution across a single year (8760 hours). In technical terms, it is formulated as a linear optimization problem, implemented in GAMS, and solved using the CPLEX solver.

2.2. Electricity Market Scenarios

In the following sections, the data used is described. All data used has been published (cf. Appendix A). The input data for Germany is based on the scenario Klimaschutzszenario 95 (KS 95) from Reference [28] and is described in Section 2.2.2. To derive the European input data, a scenario analysis based on a literature review was carried out (cf. Section 2.2.1). In Appendix D, the generation capacities per country, used as model input for the year 2050 are given.

2.2.1. European Scenario

The European scenario was determined by means of a scenario analysis of literature data, including TYNDP 2018 [5], the study eHighway 2050 [29], EU Vision Scenario 2017 [30], and EU Reference Scenario 2016 [31]. In the project Model-Based Scenario Analysis of Developments in the German Electricity System, which takes into account the European context up to 2050 in which this study was carried out. Two European electricity market scenarios were derived: an ambitious scenario in which a strong expansion of RES and a significant decline in conventional power plants are assumed, and an unambitious scenario with much slower progress in European energy transition. The unambitious scenario is based on the EU Reference Scenario 2016 [31]. Non EU28 countries are not covered in the scenario and were taken from TYNDP 2018 scenario Sustainable Transition [5].

The years 2040 and 2050 of the ambitious scenario are based on eHighway 2050 scenario 100% RES [29]. Hydro power and biomass generation capacities increase very strongly in the scenario, which does not seem comprehensible from the perspective of natural restrictions, respectively, and competing land use. Therefore, values of the eHighway 2050 Big & Market scenario [29] were used for these technologies. For hydro power generation capacities, it was further assumed that the installed capacities per country will not fall below the current level. In order to ensure that sufficient secure services are available, the size of natural gas capacities, which decrease significantly in the 100% RES scenario, was also taken from eHighway 2050 scenario Big & Market. The data for the scenario year 2030 was generated on the basis of an interpolation between TYNDP 2018 scenario Best Estimate 2020 [5] and the values of the ambitious scenario for the year 2040. In the following, the ambitious and the unambitious scenario are compared with the spread of the considered scenarios. In Appendix C, the scenarios considered are presented in more detail.

Since the European grid expansion will play an important role especially for a high RES-E scenario with large shares of wind and solar, this paper focuses on the ambitious scenario. Further results from this project, such as the effects obtained in the variation of European scenarios while maintaining the German scenario, will be published as a working paper on www.oeko.de by the end of 2019.

The following scenario presentation focuses on EU28 countries, since some of the scenarios only cover these countries. All ENTSO-E member states, except Iceland and Cyprus, were taken into account in the modeling work.

Electricity Demand

Figure 1 shows the development of electricity demand in the unambitious and the ambitious scenario when compared to the scenario spread that results from the scenarios TYNDP 2018 [5], the study eHighway 2050 [29], EU Vision Scenario 2017 [30], and the EU Reference Scenario 2016 [31]. During the period up to 2050, most of the scenarios show a significant increase in demand, which can be attributed to an overcompensation of efficiency measures by an increase of new electricity consumers, such as electric mobility or heat pumps. The unambitious and ambitious scenarios show a relatively similar trend for electricity demand and are in the midfield of the scenarios considered.

Compared to 2016, the electricity demand increases by 28% in the unambitious scenario and by 31% in the ambitious one.

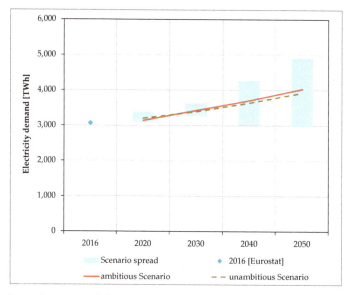

Figure 1. Comparison of annual electricity demand in EU 28 countries based on References [5,29–32].

Renewable Generation Capacities

Figure 2 shows the development of generation capacities for wind, solar, biomass, and hydro power in the unambitious and the ambitious scenario compared to the scenario spread that results from the scenarios TYNDP 2018 [5], the study eHighway 2050 [29], EU Vision Scenario 2017 [30], and EU Reference Scenario 2016 [31].

Wind and solar capacities increase significantly in all scenarios. The ambitious scenario is located at the top and the unambitious scenario is located at the bottom of the scenario funnel. In the ambitious scenario, wind capacities are more than five times higher than in 2016, and solar capacities are more than six times higher. In the unambitious scenario, wind capacities more than double compared to 2016 and solar capacities almost triple compared to 2016. In the unambitious and the ambitious scenario, both biomass capacities roughly double when compared to 2016. Compared to the scenario spread, this is a moderate increase. Hydro power capacities increase compared to 2016 by approximately 50% in the ambitious scenario and by approximately 10% in the unambitious scenario.

Conventional Generation Capacities

Figure 3 shows the development of the conventional generation technologies natural gas, coal, and nuclear power in the unambitious and the ambitious scenario when compared to the scenario spread that results from the scenarios TYNDP 2018 [5], the study eHighway 2050 [29], EU Vision Scenario 2017 [30], and the EU Reference Scenario 2016 [31]. In most scenarios, natural gas capacities show a slight decline over the next few years, which is followed by an increase until 2050 to provide for sufficient secured capacity. In the ambitious scenario, natural gas capacities in 2050 are approximately 15% above today's level. In the unambitious scenario, natural gas capacities increase by approximately 25% compared to today's level.

In all scenarios, coal capacities decline significantly from the current level, even though levels reached in the scenario year 2050 differ significantly. While the ambitious scenario assumes a European-wide phase-out of coal by 2050, the unambitious scenario assumes that coal capacities will decline to approximately 35% by 2040 compared to 2016 and to approximately 33% by 2050.

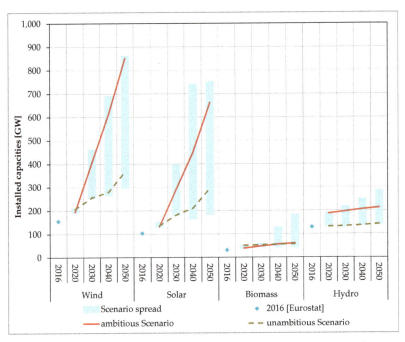

Figure 2. Comparison of RES-E capacities installed in EU28 countries based on References [5,29–31,33].

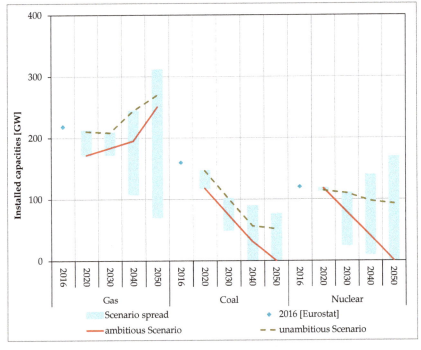

Figure 3. Comparison of conventional generation capacities installed in EU 28 countries based on References [5,29–31].

The scenarios differ even more in the assumptions on nuclear power development. While some scenarios assume an increase in nuclear power, most scenarios assume at least a slight decline. In the unambitious scenario, nuclear power capacities decline to approximately 77% for today's level. In the ambitious scenario, a European-wide nuclear phase-out is assumed.

2.2.2. German Scenario

The assumptions on the development of the German electricity market are based on scenario Klimaschutzszenario 95 (KS 95) from Reference [28]. Figure 4 shows the development of installed capacities and electricity demand for Germany. In order to end up with a more ambitious scenario in our analysis, we decided to further reduce the coal capacity for 2050 from 2.7 GW to 0 GW compared to the original scenario values. The nuclear phase-out [34] will be completed before 2030. By the year 2050, the installed wind capacity is expected to increase by a factor of 4 compared to the 2016 level and the solar capacity is expected to triple during this period. While biomass in the electricity sector will be of less importance, it is assumed that the installed capacities of hydro power (run-of-river and pumped storage) will double by 2050. Efficiency measures will dominate the development of electricity demand until 2030. After that, the demand for electricity will rise again due to new consumers such as heat consumers and electric mobility and will be about a quarter above the current level in 2050.

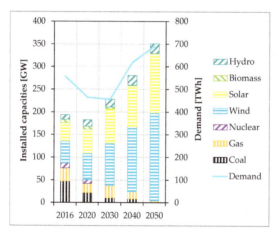

Figure 4. Electricity demand and installed capacities in Germany. Source: References [28,35].

2.3. Interconnector Scenarios

The integration of the European electricity system strongly depends on whether interconnector capacities develop, according to investment plans or whether investment hurdles slow down the process. Forecasts of net transfer capacities (NTCs) usually assume idealized developments of interconnection based on economic or technical needs, and do not explicitly take practical investment hurdles into account.

The Agency for the Cooperation of Energy Regulators (ACER) has identified significant delays for the projects of common interest (PCI). ACER [21] has shown that 75% of PCIs in the phase of "permitting" are delayed or rescheduled. Bureaucracy and a lack of social acceptance seem to be the main reasons for delays. Given high investment risks for large-scale cross-border projects, Roland Berger [19,36] has further argued that regulatory flaws and uncertainty about cost approval may present investment hurdles. A counter effect may result from economies of scale, especially learning curve effects both for investors and administration.

All these determinants of the net transfer capacities (NTC) development are more or less strongly related to the political ambitions of promoting a continued integration of the European electricity system. Accordingly, we distinguish between two integration scenarios. The high connectivity scenario reflects an ideal development of NTCs and draws on the original forecast data of eHighway 2050 scenario 100% RES [6]. Hence, in this scenario, we implicitly assume that potential investment barriers can be overcome. The lower connectivity scenario may be interpreted as a "business-as-usual" case, where issues of investment delays are not resolved. For this scenario, the original forecasts are adjusted downward to reflect slower NTC development (the methodology of how these adjustments are derived are given in Appendix B) Our adjustments lead to a regressive increase of the investment spread between the high and lower connectivity scenario (denoted ΔInv), which results in the downward-sloping curve for ΔInv, as shown in Figure 5.

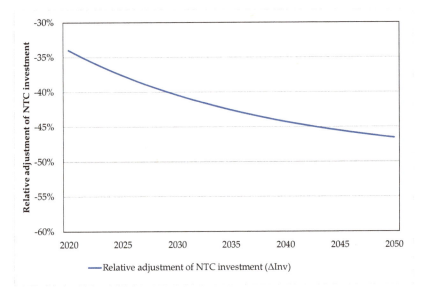

Figure 5. Development of relative NTC investment adjustment (own calculations and assumptions based on References [5,37]).

Figure 6 shows cumulated NTCs for the ENTSO-E area assumed in TYNDP 2018 [5] and eHighway 2050 [29]. In the period up to 2050, a significant increase in NTCs of up to six times of their current value is assumed. In addition to the expansion of cross-border lines, this also takes into account a higher availability of transmission lines for transnational electricity trading. According to Reference [38], the average NTC to thermal grid capacity ratio was 31% in 2016. This means that, on average, only 31% of physical cross-border transmission capacity was made available for transnational electricity trading. According to the EC's Communication on strengthening Europe's energy networks [39], at least 70% of thermal capacity must be made available to the cross-border market by 2025. If this adjustment was applied to the 2016 NTCs, the exchange capacities could be increased from approximately 57 GW to approximately 128 GW (see Figure 6).

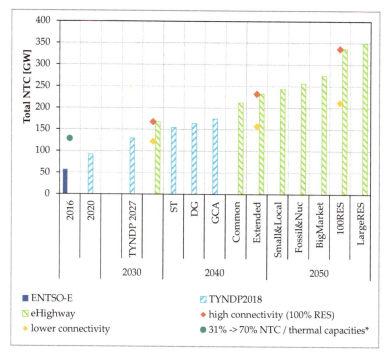

Figure 6. Development of total NTC in the ENTSO-E area [5,29]. *Increase of the NTCs due to a higher NTC to thermal grid capacity ratio: 2016: Ø 31% [38], 2025: min. 70% [39].

The high connectivity scenario is based on the values of eHighway 2050. For the scenario year 2030, there is no differentiation of NTC assumptions in this source. The extended scenario in eHighway 2050 and, thus, the scenario with the stronger NTC expansion is used for the year 2040. In the scenario year 2050, there is a clear spread between the eHighway scenarios. In this case, according to the electricity market scenario, the values of the 100% RES scenario were used. For the lower connectivity scenario, as described above, delays in the expansion of coupling capacities were transferred in accordance with the changes from TYNDP 2018 to TYNDP 2016 for the year 2020. Comparing these values with the data of TYNDP 2018, it can be seen that, in the high connectivity scenario, significantly higher values are applied, while, in the lower connectivity scenario, values are approximately at the level of TYNDP.

Figure 7 shows NTCs between the countries considered and their sum of export capacities in the high connectivity scenario for the year 2050. The cumulative increase in coupling capacities shown in Figure 3 is illustrated at country level. Germany, France, and the United Kingdom, in particular, have very strong networks with their neighboring countries, with cumulative export capacities of between approximately 70 and 120 GW.

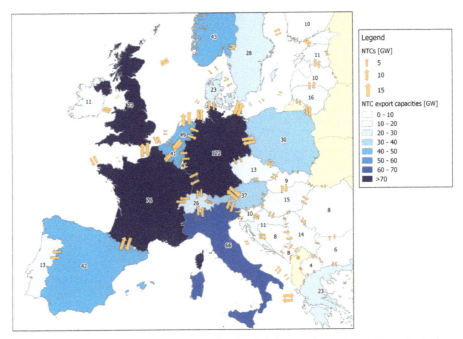

Figure 7. NTCs between the countries considered and their sum of export capacities in the high connectivity scenario for the year 2050. Source: Reference [29].

3. Results

This section presents the results of the examination of a delayed expansion of interconnector capacities. In this analysis, a strong interconnector expansion (high connectivity scenario) was compared with a delayed expansion (lower connectivity scenario), while generation capacities and electricity demand remain constant.

3.1. Import, Export, and Transit Flows

Figure 8 shows the development of electricity exchange between the modeled ENTSO-E countries and the transit flows for the lower connectivity and the high connectivity scenarios. As an indicator for electricity exchange, the sum of export flows between countries in the ENTSO-E area that was used. In line with the significant increase in NTCs, electricity flows between countries grow significantly in the scenario years. In the high connectivity scenario, the values increase to 12 times of the 2016 level by 2050. In the scenario year 2030, the reduced interconnection causes a 13% reduction in the European electricity exchange. In 2040, the reduced interconnection leads to a 25% reduction, and, in 2050, it brings a 31% reduction.

In order to determine the amounts of electricity, which are not consumed in the importing countries but are transmitted to third countries, the hours with simultaneous imports and exports per country were examined (The derivation logic is described in Appendix B). Figure 8 shows the sum of country-specific transit flows across all ENTSO-E countries considered. Transit flows through several countries, such as, for example, from Norway to Italy, are considered for each transit country. This value thus indicates the quantity of electricity that is routed through the individual countries. Transit flows in the ENTSO-E area increase significantly over the scenario years. In the high connectivity scenario, the values increase to 8.9 times the 2016 level by 2050. This increase is even more significant than the increase in the total exchange of electricity. This means that the expansion of interconnector capacities stimulates more electricity flows through transit countries. In the scenario year 2030, the reduced interconnection causes an 18% reduction of European transit flows. In 2040, it leads to a 30% reduction, and, in 2050, it brings a 36% reduction.

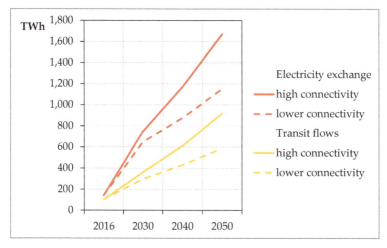

Figure 8. Electricity exchange and transit flows.

Figure 9 shows the development of electricity exchange and transit flows in relative terms to electricity demand. With this consideration, the development can be adjusted by the increase in electricity demand that is assumed in the scenarios. In the high connectivity scenario in 2050, on a country average, approximately 35% of electricity demand is traded between countries and, thus, produced abroad. The lower connectivity reduces this value by approximately 10 percentage points. A look at transit flows shows that, in 2050, in the high connectivity scenario, 20% of European electricity demand is routed through countries as transit flows, while this value amounts to only 13% with lower connectivity.

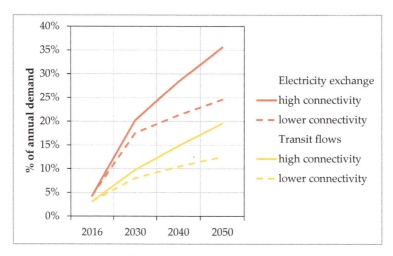

Figure 9. Electricity exchange and transit flows in relation to electricity demand.

3.2. Electricity Generation Mix

Figure 10 shows electricity generation with statistical data for 2016 and model results for the scenario years 2030, 2040, and 2050 (see Appendix D for the generation mix per country for the year 2050). By 2050, electricity generation from renewable energy technologies increases by approximately a factor of four compared to 2016. From the conventional technologies, only natural gas is used in the year 2050. Electricity generation from natural gas power plants declines in the high connectivity scenario by approximately 94% compared to 2016.

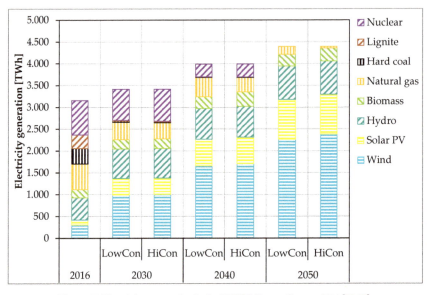

Figure 10. Electricity generation in the ENTSO-E area. Source: 2016 [32,35].

Lower connectivity leads to a reduced use of low-cost technologies such as nuclear power plants and RES technologies. In 2030, the shifts between fuels are still very small. In 2040, the missing electricity amounts are almost exclusively generated by natural gas power plants (approximately +110 TWh) and, in small quantities, by coal-fired power plants. In 2050, the delayed expansion of interconnectors leads to an increased curtailment of fluctuating RES technologies (cf. Table 1) and reduced generation of electricity from biomass. The reduced electricity production in 2050 can only be compensated by natural gas power plants (+142 TWh, cf. Figure 10).

Table 1. RES-E share and curtailment in the ENTSO-E area.

	2030		2040		2050	
	LowCon	HiCon	LowCon	HiCon	LowCon	HiCon
RES-E share of demand (%)	62%	63%	81%	84%	96%	99%
RES-E curtailment (TWh)	13	2	58	11	238	121

Figure 11 shows the change in electricity generation that results from the lower connectivity for the year 2050 on country levels. As already described in Section 3.1, the reduction in electricity exchange leads to an increased utilization of domestic electricity sources. It can be seen that the lower level of interconnectivity restricts trans-European exchange so that, in Northern Europe and Germany, renewables have to be curtailed and biomass capacities are used less, while, in Southern and Central Europe, natural gas power plants (and, in very small amounts, also biomass capacities) have to generate more electricity. Norway shows the largest decrease in RES-E integration. This can be attributed, in particular, to a significant reduction in electricity exports to Germany and the Netherlands (approximately 30%). Spain has the largest increase in electricity generation from natural gas-fired power plants. This can be attributed, in particular, to a reduction of approximately 70% of electricity imports from France.

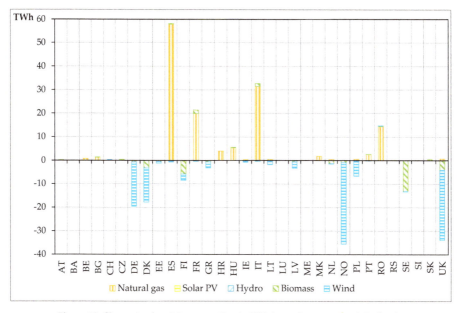

Figure 11. Change in electricity generation in 2050 due to lower connectivity levels.

3.3. CO_2 Emissions

Figure 12 shows CO_2 emissions of the electricity sector in the ENTSO-E area for 2016 and the scenario years 2030, 2040, and 2050.

By 2030, emissions in the high connectivity scenario will already have fallen by approximately 71% when compared to 2016. This significant reduction in CO_2 emissions results, in particular, from the sharp decline in coal-fired electricity generation. This decline is mainly due to the strong expansion of RES-E capacities. (A comparison with the TYNDP 2018 Sustainable Transition Scenario shows that emissions and coal electricity generation are much lower at similar coal capacities in 2030. The CO_2 prices in this study and in the Sustainable Transition scenario are at similar levels (87 € and 84 €) and cannot cause the difference. However, our study assumes a significantly faster expansion of RES-E capacities, which leads to a 10-percentage point higher RES-E share in electricity demand.) The lower connectivity leads to approximately 18.5 Mt (6%) higher CO_2 emissions, which results from a greater use of coal and natural gas power plants. This becomes necessary as more renewables are being curtailed and biomass and nuclear power plants can be used less (cf. Figure 10).

In the scenario year 2040, CO_2 emissions decrease by approximately 86% compared to 2016 (cf. Table 2). The effect of lower connectivity on CO_2 emissions, at approximately 37 Mt, is about twice as high as in 2030. In relative terms, emissions will increase by around 26% due to the lower connectivity. The reduction in the use of nuclear power plants (approximately 10 TWh) plays only a minor role compared to the decline in renewable generation (approximately 110 TWh). A similar change can be observed in fossil technologies. The decline in CO_2 neutral electricity generation is almost completely balanced out by natural gas power plants (approximately 110 TWh) and only to a marginal extent by coal-fired power plants (approximately 2 TWh) (cf. Figure 10).

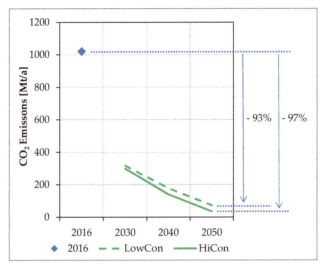

Figure 12. Development of CO_2 emissions in the ENTSO-E area. Source: 2016 [40,41].

Table 2. CO_2 emissions in the ENTSO-E area in 2016 and in the scenario years (absolute (Mt/a), effect of lower connectivity (Mt/a), and reduction compared to 2016 (%)). Source: 2016 [40,41].

	2016	2030	2040	2050
2016	1020			
LowCon (Mt/a)		317	177	72
HiCon (Mt/a)		299	140	35
LowCon-HiCon (Mt/a)		18.5	36.9	37.4
LowCon vs. 2016 (%)		69%	83%	93%
HiCon vs. 2016 (%)		71%	86%	97%

By 2050, a CO_2 reduction of approximately 97% when compared to 2016 is achieved. The effect of lower connectivity is, with approximately 37 Mt, roughly at the same level as in 2040. However, from a relative point of view, the reduced connectivity leads to more than a doubling of CO_2 emissions. This increase in emissions is caused by a shift from renewable to natural gas production of about 142 TWh.

3.4. Variable Costs of Electricity Generation

In order to evaluate the monetary impact of a delayed expansion of interconnector capacities, the variable costs of electricity generation were considered. This value is determined by the amount of electricity generated coupled with fuel and CO_2 prices. Investment costs and fixed costs are not considered in this analysis. Since no changes in the power plant fleet between the connectivity scenarios are assumed, the investment costs and the fixed costs for electricity generation also remain constant between these scenarios and can be neglected in the delta analysis.

Two opposing effects influence the development of variable costs of electricity generation over time. On the one hand, fuel and CO_2 prices rise significantly by 2050 (cf. Appendix B). On the other hand, the increasing share of renewable energies in electricity generation reduces costs. Table 3 shows the variable costs of electricity generation for the ENTSO-E area in billion €/a. Costs decline significantly over the years. Variable costs of electricity generation in the lower connectivity case are 45% lower in 2050 than in 2030, and, in the high connectivity case, the electricity generation's variable costs are 70% lower. The impact of lower interconnectivity increases from 5% higher costs in 2030 to 20% higher costs in 2040, to almost doubling the costs in 2050, caused by the less efficient use of the European power plant fleet resulting from the lower exchange of electricity described in Section 3.1. The increased use of natural gas power plants instead of renewable technologies described in Section 3.2 leads to the increase in variable costs of electricity generation, which can be seen in Table 3.

Table 3. Variable costs of electricity generation in the ENTSO-E area.

(bn €/a)	2030	2040	2050
LowCon	77.4	71.8	42.6
HiCon	73.9	59.7	22.2
LowCon-HiCon	3.5	12.1	20.5

Alternatively, the variable costs of electricity generation can also be stated per MWh of electricity generated (see Table 4). Due to the rising demand for electricity, this perspective leads to an even stronger reduction in costs over the years. In the lower connectivity scenario, costs fall by 57% between 2030 and 2050, and, in the high connectivity scenario, costs decline by 76%. The lower interconnectivity leads to an increase of variable costs of electricity generation of approximately 1 €/MWh in 2030, approximately 3 €/MWh in 2040, and approximately 4.4 €/MWh in 2050.

Table 4. Variable costs of electricity generation per MWh electricity produced in the ENTSO-E area.

(€/MWh)	2030	2040	2050
LowCon	20.9	17.4	9.1
HiCon	20.0	14.5	4.7
LowCon-HiCon	0.9	3.0	4.4

4. Discussion

This paper examines the effects of a delayed expansion of interconnector capacities between European countries. In the framework of this analysis, other input parameters, such as generation capacities and electricity demand, are not varied. In the following, approaches to compensate for a delayed grid expansion are discussed. This is followed by a detailed comparison of the results with the TYNDP 2018 "no grid" scenario.

Other studies discuss mainly two approaches as alternatives to grid expansion. More flexibility can be added to the system, or the geographical deployment of RES-E capacities can be oriented toward the distribution of electricity demand. Therefore, the question arises whether our results are due to a lack of these alternatives in our assumptions. If there is insufficient flexibility and RES-E is concentrated in specific areas, then the value of the grid expansion that we have shown could be largely driven by the assumptions.

First, with regard to the flexibility approach, METIS Study S1: Optimal flexibility portfolios for a high-RES 2050 scenario [42] provides a good benchmark. This study examined the need for flexibility in Europe with 80% RES share. Comparing the results of this study with our flexibility assumptions for the year 2040, in which an RES share of approximately 80% is achieved, it can be seen that the expansion of interconnectors is assumed to be roughly the same as in our lower connectivity scenario and that the pumped storage capacities are on a similar level. In order to avoid any restrictions resulting from a lack of flexibility, our assumptions regarding the electrolyser and battery capacities are significantly higher. In Reference [42], the demand response was considered another flexibility option, which is more than compensated for by our higher assumptions for battery capacities. The comparison of the considered flexibility options with the METIS Study indicates that flexibility options that compete with the flexibility of the grid have sufficiently been taken into account in our scenario analysis and that the effects of a lower grid expansion are not a result of a lack of such flexibility. Rather, the observed effects of a delayed expansion of interconnectors would increase further if fewer alternative flexibility options were considered. Second, a demand-driven distribution of RES-E can, to some extent, reduce the expansion needs of the European transmission grid (cf. [16]). If RES-E technologies are not distributed to the most favorable sites, this increases their levelized cost of electricity. According to Fuersch et al. [18], the higher costs for RES-E generation are not compensated for by the savings made in grid expansion, while DNV GL [16] argues that, with "decreasing costs of renewable electricity, the cost of grid expansion increasingly becomes a relevant factor, which may offset higher generation costs of RES-E that are deployed at less optimal geographical locations" (cf. [16] page 4). In the eHighway 100% RES scenario, renewables were distributed in Europe using distribution keys, which reflects both capacity factors and demand (cf. [6]). Thus, renewables were not distributed exclusively according to their generation costs, and our analysis already includes the mitigating effect on grid expansion, to a certain extent.

Our results can best be compared with the "no grid" scenario of TYNDP 2018 [24]. In this approach, for the scenario year 2040, no further grid expansion is assumed from 2020 onwards, while all other input data, such as power plant fleet or electricity demand, is correspond to the reference scenarios. Table 5 shows a comparison of the RES-E share in electricity demand and the NTC reduction between TYNDP 2018 and this study. It can be seen that, in this study, the RES-E share is comparatively high, while the relative NTC reduction is lower than in the TYNDP analysis. As has been shown in Figure 6, the planned expansion of interconnector capacity for 2040 in TYNDP 2018 is roughly at the level of the lower connectivity scenario. Therefore, in the high connectivity scenario, a significantly stronger expansion of interconnector capacities is assumed.

Table 5. Comparison of RES-E share in electricity demand and assumptions for NTC reduction in the TYNDP 2018 and this study. Source: Reference [24] and own calculation.

	Year	RES-E Share	NTC Reduction in the "No Grid" and Lower Connectivity Scenarios, Respectively
TYNDP 2018	2040	64%–80%	40%–47%
This study	2030	63%	27%
	2040	84%	32%
	2050	99%	37%

In the following, we compare our results for electricity exchange, electricity generation mix, CO_2 emissions, and variable costs of electricity generation with the TYNDP 2018 "no grid" scenario.

Our analysis shows that a reduced expansion of interconnector capacities limits European electricity trading. It reduces electricity exchange between 13% in 2030 and 31% in 2050. In the TYNDP 2018 "no grid" scenario, this analysis is given as net annual balance per region and can, therefore, not be directly compared. However, the "no grid" view also comes to the conclusion that "the enhanced grid leads to a much greater level of power transfer between countries" (cf. [24] page 19).

The electricity generation mix shifts toward technologies with higher generation costs due to the lower level of grid expansion. In our analysis, this effect is still relatively small in 2030, but increases by 2050, which is in line with the increasing RES-E expansion. This leads to an additional 47 TWh of RES-E curtailment in 2040 and 117 TWh in 2050. Gas-fired power plants compensate for the curtailed RES-E generation within Europe. In the TYNDP 2018 "no grid" analysis, the reduced grid expansion leads to approximately 156 TWh RES-E curtailment (cf. [24] page 22 f.). This stronger effect can be explained by the significantly stronger NTC reduction in the "no grid" scenario (cf. Table 5).

The changes in electricity generation lead to an increase in CO_2 emissions. Due to the small changes in the generation mix in 2030, the effect on emissions is still relatively small in this year. In our analysis, in both 2040 and 2050, the additional emissions caused by the delayed expansion of the grid amount to approximately 37 million tons. For the year 2050, this would mean a doubling of CO_2 emissions in the electricity sector. The stronger expansion of the grid can, thus, make a significant contribution toward reducing CO_2 emissions. As a result of the greater grid reduction, the TYNDP 2018 "no grid" analysis also shows a stronger increase in CO_2 emissions (+100 Mt) (cf. [24] page 23).

Due to the less efficient use of the European power plant fleet, the variable costs of electricity generation increase in the lower connectivity scenario. In our analysis, this increase amounts to 5% higher costs in 2030, 20% higher costs in 2040, and almost a doubling of costs in 2050. In addition to the overall stronger change in the electricity generation mix, this increase can be explained by two further elements. First, fuel and CO_2 prices rise over the years, so that the additional use of natural gas power plants has a greater impact on electricity generation costs. Second, the higher share of renewable energy reduces generation costs, so that the relative changes in costs are more pronounced.

If there is no grid expansion, there would be higher electricity generation costs, but, at the same time, there would also be cost savings due to lower grid expansion costs. These grid-related cost savings were not taken into account in this analysis since our focus was on the effects of grid expansion in high RES-E scenarios. It was also assumed that there would be a delay in the expansion and that the grid would, therefore, be expanded at a later date. In the TYNDP 2018 "no grid" analysis, the reduced expansion of the grid resulted in electricity prices that would lead to consumer costs about three times the cost for the additional expansion of the grid, as calculated in the baseline scenario (cf. [24] page 17).

5. Conclusions

This paper concludes that the expansion of interconnector capacities can not only ensure a more efficient use of the European power plant fleet in the European internal market and associated cost savings but can also make an important contribution toward greenhouse neutrality. These effects increase over the years. On the one hand, this is due to the assumption that the absolute capacities of delayed projects will increase over the years with increasing grid expansion, which leads, over time, to a growing difference between the high connectivity and lower connectivity scenarios. On the other hand, due to the expansion of renewables, the spatial balance made possible by the European electricity grid becomes increasingly important. This observation is also shown in the TYNDP 2018 "no grid" analysis where the strongest effects are determined for the scenario with the highest RES-E share (cf. [24] page 17). This means that grid expansions that are planned today and that may be motivated to a large extent by cost savings achievable in the internal European market, are still relevant in a future high RES-E world with ambitious CO_2 targets.

The identified effects of the delayed grid expansion can be interpreted as a conservative estimation. They would increase further with a lower level of alternative flexibilities such as batteries or power-to-gas. Compared to the assumptions in TYNDP 2018, a very strong expansion of interconnector capacities was assumed in the high connectivity scenario. As a result, the values of the lower connectivity scenario for 2030 and 2040 are approximately at the level of the TYNDP 2018 values. It can be assumed that, if the planned expansion of the grid was less pronounced, the restrictions on electricity exchange would become even more severe, and stronger effects would already become visible in the scenario year 2030.

Since both this paper as well as the TYNDP 2018 "no grid" analysis have shown the negative effects of a delayed expansion of interconnector capacities, the barriers for this expansion should be addressed. As described in Reference [20], the main obstacles are regulatory issues and acceptance problems. This is why a "simplified and standardized regulation" as well as a "strong and transparent consultation process in all stages" are proposed [20]. Bovet [43] additionally elaborates that the enforcement power of the two European legal instruments Projects of Common Interest and Ten-Year Network Development Plan should be strengthened, so that delays in the expansion of the European transmission grid can be addressed more effectively. In Reference [44], ENTSO-E and the Renewables Grid Initiative (RGI) describe how a lack of acceptance can be counteracted by "better projects." These "better projects" are characterized by "locally tailored, transparent, and participatory planning processes" [44].

Author Contributions: All authors contributed to the conceptualization of the research. D.R. took the lead in data curation, the analysis of the results, and in writing this paper. M.H. run the model software and wrote the model description in Section 2.1. R.M. developed the methodology to calculate the delay in NTC expansion and wrote the main part of Section 2.3. All authors have performed the validation of the results and have critically reviewed and edited the paper.

Funding: The German Federal Ministry for Economic Affairs and Energy, grant number 03ET4031A, funded this research.

Conflicts of Interest: The authors declare no conflict of interest. The funders had no role in the design of the study, in the collection, analyses, or interpretation of data, in the writing of the manuscript, or in the decision to publish the results.

Abbreviations

The following abbreviations are used in this paper.

a	annum (per year)
ACER	Agency for the Cooperation of Energy Regulators
bn	billion
CHP	combined heat and power plants
CO_2	carbon dioxide
EC	European Commission
ENTSO-E	European Network of Transmission System Operators for Electricity
EU	European Union
GAMS	General Algebraic Modeling System
GW	gigawatt
h	hour
HiCon	scenario high connectivity
KS 95	Klimaschutzszenario 95
LowCon	scenario lower connectivity
Mt	megaton (1 million tons)
MW	megawatt
MWh	megawatt hour
NTCs	net transfer capacities
PCI	Projects of Common Interest
PV	photovoltaic
PtG	Power-to-Gas
RES	renewable energy source
RES-E	electricity from a renewable energy source
RGI	Renewables Grid Initiative
t	ton
TWh	terawatt hour
TYNDP	Ten-Year Network Development Plan

Appendix A

Data Availability

The data sets as described in Table A1 are available in a country-specific resolution under the following link: https://zenodo.org/record/3257495.

Table A1. Fuel price (€/MWh$_{th}$) and CO$_2$ price (€/t CO$_2$) scenario.

Data	Data Type	Unit	Input/Output
Demand	Hourly profiles	MWh	Input
Variable RES-E	Hourly profiles	MWh	Input
Power plant fleet	Capacities	MW	Input
NTCs	Capacities	MW	Input
CO$_2$ emissions	Annual data	Mt	Output
Variable costs of electricity generation	Annual data	M€	Output
Variable costs of electricity generation per generation unit	Annual data	€/MWh	Output
Electricity generation	Annual data	TWh	Output
Electricity export	Annual data	TWh	Output
Electricity import	Annual data	TWh	Output
Transit flows	Annual data	TWh	Output

Appendix B

Fuel and CO$_2$ Prices

Table A2 shows the fuel and CO$_2$ prices that were used for modeling. This data is based on Klimaschutzszenario 2050 [28].

Table A2. Fuel price (€/MWh$_{th}$) and CO$_2$ price (€/t CO$_2$) scenario. Source: Reference [28].

	2030	2040	2050
Oil (€/MWh$_{th}$)	59	74	90
Gas (€/MWh$_{th}$)	34	41	50
Coal (€/MWh$_{th}$)	12	14	16
CO$_2$ Prices (€/t CO$_2$)	87	143	200

Dimensioning of Batteries and Power-to-Gas Facilities

Batteries and PtG facilities are dimensioned per country and implemented as one large plant per country, since the national grid is not considered. Table A3 shows the main characteristics of storage technologies. The assumed parameters of the batteries concerning charge, discharge, and storage capacity as well as the ratio of battery capacity to installed PV capacity are based on the scenario framework from the German Network Development Plan 2030 (2019) [45]. Deriving the electrolyser capacity of power-to-gas, a ratio of 10% concerning the generation capacity of PV and wind is assumed. No restrictions are considered either for the re-conversion into electricity as well as for the storage capacity for synthetic gas. At country level, 100% of peak load is available for re-generation and 100% of the annual demand is available as storage capacity. Total efficiency of the batteries for the coupling of charging and discharging is 95% in all scenarios. For PtG flexibility, total efficiency increases over the scenario years from 34% to 38% (calculation based on Reference [46]).

Table A3. Characteristics of storage technologies. Source: References [45,46] and own assumptions.

Technologies	Charge and Discharge Capacity	Storage Capacity	Total Efficiency
Battery	10% of installed PV capacity	10% of installed PV capacity × 1 h	95%
Power-to-Gas (PtG)	Electrolyser capacity: 10% of PV and wind generation capacity Reconversion into electricity: 100% of peak load	100% of total annual load	2030: 34% 2040: 36% 2050: 38%

Derivation of Transit Flows

As described in the following equation, the annual transit flows per country ($Trans_c$) are the sum of the hourly transit flows ($Trans_t$). Therefore, the amount of imports and exports must be distinguished on an hourly basis. If, in the respective country, more imports (Imp_t) than exports (Exp_t) are made, the export quantities can be interpreted as transit flows. If the inverse case is given, import quantities must be used.

$$Trans_t = \begin{cases} Exp_t & \text{if } Imp_t > Exp_t \\ Imp_t & \text{if } Imp_t < Exp_t \end{cases} \quad (A1)$$

$$Trans_c = \sum_{t=1}^{8760} Trans_t \quad (A2)$$

Derivation of the Lower Connectivity Scenario

To derive our lower connectivity scenario, we adjusted the original NTC forecasts–serving as the idealized high connectivity scenario–for practical investment hurdles that may slow down the actual development of interconnection capacities. Below, we describe the underlying methodology of these adjustments.

Unfortunately, existing data even for the recent past is limited, and data bases do not allow for a quantification of how overall political ambitions for system integration or specific barriers may affect future NTC delays for each of the interconnectors. Instead, we focused on data about currently known investment delays and derive future numbers based on plausible assumptions.

A comparison of NTC forecasts from TYNDPs 2016 [37] and 2018 [5] reveals that expected NTC investments have undergone a significant downward adjustment. Figure A1 shows the interpolated forecasts of the accumulated NTC investments after 2015, according to TYNDP 2016 (Inv_2016) and TYNDP 2018 (Inv_2018) for the whole ENTSO-E area until 2030.

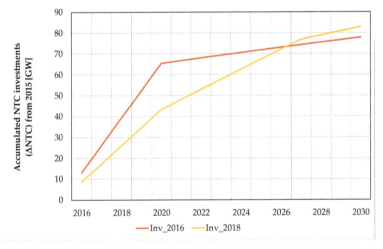

Figure A1. Accumulated NTC investments in the ENTSO-E area [5,37].

For the year 2020, the figure shows a relative reduction of accumulated investment numbers by 34%. In other words, between the two reported periods, total investment forecasts were corrected downward by one third of the original plans. Written formally, the relative adjustment of investments until 2020 (ΔInv^{2020}) is given by the equation below.

$$\Delta Inv^{2020} = \frac{Inv\_2018 - Inv\_2016}{Inv\_2016} \approx -34\% \quad (A3)$$

As the graphs show, investment forecasts in TYNDP 2018 catch up with the 2016 plans by 2026. We assume, however, that the main reason for this catch-up is that ENTSO-E calculations do not explicitly make assumptions about future investment delays. Instead of directly applying the specific numbers from the reports per year, we, therefore, decided to derive our own assumptions based on that we carry forward the relative adjustment for 2020 (ΔInv^{2020}) to later years. There are two main reasons for picking the 2020 value as a starting point. First, 2020 is the only year for which both reports provide forecasts. Hence, using 2020 avoids the uncertainty of data interpolation. Second, given that 2020 is relatively close to the TYNDP 2018 reporting period, we expect that most of the investment delays were already known when the forecasts were made and are, therefore, implicitly represented in the data.

Regarding the future development of investment delays, however, we have to rely on plausible assumptions. Drawing on the findings of ACER [21] and Roland Berger [19,36], we expect that permitting and regulatory issues are going to remain the dominant factor of investment delays and hurdles. Given that the lower connectivity scenario does not imply a strong political will to overcome administrative investment hurdles, the ambitious NTC investment plans will most likely be subject to additional delays. Hence, we assume that the spread between forecasted and actual investments will increase over time. We assume a regressive increase of the investment spread, which result in the downward-sloping curve for ΔInv shown in Figure 5 in Section 2.3.

Appendix C

For a better overview, the scenario presentations in Section 2.2.1 have been simplified. The detailed figures and data derivations are presented below.

Scenario Comparison-Electricity Demand

Figure A2 shows the development of electricity demand for selected scenarios. During the period up to 2050, most of the scenarios show a significant increase in demand, which can be attributed to an overcompensation of efficiency measures by an increase of new electricity consumers, such as electric mobility or heat pumps.

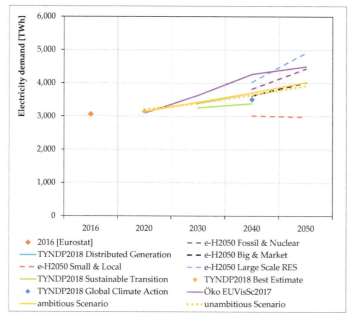

Figure A2. Annual electricity demand in EU28 countries. Sources: References [5,29–32].

Scenario Comparison-Renewable Generation Capacities

As shown in Figure A3, wind and solar capacities increase significantly in all scenarios. The ambitious scenario is located at the top and the unambitious scenario is located at the bottom of the scenario funnel. In the ambitious scenario, wind capacities are more than five times higher than in 2016, and solar capacities are more than six times higher. In the unambitious scenario, wind capacities more than double compared to 2016 and solar capacities almost triple compared to 2016.

While biomass capacities in most of the scenarios considered, double at most compared to the current level, in the scenario, 100% RES of the capacities undergo a six-fold increase. As described in Section 2.2.1, for the ambitious scenario, the values of the Big & Market scenario are used, as the increase of biomass capacities in the 100% RES scenario appears to be too strong, considering the competitive demand for land.

In most of the scenarios considered, hydro power capacities remain at about the current level or increase by half. In the 100% RES scenario, capacities more than double. In order not to overestimate the potential of hydro power, the values of the Big & Market scenario were also used here, since these are in the range of other scenarios. In addition, the assumed capacities were compared with the current level, and, for values that were lower, the current values were used. In the unambitious scenario, European hydro power generation capacities increase by approximately 10%.

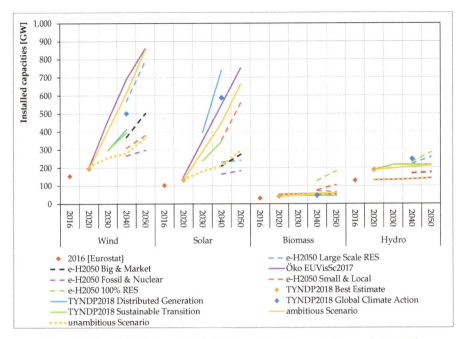

Figure A3. Installed RES-E capacities in EU 28 countries. Sources: References [5,29–31,33].

Scenario Comparison-Conventional Generation Capacities

Figure A4 shows that, in most scenarios, natural gas capacities show a slight decline over the next few years, which is followed by an increase until 2050 to provide for sufficient secured capacity. As described in Section 2.2.1, natural gas capacities in e-Highway 2050 scenario 100% RES decline significantly by 2050. Since lower biomass and hydro power generation capacities were assumed (taken from the Big & Market scenario) for the ambitious scenario as compared with the 100% RES scenario, significantly higher values—from the Big & Market scenario—were used for natural gas capacities. Thus, in the ambitious scenario, natural gas capacities in 2050 are approximately 15% above today's level. In the unambitious scenario, natural gas capacities increase by approximately 25% compared to today's level.

In all scenarios, coal capacities decline significantly from the current level, even though levels reached in the scenario year 2050 differ significantly. While the ambitious scenario assumes a European-wide phase-out of coal by 2050, the unambitious scenario assumes that coal capacities will decline to approximately 35% by 2040 compared to 2016 and to approximately 33% by 2050.

The scenarios differ even more in the assumptions on nuclear power development. While some scenarios assume an increase in nuclear power, most scenarios assume at least a slight decline. In the unambitious scenario, nuclear power capacities decline to approximately 77% of today's level. In the ambitious scenario, a European-wide nuclear phase-out is assumed.

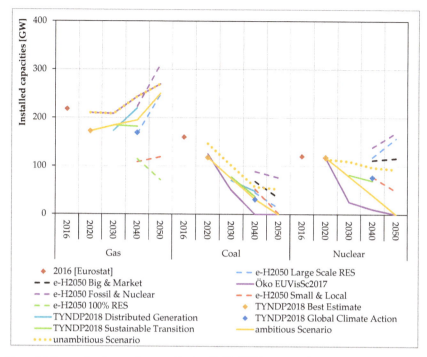

Figure A4. Conventional generation capacities installed in EU 28 countries. Sources: References [5,29–31].

Appendix D

Installed Capacities and Generation Mix 2050 per Country

In this appendix, the installed capacities (cf. Table A4) and the generation mix (cf. Tables A5 and A6) per country are presented for the scenario year 2050. As described in Section 2.2, the values for Germany are taken from Klimaschutzszenario 95 from Reference [28]. The capacities for the other countries are mainly based on scenario 100% RES from eHighway 2050 [29] (cf. Section 2.2 and Appendix C). Hydro power and biomass generation capacities increase very strongly in scenario 100% RES, which does not seem comprehensible from the perspective of natural restrictions respectively competing land use. Therefore, values of the eHighway 2050 Big & Market scenario [29] were used for these technologies. For hydro power generation capacities, it was further assumed that the installed capacities per country will not fall below the current level. In order to ensure that sufficient secure services are available, the size of natural gas capacities, which decrease significantly in the 100% RES scenario, was also taken from the eHighway 2050 scenario Big & Market. The derivation for power-to-gas and battery capacities is described in Appendix B.

Table A4. Installed capacities in GW, scenario year 2050. Source: References [28,29] and own assumptions.

	Natural Gas	Wind-On	Wind-Off	PV Solar	Bio-Mass	Hydro-Run	Hydro-Turbine	Pumped Storage	Power-to-Gas	Batteries
AT	3.5	6.9	0.0	12.1	1.3	10.1	5.4	3.4	15.0	1.3
BA	0.0	2.6	0.0	1.3	0.0	1.3	1.8	0.0	2.2	0.2
BE	21.3	10.9	3.0	24.1	2.5	0.1	1.2	1.3	21.8	2.5
BG	2.3	4.4	0.0	5.4	0.8	0.7	2.8	1.4	6.6	0.6
CH	5.3	1.4	0.0	15.0	1.5	4.1	13.6	4.2	14.0	1.7
CZ	0.5	10.2	0.0	13.0	1.0	0.6	1.1	1.2	12.6	1.3
DE	3.9	98.3	27.2	98.6	0.4	4.3	6.3	15.7	79.1	12.3
DK	0.5	18.7	25.6	2.0	3.0	0.0	0.0	0.0	7.6	0.2
EE	0.5	8.1	0.0	0.8	0.3	0.0	0.0	0.5	2.3	0.1
ES	29.3	69.4	0.0	102.5	5.0	3.6	19.1	6.0	84.2	18.6
FI	5.8	29.5	0.0	5.8	3.0	4.1	1.7	0.0	14.9	0.6
FR	16.3	124.2	0.0	106.9	7.8	13.6	11.5	8.5	130.5	14.0
GR	3.0	25.9	0.0	15.1	1.0	0.4	3.3	1.6	12.4	2.7
HR	1.8	6.3	0.0	3.8	0.0	0.5	2.5	0.3	4.6	0.4
HU	4.0	4.9	0.0	14.0	1.3	0.3	0.3	0.0	10.2	1.6
IE	1.8	13.6	0.0	3.8	0.3	0.4	0.5	0.5	7.9	0.3
IT	46.8	41.3	0.0	101.0	8.0	11.4	8.5	7.7	70.8	15.8
LT	3.3	15.2	0.0	1.3	0.5	0.3	1.1	1.1	4.8	0.1
LU	0.0	0.7	0.0	1.0	0.0	0.2	1.3	1.1	1.3	0.1
LV	1.8	13.8	0.0	1.1	0.5	1.6	0.0	0.0	3.8	0.1
ME	0.0	0.5	0.0	0.5	0.0	0.0	1.4	0.0	0.6	0.1
MK	1.0	0.4	0.0	1.4	0.0	0.6	0.7	0.0	1.7	0.2
NL	26.8	15.0	15.9	22.2	2.8	0.0	0.0	0.0	26.7	2.1
NO	0.0	0.0	3.0	5.4	0.8	4.2	48.2	0.0	18.0	0.5
PL	3.8	81.9	0.0	24.2	2.8	1.0	0.4	2.5	30.7	2.4
PT	6.0	11.9	0.0	13.8	1.0	5.1	2.8	2.0	13.4	2.5

Table A4. Cont.

	Natural Gas	Wind-On	Wind-Off	PV Solar	Bio-Mass	Hydro-Run	Hydro-Turbine	Pumped Storage	Power-to-Gas	Batteries
RO	5.8	4.8	0.0	11.0	1.5	3.8	4.0	0.0	12.9	1.2
RS	1.5	1.4	0.0	5.0	0.3	3.0	0.4	0.6	5.9	0.6
SE	0.0	24.2	3.0	8.9	2.8	0.0	18.5	0.0	23.8	0.9
SI	0.5	0.5	0.0	2.3	0.3	1.2	0.2	0.2	2.6	0.3
SK	1.8	5.2	0.0	6.9	0.5	1.8	0.4	1.3	4.4	0.7
UK	13.3	93.1	37.2	59.9	4.3	7.4	0.0	0.0	79.9	5.3
Sum	**211.4**	**757.4**	**114.9**	**690.3**	**54.6**	**85.7**	**159.0**	**60.9**	**727.2**	**91.5**

Table A5. Electricity generation in TWh, scenario year 2050 in the High Connectivity scenario. Source: own calculations.

	Natural gas	Wind-Onshore	Wind-Offshore	PV Solar	Bio-Mass	Hydro-run	Hydro-Turbine	Pumped Storage	Power-to-Gas	Batteries
AT	0.0	13.6	0.0	13.4	7.5	40.1	6.6	3.6	1.1	0.4
BA	0.0	3.4	0.0	1.6	0.0	3.6	2.1	0.0	0.3	0.1
BE	1.1	24.2	10.7	24.8	14.5	0.3	1.2	1.7	3.0	0.8
BG	0.1	7.5	0.0	6.4	4.9	5.4	5.0	2.4	0.7	0.2
CH	0.0	0.9	0.0	17.5	9.6	26.3	24.4	6.9	1.8	0.6
CZ	0.1	20.4	0.0	13.3	6.0	1.0	1.3	1.3	1.5	0.4
DE	10.6	386.9	163.7	123.4	1.6	24.7	0.0	13.6	43.9	3.2
DK	0.0	53.2	55.2	2.1	3.4	0.0	0.0	0.0	9.1	0.0
EE	0.0	15.6	0.0	0.9	0.9	0.0	0.0	0.5	0.9	0.0
ES	16.2	145.0	0.0	186.1	32.4	13.5	24.5	10.0	15.8	5.4
FI	0.0	63.5	1.1	6.0	8.6	19.4	7.7	0.0	3.5	0.2
FR	1.8	272.7	3.6	140.1	48.6	43.6	17.1	13.9	25.3	4.6
GR	0.3	63.1	0.0	26.7	6.3	3.0	5.4	3.2	4.1	0.9
HR	0.3	8.5	0.0	4.3	0.0	4.1	3.6	0.5	0.8	0.1
HU	0.7	10.9	0.0	16.2	8.2	1.0	0.9	0.0	1.3	0.5
IE	0.1	40.8	0.0	3.3	1.4	1.0	0.9	0.8	2.3	0.1
IT	3.2	72.8	0.1	158.0	51.5	42.8	15.8	14.5	11.9	5.2
LT	0.0	31.8	0.0	1.3	2.4	0.9	2.1	1.2	1.9	0.0
LU	0.0	1.3	0.0	1.0	0.0	0.8	2.4	1.0	0.1	0.0
LV	0.1	25.0	0.0	1.2	1.8	4.3	0.0	0.0	1.4	0.0
ME	0.0	0.7	0.0	0.6	0.0	0.2	1.6	0.0	0.1	0.0
MK	0.2	0.4	0.0	1.7	0.0	1.8	2.9	0.0	0.1	0.1
NL	0.0	47.8	59.7	20.6	15.5	0.1	0.0	0.0	6.3	0.6
NO	0.0	48.6	12.8	5.3	1.0	18.7	214.6	0.0	0.6	0.1

Table A5. Cont.

	Natural gas	Wind-Onshore	Wind-Offshore	PV Solar	Bio-Mass	Hydro-run	Hydro-Turbine	Pumped Storage	Power-to-Gas	Batteries
PL	0.2	128.9	0.0	23.6	14.5	4.8	0.7	2.7	9.7	0.7
PT	1.0	31.6	0.1	25.4	6.4	13.6	3.5	3.4	2.4	0.8
RO	0.8	7.5	0.0	12.4	9.8	14.6	6.0	0.0	1.1	0.4
RS	0.0	1.7	0.0	5.7	1.7	8.9	1.9	1.1	0.4	0.2
SE	0.0	49.6	12.5	8.8	14.0	0.0	76.3	0.0	1.5	0.2
SI	0.0	0.6	0.0	2.7	1.6	4.4	0.3	0.3	0.3	0.1
SK	0.2	7.0	0.0	7.4	3.3	5.4	0.8	2.3	1.1	0.3
UK	0.0	333.1	143.7	52.8	21.5	22.3	0.0	0.0	27.4	1.9
Sum	36.9	1918.4	463.1	914.4	298.5	330.7	429.6	84.9	181.5	28.1

Table A6. Electricity generation in TWh, scenario year 2050 in the Lower Connectivity scenario. Source: own calculations.

	Natural Gas	Wind-Onshore	Wind-Offshore	PV Solar	Bio-Mass	Hydro-Run	Hydro-Turbine	Pumped Storage	Power-to-Gas	Batteries
AT	0.0	13.6	0.0	13.4	7.6	40.1	6.6	4.0	1.4	0.4
BA	0.0	3.4	0.0	1.6	0.0	3.6	2.1	0.0	0.2	0.0
BE	1.9	24.2	10.7	24.8	14.4	0.3	1.2	1.9	4.0	0.8
BG	1.5	7.5	0.0	6.4	5.1	5.4	5.0	1.9	0.4	0.2
CH	0.0	0.9	0.0	17.5	9.9	26.3	24.4	5.9	1.0	0.5
CZ	0.1	20.4	0.0	13.3	6.3	1.0	1.3	1.4	1.9	0.4
DE	10.0	380.2	151.5	123.4	1.6	24.7	0.0	14.4	57.0	3.2
DK	0.0	51.6	42.4	2.1	0.1	0.0	0.0	0.0	8.9	0.0
EE	0.0	14.9	0.0	0.9	0.3	0.0	0.0	0.5	1.1	0.0
ES	74.0	144.3	0.0	186.1	32.7	13.5	24.5	8.7	9.0	5.0
FI	0.0	61.1	0.9	6.0	2.7	19.4	7.7	0.0	4.1	0.2
FR	21.7	272.3	3.5	140.1	50.0	43.6	17.1	12.1	17.4	4.0
GR	0.3	60.5	0.0	26.7	5.7	3.0	5.4	3.0	4.4	0.9
HR	4.3	8.5	0.0	4.3	0.0	4.1	3.6	0.4	0.5	0.1
HU	6.1	10.9	0.0	16.2	8.4	1.0	0.9	0.0	0.8	0.4
IE	0.6	40.1	0.0	3.3	1.2	1.0	0.9	0.8	2.2	0.1
IT	34.7	72.4	0.1	158.0	52.7	42.8	15.8	12.4	7.9	4.6
LT	0.6	30.3	0.0	1.3	2.0	0.9	2.1	1.4	2.5	0.1
LU	0.0	1.3	0.0	1.0	0.0	0.8	2.4	1.1	0.1	0.0
LV	0.0	22.4	0.0	1.2	1.2	4.3	0.0	0.0	2.0	0.0
ME	0.0	0.7	0.0	0.6	0.0	0.2	1.6	0.0	0.1	0.0
MK	2.0	0.4	0.0	1.7	0.0	1.8	2.9	0.0	0.1	0.1
NL	0.4	47.8	59.6	20.6	14.1	0.1	0.0	0.0	7.4	0.7
NO	0.0	26.9	0.0	5.3	0.0	18.7	214.6	0.0	0.0	0.0

Table A6. Cont.

	Natural Gas	Wind-Onshore	Wind-Offshore	PV Solar	Bio-Mass	Hydro-Run	Hydro-Turbine	Pumped Storage	Power-to-Gas	Batteries
PL	0.8	122.3	0.0	23.6	14.4	4.8	0.7	3.0	12.0	0.7
PT	3.6	31.5	0.1	25.4	6.5	13.6	3.5	3.1	1.7	0.7
RO	15.2	7.5	0.0	12.3	10.1	14.6	6.0	0.0	0.7	0.3
RS	0.0	1.7	0.0	5.7	1.7	8.9	1.9	0.9	0.3	0.2
SE	0.0	49.5	12.4	8.8	0.9	0.0	76.3	0.0	2.0	0.1
SI	0.0	0.6	0.0	2.7	1.7	4.4	0.3	0.3	0.1	0.1
SK	0.6	7.0	0.0	7.4	3.3	5.4	0.8	1.8	0.7	0.2
UK	0.7	329.1	118.0	52.8	17.4	22.3	0.0	0.0	30.9	1.9
Sum	179.0	1865.4	399.1	914.4	272.0	330.7	429.6	78.9	182.5	26.0

References

1. United Nations (UN). Status 7. d Paris Agreement. Available online: https://treaties.un.org/Pages/ViewDetails.aspx?src=TREATY&mtdsg_no=XXVII-7-d&Section=27&clang=_en#EndDec (accessed on 17 May 2019).
2. United Nations Framework Convention on Climate Change (UNFCCC). *Paris Agreement*; UNFCCC: Bonn, Germany, 2015.
3. European Commission (EC). 2050 Long-Term Strategy. 2018. Available online: https://ec.europa.eu/clima/policies/strategies/2050_en (accessed on 17 May 2019).
4. European Commission (EC). In-Depth Analysis in support of the commission communication com (2018) 773. A Clean Planet for All. A European Long-Term Strategic Vision for a Prosperous, Modern, Competitive and Climate Neutral Economy, Brussels. 2018. Available online: https://ec.europa.eu/clima/sites/clima/files/docs/pages/com_2018_733_analysis_in_support_en_0.pdf (accessed on 17 May 2019).
5. ENTSO-E. TYNDP 2018 Scenario Report. Data Set, Brussels. 2018. Available online: https://tyndp.entsoe.eu/maps-data/ (accessed on 8 February 2019).
6. Andersky, T.; Sanchis, G.; Betraoui, B. e-HIGHWAY 2050—Modular Development Plan of the Pan-European Transmission System 2050. Deliverable 2.1. Available online: https://www.dena.de/fileadmin/dena/Dokumente/Pdf/9013_MOB_Brochure_ehighway2050_englisch.pdf (accessed on 3 September 2018).
7. Tafarte, P.; Eichhorn, M.; Thrän, D. Capacity Expansion Pathways for a Wind and Solar Based Power Supply and the Impact of Advanced Technology—A Case Study for Germany. *Energies* **2019**, *12*, 324. [CrossRef]
8. Schlachtberger, D.P.; Brown, T.; Schramm, S.; Greiner, M. The benefits of cooperation in a highly renewable European electricity network. *Energy* **2017**, *134*, 469–481. [CrossRef]
9. Kost, C.; Längle, S. The Spatial Dimension of the Energy Transition: European Renewable Energy Sources. Local Resources and International Exchange; The European Dimension of Germany's Energy Transition. Opportunities and Conflicts. Available online: https://www.springer.com/de/book/9783030033736#otherversion=9783030033743 (accessed on 29 May 2019).
10. Hagspiel, S.; Jägemann, C.; Lindenberger, D.; Brown, T.; Cherevatskiy, S.; Tröster, E. Cost-Optimal Power System Extension under Flow-based Market Coupling; EWI Working Paper No 13/09. 2013. Available online: https://www.ewi.uni-koeln.de/cms/wp-content/uploads/2015/12/EWI_WP_13_09.pdf (accessed on 4 June 2019).
11. European Commission (EC). Energy Union and Climate: Making Energy more Secure, Affordable and Sustainable. Available online: https://ec.europa.eu/commission/priorities/energy-union-and-climate_en (accessed on 3 September 2018).
12. European Commission (EC). EU Budget: Commission Proposes Increased Funding to Invest in Connecting Europeans with High-Performance Infrastructure, Brussels. 2018. Available online: http://europa.eu/rapid/press-release_IP-18-4029_en.htm (accessed on 17 May 2019).
13. European Commission (EC). *Progress Towards Completing the Internal Energy Market*; EC: Brussels, Belgium, 2014.
14. Schmid, E.; Knopf, B. Quantifying the long-term economic benefits of European electricity system integration. *Energy Policy* **2015**, *87*, 260–269. [CrossRef]
15. Bauknecht, D.; Heinemann, C.; Koch, M.; Ritter, D.; Harthan, R.; Sachs, A.; Vogel, M.; Tröster, E.; Langanke, S. Systematischer Vergleich von Flexibilitäts- und Speicheroptionen im deutschen Stromsystem zur Integration von erneuerbaren Energien und Analyse entsprechender Rahmenbedingungen, Freiburg, Darmstadt. 2016. Available online: https://www.oeko.de/fileadmin/oekodoc/Systematischer_Vergleich_Flexibilitaetsoptionen.pdf (accessed on 19 January 2017).
16. DNV GL.; Imperial College London; NERA Economic Consulting. *Integration of Renewable Energy in Europe*; Final Report; EC: Brussels, Belgium, 2014.
17. Child, M.; Kemfert, C.; Bogdanov, D.; Breyer, C. Flexible electricity generation, grid exchange and storage for the transition to a 100% renewable energy system in Europe. *Renew. Energy* **2019**, *139*, 80–101. [CrossRef]
18. Fuersch, M.; Hagspiel, S.; Jägemann, C.; Nagl, S.; Lindenberger, D.; Tröster, E. The role of grid extensions in a cost-efficient transformation of the European electricity system until 2050. *Appl. Energy* **2013**, *104*, 642–652. [CrossRef]

19. Roland Berger. *The Structuring and Financing of Energy Infrastructure Projects, Financing Gaps and Recommendations Regarding the New TEN-E Financial Instrument*; Final Report to the European Commission; EC: Brussels, Belgium, 2011.
20. Battaglini, A.; Komendantova, N.; Brtnik, P.; Patt, A. Perception of barriers for expansion of electricity grids in the European Union. *Energy Policy* **2012**, *47*, 254–259. [CrossRef]
21. Agency for the Cooperation of Energy Regulators (ACER). *Consolidated Report on the Progess of Electricity and Gas Projects of Common Interest for the Year 2015*; ACER: Ljubljana, Slovenia, 2016.
22. Rodríguez, R.A.; Becker, S.; Andresen, G.B.; Heide, D.; Greiner, M. Transmission needs across a fully renewable European power system. *Renew. Energy* **2014**, *63*, 467–476. [CrossRef]
23. Becker, S.; Rodriguez, R.A.; Andresen, G.B.; Schramm, S.; Greiner, M. Transmission grid extensions during the build-up of a fully renewable pan-European electricity supply. *Energy* **2014**, *64*, 404–418. [CrossRef]
24. ENTSO-E. European Power System 2040 Completing the Map. The Ten-Year Network Development Plan (TYNDP) 2018 System Needs Analysis, Brussels. 2018. Available online: https://docstore.entsoe.eu/Documents/TYNDP%20documents/TYNDP2018/european_power_system_2040.pdf (accessed on 24 May 2019).
25. Koch, M.; Bauknecht, D.; Heinemann, C.; Ritter, D.; Vogel, M.; Tröster, E. Modellgestützte Bewertung von Netzausbau im europäischen Netzverbund und Flexibilitätsoptionen im deutschen Stromsystem im Zeitraum 2020–2050. *Zeitschrift für Energiewirtschaft* **2015**, *39*, 1–17. [CrossRef]
26. Koch, M.; Flachsbarth, F.; Bauknecht, D.; Heinemann, C.; Ritter, D.; Winger, C.; Timpe, C.; Gandor, M.; Klingenberg, T.; Tröschel, M. Dispatch of Flexibility Options, Grid Infrastructure and Integration of Renewable Energies Within a Decentralized Electricity System. In *Advances in Energy System Optimization: Proceedings of the first International Symposium on Energy System Optimization*; Bertsch, V., Fichtner, W., Heuveline, V., Leibfried, T., Eds.; Birkhäuser: Cham, Switzerland, 2017; pp. 67–86. ISBN 978-3-319-51794-0.
27. Bundesministerium für Umwelt, Naturschutz und nukleare Sicherheit (BMU). Projektionsbericht 2019 für Deutschland gemäß Verordnung (EU) Nr. 525/2013, 2019. Available online: https://cdr.eionet.europa.eu/de/eu/mmr/art04-13-14_lcds_pams_projections/projections/envxnw7wq/ (accessed on 25 June 2019).
28. Repenning, J.; Hermann, H.; Emele, L.; Jörß, W.; Blanck, R.; Loreck, C.; Böttcher, H.; Ludig, S.; Dehoust, G.; Matthes, F.C.; et al. Klimaschutzszenario 2050. 2. Modellierungsrunde, Berlin. 2015. Available online: https://www.oeko.de/oekodoc/2451/2015-608-de.pdf (accessed on 15 May 2017).
29. Andersky, T.; Sanchis, G.; Betraoui, B. *e-Highway 2050—Database Per Country*; Excel-Sheet; EC: Brussels, Belgium, 2016.
30. Matthes, F.C.; Blanck, R.; Greiner, B.; Zimmer, D.W. *The Vision Scenario for the European Union. 2017 Update for the EU-28*; Greens/EFA Group in the European Parliament: Brussels, Belgium, 2018.
31. European Commission (EC). *EU Reference Scenario 2016. Energy, Transport and GHG Emissions—Trends to 2050*; EC: Brussels, Belgium, 2016.
32. Eurostat. Supply, Transformation and Consumption of Electricity—Annual Data. nrg 105a. Available online: http://appsso.eurostat.ec.europa.eu/nui/show.do?dataset=nrg_105a&lang=en (accessed on 20 May 2019).
33. Eurostat. Infrastructure—Electricity—Annual Data. nrg113a. Available online: http://appsso.eurostat.ec.europa.eu/nui/show.do?dataset=nrg_113a (accessed on 20 May 2019).
34. *Gesetz über die friedliche Verwendung der Kernenergie und den Schutz gegen ihre Gefahren*; Atomgesetz; German Federal Ministry of Justice and for Consumer Protection: Berlin, Germany, 2018.
35. ENTSO-E. Transparency Platform. Available online: https://transparency.entsoe.eu/ (accessed on 29 May 2019).
36. Roland Berger. *Permitting Procedures for Energy Infrastructure Projects in the EU: Evaluation and Legal Recommendations*; Final Report to the European Commission; EC: Brussels, Belgium, 2011.
37. ENTSO-E. TYNDP 2016. Market Modelling Data. 2015. Available online: https://tyndp.entsoe.eu/maps-data/ (accessed on 3 September 2018).
38. Agency for the Cooperation of Energy Regulators (ACER). *Recommendation of the ACER No 02/2016 on the Common Capacity Calculation and Redispatching and Countertrading Cost Sharing Methodologies*; ACER: Ljubljana, Slovenia, 2016.
39. European Commission (EC). *Communication from the Commission to the European Parliament, the Council, the European Economic and Social Committee and the Committee of the Regions: Communication on Strengthening Europe's Energy Networks*; EC: Brussels, Belgium, 2017.

40. Sandbag. EU ETS Dashboard. Available online: http://sandbag-climate.github.io/EU_ETS_Dashboard.html (accessed on 29 May 2019).
41. United Nations Framework Convention on Climate Change (UNFCCC). Member States' CRF Submissions to UNFCCC. 2018. Available online: https://unfccc.int/process/transparency-and-reporting/reporting-and-review-under-the-convention/greenhouse-gas-inventories-annex-i-parties/national-inventory-submissions-2018 (accessed on 29 May 2019).
42. Bossavy, A.; Bossmann, T.; Fournié, L.; Humberset, L.; Khallouf, P. METIS Studies. Study S1: Optimal Flexibility Portfolios for a High-RES 2050 Scenario. 2018. Available online: https://publications.europa.eu/en/publication-detail/-/publication/f26e4340-67fd-11e9-9f05-01aa75ed71a1/language-en/format-PDF/source-96288622 (accessed on 4 June 2019).
43. Bovet, J. The Electricity Transmission Line Planning Process at European Level. Legal Framework and Need for Reforms; The European Dimension of Germany's Energy Transition. Opportunities and Conflicts. Available online: https://www.springer.com/de/book/9783030033736#otherversion=9783030033743 (accessed on 29 May 2019).
44. ENTSO-E.; Renewables Grid Initiative (RGI). Working Paper May 2019: Value of Timely Implementation of "Better Projects". 2019. Available online: https://docstore.entsoe.eu/Documents/Publications/Position%20papers%20and%20reports/20190517_RGI_ENTSOE_working_paper_better_projects.pdf (accessed on 24 May 2019).
45. Bundesnetzagentur (BNetzA). *Genehmigung des Szenariorahmens 2019–2030*; BNetzA: Bonn, Germany, 2018.
46. Agora Verkehrswende; Agora Energiewende. Die zukünftigen Kosten strombasierter synthetischer Brennstoffe, Berlin. 2018. Available online: https://www.agora-energiewende.de/fileadmin2/Projekte/2017/SynKost_2050/Agora_SynCost-Studie_WEB.pdf (accessed on 23 May 2018).

© 2019 by the authors. Licensee MDPI, Basel, Switzerland. This article is an open access article distributed under the terms and conditions of the Creative Commons Attribution (CC BY) license (http://creativecommons.org/licenses/by/4.0/).

Article

Capacity Expansion Pathways for a Wind and Solar Based Power Supply and the Impact of Advanced Technology—A Case Study for Germany

Philip Tafarte [1,*], Marcus Eichhorn [1] and Daniela Thrän [1,2]

[1] Helmholtz Centre for Environmental Research (UFZ), Department Bioenergy, Permoserstraße 15, 04318 Leipzig, Germany; marcus.eichhorn@ufz.de (M.E.); daniela.thraen@dbfz.de (D.T.)
[2] Deutsches Biomasseforschungszentrum gGmbH (DBFZ), Torgauer Straße 113, 04347 Leipzig, Germany
* Correspondence: philip.tafarte@ufz.de; Tel.: +49-341-97-33604

Received: 27 November 2018; Accepted: 7 January 2019; Published: 21 January 2019

Abstract: Wind and solar PV have become the lowest-cost renewable alternatives and are expected to dominate the power supply matrix in many countries worldwide. However, wind and solar are inherently variable renewable energy sources (vRES) and their characteristics pose new challenges for power systems and for the transition to a renewable energy-based power supply. Using new options for the integration of high shares of vRES is therefore crucial. In order to assess these options, we model the expansion pathways of wind power and solar photovoltaics (solar PV) capacities and their impact on the renewable share in a case study for Germany. Therefore, a numerical optimization approach is applied on temporally resolved generation and consumption time series data to identify the most efficient and fastest capacity expansion pathways. In addition to conventional layouts of wind and solar PV, our model includes advanced, system-friendly technology layouts in combination with electric energy storage from existing pumped hydro storage as promising integration options. The results provide policy makers with useful insights for technology-specific capacity expansion as we identified potentials to reduce costs and infrastructural requirements in the form of power grids and electric energy storage, and to accelerate the transition to a fully renewable power sector.

Keywords: variable renewable energy sources; wind power; solar energy; Germany; pumped hydro storage; system-friendly renewables

1. Introduction

The rapid expansion of renewable energies worldwide has resulted in a steep increase in installed capacities in recent years. Wind and solar photovoltaics (solar PV) in particular have seen a significant increase in global installed capacities and have displaced conventional sources in terms of annually added capacities worldwide. Climate protection is one of the key drivers for renewables, and especially wind and solar PV have become cost-competitive in comparison to established non-renewable sources [1].

Despite this dynamic expansion of renewables, there are several challenges ahead, since climate protection aims call for an even faster transition to keep on track with greenhouse gases (GHG) emission reduction [2]. Wind and solar PV are variable renewable energy sources (vRES). These inherently volatile sources pose major challenges for their integration into the power supply system [3–9] and the transition to a fully renewable power supply system [10–13].

Approaches to integrate the growing capacities from vRES are therefore the focus of much research. For the technical integration of vRES, three important elements have been identified: (a) electric energy storage; (b) an optimized capacity mix of different vRES; and (c) the introduction of advanced technologies in wind and solar PV systems, also called system-friendly layouts of vRES.

Electric energy storage is regarded as a key element for the integration of vRES to address the volatility of vRES, to utilize excess energy (EE) and to balance supply and demand to maintain a secure power supply [14–17]. Nevertheless, new storage technologies face either technological or economic constraints and are still not available in the required TWh range. Mature, large-scale electric energy storage solutions such as pumped hydro storage (PHS) face limitations in the physical potential of many countries, as well as restrictions due to nature conservation. In fact, electric energy storage capacities have not kept pace with vRES expansion in recent years [6,11,18–23].

A second important option is the optimization of the capacity mix of wind and solar PV [7,12,24–29]. Optimizing their shares allows exploiting the complementary production patterns of wind and solar PV over various time scales, ranging from the apparent daily patterns of solar PV production to seasonal patterns for both wind and solar PV [25,30]. In contrast, achieving high shares of vRES using either wind or solar PV alone leads to higher variability in power supply and higher EE [29,31–33] for a set renewable share (REN share) target. EE itself is likewise associated with a decline in the marginal utility of additional vRES capacities, as the energy produced in times of EE is not substituting non-renewable energy sources [3,5,10,34]. With many countries pursuing REN strategies with annual capacity targets for specific REN technologies, optimal mixes of vRES can contribute to effectively attaining these targets. Tenders for new renewable generation capacity in many countries could, in principle, allow governing the future capacity mix through the expansion pathways for each REN technology. However, there is to date little knowledge about an effective pathway for wind and solar PV regarding REN shares to achieve future REN share goals.

A third option for the integration of vRES has been identified in technologically advanced wind energy converters (WEC) and solar PV systems. Advanced technologies entail WEC with increased hub heights and low specific power ratings compared to the rotor swept area (W/m^2), as well as solar PV panels facing east or west instead of the traditionally south-facing panels in the northern hemisphere or north-facing panels in the southern hemisphere [35,36]. East-west-facing solar PV offers improved technical system integration compared to standard technology, especially when introduced in power systems with high shares of vRES [34,37,38]. The International Energy Agency (IEA) "Grid Integration of Variable Renewables" research project (GIVAR) published a report in 2014 [39] describing the contribution of advanced technologies in wind and solar PV to addressing the challenges associated with the expansion of significant vRES capacities. These "advanced technologies" [38] or "system-friendly" layouts of wind and solar PV installations [40] are important options for the improved integration of high shares of vRES into power systems [39,41–43].

Existing studies cover only one or two of the three selected options: either optimized generation mixes of vRES [11,28,44,45], the interplay of vRES with electric energy storage [15], or advanced technologies for future vRES-based power systems [38,40,46]. Among these, Killinger et al. [46] introduced advanced technology from solar PV with different azimuth and inclination angles and determined the optimal regional vRES mix regarding economic efficiency, environmental sustainability and the security of supply. This therefore covers a wide range of important options and targets. Nevertheless, the article does not include electric energy storage capacities or the expansion pathways towards the identified optimal mix from vRES. Becker et al. [28] investigated wind and solar PV build-up pathways for different regions in the United States. Their analysis covers pathways for the minimization of back-up energy as well as for economic cost. Central to the approach is the mismatch of vRES power production and power consumption. A variety of cost-minimal pathways were identified for the different regions, underlining that region-specific factors like the spatio-temporal potentials for vRES as well as power demand play an important role, meaning that the analysis has to be performed specifically for each region of interest. Unlike the approach presented in this article, two of the three identified options for the integration of vRES are not covered: storage (option a) and system-friendly technologies (option c). The incremental efficiency of every added capacity of wind and solar PV on the renewable share is likewise not directly addressed, as build-up pathways are calculated in dependence of REN shares, which are not directly linked to capacity expansion as REN shares are negatively affected by EE from vRES.

To overcome the identified limitations in the research for optimized pathways in vRES capacity expansion, the approach presented here examines the effect of all three options on the efficiency of vRES expansion pathways. This will allow identifying the most effective pathways to achieve future REN goals from an overall capacity and REN share point of view and will enable us to assess the performance of alternative configurations of vRES capacities and electric energy storage. Using capacity expansion as the basis and calculating the resulting REN share offers a direct linkage to renewable support schemes, as many countries implement technology-specific tenders that allow directly governing capacity expansion for every vRES technology.

The main objectives of this paper are therefore to (i) provide a broad picture of how wind and solar PV can be combined to achieve efficient pathways in capacity expansion to fulfill future REN targets, (ii) identify the impact of advanced technologies in wind and solar PV against baseline technology, and (iii) to investigate the impact of electric energy storage. Therefore, we developed an algorithm to assess the incremental expansion of wind and solar PV by its impact on renewable shares (REN shares). This is built on the vRES optimization model published in 2014 [38] and is extended to calculate a wide range of capacity combinations, including electric energy storage from PHS as well as the identification of efficient pathways in capacity expansion in wind and solar PV.

For our case study we selected Germany, as it is one of the countries that has already seen a large expansion of vRES since 2000, exceeding 36.2% in REN share in 2017 [47]. Renewables, excluding wind and solar, made up for 11.2% in power consumption in 2017, so that wind and solar PV will have to provide more than 85% for the transition to a 100% renewable power supply at current consumption levels. In combination with the implemented tenders for the expansion of wind and solar PV capacities, Germany is a very suitable case study region.

The paper is structured as follows: in Section 2 we describe the input data, the investigated technologies and the study cases. Section 3 provides details on the methods and modeling. The results of the study are presented in Section 4, followed by a discussion in Section 5 and our conclusions in Section 6.

2. Input Data, Technology and Study Cases

2.1. Input Data

We used hourly electricity feed-in (from onshore wind and solar PV, including capacity factors) and net load data (representing electricity demand) for the years 2012 to 2015 for Germany, provided by the Open Power System Data Platform [48]. Net load data was adjusted on an annual basis to comply with the governmental projections for power consumption of 535.4 TWh/a [49,50]. The normalized feed-in time series for wind and solar PV covers the variability in vRES production over a time period of four years, and are up-scaled in order to model the future expansion of vRES capacities [38].

2.2. Technology Options

In accordance with [38–40,51], advanced technologies or system-friendly layouts include technologically advanced WEC with low specific rated power and solar PV in a mixed setup of south, east and west-oriented systems.

2.2.1. Advanced and Baseline WECs

The technology options considered in this study included onshore WEC with low specific rated power which were developed for application in low wind regimes. In recent years, a decline in specific rated power per rotor swept area from values in the range of 380–520 W/m^2 (baseline technology) to values well below 350 W/m^2 (advanced technology) can be observed for new WEC models [38,40,43,52,53]. Larger rotor diameters and increased hub heights allow increasing the energy output per installed capacity in terms of full load hours (FLH) (this principal relation, called the Capacity Factor (CF), is another performance parameter. CF is defined as the ratio of the energy actually produced by an energy converter to the energy that could have been produced if the converter ran at its rated power over a given time period. For the period of one year, the CF can be converted to FLH by multiplying the dimensionless CF with the 8760 h of one year.). Legacy onshore WEC achieved only 1576 FLH per year on average in the 2012–2015 period according to the feed-in time series data, whereas advanced WEC enable almost double the FLH and accordingly productivity per installed capacity [54,55]. Furthermore, advanced WEC offer significant advantages in the reduction of EE generation and the required overall installed capacity to achieve set REN share goals along with reduced economic costs at high penetration rates [56,57].

Figure 1 provides an impression of the significant differences between baseline and advanced WEC based on a short period of registered wind speed data from a wind farm in Germany (a) and the effects on the annual duration curves (duration curves are created by ordering all hourly feed-in or RL values in a descending order. The highest value is located on the very left of the graph and the lowest value on the right side.) (b). It becomes apparent that although the two different WEC (Enercon E-70 and Nordex N-117) have comparable rated power of 2.3 to 2.4 MW, their temporal production characteristics (Figure 1a) and annual duration curves (Figure 1b) differ significantly, as advanced WEC deliver twice the energy per installed capacity (equivalent to the area under the curve in Figure 2b).

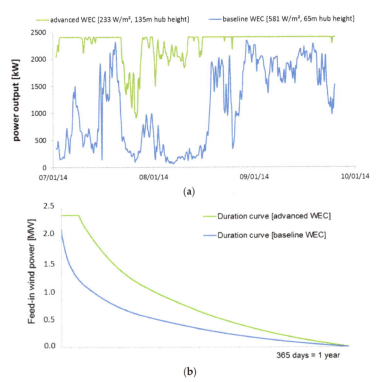

Figure 1. Comparison of the time series for power production based on actual wind and performance data from a wind farm in Germany (**a**) and generalized feed-in duration curves for baseline and advanced wind energy converters (WEC) (**b**).

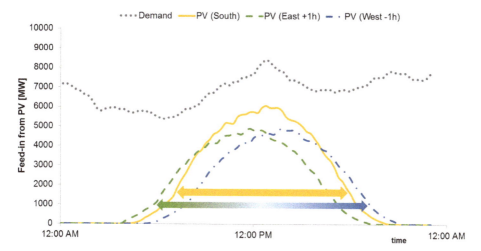

Figure 2. Comparison of normalized baseline feed-in (PV(S)) vs. modified advanced feed-in PV (E) and PV (W) installations over 24 h.

The modeling of the time series data for advanced WEC was performed according to [38] based on the registered time series of WEC feed-in in Germany. A scaling factor was iteratively determined so that the time series reach 3000. The applied modeling has been published and cross-checked [38,40,58] and a similar approach to modify feed-in time series is documented and used in the ENERGY Plan Simulation model [59].

2.2.2. Advanced and Baseline Solar PV

Advanced layouts in solar PV, especially an east or west azimuth angle of solar panels and solar PV systems, have been identified as an option to improve the integration of solar PV into the power system [39,60–63]. Solar PV modules in an east-west orientation show a positive effect on the reduction of EE as they enable a better coverage of temporal demand profiles [64] (Figure 2). With increased capacities of solar PV systems in a south-facing azimuth, instances of EE production rise at mid-day, while residual loads in the morning and evening hours remain unmet. Solar PV systems with fixed azimuth angles facing east (PV(E)) and west (PV(W)) shift the feed-in pattern towards morning PV(E) and evening PV(W) hours and therefore smooth feed-in profiles and reduce EE [65]. As a trade-off, these solar PV setups have slightly reduced FLH in comparison to south-facing setups that maximize energy production [35,36,61,66].

A composition of solar PV systems with an equal distribution of solar PV setups oriented south, east and west were selected for the modeling of advanced solar PV. Solar PV systems facing east PV(E) are modeled with feed-in one hour earlier and solar PV systems facing west PV(W) with feed-in delayed by one hour compared to south-oriented setups. East and west systems also have reduced FLHs of 869 compared to the 1000 FLHs assumed for baseline setups facing south PV(S) (see Figure 3).

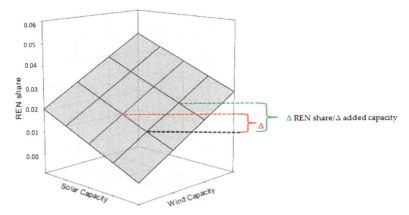

Figure 3. Illustration of the incremental evaluation of additional capacity from either wind or solar PV on the REN share surface plot with higher gradient for wind compared to solar PV (red: REN share delta solar PV, green REN share delta wind).

2.2.3. Electric Energy Storage

To implement the effect of electric energy storage [11,14] into the modeling, we included existing electric energy storage from pumped hydro storage (PHS) currently installed in Germany. For the modeling, we refered to the 9 gigawatt (GW) of PHS with a storage capacity of approximately 66 gigawatt hours (GWh) installed in Germany [14,50].

Other options for the integration of vRES, such as interconnectors for import and export or demand side management (DSM), [67] were not considered.

2.3. Study Cases

This study aims to determine efficient vRES development pathways for both "baseline" and "advanced" technologies and with and without electric energy storage from PHS. Therefore, we established four cases illustrating the respective options (Table 1).

Table 1. Introduction of the four study cases.

Case	Wind Power	Solar PV	Electric Energy Storage
Case (B)—Baseline (non-advanced) technology	380–520 W/m² 1576 FLH	oriented south 100%	no storage
Case (BS)—Baseline (non-advanced) technology + electric energy storage	380–520 W/m² 1576 FLH	oriented south 100%	PHS: 9 GW/66 GWh
Case (A)—Advanced technology	<350 W/m² 3000 FLH	east 33%, west 33%, south 33%	no storage
Case (AS)—Advanced technology + electric energy storage	<350 W/m² 3000 FLH	east 33%, west 33%, south 33%	PHS: 9 GW/66 GWh

For Cases B and BS, we used baseline or non-advanced setups from wind and solar PV, whereas in Cases A and AS we applied advanced setups [38]. Cases BS and AS also included the modeling of storage from PHS, so that EE production from wind and solar PV can be utilized and consequently contribute to achieving higher REN shares (see storage section).

The overall annual net electricity demand for Germany was set constant at the projected level of 535.4 TWh/a [50]. Other important factors for the integration of vRES into power supply systems, especially conventional Must-Run or other renewable energy sources (bioenergy, hydropower, geothermal), can be included but are not presented here [15,39,68–70], primarily because the focus of this study is on the inter-temporal patterns of demand and supply from vRES, and secondarily because the simplicity of the approach should be maintained to provide a better understanding of the basic interplay of vRES in power systems.

3. Methods

This study aims to investigate pathways for the effective capacity expansion of volatile renewable energy sources. As key indicators, we calculated the renewable energy share (REN share) and the cumulated negative RL, or simply EE. By comparing the indicators for different development pathways, we can identify efficient pathways in the sense of maximizing REN share per additionally installed capacity. All calculations were performed using MATLAB and all key components are presented in this section.

3.1. Calculation of Key Indicator Renewable Energy Share

The renewable energy share (REN share) is the amount of wind and solar PV energy generated and directly serving the power demand. EE from vRES does not contribute to the REN share in Cases B and A, whereas in Cases BS and AS we modeled electric energy storage from PHS as an integration infrastructure to make EE available to serve power demand and contribute to REN shares accordingly. The resulting direct REN share over the course of the 4-year time series was calculated for every capacity combination as:

$$REN\ share = 100 - 100 * \left(\frac{\sum RL\ pos_t}{\sum Demand_t} \right)\ [\%], \qquad (1)$$

where $REN\ share$ = renewables share, $Demand_t$ = electricity demand, $RL\ pos_t$ = positive Residual Load (see Equation (3)), t = time step of 1 h in the 2012–2015 time-series data. RL neg or EE from vRES is not accounted for. The Residual Load (RL) is the result of the scaled feed-in time series data for wind and solar PV subtracted from the hourly time series data for demand:

$$RL_t = Demand_t - (S_{wind} * Wind_t + S_{solar\ PV} * Solar\ PV_t), \qquad (2)$$

where $Wind_t$ and $Solar\ PV_t$ are the normalized time series data for wind and solar PV representing the feed-in of 3 GW installed capacity each, and scaling factors S_{wind} and $S_{solar\ PV}$ range stepwise from 1 to 100 in order to reach from 3 to 300 GW in the calculation runs (see Section 2.3 Input Data). We selected a step size of 3 GW, which is roughly equivalent to the annual capacity expansion target for wind and solar PV in Germany.

Positive and negative RL is separately accounted for over the course of the 4-year time series data:

$$\sum RL\ pos_t\ in\ case\ of\ Demand_t > (S_{wind} * Wind_t + S_{solar\ PV} * Solar\ PV_t), \qquad (3)$$

$$\sum RL\ neg_t\ *\ in\ case\ of\ Demand_t < (S_{wind} * Wind_t + S_{solar\ PV} * Solar\ PV_t). \qquad (4)$$

* or simply EE from vRES.

For the cases including electric energy storage (BS and AS), Equations (2)–(4) were extended so that the discharge from the combined electric energy storage is likewise subtracted from the hourly demand data and thus increases the REN share accordingly.

$$RL < 0\ AND\ C_{PHS} < C_{PHS\ max}\ then,$$
$$RL_t = Demand_t - (S_{wind} * Wind_t + S_{solar\ PV} * Solar\ PV_t) + P_{PHS} * \eta, \qquad (5)$$

$$RL > 0 \text{ AND } C_{PHS} > C_{PHS\ min} \text{ then}$$
$$RL_t = Demand_t - (S_{wind} * Wind_t + S_{solar\ PV} * Solar\ PV_t) - P_{PHS} * \eta. \tag{6}$$

The variables used in Equations (5) and (6) are:

C_{PHS} = energy stored in PHS. Further constraints were set for $C_{PHS\ max}$ = maximum storage capacity (=66 GWh), $C_{PHS\ min}$ = minimum storage capacity (=0 GWh), P_{PHS} = maximum storage power in/output (=9 GW) and a single cycle efficiency η of 90% [16] in the model code.

We modeled electric energy storage to identify how it enables the use of EE production from vRES which is otherwise not contributing to the REN share and progressively curtailed. The modeled PHS stores any EE in times of negative RL from vRES, and discharges the stored energy in times of positive RL to contribute to the power supply whenever vRES are not fully meeting power demand. This presented technical modeling of PHS is deterministic, so that no uncertainties are introduced. Its performance was checked by a comparison to a spreadsheet calculation and proved to be adequate for this specific approach.

All four investigated cases cover all combinations of wind and solar PV installations ranging from 0 to 300 GW with a step size of 3 GW, resulting in a 100 × 100 array with 10,000 possible capacity combinations. The calculated results for REN shares and EE were visualized as a surface plot and are given in the Results section.

3.2. Algorithm for Efficient Pathways

To identify efficient pathways, we applied an incremental evaluation of the discrete values for a REN share compared to its neighboring value in the 100 × 100 array by calculating the discrete gradient between the neighboring REN share values on the surface (7):

$$\frac{\Delta\ REN\ share_{ws}}{\Delta\ added\ capacity_{ws}}, \tag{7}$$

where w is the indexed capacity from wind power in the 100 × 100 array and s is the indexed capacity from solar PV in the 100 × 100 array.

By dividing the increase in REN share through the 3 GW of additionally installed wind or solar PV, we calculated the resulting gradient per additionally installed capacity for every neighboring grid node in the REN share array (see Figure 3). Following the highest gradients from grid node to grid node forms a pathway in capacity expansion, which results in the highest increase in REN share per installed capacity of wind or solar PV. This way, the most efficient pathways in the calculated 100 × 100 REN share array are identified, beginning at an initial point and performing an incremental assessment and selection (this approach is, in principle, also applicable to more than two RES sources. The necessary higher dimensional space needed to integrate more RES sources in one graph would be less suited for a quick visual interpretation and is therefore not realized in this study). All resulting REN share surface plots in this study show a convex or concave surface, enabling this basic algorithm to identify efficient pathways.

The necessary discrete starting point can be, for example, a combination of 0 GW of wind and 0 GW of solar PV for no initial vRES deployment, or the capacity combination of 50.5 GW of wind and 42.4 GW of solar PV installed in Germany at the end of 2017 [47]. This overall approach was used to check the various combinations in vRES technologies and identify efficient pathways, as a higher value for the gradient leads to a more efficient capacity expansion pathway compared to a lower value. In Section 4.4 we will apply this algorithm to the calculated results to identify optimal pathways and we will present residual load duration curves (RLDC) of selected results to showcase the immense impact different pathways have on the structure of the residual load and especially on EE.

4. Results

In this section, we present the results calculated for all four cases: baseline and advanced technology, with and without pumped hydro storage. The results are presented through surface plots and tables.

4.1. Baseline Technology Case B

4.1.1. Key Indicator REN Share Case B

The resulting REN share surface plot of the various capacity combinations on the 100 × 100 array forms a bi-directional concave surface. Figure 4 shows a surface plot for the resulting REN share in Case B, with REN share plotted on the vertical axis and installed capacities of wind on the horizontal right hand axis and of solar PV capacities on the horizontal left hand axis.

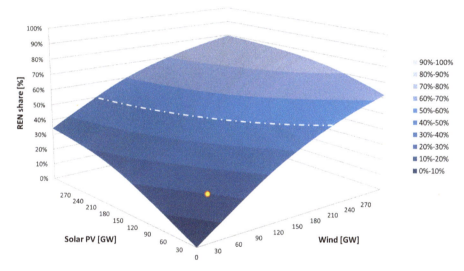

Figure 4. REN share surface plot for Case B, including the 2017 capacities from wind and solar PV (point marking), and the 50% REN share marking for various combinations resulting in a 50% REN share (mixed dotted-dashed line).

Starting either at a 0% REN share with 0 GW installed capacity for both wind and solar PV or with 50 GW of wind and 42 GW of solar PV which were installed in Germany at the end of 2017, every unit of capacity added results in an increase in REN share in the surface plot. Initially, additional wind capacities on the right hand axis of the surface plot result in a steeper increase in REN share compared to adding the same amount of solar PV capacities on the left hand axis. The initial gradient on the left hand axis, representing additional solar PV capacities, is lower (0.89% per 3 GW of solar PV) than the initial gradient for additional wind capacities (1.48% per 3 GW of wind). Furthermore, a sole solar PV deployment of 300 GW only achieves a maximum REN share of 36%, compared to the 62% for wind for the same amount of installed capacity. REN shares above 62% can only be achieved through a combination of both wind and solar PV. Overall, a declining gradient of the REN share for a sole deployment of either wind or solar becomes apparent in the surface plot, which forms a concave surface.

4.1.2. Key Indicator EE (Negative Residual Load) Case B

Figure 5 shows the development of EE production in Case B. EE is also presented as a surface plot and plotted on the vertical axis, with installed capacities of wind on the horizontal right hand axis and of solar PV capacities on the horizontal left hand axis.

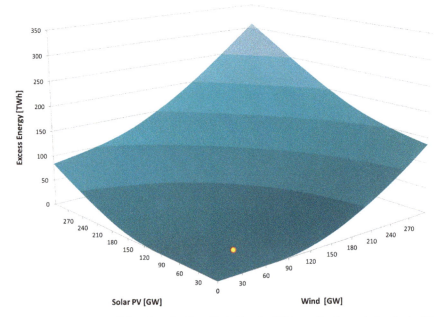

Figure 5. Excess energy (EE) surface plot Case B including the 2017 capacities from wind and solar PV (point marking).

After a threshold of roughly 20 GW from wind or solar is surpassed, a progressive production of EE is apparent in Figure 5. In contrast to the REN share surface plot in Figure 4, the EE surface plot forms a bi-directional convex surface. The convex surface of the progressive increase in EE is the reason for the concave surface of the REN share surface plot in Figure 4, as without electric energy storage EE does not contribute to serve the power demand and thus does not increase REN share.

Figure 6 demonstrates that EE is generated progressively when additional vRES capacities surpass a threshold of roughly 20 GW from wind or solar PV. This is the tipping point of the marginal improvement of additional capacities in the REN share plot given in Figure 5.

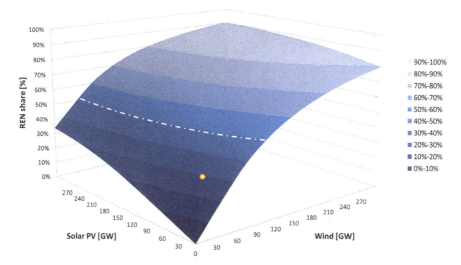

Figure 6. REN share surface plot for Case A, including the 2017 capacities from wind and solar PV (point marking), and the 50% REN share marking for various combinations resulting in a 50% REN share (mixed dotted-dashed line).

4.2. Advanced Technology Case A

4.2.1. Key Indicator REN Share Case A

The corresponding surface plot for the advanced technology case (Figure 6) shows significant differences from the baseline REN share plot (Figure 4).

While advanced solar PV again reaches about 40% REN share in a sole deployment of 300 GW, additional capacities from advanced wind power boost REN shares faster than in the baseline case, and a sole deployment of 300 GW of wind pushes REN share above 80%. The initial gradient on the left hand axis for additional solar PV capacities is significantly lower (0.78% per 3 GW of solar PV) than the gradient for additional wind capacities (2.87% per 3 GW of wind). REN shares beyond 80% are only achieved by a combination of both wind and solar PV.

The results reflect the much higher energy production per installed capacity of wind compared to solar PV in the advanced technology case (3000 FLH from advanced wind compared to 1536 FLH in the baseline case; 869 FLH for advanced solar PV compared to 1000 FLH in the baseline case). As a consequence, it is possible to achieve higher REN shares with the same installed capacities using advanced technology in wind power.

4.2.2. Key Indicator EE (Negative Residual Load) Case A

The corresponding EE surface plot (Figure 7) indicates a much higher EE production compared to the baseline case (Figure 5), especially from advanced wind power along the right hand horizontal axis. However, the higher EE production does not contradict the greater effectiveness of advanced WEC from a REN share point of view, as shown in Figure 7.

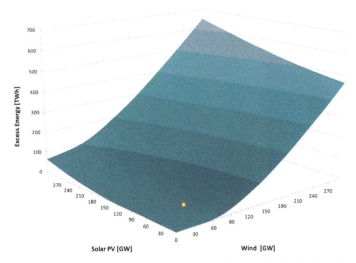

Figure 7. EE surface plot Case A including the 2017 capacities from wind and solar PV (point marking).

4.3. Cases BS and AS Including Electric Energy Storage from PHS

As described in Section 2.3, we modeled electric energy storage from PHS to identify its impact. The modeled storage enables the recovery of some of the EE from vRES, thus achieving higher REN shares from a given vRES capacity.

To visualize the results, we have chosen a surface plot showing only the differences in REN share between the cases with and without storage by subtracting the non-storage case from the storage case (and thus not providing any information about the absolute increase in REN share). The resulting differences surface plot (Figure 8) shows how storage boosts REN shares at different combinations of wind and solar PV capacities.

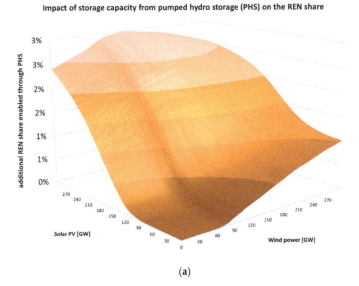

(**a**)

Figure 8. *Cont.*

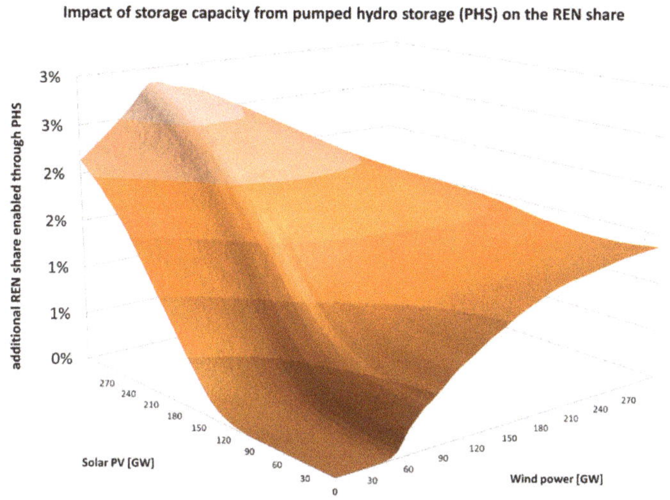

Impact of storage capacity from pumped hydro storage (PHS) on the REN share

(b)

Figure 8. Differences surface plot for REN share illustrating the additional REN share enabled by electric energy storage from pumped hydro storage (PHS); (**a**) for the differences between the baseline cases and (**b**) for the differences between the advanced technology cases.

Comparison with Cases Including Storage

For wind and solar PV capacities below the already identified threshold of 20 GW, no EE is produced and thus there is no effect from electric energy storage. For higher vRES capacities, the overall REN share increase from the modeled storage reaches up to 2.9% in the baseline case (BS) compared to the non-storage case B (Figure 8a). For high solar PV capacities, the addition of electric energy storage enables higher relative gains in REN share compared to the gains enabled for the same amount of wind capacities.

For the advanced technology case AS, a quite similar overall characteristic of the differences surface plot is obtained (Figure 8b). The higher productivity of advanced WEC leads to an earlier stabilization of the additional REN share.

The maximum additional improvement in REN share through PHS is about 2.9% at a 63% REN share provided by a wind capacity of 135 GW and a solar PV capacity of 300 GW (for the advanced technology case it is 2.8% additional REN share at 62% from 63 GW wind and 300 GW from solar PV). For lower and higher overall REN shares, this additional improvement is reduced as either less EE is available for storage or too much EE cannot be stored, either because of the limitations in installed power from PHS or storage capacity from PHS. This peak in additional improvement in REN share is therefore specific for each combination of power and storage capacity of PHS.

4.4. Efficient Pathways

Applying the algorithm for efficient pathways (see Section 3.2), the efficient capacity expansion from wind and solar can be identified and illustrated as pathways on the REN share surface plot. Efficient pathways starting from a zero wind and solar PV capacity combination are represented by the dashed red line in Figures 9 and 10, and the pathway starting at the 2017 capacities in Germany (yellow dot) is represented by the yellow dotted line. Figures 9 and 10 illustrate the identified pathways for cases BS and AS. Cases B and A without electric energy storage show only minor deviations below 3% in REN share (see Figure 9) and are therefore not depicted.

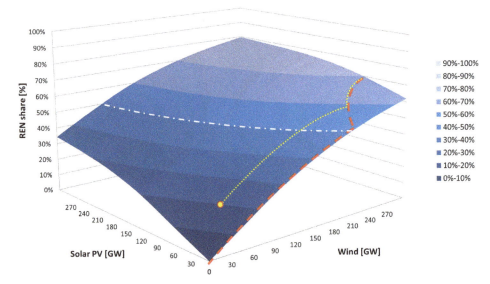

Figure 9. REN share surface plot and efficient pathway for Case BS, including the efficient pathway starting at 0 GW wind and solar PV deployment (dashed line), the efficient pathway starting at the 2017 capacities from wind and solar PV (dotted line), and the 50% REN share marking for various combinations resulting in a 50% REN share (mixed dotted-dashed line).

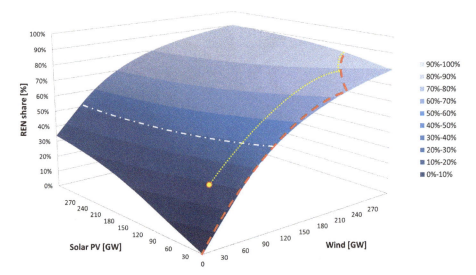

Figure 10. REN share surface plot and efficient pathway for Case AS, including the efficient pathway starting at 0 GW wind and solar PV deployment (dashed line), the efficient pathway starting at the 2017 capacities for wind and solar PV (dotted line), and the 50% REN share marking for various combinations resulting in a 50% REN share (mixed dotted-dashed line).

As apparent from Figure 9, for Case BS wind power was solely prioritized for REN share levels up to 47%. Solar PV capacity was added only before this threshold, after which an alteration of additional solar PV and wind forms the efficient pathway. When reaching the boundaries of the 100 × 100 array, the pathway for Case BS reaches 76% REN share, with wind power clearly dominating the capacity mix.

The same characteristics can be registered in Figure 10 for Case AS including advanced technology, although the first deployment of solar PV is pushed back to 76% of REN. When reaching the boundaries of the 100 × 100 array, the pathway calculated surpassed 87% REN share.

As shown in Table 2, the higher efficiency of wind power regarding the REN share per installed capacity is significant and is responsible for the initial dominance of wind power along the pathways. Efficient pathways do not include solar PV for REN shares below 47%. A comparison of Cases B and BS with Cases A and AS for a 50% REN share clearly shows that PHS can reduce the capacity requirement slightly but pushes the introduction of solar PV even further back along the efficient pathways. Interestingly, comparing baseline cases against advanced technology cases reveals that advanced wind allows for a reduction of almost 50% in required wind capacity.

Table 2. Overview of selected results from the calculated pathways.

	Case B	Case BS	Case A	Case AS
Initial Δ REN share/Δ 3 GW wind	0.89%	0.89%	1.68%	1.68%
Solar PV	0.56%	0.56%	0.51%	0.51%
REN share at which solar PV is first introduced to complement wind	47% @ 186 GW wind	49% @ 192 GW wind	74% @ 234 GW wind	76% @ 240 GW wind
Minimum capacity requirement to attain 50% in REN share	186 GW wind + 15 GW solar PV	192 GW wind + 6 GW solar PV	105 GW wind + 0 GW solar PV	102 GW wind + 0 GW solar PV

To complement the findings on pathways, we provide residual load duration curves (RLDC) in Figure 11 to add one additional aspect associated with efficient pathways and capacity mixes for vRES. The RLDC presented are directly derived from Equation (2) for three different wind and solar PV capacity combinations, each enabling a 50% REN share in Case B. The duration curves are created by ordering all hourly RL values in a descending order [14,29]. The highest RL value is located on the very left of the graph and the lowest value on the right side. Values below 0 GW indicate negative RL and the connected enclosed area between the RLDC and the zero line is equivalent to the EE produced.

On the right side of the duration curve, where excess power is located below the 0 GW RL level, significant differences become apparent. For both solar PV and wind-dominated mixes (like the case for 60 GW wind and 300 GW of solar PV in a solar PV-dominated mix or 186 GW of wind and 15 GW of solar PV in a wind-dominated mix that is also part of the efficient pathway in Case B, see Table 2), higher maximum excess power can be identified and the enclosed area under the curve (equivalent to EE) is significantly enlarged compared to a balanced mix from wind and solar PV (108 GW wind and 114 GW solar PV). Especially for the solar PV-dominated capacity mix, high EE is generated with a three-fold higher maximum excess power.

As indicated by Ueckerdt [10], the RLDC continuously becomes steeper on the right hand side of the RLDC for high shares of wind and solar PV. Wind slightly covers peak load and increasingly contributes to cover mid and base load, but also contributes to EE production, whereas a solar PV-dominated capacity mix increases excess power and EE significantly.

The examination of RLDCs makes clear that different pathways have a huge impact on the magnitude and volume of the EE produced. It is possible to deduce the energetic and temporal structure of EE from the RLDC and identify how integration options like storage, demand side management or interconnectors have to be developed in order to make use of EE from vRES.

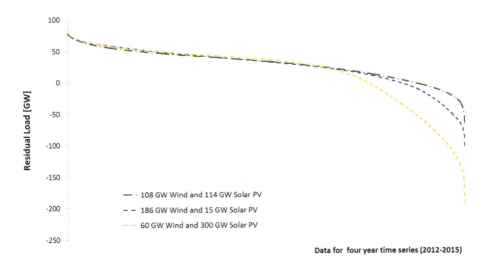

Figure 11. Residual load duration curve (RLDC) of different combinations of wind and solar PV all achieving a 50% REN share in Case B.

5. Discussion

The results provide a broader perspective on the interplay of wind, solar PV and power demand, the effect of electric energy storage form PHS, as well as pathways towards high REN shares in a case study for Germany. For power systems with a low initial REN penetration, wind power boosts REN share per installed capacity more than solar PV. This is primarily due to the higher productivity (full load hours) of wind compared to solar in the German case. Up to levels of installed wind capacity equivalent to more than 47% in REN share, wind power is more efficient from a required capacity perspective than solar PV, although significantly more EE is produced. Above this level, a mix from additional solar PV and wind shows a better performance regarding the boosting of REN shares compared to the sole addition of wind capacities. This is due to solar PV's different temporal production profile, which complements wind power to better match temporal demand patterns [20,31,32,46,71]. An indicator for this complementariness is the two-fold bend (bi-directional) concave surface of all the REN share plots, as neither wind nor solar PV alone reaches very high values for REN share (e.g., >62% in Case B), so that a combination of both sources is required. Additional renewable sources, enlarged electric energy storage, and DSM are key requirements for a fully renewable power supply.

5.1. Impact of Advanced Technology

Advanced wind power allows a significant increase of REN shares compared to the baseline technology, as apparent from the sharp gradient of the REN share surface plot in Case A (Figure 5) compared to Case B (Figure 7). In contrast, advanced solar PV, although allowing for a better coverage of daily load profiles, falls short of delivering equal benefits regarding its contribution to REN shares. Consequently, advanced solar PV is pushed back even further along the efficient pathways compared to the baseline setups and is only effective after high REN share levels of 74% are reached in Case A. Even considering the fact that EE production from advanced wind is increased, advanced wind performs better than solar PV.

Advanced wind has been identified as the most effective measure for achieving high REN shares from vRES. However, it comes at a trade-off of higher EE for REN shares at high penetration rates (Figures 6 and 8).

5.2. Effect of Electric Energy Storage

By adding storage capacities from PHS, EE from vRES can be recovered, which allows for higher REN shares compared to a progressive curtailment in the non-storage cases. The REN share differences plots showed a distinct effect of the modeled storage from PHS and that the interplay of PHS with solar PV performed better than in combination with wind power. The specific power-to-capacity ratio of the modeled PHS can be characterized as short-term electric energy storage, which is capable of integrating EE with a high frequency (several hours for a storage cycle) and high number of storage cycles but limited storage capacity. This characteristic of the existing PHS is ideal for the integration of the daily production pattern of solar PV. However, contrary to our expectation, PHS does not shift efficient pathways towards an earlier introduction of solar PV, as the generation from wind power also benefits from electric energy storage. Therefore, for all cases calculated, wind power dominated in the optimal pathways, especially in the advanced technology Cases A and AS.

5.3. Efficient Pathways

Efficient pathways for the capacity expansion of wind and solar PV show significant differences in their required overall capacities of wind and solar compared to all other possible pathways presented. The higher productivity of wind in terms of FLH in the case study region leads to wind-dominated pathways in the presented cases, regardless of whether PHS was included or not. Storage and especially advanced wind technology reduce the capacity requirement to achieve a 50% REN share, with an almost 50% reduction in overall required capacity from vRES (Table 2). As far as overall installed capacities are a criterion from an economic or technical point of view, wind power is identified as a preferable vRES source until substantial REN shares of at least 47% are reached, although it comes at the cost of increased EE production.

5.4. Transferability and Uncertainties

The presented findings cannot be fully generalized and directly transferred to other regions, as load and vRES complementarities are specific to individual regions [29,72]. For instance, the findings of Solomon [20] for the California state power system are affected by significant differences in demand and vRES production profiles. This makes it necessary to identify efficient combinations and pathways specifically for each region.

Since no field data for future cases of higher vRES shares in Germany are available, no direct comparison of the calculated outcomes is possible, but results are in line with the findings of relevant publications in the field regarding the effect of high vRES shares and the impact of electric energy storage [3,15,24,29,40,45]. Input time series data have likewise been checked by the authors, as well as by the scientific community using the data source [48]. To the best of our observation, all presented calculations are reproducible as expected due to their deterministic nature. Selected results were successfully checked based on alternative spreadsheet calculations of the modeling. Furthermore, published studies for selected elements of the approach underline the validity of the presented approach [11,25,31,40,45,59,73].

Clearly, the presented model is a simplified model in relation to the actual power system and many other relevant aspects are not considered. Consequently, the results only highlight the temporal integration aspects of vRES and do not cover other relevant aspects like economic costs, land availability, acceptance etc.

6. Conclusions

This case study for the German power system widens the existing systems analysis approaches with regard to the discourse of vRES integration in electricity systems and adds additional criteria for the transition towards a vRES-based power supply system.

The main objectives of this paper were to (i) provide a broad picture of how wind and solar PV can be combined to achieve efficient pathways in capacity expansion to fulfill future REN share targets in a storage-restricted energy system, (ii) compare the impact of advanced technologies from wind and solar PV against baseline technology, (iii) and study the impact of electric energy storage from PHS to make use of EE production from wind and solar PV. With these objectives in mind, our results indicate the following conclusions.

The results show that the higher power production from wind energy per installed capacity leads to a higher effectiveness of wind power, and effective pathways all depend on wind power in the first place, with solar PV added only after a certain REN share provided by wind is surpassed.

The positive impact of advanced technologies was confirmed for the case of wind power, as less capacity is required to achieve set REN share targets. For solar PV in a mixed setup of south, east and west-oriented systems, the lower productivity of these setups is not compensated by their better temporal matching with the demand profile from a REN share point of view.

Existing electric energy storage from PHS enables a better integration of wind and solar PV into the power system and allows for a faster achievement of REN share goals in the modeled cases. However, PHS does not result in an earlier introduction of solar PV along the efficient pathways. For all different cases calculated, wind power dominated the efficient pathways, especially in the advanced technology case, regardless of whether PHS was included or not.

To sum up: taking efficient pathways as a criterion for the future capacity expansion of vRES in the investigated case, a wind-based capacity expansion provides a faster transition towards high REN shares, even considering existing electric energy storage infrastructure from PHS in the region. Per unit of installed capacity, a considerably larger fraction of renewable energy can be provided from wind than from solar PV. Advanced wind power in particular provides higher productivity and effectiveness along with benefits regarding system integration [39,40].

Support schemes and especially tenders for renewable generation capacities should therefore ensure a steady capacity expansion of wind power, especially in the form of advanced system-friendly wind turbines. The reduced overall capacity requirement additionally offers substantial potential to reduce land use conflicts and environmental impacts, so that the results provide various connecting points for an analysis of land use implications [74], environmental impacts and economic comparison.

Specifically for the case of Germany, which has an almost equal proportion of existing wind and solar PV installations, the results underline the importance of wind power expansion in the coming years to reach the governmental goals for 2030 and beyond.

7. Outlook

The assessment of advanced technology is the focus of ongoing research [16,40,42,52,65] and an economic evaluation of the combined perspective of advanced technology and efficient pathways will be helpful to prioritize renewable policies. With specific investment costs and levelized cost of energy for wind and solar PV currently in the same order of magnitude in Europe [10,75–80], non-economic aspects are likewise relevant to decide on future capacity expansion pathways. The possibility for a quick capacity expansion of solar PV, contested public acceptance, as well as availability of sites for wind power and environmental impacts, are additional aspects to be considered. Given the mid- to long-term perspective that was taken in this case study, further advancements in technology and innovations in vRES technologies and electric energy storage will influence the outcome of efficient pathways as well.

Furthermore, a successful and fast transition to a fully renewable power supply system also depends on the extent to which other renewable sources such as bioenergy, hydro and geothermal can complement vRES in order to contribute to a secure power supply. Without additional contributions from these non-vRES sources and at current consumption levels [47], wind and solar PV have to provide more than 85% of the power supply in Germany. Therefore, additional integration options like new storage technologies, demand side management or a better coupling of the sectors for electricity, heat and mobility are key factors for integrating high shares of vRES on power supply systems.

Author Contributions: P.T. had the idea and developed the model and performed the modeling and analyzed the data and results; P.T. wrote the paper with contributions from M.E. and D.T.

Funding: This work was supported by the Helmholtz Association under the Joint Initiative "Energy System 2050 - A Contribution of the Research Field Energy."

Acknowledgments: We would like to thank the Open Power System Data platform for providing the crucial time series data used in this article.

Conflicts of Interest: The authors declare no conflict of interest.

Abbreviations

The following abbreviations are used in this manuscript:

Case A	advanced technology study case
Case AS	advanced technology + electric energy storage study case
Case B	baseline (non-advanced) technology study case
Case BS	baseline (non-advanced) technology + electric energy storage study case
DSM	demand side management
EE	excess energy (equivalent to the cumulated negative residual load)
FLH	full load hours, equivalent to the capacity factor of a power converter
GW	gigawatt
GWh	gigawatt hour
MW	megawatt
RL	residual load (power demand minus renewable feed-in; renewable feed-in is limited to wind and solar PV in the modeling)
REN	renewable energy
REN share	renewable share on power demand
solar PV	solar photovoltaics
vRES	variable renewable energy sources (primarily wind and solar PV)
WEC	wind energy converter

References

1. IEA. *World Energy Outlook 2017*; International Energy Agency (IEA): Paris, France, 2017.
2. IPCC. *Climate Change 2014: Synthesis Report*; Contribution of Working Groups I, II and III to the Fifth Assessment Report of the Intergovernmental Panel on Climate Change Geneva; IPCC: Paris, France, 2014; p. 151.
3. Edenhofer, O.; Hirth, L.; Knopf, B.; Pahle, M.; Schlömer, S.; Schmid, E.; Ueckerdt, F. On the economics of renewable energy sources. *Energy Econ.* **2013**, *40* (Suppl. 1), S12–S23. [CrossRef]
4. González-Aparicio, I.; Zucker, A. Impact of wind power uncertainty forecasting on the market integration of wind energy in Spain. *Appl. Energy* **2015**, *159*, 334–349. [CrossRef]
5. Ueckerdt, F.; Brecha, R.; Luderer, G.; Sullivan, P.; Schmid, E.; Bauer, N.; Böttger, D.; Pietzcker, R. Representing power sector variability and the integration of variable renewables in long-term energy-economy models using residual load duration curves. *Energy* **2015**, *90*, 1799–1814. [CrossRef]
6. Beaudin, M.; Zareipour, H.; Schellenberglabe, A.; Rosehart, W. Energy storage for mitigating the variability of renewable electricity sources: An updated review. *Energy Sustain. Dev.* **2010**, *14*, 302–314. [CrossRef]
7. Huber, M.; Dimkova, D.; Hamacher, T. Integration of wind and solar power in Europe: Assessment of flexibility requirements. *Energy* **2014**, *69*, 236–246. [CrossRef]
8. Schlachtberger, D.P.; Becker, S.; Schramm, S.; Greiner, M. Backup flexibility classes in emerging large-scale renewable electricity systems. *Energy Convers. Manag.* **2016**, *125*, 336–346. [CrossRef]
9. Xydis, G. On the exergetic capacity factor of a wind—Solar power generation system. *J. Clean. Prod.* **2013**, *47*, 437–445. [CrossRef]

10. Ueckerdt, F.; Hirth, L.; Luderer, G.; Edenhofer, O. System LCOE: What are the costs of variable renewables? *Energy* **2013**, *63*, 61–75. [CrossRef]
11. Rasmussen, M.G.; Andresen, G.B.; Greiner, M. Storage and balancing synergies in a fully or highly renewable pan-European power system. *Energy Policy* **2012**, *51*, 642–651. [CrossRef]
12. Becker, S.; Frew, B.A.; Andresen, G.B.; Zeyer, T.; Schramm, S.; Greiner, M.; Jacobson, M.Z. Features of a fully renewable US electricity system: Optimized mixes of wind and solar PV and transmission grid extensions. *Energy* **2014**, *72*, 443–458. [CrossRef]
13. Bussar, C.; Stöcker, P.; Cai, Z.; Moraes, L.; Alvarez, R.; Chen, H.; Breuer, C.; Moser, A.; Leuthold, M.; Sauer, D.U. Large-scale Integration of Renewable Energies and Impact on Storage Demand in a European Renewable Power System of 2050. *Energy Procedia* **2015**, *73*, 145–153. [CrossRef]
14. Child, M.; Bogdanov, D.; Breyer, C. The role of storage technologies for the transition to a 100% renewable energy system in Europe. *Energy Procedia* **2018**, *155*, 44–60. [CrossRef]
15. Schill, W.-P.; Diekmann, J.; Zerrahn, A. Power Storage: An Important Option for the German Energy Transition. 2015. Available online: https://www.econstor.eu/handle/10419/108856 (accessed on 13 April 2018).
16. Mills, A.D.; Wiser, R.H. Strategies to mitigate declines in the economic value of wind and solar at high penetration in California. *Appl. Energy* **2015**, *147*, 269–278. [CrossRef]
17. Hirth, L. The benefits of flexibility: The value of wind energy with hydropower. *Appl. Energy* **2016**, *181*, 210–223. [CrossRef]
18. Lindley, D. The energy storage problem. *Nature* **2010**, *463*, 18–20. [CrossRef] [PubMed]
19. Denholm, P.E.E.; Kirby, B.; Milligan, M. *Role of Energy Storage with Renewable Electricity Generation*; National Renewable Energy Laboratory: Golden, CO, USA, 2010.
20. Solomon, A.A.; Kammen, D.M.; Callaway, D. Investigating the impact of wind–solar complementarities on energy storage requirement and the corresponding supply reliability criteria. *Appl. Energy* **2016**, *168*, 130–145. [CrossRef]
21. Jülch, V. Comparison of electricity storage options using levelized cost of storage (LCOS) method. *Appl. Energy* **2016**, *183*, 1594–1606. [CrossRef]
22. Amirante, R.; Cassone, E.; Distaso, E.; Tamburrano, P. Overview on recent developments in energy storage: Mechanical, electrochemical and hydrogen technologies. *Energy Convers. Manag.* **2017**, *132*, 372–387. [CrossRef]
23. Nikolaidis, P.; Poullikkas, A. Cost metrics of electrical energy storage technologies in potential power system operations. *Sustain. Energy Technol. Assess.* **2018**, *25*, 43–59. [CrossRef]
24. Heide, D.; Greiner, M.; von Bremen, L.; Hoffmann, C. Reduced storage and balancing needs in a fully renewable European power system with excess wind and solar power generation. *Renew. Energy* **2011**, *36*, 2515–2523. [CrossRef]
25. Heide, D.; von Bremen, L.; Greiner, M.; Hoffmann, C.; Speckmann, M.; Bofinger, S. Seasonal optimal mix of wind and solar power in a future, highly renewable Europe. *Renew. Energy* **2010**, *35*, 2483–2489. [CrossRef]
26. Vidal-Amaro, J.J.; Østergaard, P.A.; Sheinbaum-Pardo, C. Optimal energy mix for transitioning from fossil fuels to renewable energy sources—The case of the Mexican electricity system. *Appl. Energy* **2015**, *150*, 80–96. [CrossRef]
27. Huber, M.; Weissbart, C. On the optimal mix of wind and solar generation in the future Chinese power system. *Energy* **2015**, *90 Pt 1*, 235–243. [CrossRef]
28. Becker, S.; Frew, B.A.; Andresen, G.B.; Jacobson, M.Z.; Schramm, S.; Greiner, M. Renewable build-up pathways for the US: Generation costs are not system costs. *Energy* **2015**, *81*, 437–445. [CrossRef]
29. Ueckerdt, F.; Brecha, R.; Luderer, G. Analyzing major challenges of wind and solar variability in power systems. *Renew. Energy* **2015**, *81*, 1–10. [CrossRef]
30. Zappa, W.; van den Broek, M. Analysing the potential of integrating wind and solar power in Europe using spatial optimisation under various scenarios. *Renew. Sustain. Energy Rev.* **2018**, *94*, 1192–1216. [CrossRef]
31. Kreifels, N.; Mayer, J.N.; Burger, B.; Wittwer, C. Analysis of Photovoltaics and Wind Power in Future Renewable Energy Scenarios. *Energy Technol.* **2014**, *2*, 29–33. [CrossRef]
32. Denholm, P.; Margolis, R.M. Evaluating the limits of solar photovoltaics (PV) in electric power systems utilizing energy storage and other enabling technologies. *Energy Policy* **2007**, *35*, 4424–4433. [CrossRef]

33. Lund, H. Excess electricity diagrams and the integration of renewable energy. *Int. J. Sustain. Energy* **2003**, *23*, 149–156. [CrossRef]
34. Hirth, L. The Optimal Share of Variable Renewables: How the Variability of Wind and Solar Power affects their Welfare-optimal Deployment. *Energy J.* **2015**, *36*, 149–184. [CrossRef]
35. Zipp, A. Revenue prospects of photovoltaic in Germany—Influence opportunities by variation of the plant orientation. *Energy Policy* **2015**, *81*, 86–97. [CrossRef]
36. Hartner, M.; Ortner, A.; Hiesl, A.; Haas, R. East to west—The optimal tilt angle and orientation of photovoltaic panels from an electricity system perspective. *Appl. Energy* **2015**, *160*, 94–107. [CrossRef]
37. Hirth, L. The Market Value of Solar Photovoltaics: Is Solar Power Cost-Competitive? *IET Renew. Power Gener.* **2015**, *9*, 37–45. [CrossRef]
38. Tafarte, P.; Das, S.; Eichhorn, M.; Thrän, D. Small adaptations, big impacts: Options for an optimized mix of variable renewable energy sources. *Energy* **2014**, *72*, 80–92. [CrossRef]
39. IEA. *The Power of Transformation: Wind, Sun and the Economics of Flexible Power Systems*; International Energy Agency (IEA): Paris, France, 2014; p. 238.
40. Hirth, L.; Müller, S. System-friendly wind power-How advanced wind turbine design can increase the economic value of electricity generated through wind power. *Energy Econ.* **2016**, *56*, 51–63. [CrossRef]
41. May, N. The Impact of Wind Power Support Schemes on Technology Choices. *Energy Econ.* **2017**, *65*, 343–354. [CrossRef]
42. May, N.; Karsten, N.; Frieder, B. Market incentives for system-friendly designs of wind turbines. *DIW Econ. Bull.* **2015**, *5*, 313–321.
43. Bucksteeg, M. Modelling the impact of geographical diversification of wind turbines on the required firm capacity in Germany. *Appl. Energy* **2019**, *235*, 1476–1491. [CrossRef]
44. Pforte. *Untersuchungen zur Integration der Fluktuierenden Windenergie in das System der Elektroenergieversorgung*; KIT: Karlsruhe, Germany, 2010.
45. Wagner, F. Electricity by intermittent sources: An analysis based on the German situation 2012. *Eur. Phys. J. Plus* **2014**, *129*, 20. [CrossRef]
46. Killinger, S.; Mainzer, K.; McKenna, R.; Kreifels, N.; Fichtner, W. A regional optimisation of renewable energy supply from wind and photovoltaics with respect to three key energy-political objectives. *Energy* **2015**, *84*, 563–574. [CrossRef]
47. Erneuerbare Energien in Deutschland. Daten zur Entwicklung im Jahr 2017. 2018. Available online: https://www.umweltbundesamt.de/sites/default/files/medien/376/publikationen/180315_uba_hg_eeinzahlen_2018_bf.pdf (accessed on 5 December 2018).
48. Open Power System Data: Wind and Solar Power Time Series. 2016. Available online: http://open-power-system-data.org/data-sources#8_Wind_and_solar_power_time_series2016 (accessed on 5 December 2017).
49. Schlesinger, M.; Lindenberger, D.; Lutz, C. Energieszenarien für ein Energiekonzept der Bundesregierung. 2010. Available online: https://www.prognos.com/uploads/tx_atwpubdb/100827_Prognos_Studie_Energieszenarien_fuer_ein_energiekonzept_der_Bundesregierung.pdf (accessed on 11 January 2018).
50. Netzentwicklungsplan Strom 2012. 2. Überarbeiteter Entwurf der Übertragungsnetzbetreiber. 50Hertz, Amprion, TenneT TSO, TransnetBW. 2012. Available online: https://www.netzentwicklungsplan.de/sites/default/files/nep_2012_2_entwurf_teil_1_kap_1_bis_8.pdf (accessed on 21 April 2018).
51. May, N.; Neuhoff, K.; Borggrefe, F. *Marktanreize für Systemdienliche Auslegungen von Windkraftanlagen*; DIW Wochenbericht: Wirtschaft, Politik, Wissenschaft; DIW Berlin: Berlin, Germany, 2015; pp. 555–564.
52. Molly, P. Design of Wind Turbines and Storage: A Question of System Optimisation. 2012. Available online: https://www.dewi.de/dewi_res/fileadmin/pdf/publications/Magazin_40/04.pdf (accessed on 23 April 2017).
53. Molly, P. Rated Power of Wind Turbines: What is Best? 2011. Available online: https://www.dewi.de/dewi_res/fileadmin/pdf/publications/Magazin_38/07.pdf (accessed on 12 November 2018).
54. IWES. *Entwicklung der Windenergie in Deutschland—Eine Beschreibung von aktuellen und zukünftigen Trends und Charakteristika der Einspeisung von Windenergieanlagen*; IWES: Kassel, Germany, 2013; p. 28.
55. Durstewitz, M.; Berkhout, V.; Hirsch, J.; Pfaffel, S.; Rohrig, K.; Adam, F.; Bange, J.; Bergmann, D.; Cernusko, R.; Faulstich, S. *Windenergie Report Deutschland 2016*; Fraunhofer Institut für Windenergie und Energiesystemtechnik (IWES): Stuttgart, Germany, 2017.

56. FfE. *Verbundforschungsvorhaben Merit Order der Energiespeicherung im Jahr 2030 Teil 1: Hauptbericht Endbericht*; Forschungsstelle für Energiewirtschaft FfE: München, Germany, 2016; p. 350.
57. Buck, P. Ökonomische Bewertung Systemfreundlich Optimierter Erneuerbarer Stromerzeugungstechnologien. Master's Thesis, Munich, Germany, 2016.
58. Tafarte, P.; Buck, P. Integration of wind power—Challenges and options for market integration and its impact on future cross-sectorial use. In Proceedings of the 14th International Conference on the European Energy Market (EEM), Dresden, Germany, 6–7 June 2017; pp. 1–5.
59. Lund, H. EnergyPLAN Advanced Energy Systems Analysis. 2012. Available online: http://energy.plan.aau.dk/EnergyPLAN%20documentation.pdf (accessed on 12 December 2017).
60. Matthes, F. Erneuerbare-Energien-Gesetz 3.0 (Langfassung). In *Studie im Auftrag von Agora Energiewende*; Öko-Institut: Freiburg, Germany, 2014.
61. Fraunhofer_ISE. *Effekte Regional Verteilter Sowie Ost-/West-Ausgerichteter Solaranlagen*; Fraunhofer_ISE: Freiburg, Germany, 2014.
62. Hafez, A.Z.; Soliman, A.; El-Metwally, K.A.; Ismail, I.M. Tilt and azimuth angles in solar energy applications—A review. *Renew. Sustain. Energy Rev.* **2017**, *77*, 147–168. [CrossRef]
63. Deetjen, T.A.; Garrison, J.B.; Rhodes, J.D.; Webber, M.E. Solar PV integration cost variation due to array orientation and geographic location in the Electric Reliability Council of Texas. *Appl. Energy* **2016**, *180*, 607–616. [CrossRef]
64. Hummon, M.; Denholm, P.; Margolis, R. Impact of photovoltaic orientation on its relative economic value in wholesale energy markets. *Prog. Photovolt. Res. Appl.* **2013**, *21*, 1531–1540. [CrossRef]
65. Achner, S.; Brühl, S.; Krzikalla, N. *Möglichkeiten zum Ausgleich Fluktuierender Einspeisungen aus Erneuerbaren Energien*; BET Büro für Energiewirtschaft und Technische Planung GmbH: Aachen, Germany, 2013.
66. Li, G.; Jin, Y.; Akram, M.W.; Chen, X.; Ji, J. Application of bio-inspired algorithms in maximum power point tracking for PV systems under partial shading conditions—A review. *Renew. Sustain. Energy Rev.* **2018**, *81*, 840–873. [CrossRef]
67. Salpakari, J.; Mikkola, J.; Lund, P.D. Improved flexibility with large-scale variable renewable power in cities through optimal demand side management and power-to-heat conversion. *Energy Convers. Manag.* **2016**, *126*, 649–661. [CrossRef]
68. Szarka, N.; Eichhorn, M.; Kittler, R.; Bezama, A.; Thrän, D. Interpreting long-term energy scenarios and the role of bioenergy in Germany. *Renew. Sustain. Energy Rev.* **2017**, *68*, 1222–1233. [CrossRef]
69. Szarka, N.; Scholwin, F.; Trommler, M.; Fabian Jacobi, H.; Eichhorn, M.; Ortwein, A.; Thrän, D. A novel role for bioenergy: A flexible, demand-oriented power supply. *Energy* **2013**, *61*, 18–26. [CrossRef]
70. Thrän, D.; Eichhorn, M.; Krautz, A.; Das, S.; Szarka, N. Flexible power generation from biomass—An opportunity for a renewable sources based energy system? In *Transition to Renewable Energy System*; Stolten, D., Scherer, V., Eds.; Whiley-VCH: Weinheim, Germany, 2013.
71. Schill, W.-P. Residual load, renewable surplus generation and storage requirements in Germany. *Energy Policy* **2014**, *73*, 65–79. [CrossRef]
72. Solomon, A.; Kammen, D.; Callaway, D. The role of large-scale energy storage design and dispatch in the power grid: A study of very high grid penetration of variable renewable resources. *Appl. Energy* **2014**, *134*, 75–89. [CrossRef]
73. Petrakopoulou, F.; Robinson, A.; Loizidou, M. Exergetic analysis and dynamic simulation of a solar-wind power plant with electricity storage and hydrogen generation. *J. Clean. Prod.* **2016**, *113*, 450–458. [CrossRef]
74. Lund, H. Large-scale integration of optimal combinations of PV, wind and wave power into the electricity supply. *Renew. Energy* **2006**, *31*, 503–515. [CrossRef]
75. Eichhorn, M.; Tafarte, P.; Thrän, D. Towards energy landscapes—"Pathfinder for sustainable wind power locations". *Energy* **2017**, *134*, 611–621. [CrossRef]
76. Moné, C.; Maples, A.S.B.; Hand, M. *2013 Cost of Wind Energy Review*; NREL (National Renewable Energy Laboratory): Golden, CO, USA, 2015; p. 94.
77. Reichelstein, S.; Yorston, M. The prospects for cost competitive solar PV power. *Energy Policy* **2013**, *55*, 117–127. [CrossRef]
78. Aisma, V. *IEA Wind Task 26: Wind Technology, Cost, and Performance Trends in Denmark, Germany, Ireland, Norway, the European Union, and the United States: 2007–2012*; NREL: Golden, CO, USA, 2015.

79. Wiser, R.; Bolinger, M. *2013 Wind Technologies Market Report*; U.S. Department of Energy: Washington, DC, USA, 2014.
80. Fraunhofer_ISE. Current and Future Cost of Photovoltaics. In *Long-term Scenarios for Market Development, System Prices and LCOE of Utility-Scale PV Systems*; Study on behalf of Agora Energiewende; Fraunhofer-Institute for Solar Energy Systems: Freiburg, Germany, 2015.

 © 2019 by the authors. Licensee MDPI, Basel, Switzerland. This article is an open access article distributed under the terms and conditions of the Creative Commons Attribution (CC BY) license (http://creativecommons.org/licenses/by/4.0/).

Article

Resilient and Immune by Design Microgrids Using Solid State Transformers

Mihai Sanduleac [1,*], João F. Martins [2], Irina Ciornei [3], Mihaela Albu [3], Lucian Toma [1], Vitor Fernão Pires [4], Lenos Hadjidemetriou [5] and Rooktabir Sauba [6]

1. Faculty of Power Engineering, Politehnica University of Bucharest, 060042 Bucharest, Romania; lucian.toma@upb.ro
2. Faculty of Sciences and Technology, Universidade NOVA de Lisboa, CTS-UNINOVA, 2829-516 Caparica, Portugal; jf.martins@fct.unl.pt
3. Faculty of Electrical Engineering, Politehnica University of Bucharest, 060042 Bucharest, Romania; irina.ciornei@upb.ro (I.C.); albu@ieee.org (M.A.)
4. Polytechnic Institute of Setúbal, INESC-ID Lisboa, 2910-761 Setúbal, Portugal; vitor.pires@estsetubal.ips.pt
5. KIOS Research and Innovation Center of Excellence, University of Cyprus, 2109 Nicosia, Cyprus; hadjidemetriou.lenos@ucy.ac.cy
6. DNV-GL, 6812 AR Arnhem, The Netherlands; ganesh.sauba@dnvgl.com
* Correspondence: m.sanduleac.ro@ieee.org or mihai.sanduleac@gmail.com; Tel.: +40-722-315-123

Received: 1 November 2018; Accepted: 29 November 2018; Published: 3 December 2018

Abstract: Solid State Transformers (SST) may become, in the near future, key technological enablers for decentralized energy supply systems. They have the potential to unleash new technologies and operation strategies of microgrids and prosumers to move faster towards a low carbon-based economy. This work proposes a paradigm change in the hierarchically and distributed operated power systems where SSTs are used to asynchronously connect the many small low voltage (LV) distribution networks, such as clusters of prosumers or LV microgrids, to the bulk power system. The need for asynchronously coupled microgrids requires a design that allows the LV system to operate independently from the bulk grid and to rely on its own control systems. The purpose of this new approach is to achieve immune and resilient by design configurations that allow maximizing the integration of Local Renewable Energy Resources (L-RES). The paper analyses from the stability point of view, through simplified numerical simulations, the way in which SST-interconnected microgrids can become immune to disturbances that occur in the bulk power system and how sudden changes in the microgrid can damp out at the Point of Common Coupling (PCC), thus achieving better reliability and predictability in both systems and enabling strong and healthy distributed energy storage systems (DESSs). Moreover, it is shown that in a fully inverter-based microgrid there is no need for mechanical or synthetic inertia to stabilize the microgrid during power unbalances. This happens because the electrostatic energy stored in the capacitors connected behind the SST inverter can be used for a brief time interval, until automation is activated to address the power unbalance for a longer term.

Keywords: microgrid; microgrid by design; energy community; net metering; prosumer; regulation; resilience; immunity; Solid State Transformer; electrostatic-driven inertia

1. Introduction

Background

Today the power systems operate under the paradigm of bulk networks, synchronously interconnected over wide areas (e.g., the continental zone of ENTSO-E), where a disturbance that occurs at the highest voltage level can be experienced down to the low voltage level. In the 20th century, the electricity sector was driven by the expansion of long-distance transmission lines to allow power transmission from large power plants to any remote consumer. Under these conditions, wide area stability and control became the necessary coordination strategy in ensuring the quality of the electrical energy supplied to the customers [1]. With the advent of power electronics and IT&C technologies, the supply of electrical energy can be seen as a service [2], and the reliable operation of the grid is mandatory in ensuring the quality.

The microgrid concept was developed, similar to other smart grid concepts, as a solution for power system decentralization designed to enhance the controllability within local communities and to mitigate the technical problems that affect the synchronously interconnected power systems [3,4]. Microgrids are decentralized energy supply systems that could form the cells of a smart, adaptive and resilient power grid of the future [5]. Furthermore, microgrids are recognized as innovative environments able to maximize the integration of Local Renewable Energy Resources (L-RES) [6]. Their role is motivated by more and more stringent challenges on a global scale: climate change, economies in need for higher efficiency, resilience, sustainability of energy policies and capacity to mitigate disturbances in the energy supply [7]. However, the unpredictability of the power generation from RES is a barrier in advancing towards 100% clean energy [8], along with other aspects, such as reduced or no inertia, which is a consequence of higher share of power electronic converters mediated energy transfer (and less rotating generators) [9]. Moreover, there is also an increased need for addressing the power system resilience following the increasing frequency of occurrence of the natural or man-induced extreme phenomena [10]. In fact, resilience is one of the characteristics recognized as an essential value of the future energy grids [11] and the mission orientated goal for Europe is formulated as "A secure, efficient and digitalized European energy system, fully decarbonized by 2050, coupling all energy sectors." [12].

In line with this latter challenge, DC medium and low voltage power distribution systems are also on the verge of research and development interests from both academia [13,14] and global industry players, such as Mitsubishi Electric or Siemens [15,16]. For instance, the distribution system operator from Finland carried out a feasibility study that concluded that low voltage DC (LVDC) electrical lines with lengths up to 8 km long can replace the existing AC infrastructure, with several advantages, among which, to increase the power transfer capacity up to 20% [17]. Other specialists concluded also that replacing medium voltage (MV) AC lines with DC lines can result in significant investment savings because of fewer induction transformers needed in the distribution grid [18]. Such vision is also a strong reason for deploying SSTs in future grid configurations, because they could easily allow access to a DC link.

A bottom-up development into an adaptive and resilient power system architecture implies a wide spread of low-voltage microgrids. A set of emerging technologies allows the implementation of multiple low-voltage microgrids, connected asynchronously with the main grid through SSTs. These technologies envisage distributed energy resources, especially renewables, and are derived from more recent trends in large adoption of storage (especially electrochemical type), while the core component for a seamless integration with the main grids is the solid-state transformer [19].

SST technology has been enabled by the advancements in power electronics. Power electronics got relevant importance in the energy domain especially for high voltage, when first High Voltage Direct Current (HVDC) lines were constructed, and Flexible Alternating Current Transmission Systems (FACTS) applications proved to be also needed especially in long distance power systems [20,21]. The development of renewables and lately of electrical vehicles brought the economy of scale and new technologies, such as Silicon Carbide (SIC) switching devices, thus enabling the integration of low cost and high-quality devices in their designs [22].

For more information about SST technologies and power electronics possible configurations the reader may consult [23] and a comprehensive state of the art literature review from [24].

Even if the SST technology is not yet on the market, recent projects report on SST being demonstrated in pre-commercial stages, which can advocate that the SSTs need only a final push to arrive on the market. In this respect, proven SST prototypes are already reported in the project "The Highly Efficient and Reliable Smart Transformer, a new Heart for the Electric Distribution System" (HEART) for smart grid applications developed by Kiel and Aalborg Universities [25], in ETH Zurich, application of SSTs is targeting locomotives and fast charging for electrical transportation [26], or from North Carolina State University [27] where the first target already achieved is fast charging and direct connection to (MV) networks. Furthermore, SST efficiencies of 97% and 98% are already reported in References [26,27], while in Reference [26] the SIC technology is particularly mentioned as one of the reasons for improvement. New enablers are a prerequisite for new paradigms. Some of the most important are indeed decentralized deployments of RES and distributed storage clustered in microgrids configurations. However, none of these works investigate an architecture where the SST could play a crucial role in providing stability for low inertia microgrids. They are rather application specific, either on traction systems or on fast charging capabilities.

Although the L-RES can contribute to supply the load during some time periods, one major drawback of RES is the intermittent behavior which requires additional solutions. This problem has been addressed until now through wide area balancing solutions [28].

The problem of matching the local generation and load are about to be solved, as the new storage technologies, especially based on Li-Ion batteries, are gaining momentum and the prices are in continuous decline [29]. The 129 MWh battery recently commissioned in Australia [30] and the plans for large new storage facilities in Hawaii [31] are only some of the many examples of battery applications used today at large scale.

In the case of microgrids, however, a usual approach for an islanded operation mode is possible only after disconnection from the main grid, which inevitably implies a short period of interruption, which can take a period from seconds to minutes. This is because the energy sources in microgrids are connected with anti-islanding protections required by the actual grid codes [32]. Also, it is because the inverter-based sources are designed to operate in a "grid following" mode, which means that they can be synchronized to the grid only if the frequency and its voltage are provided by an external part, which normally is the bulk grid.

The possibility of mitigating on short to medium term a match between production and consumption during the post-disconnection moment (when starting to work in islanding operation mode) are discussed in recent works [33]. In this case, the under investigation micro-grid was considering a diesel generator as a master in order to keep the stability of the microgrid while the photovoltaic (PV) and storage was in a grid or generator follower mode. However, in full inverter-based networks able to commute to island mode is not yet fully considered for most of today's microgrids.

Moreover, there is yet an unclear technical solution to be pursued for microgrids in the case of high system stability threats, such as the case of inertia reduction in large power systems (due to reduced rotational inertia capable to inject or absorb energy), which may bring instability and even collapse during unbalance transients. The microgrids are facing, in most cases, zero rotational energy source inertia, as they may include only grid-follower inverters. Therefore, their stability problem is even worse in the case of emergency islanding from the main grid.

As a consequent drawback of these uncertainties, there is yet no "microgrid by design architecture" in place, to be used for mediating large quantities of renewables and resilience or even immunity for the grid end-users. The key vision of the paper is that the SST allows an asynchronous interconnection between the bulk power system and the many small low voltage (LV) distribution networks. This enables implementing local optimization strategies of the energy supply service while meeting the requirements for relying more and more on clean energy production at the local level. The purpose of this new approach is to achieve immune and resilient by design configurations that allow maximizing the integration of Local Renewable Energy Resources (L-RES). The need for asynchronously coupled microgrids requires a design that allows the LV system to operate independently from the bulk grid and rely on its own control systems. Therefore, all necessary design measures are to be taken, such as generation-load balancing, local demand-response, local energy markets or other similar energy services. Such a microgrid is not intended to have an installed generation capacity capable to fully cover the load, and thus the power difference can be supplied from the bulk power systems through the SST, which is the only point of connection of the microgrid to the bulk grid, based on an ex-ante schedule. Moreover, today electronics are capable to address complex equipment such as, SSTs in a more cost-effective way, thus allowing SST to become a standard equipment, which improves the microgrids functionality, surpassing the classic transformer through functionalities, which are not possible with traditional solutions, such as flexible coupling between the medium and the low voltage networks, possibility to enable an additional DC grid by design and other advantages to be developed in next section.

The main contributions of this work are summarized below:

1. Proposing a new architecture for interconnections between the main grid and the LV distribution grids by eliminating the need for synchronicity and by obtaining microgrids by design (always operating in island mode versus the main grid, which only injects a constant power in the SST DC busbar); it is shown that the architecture brings resilience and immunity by design in the microgrid;
2. Proposing suitable test cases for the evaluation of the proposed architecture in terms of microgrid stability, in a situation with power electronics-only energy injection and no classical mechanical inertia (no rotating machines to stabilize the grid); the test cases are also showing that the microgrid has resilience and immunity, which is supported by the proposed design;
3. Showing with the selected test cases that in microgrids with power electronics only generation, the microgrid stability is based on electrostatic energy in the capacitors behind the inverters. Thus, a different stability principle applies compared with the classical main grid mechanical-inertia dependent principle. This is the most important contribution, as in most of the studies one tries to keep an acceptable mechanical or mechanical-simulated inertia within the grid, in order to keep the frequency around the nominal value;
4. Summarizing the possible multiple roles of SSTs to ensure resilience, sustainability, adaptability and expandability of the architecture in a smart grid vision with SST separated LV microgrids.

The rest of this paper is organized as follows. In Section 2, the description of the new architectures based on SST enabled microgrids are presented. Section 3, describes the test-cases used for simulations, while Section 4 details the simulations, interpret and discusses the results, while the conclusive remarks are given in Section 5.

2. New Architectures Based on SST Connected Microgrids

Solid State Transformers (SSTs) or smart transformers are key technological enablers for several types of applications, such as traction systems, distribution electricity networks, including microgrids, storage deployment etc.). They have attracted significant attention during the last two decades, especially due to needs related to the smooth integration of RES into the main power grid [34]. SSTs are devices that use power electronics to ensure power flow from a voltage level (focus on MV) to another voltage level (focus on low voltage) by using high frequency transformer (HFT) coupling (e.g., 5 kHz to 50 kHz) instead of standard industrial frequency (50 or 60 Hz). Several topologies can be considered, going from single stage to multi stage or considering, or not, the existence of an intermediate DC bus. Being potentially highly modular, SST can be described using Power Electronics Building Blocks (PEBBs) as described in Reference [34].

The idea of using SSTs as an interface between the MV grid and a microgrid based on local RES generation is not new [35]. In Reference [36], one of the promoted features of this architecture was related to control capabilities of the power flow exchange. However, the stability of the microgrid under these architectures was not investigated.

The most feasible SST topology is the three-stage configuration, where both MV and LV DC-links available [37]. An adaptation of this type of architecture is presented in Figure 1.

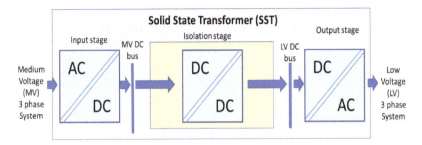

Figure 1. Solid state transformer design example.

Figure 1 shows that the HFT works between an MV DC bus and a LV DC bus, while the AC grid compatibility is solved with rectifiers (one direction, as shown in Figure 1, or bidirectional in general case, with the later not addressed in this paper) and three-phased inverters. The internal graphical representation of the three blocks is generic. The most feasible SST topology is the three-stage configuration, where both MV and LV DC-links available, and it can be implemented in different ways (e.g., the rectifier can be a more complex Vienna rectifier) and with different topologies (e.g., HFT can be mono or with three phases etc.). Even if the arrow demonstrating the power flow is monodirectional—which is a proposed situation which only allows the absorption of energy towards LV—as a friendly approach in the business as usual frame (the "sponge" model), a general design allows also bidirectional energy exchange. This particular SST architecture has, by nature, a MV DC bus and a LV DC bus. By adding suitable internal connection and protection devices and making available the DC buses, additional DC grids can be developed outside the SST, with minimal added complexity inside it. This architecture is presented in Figure 2.

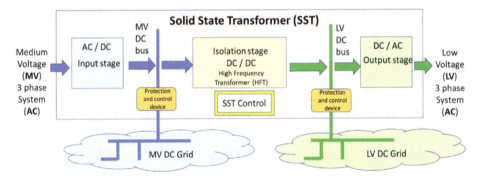

Figure 2. Solid State Transformers (SST) enabling DC grids (medium and low voltage).

Figure 2 shows that new DC grids can be deployed from an SST, starting from the internal DC buses (the one-way energy flow continues to be pursued, for keeping the business as usual consumption only power flow, for which the existing distribution grids have been designed). Thus, it provides the first steps in solving the "chicken-egg problem", by making available both, the AC and the DC, connections on each voltage level.

A third natural extension is the provision of storage means connected at one or at both DC buses, as it can be observed in Figure 3.

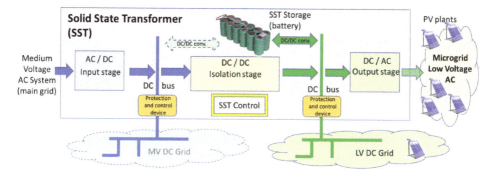

Figure 3. SST with a flexible connection through storage included by design. Example for unidirectional power flow.

Figure 3 depicts the potential to include storage connected at any of the two DC buses, however, as microgrids are essential for achieving resilience and large-scale integration of geographically distributed renewable energy sources, the first place for storage to be considered is at the LV side of the DC bus.

The architecture described in Figure 3 does not use the low voltage DC grid (but stays as an expandable feature). However, the microgrid can be supported by several features, which have been pointed before as challenges, such as:

- The balancing between the microgrid consumption and locally connected production (renewable, mainly PV) is now possible locally with the means of storage within the SST, acting as an equilibrium node of the whole microgrid;
- The SST LV AC connection module can operate as grid forming device, thus giving the frequency and the nominal voltage signals, while all other RES can act in the standard grid-following mode;
- Intense disturbances of the main grid cannot actually affect the microgrid, due to the SST AC/DC/AC interconnection. Further, intense variations, voltage sag events, low power quality in the main grid are smooth out by the SST and thus, the microgrid resilience and power quality can be enhanced (and it is decoupled from the resilience/quality of the main grid)
- The connection with the main grid (MV network) becomes buffered, which can be translated into flexible, predictable and even constant power flow, thus drastically reducing the uncertainty in system operation (which may remain only on special cases), and asking for less ancillary services while improving the stability in the main grid;
- The buffered energy in the SST (or associated with SST, as the battery can be physically outside SST, but logically integrated), allows setting different degrees of resilience and even immunity, as the microgrid may be able to supply energy to loads even in the case of main grid outages;
- Finally, the microgrid becomes an independent system by design, being able to operate as an island (a system by itself, with its own balancing means and not depending on the main grid synchronicity) or connected (through a back-to-back elastic connection).

An important aspect remains if SST could provide, besides being a microgrid former, the local grid stability during unbalance transients, which is now missing in the traditional interconnection, and which is provided by the main grid. Numerical simulations, presented in Section 4, show that grid stability, based on mechanical inertia transformed in needed energy by decreasing or increasing the rotation speed, thus the system frequency, is not anymore necessary in a fully inverter-based small system. In the next chapter it is demonstrated that transient generation-load unbalance is covered by the inertia coming from electrostatic energy in the SST capacitors, thus bridging the gap between disturbance and the automated balance implemented by means, such as voltage source control or droop control. It shows that the main grid type of inertia is not a concern for microgrids and that these can achieve a stable operation based on voltage recovery level, by combining both natural (immediate, based on physics laws, as it is the mechanical inertia working in large grids) and artificial means.

The scenarios developed in the following Sections emphasize the value of power balancing in the microgrid, addressing the system stability under unbalanced disturbances, and the ability of not propagating disturbances from the main grid towards the microgrid and vice-versa.

3. Numerical Simulation Scenarios

Within this section we define meaningful design and operation scenarios to show the main advantages for both the main (external) grid and the SST connected microgrid. Simulation cases based on these scenarios will be then tested and discussed in the next section.

For the implementation of the simulation cases several control systems were employed, namely for the inverter of the smart-transformer, for the DC/DC converter of the storage system and for the inverter of the PV system. The smart-transformer inverter is controlled by means of a sliding mode controller associated with a voltage vectorial modulator (Figure 4a). This controller was implemented with the purpose to control the voltages ($V_{cf\ 123}$) of the LC filter capacitors (grid voltage). For the battery system, a cascade control was used, as shown in Figure 4c. Since the battery is used to keep the direct voltage stable, a PI regulator associated with this voltage (V_{Co}) was used for the outer loop, whereas for the inner loop a hysteretic controller was used. The inverter of the PV system is also controlled by a cascaded system (Figure 4b). However, in this model, a voltage (PI type) controller was employed within the outer loop (to maintain the direct voltage of the inverter stable around its reference value), and a current controller (hysteretic type) was used in the inner loop (to inject three-phase currents in phase with the grid voltages).

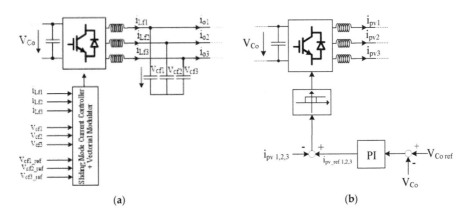

Figure 4. *Cont.*

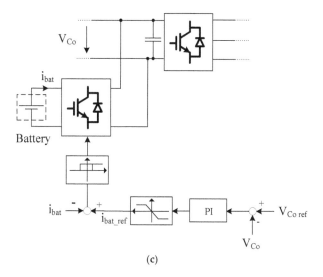

(c)

Figure 4. Control systems for (**a**) inverter of the smart-transformer; (**b**) inverter of the PV system; (**c**) DC/DC converter of the storage system.

As the DSOs and the TSO need planning and predictable operation when connecting prosumers and microgrids, there are needs for new models and operation features when promoting MG architectures. To help mitigating this situation, model considerations and desired operation features of the promoted microgrid (MG) architectures are summarized below:

- The profile of the power absorbed by the microgrid from the main grid shall be either set and known in advance (contractually bind) or schedulable. Therefore, in the proposed scenarios, we assume a constant power injection from the DSO towards the microgrid (P_{grid} = constant).
- Microgrid operation is set to "island operation mode". In other words, as long as the grid provides only scheduled power/energy, the real-time balancing of the MG is performed internally. Thus, the real-time power control remains essential and can to be done by means of one or more of the following resources:

    ○ storage units (e.g., battery) injects/absorbs power through the DC bus of the SST depending on the balancing needs of the SST (ΔP);

    ○ LV inverter of the SST acts as *grid former*, which means that it provides the frequency signal and sets the operation point for the battery;

    ○ in order to allow powers balancing, co-participation of PVs in the microgrid, in addition to its power modulation, the grid former can alter the frequency in a band centered on the nominal value (50 Hz) to allow primary control, in response to what the PVs can provide in real-time; note that all PVs operate in droop control mode. Therefore, frequency is only an information signal to show that a balancing reaction from the grid followers is needed (not anymore a physical consequence of unbalance, as it is in the main systems driven by large rotating machines), information that is easy to be spread over the whole microgrid through the same wires used for transmitting power.

The basic configuration of the SST, interfacing asynchronously (with back-to-back interconnection) the microgrid with the bulk power system, is presented in Figure 5.

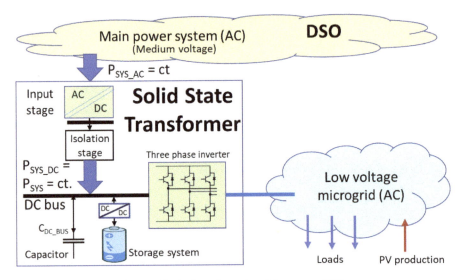

Figure 5. The basic configuration of the proposed SST.

Two use-case scenarios are defined based on the above-mentioned assumptions.

Use case 1. *A power unbalance occurs inside the microgrid, caused by the variation of local generation (PVs) and/or by the microgrid load. The balancing is provided by the SST through the battery and the capacitor connected to the SST LV busbar, while the set point of the power exchanged between the microgrid and the DSO remains unchanged.*

Use case 2. *A disturbance is assumed to occur on the DSO side, which affects the power exchanged between DSO and MG. The internal balancing mechanism of the MG provides the necessary balancing by using the same mechanisms, i.e., battery/storage plus distributed droop control. This case is assumed in our simulations as a sudden decrease in the power provided by the grid (DSO), i.e., 10 kW or ~25% of the requested/scheduled power, or even complete loss of power due to a DSO grid short interruption or due to a blackout. Such a short interruption is considered in use case 2.*

Figure 6 shows the sequence of events simulated to test the propose the microgrid interconnection solution in both use-cases.

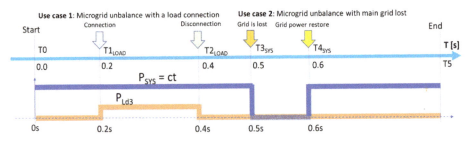

Figure 6. The simulated sequence of events.

The unbalance simulated in the first use-case is performed by connecting then disconnecting a load (P_{Load}) at the time instants $T1_{LOAD}$ and $T2_{LOAD}$, whereas in the second use-case the DSO disturbance is simulated by disconnecting then reconnecting the link with the DSO grid at the time instants $T3_{GRID}$ and $T4_{GRID}$.

4. Simulations and Results

The purpose of this section is to show, by numerical simulations, the effectiveness of the SST-based microgrid interfacing proposed solution, as well as the win-win outcomes for both the microgrid actors and the DSO. A simple microgrid scheme, together with a SST/inverter configuration, was simulated in Matlab/Simulink (Figure 7). The main variables are also illustrated in the figure.

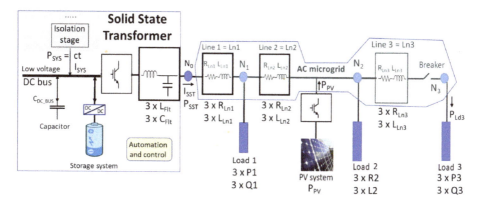

Figure 7. The one-line diagram of the SST interfaced microgrid.

The operation of the storage unit is coordinated through an SST that plays the role of an energy router both internally (within the MG infrastructure) and externally (between the DSO and the MG). The interplay between SST and the storage unit is intended to supply the necessary power/energy to compensate any type of perturbation coming from inside the MG or external (e.g., coming from perturbations/fault propagations taking place upstream of the DSO).

Due to the complexity of the studied network, accurate simplified models were considered for the AC main grid, as well as for rectifier and DC/DC High Frequency Transformer inside the SST. Those components were modelled through a controlled DC current source, controlled in power mode which is the way that the smart-transformer is normally controlled. The remaining components of the smart-transformer were simulated in a more detailed way. This will allow for the study the dynamic behavior of the smart-transformer when there are perturbations on the main grid side and how to react in order to maintain the secondary side stable (microgrid side).

The SST has been modeled by the following components:

- The SST DC bus and its associated capacitor;
- The DSO grid is modeled as a constant power source with P_{SYS} = 35 kW, except the time interval [0.5s, 0.6s] when the loss the connection of the MG with main power system is simulated. P_{SYS} is simulated as a power injection from the isolation stage of SST in the low voltage DC bus bar of SST, as per Figure 7;
- One storage system (it can be also seen as a virtual aggregation of several storage units) connected to the SST DC bus through a DC/DC converter. The storage system is represented by a standard battery (model provided by the Simulink library), connected to the DC/DC converter. For the DC/DC converter, the classical bidirectional Buck/Boost converter was used [38]. The battery is also used to control the inner DC bus voltage, for which a PI controller was used. The time-response of the PI controller is defined by its variables kp and ki. The parameters of the battery are 725 V and 60 Ah;
- An IGBT three-phase voltage source bridge inverter;
- An LC low-pass filter, with L_{Flt} = 5 mH (series) and C_{Flt} = 10 µF (parallel), is employed on the AC side of the inverter to filter out higher frequency harmonics produced by the inverter.

The storage system is emulated with its internal capacitance and the time-response variables of its corresponding control system.

The scenarios are defined focusing on the DC bus capacitor and the parameters of the storage system PI controller. They are the most representative components of the simulated model in order to emphasize the model dynamics. Therefore, two scenarios are identified:

(a) The capacitor on the SST DC bus is $C_{DC\_BUS} = 10$ mF, and the parameters of the proportional-integral (PI) controller associated with the storage system are $kp = 2$ and $ki = 10$, respectively (these are corresponding to a relatively fast response to disturbances).

(b) The capacitor connected to the SST DC bus is much lower ($C_{BAT} = 1$ mF), while the parameters of its PI controller are also slower ($kp = 0.5$ and $ki = 0.5$, respectively).

The microgrid components are:

- **Electrical lines:** Line 1 (Ln1) has $R_{Ln1} = 0.4\ \Omega$, $L_{Ln1} = 50\ \mu H$, Line 2 (Ln2) has $R_{Ln2} = 0.3\ \Omega$, $L_{Ln2} = 50\ \mu H$, Line 3 (Ln3) has $R_{Ln3} = 0.5\ \Omega$, $L_{Ln3} = 50\ \mu H$.
- **Loads:** Load 1 has $P_1 = 3 \times 2500$ W, $Q_1 = 3 \times 2000$ var at nominal voltage U = 230 V AC; Load 2 has $R_2 = 50\ \Omega$, $L_2 = 1$ mH on each phase; Load 3 has $P_3 = 3 \times 3000$ W, $Q_3 = 3 \times 2000$ var at nominal voltage U = 230 V AC.
- **PV generation unit:** It is connected in node 2, in parallel with load 2 and is generating a constant power of $3 \times 1500 = 4500$ W. Its characteristics have been extrapolated from a real PV system consisting of a set of Sunmodule Plus SW 300 mono PV panels [39] with a total power under STC conditions of 24.2 kW. The PV unit is connected to the microgrid via a classical three-phase inverter. This PV system was implemented in Matlab/Simulink trough the Simscape toolbox elements.

As presented above, the scenarios are defined with two different dimensioning and parameterizations in the SST (C_{DC_BUS} and controller parameters), in order to show their importance in maintaining the microgrid stability in the case of the most severe perturbations, i.e., power unbalance inside the microgrid (use-case 1) and loss or power supply from the main grid outage (short term or blackouts as use-case 2). Note that this work does not focus also on short-circuit type disturbances because they need a more detailed analysis of the microgrid architecture and protection solutions. The scenarios capture the capability of the microgrid to achieve immunity and resilience against system disturbances and blackouts.

Scenario 1: Use-cases 1 and 2 are tested with a favorable dynamic inside the SST, as both grid former and controller for the microgrid: A normal capacitor connected to the SST DC bus ($C_{DC\_BUS} = 10$ mF) and fast response of the SST DC bus controller ($kp = 2$ and $ki = 10$ for the PI controller).

The following sequence of events for the two use-cases is considered: (i) at time instant t = 0.2 s, Load3 ($3 \times (3$ kW $+ j\ 2$ kvar)) is connected; then, at time instant t = 0.4 s, Load3 is disconnected; (ii) at time instant t = 0.5 s the power supply from the main grid is lost ($P_{SYS} = 0$,), then at time instant t = 0.6 s the grid supply is restored to the scheduled value ($P_{SYS} = 35$ kW). The results of this simulation are presented in Figure 8a–d.

As mentioned before, the power supplied by the main grid is maintained constant, and equal to a scheduled value. After the first perturbation ($T1_{LOAD} = 0.2$ s), the power required by the loads is higher (a new load is connected, *Load3*). When the second perturbation occurs ($T3_{GRID} = 0.5$ s), the power supplied by the grid is completely lost (unscheduled perturbation at the grid side, see Figure 7b). In both cases the battery will provide all the needed energy (instant power) required by the microgrid, with minimum or no intervention in load reduction.

Analyzing the AC currents injected by the SST (see Figure 8c), we can see that there is only a slight change in the amplitude of the load currents, which shows that in the case of a grid outage, the microgrid is capable of maintaining its normal operation and to ensure the power balancing without any need for load shedding (the current amplitude remains almost unchanged because the battery provides the required support).

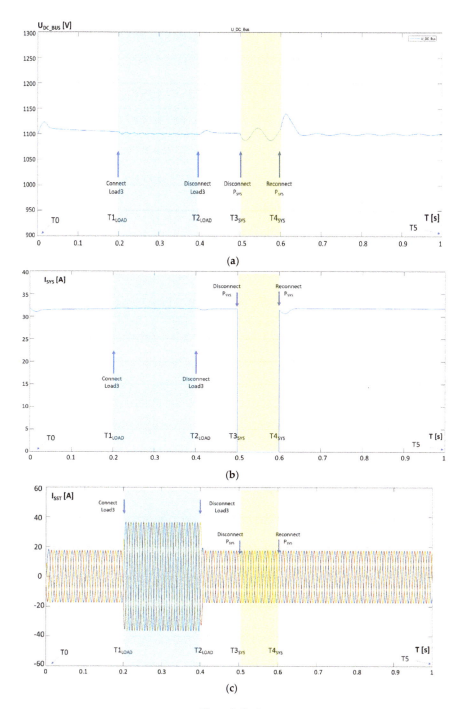

Figure 8. *Cont.*

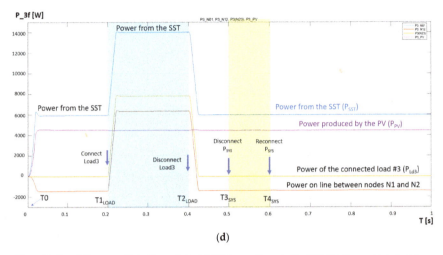

(d)

Figure 8. Simulations results in Scenario 1. (**a**) DC bus voltage in the SST; (**b**) Current injected from the main grid in the DC bus of the SST; (**c**) The output currents of the SST (ISST), injected into the microgrid; (**d**) Active power evolution in different parts of the AC microgrid.

Figure 8d illustrates the power flows in different sections of the microgrid. It can be seen that between T3$_{GRID}$ = 0.5 s and T4$_{GRID}$ = 0.6 s there is no observable power flow difference, as SST is taking the role to cover the missing P$_{SYS}$ during this outage, showing immunity during the period when the main grid is lost.

Scenario 2: Use-cases 1 and 2 are tested with a smaller capacitance connected to the SST DC bus (C$_{DC\_BUS}$ = 1 mF) and fast response of the PI controller (*kp* = 0.5 and *ki* = 0.5, respectively).

This test case is similar to the previous one with the only exception that the capacitance of the storage unit is ten times smaller. The results are presented in Figure 9a–d.

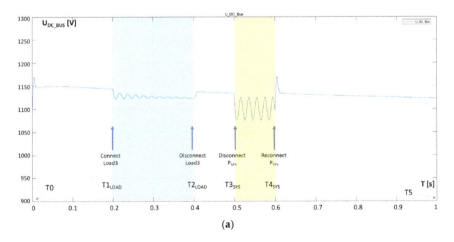

(a)

Figure 9. *Cont.*

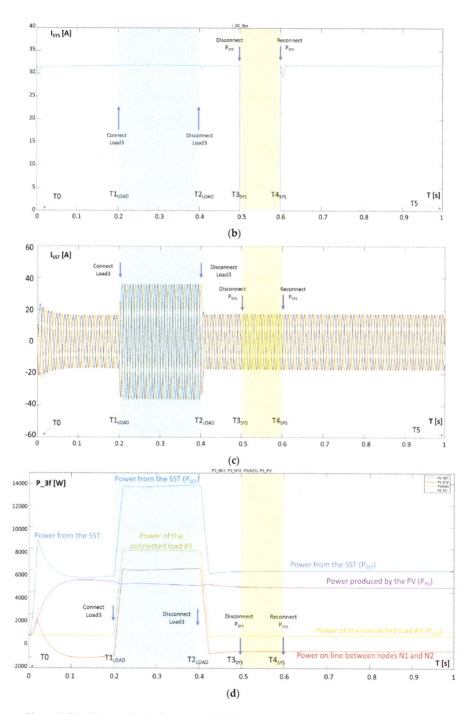

Figure 9. Simulation results in Scenario 2. (**a**) DC bus voltage in the SST; (**b**) Current injected from the main grid in the DC bus of the SST; (**c**) Output currents of the SST (ISST), towards the microgrid (real-time values); (**d**) Active power evolution in different parts of the AC microgrid.

As it can be noticed, the results of this use-case look pretty much the same as in the previous case. These simulations show also the high level of immunity inherited by the microgrid within the proposed solution. The microgrid achieves stable operation after transient disturbances. The difference from Scenario 1 consists is in the inertia of the system based on the energy in the SST capacitor, influencing the amplitude transients of DC voltage on the SST capacitor following the perturbations, which is higher (as expected, since the capacity of the capacitor is smaller). To emphasize the difference between the two scenarios, the voltage resulted on the DC bus of the SST is shown in Figure 10. The blue zone is the DC voltage variation resulted from the disturbance caused by *Load3*, whereas the yellow zone is the DC voltage variation resulted from *the loss of the main grid supply*.

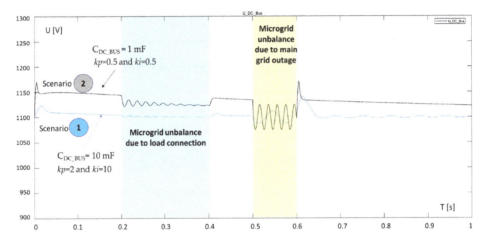

Figure 10. Superposition of the SST DC bus voltage variation in both scenarios (1 and 2).

In this figure it can be seen that in Scenario 1, besides the time delay due to storage response, there is also a time delay from the physical part of the power converter that is much faster than the one caused by the controller of the storage. In fact, when there is a sudden change in the reference the rate-of-change-of-current is limited by the inductor inside the storage device. Note that the power converter used for the simulations in this study consists of an inductor and two switches (the classical bidirectional buck-boost converter was used for operating the charging and discharging of the storage device). During that transition, the capacitor connected on the SST DC bus is the component that must support the disturbance, while keeping an acceptable voltage variation until the storage unit control becomes effective. However, since the energy that is stored in this capacitor connected to the SST DC bus is small, then the voltage in the DC bus decreases slightly, as shown in Figure 9 with the blue line voltage evolution.

In the case of Scenario 2, the perturbation at SST DC bus level is higher. Therefore, it is easier to see the limitation effect of the grows in the rate of current. When there is a sudden transition, the battery current does not follow the reference, since its rate of growth is limited by the inductor, which affects more the voltage level on the SST DC bus. However, for the studied use-cases, the microgrid operation remains stable, showing the SST, as microgrid former, keeps well the microgrid stability during the disturbances.

5. Conclusions

The paper proposes an analysis, from the point of view of stability, of microgrid operation in the case of grid-connection via SST, which can be seen as an essential enabler of microgrids-by-design. This solution allows by design, the accommodation of large quantities of distributed renewables production, the friendly connection to the main grid (predictability and no disturbance propagation in both directions), while enhancing the resilience or even reaching immunity for the end-users supplied by the respective microgrid.

The advantages have been analyzed with two test scenarios, each with two types of disturbances in the microgrid—one considering the sudden connection of a load, and another one introduced by the sudden loss of a constant power supplied from the main grid. The simulations were performed in Matlab/Simulink version R2017b. A simplified microgrid was assumed, with only three loads (two modelled as constant real power P and modelled as constant impedance Z) and one PV plant assumed to produce constant power (P_{PV} = ct.), all connected to a low voltage line, as depicted in Figure 7. The microgrid is connected to the bulk power system through an SST, consisting of the grid-connected inverter and the DC bus where the capacitor is connected, and the battery based storage system. The control of the SST output was also considered, namely through a cascaded controller in which the AC voltages (filter capacitors) and AC currents (inductor of the filter) are controlled. A controller for the PV system was also considered. In this case was again adopted a cascade structure, but what is controlled is the DC voltage of the inverter and their AC currents. The bulk power system is modeled as a power source that supplies a constant P to the DC bus-bar. Future work will consider more complex situations—requiring eventually for further elaboration of algorithms; however, the proof of concept has been demonstrated with the simplified grid. Moreover, future work will consider microgrid stabilization in wider time frames (minutes, hours or more), as being related to the battery and PV (microgrid local production) resources size in the microgrid.

The results of the numerical simulations consider a Decentralized Energy Supply System based on the SST connected microgrid which becomes immune and resilient towards power supply short failures and for blackouts. The simulation shows the level of resilience of the microgrid in this situation and the capacity to remain stable without mechanical inertia, but based on the electrostatic energy in capacitors behind the inverters, acting as system inertia to absorb the unbalance between loads and production. One important lesson is that the role of the mechanical inertia in the main grids is taken in the full inverter-based microgrid by the energy in the capacitors on the DC busbar behind the inverters, especially from the SST as grid former, and that the dimension of this capacitor needs to be chosen in order to cope with the disturbance level. In the studied microgrids, there is no frequency dependency for the grid stability, but only voltage control in the DC bus-bars of the injection points (SST and PVs injecting power in the microgrid used in our test cases), which allows to keep stability during the transients based on the released energy from the capacitors on the DC bus-bars behind the inverters. The two scenarios show that bigger capacitors give better stability of DC busbar voltage and of the microgrid, while smaller capacitors are still able to maintain stability against disturbances, even if the DC busbar voltage has a higher variation. We extend the simulation case studies: To address some variations regarding the PV generation, and also to examine how some disturbances for the grid side are observed in the microgrid side. In that way, we can claim that the main transient events that can occur in the daily operation of the microgrid have been adequately examined. These critical transient events are not a problem considering a wider time frame because in this case the stability of the system is only dependent on the battery and PV size.

Future work will expand the idea on the applicability and efficacy of shared resources for ad-hoc formed clusters of sub-microgrids connected physically or by cyber connection links. Moreover, more complex use-cases in terms of microgrid complexity and with more types of disturbances will be further analyzed, also by using new methods of enhancing its real-time balancing and stability.

Author Contributions: M.S. and J.F.M. are the main contributors of the paper, by understanding and refining the concepts and by demonstrating through simulations the stability of islanded microgrids with inverter-only energy sources connection, based on capacitors and storage means, with no need of frequency involvement. They are also main contributors for considering Solid State Transformers as essential devices in the microgrid-by-design architecture and for the resilience approach. I.C. contributed to the overall writing of the paper, on the simulations and analysis of results. M.A. contributed to the overall writing of the paper, with discussions on the subject and with the resilience approach. L.T. contributed to the overall writing of the paper, on the simulations and analysis of results. V.F.P. has contributed with the detailed simulation model based on real-time waves modeling, providing the essential tools for the analysis by simulation. L.H. contributed to the overall writing of the paper and with analysis against current microgrid approach. R.S. contributed to the overall writing, analysis and suggestions for improving the paper content. Conceptualization, M.S. and J.F.M.; Formal analysis, M.S., J.F.M., I.C., M.A., L.T. and L.H.; Investigation, M.S., I.C., M.A., V.F.P. and R.S.; Methodology, M.A.; Software, M.S., J.F.M., L.T. and V.F.P.; Validation, M.S., J.F.M., L.T. and V.F.P.; Writing—original draft, M.S.; Writing—review and editing, M.S., J.F.M., I.C., M.A., L.T., L.H. and R.S.

Funding: This work has been undertaken within the framework of the European Union's Horizon 2020 research and innovation programme under the Storage4Grid project grant agreement No. 731155 and RESERVE project grant agreement No. 727481, by Portugal national funds through FCT—Fundacão para a Ciência e a Tecnologia, under projects UID/CEC/50021/2013 and UID/EEA/00066/2013, by DCNextEve project grant agreement No. 708844 and by KIOS CoE project grant agreement No. 739551.

Acknowledgments: Authors gratefully thank also to Professor Nicolae Golovanov for the vision of having SST as important new devices in the network, to Prof Emeritus Mircea Eremia for valuable discussions regarding the viability of the simulated microgrid, and to Prof. Goran Andersson, for valuable discussions on the overall subject. Prof Golovanov and Eremia are from Politehnica University of Bucharest, Romania and Prof. Andersson is from ETH Zurich, Switzerland.

Conflicts of Interest: The authors declare no conflicts of interest.

References

1. Terzija, V.; Valverde, G.; Cai, D.; Regulski, P.; Madani, V.; Fitch, J.; Skok, S.; Begovic, M.M.; Phadke, A. Wide-Area Monitoring, Protection, and Control of Future Electric Power Networks. *Proc. IEEE* **2011**, *99*, 80–93. [CrossRef]
2. Faruque, M.A.A.; Vatanparvar, K. Energy Management-as-a-Service Over Fog Computing Platform. *IEEE Internet Things J.* **2016**, *3*, 161–169. [CrossRef]
3. Eremia, M.; Shahidehpour, M. (Eds.) *Handbook of Electrical Power System Dynamics: Modeling, Stability, and Control*; Power Engineering Series; Wiley & IEEE Press: New York, NY, USA, 2013.
4. Hatziargyriou, N. *MicroGrids*; Wiley-IEEE Press: New York, NY, USA, 2014; ISBN 1-118-72067-9.
5. El-Hawary, M.E. The Smart Grid—State-of-the-art and Future Trends. *Electr. Power Compon. Syst.* **2014**, *42*, 239–250. [CrossRef]
6. Hirsch, A.; Parag, Y.; Guerrero, J. Microgrids: A review of technologies, key drivers, and outstanding issues. *Renew. Sustain. Energy Rev.* **2018**, *90*, 402–411. [CrossRef]
7. European Climate Foundation. 2010. Available online: https://www.solarworld.de/en/home/ (accessed on 20 October 2018).
8. International Renewable Energy Agency (IRENA). *Renewable Energy Policies in a Time of Transition*; IRENA: Bonn, Germany, 2018.
9. Vandoorn, T.L.; Meersman, B.; Kooning, J.D.M.D.; Vandevelde, L. Directly-Coupled Synchronous Generators with Converter Behavior in Islanded Microgrids. *IEEE Trans. Power Syst.* **2012**, *27*, 1395–1406. [CrossRef]
10. Ciornei, I.; Heracleous, C.; Kyriakou, M.; Eliades, D.; Constantinou, C.K.; Kyriakides, E. Test System for Mapping Interdependencies of Critical Infrastructures for Intelligent Management in Smart Cities. In *Smart Cities in the Mediterranean*; Progress in IS; Springer: Cham, Switzerland, 2017; pp. 355–377. ISBN 978-3-319-54557-8.
11. Monti, A.; Huitema, G.; Sayed-Mouchawe, M.; Amezua, A.S.A. *Digitalization of the Electricity System and Customer Participation*; European Commission ETIP-SNET: Brussels, Belgium, 2018.
12. European Technology and Innovation Platform for Smart Networks in Energy Transition ETIP SNET Decarbonizing Europe by 2050: EU Energy Players Propose One Broad Ambitious Mission for Europe. 2018. Available online: https://www.solarworld.de/en/home/ (accessed on 20 October 2018).
13. Hailu, T.G.; Mackay, L.; Ramirez-Elizondo, L.M.; Ferreira, J.A. Voltage Weak DC Distribution Grids. *Electr. Power Compon. Syst.* **2017**, *45*, 1091–1105. [CrossRef]

14. Gavriluta, C.; Caire, R.; Gomez-Exposito, A.; Hadjsaid, N. A Distributed Approach for OPF-Based Secondary Control of MTDC Systems. *IEEE Trans. Smart Grid* **2016**. [CrossRef]
15. Mitsubishi Electric Corporation. *Mitsubishi Electric Launches D-Smiree System for Medium- and Low-Voltage DC Distribution*; Mitsubishi Electric Corporation: Tokyo, Japan, 2016.
16. Prötzsch, M. MVDC Plus. Available online: https://www.siemens.com/global/en/home/products/energy/medium-voltage/solutions/mvdc.html (accessed on 5 March 2018).
17. Hakala, T.; Lähdeaho, T.; Järventausta, P. Low-Voltage DC Distribution—Utilization Potential in a Large Distribution Network Company. *IEEE Trans. Power Deliv.* **2015**, *30*, 1694–1701. [CrossRef]
18. Lassila, J.; Kaipia, T.; Haakana, J.; Partanen, J.; Koivuranta, K. Potential and strategic role of power electronics in electricity distribution systems. In Proceedings of the CIRED 2009—The 20th International Conference and Exhibition on Electricity Distribution, Prague, Czech Republic, 8–11 June 2009; Part 2. p. 1.
19. She, X.; Burgos, R.; Wang, G.; Wang, F.; Huang, A.Q. Review of solid state transformer in the distribution system: From components to field application. In Proceedings of the 2012 IEEE Energy Conversion Congress and Exposition (ECCE), Raleigh, NC, USA, 15–20 September 2012; pp. 4077–4084.
20. Eremia, M.; Liu, C.-C.; Edris, A.-Y. (Eds.) *Advanced Solutions in Power Systems: HVDC, FACTS, and Artificial Intelligence*; Power Engineering Series; Wiley & IEEE Press: New York, NY, USA, 2016.
21. Hammons, T.J.; Lescale, V.F.; Uecker, K.; Haeusler, M.; Retzmann, D.; Staschus, K.; Lepy, S. State of the Art in Ultrahigh-Voltage Transmission. *Proc. IEEE* **2012**, *100*, 360–390. [CrossRef]
22. Spagnuolo, G.; Petrone, G.; Araujo, S.V.; Cecati, C.; Friis-Madsen, E.; Gubia, E.; Hissel, D.; Jasinski, M.; Knapp, W.; Liserre, M.; et al. Renewable Energy Operation and Conversion Schemes: A Summary of Discussions During the Seminar on Renewable Energy Systems. *IEEE Ind. Electron. Mag.* **2010**, *4*, 38–51. [CrossRef]
23. Kolar, J.W.; Huber, J.E. Solid-State Transformers—Key Design Challenges, Applicability, and Future Concepts. In *Conference Guide*; IEEE: New York, NY, USA, 2016; p. 26.
24. Abu-Siada, A.; Budiri, J.; Abdou, A.F. Solid State Transformers Topologies, Controllers, and Applications: State-of-the-Art Literature Review. *Electronics* **2018**, *7*, 298. [CrossRef]
25. Intelligent COMPONENTs for the Power Grid of the Future. Available online: https://phys.org/news/2018-04-intelligent-components-power-grid-future.html (accessed on 20 October 2018).
26. Smart Transformer for the Energy Turnaround. Available online: https://techxplore.com/news/2018-09-smart-energy-turnaround.html (accessed on 20 October 2018).
27. New Electric Car Charger Is More Efficient, 10 Times Smaller Than Current Tech. Available online: https://techxplore.com/news/2018-10-electric-car-charger-efficient-smaller.html (accessed on 21 October 2018).
28. Zacharia, L.; Hadjidemetriou, L.; Kyriakides, E. Integration of Renewables into the Wide Area Control Scheme for Damping Power Oscillations. *IEEE Trans. Power Syst.* **2018**, *33*, 5778–5786. [CrossRef]
29. Berckmans, G.; Messagie, M.; Smekens, J.; Omar, N.; Vanhaverbeke, L.; Van Mierlo, J.; Berckmans, G.; Messagie, M.; Smekens, J.; Omar, N.; et al. Cost Projection of State of the Art Lithium-Ion Batteries for Electric Vehicles Up to 2030. *Energies* **2017**, *10*, 1314. [CrossRef]
30. Ayre, J. Tesla Completes World's Largest Li-ion battery (129 MWh) in South Australia. 2017. Available online: https://cleantechnica.com/2017/11/23/tesla-completes-worlds-largest-li-ion-battery-129-mwh-energy-storage-facility-south-australia-notfree/ (accessed on 16 November 2018).
31. Colthorpe, A. Big Solar-Plus-Storage Project Will be One of Hawaii Utility's Lowest-Cost Power Sources. 2018. Available online: https://www.pv-tech.org/news/big-solar-plus-storage-project-will-be-one-of-hawaii-utilitys-lowest-c/ (accessed on 16 November 2018).
32. ENTSO-E. *Network Code on Requirements for Grid Connection Applicable to all Generators*; ENTSO-E: Brussels, Belgium, 2016.
33. Zacharia, L.; Kyriakou, A.; Hadjidemetriou, L.; Kyriakides, E.; Azzopardi, C.P.B.; Martensen, N.; Borg, N. Islanding and Resynchronization Procedure of a University Campus Microgrid. In Proceedings of the 2018 International Conference on Smart Energy Systems and Technologies (SEST), Sevilla, Spain, 10–12 September 2018; pp. 1–6.
34. Huber, J.E.; Kolar, J.W. Solid-State Transformers: On the Origins and Evolution of Key Concepts. *IEEE Ind. Electron. Mag.* **2016**, *10*, 19–28. [CrossRef]

35. Roasto, I.; Romero-Cadaval, E.; Martins, J.; Smolenski, R. State of the art of active power electronic transformers for smart grids. In Proceedings of the IECON 2012—38th Annual Conference on IEEE Industrial Electronics Society, Montreal, QC, Canada, 25–28 October 2012; pp. 5241–5246.
36. Huang, A.Q.; Crow, M.L.; Heydt, G.T.; Zheng, J.P.; Dale, S.J. The Future Renewable Electric Energy Delivery and Management (FREEDM) System: The Energy Internet. *Proc. IEEE* **2011**, *99*, 133–148. [CrossRef]
37. Rodriguez, J.R.; Dixon, J.W.; Espinoza, J.R.; Pontt, J.; Lezana, P. PWM regenerative rectifiers: State of the art. *IEEE Trans. Ind. Electron.* **2005**, *52*, 5–22. [CrossRef]
38. Fernão Pires, V.; Romero-Cadaval, E.; Vinnikov, D.; Roasto, I.; Martins, J.F. Power converter interfaces for electrochemical energy storage systems—A review. *Energy Convers. Manag.* **2014**, *86*, 453–475. [CrossRef]
39. SolarWorld Sunmodule Plus SW 300 mono. Available online: https://www.solarworld.de/en/home/ (accessed on 12 November 2018).

© 2018 by the authors. Licensee MDPI, Basel, Switzerland. This article is an open access article distributed under the terms and conditions of the Creative Commons Attribution (CC BY) license (http://creativecommons.org/licenses/by/4.0/).

Article

Global Transportation Demand Development with Impacts on the Energy Demand and Greenhouse Gas Emissions in a Climate-Constrained World

Siavash Khalili *, Eetu Rantanen, Dmitrii Bogdanov and Christian Breyer *

School of Energy Systems, LUT University, Yliopistonkatu 34, 53850 Lappeenranta, Finland;
eetu.rantanen@lut.fi (E.R.); dmitrii.bogdanov@lut.fi (D.B.)
* Correspondence: siavash.khalili.maybodi@lut.fi (S.K.); christian.breyer@lut.fi (C.B.);
  Tel.: +358-41-750-4243 (S.K.)

Received: 1 September 2019; Accepted: 10 October 2019; Published: 12 October 2019

Abstract: The pivotal target of the Paris Agreement is to keep temperature rise well below 2 °C above the pre-industrial level and pursue efforts to limit temperature rise to 1.5 °C. To meet this target, all energy-consuming sectors, including the transport sector, need to be restructured. The transport sector accounted for 19% of the global final energy demand in 2015, of which the vast majority was supplied by fossil fuels (around 31,080 TWh). Fossil-fuel consumption leads to greenhouse gas emissions, which accounted for about 8260 MtCO$_{2eq}$ from the transport sector in 2015. This paper examines the transportation demand that can be expected and how alternative transportation technologies along with new sustainable energy sources can impact the energy demand and emissions trend in the transport sector until 2050. Battery-electric vehicles and fuel-cell electric vehicles are the two most promising technologies for the future on roads. Electric ships and airplanes for shorter distances and hydrogen-based synthetic fuels for longer distances may appear around 2030 onwards to reduce the emissions from the marine and aviation transport modes. The rail mode will remain the least energy-demanding, compared to other transport modes. An ambitious scenario for achieving zero greenhouse gas emissions by 2050 is applied, also demonstrating the very high relevance of direct and indirect electrification of the transport sector. Fossil-fuel demand can be reduced to zero by 2050; however, the electricity demand is projected to rise from 125 TWh$_{el}$ in 2015 to about 51,610 TWh$_{el}$ in 2050, substantially driven by indirect electricity demand for the production of synthetic fuels. While the transportation demand roughly triples from 2015 to 2050, substantial efficiency gains enable an almost stable final energy demand for the transport sector, as a consequence of broad electrification. The overall well-to-wheel efficiency in the transport sector increases from 26% in 2015 to 39% in 2050, resulting in a respective reduction of overall losses from primary energy to mechanical energy in vehicles. Power-to-fuels needed mainly for marine and aviation transport is not a significant burden for overall transport sector efficiency. The primary energy base of the transport sector switches in the next decades from fossil resources to renewable electricity, driven by higher efficiency and sustainability.

Keywords: transport sector; transportation demand; final energy demand; road; rail; marine; aviation; levelized cost of mobility; greenhouse gas emissions; electrification

---

1. Introduction

Besides power and heat generation and industrial activities, transport is one of the major energy-demanding sectors. In 2015, the global transport sector consumed approximately 31,310 TWh of final energy [1] and represented around 14% of global greenhouse gas (GHG) emissions. To meet the goals of the Paris Agreement [2], this value must be shrunk to zero by mid of the 21st century across all energy sectors. Fossil oil plays an integral role in all means of transport including road, rail, marine, and aviation with roughly 28,840 TWh final energy consumption in 2015 [1]. Over 92% of the energy for transport is provided by oil, 3% by natural gas (NG), 1% by electricity, and other fuels contribute 4%. These values encompass all transport modes, passengers and freights [1]. Some major suppliers of fossil fuels for the transport sector expect no major changes of fossil-fuel demand in the decades to come [3], despite the fact that fossil-fuel use is the main reason for anthropogenic climate change and hazardous air pollution.

Transport demand is rapidly increasing and, with such high dependence on fossil fuels, there would be serious consequences for human health and energy security-related issues [4] as long as this trend continues. Nonetheless, a couple of vital changes towards mobility are anticipated. These changes will be alternative fuel penetration, e.g., electricity, hydrogen, and renewable fuels such as synthetic fuels, but also biofuels to lessen conventional fuel usage [5]. Technological efficiency and demand-side solutions are additional changes that are expected for the transport sector [6]. Electricity can be used in direct form in all transport modes, though, with distinct emergence in each mode: in road and rail modes to a greater extent, and in marine and aviation to a lesser extent. Direct electricity-based transportation is one of the most promising technologies with high reliability, safety, and efficiency for mobility. Baronti et al. [7] identified the main drawbacks for direct electricity-based road transportation as charging infrastructure immaturity and range limit. Hydrogen as fuel for the transport sector can be produced from electricity or fossil fuels and does not produce GHG emissions directly by usage. Hydrogen as an energy carrier can be based on renewable electricity via water electrolysis, but at present it is mainly based on NG and converted via steam methane reforming (SMR), which does not make it automatically a sustainable fuel [8]. Hydrogen will exist in all transport segments due to its flexible usage via fuel cells. Biofuels such as bioethanol, biomethanol, and biodiesel produced from biomass sources can directly substitute current fossil-fuel demand. Electricity and hydrogen are emerging sources of energy for transportation, representing 2% of the final energy supply in the transport sector in 2015.

The road mode is one of the most attractive transport segments to be electrified. Battery-electric vehicles (BEV), hybrid electric vehicles (HEV), and plug-in hybrid electric vehicles (PHEV) have shown high growth rates in recent times [9]. It is expected that these vehicle types will encounter substantial growth in upcoming decades [10,11]. The internal combustion engine (ICE) is the dominating power train as of today, but the limited efficiency of around 30% [12] reduces the competitiveness of this type drastically, in addition to the rising concerns about air pollution [9,13,14]. HEV has almost the same complexity as ICE with an electric motor/generator and a battery to improve the efficiency of the system. This hybridization makes it feasible to benefit from regenerative braking to generate electricity and charge the battery, which improves the efficiency to some extent. In this research, there is no focus on HEV, though PHEV is regarded. PHEV has the same features as a HEV, but the battery is generally larger and can be charged from the power grid for a range of typically up to 50–80 km [15]. Therefore, it would be possible to use PHEV daily mainly on an electricity basis for reducing the overall fuel cost, and hence improving fuel economy. PHEVs are not zero-emission vehicles, since fossil fuel is still used, but it has been observed that about 70% of all driven kilometers could be electric and only 30% are typically based on fossil fuels [16,17], which can drastically reduce GHG emissions, in particular if fossil-fuel-free electricity is used. BEVs are vehicles type that rely solely on electric propulsion and consist of comparable components to PHEV, though without the ICE and higher battery capacity, and it could use a more powerful electric engine. Most BEVs currently offered to the market have a range of 100–250 km on a single charge [18,19] with the highest range up to 550 km [20]. Charging time is a peculiar drawback for BEV, depending on charger configuration, its infrastructure, and operating power levels [21,22]. Similar to BEVs, a fuel-cell electric vehicle (FCEV) uses an electric drive train, wherein the vehicle is powered by a fuel cell, typically using hydrogen to generate electricity that flows to the power module (electric motor) to turn the wheels. Therefore, both BEVs and FCEVs operate by electricity running the vehicle, though battery for BEVs and hydrogen for FCEVs are the supply sources. FCEVs can be refueled in roughly 5 min for a 480 km range [23]. On the contrary, lack of refueling infrastructure and impossibility for FCEVs to be charged at most residential homes is a key demerit [24–26]. Efficiency and cost remain controversial for the future of BEVs and FCEVs to determine which technology exceeds the other, but indications can be found, which favor BEVs [27–30].

The rail mode is less environmentally critical, more energy efficient, and may enable a faster transportation compared with other transport modes. These virtues also pose economic attractiveness and contribute to societal benefits. Electric trains have a higher final energy efficiency than conventional ICE trains. To achieve a higher overall efficiency for the rail mode, the share of electrical rail transportation should be increased, as has been already achieved or targeted in many countries [31–33]. Renewable electricity leads to an even higher level of sustainability in also increasing the primary energy efficiency and reducing respective indirect GHG emissions. Currently, the shares of rail passenger and freight based on liquid-fuel operation are 55% and 61%, respectively, in global averages [34]; the rest is electricity. It is expected to change to higher electricity supply shares in the decades to come [31–33]. In 2018, the first commercial fleet of hydrogen-based trains started their operations [35]; however, in this study, hydrogen-based trains are not considered.

Marine transportation is a central element for global freight distribution. The compelling reasons are, first, higher capability to carry bulk goods over long distances. Second, merchandise shipping is the most energy-effective approach to transport goods and thus an economically beneficial transport mode. Marine represents about 2.6% of the global GHG emissions. Almost all ships in operation for passenger and freight transportation are based on liquid fuels. However, hydrogen is expected to play a key role in the future of shipping, with LNG and electricity to a lesser extent. Hydrogen-based ships may compete with other alternatively powered ships [36–39]. Hydrogen-powered ships can play a significant role in reducing shipping emissions [40]. Full electric ships will become an attractive solution for marine transportation with shorter distances to decrease the energy consumption [41–43]. The other considerable benefit of electric propulsion ships, similar to other electric transport modes, is to minimize GHG emissions and further reduce cost [44,45]. However, the important question that remains is to what extent ships and ferries can be fully electrified.

Airplanes are operated solely by liquid fuels at present, while it is expected that this solitary propulsion system will be complemented by electricity and hydrogen in the upcoming decades to meet the emissions reduction goal [46,47]. The aviation industry is responsible for 12% of transport-related GHG emissions and 2–3% of the entire anthropogenic GHG emissions [48]. GHG emissions can be reduced by either defossilizing the used jet fuel [49], or by using alternative fuels without GHG emissions [50]. Hydrogen, used in compressed or liquid form, may be a solution to achieve the emissions reduction target in the aviation industry. Liquid hydrogen (LH_2)-fueled airplanes weigh less than conventional kerosene-fueled planes due to the higher gravimetric energy density of LH_2, which leads to a better energy efficiency as pointed out by Kadyk et al. [48]. Electric aviation is another option to increase efficiency and reduce emissions [51–53]. Hepperle [54] calculates the total energy efficiency of battery-electric planes to be 73%, substantially more than hydrogen-based fuel-cell planes with 44% and conventional kerosene-fueled turboprop planes with 39%. This excellent efficiency merit would offset the propulsion system, the increased airplane mass due to batteries, and to some extent aerodynamic features.

Power-to-gas (PtG) and even more so power-to-liquids (PtL) are expected to play a significant role in the transport sector. PtL and PtG solely take electricity from renewable energy sources and convert electricity to liquid or gaseous fuels [55]. Synthetic fuels such as Fischer-Tropsch-based fuels, methanol (CH_3OH), dimethyl ether (DME), methane (CH_4), and other hydrocarbons can substitute fossil fuels. These are zero-emission fuels, since no fossil fraction is included, and they are used in the transport sector [56].

The core aim of this study is to present a detailed framework for a 100% renewable transition scenario for the global transport sector in high technological and regional resolution. This will comprise all used inputs, assumptions, parameters, and respective references. The used methods will allow applicability to comparable research questions. It is not intended to compare several scenarios within this framework, but to present a stringent scenario which fulfills the aims of the Paris Agreement in the highest possible sustainability, reflecting the ambitious requirements for a 1.5 °C scenario, also respecting sustainability guardrails [57].

The paper is organized as follows: Methods and Data (Section 2) outline the methods for transportation demand, assumed technology shares with respective consequences on specific energy demand, and specific GHG emissions. This is followed by the Results (Section 3) for transportation demand, energy demand, GHG emissions, and cost considerations, which are discussed in Section 4 and concluded in Section 5.

2. Methods and Data

The methodology is divided into 7 subsections: First, transportation activity and respective demand is investigated for all transport modes. Second, specific energy demand, also known as energy intensity or efficiency, for all modes with different technologies is defined. Third, the fuel-share options are linked to the transport modes. Fourth, economic considerations for the road mode are presented. Fifth, calculations of final energy consumption for all transport modes are defined. Sixth, GHG emissions are linked to the transport segments. Seventh, well-to-wheel efficiency and insights on efficiency drivers for the transport sector are considered.

2.1. Transportation Demand Data

The four transport modes—road, rail, marine, and aviation—are considered for the total transportation demand. The transportation demand is driven by activities for passenger and freight per mode. The transportation activity is measured in passenger kilometers (p-km), which is the movement of passengers for the kilometers of a journey, and in (metric) ton kilometers (t-km), which is the movement of freight for the kilometers carried. Therefore, the transportation activities need to be investigated for the four modes and each for passenger and freight.

2.1.1. The Role of Gross Domestic Product (GDP) and Population in Transportation Demand Projections

It is projected that transport activities benefit from prosperous economic development in the decades to come, which may lead to an average increase in global transportation activity of around 2.7% and 2.3% per annum for passengers and freight, respectively. The driving forces for the demand development in transportation are, according to Ribeiro et al. [58] and Royal Automobile Club Foundation [59] industrialization, globalization, and urbanization. The two dominating factors, which affect the growth in transportation activities are economic activity and population development. Economic activity is measured as gross domestic product (GDP), often referred to as GDP per capita (GDP_{cap}) to indicate the specific economic activity per population for a country [60]. The development of population is used to project the transportation demand for a country or region. The transportation supply side consists of complete operations performed to provide transportation services, while the demand side includes final demand and intermediate demand that act with the aim of satisfying the transportation needs. The transport sector contributes to the GDP via provided services. The demand side has direct effects on GDP through reverse linkages to all supply sides of the economy and GDP generation [60]. The demand side of transportation is the scope of this research. Transportation activities and their future growth mostly depend on the growth of GDP per capita and population [61]. In this study, population and GDP numbers are mainly used to disaggregate regional transportation demand to a country level. The population growth is based on United Nations' Medium scenario [62] and GDP/capita development is taken from Toktarova et al. [63] reflecting the central United Nations target of equal standards of living, to be achieved in the year 2100, which leads to further very strong GDP/capita increase in the second half of the 21st century, which is beyond the period analyzed in this paper. Strong GDP/capita demand increase stabilizes population as documented in developed countries all around the world [62], which is reflected in the assumed major trends for GDP/capita and population in this manuscript.

2.1.2. Road and Rail Transportation Activity

The International Council on Clean Transportation (ICCT) roadmap data [64] is used to investigate transportation demand in road and rail segments from 2000 to 2050 for passenger and freight. Transportation activities in ICCT data are provided for several countries, such as United States, Canada, China, India, Russia and some others, and the rest for regions such as Africa, Middle East, 27 European countries, Asia-Pacific 40, Non-European countries, and Latin America. For the road mode, transportation demand per country and region is split into the passenger segments, including light duty vehicles (LDV), buses (BUS) and two and three wheelers (2W/3W) and into the freight segments, which includes light heavy-duty trucks (LHDT), medium heavy-duty trucks (MHDT) and heavy heavy-duty trucks (HHDT). For this research LHDT and MHDT are merged into medium duty vehicles (MDV) and HHDT is renamed to heavy-duty vehicles (HDV). Transportation road activity for passenger and freight is summarized in Table 1. Rail transportation activity is provided for passenger and freight in the ICCT roadmap [64].

Table 1. Global aggregation of LDV, 2W/3W, BUS, MDV and HDV for all given countries and regions for 2015 to 2050 [64].

Vehicle	Unit	2015	2020	2025	2030	2035	2040	2045	2050
LDV	b p-km	23,137	27,482	31,438	36,145	41,356	47,458	54,535	62,942
2W/3W	b p-km	4370	5606	6634	7750	8780	10,164	12,067	15,232
BUS	b p-km	18,619	21,653	24,235	27,240	30,440	34,295	38,684	42,498
MDV	b t-km	2919	3433	3894	4438	5065	5835	6694	7617
HDV	b t-km	9787	11,398	12,889	14,628	16,601	19,021	21,691	24,539

For all countries being part of one of the aforementioned regions, a disaggregation method is required. As a best proxy, the GDP has been chosen, reflecting the correlation between GDP_{cap} and population with transportation activity. Equation (1) represents the method used to disaggregate the passenger and ton kilometers from a particular country j and a segment k out of its region.

$$(p\text{-}km)_{i,k} = \frac{(GDP_i\ cap \cdot P_i)}{(GDP_j\ cap \cdot P_j)} \cdot (p\text{-}km)_{j,k} (t\text{-}km)_{i,k} = \frac{(GDP_i\ cap \cdot P_i)}{(GDP_j\ cap \cdot P_j)} \cdot (t\text{-}km)_{j,k} \quad (1)$$

wherein, $(p\text{-}km)_{i,k}$ is road passenger transportation activity for country i and segment k, $GDP_i\ cap$ and P_i is the GDP_{cap} and population of country i, the subscript j represents the respective region. $(t\text{-}km)_{i,k}$ is road freight transportation activity for country i and segment k. $GDP_i\ cap$, P_i and $GDP_j\ cap$, P_j are the same values as for passenger transport.

Detailed numbers for all countries can be found in the Supplementary Material (spreadsheet).

Transportation activity values for the road mode can also be categorized in road passenger (sum of LDV, 2W/3W and BUS) and road freight (sum of MDV and HDV). Table 2 summarizes transportation activities for road passenger and freight, as well as rail passenger and freight. Detailed numbers for all countries can be found in the Supplementary Material (Table S1).

Table 2. Global transportation activity for road and rail modes separated for passenger and freight for 2015 to 2050 [64].

Transport Modes	Unit	2015	2020	2025	2030	2035	2040	2045	2050
Road Passenger	b p-km	46,104	54,713	62,247	71,100	80,546	91,899	105,297	120,739
Road Freight	b t-km	12,708	14,832	16,783	19,066	21,665	24,856	28,385	32,156
Rail Passenger	b p-km	3821	4573	5171	5792	6280	6854	7504	8193
Rail Freight	b t-km	11,141	12,302	13,333	14,520	15,898	17,591	19,566	21,857

2.1.3. Marine Transportation Activity

The third International Marine Organization (IMO) greenhouse gas study 2014 [65] is used as the main data source. IMO provides data extracted from the United Nation Conference on Traded and Development (UNCTAD) that produces global data on seaborne transport of freight from 1970 to 2012 in billion ton-miles. This data includes the following freight kinds: crude oil, other oil, iron ore, coal, grain, bauxite, and alumina, phosphate, and other dry cargoes. This classification can be categorized into total oil, coal, total (non-coal) bulk dry goods and total dry goods. It was extracted that total bulk dry goods in form of non-coal bulk cargo is 9400 billion ton-miles (t-mi), other dry cargoes in form of unitized cargo is 14,500 billion t-mi, total oil transported in the form of liquid bulk is 12,100 billion t-mi and coal transported in the form of bulk coal is 5000 t-mi. In total 41,000 t-mi for 2012 is regarded as the global goods shipped via seawater. To analyze the growth trend for the obtained value by 2050, scenario projections by IMO are used. For non-coal bulk cargo and unitized cargo the SSP5 scenario and for liquid bulk and bulk coal the RCP2.6 scenario are used. This is to reflect a growing global economy, which intends to reduce the dependence on fossil fuels, still taking into account that fuels must be transported, such as synthetic fuels in later periods [66–68]. The methods of SSP and RCP, explained in detail in the 5th Assessment Report of the IPCC [69], are not further used in this study, but the respective framework matches the requirements of this study. From 2012 to 2050, linear approximation is applied for bulk goods, oil transported, and coal freight, and exponential growth for other dry cargoes is assumed. The sum of the four major cargo categories is projected to a marine transportation activity of 149,500 billion t-mi for 2050, which translates to about 276,880 billion t-km. For the statistics on marine passenger activity, the European Commission data is used [70], which provides data for marine passenger and freight for the EU 27, the United States, Japan, China, and Russia. The passenger and ton kilometers for all given data are transformed into energy units. This has been done by using specific energy demand values that are introduced later. This delivers the share of energy demand for marine passenger and marine freight, for the listed countries. The share of marine freight of marine energy demand is found to be 96.8%, thus 3.2% of marine energy demand is to be allocated for marine passenger. This average factor has been used to estimate marine passenger energy demand based on better accessible data on marine freight on a country wise basis, according to Equation (2).

$$E_{p,i} = E_{f,i} \cdot \frac{0.032}{1 - 0.032} \tag{2}$$

wherein, E_p is the energy consumption of each country i for marine passenger and E_f is the energy consumption of marine freight of the same country i, based on the accessible data for 2012. The energy consumption data is re-converted to data for marine passenger activity. Finally, for each country the marine passenger demand is developed until 2050 by Equation (3).

$$(p\text{-}km)_{i,t+1} = \frac{(GDP_{i,t+1} - GDP_{i,t})}{(GDP_{j,t+1} - GDP_{j,t})} \cdot (p\text{-}km)_{i,t} \tag{3}$$

wherein, $(p\text{-}km)_{i,t+1}$ represents the marine passenger demand for a country i for the following time steps, which is typically an interval of 5 years in this research, $(GDP_{i,t+1} - GDP_{i,t})$ is the difference of the GDP of a country i for the respective time steps, whereas $(GDP_{j,t+1} - GDP_{j,t})$ is the difference of the GDP of a region j to which the country belongs. Landlocked countries are excluded in the calculation. Table 3 summarizes the global marine transportation activity for passenger and freight for the period 2015 to 2050. Detailed numbers for all countries can be found in the Supplementary Material (Table S1).

Table 3. Global transportation activity for marine passenger and freight from 2015 to 2050 [65,70].

Transport Modes	Unit	2015	2020	2025	2030	2035	2040	2045	2050
Marine Passenger	b p-km	126	151	185	226	278	340	411	491
Marine Freight	b t-km	83,961	98,980	116,550	137,402	162,472	192,967	230,438	276,879

2.1.4. Aviation Transportation Activity

For the aviation passenger activity, the ICCT roadmap [64] from 2000 to 2050 is used. The metric used by ICCT is revenue passenger kilometers (rp-km), which is almost identical to the used p-km metric, not accounting for pilot and flight attendants, which seems acceptable as a first order proxy. Thus, rp-km has an identical concept as p-km from a statistical standpoint and it is used as passenger demand. The aviation t-km demand is excluded in the ICCT roadmap, but extracted from the International Civil Aviation Organization (ICAO) [71]. Based on ICAO, 197,549 million t-km transportation demand has been handled in the global aviation industry in 2015. Airfreight demand is projected to grow by 6% per year until 2035 according to ICAO [72]. From 2040 to 2050, annual growth rates of 6.4% and 6.0% and 5.5% for 2040, 2045, and 2050, respectively, are considered to be it was evaluated that the global GDP may grow approximately 4–5% per year in that period, as also adopted by Toktarova et al. [63] and airfreight demand experiences a moderately swifter growth rate than GDP.

Equation (4) indicates how aviation freight transportation demand is projected to develop in the period 2015 to 2050.

$$(t\text{-km})_{G,t+1} = (t\text{-km})_{G,t}(1+GR)^{\,year_{t+1}-year_t} \qquad (4)$$

wherein, $(t\text{-km})_{G,t+1}$ is the global aviation freight transportation demand for the following time steps, which is typically an interval of 5 years in this research, GR is the growth rate for aviation freight transportation demand, $year_{t+1}$ and $year_t$ represent the concrete years of each step. The aviation freight transportation demand from 2015 to 2050 is distributed across countries to obtain the freight transportation demand for each country individually, as indicated in Equation (5).

$$(t\text{-km})_{i,t} = (t\text{-km})_{G,t} \cdot \frac{(GDP_{i,t}\,cap \cdot P_{i,t})}{(GDP_{G,t}\,cap \cdot P_{G,t})} \qquad (5)$$

wherein, $(t\text{-km})_{i,t}$ is a freight demand of a country i for a point t in time, $GDP_{i,t}\,cap$ and $P_{i,t}$ is the GDP_{cap} and population of country i for a point t in time, the subscript G, represents the respective global. The regarded time period is from 2015 to 2050 and typically applied for intervals of 5 years. Table 4 summarizes the transportation demand values for passenger and freight in the aviation industry during the transition period until 2050, in 5-year intervals. Detailed numbers for all countries can be found in the Supplementary Material (Table S1).

Table 4. Global transportation activity for aviation passenger [64] and freight [71,72] from 2015 to 2050.

Transport Modes	Unit	2015	2020	2025	2030	2035	2040	2045	2050
Aviation Passenger	b p-km	5629	6866	8335	10,665	13,131	17,024	21,520	26,363
Aviation Freight	b t-km	198	264	354	473	634	863	1157	1514

The total global passenger transportation demand and freight transportation demand through the transition from 2015 to 2050, summarizing Tables 2–4 is shown in Figure 1.

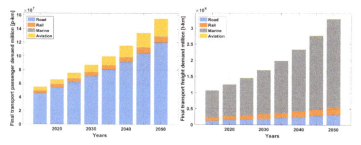

Figure 1. Development of global passenger transportation demand (**left**) and freight transportation demand (**right**) from 2015 to 2050.

2.2. Specific Energy Demand

Specific energy demand of each segment is the next step to finally derive energy demand in the transport sector. Energy demand is expressed in electrical ($-_{el}$) and thermal ($-_{th}$) units, followed by a fuel specification for thermal units, such as $TWh_{th,H2}$, $TWh_{th,CH4}$, $TWh_{th,liq}$, for hydrogen, methane, and liquid fuels, respectively. All thermal energy units are provided and used in lower heating values (LHV). Specific energy demand units can be in (MJ, kWh)/(p-km, t-km). Specific energy demand estimations are analyzed for each transport mode, segment, and power train for the transition period.

2.2.1. Road Specific Energy Demand

Heywood et al. [73] provide estimates for LDV fuel consumption in (liters/100 km) and in (kWh/100 km) for all power trains until 2050. The vehicle specific demand is linked to the number of passengers per vehicle, so that the specific energy demand in units of kWh/p-km is derived. Vehicle numbers and its occupancy known as load factor, or average people per vehicle and average freight in ton per vehicle, is extracted from Greenpeace [34] and ICCT [64], for the period until 2050. The global weighted average of load factors is calculated by the global summation of vehicle occupancy multiplied by the respective vehicle numbers of a country and then divided by the total global number of respective vehicles. The units used in this research for the specific energy demand are kWh_{th}/p-km, kWh_{el}/p-km, and kWh_{H2}/p-km for ICE, BEV, and FCEV, respectively. In case of PHEV, the electric driving range also influences the utility factor, also called electric driving share, as described by Plötz et al. [17,74]. The utility factor is calculated to be 0.7 for the battery-electric range of current vehicles with about 10 kWh of battery capacity [19] and is expected to grow to 0.78 by 2050. The specific energy demand for the thermal and electric parts of PHEV is based on the values for ICE and BEV. The number of passengers per vehicle is not varied for LDV of different power trains.

The energy consumption for 2W/3W BEV is estimated to be around 3–5 kWh_{el}/100 km for present vehicles according to [9], which is considered to be a constant value for the entire transition period. Mendes et al. [75] show that the specific energy consumption for 2W/3W ICE is 65% higher than for the BEV power train, and is also assumed constant throughout the transition period, and provided in units of kWh_{th}/p-km. The global weighted average of vehicle occupancy for 2W/3W is calculated in a comparable way as for LDV.

The specific energy consumption for BUS is taken from CIVITAS [76], in units of kWh/km for all power trains. The projection is available until 2030 and from then on is extrapolated based on the decrease rate from 2015 to 2030 for all power trains, excluding BUS PHEV, which is composed by BUS ICE and BUS BEV. The utility factor for BUS PHEV is taken from [77] as a constant value of 0.5 throughout the transition period. The specific energy demand for BUS PHEV is composed of the respective BEV and ICE values. Equations (6a) and (6b) show the extrapolation.

$$DR = \left(\frac{SED_{t_m}}{SED_{t_0}}\right)^{\frac{1}{t_m-t_0}} - 1 \tag{6a}$$

$$SED_{t_k} = SED_{t_{k-1}} \cdot (1+DR)^{t_k-t_{k-1}} \tag{6b}$$

wherein, DR is the decline rate, SED is the specific energy demand, t_m is the year with the last provided data, t_0 is the beginning of the transition period, t_k is a year within the transition period. The BUS occupancy and its projection until 2050 is done similarly to LDV.

The specific energy consumption of MDV BEV and HDV BEV is estimated to be 100 kWh/100 km and 200 kWh/100 km in 2012, according to Boer et al. [78]. The specific energy demand is projected according to Equation (6a) and (6b) using decline rates from LDV BEV. Specific energy demand for MDV ICE and HDV ICE is 4.8 and 1.6 MJ/t-km for 2015 and 2.7 and 0.8 MJ/t-km for 2050, adopted from [34]. Fulton [79] investigated that FCEV trucks have 40% lower consumption compared with ICE trucks. Load factors for MDV and HDV to translate kWh/km units to kWh/t-km units are obtained in a similar way as the passenger number per LDV, though here for ton per MDV and HDV. The utility factors for MDV PHEV and HDV PHEV are considered from [77] as a constant value of 0.4 and 0.3, respectively, throughout the transition period. The specific energy demand for MDV PHEV and HDV PHEV is composed of the respective ICE and BEV values. Table 5 summarizes the used references for the specific energy consumption and load factors of road vehicles.

Table 5. Sources for the specific energy consumption and load factors of road vehicles. Detailed numbers for all assumptions can be found in the Supplementary Material (Table S1).

Vehicle	Item	Unit	Reference
LDV	Energy consumption	kWh/100 km	[73]
	Load factor	passengers per vehicle	[34,64]
2W/3W	Energy consumption	kWh/100 km	[9,75]
	Load factor	passengers per vehicle	[64]
BUS	Energy consumption	kWh/km	[76]
	Load factor	passengers per vehicle	[1]
MDV	Energy consumption	kWh/km	[34,78,79]
	Load factor	ton per vehicle	[64]
HDV	Energy consumption	kWh/km	[34,78,79]
	Load factor	ton per vehicle	[64]

2.2.2. Rail Specific Energy Demand

Trains are divided into two power trains, electric and diesel, and this is applied for passenger and freight transport. Schäfer et al. [80] introduced a specific energy demand scenario for passenger and freight electric trains and provide specific energy demand for the years 2010 and 2050, which is considered for this research. They have also investigated that electric trains are between 45–50% more energy efficient than diesel-fueled trains, which is applied in this research. It is assumed that the specific energy demand for trains declines in a linear rate, so that all periods between 2010 and 2050 can be linearly interpolated.

2.2.3. Marine Specific Energy Demand

Marine transportation is taken into account with three power trains ICE, battery electric, and fuel-cell electric, whereas ICE can be fueled by diesel and LNG, and the fuel cells by hydrogen. For the specific energy demand for marine freight, IMO [65] introduced the absolute fuel consumption of all vessel types for 2012, which is accounted to 274,700 kt of bunker fuel, for both domestic and international shipping. Calorific values in kJ/g for heavy fuel oil, marine diesel and gas oil are provided by DNV GL [81]. Marine freight transportation demand is adopted from Section 2.1.3 and adjusted to 2012 values, so that the specific energy consumption is obtained. Horvath et al. [36] provide efficiency values for marine diesel engines for 2030 and 2040 to be 46% and 47%, respectively, and for 2050, 48% is assumed. This efficiency development is used for specific energy demand projection.

A comparison between the mechanical and electrical drives in ships is presented by Fireman and Arbor [51], introducing relative drag coefficients and propeller efficiency for both propulsion options, leading to about 65–70% efficiency. This is linked to a fuel-to-power efficiency of 40% [36] and battery full charge cycle efficiency of 92%, resulting in a total power train efficiency of about 28% and 60% for ICE and battery-electric ships, respectively for 2015. The ratio of battery electric to ICE efficiency develops from 2.16 to 1.80 from 2015 to 2050. This ratio of relative efficiency can be used to obtain the specific energy consumption for freight battery-electric ships. The same procedure is adopted for hydrogen-based fuel-cell ships, though fuel-to-H_2 efficiency is assumed to increase from 53% to 65%, from 2030 to 2050, based on [36]. The respective ratio of fuel-cell to ICE efficiency for ships develops from 1.08 to 1.27, from 2030 to 2050. In terms of marine passenger specific energy demand, Becken [82] indicated that for a couple of marine passenger transport types, including ferries and cruise ships, the average value is about 2.5 MJ$_{th}$/p-km for 2010. The marine passenger specific energy demand is projected in comparable correlation as freight marine, for battery electric and fuel-cell electric ships.

2.2.4. Aviation Specific Energy Demand

The specific energy consumption of ICE, battery electric and FC planes for passenger and freight transportation is estimated. The ICCT roadmap provides aviation data in units of (revenue passenger km) rp-km/kg jet fuel consumption. As a first order approximation rp-km/kg is considered to be p-km/kg. Net calorific value is defined for jet fuels in [83], which is regarded in units of MJ/kg. ICCT [64] provides data for kg of jet fuel needed to enable respective p-km, which leads to the desired specific energy demand for ICE planes in MJ/p-km.

For electric airplanes, there is a need to use batteries for power supply, which leads to an efficiency enhancement from 30% to 80% from turboprop engine to a full battery-electric system, according to Mueller et al. [84]. They also investigate the efficiency increase of ICE to hydrogen-based FC and obtain a development from 30% to 41.7% overall efficiency. The specific energy demand for battery electric and FC planes is estimated by these efficiency ratios of battery electric and FC planes to ICE planes. Table 6 summarizes all references used to derive specific energy demand for the transport modes rail, marine, and aviation.

Table 6. Sources to calculate the specific energy demand for the transport modes rail, marine, and aviation. Detailed numbers for all assumptions can be found in the Supplementary Material (Table S1).

Modes	Item	Unit	Reference
Rail	Specific energy demand	MJ$_{el}$/p-km	[80]
	Specific energy demand	MJ$_{el}$/t-km	[80]
Marine	Bunker fuel consumption	kilo ton	[65]
	Calorific value	kJ/g	[81]
	Efficiency	%	[36,51]
	Specific energy demand	MJ$_{th}$/p-km	[82]
	Specific energy demand	MJ$_{th}$/t-km	[82]
Aviation	Calorific value	MJ$_{th}$/kg	[83]
	Efficiency	%	[84]
	Specific energy demand	MJ$_{th}$/p-km	[83,84]
	Specific energy demand	MJ$_{th}$/t-km	[83,84]

2.3. Fuel-Share Distribution of Transport Modes

The above-mentioned approaches are used to collect and calculate the transportation demand and specific energy demand for each transport mode. Thereafter, transportation demand is converted to energy demand with estimated fuel shares for the transition from the current form to sustainable and zero GHG emitting fuels throughout, until 2050. Sustainable production routes for all required fuels are established to link primary energy supply to final energy fuel demand. The following fundamental fuel types and its sustainable production routes are taken into consideration and depicted in Figure 2:

- Road: electricity, hydrogen, liquid fuels (liquid hydrocarbons)
- Rail: electricity, liquid fuels (liquid hydrocarbons)
- Marine: electricity, hydrogen, methane, liquid fuels (liquid hydrocarbons)
- Aviation: electricity, hydrogen, liquid fuels (liquid hydrocarbons)

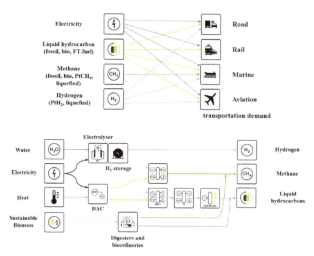

Figure 2. Transport modes and fuels (**top**) and value chain elements for sustainable fuels (**bottom**).

Road transport can be powered by electricity, liquid fuels, and hydrogen. These fuels contribute with different shares through the years and complement each other. Share of each transport vehicle type within newly sold vehicles portfolio is estimated based on expected levelized cost of mobility (LCOM). The vehicles stock numbers are based on the historic structure and vehicles lifetimes, whereas newly sold vehicles substitute the existing stock at the end of their lifetimes, plus additional vehicles to satisfy a potentially growing transportation demand. Conversion to stock numbers is performed based on these newly sold vehicle shares and estimation of the total number of vehicles needed to satisfy the respective transportation demand. To calculate country wise vehicles portfolios, the respective country transportation demand is divided by respective passengers per vehicle (or freight per MDV/HDV), and average annual distance per vehicle (Equation (7a)). The number of newly sold vehicles for a respective year is comprised by the growth of the entire vehicle fleet and the reinvested vehicles (Equation (7b)). Vehicles fleet growth is calculated in comparison to the previous period (Equation (7c)). Reinvestment of vehicles is equal to vehicles expected to be decommissioned at the end of their lifetimes and respective need for substitution (Equation (7d)). The number of new vehicles of each type is the product of the share of vehicle type in newly sold vehicles and the respective number of new vehicles added in that period. Stock numbers are the sum of newly sold vehicles during the expected lifetime of vehicles. Detailed numbers for all assumptions and countries can be found in the Supplementary Material (Table S1).

$$TF_{i,j,t} = \frac{D_{i,j,t}}{PPV_{i,j,t} \cdot DPV_{i,j,t}} \quad (7a)$$

$$NV_{i,j,t} = FG_{i,j,t} + FR_{i,j,t} \quad (7b)$$

$$FG_{i,j,t} = TF_{i,j,t} - TF_{i,j,t-1} \quad (7c)$$

$$FR_{i,j,t} = FG_{i,j,t-lifetime_j} \quad (7d)$$

wherein, $TF_{i,j,t}$ is the total fleet per road segment j and country i and year t as an integer, $D_{i,j,t}$ is the transportation demand, $PPV_{i,j,t}$ is passengers (or freight) per vehicle, $DPV_{i,j,t}$ is average annual distance per vehicle, $NV_{i,j,t}$ is the number of newly sold vehicles in the total fleet, $FG_{i,j,t}$ is the number of newly sold vehicles to satisfy the growth of the vehicle fleet, $FR_{i,j,t}$ is the number of newly sold vehicles to substitute decommissioning of vehicles, t is the respective year, $t - 1$ is the previous period, *lifetime* is the lifetime of vehicles. Road segments j are: LDV, 2W/3W, BUS, MDV, and HDV. The countries i are all countries in the world. The years t are from 2015 to 2050, in intervals of 5 years.

Rail transportation is based on the fuel types, electricity, and liquid fuels, applied to the shares of passenger and freight transport. The applied electricity and liquid-fuel shares for the rail mode until 2050 are taken from Greenpeace [34]. This leads to electricity and liquid fuel shares for the rail modes in 2050 of 86% and 14%, respectively.

Presently, the marine mode is practically powered solely by liquid fuels for both passenger and freight transport, neglecting small shares of methane-based LNG [85] and electric ships [86]. From 2020 onwards electricity, methane, and hydrogen will play an increasing role as alternative fuels. For electric ships, a mileage limitation to maximum of 100 km on a single charge of lithium batteries is expected [87,88]. Hydrogen and methane-based LNG are not limited in mileage. The transportation share of low range trips for ships is evaluated for deriving the electricity contribution for the marine mode. Based on GHG emissions shares of international and domestic shipping [89], it is obtained that 11% of the total shipping is domestic and it is assumed that 80% of all domestic shipping is within a range for electrification. The assumed phase-in of electric domestic ships is visualized in Figure 3. In accordance with this assumption and marine transportation demand, the share of electric shipping is calculated.

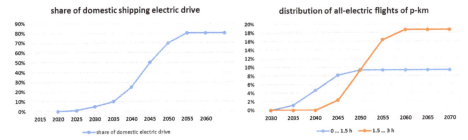

Figure 3. Projected phase-in of all-electric domestic shipping as a percentage of all domestic shipping (**left**) and flights for ranges up to 3 h as a percentage of all domestic and international flights in passenger kilometers (**right**).

Currently, aviation transportation is entirely based on liquid fuels. This will have to change in the upcoming decades for responding to the climate emergency but also due to economic reasons. From around 2035 onwards, it is assumed that hydrogen and electricity start to gain market shares for powering airplanes, as documented by first policies for all-electric flights in Norway with up to 1.5 h range [52] and expectations in technology enhancement for flights up to 3 h [90]. Electric airplanes are limited in range due to the limited energy density of lithium batteries. Short haul flights up to 1.5 to 3 h with utmost 100 passengers have the potential to be electrified according to Wilkerson et al. [91] and Mueller et al. [80]. Consequently, this research assumes for 2050 that 18.7% of the flights measured in passenger kilometers representing short haul flights of less than 1.5 h and half of the flights between 1.5 and 3 h will be electric and twice that is assumed to be contributed by fuel-cell-based flights fueled by hydrogen (37.4%), while the rest representing the majority of all p-km for flights is projected to remain powered with jet fuel. The phase-in of all-electric flights is visualized in Figure 3, and based on the estimate of 11.7% of all p-km for flights up to 1.5 h and 23.4% of all p-km for flights within 1.5 and 3 h, whereas 80% of these flights should be served by all-electric flights in the longer term, which is projected to be achieved between 2050 and 2060. The assumed progress in aviation technology and respective implementation is based on today's understanding of technological options [84,90,91], first respective policies [52] and the enormous pressure to react on climate emergency [2,69,92,93], while economics may be attractive and first leading technology providers and airlines push the development to introduce all-electric flights by 2030 [94].

2.4. Capital Expenditures, Operational Expenditures, and Lifetimes for Road Vehicles

In this paper, the LCOM for road vehicles is used to obtain the evolution of the vehicle types. Capital expenditures (capex) for the vehicle types of LDV, BUS, MDV, and HDV and their respective projections from 2015 to 2050 are considered. This evaluation is done for four mentioned segments and the following power trains: ICE, BEV, PHEV, and FCEV. In addition, operational expenditures (opex) for all vehicle types and lifetimes are considered.

Capex, opex, lifetime and weighted average cost of capital (WACC) form the key performance unit LCOM, so that all vehicle types within a vehicle class can be compared. LCOM is defined in Equation (8). Opex variable is defined in Equation (9). The capital recovery factor (crf) used for LCOM is defined in Equation (10). WACC is set at 7% in this study. GHG emissions cost (GHG$_{cost}$) are adopted from Bogdanov et al. [95].

$$LCOM = \frac{\left[(capex_{tot} - capex_{bat}) \cdot crf_{tot} + capex_{bat} \cdot crf_{bat} + opex_{fix}\right]}{mileage} + opex_{var} \quad (8)$$

$$opex_{var} = E_{cons} \cdot E_{cost} + GHG_{emit} \cdot GHG_{cost} \quad (9)$$

$$crf = \frac{WACC \cdot (1 + WACC)^N}{(1 + WACC)^N - 1} \quad (10)$$

wherein, $capex_{tot}$ is total capital expenditure of vehicle, $capex_{bat}$ is battery capex of vehicle, $opex_{fix}$ is the fixed operational expenditure of vehicle, $mileage$ is the annual mileage of vehicle, $opex_{var}$ is the variable operational expenditure of vehicle, E_{cons} is the specific energy demand per km of vehicle, E_{cost} is the specific cost of fuels used by vehicle, GHG_{emit} is the specific emitted GHG emissions per km, GHG_{cost} is the applied CO_{2eq} price, and $mileage$ is the annual mileage of vehicle.

2.4.1. Capital Expenditures

Vliet et al. [96] investigated the regular diesel and gasoline prices in euros for LDV ICE vehicles. Vehicles consist of two major parts: platform and power train. The two liquid-fuel LDV types are averaged in the following, and constant cost for LDV ICE platform and power train are assumed over the entire transition period. The capex of LDV BEV are split into three main components: platform, electrical drive, and battery. The specific cost of the battery is high in the beginning, but a continued and drastic cost reduction is factored in, based on Bloomberg New Energy Finance (BNEF) [97] and UBS [19]. The starting specific cost of the battery is 198 €/kWh$_{cap}$ in 2017 [19,97]. A cost reduction of 7.9% per year is assumed until 2030, based on BNEF and UBS assumptions, and 2% per year until 2050. The obtained specific battery cost for 2030 is confirmed by Nguyen and Ward [98]. The power train cost reduction is assumed at 7.9% per year until 2030 and 2% per year then onwards [19,97]. LDV PHEV is composed by ICE and BEV components, but with lower battery capacity. The cost reduction of the power train and battery is assumed to follow the same percentage as for LDV BEV. The battery capacity for BEV and PHEV is calculated to be 70 and 10 kWh, respectively by multiplying all-electric range km of the vehicle to its specific efficiency in kWh/km [19]. LDV FCEV vehicles consist of the major components: platform, power train (fuel cell and electric motor) and hydrogen energy storage. The platform cost is adopted from Vliet et al. [96], with a fuel-cell power of 100 kW and a range of about 500 km, leading to a hydrogen storage capacity of 140 kWh$_{H2}$. Assumptions for the power train and hydrogen storage are considered from Bubeck et al. [99]. The fuel tank capex is considered to be fixed at 1.9 €/kWh$_{H2}$, whereas the power train capex declines from 284 €/kW in 2015 to 48 €/kW in 2050, according to estimates of UBS [19].

BUS ICE capex is adopted from Lajunen and Lipman [100] and constant capex for the entire transition period is assumed. The platform cost share of BUS ICE is extracted from LDV platform cost share, according to Vliet et al. [96] and found to be 74% of the total capex, so that the other BUS power train types can be investigated. BUS BEV is composed of the platform capex plus the power train and battery. The platform cost of BUS BEV is identical to BUS ICE, and the BUS BEV battery cost is calculated by multiplying the battery capacity in kWh [100] with the specific battery cost. The reduction of battery cost for the BUS BEV by 2050 is according to the LDV method. BUS BEV power train capex is the same value as for BUS PHEV, which is described in Equation (11). BUS BEV battery capacity is set to 333 kWh, according to Lajunen and Lipman [100], assuming the identical specific battery capex cost reduction as in LDV BEV. BUS PHEV capex components are split to the components: platform, battery, and power train (ICE and BEV). The platform cost is identical for all BUS vehicle types. Battery capacity is set to 49.7 kWh, according to Lajunen et al. [101] and the specific battery capex cost decline is assumed to be identical to LDV BEV. The BUS PHEV power train is calculated according to the respective development of LDV, but based on BUS assumptions, as detailed in Equation (11), which can be applied for all years of the transition period.

$$capex_{power\ train,\ BUS\ PHEV,\ year} = \left(capex_{total,\ BUS\ ICE} - capex_{platform,\ BUS\ ICE}\right) \cdot \frac{capex_{powertrain,\ LDV\ PHEV,\ year}}{capex_{powertrain,\ LDV\ ICE,\ year}} \quad (11)$$

wherein, *capex* is capital expenditures for the *power train*, the entire bus, *total*, and the *platform.*, and *year* indicates the considered year in the transition period.

Current BUS FCEV capex are adopted from Lajunen [101], leading to a cost decline of the vehicle, excluding the platform, of 5% per year up to 2030, based on Vliet et al. [96]. As technological similarities exist, a further cost decline of 2% from 2030 to 2050 is presumed. Finally, the aggregation of all components per BUS type leads to the total capex for each year within the transition period.

MDV ICE capex is assumed to stay stable, according to Yeon and Thomas [102], from which the class 6 vehicle is regarded. In analogy to BUS, the LDV platform share of 74% is also applied for MDV vehicles. MDV BEV capex is composed of three capex contributions from the platform, power train, and battery. The platform capex is identical to MDV FCEV. MDV BEV power train is estimated as the ratio of LDV BEV power train capex to LDV BEV platform capex, applied to the MDV BEV platform capex. The specific battery capex is assumed identical to LDV BEV, but for a battery capacity of 120 kWh [103]. The MDV PHEV capex is composed with the same logic as in LDV PHEV and MDV in general. The MDV PHEV platform capex is identical to MDV BEV, i.e., 74% of the total capex of MDV ICE. MDV PHEV power train capex is calculated similarly to Equation (11). The MDV PHEV battery capacity is taken as the MDV BEV battery capacity multiplied by the ratio of the battery capacities of LDV PHEV to LDV BEV, while the identical specific battery capex is assumed. MDV FCEV electric motor is set to 170 kW for the class 6 vehicle, according to Kast et al. [104], and the respective capex decline follows the percentage of LDV FCEV. The MDV FCEV hydrogen storage capacity is scaled according to the specific energy demand of MDV FCEV versus LDV FCEV and the identical specific hydrogen storage capex is assumed. The sum of the three capex components yields the total capex of MDV FCEV, which is then applied for all years within the transition period.

Capex for HDV ICE is regarded as the average capex of several heavy-duty trucks, according to Laitila et al. [105]. The method is identical to MDV. Specific values are HDV FCEV electric motor of 250 kW [104] with a capex decline according to MDV FCEV. Tesla [106] claims that by 2020 there will be 900 kWh battery capacity for their HDV BEV for 143 €/kWh$_{cap}$, which is set as a reference, while the relative battery capex decline is assumed to be according to LDV BEV. The battery capacity for HDV PHEV is estimated according to the same method as in MDV PHEV, as also for the other components.

2.4.2. Operational Expenditures

Opex fixed comprises of insurance and maintenance cost for the vehicles, and no change in the insurance cost is assumed throughout the transition period. The annual insurance cost for LDV ICE [107] is assumed to be the same for all LDV types. LDV BEV maintenance cost is lower than for LDV ICE due to reduced complexity [108]. LDV ICE and LDV BEV maintenance costs are assessed in [53] and used in this study. LDV PHEV maintenance cost is comprised of the full LDV ICE maintenance cost plus half the maintenance cost of LDV BEV. LDV FCEV maintenance cost is assumed to be comparable to ICE and BEV, thus comprising half of each.

Insurance cost for BUS is taken from [109] and assumed to be identical for all BUS types. BUS ICE maintenance cost is taken from [100], as 0.16 €/km for an annual distance of 66,667 km. Maintenance costs for BUS BEV, PHEV, and FCEV are based on BUS ICE and scaled according to the LDV types. Insurance costs for MDV ICE and HDV ICE are taken from [110], whereas the respective classifications for MDV and HDV are taken from [104]. MDV ICE maintenance costs for diesel MDV is estimated to be between 300 to 600 USD/month, therefore 450 USD/month are applied and converted by long-term average currency exchange rate of 1.3 USD/€. Other MDV type maintenance cost is scaled in accordance to LDV. HDV ICE insurance cost is set identical to all HDV types and taken from Bento et al. [111]. HDV maintenance cost is set to be identical to BUS for all HDV types.

Table 7 provides all sources used for capex and opex for all road vehicle types. The calculations of vehicle, battery and hydrogen storage capex as well as maintenance and insurance costs are presented in the Supplementary Material (Table S1).

Table 7. Sources used for vehicle, battery, and hydrogen storage prices as well as maintenance and insurance costs.

Vehicle	Item	Unit	Reference
LDV	Vehicle price	€	[96]
	Battery/hydrogen price	€/kWh	[19,97–99]
BUS	Vehicle price	€	[100]
	Battery/hydrogen price	€/kWh	[100,101]
MDV	Vehicle price	€	[102]
	Battery/hydrogen price	€/kWh	[104]
HDV	Vehicle price	€	[105]
	Battery/hydrogen price	€/kWh	[104,106]
All types	Insurance	€/vehicle	[107,109,110]
	Maintenance	€/vehicle	[19,100,108]

2.4.3. Lifetime

Vehicle lifetime is determined as an average vehicle age from starting operation to scrappage stage. Vehicle lifetimes for all vehicle types are assumed to stay constant until 2050. Battery lifetime must be considered for all BEV and PHEV road segments. Changes in scrappage patterns for LDV and the consequence of a higher average lifetime is discussed by Bento et al. [105]. However, Dun et al. [112] point out that vehicle lifetime heavily depends on annual mileage, which is assumed to be roughly 10,000 km for LDV. Battery lifetime is assumed to be identical for BEV and PHEV, as discussed by Guenther et al. [113]. Laver et al. [114] discuss the concept of useful lifetime for BUS, which is concluded to be between 12 and 14 years. In this study, the planned useful lifetime chosen is a bit longer to also cover the period until decommissioning. Lajunen [101] describes 80,000 km for the BUS battery lifetime in case of city operation, which can be translated to 3000–12,000 full charge cycles or 5–10 years [115–117]. 2W/3W vehicles lifetimes are taken from [9]. Battery installed in 2W/3W vehicles can be valve-regulated lead-acid (VRLA) or lithium-ion battery with different lifetimes, whereas lithium-ion technology is assumed as the standard, also due to more promising future and longer lifetime in mobile applications, according to Weinert et al. [118]. MDV lifetime is similar to LDV decommissioning age, and average age of MDV is taken from [119]. HDV lifetime is slightly longer than that of MDV or LDV [114,119]. Tables 8 and 9 summarize the vehicle and battery lifetimes for all road segments and vehicle types.

Table 8. Vehicle lifetime for all road segments.

Vehicle	Unit	2015–2050	Reference
LDV	years	15	[111,112]
2W/3W	years	10	[9]
BUS	years	15	[114]
MDV	years	15	[119]
HDV	years	16	[114,119]

Table 9. Battery lifetime for all technologies on the road.

Vehicle Type	Unit	2015–2050	Reference
LDV BEV	years	10	[113]
LDV PHEV	years	10	[113]
2W/3W BEV	years	9	[9]
BUS BEV	years	9	[101]
BUS PHEV	years	6	[101]
MDV BEV	years	10	[113]
MDV PHEV	years	5	[113]
HDV BEV	years	10	[113]
HDV PHEV	years	5	[113]

2.4.4. Annual Kilometers for the Road Segment

The annual kilometers driven per vehicle type is the weighted average kilometers of vehicle types with their occupancy and number of vehicles for all countries globally. Table 10 summarizes the annual kilometers for all road vehicles. Detailed numbers for all countries can be found in the Supplementary Material (Table S1).

Table 10. Annual kilometers per vehicle.

Vehicle Type	Unit	2015	2020	2025	2030	2035	2040	2045	2050
LDV	km/a	14,603	14,004	13,357	12,993	12,728	12,468	12,217	11,971
2W/3W	km/a	7224	7380	7453	7494	7435	7427	7480	7702
BUS	km/a	64,744	67,178	68,854	70,810	72,610	74,503	76,293	77,465
MDV	km/a	25,389	26,154	26,631	27,140	27,601	28,058	28,416	28,655
HDV	km/a	54,541	53,521	52,941	52,582	52,188	51,747	51,312	50,866

2.5. Global Final Energy Demand in the Transport Sector

The final energy demand for the transport sector can be derived on basis of transportation activities, specific energy demand for each transport mode with all transport segments and vehicle types, and the respective fuel-share distribution. The GHG emission intensity of the used fuels further determine the GHG emissions of the transport sector. An overview diagram of the key factors, from transportation activity to total final energy demand and GHG emissions via specific energy demand and fuel-share distribution is visualized in Figure 4.

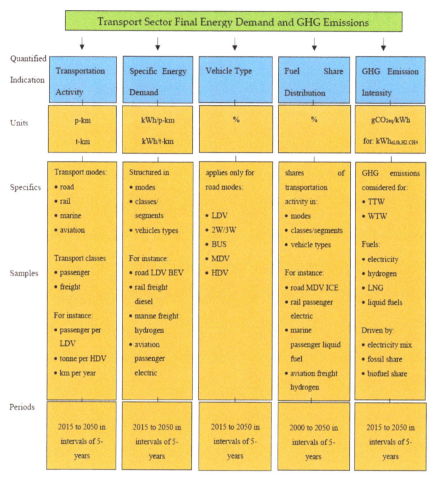

Figure 4. Process flow for deriving final energy demand and respective GHG emissions for the transport sector.

The final energy demand is calculated according to Equation (12), which allows a detailed consideration of all transport activities of the different transport modes and segments, the differentiation of vehicle types, the evolution of fuel shares and the development of the specific energy demand per vehicle type, fuel, and segment. The structure of Equation (12) is also visualized in Figure 4. This calculation can be carried out per geographic entity, for instance a country, and then aggregated to larger regions, continents, and the world. Detailed numbers for all input data can be found in the Supplementary Material (Table S1).

$$E_{FD,year} = \sum_{i,s,v,f} TA_{i,s} \cdot VT_v \cdot F_{i,s,v,f} \cdot ED_{i,s,v,f} \qquad (12)$$

wherein, E_{FD} is the final energy demand, $year$ is the considered year within the transition period, TA is the transport activity, VT is the vehicle type, F is the fuel-share distribution, ED is the specific energy demand and the indices are i for the transport mode (road, rail, marine, aviation), s for the transport segment (passenger, freight; for road: LDV, 2W/3W, BUS, MDV, HDV), v for the vehicle type (road: ICE,

BEV, PHEV, FCEV) and f for the fuel type (electricity, hydrogen [electricity, fossil], methane [electricity, fossil], liquid fuels [electricity, biofuel, fossil]).

The final energy demand according to Equation (12) can be categorized in different ways, e.g., as the global total for all countries and all transport activities, or per country for a transport mode or transport segment, or for a specific fuel type.

The analysis can be further differentiated for the total primary energy demand of the transport sector. This requires the consideration of the conversion of primary energy sources to the final energy forms of required fuels. Figure 2 indicates this for modern synthetic fuels. For deriving the full primary energy demand, an energy supply scenario is required reflecting the development of the electricity mix, the applied hydrogen production technology, in particular electricity-based electrolysis and steam methane reforming based on fossil natural gas, the methane supply mix, in particular fossil natural gas and power-to-gas, liquid-fuel mix based on fossil fuels, biofuels, and electricity-based Fischer-Tropsch fuels. This is detailed in Section 2.7.

2.6. GHG Emissions from the Transport Sector

Well-to-wheel (WTW) GHG emissions analysis for the various fuels used is the decisive metric, since it considers the fuel value chain from primary energy to final use. WTW consists of well-to-tank (WTT) comprising fuel refining and logistic requirements from primary energy to final energy and tank-to-wheel (TTW), which comprises the GHG emissions of the final energy fuels used. GHG emission factors for fuels are taken from IPCC [120], using average values for liquid fuels comprised of diesel, gasoline, jet fuel, residual fuel oil and biofuel for the TTW balance, and fossil natural gas for LNG TTW emissions. The TTW values for hydrogen and electricity as a final energy fuel are zero. The TTW GHG emission values for LNG and liquid fuels will decline until 2050 based on the applied energy transition scenario, which can imply an electricity share for methane via power-to-gas and a renewable electricity (RE) share for liquid fuels, comprised of biofuels and electricity-based FT fuels. The shares of the various sustainable fuels are according to Sections 2.3 and 3.2.3. WTW GHG emission intensity for liquid fossil fuels are taken from Rahman et al. [121], who averaged five North American conventional crudes, and derived values for gasoline, diesel, and jet fuel, which have been averaged for liquid fossil fuels, as used in this analysis. WTW GHG emissions from sugarcane and corn as bioethanol feedstock are taken from Wang et al. [122]. GHG emissions from palm oil as biodiesel feedstock are taken from Nylund and Koponen [123]. The finally used emission value for biofuel is the weighted average of bioethanol and biodiesel with their available market shares and represented by the main producers the USA and Brazil, as taken from [124]. WTW GHG emissions for fossil LNG is 300 gCO_{2eq}/kWh$_{th}$ in the 100-year GWP consideration of methane emissions, as suggested by IPCC in its 5th Assessment Report and discussed here [125]. The WTW emission intensity of liquid fuels and LNG declines because of the applied energy transition scenario through an expected increase of RE shares used for these final energy fuels. Presently, hydrogen production is dominated by fossil natural gas-based SMR, leading to a WTW GHG emission of 380 gCO_{2eq}/kWh$_{H2}$. Similar to liquid fuels and LNG, these emissions decline as the share of used RE increases, because of the energy transition. Hydrogen from SMR is expected to be substituted by hydrogen from renewable electricity-based electrolysis, as discussed in Fasihi et al. [126] and Elgowainy et al. [127]. Electricity WTT GHG emissions, better called well-to-grid (WTG) GHG emissions, depend on the used electricity supply mix and its composition with primary fuels such as coal, fossil natural gas, fuel oil, nuclear, and the various forms of renewables. The GHG emission values of fossil oil and fossil natural gas used for the final energy fuels are also used for the electricity supply. GHG emission values for lignite coal (400 gCO_{2eq}/kWh$_{th}$) and hard coal (390 gCO_{2eq}/kWh$_{th}$) are taken from Schuller [128]. The two coal emission factors are weighted into a unified GHG emission value, based on their total global production, according to Skone [129]. The specific GHG emission values in thermal energy units are converted to the average efficiency of thermal power plants used for electricity generation. The considered thermal power plants are oil-based ICE generators, coal power plants, and open cycle and combined cycle gas turbines. All efficiency values and the assumed energy transition scenario is taken from Bogdanov et al. [95]. The energy transition scenario for the final energy fuels is according to Sections 2.7 and 3.5. GHG emission intensities of the considered final energy fuels during the energy transition period, as obtained by applying the energy transition scenario is summarized in Table 11 for TTW and WTW considerations, which also allows a WTT analysis, if required.

Table 11. GHG emission intensity for all applied final energy fuels for TTW and WTW consideration. The remaining GHG emissions in 2050 are from biofuels and mainly due to indirect GHG emissions.

Fuel	Method	Unit	2015	2020	2025	2030	2035	2040	2045	2050
Electricity	TTW	gCO_{2eq}/kWh_{el}	0	0	0	0	0	0	0	0
Hydrogen	TTW	gCO_{2eq}/kWh_{H2}	0	0	0	0	0	0	0	0
LNG	TTW	gCO_{2eq}/kWh_{CH4}	237	237	237	230	194	135	54	0
Liquid fuel	TTW	gCO_{2eq}/kWh_{th}	266	266	266	258	218	151	71	10
Electricity	WTW	gCO_{2eq}/kWh_{el}	513	373	140	47	15	6	2	0
Hydrogen	WTW	gCO_{2eq}/kWh_{H2}	389	395	334	223	148	65	21	0
LNG	WTW	gCO_{2eq}/kWh_{CH4}	300	300	300	294	251	176	71	0
Liquid fuel	WTW	gCO_{2eq}/kWh_{th}	368	366	366	358	305	211	96	8

The total GHG emissions of the transport sector on different levels of aggregation and for different years can be calculated according to Equation (13), which is closely linked to Equation (12). The structure of Equation (13) is also visualized in Figure 4. This calculation can be carried out per geographic entity, for instance a country, and then aggregated to larger regions, continents, and the world, in the same way as for the final energy demand. The TTW, WTW, or WTT GHG emissions can be analyzed separately, by applied respective values according to Table 11. Detailed numbers for all input data can be found in the Supplementary Material (Table S1).

$$GHG_{total,b,year} = \sum_{i,s,v,f} TA_{i,s} \cdot VT_v \cdot F_{i,s,v,f} \cdot ED_{i,s,v} \cdot GHG_{f,b} \qquad (13)$$

wherein, GHG_{total} is the total GHG emissions, b is the balancing of WTT, TTW, or WTW, $year$ is the considered year within the transition period, TA is the transportation activity, VT is the vehicle type, F is the fuel-share distribution, ED is the specific energy demand, GHG_f is the specific GHG emission per final fuel, and the indices are i for the transport mode (road, rail, marine, aviation), s for the transport segment (passenger, freight; for road: LDV, 2W/3W, BUS, MDV, HDV), v for the vehicle type (road: ICE, BEV, PHEV, FCEV), and f for the fuel type (electricity, hydrogen, LNG, liquid fuels).

The total GHG emissions according to Equation (13) can be categorized in different ways, e.g., as total global for all countries and all transport activities, or per country for a transport mode or transport segment, or for a specific fuel type.

2.7. Primary Energy Demand and Well-to-Wheel Efficiency

WTW efficiency analysis for various fuels and vehicle types used is a key metric for the transport sector, since it considers the entire energetic value chain from primary energy to final mechanical use. The WTW concept consists of WTT, comprising the fuel production chain from primary energy to final energy fuels, and TTW, which comprises the final energy fuels used in vehicles. For WTT, the full life cycle chain of the fuels is evaluated for analyzing the fuel efficiency. The conversion steps comprise the principle routes from primary input to final energy fuels, as characterized in Table 12. Primary energy is defined as the first form of energy provided by an extraction technology from nature. This applies to fossil fuels (coal, natural gas and crude oil), nuclear fuels (uranium), biofuels (biomass) and renewable electricity (solar PV, wind electricity, hydropower). Losses of power transmission and distribution are considered for all electricity generation. For renewable electricity, there are two further loss types, which are considered for the WTT value chain: curtailment and storage. Curtailment and storage losses related to renewable electricity are taken from Bogdanov et al. [95] and overall power transmission losses are taken from Sadovskaia et al. [130].

Table 12. Overview of conversion processes from primary input to final energy fuels for the WTT perspective.

Primary Input	Conversion	Final Energy Fuel
Fossil fuels	Refinery	liquid hydrocarbons, diesel, gasoline
Fossil fuels	Power plants (coal, gas, oil)	electricity
Fossil fuels	Steam methane reforming	hydrogen
Nuclear fuels	Nuclear power plant	electricity
Electricity	Fischer-Tropsch	liquid hydrocarbons
Electricity	Electrolysis	hydrogen
Hydrogen	Methanation	methane
Methane	Liquefaction	LNG
Biomass	Biorefinery	biofuels, liquid hydrocarbons, biodiesel, bioethanol

For example, if the final energy fuel is LNG, the efficiency chain from raw material extraction to the vehicle tank has to be taken into account, and in the case of renewable electricity, the electricity generation, the conversion steps, electrolyzer, methanation, and liquefaction are required and the losses due to power transmission, curtailment, and storage have to be considered. Table 13 details the WTT efficiencies taken into account for all final energy fuels. The references indicated are used for the respective efficiencies.

Table 13. WTT efficiency values for all final energy fuels. Renewable electricity (RE) is mainly composed of solar PV, wind electricity, and hydropower. Conversion of fossil fuels to electricity is volume averaged for the power plant types of coal, combined cycle gas turbines, open cycle gas turbines, and internal combustion engines.

Primary Origination	Fuel Type	WTT Efficiency	2015	2020	2025	2030	2035	2040	2045	2050
Fossil	Diesel [131,132]	%	83	84	85	85	86	87	87	88
Fossil	Gasoline [131,132]	%	85	86	86	87	88	88	89	90
Fossil	Liquid Hydrocarbons	%	84	85	85	86	87	87	88	89
RE	Liquid Hydrocarbons [133]	%	n/a	n/a	n/a	53	53	53	53	53
Fossil	Electricity [95]	%	44	46	47	48	47	46	46	0
Nuclear	Electricity [95]	%	33	33	33	33	37	37	37	38
RE	Electricity [95]	%	100	100	100	100	100	100	100	100
Fossil	Hydrogen [134]	%	85	85	85	85	85	85	85	85
RE	Hydrogen [95]	%	84	84	84	84	84	84	84	84
Fossil	LNG [135]	%	85	85	85	85	85	85	85	85
RE	LNG [135]	%	57	57	57	57	57	57	57	57
Corn	Bioethanol [131]	%	61	61	61	61	61	61	61	61
Sugarcane	Bioethanol [131]	%	48	48	48	48	48	48	48	48
Palm	Biodiesel [131]	%	80	80	80	80	80	80	80	80
Biomass	Liquid Hydrocarbons	%	60	60	60	60	60	60	60	60

Fossil liquid hydrocarbons is an average of diesel and gasoline in the ratio 1:1. Similarly, biomass-based liquid hydrocarbons is the weighted average of the two main biofuels, composed by 79% of bioethanol and 21% of biodiesel [136]. Hydrogen and LNG are considered from fossil fuels and renewable electricity with changing shares during the transition period. Electricity is supplied from renewable sources, nuclear, and fossil fuels with changing shares during the transition period from 2015 to 2050. Production route shares for the final energy fuels are indicated in Table 14, in case more than only one route exists. Electricity is factored in according to the generation mix of the respective period.

Table 14. Shares of final energy production routes.

Final Energy Fuel	Input	Contribution Share	2015	2020	2025	2030	2035	2040	2045	2050
	Fossil	%	68	50	19	7	2	1	0	0
Electricity	Nuclear	%	10	10	7	4	2	1	1	0
	Renewable	%	22	40	74	89	96	98	99	100
Hydrogen	Fossil	%	100	90	75	50	35	15	5	0
	Electricity	%	0	10	25	50	65	85	95	100
LNG	Fossil	%	100	100	100	97	82	57	23	0
	Electricity	%	0	0	0	3	18	43	77	100
	Biofuel	%	3	4	4	4	4	4	4	4
Liquid hydrocarbons	FT fuels	%	0	0	0	3	18	43	73	96
	Fossil	%	97	96	96	93	78	53	23	0

TTW efficiency for the four transport modes is calculated to represent how much final energy can be converted by the power trains to mechanical energy and the rest is allocated as loss. Table 15 shows the TTW efficiencies for the road transport segments, while Table 16 shows the TTW efficiencies for the transport modes rail, marine, and aviation.

Table 15. TTW efficiencies of all vehicle types for road transport.

Vehicle	Type	TTW Efficiency	2015	2020	2025	2030	2035	2040	2045	2050
	ICE [137]	%	20	22	24	26	26	27	27	28
	BEV [138]	%	74	77	81	84	86	87	89	91
LDV	PHEV—ICE	%	20	22	24	26	26	27	27	28
	PHEV—EV	%	74	77	81	84	86	87	89	91
	FCEV [131]	%	30	34	39	43	45	47	48	50
2W/3W [139]	ICE	%	12	13	14	16	16	16	16	17
	BEV	%	44	46	48	50	51	52	53	54
	ICE	%	33	33	34	35	35	36	36	37
	BEV	%	73	76	79	83	85	86	88	90
BUS [140]	PHEV—ICE	%	33	33	34	35	35	36	36	37
	PHEV—EV	%	73	76	79	83	85	86	88	90
	FCEV	%	44	46	48	50	52	54	56	58
	ICE [141]	%	32	32	33	33	34	34	35	35
	BEV [142]	%	73	76	79	83	85	86	88	90
MDV	PHEV—ICE	%	32	32	33	33	34	34	35	35
	PHEV—EV	%	73	76	79	83	85	86	88	90
	FCEV [142]	%	45	47	49	51	53	55	57	59
	ICE [141]	%	41	42	43	43	44	45	45	46
	BEV [142]	%	73	76	79	83	85	86	88	90
HDV	PHEV—ICE	%	41	42	43	43	44	45	45	46
	PHEV—EV	%	73	76	79	83	85	86	88	90
	FCEV [142]	%	45	47	49	51	53	55	57	59

Table 16. TTW efficiencies for the transport modes rail, marine, and aviation.

Modes	Type	TTW Efficiency	2015	2020	2025	2030	2035	2040	2045	2050
Rail, trains [143]	Electric	%	76	77	78	79	80	81	82	83
	Diesel	%	31	33	34	35	36	36	37	37
	Electric	%	62	63	64	64	65	66	67	68
Marine, ships [36,144]	Hydrogen	%	45	48	51	54	56	57	59	60
	LNG	%	45	46	48	49	50	50	51	51
	Diesel	%	42	43	45	46	47	47	48	48
Aviation, airplanes [54]	Electric	%	73	74	75	76	77	78	79	81
	Hydrogen	%	44	46	47	49	50	52	54	55
	Jet fuel	%	39	40	41	42	43	44	44	45

3. Results

3.1. Global, Regional, and Country Level Transportation Demand

The transportation demand is structured into the four transport modes, road, rail, marine, and aviation, each for passenger and freight transportation, as detailed in Section 2.2. The geographic structuring of the global results are in accordance to Bogdanov et al. [95], for the nine major regions: Europe, Eurasia, Middle East Northern Africa (MENA), Sub-Saharan Africa, South Asian Association for Regional Cooperation (SAARC), Northeast Asia, Southeast Asia, North America, and South America. The scaling of the geographic results and aggregation is visualized in Figure 5 for the global road passenger and freight transportation demand during the entire energy transition period. The European aviation transportation demand for passenger and freight is shown in Figure 6. The marine transportation demand in France for passengers and freight is depicted in Figure 7. The disaggregated values for all countries, transport modes, and transport segments can be found in the Supplementary Material (Table S1). The global transportation demand for the transport modes rail, marine, and aviation across the nine major regions during the transition period is presented in Figures 8–10. All transport modes are faced with strong global transportation demand growth, as also mentioned in Section 2.1. More detailed diagrams for the four transport modes across the nine major regions and on the country level is presented in the Supplementary Material (Figures S1–S5). All numeric details are part of the comprehensive tables in the Supplementary Material (Table S1), which allow further analyses.

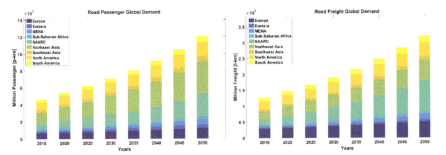

Figure 5. Global road transportation demand for passenger and freight in the nine major regions in resolution of 5-year intervals from 2015 to 2050.

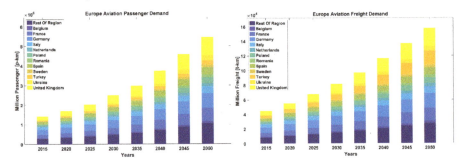

Figure 6. European aviation transportation demand for passenger and freight in the country resolution for the years 2015 to 2050.

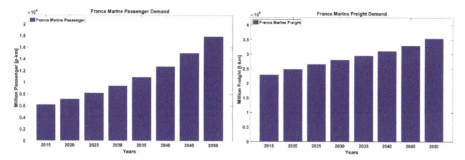

Figure 7. France marine transportation demand for passenger and freight for the years 2015 to 2050.

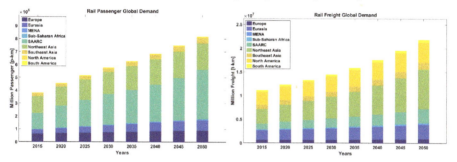

Figure 8. Global rail transportation demand for passenger and freight in the nine major regions for the years 2015 to 2050.

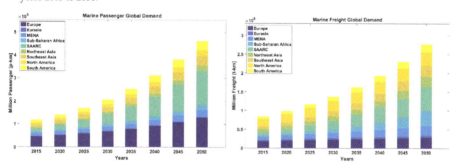

Figure 9. Global marine transportation demand for passenger and freight in the nine major regions for the years 2015 to 2050.

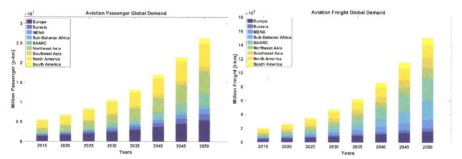

Figure 10. Global aviation transportation demand for passenger and freight in the nine major regions for the years 2015 to 2050.

3.2. Specific Energy Demand, Road LCOM, and Shares of Vehicle and Fuel Types

3.2.1. Specific Energy Demand

The specific energy demand and energy intensity values for all transport modes are calculated according to the methods introduced and are presented in detail in this section. Values for specific energy demand for the road transport mode are presented in greater detail in Table 17 with a variety of segments (LDV, 2W/3W, BUS, MDV, HDV) and vehicle technologies (ICE, BEV, PHEV, FCEV). The values of specific energy demand for the transport modes rail, marine, and aviation are presented in Table 18, also comprising differentiation according to passenger and freight transportation and the fuel options.

Table 17. Specific energy demand for the transport mode road. The values are detailed according to the road transportation segments, vehicle types for the years 2015 to 2050.

Vehicle	Type	Unit	2015	2020	2025	2030	2035	2040	2045	2050
LDV	ICE	kWh_{th}/p-km	0.485	0.456	0.413	0.368	0.336	0.308	0.260	0.211
	BEV	kWh_{el}/p-km	0.113	0.101	0.089	0.078	0.072	0.067	0.061	0.055
	PHEV	kWh_{th}/p-km	0.145	0.114	0.091	0.081	0.074	0.068	0.057	0.046
	PHEV	kWh_{el}/p-km	0.079	0.075	0.069	0.061	0.056	0.052	0.048	0.043
	FCEV	kWh_{H2}/p-km	0.172	0.164	0.136	0.130	0.119	0.118	0.097	0.091
2W/3W	ICE	kWh_{th}/p-km	0.126	0.126	0.126	0.126	0.125	0.125	0.125	0.125
	BEV	kWh_{el}/p-km	0.044	0.044	0.044	0.044	0.044	0.044	0.044	0.044
BUS	ICE	kWh_{th}/p-km	0.233	0.224	0.210	0.210	0.205	0.199	0.193	0.189
	BEV	kWh_{el}/p-km	0.107	0.101	0.095	0.091	0.087	0.083	0.079	0.076
	PHEV	kWh_{th}/p-km	0.116	0.112	0.105	0.105	0.102	0.100	0.097	0.095
	PHEV	kWh_{el}/p-km	0.053	0.050	0.048	0.045	0.043	0.041	0.039	0.038
	FCEV	kWh_{H2}/p-km	0.178	0.166	0.156	0.147	0.139	0.132	0.124	0.118
MDV	ICE	kWh_{th}/t-km	1.334	1.229	1.132	1.043	0.961	0.885	0.815	0.751
	BEV	kWh_{el}/t-km	0.549	0.479	0.419	0.367	0.333	0.302	0.275	0.251
	PHEV	kWh_{th}/t-km	0.801	0.737	0.679	0.626	0.576	0.531	0.489	0.450
	PHEV	kWh_{el}/t-km	0.220	0.191	0.168	0.147	0.133	0.121	0.110	0.101
	FCEV	kWh_{H2}/t-km	0.801	0.737	0.679	0.626	0.576	0.531	0.489	0.450
HDV	ICE	kWh_{th}/t-km	0.445	0.403	0.365	0.330	0.299	0.271	0.246	0.222
	BEV	kWh_{el}/t-km	0.237	0.207	0.181	0.159	0.144	0.130	0.119	0.108
	PHEV	kWh_{th}/t-km	0.311	0.282	0.255	0.231	0.210	0.190	0.172	0.156
	PHEV	kWh_{el}/t-km	0.071	0.062	0.054	0.048	0.043	0.039	0.036	0.032
	FCEV	kWh_{H2}/t-km	0.267	0.242	0.219	0.198	0.180	0.163	0.147	0.133

The load factor for each transport segment is assumed to be identical within each vehicle category. For example, in the case of LDV BEV, the same average number of passengers in the vehicle as in LDV ICE is assumed. The load factor for MDV and HDV is measured in tons per vehicle, and it is assumed to be identical, independent of the vehicle type. The values in Table 18 show the energy required to transport one passenger or one ton over one kilometer, depending on the road transport segment, the vehicle type, and fuel used. The specific energy demand declines over time for all road transport segments and vehicle types, due to enhancements in vehicle technology. The relative efficiency of the vehicle types is a structural element of the results, since the least specific final energy demand is required for BEV, followed by FCEV, PHEV, and finally, ICE. PHEV mixes ICE and BEV, so that both fuels, electricity, and liquid fuels, are required. By 2050, all values decline to its minimum value, since no reduction in efficiency is assumed. 2W/3W BEV appears to be the most efficient vehicles for passenger transportation in the road transport mode with 0.044 kWh_{el}/p-km and MDV ICE, the least efficient with a consumption of 0.751 kWh_{th}/t-km, as it requires more energy with less ton capacity.

Table 18. Specific energy demand for the transport modes rail, marine, and aviation. The values are detailed according to the segment's passenger and freight transportation, and the assumed fuels for the years 2015 to 2050.

Modes	Type	Unit	2015	2020	2025	2030	2035	2040	2045	2050
Rail	Electricity	kWh_{el}/p-km	0.068	0.065	0.063	0.060	0.058	0.055	0.053	0.050
	Diesel	kWh_{th}/p-km	0.105	0.104	0.102	0.101	0.099	0.097	0.096	0.094
	Electricity	kWh_{el}/t-km	0.034	0.032	0.030	0.028	0.026	0.024	0.022	0.019
	Diesel	kWh_{th}/t-km	0.065	0.063	0.060	0.058	0.056	0.054	0.052	0.050
Marine	Electricity	kWh_{el}/p-km	0.315	0.319	0.323	0.325	0.325	0.325	0.325	0.325
	Diesel	kWh_{th}/p-km	0.680	0.657	0.634	0.612	0.605	0.599	0.592	0.586
	LNG	kWh_{CH4}/p-km	0.680	0.657	0.634	0.612	0.605	0.599	0.592	0.586
	Hydrogen	kWh_{H2}/p-km	n/a	n/a	n/a	0.566	0.521	0.484	0.472	0.461
	Electricity	kWh_{el}/t-km	0.019	0.020	0.020	0.020	0.020	0.020	0.020	0.020
	Diesel	kWh_{th}/t-km	0.042	0.041	0.039	0.038	0.037	0.037	0.037	0.036
	LNG	kWh_{CH4}/t-km	0.042	0.041	0.039	0.038	0.037	0.037	0.037	0.036
	Hydrogen	kWh_{H2}/t-km	n/a	n/a	n/a	0.035	0.032	0.030	0.029	0.029
Aviation	Electricity	kWh_{el}/p-km	0.204	0.194	0.184	0.175	0.166	0.157	0.149	0.141
	Jet fuel	kWh_{th}/p-km	0.545	0.517	0.490	0.465	0.442	0.419	0.398	0.377
	Hydrogen	kWh_{H2}/p-km	0.392	0.372	0.353	0.335	0.318	0.302	0.286	0.271
	Electricity	kWh_{el}/t-km	0.053	0.050	0.048	0.045	0.043	0.041	0.039	0.037
	Jet fuel	kWh_{th}/t-km	0.142	0.134	0.128	0.121	0.115	0.109	0.104	0.098
	Hydrogen	kWh_{H2}/t-km	0.102	0.097	0.092	0.087	0.083	0.079	0.075	0.071

In the transport mode rail, the specific final energy demand of electric trains is lower than their diesel (liquid-fuel) counterparts in 2015, with a trend of increasing energy efficiency for both power trains. The highest energy efficiency of freight transportation is enabled by ships. The relative specific final energy demand for freight transportation in 2015 for marine (0.042 kWh_{th}/t-km), rail (0.065 kWh_{th}/t-km), aviation (0.142 kWh_{th}/t-km), clearly indicates that bulk transportation is most energy efficient by ships, followed by trains, and only highly valuable cargo to be transported in airplanes, as a consequence of relative efficiency. The longer the transport distances, the more relative efficiency matters. Another clear trend that can be observed in the relative specific final energy demand values for all transport modes for fuels. Electricity-based transportation is for all transport modes the most energy efficient option, but currently only accessible for railways in substantial volumes. As soon as more electricity-based ships and airplanes are available, the relative transportation share can be expected to rise, because of efficiency gains. Since energy density for long-distance transportation is a severe challenge for batteries, hydrogen appears as a valuable option for the energy transition in the transport sector. The conclusions of Horvath et al. [36] confirm this observation. The final energy fuel hydrogen is emission-free, the fuel can be based on sustainable electricity and the relative end-use efficiency places hydrogen-based solutions between direct electricity-based options and liquid-fuel options, which are currently in use. The fundamental insights for the relative efficiencies of electricity, hydrogen, and liquid-fuel-based options can be observed in all four transport modes.

3.2.2. Road LCOM

LCOM is considered for the road transport mode, so that the fuel shares and vehicle types can be better derived for the road transport segments. The fuel shares for the other transport modes are obtained from other sources, and are described in Section 3.2.3. LCOM is comprised of capex and opex fixed, as detailed in Equation (8). The capex values for all road vehicle types for the energy transition period are derived according to Section 2.4 and summarized in Table 19. The respective opex fixed values for the LCOM are calculated according to Section 2.4 and summarized in Table 20. The opex variable values are based on assumptions shown in Table 21 and summarized in Table 22, for all road transport segments and vehicle types, separated for the cost of energy and cost of GHG emissions.

The energy scenarios presented by Bogdanov et al. [95] and Breyer et al. [145] are considered. LCOM for all road transport segments and vehicle types are presented in Table 23 and visualized in Figure 5.

Table 19. Capex for all road transport segments and vehicle types for 2015 to 2050. More details on the capex composition can be found in the Supplementary Material (Table S1).

Vehicle	Type	Unit	2015	2020	2025	2030	2035	2040	2045	2050
LDV	ICE	€/unit	20,260	20,260	20,260	20,260	20,260	20,260	20,260	20,260
	BEV	€/unit	50,070	30,126	25,805	22,850	22,279	21,756	21,279	20,843
	PHEV	€/unit	25,466	23,874	22,593	21,679	21,510	21,296	21,153	20,974
	FCEV	€/unit	46,396	35,144	28,199	23,896	23,199	22,572	22,006	21,496
BUS	ICE	€/unit	225,000	225,000	225,000	225,000	225,000	225,000	225,000	225,000
	BEV	€/unit	289,735	254,988	230,663	213,534	210,143	207,020	204,142	201,489
	PHEV	€/unit	255,089	242,750	233,279	225,952	224,403	222,946	221,573	220,280
	FCEV	€/unit	742,500	612,085	511,172	433,088	413,592	395,519	378,765	363,234
MDV	ICE	€/unit	78,950	78,950	78,950	78,950	78,950	78,950	78,950	78,950
	BEV	€/unit	102,177	89,739	81,039	74,918	73,707	72,592	71,565	70,618
	PHEV	€/unit	89,458	85,136	81,813	79,237	78,692	78,179	77,695	77,240
	FCEV	€/unit	111,138	92,009	80,203	72,888	71,703	70,637	69,676	68,808
HDV	ICE	€/unit	152,000	152,000	152,000	152,000	152,000	152,000	152,000	152,000
	BEV	€/unit	337,364	265,925	217,695	185,132	178,896	173,219	168,051	163,343
	PHEV	€/unit	172,922	164,376	157,833	152,784	151,718	150,715	149,772	148,883
	FCEV	€/unit	189,358	161,228	143,866	133,108	131,365	129,797	128,384	127,108

Table 20. Opex fixed for all road transport segments and vehicle types for 2015 to 2050. More details on the opex fixed composition can be found in the Supplementary Material (Table S1).

Vehicle	Type	Unit	2015	2020	2025	2030	2035	2040	2045	2050
LDV	ICE	€/year	1207	1207	1207	1207	1207	1207	1207	1207
	BEV	€/year	898	898	898	898	898	898	898	898
	PHEV	€/year	1318	1318	1318	1318	1318	1318	1318	1318
	FCEV	€/year	1053	1053	1053	1053	1053	1053	1053	1053
BUS	ICE	€/year	36,983	36,983	36,983	36,983	36,983	36,983	36,983	36,983
	BEV	€/year	30,775	30,775	30,775	30,775	30,775	30,775	30,775	30,775
	PHEV	€/year	39,212	39,212	39,212	39,212	39,212	39,212	39,212	39,212
	FCEV	€/year	33,879	33,879	33,879	33,879	33,879	33,879	33,879	33,879
MDV	ICE	€/year	15,461	15,461	15,461	15,461	15,461	15,461	15,461	15,461
	BEV	€/year	13,098	13,098	13,098	13,098	13,098	13,098	13,098	13,098
	PHEV	€/year	16,310	16,310	16,310	16,310	16,310	16,310	16,310	16,310
	FCEV	€/year	14,280	14,280	14,280	14,280	14,280	14,280	14,280	14,280
HDV	ICE	€/year	33,468	33,468	33,468	33,468	33,468	33,468	33,468	33,468
	BEV	€/year	27,260	27,260	27,260	27,260	27,260	27,260	27,260	27,260
	PHEV	€/year	35,697	35,697	35,697	35,697	35,697	35,697	35,697	35,697
	FCEV	€/year	30,364	30,364	30,364	30,364	30,364	30,364	30,364	30,364

Table 21. Opex variable assumptions for all road transport segments and vehicle types for 2015 to 2050.

Quantity	Unit	2015	2020	2025	2030	2035	2040	2045	2050
Electricity price excluding distribution	€/kWh$_{el}$	0.070	0.067	0.063	0.060	0.057	0.054	0.052	0.049
Electricity price including distribution	€/kWh$_{el}$	0.093	0.088	0.084	0.080	0.076	0.072	0.069	0.065
Fuel price excluding distribution	€/kWh$_{th}$	0.070	0.075	0.081	0.088	0.094	0.102	0.109	0.118
Fuel price including distribution	€/kWh$_{th}$	0.079	0.085	0.092	0.099	0.106	0.115	0.123	0.133
Hydrogen price excluding distribution	€/kWh$_{H2}$	0.139	0.130	0.120	0.110	0.104	0.099	0.094	0.089
Hydrogen price including distribution	€/kWh$_{H2}$	0.181	0.170	0.156	0.144	0.137	0.130	0.123	0.117
CO_2 price	€/t	9.000	28.00	52.00	61.00	68.00	75.00	100.00	150.00
Fuel price	€/l	0.700	0.750	0.812	0.875	0.943	1.016	1.094	1.179

Table 22. Opex variable for all road transport segments and vehicle types for 2015 to 2050. *E* and *GHG* indicate the energy-related and GHG-related opex variable, respectively.

Vehicle	Type		Unit	2015	2020	2025	2030	2035	2040	2045	2050
LDV	ICE	E	€/km	0.062	0.064	0.063	0.061	0.060	0.060	0.055	0.049
		GHG	€/km	0.002	0.006	0.009	0.010	0.008	0.006	0.003	0.001
	BEV	E	€/km	0.017	0.015	0.012	0.010	0.009	0.008	0.007	0.006
		GHG	€/km	0.000	0.000	0.000	0.000	0.000	0.000	0.000	0.000
	PHEV	E	€/km	0.030	0.027	0.024	0.022	0.020	0.019	0.018	0.016
		GHG	€/km	0.001	0.001	0.002	0.002	0.002	0.001	0.001	0.000
	FCEV	E	€/km	0.050	0.046	0.035	0.031	0.027	0.026	0.020	0.018
		GHG	€/km	0.000	0.000	0.000	0.000	0.000	0.000	0.000	0.000
BUS	ICE	E	€/km	0.323	0.342	0.363	0.384	0.407	0.431	0.457	0.484
		GHG	€/km	0.010	0.030	0.055	0.061	0.057	0.043	0.026	0.006
	BEV	E	€/km	0.174	0.160	0.146	0.134	0.123	0.113	0.104	0.095
		GHG	€/km	0.000	0.000	0.000	0.000	0.000	0.000	0.000	0.000
	PHEV	E	€/km	0.248	0.251	0.249	0.259	0.265	0.272	0.280	0.289
		GHG	€/km	0.005	0.015	0.026	0.031	0.028	0.021	0.013	0.003
	FCEV	E	€/km	0.566	0.507	0.446	0.392	0.355	0.322	0.291	0.264
		GHG	€/km	0.000	0.000	0.000	0.000	0.000	0.000	0.000	0.000
MDV	ICE	E	€/km	0.179	0.183	0.185	0.187	0.189	0.192	0.194	0.194
		GHG	€/km	0.002	0.006	0.010	0.010	0.009	0.006	0.004	0.001
	BEV	E	€/km	0.087	0.074	0.063	0.053	0.047	0.041	0.036	0.032
		GHG	€/km	0.000	0.000	0.000	0.000	0.000	0.000	0.000	0.000
	PHEV	E	€/km	0.142	0.139	0.136	0.134	0.132	0.132	0.131	0.129
		GHG	€/km	0.003	0.010	0.017	0.018	0.016	0.011	0.007	0.001
	FCEV	E	€/km	0.247	0.219	0.189	0.164	0.146	0.130	0.116	0.102
		GHG	€/km	0.000	0.000	0.000	0.000	0.000	0.000	0.000	0.000
HDV	ICE	E	€/km	0.277	0.277	0.276	0.275	0.273	0.272	0.271	0.268
		GHG	€/km	0.004	0.012	0.021	0.021	0.018	0.013	0.008	0.001
	BEV	E	€/km	0.174	0.148	0.125	0.107	0.094	0.083	0.073	0.064
		GHG	€/km	0.000	0.000	0.000	0.000	0.000	0.000	0.000	0.000
	PHEV	E	€/km	0.246	0.238	0.231	0.224	0.220	0.215	0.211	0.207
		GHG	€/km	0.006	0.017	0.029	0.031	0.027	0.019	0.011	0.002
	FCEV	E	€/km	0.382	0.332	0.282	0.241	0.211	0.185	0.162	0.141
		GHG	€/km	0.000	0.000	0.000	0.000	0.000	0.000	0.000	0.000

Table 23. LCOM for all road transport segments and vehicle types for 2015 to 2050.

Vehicle	Type	Unit	2015	2020	2025	2030	2035	2040	2045	2050
LDV	ICE	€/km	0.299	0.314	0.329	0.335	0.340	0.345	0.347	0.350
	BEV	€/km	0.491	0.340	0.309	0.285	0.283	0.282	0.281	0.281
	PHEV	€/km	0.318	0.313	0.312	0.310	0.313	0.316	0.319	0.322
	FCEV	€/km	0.471	0.396	0.346	0.314	0.310	0.309	0.304	0.303
BUS	ICE	€/km	1.286	1.291	1.314	1.319	1.326	1.335	1.364	1.426
	BEV	€/km	1.196	1.070	0.986	0.918	0.881	0.847	0.815	0.793
	PHEV	€/km	1.310	1.258	1.225	1.200	1.183	1.168	1.166	1.184
	FCEV	€/km	2.348	2.012	1.753	1.542	1.447	1.359	1.280	1.216
MDV	ICE	€/km	1.240	1.233	1.193	1.169	1.144	1.132	1.125	1.128
	BEV	€/km	1.190	1.083	0.973	0.904	0.866	0.841	0.816	0.794
	PHEV	€/km	1.312	1.263	1.190	1.144	1.111	1.091	1.075	1.067
	FCEV	€/km	1.405	1.263	1.127	1.042	0.993	0.957	0.923	0.893
HDV	ICE	€/km	1.194	1.227	1.254	1.263	1.270	1.278	1.295	1.323
	BEV	€/km	1.458	1.271	1.134	1.037	1.015	0.996	0.980	0.967
	PHEV	€/km	1.263	1.261	1.259	1.249	1.250	1.252	1.262	1.279
	FCEV	€/km	1.306	1.218	1.143	1.086	1.059	1.037	1.018	1.002

The steep decline in the capex of batteries can be observed for all road transport segments. For instance, capex for LDV BEV is the highest among all LDV options in 2015, but second lowest in 2050, close to LDV ICE. BUS FCEV has by far the highest capex in 2015, which still remains the highest capex in 2050, but at a much smaller relative difference. BUS BEV starts in 2015 as the second-highest next to BUS FCEV, but it becomes the least capex option from 2030 onwards. MDV FCEV starts as the highest capex option for MDV in 2015, but emerges as the least capex option for MDV from 2030 onwards. A similar trend is found in HDV, for which HDV FCEV may be the most attractive capex option from 2025 onwards.

The structural results show that the opex fixed of PHEV is the highest, since the maintenance cost is the highest, as two different power trains for the ICE and the BEV must be maintained, leading to higher complexity. This can be observed for all transport segments. Second-highest opex fixed can be observed in ICE vehicles, due to the maintenance cost, which is a consequence of the relatively high complexity of ICE, compared to the lower complex FCEV and in particular, BEV. BEV shows the least opex fixed of all road transport segments.

The LCOM for all road transport segments are summarized in Table 23. All results for capex, opex fixed, opex variable, and input data for lifetimes, WACC, and annual average mileage are used to calculate the LCOM, according to Equation (8) for the transport segments LDV, 2W/3W, BUS, MDV, and HDV and the vehicle types ICE, BEV, PHEV, and FCEV. The results for LDV, identify LDV ICE as the least cost type in 2015, but from 2025 onwards, LDV BEV is the least LCOM option for LDV. For BUS, the BEV option is already in 2015 slightly lower in LCOM than BUS ICE and BUS BEV remains the least LCOM option for BUS. This fundamental insight seems to be recognized in China, since there are by far the highest number of BUS BEV operating in China [146], with Shenzhen in the lead, at the end of 2017, all city buses have switched to the BUS BEV option [147,148]. The results for MDV reveal a similar dynamic as in BUS; however, this has not yet been observed in the market. The results for HDV show similarities to LDV; however, the HDV BEV and HDV FCEV LCOM are very close, so that a co-existence of both vehicle types may occur.

The results of Table 23 are further visualized in Figure 11 for a more detailed discussion of the important road transport mode. The structural result is that for all transport segments, the BEV option shows the least LCOM from 2025 onwards, which is a very strong indication that practically all road vehicles will have a strong tendency to transition towards the BEV option. However, for LDV and in particular HDV, the FCEV option is rather close, so that a technological co-existence of both vehicle types seems to be rather likely. For BUS, the BEV option is by far the least LCOM option, so it may be expected that the other vehicle types may not play a significant role in the years to come. The PHEV option outperforms the ICE option for all road transport segments form 2025 onwards, clearly indicating that the ICE option will decline in newly sold market shares rapidly, across all transport segments. PHEV is the second-highest LCOM option; however, it may be still competitive in many parts of the world, since this option can overcome infrastructure restrictions for electricity supply in developing and emerging countries, as liquid fuels can still be used, as a kind of backup for weak electricity supply grids.

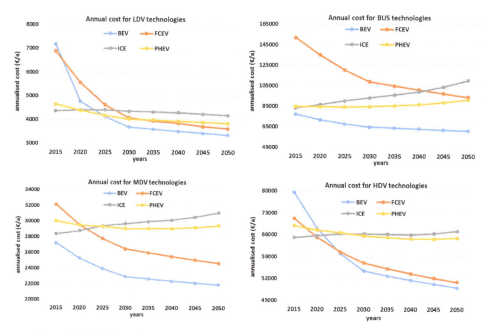

Figure 11. LCOM for road transport segments LDV (**top left**), BUS (**top right**), MDV (**bottom left**) and HDV (**bottom right**) for the vehicle types ICE, BEV, PHEV, and FCEV for the years 2015 to 2050.

3.2.3. Vehicles and Fuel Type Shares

Liquid fuels, electricity, and hydrogen are used in the transport modes of road and aviation. Marine mode uses in addition, LNG. The rail mode uses only liquid fuels and electricity. Figure 12 presents the fuel shares of the road mode for LDV, BUS, MDV, HDV and 2W/3W, and the fuel shares for the modes rail, marine, and aviation. In 2015, LDV operate fully on liquid fuels. Meanwhile, electricity dominates the final energy demand with 82.2% in 2050. Hydrogen used for LDV reaches a maximum share of 8.6% in 2050. Similar to LDV, MDV and HDV are operated by liquid fuels in the beginning of the transition period with a negligible share of electricity. This is expected to change, so that the electricity demand for MDV and HDV will be 82.4% and 54.7% in 2050, respectively, taking into account the BEV share plus the PHEV share with the respective utility factor. The electricity share of BUS is expected to be around 10% in 2020, which is the highest for road vehicles and is expected to reach 93% in 2050. Electricity, liquid fuels, and hydrogen contribute with different shares through the years. LCOM is used to calculate the shares of each type of road transport vehicle in the newly sold vehicles portfolio. Newly sold vehicles replace decommissioned vehicles in the existing stock at the end of their lifetimes. Table 24 shows the stock shares of all road vehicle types.

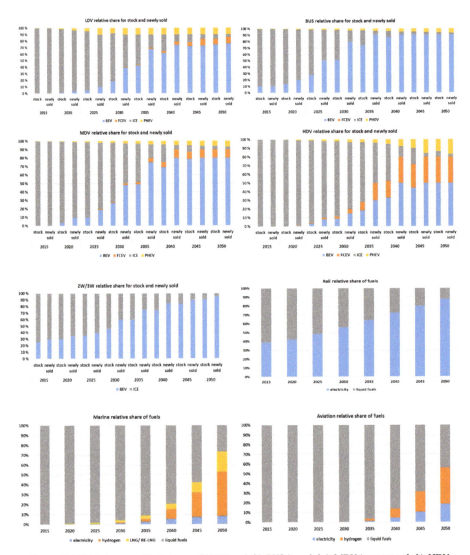

Figure 12. Vehicle types and fuel shares of LDV (**top left**), BUS (**top right**), MDV (**center top left**), HDV (**center top right**), 2W/3W (**center bottom left**), rail (**center bottom right**), marine (**bottom left**), and aviation (**bottom right**) for the years 2015 to 2050.

Table 24. Stock shares of all the vehicles from 2015 to 2050.

Vehicle	Type	Unit	2015	2020	2025	2030	2035	2040	2045	2050
LDV	ICE	%	99.6	97.3	90.4	72.6	46.3	25.3	12.1	6.9
	BEV	%	0.2	1.3	4.8	19.1	42.5	61.9	71.8	74.4
	PHEV	%	0.2	1.3	4.8	7.9	10.0	10.0	10.0	10.0
	FCEV	%	0.0	0.0	0.0	0.4	1.1	2.8	6.0	8.6
2W/3W	ICE	%	74.3	69.5	64.6	53.9	40.2	25.6	15.9	9.3
	BEV	%	25.7	30.5	35.4	46.1	59.8	74.4	84.1	90.7
BUS	ICE	%	89.4	85.7	71.1	46.3	22.7	8.9	4.8	3.9
	BEV	%	10.0	13.5	27.6	51.5	74.2	86.9	90.0	90.0
	PHEV	%	0.5	0.7	1.2	2.1	3.0	4.1	5.1	6.0
	FCEV	%	0.1	0.1	0.1	0.1	0.1	0.1	0.1	0.1
MDV	ICE	%	99.6	95.8	88.1	69.9	45.3	20.9	7.8	3.9
	BEV	%	0.2	3.7	10.4	26.9	48.9	68.9	78.6	80.
	PHEV	%	0.2	0.5	1.1	2.1	3.1	4.1	5.1	6.1
	FCEV	%	0.0	0.0	0.4	1.1	2.8	6.0	8.6	10.0
HDV	ICE	%	100	99.1	94.7	86.6	69.2	42.4	18.7	6.1
	BEV	%	0.0	0.4	3.3	8.6	18.3	33.1	44.3	50.0
	PHEV	%	0.0	0.4	1.1	2.1	3.1	5.2	9.9	13.9
	FCEV	%	0.0	0.2	0.9	2.7	9.5	19.3	27.1	30.0

At present, the rail mode has the highest electricity share in all transport modes with 45% for passenger and 39% for freight. Electricity will contribute approximately 87% of the energy demand from the rail mode leaving the rest for liquid fuels in 2050.

Marine uses only liquid fuels in 2015. Meanwhile, from 2020 onwards LNG is projected to contribute more for marine passenger. By 2050, the fuel shares in the marine mode are comprised of 20% LNG, 45% hydrogen, 26% liquid fuel, and 9% electricity, which is used for domestic shipping.

Currently, aviation operates with 100% liquid fuels, while from 2035 onwards, electricity and hydrogen penetration is expected, but still on very small shares. Liquid fuels will play an important role in the aviation of passenger and freight with 44% and 63%, respectively in 2050.

3.3. Global Final Energy Demand for the Transport Sector

Global final energy demand for the transport sector is calculated according to Equation (12), applying the results for the vehicle and fuel shares and the inputs of the transportation activity and specific energy demand per transport mode, segment, and vehicle type. Such a scenario will reflect the ambitious 1.5 °C target of the Paris Agreement [2] and sustainability guardrails [57]. It is not intended to compare different scenarios within the framework presented in this paper. The results are shown per transport mode and segment in Figure 13, and the fuels for covering the final energy demand, as summarized in Table 25. The final energy fuels are electricity, hydrogen, LNG, and liquid fuels.

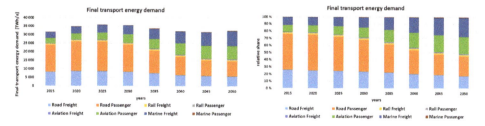

Figure 13. Final global transport energy demand in absolute (**left**) and relative (**right**) values for the years 2015 to 2050.

Table 25. Total global final energy demand of the transport sector aggregated into the four fuel types.

Fuels	Unit	2015	2020	2025	2030	2035	2040	2045	2050
Electricity	TWh$_{el}$/a	531	878	1787	3861	6432	8506	10,046	11,462
Hydrogen	TWh$_{H2}$/a	3	9	42	182	685	2027	4518	8197
LNG	TWh$_{CH4}$/a	0	21	47	107	188	368	869	2067
Liquid fuels	TWh$_{th}$/a	31,079	33,891	33,973	31,459	26,456	21,275	16,325	10,816
Total	TWh/a	31,613	34,799	35,848	35,609	33,761	32,177	31,758	32,542

The road transport mode dominates the total final energy demand of about 31,613 TWh in 2015 with 76%, in which road passenger transportation contributes the major share. The final energy demand of about 32,540 TWh in 2050 is roughly the same as in 2015, which is a result of the strong shift towards higher efficient vehicle types and fuels, since the transportation demand triples, as presented in Figure 1. Not all transport modes benefit from the strong shift towards direct electricity, as for marine and aviation. Therefore, a bit more than 50% of all final energy demand in 2050 is needed to cover marine and aviation transportation. From about 2025 onwards and more prominently from 2030 onwards, the relative final energy demand of the road mode declines, because of strong direct electrification with BEV in all road transport modes.

Liquid fuels dominate the total final energy demand with 98% in 2015, and can still contribute 33% of the final energy demand in 2050, which is mainly for marine and aviation transportation. Electricity grows from a final energy demand supply of 2% in 2015 to 35% in 2050. In 2015 most of the electricity is used for already electrified rail transportation, but most direct electricity is needed in 2050 for road transportation. Hydrogen is practically not used at present, but it can contribute 25% in 2050, meeting the demand form the transport modes road, marine, and aviation. Whether hydrogen will dominate the marine transport mode as fuel in 2050 is still uncertain. However, LNG is currently introduced in marine transportation as a fuel, which could contribute higher shares in 2050 with about 6% of the total transport sector final energy demand, mainly based on the power-to-gas option, as indicated by Horvath et al. [36] and Breyer et al. [145].

3.4. Total GHG Emissions in the Transport Sector

GHG emissions in the transport sector are investigated using the method and parameters introduced in Section 2.7. In the following, the TTW and WTW GHG emissions are presented. The most GHG emissions of combustible vehicles happen at TTW (downstream), while emissions of alternative fuels mostly happen in WTT (upstream) [149]. Figure 14 depicts the GHG emissions of the entire transport sector and highlights the road transport mode, as the dominant transport mode, not only in terms of final energy demand, but also in GHG emissions. The road mode can be defossilized by transitioning to alternative fuels such as electricity, synthetic fuels, mainly hydrogen, and biofuels [150]. Road passenger LDV is the dominant segment for GHG emissions. This high share of more than one third in 2015 declines to small shares from 2040 onwards, as a consequence of high efficiency gains due to massive electrification and in addition due to defossilization of the electricity supply, as indicated by Bogdanov et al. [95]. Aviation passenger and marine freight will evolve as the main GHG emission contributing transport segments, from around 2035 to 2040 onwards. These results clearly indicate that the pressure on airlines and ship operators will dramatically increase to curb their GHG emissions, to comply with the targets of the Paris Agreement.

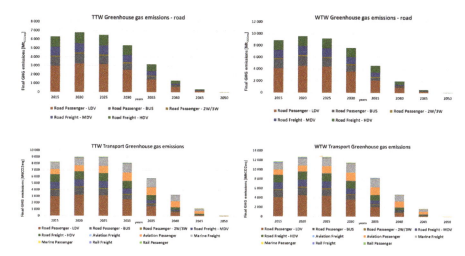

Figure 14. GHG emissions of the entire transport sector (**bottom**) and road transport mode (**top**) for the TTW (**left**) and WTW (**right**) for the years 2015 to 2050 for all transport segments.

3.5. Primary Energy Demand and Well-to-Wheel Efficiency

The WTW efficiency covers all conversions from primary energy to final mechanical energy. There are two phases of losses: first, losses that are induced by conversion of primary energy sources to final energy fuels (WTT efficiency) and second, from the fuel conversion of final energy to mechanical energy by the vehicles (TTW efficiency).

The energy flow for the WTT and TTW efficiency in the global transport sector is depicted in Figure 15 for 2015 (fossil-fuel-dominated) and 2050 (renewable-electricity-dominated), and summarized in Table 26. In 2015, almost all losses are related to the combustion of fuels, while for 2050, relatively more losses are for the conversion of primary energy to final energy fuels and substantially reduced combustion processes and related losses. The overall efficiency in the transport sector is drastically increased from 26% in 2015 to 39% in 2050, i.e., by 50%, measured in mechanical energy at the vehicles versus the total primary energy input for the global transport sector. The conversion efficiency from primary energy to final energy fuels decreases from 82% in 2015 to 62% in 2050, which is mainly caused by synthetic fuel production for the marine and aviation transport modes, whereas the conversion efficiency from final energy fuels to mechanical energy is drastically increased from 31% in 2015 to 62% in 2050. This doubling in TTW efficiency is mainly driven by direct electrification of the road transport mode.

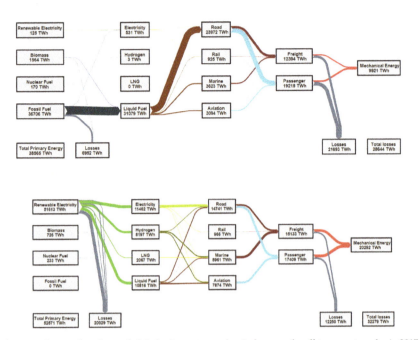

Figure 15. Energy flow for total global primary to mechanical energy for all transport modes in 2015 (**top**) and 2050 (**bottom**).

Table 26. WTW energy demand for the global transport sector and respective transport activities for passenger and freight for 2015 and 2050.

Year	Primary Energy	Final Energy	Mechanical Energy	Transport Activity Passenger	Transport Activity Freight
	TWh	TWh	TWh	b p-km	b t-km
2015	38,565	31,613	9921	181,273	108,006
2050	52,571	32,542	20,292	646,522	332,405
relative change	36.3%	2.9%	104.5%	257%	208%

The transport activity increases from 2015 to 2050 by about 210% (freight) and 260% (passenger) (Tables 2–4 and Figure 1), which requires about 105% more mechanical energy for which only about 3% more final energy fuels are needed, but for 36% more primary energy demand. These numbers reveal not only a higher efficiency of used mechanical energy, but also an enormous gain in efficiency from final energy to mechanical energy, which is a consequence of drastically reduced combustion processes and use of electric power trains, fueled by electricity and hydrogen. The increase in primary energy demand is attributed to more electricity demand for synthetic fuels. Figure 15 also reveals that the primary energy base for the transport sector is fully exchanged during the transition process, from 95% fossil-fuel dominance in 2015 to 98% renewable electricity dominance in 2050.

4. Discussion

4.1. Data Analysis

The transportation demand drastically grows by about 210% to 260% from 2015 to 2050, as shown in Figure 1. This growth can be observed for all transport modes and transport segments on a global scale. While some countries grow stronger, in particular developing and emerging countries, others, mainly developed industrialized countries, grow slower or even stagnate in transportation demand. This strong transportation demand is not translated into final energy demand, which remains roughly constant as a consequence of massive fuel shift towards higher efficient fuels, such as direct electricity and hydrogen conversion, also supported by further efficiency increase in existing power trains.

The most prominent decline is that of specific energy demand for the road mode, as summarized in Table 11. All road vehicle types are expected to further increase efficiency, which is further improved by a shift from ICE to BEV and some FCEV, wherein the two latter lead to higher efficiency for the road mode, in particular BEV. These two fundamental trends can be also observed for the three other transport modes, as summarized in Table 12, i.e., higher efficiency of all power trains, and in addition, a shift from liquid fuels towards hydrogen and direct electricity, where applicable.

These efficiency trends and rise of alternative power trains are clearly documented by the shift of fuels for covering the final energy demand, which is presented in Table 16. The total final energy demand peaks around 2025 to 2030 and declines in the following years by about 9% until 2050, despite the continued growth of transportation demand. Interestingly, if all the 2050 technologies could be used at present, the final energy demand for the transport sector would reduce from about 31,610 TWh to about 21,370 TWh. Even more interesting, using today's technology status for the transportation demand in 2050, the energy demand would drastically rise to about 90,500 TWh, which is about 280% of the final energy demand derived with technological progress and fuel shift, as projected in this research.

The dominant role of the road mode in 2015 with a final energy demand of about 76% is substantially reduced to about 45% in 2050, due to a massive shift towards higher efficient BEV. As long-distance shipping and flights cannot be directly electrified, the two transport modes marine and aviation cannot benefit from the efficiency gains of electric ships and planes, which are projected to proliferate in short distance transport of up to 100 km for ships and up to 1500 km for flights. This leads to a substantial increase in final energy demand of marine, growing from 11.5% to 27.5% and of aviation growing from 9.8% to 24.2% for 2015 and 2050, respectively.

The full LCOM is only considered for the road mode, so that the vehicle type and fuel shift of the most important road mode can be better understood and discussed in greater detail. All road transport segments show the same fundamental result: dominance of BEV, which is driven by high efficiency power trains, competitive fuel costs, declining GHG emissions, projected rapid cost decline of batteries and finally a lower level of complexity compared to ICE vehicles, leading to lower maintenance costs. The first road transport segment for which BEV is the least LCOM solution is BUS, which is indicated by the fast ramp-up of BUS BEV in China [146] and already full 100% BUS BEV penetration in Shenzhen [147,148]. Other world regions may follow quite soon. LDV BEV may grow even faster for end users that have the opportunity for solar PV self-consumption, since it accelerates LDV BEV phase-in, due to enhanced economic performance of even lower costing electricity supply and even higher storage flexibility, all over the world [151], and also for tenements, as analyzed for the case of Germany [152]. FCEV emerges as the second least LCOM in all road transport segments, and HDV and LDV FCEV may evolve as a second option, or at least a backup solution, in case BEV does not develop as fast as projected. Robinius et al. [153] have investigated in a low market penetration scenario, the cost of infrastructure for both LDV BEV and LDV FCEV and found comparable costs. Nevertheless, if 20 million vehicles appear in a scenario for a country such as Germany, an investment for the battery charging infrastructure may roughly cost 51 b€ and the hydrogen infrastructure may cost 40 b€, according to Robinius et al. [153]. However, the total transport segment cost should include the energy system cost for fueling the LDV FCEV and the LDV BEV, which has to take into account the relative efficiencies that are substantially higher for LDV BEV and may balance out a potential infrastructure cost drawback.

From 2025 onwards, ICE is the highest LCOM option resulting in a massive decline of newly sold ICE vehicles. PHEV may be a compromise in developing and emerging countries, even though they are the second-highest LCOM. PHEV can use the higher efficient electric power train, but still can use liquid fuels as a backup in case of lack of electricity supply and weak grids.

The least LCOM of BEV is from the 2020s onward and enables GHG emissions reduction benefits if powered by renewable electricity. The levelized cost of electricity in the power sector is expected to decline, as the renewable energy share increases, which is pointed out by Bogdanov et al. [95]. Since renewable electricity powered BEV shows a highly attractive GHG emission profile close to zero GHG emissions [154], not only BEV LCOM are lower than those of ICE vehicles, but also GHG emissions, leading to GHG emissions reduction benefits, as found earlier in different regions and for different applications due to solar PV in the power sector [155].

The two fuels gaining most ground are electricity and hydrogen, both due to the higher efficiencies compared to current power train options. Hydrogen may only complement direct electricity in the road mode; however, in marine and aviation, hydrogen would have the potential to emerge as the dominant fuel for long-distance transportation [36], in case existing technical challenges are overcome. Hydrogen produced via SMR still causes GHG emissions and may not have much market chances in a climate-constrained energy system. However, renewable electricity-based electrolysis can provide clean and low-cost hydrogen [126], also improving the overall economics of hydrogen as a fuel for the transport sector.

Hydrocarbon fuels can still be used in the transport sector, but they have to be defossilized, which can be achieved by biofuels that are volume constrained and can cause sustainability issues, such as for palm oil, or by electricity-based liquid fuels. Creutzig et al. [156] clearly point out that the total available sustainable biomass potential for the energy sector is about 100 EJ (27,780 TWh) without compromising sustainability constraints, such as sustainability guardrails [57], and thus could provide biofuels of about 16,670 TWh according to the efficiency of about 60% of biomass-to-biofuel conversion. This compares to the 12,880 TWh of LNG and liquid hydrocarbon demand identified in this research. This means that 77% of all sustainably available biomass would be needed to only cover the remaining LNG and liquid hydrocarbon demand in the transport sector in 2050, and thus massively limiting the available biomass resource potential for the other energy sectors. Already, this clearly emphasizes the massive requirement to directly electrify all transport modes, as much as possible. In addition, electricity-based liquid fuels are an option for power-to-gas-based LNG in marine transportation and in particular for Fischer-Tropsch-based jet fuel in the aviation sector, so that the biofuel demand can be reduced to a minimum level and thus releasing more limited potential for other energy sectors. LNG as a marine fuel suffers from the possibility of methane leakage, which is a major threat for this fuel option due to the very high global warming potential of methane emissions. This may reduce the economic potential of renewable-based LNG as a major fuel option for the marine mode.

A full defossilization of the transport sector can be achieved by direct and indirect electrification and the respective transition towards sustainable fuels [36,145]. A first modeling in full hourly resolution of a zero GHG emission transport sector is presented by Ram et al. [157], which further demonstrates the technical feasibility and economic viability of a zero GHG emission transport sector. GHG emissions in the transport sector are projected to peak between 2020 and 2025 and then decline to zero in 2050, based on the applied energy transition scenarios for the power sector and transport sector. About 76% of all GHG emissions are contributed by the road mode in 2015, as shown in Figure 7. However, form 2040 onwards the GHG emissions are dominated by more than 50% by marine and aviation, which is also a consequence of hard-to-abate long-distance transportation. The consequence may be that as soon as the road mode shifts for newly sold vehicles to BEV or sustainable hydrogen-based FCEV options, the pressure on ship operators and airlines grows fast for ambitious defossilization measures. The pressure for airlines may be more drastic, as recent research indicates that zero GHG emissions for the aviation sector may not be possible with fuel measures alone, since contrail–cirrus formation cannot be reduced to zero [158]. Lund et al. [158] conclude that the 100 years of global temperature change impact of contrail–cirrus formations is about 12% of the aviation CO_2 emissions. Burkhardt et al. [159] point out that 80% reduction in atmospheric ice crystals can reduce the global contrail–cirrus radiative forcing by 50%. Synthetic fuels are an effective means to reduce soot and thus atmospheric ice crystals in the required amount. A remaining net positive GHG emissions impact of the aviation mode would have to be balanced by negative CO_2 emissions technologies, such as enabled by CO_2 direct air capture [160] and broadly discussed by Fuss et al. [161].

In 2015, 95% of primary energy need for the transport sector is supplied by fossil fuels. Only 4% is contributed by biofuels and the rest is renewable and nuclear electricity. Meanwhile, in 2050, renewable electricity supplies 98% of the energy need for the transport sector via direct and indirect electrification. The relative losses for freight and passenger transportation in 2015 are 74%, while this can be reduced to losses of 61% in 2050, measured in the WTW perspective. The much lower relative loss in 2050 is mainly driven by direct electrification of the road transport mode, while the penalty of power-to-fuels for the marine and aviation transport mode does not limit dramatically the overall increase in transport sector efficiency. The overall transport sector WTW efficiency can be increased by 50% from 26% in 2015 to 39% in 2050, which is a clear benefit of overall direct and indirect electrification of the transport sector, which is further supported by a fuel switch from less efficient liquid hydrocarbon combustion to higher efficient hydrogen use in fuel cells and highly efficient use of electricity in electric drives. There are several trends observable for efficiency change: first, mechanical energy demand grows by 105%, while transport activities grow to nearly 210% to 260% (Table 26), indicating further substantial improvements in efficiencies of transport vehicles. The fuel and power train switch from liquid fuels to hydrogen and in particular electricity allows that a growth of only 3% in final energy fuels enables a 105% growth in mechanical energy, documenting the low efficiency of combustion processes. The requirement of electricity-based synthetic fuels leads to an increase in primary energy demand of 36%, which seems to be moderate from energetic point of view and attractive from economic point of view. Renewable electricity costs further decline [95], and thereof solar PV is projected to continue the outstanding cost decline to historically unrivalled levels [162] enabling multiple power-to-X processes [163]. Meanwhile, fossil fuels are expected to increase [164,165]. The conversion efficiency of electricity to liquid hydrocarbons of about 53% can well compete with biomass to liquid hydrocarbons of 48–80%, while the latter is mainly based on area limited energy crops, whereas the area for renewable electricity based on solar and wind resources is practically not limited on a global scale. The drastic primary energy switch from 95% fossil sources in 2015 to 98% renewable electricity in 2050 is a consequence of several major trends, such as drastically declining renewable electricity and battery cost, enabling not only a massive road transport electrification, but also affordable synthetic fuels, and finally the requirement of a zero GHG emission energy system according to the Paris Agreement, which is not possible with fossil-fuel combustion in mobile vehicles.

4.2. Comparison to Other Results

In this study, the total final energy demand for the transport sector is calculated for the years 2015 to 2050 in 5-year intervals, in a way that the ambitious 1.5 °C target of the Paris Agreement [2] can be achieved, while the sustainability guardrails [57] are respected. In the following, these findings are compared to results of comparable studies on the transition in the transport sector on a global scale. Table 27 illustrates the results of the final energy demand found in other major studies. Table 27 also shows the total final energy fuel demand share for all transport sector scenarios in 2050. All known global 100% renewable energy studies presenting details for the transport sector are included [166]. García-Olivares et al. [167] do not specify when exactly their 'future' 100% renewable transport sector would be, thus it is estimated by 2050. Brown et al. [168] discuss standard claims against 100% renewable energy studies and debunk these standard myths. In case several scenarios are offered by a reference, then the most progressive scenario of a set of scenarios is included.

Table 27. Total global final energy demand of the transport sector for the years 2015 to 2050 in the referenced scenarios. Various kinds of energy units are converted to TWh for comparability. Total final energy fuel demand shares in 2050 of all transport sectors are listed in the right part of the table. For International Energy Agency (IEA), BP, ExxonMobil, and US DoE EIA scenarios the fuel-share values for 2040 are considered.

Global Transport Sector Scenarios		Final Energy Demand of Transport Sector in TWh/a								Final Energy Fuel Shares in 2050 [%]			
Source	Publ. Year	2015	2020	2025	2030	2035	2040	2045	2050	Fossil Fuels	Biofuels	Synthetic Fuels	Electricity
this study	2019	31,613	34,799	35,848	35,609	33,761	32,177	31,758	32,542	0	1	63	35
Greenpeace [E]R [34]	2015	-	26,129	25,599	25,070	-	21,808	-	19,159	29	14	20	38
Greenpeace [E]R adv. [34]	2015	-	25,850	24,897	23,207	-	18,020	-	14,836	0	14	35	51
Teske, 1.5 °C [169]	2019	30,752	-	29,411	25,606	-	19,604	-	17,001	0	16	36	48
Teske, 2 °C [169]	2019	30,752	-	26,142	20,371	-	15,919	-	14,279	0	25	29	46
Jacobson et al. [170]	2018	-	-	-	-	-	-	-	13,113	0	0	33	67
Löffler et al. [171]	2017	31,298	32,434	28,910	24,069	20,258	16,706	13,326	10,414	0	15	44	41
Pursiheimo et al. [172]	2019	-	-	-	-	-	-	-	23,480	0	30	33	37
García-Olivares et al. [167]	2018	-	-	-	-	-	-	-	28,383	n/a	n/a	n/a	n/a
WWF [173]/Deng et al. [174]	2011	29,102	29,598	28,714	25,940	24,420	19,533	17,998	17,741	0	74	0	26
World Energy Council [175]	2019	34,203	-	33,820	33,413	-	34,448	-	33,134	62	12	9	17
DNV GL [29]	2019	29,861	33,333	35,416	34,027	32,638	31,250	30,555	30,000	49	12	6	33
IEA, WEO NPS [176]	2018	31,308	-	36,564	38,530	40,088	42,065	-	-	90	6	0	4
IEA, WEO SDS [176]	2018	31,308	-	34,250	33,668	-	30,703	-	-	73	13	0	14
Luderer et al. B200 [177]	2018	-	-	-	-	-	-	-	31,945	32	29	18	21
Luderer et al. B800 [177]	2018	-	-	-	-	-	-	-	36,110	47	26	12	15
Shell, Sky [178]	2018	30,812	33,019	34,989	34,611	36,290	37,686	38,837	40,630	67	13	2	18
BP Energy Outlook [179]	2019	29,656	32,564	34,890	36,053	37,216	37,099	-	-	89	7	0	4
ExxonMobil [3]	2017	32,530	-	36,633	-	-	40,736	-	-	94	4	0	2
US DoE EIA [180]	2017	32,823	33,703	35,168	37,806	40,736	44,400	-	-	98	0	0	2

The Greenpeace E[R] scenario [34] defines a high RE penetration in its scenario, which leads to a very low final energy demand for each time step. The Greenpeace E[R] advanced scenario [34] introduces extremely high RE penetration to its transport sector scenario achieving a 100% RE share in 2050, leading to merely 15,703 TWh final energy demand in 2050, which demonstrates a very high level of ambition. Electricity and hydrogen represent a final energy demand of 8122 TWh (51.7%) and 3900 TWh (24.8%), respectively, complemented by biofuels (13.9%) and synthetic fuels (9.5%).

Teske [169] defines three scenarios out of which 1.5 °C and 2 °C are selected for comparison. By around 2030, electricity is projected to supply 12% of the transport sector's total final energy demand in the 2 °C scenario, while in 2050, the share is expected to be 47%. In the 1.5 °C scenario, the annual electricity demand shall be 38% in 2050. Hydrogen contributes 13% and 14% for the 2 °C and 1.5 °C scenarios, respectively, by 2050. Biofuel is also used as complementary renewable option with around 19% and 20% for the 2 °C and 1.5 °C scenarios by 2050.

Jacobson et al. [170] projects 16,638 TWh for 2050, which is a very ambitious target. The scenario aims to only use electricity and hydrogen as a final energy fuel for all transport modes.

Löffler et al. [171] show the most ambitious scenario with the least final energy demand for the transport sector among all scenarios of around 10,410 TWh in 2050. The final energy share of electricity and synthetic fuels is 41% and 44%, respectively, and the rest is supplied by biofuels (15%).

Pursiheimo et al. [172] define a scenario with an ambitious final energy demand of around 23,480 TWh in 2050. The reason for such a low value is to replace fossil fuels fully with biofuels, synthetic fuels and electricity with 30%, 33% and 37%, respectively.

Deng et al. [174] and WWF [173] indicate 26% electricity share in 2050, and the rest of the fuel share stays with biofuels, which is the highest biofuel share of all scenarios.

The World Energy Council [175] projects a couple of scenarios with various fuel shares and consequently different final energy demands. In the most ambitious scenario, named Unfinished Symphony, opted for this study, electricity contributes only 2.4% and 17% for 2025 and 2050, respectively. The hydrogen share is 0.04% and 1.66% for the same period, respectively. Biofuels contribute 15% in 2050. The fossil-fuel share is still 78% in 2050, leading in total to a final energy demand of 37,169 TWh.

DNV GL [29] shows a reduction of the fossil-fuel share from 99% in 2015 to 49% in 2050. Biomass and electricity are projected to reach 12% and 33% by 2050 with a negligible hydrogen share.

The World Energy Outlook of the International Energy Agency (IEA) [176] projects in a very similar way in the New Policy Scenario as ExxonMobil a high fossil-fuel demand (90%) and low electricity penetration in the total final energy demand, which leads to a strong demand increase until 2040, which is about a quarter higher than in this study. The same source, but in the Sustainable Development Scenario projects 30,703 TWh final energy demand for the transport sector for 2040. This energy demand is provided by 73% fossil fuels, complemented by electricity (14%) and biofuels (13%).

Luderer et al. [177] define a couple of different scenarios generated by integrated assessment models, of which the scenarios B200 and B800 from the used GCAM model are selected. The B200 and B800 scenarios require final energy for the transport sector of 31,945 TWh and 36,110 TWh, respectively, for 2050. Energy demand in B800 scenario is more than B200 due to a higher share of fossil fuels. The two scenarios assume a fossil-fuel share of 34.7% and 49.6% for the B200 and B800, respectively, which is hardly in line with the targets of the Paris Agreement.

Shell [178] indicates the share of fossil hydrocarbon fuels in 2015 at around 98.8%. This share dwindles moderately to 80% in 2050. Electricity and hydrogen shares are projected to reach 17.6% and 2.4%, respectively by 2050, and the reason for the high final energy demand is the low level of electrification.

The BP Energy Outlook [179] provides a scenario with liquid fuels, LNG, and electricity as fuel supply. In 2040 energy demand is expected to be more or less high due to low appearance of RE and in particular electricity, since a major part (86%) of all final energy demand is still expected to be supplied by fossil oil, which blocks more efficient fuel and vehicle options.

ExxonMobil [3] projects a total global final energy demand, which is very similar to the projection of US DoE EIA, in assuming 88.5% of fossil-fuel supply for the transport sector energy demand. The 2040 total global final energy demand is the highest of all compared scenarios, with about 40% higher final energy demand as in this study, mainly driven by assuming a very slow rise of alternative fuels and vehicle types, in particular BEV in the road mode.

The Energy Information Administration [180], part of US Department of Energy, projects the total global transport sector final energy demand until 2040 and finds a continuous final energy demand increase. The 2040 final energy demand of 44,400 TWh in 2040 is the highest of all compared studies. This may be a consequence of practically ignoring the opportunities provided by more sustainable fuels and more efficient vehicle types. The fossil-fuel share in 2040 is 98.3% of the total global final energy demand in the transport sector.

4.3. Outlook and Further Investigations

Indications of this study and also results by Jacobson et al. [170], Teske [169] and Pursiheimo et al. [172] clearly indicate a massive increase in electricity demand for a sustainable transport sector, whereas this study and Jacobson et al. [170] project a transport sector practically fully based on electricity in 2050, via direct and indirect electrification, and thus avoiding sustainability conflicts of biofuels, respecting sustainability guardrails [57]. It remains a research question to investigate what this means for a fully sector coupled energy system. The high dynamic flexibility of electrolyzers [181] in conjunction with decreasing capex [95,126] allows a most valuable demand response leading to a very effective energy system integration of variable renewables, in particular solar PV and wind energy, thus reducing curtailment, higher costing storage demand and total system cost. These effects require more analyses. In addition, the enormous fleet of BEV in road transport allows another form of large-scale demand response in the form of smart charging and vehicle-to-grid, both leading to optimized variable renewable electricity system integration [182,183]. This is confirmed by Mathiesen et al. [184] who point out that variable renewable energy can be linked to new sources of flexibility, such as synthetic fuel storage and BEV in a Smart Energy System design, which may even allow a bioenergy-free 100% renewable energy system. Brown et al. [185] find fast defossilizing road and rail transport modes due to high efficiency and attractive economics, further supported by high flexibility benefits due to smart charging and vehicle-to-grid services.

Further analyses are required to better understand the financial parameter setup needed to phase-in all elements required for a fully sustainable transport sector. The road transport mode has been investigated in this study with clear results that in the 2020s the road mode switches to BEV solutions at a high level of probability, driven by least LCOM. However, synthetic fuels required for the marine and aviation mode need very low-cost electricity, high GHG emissions cost, and further scaled synthesis processes. Demand centers for synthetic fuels are often in regions of moderate solar and wind resource conditions, which may be bypassed by imports of synthetic fuels from solar and wind resource rich regions, such as Patagonia [63,65], Maghreb [64], Horn of Africa or Western Australia [186]. The generated value of additional energy system flexibility with electrolyzers, BEV smart charging, and vehicle-to-grid needs to be better quantified and analyzed. More research is required to better understand the key drivers for a cost-effective and rapid phase-in of synthetic fuels.

Material resource limitations must be investigated in a substantially improved manner. Junne et al. [187] found in a very first comparative study on highly renewable energy systems indications for very challenging resource limitations for the transport sector, in particular due to the materials neodymium, dysprosium, lithium, and cobalt, needed for electric motors and lithium-ion batteries. Greim et al. [188] conclude that a continuously growing road transport mode cannot be matched with the economically extractable lithium resource availability leading to an entirely depletion of expected resource in the 2060s, but even earlier if recycling rates and collection rates of end-of-life batteries would not be very close to 100%. Grandell et al. [189] conclude that silver would be the most critical metal for a global energy transition, and thus also highly critical for the transport sector, since solar PV is the dominant source of energy for the transport sector as discussed by Breyer et al. [81]. Detailed research by solar PV experts cannot confirm this concern as the specific silver demand can be further reduced [190] so that the present silver cost level can be prolonged, and furthermore silver can be substituted by copper so that an effective substitution is in place and applied as soon as required [190–192].

Ramp-up of renewables has continuously generated new jobs in recent years as monitored by IRENA [193]. Highly renewable energy scenarios have been coupled to analyze the impact on jobs, as done since several editions for the Greenpeace scenarios [34], but also by Jacobson et al. [90] and recently by Ram et al. [194] who integrated for the first time jobs related to electricity storage. Consequences for jobs for a transport sector flipping from more than 95% fossil-fuel supply in 2015 to an entirely renewable energy supply in 2050, almost fully based on electricity and requiring massive power-to-fuel capacities are of highest interest. The chances are high that more jobs can be generated for the energy supply of a fully sustainable transport sector, compared to a fossil-fuel-based transport sector as of 2015.

The fast progressing anthropogenic climate change [195] requires a fast and drastic response in radical GHG emission reductions to zero, the sooner the better, so that the temperature rise can be limited to 1.5 °C compared to pre-industrial levels. Progress in tackling this historic challenge is much too slow and GHG emissions reduction is not on track at all [196]. The Fridays For Future global youth movement has created a massive momentum within a very short period of time, started in August 2018 by Greta Thunberg. Scientists all around the world have confirmed that the claims and concerns of the global youth are more than justified [92,93], and a massive and radical response is required to avoid a collapse of civilization. Climate change mitigation requires a societal tipping point, so that a drastic response to tackle the climate crisis can be initiated. A new consciousness of humans is needed to respect and rebalance within the planetary boundaries [197]. The impact on the transport sector may be that a drastic reaction may require zero GHG emissions for 2040 or even earlier, implying substantially more ambitious measures than discussed in this paper. The presented transition in the transport sector in this paper is technically and economically possible, however, this has to be driven by societal will for change, which leads to a likelihood whether the proposed scenario can be achieved. In the following a brief discussion on transition dynamics and change processes is provided.

Research on transition dynamics indicate that the speed of transition assumed in this research is possible and not out of reach. Several research teams [169–172] find similar results to this research for the transition in the transport sector as summarized in Table 27. Smith et al. [198] apply socio-economic constraints for an overall energy transition and conclude that a phase-out of carbon-intensive infrastructure at the end of its design lifetime enables a 1.5°C scenario at a 64% chance, which is close to the 67% probability used typically, and in agreement to this research. Smith et al. [198] do not assume stranded assets in the energy system which can accelerate the transition substantially as pointed out by Kalkuhl et al. [199], since vested interests and lobbying power of owners of fixed factors such as fossil resources cannot be ignored. Carbon Tracker International [200] has indicated a stranded asset potential of the fossil oil and gas industry of more than 20 trillion USD, due to non-adaptive strategies of most players in this industry, which has a strong impact on the transport sector, as this is the largest demand sector for fossil oil at present. Geels et al. [201] emphasize that techno-economic analyses are crucial for analyzing and managing low-carbon transitions, but social, political and cultural processes have to be integrated for a multi-level perspective to capture dynamics in broad, since dynamic policy mixes are required, politics are as important as policy and phase-out processes have to be actively managed besides phase-in processes of new solutions. Geels [202] points out further that this requires a full regime change, which indeed goes far beyond techno-economic solutions, since resistance by incumbent regime actors have to be overcome. Therefore, techno-economic approaches have to be coupled to frameworks addressing the socio-technical dynamics [201,202] so that the ambitious targets of the Paris Agreement can be achieved. Existing lock-in elements have to be further investigated in future research in a more socio-economic perspective and social acceptance of any transition in the transport sector requires more research efforts for a broader societal discourse.

5. Conclusions

Transportation demand will drastically expand due to population growth, urbanization, globalization, and overall economic development. The central finding of this study is that a by about 210% (freight) and 260% (passenger) increased global transportation demand by 2050 can be managed by a stable final energy demand compared to 2015. This surprising result is driven by ongoing efficiency increase of all vehicle types, a consequent shift to fuels enabling more efficient transportation and in particular a massive direct electrification of the road mode in all road transport segments. This leads to a decline of the road final energy demand share of about 80% in 2015 to about 50% in 2050. Long-distance transport by marine and aviation suffers from the inability to switch to direct electric propulsion due to the too low energy density of batteries for long distances. For shorter distances direct electric transportation is also projected for marine and aviation.

Economic analyses for the road mode have revealed that electricity-based BEV will become the dominant newly sold vehicle type from 2025 onwards due to least LCOM of all vehicle options. Hydrogen-based FCEV are close to BEV and therefore may receive some market shares and can be regarded as major backup option in case of slower than expected BEV development. Form 2025 onwards, the ICE vehicles are the highest LCOM option and thus will lose quickly market shares of newly sold vehicles and with a lifetime-dependent delay this will also have a strong impact on the vehicle stock, which is expected to mainly switch from ICE to BEV by 2035 to 2040.

The GHG emissions in the transport sector are projected to peak between 2025 and 2030. Then more BEV are based on electricity which is assumed to be also switched to renewable electricity, thus drastically reducing the GHG emissions in the road mode. This will lead in 2035 and 2040 to a majority GHG emission contribution of marine and aviation transportation which may induce a fast-accelerating pressure on ship operators and airlines to drastically reduce their GHG emissions by fuel switch to defossilized fuels.

The most important fuels for the transport sector during the energy transition will be electricity, then based on renewable electricity, and hydrogen, which can be also produced with low-cost renewable electricity. Hydrogen could also become the dominant fuel for long-distance marine and aviation transportation, but existing technical challenges may be backed by electricity-based synthetic hydrocarbon fuels, such as jet fuel produced in Fischer-Tropsch units.

Direct and indirect electrification of the transport sector increases substantially the well-to-wheel efficiency from 26% in 2015 to 39% in 2050, despite the more energy intensive production processes of electricity-based liquid hydrocarbon fuels. This reduction in relative losses should enable a cost-effective energy transition of the transport sector to full sustainability. The well-to-wheel efficiency of biofuels is comparable to electricity-based synthetic fuels, whereas the latter are not restricted much by area or other sustainability issues. The primary energy base of the transport sector is practically entirely switched from fossil fuels to renewable electricity.

The global transport sector can achieve zero GHG emissions by 2050 fully supporting the ambitious 1.5 °C target of the Paris Agreement from a technological perspective supported by fast improving economics. The socio-technical dynamics require more emphasize in research and societal discourse. This includes not only demanding policies for the transport sector transition, but also a public insisting on achieving the targets, identification and overcoming of barriers, integrated in an overall societal discourse on the transition in the transport sector. All required major technologies are known, or already introduced to markets. Renewable electricity will be the low-cost basis for direct and indirect electrification of the global transport sector.

Supplementary Materials: The following are available online at http://www.mdpi.com/1996-1073/12/20/3870/s1, Figures S1–S5: Transportation demand for Global, Major Regions and Countries, Table S1: Detailed Data for Transport Sector.

Author Contributions: S.K. carried out the research, including collecting input data, implementing the transition modeling, analyzing the transition, calculating, generating and analyzing the results, visualizing the figures, tables, and writing the manuscript. E.R. carried out some of the research, including collecting input data. D.B. did some parts of the calculations in this research, supported the implementing the transition modeling, and wrote parts of the manuscript. C.B. framed the research questions and the scope of work, checked results and data, facilitated discussions, wrote parts of the manuscript, and reviewed in detail the entire paper.

Funding: This research received no external funding.

Acknowledgments: The authors gratefully acknowledge the public financing of Tekes, the Finnish Funding Agency for Innovation, for the "Neo-Carbon Energy" project under the number 40101/14. The authors would like to thank Manish Ram for proofreading.

Conflicts of Interest: The authors declare no conflict of interest. The founding sponsors had no role in the design of the study; in the collection, analyses, or interpretation of data; in the writing of the manuscript, and in the decision to publish the results.

Abbreviations

BEV	battery-electric vehicle
BUS	buses
COP	conference of parties
CAGR	compound annual growth rate
Capex	capital expenditure
eq	equivalence
€	euro
FCET	fuel-cell electric truck
FCEV	fuel-cell electric vehicle

GHG	greenhouse gas
GDP	growth domestic product
HEV	hybrid electric vehicle
HHDT	heavy heavy-duty truck
HDV	heavy-duty vehicle
ICE	internal combustion engine
ICAO	International Civil Aviation Organization
ICCT	International Council on Clean Transportation
IPCC	Intergovernmental Panel on Climate Change
IMO	International Marine Organization
GR	growth rate
LDV	light duty vehicles
LCOM	levelized cost of mobility
LHDT	light heavy-duty truck
LH_2	liquid hydrogen
LNG	liquefied natural gas
MDV	medium duty vehicle
MHDT	medium heavy-duty truck
NG	natural gas
Opex	operational expenditure
PHEV	plug-in hybrid electric vehicle
p-km	passenger kilometer
RP-km	revenue passenger kilometers
PtG	power-to-gas
PtL	power-to-liquids
SMR	steam methane reforming
t-km	ton kilometers
t-mi	ton-miles
TTW	Tank-to-Wheel
TWh	Terawatt hour
UF	utility factor
UNCTAD	United Nation Conference on Traded and Development
WTW	Well-to-Wheel
WTT	Well-to-Tank
WTG	Well-to-Grid
WACC	weighted average cost of capital
2W	two wheelers
3W	three wheelers
Subcripts	
el	Electric units
th	Thermal units
H_2	Hydrogen units
CH_4	Methane units
DME	Dimethyl ether units

References

1. International Energy Agency (IEA). *World Energy Outlook 2017*; International Energy Agency: Paris, France, 2017.
2. United Nations Framework Convention on Climate Change (UNFCCC). Adaptation of the Paris Agreement, COP21. United Nations Framework Convention on Climate Change: Paris, France, 2015. Available online: https://unfccc.int/resource/docs/2015/cop21/eng/l09r01.pdf (accessed on 13 August 2016).
3. ExxonMobil. 2017 Outlook for Energy: A View to 2040. ExxonMobil: Irvine, CA, USA, 2017. Available online: https://cdn.exxonmobil.com/~{}/media/global/files/outlook-for-energy/2017/2017-outlook-for-energy.pdf (accessed on 5 February 2018).

4. International Transport Forum (ITF). *ITF Transport Outlook 2019*; International Transport Forum: Paris, France, 2019. Available online: http://doi.org/10.1787/25202367 (accessed on 23 March 2019).
5. Hua, J.; Wu, Y.H.; Jin, F.P. Prospects for renewable energy for seaborne transportation—Taiwan example. *Renew. Energy* **2008**, *33*, 1056–1063. [CrossRef]
6. Creutzig, F. Evolving narratives of low-carbon futures in transportation. *Transp. Rev.* **2015**, *36*, 341–360. [CrossRef]
7. Baronti, F.; Chow, M.Y.; Ma, C.; Rahimi-Eichi, H.; Saletti, R. E-transportation: The role of embedded systems in electric energy transfer from grid to vehicle. *EURASIP J. Embed. Syst.* **2016**, *2016*, 11. [CrossRef]
8. Royal Belgian Council of Applied Science. Hydrogen as an Energy Carrier. Royal Belgian Council of Applied Science: Belgium, 2006. Available online: http://www.kvab.be/sites/default/rest/blobs/1125/tw_BACAS_hydrogen_as_an_energy_carrier.pdf (accessed on 11 July 2017).
9. International Energy Agency (IEA). *Global EV Outlook 2018. Towards Cross-Model Electrification*; International Energy Agency: Paris, France, 2018.
10. German Aerospace Center. Development of the Car Fleet in EU28+2 to Achieve the Paris Agreement Target to Limit Global Warming to 1.5 °C. Cologne, Germany, 2018. Available online: https://www.greenpeace.de/sites/www.greenpeace.de/files/publications/20180907_gp_eucarfleet_1.5.pdf (accessed on 5 June 2019).
11. International Energy Agency (IEA). *Hybrid and Electric Vehicles, IA-HEV, The Electric Drive Delivers*; International Energy Agency: Paris, France, 2015.
12. Liu, H.; MA, J.; Tong, G.; Zheng, Z.; Yao, M. Investigation on the potential of high efficiency for internal combustion engines. *Energies* **2018**, *11*, 513. [CrossRef]
13. Transport and Environment. *Don't Breathe Here, Beware the Invisible Killer*; Transport and Environment: Brussels, Belgium, 2015. Available online: https://www.transportenvironment.org/sites/te/files/publications/Dont_Breathe_Here_exec_summary_FINAL.pdf (accessed on 15 August 2018).
14. International Energy Agency (IEA). *Energy and Air Pollution*; World Energy Outlook: Paris, France, 2016.
15. Singer, M. *Consumer Views on Plug-in Electric Vehicles-National Benchmark Report*; National Renewable Energy Laboratory (NREL): Golden, CO, USA, 2016. Available online: https://www.nrel.gov/docs/fy17osti/67107.pdf (accessed on 11 August 2017).
16. Zhang, Q.; Ou, X.; Yan, X.; Zhang, X. Electric vehicle market penetration and impacts on energy consumption and CO_2 emissions in the future: Beijing case. *Energies* **2017**, *10*, 228. [CrossRef]
17. Plötz, P.; Funke, S. *Real-World Fuel Economy and CO2 Emissions of Plug-in Hybrid Electric Vehicles*; Fraunhofer Institute for Systems and Innovation Research: Karlsruhe, Germany, 2015. Available online: https://www.isi.fraunhofer.de/content/dam/isi/dokumente/sustainability-innovation/2015/WP01-2015_Real-world-fuel-economy-and-CO2-emissions-of-PHEV_Ploetz-Funke-Jochem-Patrick.pdf (accessed on 9 March 2017).
18. Varga, B.; Sagoian, A.; Mariasiu, F. Prediction of electric vehicle range: A comprehensive review of current issues and challenges. *Energies* **2019**, *12*, 946. [CrossRef]
19. Hummel, P. *Evidence Lab Electric Car Teardown—Disruption Ahead?* UBS: Zurich, Switzerland, 2017. Available online: https://neo.ubs.com/shared/d1wkuDlEbYPjF/ (accessed on 29 February 2018).
20. Schmidt, B. Tesla Extends Range to Near 600 km, Says New Batteries Will Last 1.6 Million Kms. 2019. Available online: https://thedriven.io/2019/04/24/tesla-extends-range-to-near-600km-says-new-batteries-will-last-1-6-million-kms/ (accessed on 12 April 2018).
21. Emadi, A. Transportation 2. *IEEE Power Energy Mag.* **2011**, *9*, 18–29. [CrossRef]
22. Un-Noor, F.; Padmanaban, S.; Mihet-popa, L.; Mollah, M.; Hossain, E. A Comprehensive Study of Key Electric (EV) Components, Technologies, Challenges, Impacts, and Future Direction of Development. *Energies* **2017**, *10*, 1217. [CrossRef]
23. Kurtz, J.; Sprik, S.; Saur, G.; Onorato, S. On-Road Fuel Cell Electric Vehicles Evaluation: Overview. National Renewable Energy Laboratory (NREL): Golden, CO, USA, 2018. Available online: https://www.nrel.gov/docs/fy19osti/73009.pdf (accessed on 3 March 2019).
24. FuelCellToday. *Fuel Cell Electric Vehicles*: The Road Ahead. FuelCellToday: London, UK, 2013. Available online: http://www.fuelcelltoday.com/media/1711108/fuel_cell_electric_vehicles_-_the_road_ahead_v3.pdf (accessed on 13 June 2016).
25. Lee, D.; Elgowainy, A.; Kotz, A.; Vijayagopal, R. Marcinkoski. Life-cycle implications of hydrogen fuel cell electric vehicle technology for medium- and heavy-duty trucks. *J. Power Sour.* **2018**, *393*, 217–229. [CrossRef]

26. Lipman, T.; Elke, M.; Lidicker, J. Hydrogen fuel cell electric vehicle performance and user-response assessment: Results of an extended driver study. *Int. J. Hydrog. Energy* **2018**, *43*, 12442–12454. [CrossRef]
27. Kaa, G.V.D.; Scholtan, D.; Rezaei, J.; Milcharm, C. The battle between battery and fuel cell powered electric vehicle: A BWM approach. *Energies* **2017**, *10*, 1707. [CrossRef]
28. Transport and Environment. *Electric Surge: Carmakers' Electric Car Plans Across Europe 2019–2025*; Transport and Environment: Brussels, Belgium, 2019. Available online: https://www.transportenvironment.org/sites/te/files/publications/2019_07_TE_electric_cars_report_final.pdf (accessed on 10 November 2018).
29. DNV. GL. *Energy Transition Outlook 2019, A Global and Regional Forecast to 2050*; London, UK. Available online: https://eto.dnvgl.com/2019#ETO2019-top (accessed on 12 September 2019).
30. Schmitt, B. German Auto Industry Battles Over the Electric Future. 2019. Available online: https://www.thedrive.com/tech/27841/german-auto-industry-battles-over-the-electric-future (accessed on 30 May 2019).
31. International Energy Agency (IEA). *Railway Handbook 2017. Energy Consumption and CO2 Emissions, Focus on Passenger Rail Services*; International Energy Agency: Paris, France, 2017.
32. International Union of Railways (UCI). *Technologies and Potential Development for Energy Efficiency and CO2 Reductions in Rail Systems*; International Union of Railways: Paris, France, 2016. Available online: https://uic.org/IMG/pdf/_27_technologies_and_potential_developments_for_energy_efficiency_and_co2_reductions_in_rail_systems._uic_in_colaboration.pdf (accessed on 19 April 2018).
33. International Energy Agency (IEA). *The Future of Rail Opportunities for Energy and The Environment*; International Energy Agency (IEA): Paris, France, 2019.
34. Greenpeace. Energy [r] Evolution. *A Sustainable World Energy Outlook 2015, 100% Renewable Energy for All*; Greenpeace. Energy [r] Evolution: Amsterdam, The Netherlands, 2015. Available online: https://www.greenpeace.de/sites/www.greenpeace.de/files/publications/greenpeace_energy-revolution_erneuerbare_2050_20150921.pdf (accessed on 12 April 2018).
35. Petzinger, J. The World's First Hydrogen-Powered Train Hits the Tracks in Germany. 2018. Available online: https://qz.com/1392287/the-worlds-first-hydrogen-powered-train-hits-the-tracks-in-germany/ (accessed on 23 December 2018).
36. Horvath, S.; Fasihi, M.; Breyer, C. Techno-economic analysis of a decarbonized shipping sector: Technology suggestions for a fleet in 2030 and 2040. *Energy Convers. Manag.* **2018**, *164*, 230–241. [CrossRef]
37. Grenzeback, L.R.; Brown, A.; Fischer, M.J.; Hutson, N.; Lamm, C.R.; Pei, Y.L.; Vimmerstedt, L.; Vyas, A.D.; Winebrake, J.J. *Freight Transportation Demand: Energy-Efficient Scenarios for a Low-Carbon Future*; Transportation Energy Future Series; DOE/GO-102013-3711; Cambridge Systematics, Inc.: Cambridge, UK; National Renewable Energy Laboratory: Golden, CO, USA; U.S. Department of Energy: Washington, DC, USA, 2013; 82. Available online: https://www.nrel.gov/docs/fy13osti/55641.pdf (accessed on 19 May 2017).
38. International Transport Forum (ITF). *Reducing Shipping Greenhouse Gas Emissions: Lessons from Port-Based Incentives*; International Transport Forum: Paris, France, 2018. Available online: https://www.itf-oecd.org/sites/default/files/docs/reducing-shipping-greenhouse-gas-emissions.pdf (accessed on 23 December 2018).
39. Bakhtov, A. Alternative Fuels for Shipping in the Baltic Sea Region (HELCOM 2019). Available online: http://www.helcom.fi/Lists/Publications/HELCOM-EnviSUM-Alternative-fuels-for-shipping.pdf (accessed on 12 April 2018).
40. Raucci, C. The Potential of Hydrogen to Fuel International Shipping. UCL Energy Institute. Ph.D. Thesis, University College London, London, UK, February 2017. Available online: http://discovery.ucl.ac.uk/1539941/1/PhD%20Thesis%20Carlo%20Raucci%20Final.pdf (accessed on 2 May 2018).
41. Jafarzadeh, S.; Schjolberg, I. Operational profiles ships in Norwegian water: An activity-based approach to assess the benefits of hybrid and electric propulsion. *Transp. Res. Part D* **2018**, *65*, 500–523. [CrossRef]
42. Yu, J.; Vob, S.; Tang, G. Strategy development for retrofitting ships for implementing shore side electricity. *Transp. Res. Part D* **2019**, *74*, 201–213. [CrossRef]
43. Lim, C.; Park, B.; Lee, J.; Kim, E.S.; Shin, S. Electric power consumption predictive modeling of an electric propulsion ship considering the marine environment. *Int. J. Nav. Archit. Ocean Eng.* **2019**, *11*, 765–781. [CrossRef]
44. Kanellos, F.; Moghaddam, A.A.; Guerrero, J.M. A cost-effective and emission-aware power management system for ships with integrated full electric propulsion. *Electr. Power Syst. Res.* **2017**, *150*, 63–75. [CrossRef]

45. Moore, R. World's Most Powerful All-Electric Ferry to Enter Operations. 2019. Available online: https://www.rivieramm.com/news-content-hub/worldrsquos-most-powerful-all-electric-ferry-to-enter-operations-55117 (accessed on 28 June 2018).
46. International Air Transport Association (IATA). *IATA 2015 Report on Alternative Fuels*; International Air Transport Association: Geneva, Switzerland, 2015. Available online: https://www.iata.org/publications/Documents/2015-report-alternative-fuels.pdf (accessed on 16 July 2017).
47. Han, H.; Yu, J.; Kim, W. An electric airplane: Assessing the effect of travelers' perceived risk, attitude, and new product knowledge. *J. Air Transp. Manag.* **2019**, *78*, 33–42. [CrossRef]
48. Kadyk, T.; Winnefeld, C.; Hanke-Rauschenbach, R.; Krewer, U. Analysis and Design of Fuel Cell Systems for Aviation. *Energies* **2018**, *11*, 375. [CrossRef]
49. German Environment Agency (UBA). *Power-To-Liquids. Potential and Perspectives for the Future Supply of Renewable Aviation Fuel*; German Environment Agency (UBA): Berlin, Germany, 2016. Available online: http://www.lbst.de/news/2016_docs/161005_uba_hintergrund_ptl_barrierrefrei.pdf (accessed on 12 July 2018).
50. Baroutaji, A.; Wilberforce, T.; Ramadan, M.; Olabi, A.G. Comprehensive investigation on hydrogen and fuel cell technology in the aviation and aerospace sectors. *Renew. Sustain. Energy Rev.* **2019**, *106*, 31–40. [CrossRef]
51. Fireman, H.; Arbor, A. Designing All Electric Ships. Ninth International Marine Design Conference 2006, University of Michigan, Department USA. NA&ME, Designing All Electric Ships, IMDC'06, 16 May 2006, NAVSEA. Available online: https://pdfs.semanticscholar.org/presentation/1291/50a6ce6311ca5cf489f48081d249f0a87f5c.pdf (accessed on 28 June 2018).
52. The Guardian. Norway Aims for All Short-Haul Flights to Be 100% Electric by 2040. The Guardian: London, UK, 2018. Available online: https://www.theguardian.com/world/2018/jan/18/norway-aims-for-all-short-haul-flights-to-be-100-electric-by-2040 (accessed on 17 March 2018).
53. Reimers, J.O. Introduction of Electric Aviation in Norway. Green Future: Norway, 2018. Available online: https://avinor.no/contentassets/c29b7a7ec1164e5d8f7500f8fef810cc/introduction-of-electric-aircraft-in-norway.pdf (accessed on 12 May 2017).
54. Hepperle, M. Electric Flight—Potential and Limitation. NATO, OTAN, German Aerospace Center Sto-MP-AVT-209. Available online: https://www.mh-aerotools.de/company/paper_14/MP-AVT-209-09.pdf (accessed on 11 February 2018).
55. Colbertaldo, P.; Guandalini, G.; Campanari, S. Modelling the integrated power and transport energy system: The role of power-to-gas and hydrogen in long-term scenarios for Italy. *Energy* **2018**, *154*, 592–601. [CrossRef]
56. Bellocchi, S.; Falco, M.D.; Gambini, M.; Manno, M.; Stilo, T.; Vellini, M. Opportunities for power-to-Gas and Power-to-liquid in CO2-reduced energy scenarios: The Italian case. *Energy* **2019**, *175*, 847–861. [CrossRef]
57. Child, M.; Koskinen, O.; Linnanen, L.; Breyer, C. Sustainability guardrails for energy scenarios of the global energy transition. *Renew. Sustain. Energy Rev.* **2018**, *91*, 321–334. [CrossRef]
58. Kahn Ribeiro, S.; Kobayashi, S.; Beuthe, M.; Gasca, J.; Greene, D.; Lee, D.S.; Muromachi, Y.; Newton, P.J.; Plotkin, S.; Sperling, D.; et al. Transport and its infrastructure. In *Climate Change 2007: Mitigation; Contribution of Working Group III to the Fourth Assessment Report of the Intergovernmental Panel on Climate Change*; Cambridge University Press: Cambridge, UK, 2007.
59. Royal Automobile Club Foundation. Travel Demand and its Causes. Motoring towards 2050-Roads and Reality. Royal Automobile Club Foundation: London, UK, 2008. Available online: https://www.racfoundation.org/assets/rac_foundation/content/downloadables/roads%20and%20reality%20-%20bayliss%20-%20travel%20demand%20and%20its%20causes%20-%20150708%20-%20background%20paper%203.pdf (accessed on 12 March 2017).
60. Fang, B.; Han, X. *Relating Transportation To GDP: Concepts, Measures, and Data*; MacroSys Research and Technology. MacroSys: Washington, DC, USA. Available online: http://www.e-ajd.net/source-pdf/nouveau/ajd-41-fang-han-4-december-2000.pdf (accessed on 16 March 2018).
61. Garcia, C.; Levy, S.; Limão, S.; Kupfer, F. Correlation Between Transport Intensity and GDP in European Regions: A New Approach, 8th Swiss Transport Research Conference, Monte Verit/Ascona. 2008. Available online: http://www.strc.ch/2008/2008_Garcia_Levy_Limao_Kupfer_TransportIntensity_GDP.pdf (accessed on 14 May 2017).

62. United Nations, Department of Economic and Social Affairs, Population Division. World Population Prospects: The 2015 Revision, Key Findings and Advance Tables. Working Paper No. ESA/P/WP.241. New York. Available online: https://population.un.org/wpp/DataQuery/ (accessed on 24 December 2017).
63. Toktarova, A.; Gruber, L.; Hlusiak, M.; Bogdanov, D.; Breyer, C. Long term load projection in high resolution for all countries globally. *Int. J. Electr. Power Energy Syst.* **2019**, *111*, 160–181. [CrossRef]
64. International Council on Clean Transportation (ICCT). *Global Transportation Roadmap*; International Council on Clean Transportation: Washington, DC, USA, 2012. Available online: www.theicct.org/transportation-roadmap (accessed on 26 July 2016).
65. International Marine Organization (IMO). *Third IMO Greenhouse Gas Study 2014*; International Marine Organization: Suffolk, UK, 2014. Available online: http://www.imo.org/en/OurWork/Environment/PollutionPrevention/AirPollution/Documents/Third%20Greenhouse%20Gas%20Study/GHG3%20Executive%20Summary%20and%20Report.pdf (accessed on 25 October 2017).
66. Fasihi, M.; Bogdanov, D.; Breyer, C. Techno-economic assessment of power-to-liquid (PtL) fuels production and global trading based on Hybrid PV-Wind power plants. *Energy Procedia* **2016**, *99*, 243–268. [CrossRef]
67. Fasihi, M.; Bogdanov, D.; Breyer, C. Long-term hydrocarbon trade options for the Maghreb region and Europe—renewable energy based synthetic fuels for a net zero emissions world. *Sustainability* **2016**, *9*, 306. [CrossRef]
68. Heuser, P.M.; Ryberg, D.S.; Grube, T.; Robinius, M.; Stolten, D. Techno-economic analysis of a potential energy trading link between Patagonia and Japan based on CO2 free hydrogen. *Int. J. Hydrog. Energy* **2019**, *44*, 12733–12747. [CrossRef]
69. The Intergovernmental Panel on Climate Change (IPCC). IPCC 5th Assessment report: Working Group III—Mitigation of Climate Change. Geneva, Switzerland, 2014. Available online: http://www.ipcc.ch/ (accessed on 10 November 2017).
70. European Commission (EC). EU Transport in Figures, Statistical Pocketbook 2012. European Commission: Brussels, Belgium, 2012. Available online: https://ec.europa.eu/transport/sites/transport/files/facts-fundings/statistics/doc/2012/pocketbook2012.pdf (accessed on 22 March 2016).
71. International Civil Aviation Organization (ICAO). *Appendix 1. Tables Relating to the World of Air Transport in 2015*; International Civil Aviation Organization: Montreal, QC, Canada, 2015. Available online: https://www.icao.int/annual-report-2015/Documents/Appendix_1_en.pdf (accessed on 13 April 2017).
72. International Civil Aviation Organization (ICAO). *Committee on Aviation Environmental Protection (CAEP), Agenda Item 3: Forecasting and Economic Analysis Support Group (FESG)*; International Civil Aviation Organization: Lima, Peru, 2008. Available online: http://s3.amazonaws.com/zanran_storage/www.icao.int/ContentPages/108603156.pdf (accessed on 26 March 2018).
73. Heywood, J.; Mackenzie, D. On the Road Toward 2050: Potential for Sustainable Reductions in Light-Duty Vehicles Energy Use and Greenhouse Gas Emissions. Available online: http://web.mit.edu/sloan-auto-lab/research/beforeh2/files/On-the-Road-toward-2050.pdf (accessed on 18 June 2017).
74. Plötz, P.; Funke, S.A.; Jochem, P. Emprirical fuel consumption and CO2 emissions of plug-in hybrid electric vehicles. *J. Ind. Ecol.* **2017**, *22*, 4. [CrossRef]
75. Mendes, M.; Duarte, G.; Baptista, P. Introducing specific power to bicycle and motorcycles: Application to electric mobility. *Transp. Res. Part C Emerg. Technol.* **2015**, *51*, 120–135. [CrossRef]
76. CIVITAS. Cleaner and Smarter Transport in Cities. Smart Choices for Cities. Policy Note, Clean Buses for City, CIVITAS: Belgium, 2013. Available online: http://civitas.eu/sites/default/files/civ_pol-an_web.pdf (accessed on 9 January 2018).
77. Transportation Research Center—University of Vermont (UVM TRC). Plug-in Hybrid Electric Vehicle Research Project: Phase II Report. Available online: http://www.greenmtn.edu/wordpress/wp-content/uploads/phev-final-report-april2010.pdf (accessed on 15 April 2018).
78. Boer, E.D.; Aarnink, S. Zero Emissions Trucks, An Overview of State-Of-The-Art Technologies and Their potential. DLR, D-70569. Available online: https://www.theicct.org/sites/default/files/publications/CE_Delft_4841_Zero_emissions_trucks_Def.pdf (accessed on 1 July 2017).
79. Fulton, L.; Eads, G. IEA/SMP Model Documentation and Reference Case Projection. Paris, France, 2004. Available online: http://www.libralato.co.uk/docs/SMP%20model%20guidance%202004.pdf (accessed on 16 March 2018).

80. Schäfer, A.; Dray, L.; Andersson, E.; Ben-Akiva, M.E.; Berg, M.; Boulouchos, K.; Dietrich, P.; Fröidh, O.; Graham, W.; Kok, R.; et al. TOSCA Project Final Report: Description of the Main S&T Results/Foregrounds. California, 2011. TOSCA, EC FP7 Project. Available online: http://www.transport-research.info/sites/default/files/project/documents/20120406_000154_97382_TOSCA_FinalReport.pdf (accessed on 14 May 2017).
81. DNV GL. Fuels & Fuel Converters (Future). Maritime Academy. NTNU, Norwegian University of Science and Technology: Trondheim, Norway. Available online: https://www.ntnu.edu/documents/20587845/1266707380/01_Fuels.pdf/1073c862-2354-4ccf-9732-0906380f601e (accessed on 3 December 2017).
82. Becken, S. *Tourism and Oil, Preparing for the Challenge*; Channel View Publications; Tourism Essential: Bristol, UK, 2015.
83. Air, B.P. Handbook of Products. Air BP Ltd.: London, UK, 2000. Available online: https://web.archive.org/web/20110608075828/http://www.bp.com/liveassets/bp_internet/aviation/air_bp/STAGING/local_assets/downloads_pdfs/a/air_bp_products_handbook_04004_1.pdf (accessed on 2 May 2018).
84. Mueller, J.K.; Bensmann, A.; Bensmann, B. Design Considerations for the Electrical Power Supply of Future Civil Aircraft with Active High-Lift Systems. *Energies* **2018**, *11*, 179. [CrossRef]
85. Parfomak, P.W.; Frittelli, J.; Lattanzio, R.K.; Patner, M. LNG as a Marine Fuel: Prospects and Policy. Congressional Research Service: Washington, DC, USA, 2019. Available online: https://fas.org/sgp/crs/misc/R45488.pdf (accessed on 19 October 2017).
86. Misyris, G.S.; Marinopoulos, A.; Doukas, D.I.; Tengner, T.; Labridis, D.P. On battery state estimation algorithms for electric ship applications. *Electr. Power Syst. Res.* **2017**, *151*, 115–124. [CrossRef]
87. National Post. Norway is Building Some of the World's first Battery-Powered Ferries. Will They Lead the Way in Cutting Maritime Pollution? Toronto, Ontario, 2018. Available online: https://nationalpost.com/news/world/will-new-electric-ferries-lead-the-way-in-cutting-maritime-pollution (accessed on 18 September 2018).
88. Newsweek. World's First Electric Ships Now Sailing in China-and Hauling Coal. USA, 2017. Available online: https://www.newsweek.com/worlds-first-electric-ship-now-sailing-china-and-hauling-coal-740015 (accessed on 28 April 2018).
89. International Council on Clean Transportation (ICCT). *Greenhouse Gas Emissions from Global Shipping, International Council on Clean Transportation, 2013–2015*; International Council on Clean Transportation: Washington, DC, USA, 2017. Available online: https://www.theicct.org/sites/default/files/publications/Global-shipping-GHG-emissions-2013-2015_ICCT-Report_17102017_vF.pdf (accessed on 21 January 2018).
90. Jacobson, M.Z.; Delucchi, M.A.; Bauer, Z.A.; Goodman, S.C.; Chapman, W.E.; Cameron, M.A.; Bozonnat, C.; Chobadi, L.; Clonts, H.A.; Enevoldsen, P.; et al. 100% Clean and Renewable Wind, Water, and Sunlight All-Sector Energy Roadmaps for 139 Countries of the World. *Joule* **2017**, *1*, 1–14. [CrossRef]
91. Wilkerson, J.; Jacobson, M.Z.; Malwitz, A.; Wayson, R.; Naiman, A.D.; Lele, S.K.; Balasubramanian, S.; Fleming, G. Analysis of emission data from global commercial aviation: 2004 and 2006. *Atmos. Chem. Phys.* **2010**, *10*, 6391–6408. [CrossRef]
92. Hagedorn, G.; Kalmus, P.; Mann, M.; Vicca, S.; Berge, J.V.D.; Van Ypersele, J.-P.; Bourg, D.; Rotmans, J.; Kaaronen, R.; Rahmstorf, S.; et al. Concerns of young protesters are justified. *Science* **2019**, *364*, 139–140. [CrossRef] [PubMed]
93. Hagedorn, G.; Loew, T.; Seneviratne, S.I.; Lucht, W.; Beck, M.-L.; Hesse, J.; Knutti, R.; Quaschning, V.; Schleimer, J.-H.; Mattauch, L.; et al. The concerns of the young protesters are justified: A statement by scientists for future concerning the protests for more climate protection. *GAIA* **2019**, *28*, 79–87. [CrossRef]
94. Thomson, R. EasyJet CEO Johan Lundgren: Electric Planes within 10 years—Electrical Propulsion Reduces Environmental Footprint, Point of Views. Roland Berger: London, UK, 2018. Available online: https://www.rolandberger.com/en/Point-of-View/easyJet-CEO-Johan-Lundgren-Electric-planes-within-10-years.html (accessed on 20 September 2019).
95. Bogdanov, D.; Farfan, J.; Sadovskaia, K.; Aghahosseini, A.; Child, M.; Gulagi, A.; Oyewo, A.S.; Barbosa, L.D.S.N.S.; Breyer, C. Radical transformation pathway towards sustainable electricity via evolutionary steps. *Nat. Commun.* **2019**, *10*, 1077. [CrossRef]
96. Vliet, O.; Brouwer, A.S.; Kuramochi, T.; Brok, M.V.D.; Faaij, A. Energy use, cost and CO2 emissions of electric cars. *J. Power Sources* **2010**, *196*, 2298–2310. [CrossRef]

97. Curry, C. Lithium-Ion Battery Cost and Market. Lithium-Ion Battery Cost and Market. Squeezed Margins Seek Technology Improvements & New Business Models. Bloomberg New Energy Finance: New York, NY, USA, 2017. Available online: https://data.bloomberglp.com/bnef/sites/14/2017/07/BNEF-Lithium-ion-battery-costs-and-market.pdf (accessed on 12 July 2018).
98. Nguyen, T.; Ward, J. Life-Cycle Costs of Mid-Size Light-Duty Vehicles, Program Record (Office of Vehicle Technologies & Fuel Cell Technologies). Washington, DC, USA, 2013. Available online: https://www.hydrogen.energy.gov/pdfs/13006_ldv_life_cycle_costs.pdf (accessed on 11 March 2018).
99. Bubeck, S.; Tomaschek, J.; Fahl, U. Perspective of electric mobility: Total cost of ownership of electric vehicles in Germany. *Transp. Policy* **2016**, *50*, 63–77. [CrossRef]
100. Lajunen, A.; Lipman, T. Lifecycle cost assessment and carbon dioxide emissions of diesel natural gas, hybrid electric, fuel cell hybrid and electric transit buses. *Energy* **2016**, *106*, 329–342. [CrossRef]
101. Lajunen, A. Evaluation of battery requirements for hybrid and electric city buses. *World Electr. Veh. J.* **2012**, *5*, 340–349. [CrossRef]
102. Yeon, L.D.; Thomas, V.M. Parametric modeling approach for economic and environmentally life cycle assessment of medium-duty truck electrification. *J. Clean. Prod.* **2017**, *142*, 3300–3321. [CrossRef]
103. Lee, A.H.; Kim, N.W.; Jeong, J.R.; Park, Y.I.; Cha, A.W. Component sizing and engine optimal operation line analysis for a plug-in hybrid electric transit bus. *J. Clean. Prod.* **2013**, *14*, 459–469. [CrossRef]
104. Kast, J.; Vijayagopal, R.; Gangloff, J.J.; Marcinkoski, J. Clean commercial transportation: Medium and heavy duty fuel cell electric trucks. *Int. J. Hydrog. Energy* **2017**, *42*, 4508–4517. [CrossRef]
105. Laitila, J.; Asikainen, A.; Ranta, T. Cost analysis of transporting forest chips and forest industry by-product with large truck-trailers in Finland. *Biomass Bioenergy* **2016**, *90*, 252–261. [CrossRef]
106. Ars Technica. Tesla Announce Truck Prices Lower than Experts Predicted. 2017. Available online: https://arstechnica.com/cars/2017/11/teslas-expected-truck-prices-are-much-lower-than-experts-predicted/ (accessed on 24 October 2017).
107. DMV.ORG. Average Car Insurance Rates. USA. Available online: https://www.dmv.org/insurance/average-car-insurance-rates.php (accessed on 17 November 2017).
108. EZ-EV. Electric Cars vs. Gas Cars: Comparing Maintenance & Battery Costs. Available online: https://ez-ev.com/tips/electric-cars-vs-gas-maintenance-battery-cost (accessed on 25 February 2018).
109. Trusted Choice. How Much Does Commercial Vehicle Insurance Cost? USA. Available online: https://www.trustedchoice.com/commercial-vehicle-insurance/compare-coverage/rate-cost/ (accessed on 13 May 2018).
110. Trusted Choice. Commercial Truck Insurance Light, Medium, Heavy & Extra Heavy. USA. Available online: https://truckinsurance.mobi/ (accessed on 26 March 2017).
111. Bento, A.; Roth, K.; Zou, Y. Vehicle Lifetime Trend and Scrappage Behavior in the U.S. Used Car Market. *Energy J. Int. Assoc. Energy Econ.* **2016**, *39*. [CrossRef]
112. Dun, C.; Horton, G.; Kollamthodi, S. Improvements to the Definition of Lifetime Mileage of Light Duty Vehicles. Ricardo-AEA: London, UK, 2015. Available online: https://ec.europa.eu/clima/sites/clima/files/transport/vehicles/docs/ldv_mileage_improvement_en.pdf (accessed on 24 August 2018).
113. Guenther, C.; Schott, B.; Hennings, W.; Waldowski, P.; Danzer, A.M. Model-based investigation of electric vehicle aging by means of vehicle-to-grid scenario simulations. *J. Power Sour.* **2013**, *239*, 604–610. [CrossRef]
114. Laver, R.; Schneck, D.; Skorupski, D.; Brady, S.; Cham, L. *Useful Life of Transit Buses and Vans*; Report No. FTA VA-26-7229-07.1; U.S. Department of Transportation Federal Transit Administration: Washington, DC, USA, 2007. Available online: https://www.transitwiki.org/TransitWiki/images/6/64/Useful_Life_of_Buses.pdf (accessed on 23 September 2017).
115. Vilppo, O.; Markkula, J. Feasibility of electric buses in public transport. *World Electr. Veh. J.* **2015**, *7*, 357–365. [CrossRef]
116. Norregaard, K.; Johsen, B.; Gravesen, C.H. Battery Degradation in Electric Buses. Danish Technological Institute: Taastrup, Denmark, 2016. Available online: https://www.trafikstyrelsen.dk/~{}/media/Dokumenter/06%20Kollektiv%20trafik/Forsogsordningen/2013/Elbusser/Battery%20degradation%20in%20electric%20buses%20-%20final.pdf (accessed on 12 March 2018).
117. Martinez-Laserna, E.; Herrera, V.; Gandiaga, I.; Milo, A.; Sarasketa-Zabala, E.; Gaztañaga, H. Li-Ion battery lifetime Model's influence on the economic assessment of a hybrid electric bus's operation. *World Electr. Veh. J.* **2018**, *9*, 28. [CrossRef]

118. Weinert, J.; Ogden, J.; Sperling, D.; Burke, A. The future of electric two-wheelers and electric vehicle in China. *Energy Policy* **2008**, *36*, 2544–2555. [CrossRef]
119. European Environment Agency (EEA). Average Age of the Vehicle Fleet. European Environment Agency: Copenhagen, Denmark, 2016. Available online: https://www.eea.europa.eu/data-and-maps/indicators/average-age-of-the-vehicle-fleet/average-age-of-the-vehicle-8 (accessed on 5 August 2018).
120. International Panel on Climate Change (IPCC). Energy. 1996 IPCC. Guidelines for National Greenhouse Gas Inventories: Reference Manual, Chapter 1 Energy. Italy. Available online: https://www.ipcc-nggip.iges.or.jp/public/2006gl/ (accessed on 18 January 2017).
121. Rahman, M.M.; Canter, C.; Kumar, A. Well-to-wheel life cycle assessment of transportation fuels derived from different North American conventional crudes. *Appl. Energy* **2015**, *156*, 159–173. [CrossRef]
122. Wang, M.; Han, J.; Dunn, J.B.; Cai, H.; Elgowainy, A. Well-to-wheels energy use and greenhouse gas emissions of ethanol from corn, sugarcane and cellulosic biomass for US use. *Environ. Res. Lett.* **2012**, *7*, 045905. [CrossRef]
123. Nylund, N.O.; Koponen, K. Fuel and Technology Alternatives for Buses: Overall Energy Efficiency and EMISSION performance. VTT Technology: Espoo, Finland, 2012. Available online: https://www.vtt.fi/inf/pdf/technology/2012/T46.pdf (accessed on 11 June 2018).
124. Renewable Energy Policy Network for the 21st Century (REN21), Renewables 2018 Global Status Report. REN21: Paris, France. Available online: https://www.renewable-ei.org/pdfdownload/activities/S1_Arthouros%20Zervos.pdf (accessed on 21 July 2018).
125. Delgado, O.; Muncrief, R. Assessment of Heavy-Duty Natural Gas Vehicle Emissions: Implications and Policy Recommendations. White Paper; International Council on Clean Transportation (ICCT): Washington, DC, USA, 2015. Available online: https://www.theicct.org/sites/default/files/publications/ICCT_NG-HDV-emissions-assessmnt_20150730.pdf (accessed on 24 March 2018).
126. Fasihi, M.; Breyer, C. Baseload electricity and hydrogen supply based on hybrid PV-Wind power plants. *J. Clean. Prod.* **2020**, *243*, 118466. [CrossRef]
127. Elgowainy, A.; Dai, Q.; Han, J.; Wang, M. Life Cycle Analysis of Emerging Hydrogen Production Technologies. Annual Progress Report; Argonne National Laboratory, 2016. Available online: https://www.hydrogen.energy.gov/pdfs/progress16/ix_5_elgowainy_2016.pdf (accessed on 27 July 2018).
128. Schuller, O. Greenhouse Gas Intensity of Natural Gas. Think Step AG: Germany, 2017. SOL 16-043.1. Available online: http://gasnam.es/wp-content/uploads/2017/11/NGVA-thinkstep_GHG_Intensity_of_NG_Final_Report_v1.0.pdf (accessed on 14 September 2017).
129. Skone, T.J. Life Cycle Greenhouse Gas Perspective on Exporting Liquefied Natural Gas from the United States. NETL, National Energy Technology Laboratory: USA, 2014. Available online: https://www.energy.gov/sites/prod/files/2014/05/f16/Life%20Cycle%20GHG%20Perspective%20Report.pdf (accessed on 19 November 2017).
130. Sadovskaia, K.; Bogdanov, D.; Honkapuro, S.; Breyer, C. Power transmission and distribution losses—A model based on available empirical data and future for all countries globally. *Electr. Power Energy Syst.* **2019**, *107*, 98–109. [CrossRef]
131. European Commission. Well-To-Wheels Analysis of Future Automotive Fuels and Powertrains in the European Context. Well-To-Tank Report Version4. Luxembourg. 2013. Available online: https://ec.europa.eu/jrc/en/publication/eur-scientific-and-technical-research-reports/tank-wheels-report-version-4a-well-wheels-analysis-future-automotive-fuels-and-powertrains (accessed on 8 November 2017).
132. Dehaghani, E.S. Well-To-Wheels Energy Efficiency Analysis of Plug-in Electric Vehicles Including Varying Charging Regimes. M.Sc. Thesis, Concordia University, Montreal, QC, Canada, 2013. Available online: https://pdfs.semanticscholar.org/20bb/5e329521fde98163b406c2f44951f5dbed99.pdf (accessed on 28 November 2017).
133. Fasihi, M.; Bogdanov, D.; Breyer, C. Overview on PtX Options Studied in NCE and Their Global Potential Based on Hybrid PV-Wind Power Plants. Presentation. Neo-Carbon Energy Seminar: Lappeenranta, Finland, 2017. Available online: http://www.neocarbonenergy.fi/wp-content/uploads/2016/02/13_Fasihi.pdf (accessed on 11 May 2018).
134. Prieur, P.; Fareau, D.; Vinot, S. Well to Tank Technology Pathways and Carbon Balance. Luxembourg, 2009. Available online: http://s3.amazonaws.com/zanran_storage/www.roads2hy.com/ContentPages/2498021066.pdf (accessed on 1 November 2017).

135. Wang, M.; Elgowainy, A. Well-To-Wheels GHG Emissions of Natural Gas Use in Transportation: CNGVs, LNGVs, EVs, and FCVs. Washington, DC, USA, 2014. Available online: https://www.google.com/url?sa=t&rct=j&q=&esrc=s&source=web&cd=1&cad=rja&uact=8&ved=2ahUKEwie35zmio3kAhXtiIsKHU_IAhwQFjAAegQIAhAC&url=https%3A%2F%2Fgreet.es.anl.gov%2Ffiles%2FEERE-LCA-NG&usg=AOvVaw3aBA3Xrrz_O4NhNXbFZkqy (accessed on 8 December 2017).
136. Organisation for Economic Co-Operation and Development—Food and Agriculture (OECD-FAO). *Agricultural Outlook*; Dataset; FAO: Rome, Italy; OECD: Paris, France, 2016. Available online: https://www.oecd-ilibrary.org/agriculture-and-food/data/oecd-agriculture-statistics_agr-data-en (accessed on 9 May 2017).
137. Washing, E.M.; Pulugurtha, S. Well-To-Wheel analysis of electric and hydrogen light rail. *J. Public Transp.* **2015**, *18*, 74–88. [CrossRef]
138. Serpa, D. Tank to Wheel Efficiency. After Oil EV, 2011. Available online: http://www.afteroilev.com/Pub/EFF_Tank_to_Wheel.pdf (accessed on 8 November 2018).
139. Auto Tech Review. Making Sense of Two-Wheeler Fuel Efficiencies. Auto Tech Review: New Delhi, 2016. Available online: https://autotechreview.com/technology/tech-update/making-sense-of-two-wheeler-fuel-efficiencies (accessed on 14 March 2018).
140. Schwertner, M.; Weidmann, U. Comparison of Well-to_wheel efficiencies for different drivetrain configurations of transit buses. *Transp. Res. Rec. J. Transp. Res. Board* **2016**, *2539*, 55–64. [CrossRef]
141. Thiruvengadam, A.; Pradhan, S.; Besch, M.; Carder, D. Heavy-Duty Vehicle Design Engine Efficiency Evaluation and Energy Audit. CAFEE, Center for Alternative Fuels, Engines and Emissions; West Virginia University: Morgantown, WV, USA, 2014. Available online: https://theicct.org/sites/default/files/publications/HDV_engine-efficiency-eval_WVU-rpt_oct2014.pdf (accessed on 1 May 2018).
142. Gruber, C.; Wurster, R. Hydrogen-Fueled Buses: The Bavarian Fuel Cell Bus Project. MAN Nutzfahrzeuge, Munich; L-B-Systemtechnik, Ottobrunn. Available online: http://ieahydrogen.org/pdfs/Case-Studies/bavarian_proj.aspx (accessed on 19 May 2018).
143. Hoffrichter, A. Hydrogen as an Energy Carrier for Railway Traction. Ph.D. Dissertation, University of Birmingham, Birmingham, UK, 2013. Available online: https://etheses.bham.ac.uk/id/eprint/4345/9/Hoffrichter13PhD1.pdf (accessed on 15 April 2018).
144. Vodovozov, V.; Lehtla, T. Power Accounting for Ship Electric Propulsion. Closing Conference of Doctoral School of Energy and Geotechnology II, Pärnu, Estonia. 2015. Available online: https://pdfs.semanticscholar.org/6663/89cd6ba20958fb5e92e46d78683f66fecf89.pdf (accessed on 19 April 2017).
145. Breyer, C.; Khalili, S.; Bogdanov, D. Solar Photovoltaic Capacity Demand for a fully sustainable Transport Sector—How to fulfill the Paris Agreement by 2050. *Prog. Photovolt. Res. Appl.* **2018**, 1–12. [CrossRef]
146. Du, J.; Li, F.; Li, J.; Wu, X.; Song, Z.; Zou, Y. Evaluating the technological evolution of battery electric buses: China as a case. *Energy* **2019**, *176*, 309–319. [CrossRef]
147. Transport and Environment. Electric Buses Arrive on Time. Market Place, Economy, Technology, Environmental and Policy Perspectives for Fully Electric Buses in the UE. Transport and Environment: Brussels, Belgium, 2018. Available online: https://www.transportenvironment.org/sites/te/files/publications/Electric%20buses%20arrive%20on%20time.pdf (accessed on 1 May 2019).
148. Zart, N. 100% Electric Bus Fleet for Shenzhen (Population 11.9 Million) by End of 2017. Clean Technica: El Cerrito, CA, USA, 2017. Available online: https://cleantechnica.com/2017/11/12/100-electric-bus-fleet-shenzhen-pop-11-9-million-end-2017/ (accessed on 22 May 2017).
149. Creutzig, F.; McGlynn, E.; Minx, J.; Edenhofer, O. Climate policies for road transport revisited (I): Evaluation of the current framework. *Energy Policy* **2011**, *39*, 2396–2406. [CrossRef]
150. Creutzig, F.; Jochem, P.; Edelenbosch, O.Y.; Mattauch, L.; Vuuren, D.P.V.; Mccollum, D.; Minx, J.C. Transport: A roadblock to climate change mitigation? *Science* **2015**, *350*, 911–912. [CrossRef]
151. Keiner, D.; Ram, M.; Barbosa, L.D.S.; Bogdanov, D.; Breyer, C. Cost optimal self-consumption of PV prosumers with stationary batteries, heat pumps, thermal energy storage and electric vehicle across the world up to 2050. *Sol. Energy* **2019**, *185*, 406–423. [CrossRef]
152. Keiner, D.; Breyer, C.; Sterner, M. Cost and self-consumption optimized residential PV prosumer system in Germany covering residential electricity, heat and mobility demand. *Int. J. Sustain. Energy Plan. Manag.* **2019**, *21*, 35–58. [CrossRef]

153. Robinius, M.; Linßen, J.; Grube, T.; Reuß, M.; Stenzel, P.; Syranidis, K.; Kuckertz, P.; Stolten, D. Comparative Analysis of Infrastructures: Hydrogen Fueling and Electric Charging of Vehicles. Forschungszentrum Jülich: Jülich, Germany, 2018. Available online: https://content.h2.live/wp-content/uploads/2018/01/Energie-und-Umwelt_408_Robinius-final.pdf (accessed on 17 July 2018).
154. Hoekstra, A. The understanding potential of battery electric vehicles to reduce emissions. *Joule* **2019**, *3*, 1404–1414. [CrossRef]
155. Breyer, C.; Koskinen, O.; Blechinger, P. Profitable climate mitigation: The case of greenhouse gas emission reduction benefits enabled by solar photovoltaic systems. *Renew. Sustain. Energy Rev.* **2015**, *49*, 610–628. [CrossRef]
156. Creutzig, F.; Ravindranath, N.H.; Berndes, G.; Bolwig, S.; Bright, R.; Cherubini, F.; Chum, H.; Corbera, E.; Delucchi, M.; Faaij, A.; et al. Bioenergy and climate change mitigation: An assessment. *Glob. Change Biol. Bioenergy* **2015**, *7*, 916–944. [CrossRef]
157. Ram, M.; Bogdanov, D.; Aghahosseini, A.; Gulagi, A.; Oyewo, A.S.; Child, M.; Caldera, U.; Sadovskaia, K.; Farfan, J.; Barbosa, L.S.N.S.; et al. Global Energy System Based on 100% Renewable Energy—Power, Heat, Transport and Desalination Sectors. Lappeenranta University of Technology and Energy Watch Group: Lappeenranta, Finland; Berlin, Germany, 2019. Available online: http://energywatchgroup.org/wp-content/uploads/EWG_LUT_100RE_All_Sectors_Global_Report_2019.pdf (accessed on 12 July 2019).
158. Lund, M.T.; Aamaas, B.; Berntsen, T.; Bock, L.; Burkhardt, U.; Fuglestvedt, J.S.; Shine, K.P. Emission metrics for quantifying regional climate impacts of aviation. *Earth Syst. Dyn.* **2017**, *8*, 547–563. [CrossRef]
159. Burkhardt, U.; Bock, L.; Bier, A. Mitigating the contrail cirrus climate impact by reducing aircraft soot number emissions. *NPJ Clim. Atmos. Sci.* **2018**, *1*, 37. [CrossRef]
160. Breyer, C.; Fasihi, M.; Bajamundi, C.; Creutzig, F. Direct air capture of CO2—A key technology for ambitious climate change mitigation. *Joule* **2019**, *3*, 2053–2057. [CrossRef]
161. Fuss, S.; Lamb, W.F.; Callaghan, M.W.; Hilaire, J.; Creutzig, F.; Amann, T.; Beringer, T.; Garcia, W.D.O.; Hartmann, J.; Khanna, T.; et al. Negative emissions—Part 2: Costs, potentials and side effects. *Environ. Res. Lett.* **2018**, *13*, 063002. [CrossRef]
162. Vartiainen, E.; Masson, G.; Breyer, C.; Moser, D.; Medina, E.R. Impact of Weighted Average Cost of Capital, Capital Expenditure and Other Parameters on Future Utility-Scale PV Levelised Cost of Electricity. *Prog. Photovolt. Res. Appl.* **2019**, in press. [CrossRef]
163. Haegel, N.M.; Atwater, H.; Barnes, T.; Breyer, C.; Burrell, A.; Chiang, Y.M.; De Wolf, S.; Dimmler, B.; Feldman, D.; Glunz, S.; et al. Terawatt-scale photovoltaics: Transform global energy. *Science* **2019**, *364*, 836–838. [CrossRef]
164. International Energy Agency (IEA). *World Energy Outlook 2015*; International Energy Agency: Paris, France, 2015.
165. Bloomberg New Energy Finance. New Energy Outlook 2015. Long-Term Projections of the Global Energy Sector. BNEF: London, 2015. Available online: Catskillcitizens.org/learnmore/BNEF-NEO2015_Executive-summary.pdf (accessed on 19 March 2018).
166. Hansen, K.; Breyer, C.; Lund, H. Status and perspectives on 100% renewable energy systems. *Energy* **2019**, *175*, 471–480. [CrossRef]
167. García-Olivares, A.; Sole, J.; Osychenko, O. Transportation in a 100% renewable energy system. *Energy Convers. Manag.* **2018**, *158*, 266–285. [CrossRef]
168. Brown, T.W.; Bischof-Niemz, T.; Blok, K.; Breyer, C.; Lund, H.; Mathiesen, B.V. Response to 'Burden of proof: A comprehensive review of the feasibility of 100% renewable-electricity systems'. *Renew. Sustain. Energy Rev.* **2018**, *92*, 834–847. [CrossRef]
169. Teske, S. *Achieving the Paris Climate Agreement Goals, Global and Regional 100% Renewable Energy Scenarios with Non-Energy GHG Pathways for +1.5 °C and +2 °C*; Springer: Basel, Switzerland, 2019.
170. Jacobson, M.Z.; Delucchi, M.A.; Cameron, M.A.; Mathiesen, B.V. Matching demand with supply at low cost in 139 countries among 20 world regions with 100% intermittent wind, water, and sunlight (WWS) for all purposes. *Renew. Energy* **2018**, *123*, 236–248. [CrossRef]
171. Löffler, K.; Hainsch, K.; Burandt, T.; Oei, P.Y.; Kemfert, C.; Hirschhausen, C.V. Designing a model for the Global energy system-GENeSYS-MOD: An Application of the Open-Source energy modeling system (OSeMOSYS). *Energies* **2017**, *10*, 1468. [CrossRef]

172. Pursiheimo, E.; Holttinen, H.; Koljonen, T. Inter-sectoral effects of high renewable energy share in global energy system. *Renew. Energy* **2019**, *136*, 1119–1129. [CrossRef]
173. World Wildlife Fund (WWF). *The Energy Report 100% Renewable Energy by 2050*; World Wildlife Fund (WWF): Washington, DC, USA, 2011. Available online: https://www.google.com/search?client=firefoxbe&q=World+Wildlife+Fund+%28WWF%29.+The+energy+report+100%25+renewable+energy+by+2050.+2011%2C+Washington+DC%2C+USA.+Available+online%3A (accessed on 19 May 2018).
174. Deng, Y.Y.; Blok, K.; Der Leun, K.V. Transition to a fully sustainable global energy system. *Energy Strategy Rev.* **2012**, *1*, 109–121. [CrossRef]
175. World Energy Council. *World Energy Scenarios 2019. Exploring Innovation Pathways to 2040*; World Energy Council: London, UK, 2019. Available online: https://www.worldenergy.org/assets/downloads/European_Scenarios_FINAL_for_website.pdf (accessed on 10 September 2019).
176. International Energy Agency (IEA). *World Energy Outlook 2018*; International Energy Agency: Paris, France, 2018.
177. Luderer, G.; Vrontisi, Z.; Bertram, C.; Edelenbosch, O.Y.; Pietzcker, R.C.; Rogelj, J.; De Boer, H.S.; Drouet, L.; Emmerling, J.; Fricko, O.; et al. Residual fossil CO2 emissions in 1.5–2 °C pathway. *Nat. Clim. Change* **2018**, *8*, 626–633. [CrossRef]
178. Shell International B.V. Sky Scenario. The Hague, The Netherlands, 2018. Available online: https://www.shell.com/energy-and-innovation/the-energy-future/scenarios/shell-scenario-sky.html (accessed on 20 August 2019).
179. BP Energy Outlook. BP Energy Economics: UK, 2019. Available online: https://www.bp.com/content/dam/bp/business-sites/en/global/corporate/pdfs/energy-economics/energy-outlook/bp-energy-outlook-2019.pdf (accessed on 8 March 2018).
180. Energy Information Administration (EIA). Global Transportation Energy Consumption: Examination of Scenarios to 2040 Using ITEDD. Energy Information Administration: Washington, DC, USA, 2017. Available online: https://www.eia.gov/analysis/studies/transportation/scenarios/pdf/globaltransportation.pdf (accessed on 12 May 2018).
181. Breyer, C.; Tsupari, E.; Tikka, V.; Vainikka, P. Power-to-Gas as an Emerging profitable business through creating an integrated value chain. *Energy Procedia* **2015**, *73*, 182–189. [CrossRef]
182. Child, M.; Nordling, A.; Breyer, C. The impacts of high V2G participation in a 100% renewable Åland energy system. *Energies* **2018**, *11*, 2206. [CrossRef]
183. Meschede, H.; Child, M.; Breyer, C. Assessment of sustainable energy system configuration for a small Canary island in 2030. *Energy Convers. Manag.* **2018**, *165*, 363–372. [CrossRef]
184. Mathiesen, B.V.; Lund, H.; Connolly, D.; Wenzel, H.; Østergaard, P.A.; Möller, B.; Nielsen, S.; Ridjan, I.; Karnøe, P.; Sperling, K.; et al. Smart energy systems for coherent 100% renewable energy and transport solutions. *Appl. Energy* **2015**, *145*, 139–154. [CrossRef]
185. Brown, T.; Schäfer, M.; Greiner, M. Sectoral interactions as carbon dioxide emissions approach zero in a Highly-Renewable European energy system. *Energies* **2019**, *12*, 1032. [CrossRef]
186. Gulagi, A.; Bogdanov, D.; Fasihi, M.; Breyer, C. Can Australia power the energy-hungry Asia with renewable energy? *Sustainability* **2017**, *9*, 233. [CrossRef]
187. Junne, T.; Wulff, N.; Breyer, C.; Naegler, T. Critical materials in global low carbon energy scenarios: The case of dysprosium, neodymium, lithium and cobalt. 2019; submitted.
188. Greim, P.; Solomon, A.A.; Breyer, C. Availability of lithium for the global transition towards renewable based energy supply with focus on power and mobility. 2019; submitted.
189. Grandell, L.; Lehtilä, A.; Kivinen, M.; Koljonen, T.; Kihlman, S. Role of critical metals in the future markets of clean energy technologies. *Renew. Energy* **2016**, *95*, 53–62. [CrossRef]
190. Altermatt, P.P.; Chen, Y.; Feng, Z. Riding the workhorse of the industry: PERC. *Photovolt. Int.* **2018**, *41*, 46–54.
191. Köntges, M.; Jung, V. Al/Ni: V/Ag metal stacks as rear-side metallization for crystalline silicon solar cells. *Prog. Photovolt. Res. Appl.* **2012**, *21*, 876–883. [CrossRef]
192. Hsiao, P.-C.; Song, N.; Wang, X.; Shen, X.; Phua, B.; Colwell, J.; Romer, U.; Johnston, B.; Lim, S.; Shengzhao, Y.; et al. 266-nm ps laser ablation for copper-plated p-type selective emitter PERC silicon solar cells. *IEE J. Photovolt.* **2018**, *8*, 4. [CrossRef]

193. International Renewable Energy Agency (IRENA). Renewable Energy and Jobs. Abu Dhabi, United Arab Emirates, 2019. Available online: https://www.irena.org/-/media/Files/IRENA/Agency/Publication/2019/Jun/IRENA_RE_Jobs_2019-report.pdf (accessed on 1 May 2018).
194. Manish, R.; Aghahosseini, A.; Breyer, C. Job creation during the global energy transition towards 100% renewable power system by 2050. *Tech. Forecast. Soc. Chang.* **2019**. [CrossRef]
195. Intergovernmental Panel on Climate Change (IPCC). *Global Warming of 1.5 °C*; Intergovernmental Panel on Climate Change (IPCC): Geneva, Switzerland, 2018. Available online: https://report.ipcc.ch/sr15/pdf/sr15_spm_final.pdf (accessed on 6 April 2018).
196. Pahle, M.; Burtraw, D.; Flachsland, C.; Kelsey, N.; Biber, E.; Meckling, J.; Edenhofer, O.; Zysman, J. Sequencing to ratchet up climate policy stringency. *Nat. Clim. Change* **2018**, *8*, 861–867. [CrossRef]
197. Breyer, C.; Heinonen, S.; Ruotsalainen, J. New consciousness: A societal and energetic vision for rebalancing humankind within the limits of planet earth. *Technol. Forecast. Soc. Change* **2017**, *114*, 7–15. [CrossRef]
198. Smith, C.J.; Forster, P.M.; Allen, M.; Fuglestvedt, J.; Miller, R.J.; Rogelj, J.; Zickfeld, K. Current fossil fuel infrastructure does not yet commit us to 1.5°C warming. *Nat. Commun.* **2019**, *10*, 101. [CrossRef] [PubMed]
199. Kalkuhl, M.; Steckel, J.; Edenhofer, O. All or nothing: Climate policy when assets can become stranded. *J. Environ. Econ. Manag.* **2019**, in press. [CrossRef]
200. Cabon Tracker Initiative. 2020 Vision: Why You Should See Peak Fossil Fuels Coming. London, 2018. Available online: https://www.carbontracker.org/reports/2020-vision-why-you-should-see-the-fossil-fuel-peak-coming/ (accessed on 20 September 2019).
201. Geels, F.W.; Sovacool, B.K.; Schwanen, T.; Sorrell, S. The Socio-Technical Dynamics of Low-Carbon Transitions. *Joule* **2017**, *1*, 463–479. [CrossRef]
202. Geels, F.W. Regime resistance against low-carbon energy transitions: Introducing politics and power in the multi-level perspective. *Theory Cult. Soc.* **2014**, *31*, 21–40. [CrossRef]

© 2019 by the authors. Licensee MDPI, Basel, Switzerland. This article is an open access article distributed under the terms and conditions of the Creative Commons Attribution (CC BY) license (http://creativecommons.org/licenses/by/4.0/).

Article

The Impacts of High V2G Participation in a 100% Renewable Åland Energy System

Michael Child [1,*], Alexander Nordling [2] and Christian Breyer [1]

1. School of Energy Systems, Lappeenranta University of Technology, 53850 Lappeenranta, Finland; Christian.Breyer@lut.fi
2. Faculty of Science and Engineering, Åbo Akademi, 20500 Turku, Finland; alnordli@abo.fi
* Correspondence: Michael.Child@lut.fi; Tel.: +358-40-829-7853

Received: 27 July 2018; Accepted: 22 August 2018; Published: 23 August 2018

Abstract: A 100% renewable energy (RE) scenario featuring high participation in vehicle-to-grid (V2G) services was developed for the Åland islands for 2030 using the EnergyPLAN modelling tool. Hourly data was analysed to determine the roles of various energy storage solutions, notably V2G connections that extended into electric boat batteries. Two weeks of interest (max/min RE) generation were studied in detail to determine the roles of energy storage solutions. Participation in V2G connections facilitated high shares of variable RE on a daily and weekly basis. In a Sustainable Mobility scenario, high participation in V2G (2750 MWh$_e$) resulted in less gas storage (1200 MWh$_{th}$), electrolyser capacity (6.1 MW$_e$), methanation capacity (3.9 MWh$_{gas}$), and offshore wind power capacity (55 MW$_e$) than other scenarios that featured lower V2G participation. Consequently, total annualised costs were lower (225 M€/a). The influence of V2G connections on seasonal storage is an interesting result for a relatively cold, northern geographic area. A key point is that stored electricity need not only be considered as storage for future use by the grid, but V2G batteries can provide a buffer between generation of intermittent RE and its end-use. Direct consumption of intermittent RE further reduces the need for storage and generation capacities.

Keywords: energy system modelling; storage solutions; 100% renewable energy; Åland; vehicle-to-grid; power-to-gas

---

1. Introduction

Driven by efforts to eliminate dependency on imported fossil fuels and increase overall sustainability, island nations and regions of archipelago may encounter higher shares of renewable energy in their energy systems much faster than their continental counterparts. In doing so, these regions will be the first to determine optimal levels of various energy storage solutions needed as higher shares of intermittent renewable energy (RE) resources are assimilated [1]. Furthermore, island groups represent interesting case studies of transitions as their energy systems are relatively compact, homogeneous, and less complex. For these reasons, such regions may offer potential blueprints or test-beds for energy system transitions toward sustainability that will happen on a wider scale in the future [2].

In order to encourage a transition away from fossil fuels and toward sustainability on the Aegean Archipelago Islands, Kadellis et al. [3] suggest that island energy systems based on RE and appropriate Energy Storage Solutions (ESS) can aid in achieving both environmental goals and result in financial advantages. Further, Hlusiak et al. [4] highlight how utilising the storage potential of battery electric vehicles (BEV) can contribute to island grid stability while not imposing significant restrictions on electric vehicle range. The potential coupling of RE generation and electrified mobility, therefore, seems promising.

Over the past two decades, there has been considerable research interest in the idea that electrified vehicles could offer benefits to both the transport and power sectors when a sector coupling is achieved [5,6]. In essence, the concept of vehicle-to-grid (V2G) involves the bidirectional flow of electricity between power grids and various forms of transport in a manner that is mutually beneficial. It includes the idea that electrified forms of transport will have batteries that can offer flexibility to energy systems, thereby improving efficiency and profitability of power grids, enabling higher shares of renewable energy, reducing greenhouse gas (GHG) emissions for the transport sector, and offering potential income for vehicle owners [6]. This flexibility will come in the form of so-called smart charging or enabling vehicles to charge when electricity is abundant or when demands are otherwise low and from discharging batteries back to the grid at times when demand exceeds supply. This flexibility becomes more relevant in energy systems that feature high shares of variable renewable energy, such as solar photovoltaics (PV) and wind turbines. Zhang et al. [7] show how smart charging of BEVs can positively affect power systems through valley-filling and peak shaving of load profiles. Further, several studies have demonstrated how broader use of electric vehicles can be an effective means of managing variable renewable energy resources [8,9]. Further, smart charging need not place unnecessary burdens on power systems if properly managed [10,11], and the lifetimes of lithium-ion vehicle batteries could be extended through optimal V2G strategies [12].

The Åland Islands are an archipelago situated in the Gulf of Bothnia of the Baltic Sea between Finland and Sweden. Åland is composed of 6757 islands, 60 of which are populated by 28,916 inhabitants [13]. Åland is an autonomous region of Finland yet also has strong trade, cultural, and linguistic ties with Sweden. Currently, the Government of Åland aims to identify actions that can be taken to achieve sustainable growth goals by 2051 [14]. These goals are defined by sustainability principles outlined within a Framework for Strategic Sustainable Development [15]. In turn, the Åland Smart Energy Platform has emerged as a group dedicated to envisioning and demonstrating how a fully sustainable energy system could be developed for the region, one that enables the delivery of reliable, cost competitive, and quality energy services to end users which are free of fossil fuels [16].

Previous work for the whole of Finland suggested that a combination of 100% RE and an appropriate mix of energy storage solutions (ESS) could provide the basis of a sustainable and affordable energy system for the entire country by 2050 [17]. In addition, Child and Breyer [18] showed how storage technologies could play support high shares of solar PV and wind power at high northern latitudes. However, as the geography and energy system of Åland represent unique contexts within the Finnish system, a more specific and local analysis was required. In addition, following the idea that energy system transition towards high shares of renewables could be achieved on islands and regions of archipelago sooner than continents, an accelerated timeframe for Åland was needed for investigation. The transition towards a sustainable island energy system will require a variety of complementary energy generation and storage solutions. Past research [19] indicates that electricity storage will be required after 50% of electricity is generated from variable RE, and that seasonal storage will be required after that level exceeds 80% [20,21]. Currently, a variety of flexibility measures are available which support high levels of variable RE [22].

For these reasons, several sustainable energy scenarios were investigated for Åland [23]. In total, six scenarios were developed and compared to a Business as Usual scenario for the year 2030. The Sustainable Mobility—High Electrification (2030 SM El) scenario emerged as a highly cost-competitive option for Åland. This scenario featured a highly electrified transport sector, which included both land and water-based forms of mobility. Cost savings were observed as high capacities of BEV battery storage and V2G connections resulted in lower requirements of seasonal storage, synthetic fuel production, and offshore wind installed capacity. As reported in [23], the effect of high V2G participation resulting in less need for a form of seasonal storage, in this case Power-to-Gas (PtG), has never before been reported, and represents a novelty that merits further investigation. Another novelty of the scenario is that it extended V2G participation beyond automobiles and featured the use of batteries of electrified watercraft. The significance of such batteries is that they often stay unused for transport purposes during much of the winter season, offering a source of flexibility not previously considered.

The purpose of this current study is to explain the roles of ESS in more detail in the Åland context. Included in this analysis are gas storage, PtG technologies, Thermal Energy Storage (TES), stationary batteries, and V2G connections. Several key questions will be answered to aid in determining the significance of ESS in this future energy system.

- To what extent are wind and solar PV power used directly?
- How much do storage technologies contribute to annual energy demand?
- What is the amount of stored energy arising from V2G connections?
- What is the amount of stored energy arising from TES?
- What is the amount of stored energy arising from gas storage?

2. Materials and Methods

The EnergyPLAN tool is an advanced energy system analysis computer model [24], and was employed to simulate a 100% RE scenario with a highly electrified mobility sector for Åland in 2030. The chosen scenario was one of nine developed in the study by Child et al. [23], and was chosen because it was the most cost competitive of the scenarios studied. A full description of the tool used, scenario parameters, and the main inputs to EnergyPLAN for the 2030 SM El scenario can be found in [23] as well as in its detailed supplementary materials. A summary table of main inputs is provided in Table 1. In addition, an annual energy flow diagram is provided in Figure 1.

The EnergyPLAN modelling tool was designed at Aalborg University in 1999 and has seen continued development since that time. Version 12.4 was used for this study and was the most recent version available at the moment the study began. The model has been formally described as a simulation model, which compares options or scenarios that can differ between key input parameters, such as costs, emission factors, energy generation technologies, storage options, and many others [25]. The model has typically been used to simulate national energy systems but can also be used for smaller regions. Simulation models differ in nature to optimisation models, which generally establish an optimal strategy based purely on quantitative analyses according to one criteria. Instead, simulation models allow several criteria to be compared through the creation of unique scenarios [25]. The strengths and weaknesses of scenarios can then be compared and discussed. A comparative discussion and overview of the many modelling tools available can be found in [26].

As stated above, this current study examines one scenario in greater detail to determine the roles of various forms of ESS, and to elaborate on the finding in [23] that V2G participation could not only aid in enabling higher shares of RE but could preclude the need for other forms of storage, most notably seasonal energy storage. The 2030 SM El scenario under analysis featured a special focus on the mobility sector, whereby electrification of passenger vehicles was assumed to reach 100%. In addition, an extra 350 MWh$_e$ of V2G battery capacity was added to represent a capacity of marine transport batteries. This value was deemed sufficient to represent the more than 7000 marine watercraft, from recreational boats to large Roro vessels and ferries, that are found in Åland [13] and the level of electrification that might be possible. However, complete electrification of transport was not assumed. For this reason, 31 GWh of biodiesel and 9 GWh of synthetic diesel were produced to satisfy the remaining transport demand. In this scenario, it was also assumed that V2G and flexible charging participation would be limited to 75% of vehicles, with the remainder of electric vehicles being charged during the evening hours.

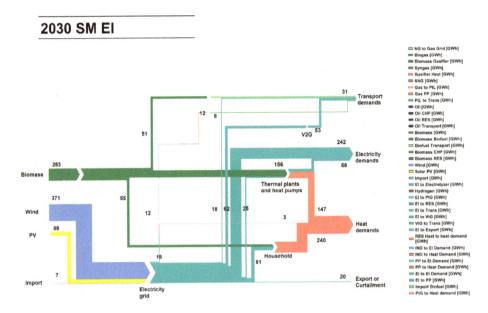

Figure 1. Simplified annual energy flows (in GWh) for the 2030 SM El scenario. Data source: [23].

From the EnergyPLAN outputs, data was collected and processed to show the workings of the energy system components in hourly resolution. EnergyPLAN provides hourly resolved output data related to demand, production, and storage of electricity, district heat and grid gas (or PtG methane). This data is organized from the first hour of a calendar year beginning 1 January, to the 8784th h of the year on 31 December. EnergyPLAN assumes that all years are leap years, which therefore include values for 29 February. This explains the divergence from a standard year of 8760 h. The annual graphics showed two periods of interest and illustrated in greater detail how various forms of energy were generated, how energy was stored, and how it was ultimately consumed. Although hourly results of combustion/boiler-based home heating are not available from EnergyPLAN, the three categories of electricity use, district heating and grid gas were used to provide an overview of energy supply, consumption, and storage to enable an interpretation of results. It was deemed interesting to see how the energy system would function at times of both high and low variable renewable energy generation, characterised by the sum of solar PV, onshore wind and offshore wind. These moments could be times of high inflow of energy to and outflow of energy from storage, respectively.

Periods of study were chosen as the weeks surrounding these moments of interest, with the moments of interest close to the midway point of the study periods. At the same time, the starts of the study periods were maintained as the first hour of the calendar day and week (Sunday 00:00–01:00) and the final hour of the study periods as the final hour of a calendar day (Saturday 23:00–00:00). The two weeks chosen for analysis are 26 March–1 April (Hours 2107–2185), and November 19–25 (Hours 7776–7944). Afterward, results were further processed and analyzed.

Table 1. Main input parameters for the 2030 SM El scenario.

Parameter		Unit	Value
RE generation capacity			
	Wind onshore	MW$_e$	70
	Wind offshore	MW$_e$	55
	Solar PV—Rooftop	MW$_e$	28
	Solar PV—Ground mounted	MW$_e$	55
Thermal plant capacity			
	Condensing PP	MW$_e$	10
	CHP	MW$_e$	20
	DH Boilers	MW$_{th}$	15.3
	DH Heat pumps	MW$_e$	5
Storage capacities			
	Heat storage	MWh$_{th}$	1100
	V2G electric storage	MWh$_e$	2750
	Methane storage	MWh$_{th}$	1200
PtG capacities			
	Electrolysis	MW$_e$	6.1
	Methanation	MWh$_{gas}$	3.9
Annual electricity demand		GWh$_e$	451.54
Annual district heating demand		GWh$_{th}$	135
Annual individual heating total		GWh$_{th}$	240.05
	Biomass	GWh$_{th}$	50.05
	Heat pump	GWh$_{th}$	150
	Electricity	GWh$_{th}$	40
Annual fuel for transport		M km	415
	Biodiesel	GWh$_{th}$	30.73
	Synthetic diesel	GWh$_{th}$	9.27
	Electricity (Dump charge)	GWh$_e$	17.8
	Electricity (Smart charge)	GWh$_e$	51.2

To explore a broader context, several the hourly profiles were examined for the duration of year. These included annual electricity supply and consumption by category as well as the state of charge of electric, DH, and gas storage. Hourly end-user demand data for Åland were based on real values from 2014 obtained from Kraftnät Åland, the Åland transmission system operator. A district heat demand and wind energy generation profiles were provided by a local energy company (Mariehamns Energi). Each profile was based on real data from 2014. Solar PV production data was derived from 2005 data originating from [27,28], as suitable, real production data was not available for 2014. All original data is available in [23].

To calculate the various contributions of ESS options employed in this study, total energy demand was calculated based on electric and thermal energy end-user consumption, which represent to EnergyPLAN inputs. In total, 797 GWh of energy was consumed for the year, represented by 422 GWh of electricty and 375 GWh of heat. A number of annual and hourly outputs from EnergyPLAN were available, including discharge values from V2G, stationary battery, and thermal energy storage. At the same time, values for the annual electricity and heat that came from stored gas were calculated using the equations listed in [18].

The direct usage of solar PV and wind energy was calculated as the sum of the categories of supply (onshore wind + offshore wind + solar PV) divided by the sum of electricity supply from all sources. To calculate the amount of wind and solar PV power that was consumed directly, this ratio was multiplied by the level of total electricity. The ratio was also multiplied by the sum of power going to electricity storage (V2G batteries + stationary batteries + PtG electrolysers) to calculate the amount of wind and solar being transferred to storage. The share of directly consumed solar PV and wind energy is the ratio of solar PV and wind energy which was directly consumed to the consumption of total electricity by all sources. These calculations were made for all hours and then added to determine annual totals. Further compilation, tabulation and analysis of the results were performed.

3. Results

Annual results are shown in Figures 2–6 for electricity supply, electricity demand, electricity storage, thermal storage and grid gas storage in the energy system. Calculation results are shown in Figure 7 and Table 2. Hourly results are compiled for the two study periods in Figures 8–13 for the electricity, district heating and gas components of the energy scenario.

Electricity consumption and supply are shown in Figures 2 and 3. Generation from solar PV is more concentrated during the late spring to early autumn months and is seen to be variable at an hourly resolution. Wind energy, especially offshore wind, is less variable, and shows more concentration during the period of late autumn to early spring. This represents a somewhat natural seasonal complement of the two resources, which reduces the variability of RE in more general terms. At the same time, Combined Heat and Power (CHP) plants are available to maintain the balance between supply and consumption. The balancing offered by V2G and flexible demands also contributes to system stability through peak shaving and valley-filling during times of extreme highs and lows. Some curtailment of wind and solar is necessary when generation from RE is highest, but this is limited to less than 3.5% of total generation.

Figures 4–6 demonstrate the nature of different types of storage. In general, storage of gas and thermal energy appears to follow a typical pattern of charging during the period of late spring to autumn as excess electricity predominantly from solar PV is converted to other energy carriers that can be utilised during the colder months of the year when demands for energy are higher. In addition, it is seen that electric vehicle batteries generally show daily and multi-day charging and discharging cycles. However, there is a longer period during the winter months (roughly hours 400–1200, corresponding to late January to mid-February) when the use of batteries is significant, and they are a major source of power in the system. At the same time, thermal and gas storage levels are at annual low levels, suggesting that the large capacity of V2G batteries also have a role as a storage technology that can contribute to balancing over a longer time period. This is also supported by the observation in [23] that lower overall capacities of PtG technologies were needed compared to other scenarios. Discharge of V2G batteries totals 78 GWh and represents 17% of annual electricity generation.

Table 2. Summary of calculations related to storage discharge and consumption.

Parameter	Unit	Value
Consumption of electricity	GWh_e	452
Consumption of heat	GWh_{th}	375
Consumption of total energy	GWh	827
Discharge from V2G	GWh_e	78
Electricity from stored gas	GWh_e	0
Heat from stored gas	GWh_{th}	0
DH storage discharge	GWh_{th}	7
Direct consumption of Solar PV and wind	GWh_e	273
as% of total solar PV and wind production		67%
as% of total electricity production		53%
as% of final electricity consumption		60%
Solar PV and wind to electric storage	GWh_e	115
as% of total solar PV and wind production		29%
Solar PV and wind to curtailment	GWh_e	20
as% of total solar PV and wind production		4%
Total storage discharge	GWh	85
as% of total consumption		10%
Electricity storage discharge	GWh_e	78
as% of electricity consumption		17%
V2G discharge	GWh_e	78
as% of all electricity storage discharge		100%
Thermal storage discharge	GWh_{th}	7
as% of heat consumption		2%
Gas storage discharge	GWh_{gas}	4
as% of grid gas consumption		31%

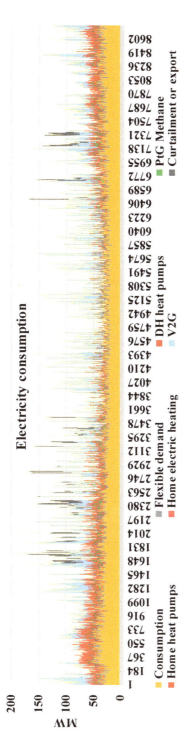

Figure 2. Annual hourly power demand by category (MW$_e$). Flexible demand and electric vehicle charging enables a reduction in high peaks of electricity demand and fills valleys in demand during midday and night hours. Total curtailment of electricity is less than 3.5%.

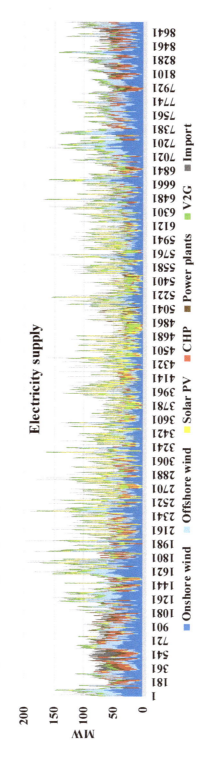

Figure 3. Annual hourly power supply by category (MW$_e$). A seasonal complement can be observed between solar PV and CHP electricity production. Solar PV is also seasonally complemented by wind power to a lesser extent.

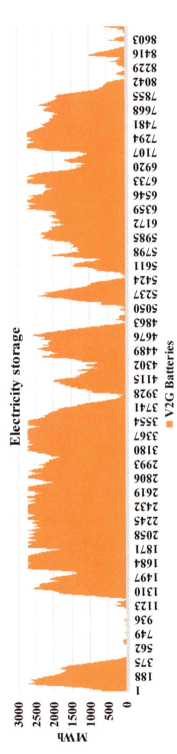

Figure 4. Hourly electric storage levels (MWh$_e$) for the year. Maximum storage capacity is 2750 MWh$_e$. V2G batteries had a significant role in the energy system, providing flexibility on a daily and multi-day level. High capacities of V2G led to reduced need for seasonal gas storage.

Figure 5. Hourly thermal storage levels (MWh$_{th}$) for the year. Maximum storage capacity is 1100 MWh$_{th}$. Thermal storage has a strong coupling with heat pump use in the district heating system, thereby allowing excess electricity to be stored as heat in long-term storage.

Energies **2018**, *11*, 2206

Figure 6. Hourly grid gas storage levels (MWh$_{gas}$) for the year. Maximum storage capacity is 1200 MWh$_{gas}$. High levels of gas storage appear to be associated with higher generation of wind power. Gas storage becomes lower during the summer months when solar PV generation is at its maximum.

Figure 7. Amount of solar PV, onshore wind and offshore wind that is directly consumed (%). Values are in the range of 0–85% with a mean of 73%. As a result of high direct utilization of RE and extensive use of V2G storage, there was noticeably less need for gas and thermal storage.

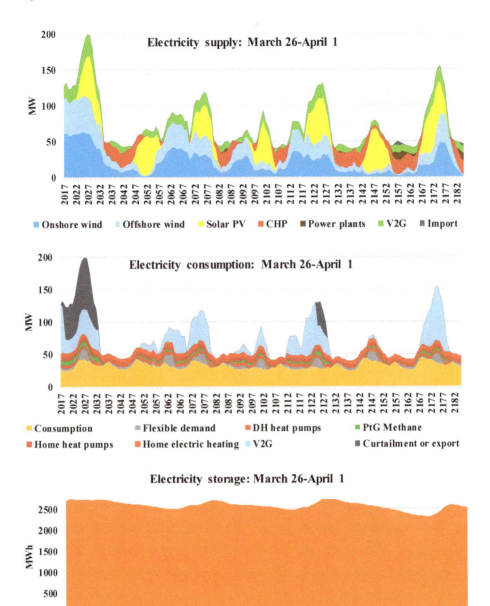

Figure 8. Electricity supply (**Top**), consumption (**Centre**), and storage (**Bottom**) for the first study period: 26 March–1 April. The beginning of the week shows the highest amount of variable RE generation. As storage options reached their capacities, some curtailment was needed. Daily cycles of charging and discharging of V2G storage are apparent over the week. These cycles are somewhat more prominent during days of lower wind generation. V2G charging is highly associated with solar PV generation throughout the week, creating a buffer between RE generation and end-use.

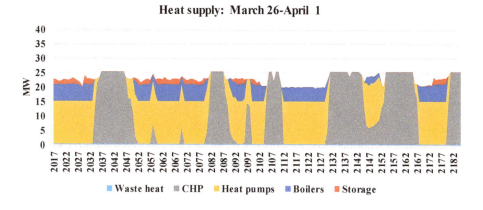
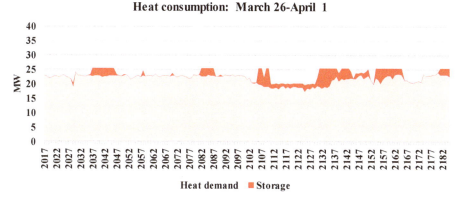
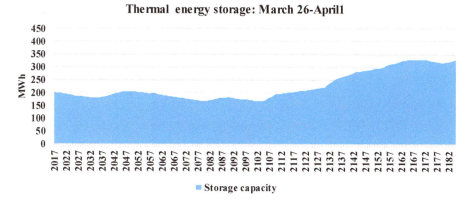

Figure 9. District heat supply (**Top**), consumption (**Centre**), and storage (**Bottom**) for the first study period: 26 March–1 April. Heat pump use is maximized during times of high variable RE generation. CHP plant production satisfies needs for both electricity and heat during evening hours. Utilisation of storage is minimal. Total thermal storage capacity is 1100 MWh$_{th}$. Thermal storage levels are relatively low at the end of the winter months.

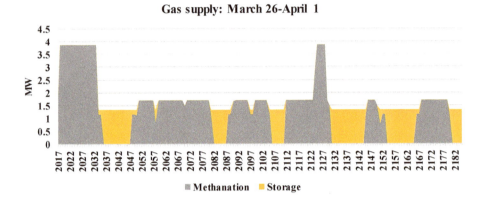

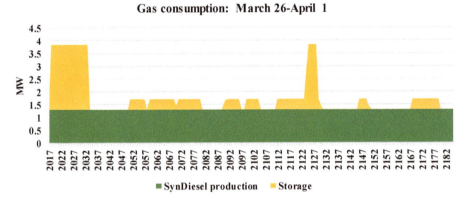

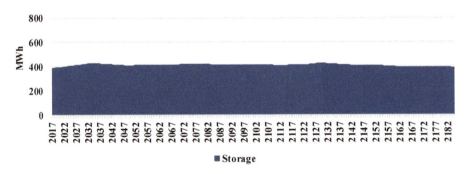

Figure 10. Gas supply (**Top**), consumption (**Centre**) and storage (**Bottom**) for the first study period: 26 March–1 April. Methanation occurs during periods of high variable RE generation and seems somewhat more associated with periods of high wind. Produced methane is stored for later use in synthetic liquid fuel production for the mobility sector only and was not needed for power or heat generation. Seasonal gas storage for these sectors was not needed in a system with high levels of V2G and thermal storage, which led to reduced system costs.

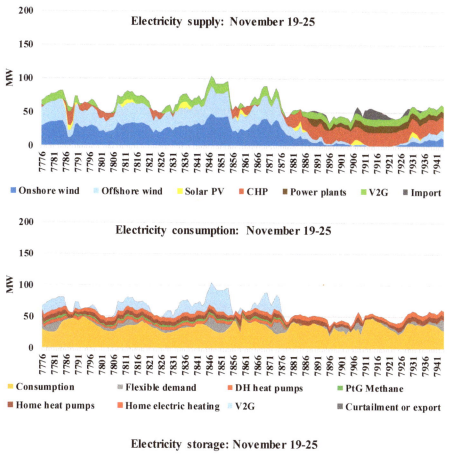

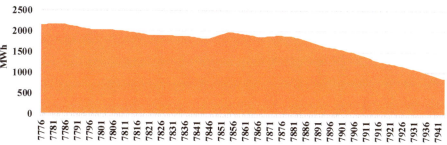

Figure 11. Electricity supply (**Top**), consumption (**Centre**), and storage (**Bottom**) for the second study period: 19–25 November. The end of the week showed the lowest levels of variable RE generation during the year and was the most challenging period for the energy system. However, use of electric storage, thermal power plants, and a small amount of imported electricity was sufficient to satisfy demand. V2G batteries experienced net discharge over the week but still maintained more than 25% capacity.

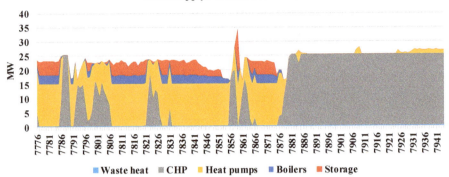

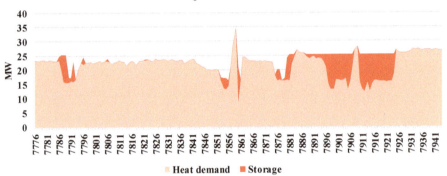

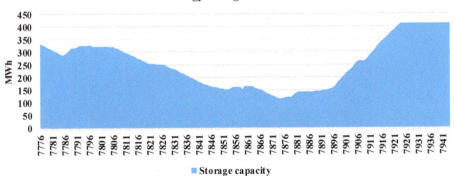

Figure 12. District heat supply (**Top**), consumption (**Centre**), and storage (**Bottom**) for the second study period: 19–25 November. High power requirements toward the end of the week led to oversupply of heat originating from CHP plants. Thermal storage levels increased toward the end of this study period accordingly. Heat pumps use early in the week occurred at times of relatively higher variable RE production.

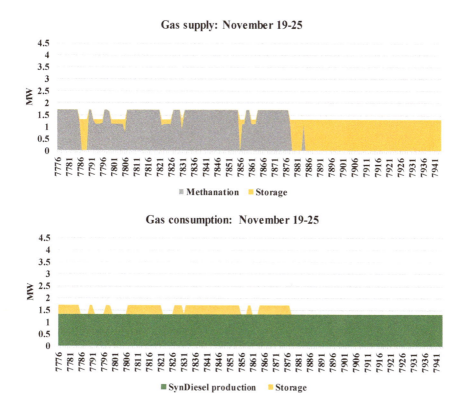

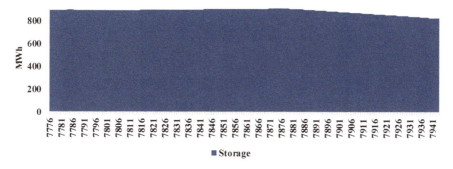

Figure 13. Gas supply (**Top**), consumption (**Centre**), and storage (**Bottom**) for the second study period: 19–25 November. Relatively high levels of variable RE generation at the beginning of the week led to high levels of methane production. This ended later in the week as demands for power were high and variable RE generation was at its lowest. Gas needed for synthetic fuel production came from storage, which declined near the end of the week, but was still at more than 75% capacity.

Table 2 and Figure 7 indicate that there is relatively high direct usage of electricity from solar PV and wind, approximately 67% of total production. Approximately 29%, or 115 GWh goes to electric storage, which can be in the form of batteries or PtG. It appears, however, that the majority of this excess goes to battery storage, as the output of V2G batteries to the grid is 78 GWh$_e$ and the output of gas storage is relatively small (4 GWh$_{gas}$). Further, this stored gas is used only for the production of liquid synthetic transport fuels and is not converted back to electricity for use in the grid. This also suggests that electric storage plays a more dominant role in the energy system.

In total, 139.82 TWh of electricity went from the grid to charge V2G batteries, and 78.12 TWh was discharged back to the grid (56%). Mobility demand for those V2G vehicles represented 50.54 GWh, or 36% of the total electricity charge, leaving losses due to charging and discharging at approximately 8%. This suggests that the utility of V2G batteries could be greater for the power sector than for the mobility sector.

4. Discussion

Variable RE in the form of solar PV and wind power contribute 60% to final electricity consumption and represent 53% of the total electricity generation. Importantly, this generation is seen to be highly variable throughout the year. Moreover, it is sometimes concentrated during daytime, creating a need for both short and long-term storage. In total about 67% of variable RE is directly utilized, with the remainder going to storage (28%) and a much smaller amount to curtailment (5%). Electric storage discharge totalled 78 GWh$_e$, or 17% of end-user consumption. V2G batteries have a very strong role in the energy system and provided 100% of electric storage. Extending V2G storage to a greater range of transport types, in particular the more than 7000 personal watercraft in Åland, appears to be of great benefit to the energy system. At the same time, the EnergyPLAN modelling tool was not fully able to harness all the flexibility that could be offered by boats. One limitation of the model is that it could not distinguish between vehicles and boats in terms of their electricity demands nor their variable seasonal availability. Indeed, a large portion of personal watercraft would be completely idle during winter months and their batteries could offer greater storage than was represented by EnergyPLAN. Likewise, demands for electricity during summer months could be noticeably higher than what has been represented. Further study is needed to determine the full range of benefits and operational challenges related to extending V2G services to such a high number of vehicles and other devices. Such devices could include other aquatic craft that are fully or partially electrified such as ferries, fishing vessels and larger ships. A wide range of support vehicles may also be possible to include such as forklifts, tractors, forestry machines and golf carts. In addition, there may be a role for stationary batteries in reality that was not supported by this analysis.

The results of this study suggest that V2G batteries may serve a greater role in the power sector than even in the mobility sector, as 56% of the electricity that flowed into the V2G batteries eventually went back to the grid, while only 36% was used for mobility demand. This effect is enabled by the relatively large size of batteries that may be demanded in the future in order to ensure sufficient range of driving. The largest available battery is currently found in the Tesla Model S, at 100 kWh [29]. The average battery sizes for 2030 assumed for this study were more conservative, at 75 kWh for road vehicles and 50 kWh for watercraft. Larger average battery sizes may offer greater flexibility to the energy system than is assumed here.

At the same time, it must be remembered that vehicles and watercraft are items of personal ownership, and utilisation of their batteries is subject to the desires of their owners. It is one thing to conclude that there is technical feasibility and economic benefit to the utilisation of V2G batteries for the benefit of the energy system. It is quite another to assume that this would be a desirable outcome for battery owners. Some form of motivation must be considered. Kiviluoma [30] cautions that the marginal benefits for plug-in hybrid electric vehicle owners would decrease with higher participation in V2G services. In essence, a larger number of participants would be sharing limited benefits as there are finite demands for power system reserves and system flexibility.

There are several studies that suggest that V2G participation can be of benefit to both vehicle owners and save costs in the power system. First, V2G can reduce transmission system losses and the overall costs of grid operation [31]. Second, both vehicle owners and grid operators were reported to be able to reduce costs through optimised vehicle charging [7]. Third, Zakariazadeh et al. [9] suggest that effective scheduling of charging and discharging of EVs can result in mutual benefits for vehicle owners, distribution system operators and the service providers or aggregator elements that may bring them together.

These observations are also summarised in a review by Sovacool et al. [6]. However, the authors point out that the social dimension of V2G is greatly overlooked in scientific studies. They conclude that meaningful sociotechnical advantages and disadvantages to V2G systems remain unexplored. Designing V2G systems based purely on technical and economic feasibility would be premature without addressing obvious research gaps related to overall environmental performance, financing and business models, user behaviour, use of natural resource, visions and narratives, concerns about social justice, gender norms, and urban resilience.

PtG technology has only a limited role in the 2030 SM El scenario analysed. The only purpose of PtG had been in the production of synthetic transport fuels, which EnergyPLAN generates in a Power-to-Gas-to-Liquid sequence. Gas storage arising from PtG amounts to 4 GWh$_{gas}$, or 31% of annual gas usage. On a daily and weekly level, PtG technology provides a buffer between high levels of variable RE generation and the creation of synthetic fuels for transport. This result is interesting when considering that PtG played a very important seasonal storage role in an analysis of Finland as a whole [17,18]. The contrasting result appears partially due to the less variable wind conditions in the Åland archipelago, but also due to extensive V2G storage. In this regard, this study may be the first to show that while V2G services provide rather short-term storage on a daily and multi-day level, extending these services may greatly result in less need for seasonal storage. In this scenario, lack of seasonal storage is represented by no need for synthetic gas for electricity or heat production. At the same time, other scenarios from a broader study [23] emphasise the structural findings obtained here. These scenarios also showed little need for seasonal storage in the form of PtG outside of liquid fuel production. In fact, PtG seasonal storage was only needed in the two scenarios that featured Åland in complete island mode, and exports of energy carriers were not allowed by scenario design.

Thermal energy storage in Åland appears to have a less significant role when annual numbers are considered. Thermal storage discharge totalled 7 GWh$_{th}$, representing just 2% of end-user heat demand. At the same time, this role would be expected to be more significant during colder months and in more urban areas. Thermal storage is relatively inexpensive and complements the extensive use of heat pumps seen in the 2030 SM El scenario. Having sufficient thermal storage allows excess variable RE power generation to be utilized by heat pumps at a much greater extent.

The variability of RE energy generation in Åland seems manageable by the storage technologies employed in this study. In all, 89 GWh of electricity and heat are discharged from storage, totalling 11% of end-user consumption.

5. Conclusions

Developing a fully sustainable scenario for any region merits proper consideration of the appropriate mix of these measures for each context. In this work, the right mix of technologies for Åland was influenced by high levels of direct consumption of variable RE and expanded use of V2G storage on Åland. In turn, the energy system required lower installed capacities of offshore wind generation, and the need for both PtG and seasonal storage of gas was eliminated. To this end, V2G services seem to offer a key flexibility for future energy systems, provided that charging and discharging is optimised. Expanding such services to a wider range of electrified transportation modes (boats, bikes, motorcycles, etc.) appears to be an interesting area of future research that merits considerable attention. Such attention could even be directed toward other types of commercial vehicles, such as electrified carts, forklifts, forestry machines, etc. Variable RE and ESS can play significant roles in a fully sustainable future energy system for Åland. V2G services should therefore be investigated as a significant electricity storage option for islands and regions of archipelago. However, the social dimensions of V2G systems need further research to determine a further range of advantages and disadvantages to society.

Author Contributions: A.N. conceived and designed the simulations for the Åland energy system under the supervision of M.C. and C.B.; M.C. performed the numerical analysis of hourly energy system data; C.B. and M.C. were involved in further interpretation of the data; M.C. wrote the paper under the supervision of C.B.

Funding: The authors gratefully acknowledge the public financing of Tekes, the Finnish Funding Agency for Innovation, for the 'Neo-Carbon Energy' project under the number 40101/14.

Conflicts of Interest: The authors declare no conflict of interest.

Abbreviations

BEV	battery electric vehicle
CHP	combined heat and power
DH	district heating
ESS	energy storage solution
GHG	greenhouse gas
GWh	gigawatt hour
M	million
MW	megawatt
MWh	megawatt hour
RE	renewable energy
PV	photovoltaics
PtG	Power-to-gas
TES	thermal energy storage
V2G	vehicle-to-grid
e	electric units
th	thermal units
gas	gas units

References

1. Franzen, E.; Strauch, N.; Triebel, C.; Bosch, E.; Richards, B. Switching off the generator: Technical and economic approach for storage based renewable energy systems for islands. *WIT Trans. Ecol. Environ.* **2013**, *176*, 3–13.
2. Blechinger, P.; Cader, C.; Bertheau, P.; Huyskens, H.; Seguin, R.; Breyer, C. Global analysis of the techno-economic potential of renewable energy hybrid systems on small islands. *Energy Policy* **2016**, *98*, 674–687. [CrossRef]
3. Kaldellis, J.K.; Zafirakis, D.; Kavadias, K. Techno-economic comparison of energy storage systems for island autonomous electrical networks. *Renew. Sustain. Energy Rev.* **2009**, *13*, 378–392. [CrossRef]
4. Hlusiak, M.; Arnhold, O.; Breyer, C. Optimising a Renewables Based Island Grid and Integrating a Battery Electric Vehicles Concept on the example of Graciosa Island, Azores Archipelago. In Proceedings of the 6th European Conference on PV-Hybrids and Mini-Grids, Chambery, France, 26–27 April 2012.
5. Sovacool, B.; Axsen, J.; Kempton, W. Tempering the Promise of Electric Mobility? A Sociotechnical Review and Research Agenda for Vehicle-Grid-Integration (VGI) and Vehicle-to-Grid (V2G). *Annu. Rev. Environ. Resour.* **2017**, *42*, 16.1–16.30. [CrossRef]
6. Sovacool, B.K.; Noel, L.; Axsen, J.; Kempton, W. The neglected social dimensions to a vehicle-to-grid (V2G) transition: A critical and systematic review. *Environ. Res. Lett.* **2018**, *13*, 013001. [CrossRef]
7. Zhang, K.; Xu, L.; Ouyang, M.; Wang, H.; Lu, L.; Li, J.; Li, Z. Optimal decentralized valley-filling charging strategy for electric vehicles. *Energy Convers. Manag.* **2014**, *78*, 537–550. [CrossRef]
8. Morais, H.; Sousa, T.; Vale, Z.; Faria, P. Evaluation of the electric vehicle impact in the power demand curve in a smart grid environment. *Energy Convers. Manag.* **2014**, *82*, 268–282. [CrossRef]
9. Zakariazadeh, A.; Jadid, S.; Siano, P. Integrated operation of electric vehicles and renewable generation in a smart distribution system. *Energy Convers. Manag.* **2015**, *89*, 99–110. [CrossRef]
10. Lassila, J.; Koivuranta, K. Network effects of electric vehicles—Case from Nordic country. In Proceedings of the CIRED 21st International Conference on Electricity Distribution, Frankfurt, Germany, 6–9 June 2011.

11. Lassila, J.; Tikka, V.; Haakana, J.; Partanen, J. Electric cars as part of electricity distribution—Who pays, who benefits? *IET Electr. Syst. Transp.* **2012**, *2*, 186–194. [CrossRef]
12. Uddin, K.; Jackson, T.; Widanage, W.D.; Chouchelamane, G.; Jennings, P.A.; Marco, J. On the possibility of extending the lifetime of lithium-ion batteries through optimal V2G facilitated by an integrated vehicle and smart-grid system. *Energy* **2017**, *133*, 710–722. [CrossRef]
13. Statistics and Research Åland Statistical Yearbook of Åland 2017. 2017. Available online: https://www.asub.ax/sites/www.asub.ax/files/attachments/page/statistisk_arsbok_for_aland17.pdf (accessed on 7 August 2018).
14. Nedergård, A. Utvecklings- och Tillväxtplan för Ett Hållbart Åland 2015–2017. 2015. Available online: http://www.atc.ax/files/utvecklingsplan_an_eng2_1492015_website.pdf (accessed on 2 June 2016).
15. Alliance for Strategic Sustainable Development Framework for Strategic Sustainable Development. 2010. Available online: http://www.alliance-ssd.org/framework-for-strategic-sustainable-development-fssd/ (accessed on 8 August 2018).
16. Ålands Teknologi- och Energicentrum The World's Most Advanced Flexible Energy System of the Future—Case Åland. 2015. Available online: http://www.atc.ax/files/press_release_smart_energy_aland_20150911_eng.pdf (accessed on 8 August 2018).
17. Child, M.; Breyer, C. Vision and initial feasibility analysis of a recarbonized Finnish energy system for 2050. *Renew. Sustain. Energy Rev.* **2016**, *66*, 517–536. [CrossRef]
18. Child, M.; Breyer, C. The role of energy storage solutions in a 100% renewable Finnish energy system. *Energy Procedia* **2016**, *99*, 25–34. [CrossRef]
19. Sterner, M.; Thema, M.; Eckert, F.; Moser, A.; Schäfer, A.; Drees, T. *Stromspeicher in der Energiewende*; Agora Energiewende: Berlin, Germany, 2014.
20. Bogdanov, D.; Breyer, C. The Role of Solar Energy towards 100% Renewable Power Supply for Israel: Integrating Solar PV, Wind Energy, CSP and Storages. In Proceedings of the 19th Sede Boqer Symposium on Solar Electricity Production, Sede Boqer, Israel, 23–25 February 2015.
21. Weitemeyer, S.; Kleinhans, D.; Vogt, T.; Agert, C. Integration of Renewable Energy Sources in future power systems: The role of storage. *Renew. Energy* **2015**, *75*, 14–20. [CrossRef]
22. Lund, P.D.; Lindgren, J.; Mikkola, J.; Salpakari, J. Review of energy system flexibility measures to enable high levels of variable renewable electricity. *Renew. Sustain. Energy Rev.* **2015**, *45*, 785–807. [CrossRef]
23. Child, M.; Nordling, A.; Breyer, C. Scenarios for a sustainable energy sytem in the Åland Islands in 2030. *Energy Convers. Manag.* **2017**, *137*, 49–60. [CrossRef]
24. Lund, H.; EnergyPLAN. Advanced Energy System Analysis Computer Model. 2015. Available online: http://www.energyplan.eu/ (accessed on 8 August 2018).
25. Lund, H.; Arler, F.; Østergaard, P.A.; Hvelplund, F.; Connolly, D.; Mathiesen, B.V.; Karnøe, P. Simulation versus optimisation: Theoretical positions in energy system modelling. *Energies* **2017**, *10*, 840. [CrossRef]
26. Connolly, D.; Lund, H.; Mathiesen, B.V.; Leahy, M. A review of computer tools for analysing the integration of renewable energy into various energy systems. *Appl. Energy* **2010**, *87*, 1059–1082. [CrossRef]
27. Stackhouse, P. Surface Meteorology and Solar Energy (SSE). Release 6.0. Available online: https://eosweb.larc.nasa.gov/sse/ (accessed on 17 November 2014).
28. Stetter, D. Enhancement of the REMix Energy System Model: Global Renewable Energy Potentials, Optimized Power Plant Siting and Scenario Validation. Ph.D. Thesis, Institue of Thermodynamics and Thermal Engineering, University of Stuttgart, Stuttgart, Germany, 2012.
29. Golson, J. Tesla's new 100kWh battery makes Ludicrous Mode even more ludicrous. *Verge*. 2016. Available online: http://www.theverge.com/2016/8/23/12611466/tesla-battery-upgrade-p100d-model-s-x-ludicrous (accessed on 8 August 2018).
30. Kiviluoma, J. Managing Wind Power Variability and Uncertainty Through Increased Power System Flexibility. Ph.D. Thesis, School of Science, Aalto University, Espoo, Finland, 2013.
31. Panwar, L.K.; Reddy, K.S.; Kumar, R.; Panigrahi, B.K.; Vyas, S. Strategic Energy Management (SEM) in a micro grid with modern grid interactive electric vehicle. *Energy Convers. Manag.* **2015**, *106*, 41–52. [CrossRef]

© 2018 by the authors. Licensee MDPI, Basel, Switzerland. This article is an open access article distributed under the terms and conditions of the Creative Commons Attribution (CC BY) license (http://creativecommons.org/licenses/by/4.0/).

Article

Assessing Financial and Flexibility Incentives for Integrating Wind Energy in the Grid Via Agent-Based Modeling

Amtul Samie Maqbool [1,*], Jens Baetens [1], Sara Lotfi [2], Lieven Vandevelde [1] and Greet Van Eetvelde [1]

[1] Electrical Energy Laboratory (EELAB), Department of Electromechanical, Systems and Metal Engineering, Ghent University, Tech Lane Ghent Science Park—Campus A, Technologiepark-Zwijnaarde 131, 9052 Ghent, Belgium; j.baetens@ugent.be (J.B.); lieven.vandevelde@ugent.be (L.V.); greet.vaneetvelde@ugent.be (G.V.E.)
[2] Sharif Policy Research Institute (SPRI), Sharif University of Technology, Tehran 1459986131, Iran; Sara.Lotfi@Outlook.com
* Correspondence: samie.maqbool@ugent.be

Received: 12 September 2019; Accepted: 7 November 2019; Published: 12 November 2019

Abstract: This article provides an agent-based model of a hypothetical standalone electricity network to identify how the feed-in tariffs and the installed capacity of wind power, calculated in percentage of total system demand, affect the electricity consumption from renewables. It includes the mechanism of electricity pricing on the Day Ahead Market (DAM) and the Imbalance Market (IM). The extra production volumes of Electricity from Renewable Energy Sources (RES-E) and the flexibility of electrical consumption of industries is provided as reserves on the IM. Five thousand simulations were run by using the agent-based model to gather data that were then fit in linear regression models. This helped to quantify the effect of feed-in tariffs and installed capacity of wind power on the consumption from renewable energy and market prices. The consumption from renewable sources, expressed as percentage of total system consumption, increased by 8.17% for every 10% increase in installed capacity of wind power. The sharpest increase in renewable energy consumption is observed when a feed-in tariff of 0.04 €/kWh is provided to the wind farm owners, resulting in an average increase of 9.1% and 5.1% in the consumption from renewable sources while the maximum installed capacity of wind power is 35% and 100%, respectively. The regression model for the annualized DAM prices showed an increase by 0.01 €cents/kWh in the DAM prices for every 10% increase in the installed wind power capacity. With every increase of 0.01 €/kWh in the value of feed-in tariffs, the mean DAM price is lowered as compared to the previous value of the feed-in tariff. DAM prices only decrease with increasing installed wind capacity when a feed-in tariff of 0.04 €/kWh is provided. This is observed because all wind power being traded on DAM at a very cheap price. Hence, no volume of electricity is being stored for availability on IM. The regression models for predicting IM prices show that, with every 10% increase in installed capacity of wind power, the annualized IM price decreases by 0.031 and 0.34 €cents/kWh, when installed capacity of wind power is between 0 and 25%, and between 25 and 100%, respectively. The models also showed that, until the maximum installed capacity of wind power is less than 25%, the IM prices increase when the value of feed-in tariff is 0.01 and 0.04 €/kWh, but decrease for a feed-in tariff of 0.02 and 0.03 €/kWh. When installed capacity of wind power is between 25 and 100%, increasing feed-in tariffs to the value of 0.03 €/kWh result in lowering the mean IM price. However, at 0.04 €/kWh, the mean IM price is higher, showing the effect of no storage reserves being available on IM and more expensive reserves being engaged on the IM. The study concludes that the effect of increasing installed capacity of wind power is more significant on increasing consumption of renewable energy and decreasing the DAM and IM prices than the effect of feed-in tariffs. However, the effect of increasing values of both factors on the profit of RES-E producers with storage facilities is not positive, pointing to the need for customized rules and incentives to encourage their market participation and investment in storage facilities.

Keywords: agent-based modelling; flexibility; renewable energy; electricity markets

1. Introduction

In 2017, with 17% contribution of renewables in the total energy needs, the EU was well on the way to achieve the 2020 target of 20% renewables [1]. As the EU Renewable Energy Directive aims to increase this number to 32% in 2030 [2], considerable investments and infrastructural changes are needed in the European member states to accommodate renewables in the energy mix. In 2018, 26.7 billion Euros were spent alone on wind energy projects, of which 16.4 billion was spent solely on onshore wind energy [3].

Different market integration schemes and support mechanisms have been developed for increasing the injection of Electricity from Renewable Energy Sources (RES-E) in the grid and to restrict the costs induced by the variability and limited predictability of RES-E generation. In liberalized power markets, these costs occur as imbalance costs, which may be defined as a penalty for deviating from the submitted production and consumption plan [4]. In extreme cases, the unpredictable RES-E that are protected from the market effects by different financial incentives, like the tradable green certificates and the feed-in tariffs contribute to causing a negative market price [4–6]. Investment grants, RES-E quotas, feed-in-tariffs, green certificates, etc. also generate incentives to invest, which indirectly increase competition and improve technology leading to cost reductions and volume growth [7]. Eventually, the RES-E push the expensive systems like nuclear and gas fired power plants out of the market and lower the market price due to their negligible marginal costs. However, this increases price volatility on the market. Extremely high prices are caused when demand peaks as compared to the supply.

Traditionally, established technologies of power production, e.g., coal-fired, gas-fired or nuclear power plants, were used to provide the needed ancillary services to the grid, maintaining a safe operation. However, since renewables have successfully entered the electricity market, the need for system security has increased. It is estimated that, for every 8 MW of wind power installed, a 1 MW of peaking plant is required [8], whereas, it is also estimated that most of the peaking gas units today operate at below 20% utilization rates [9]. Use of demand side response (DSR) as a grid balancing strategy is a recent phenomenon [10], but it shows promising potential, especially when coupled with increased wind power injection [11]. DSR is a set of measures that uses loads, local generation, and storage to support network operations and also to enhance the quality of power supply [12]. DSR has been proven to reduce the needed conventional generation capacity, to maximize the low carbon generation, to contribute to short-term system balancing and to defer the network reinforcements [13]. This article studies the effect of limited generational flexibility of the wind farms that receive a feed-in tariff for each kWh of renewable power they inject in the grid, against the reserves provided by the industries and other technologies as flexible demand.

Electricity grid and markets are composed of multiple actors, who are engaged in consumption/production of electricity that fulfill their own needs and businesses. Their interactions via the market and the electricity grid results in impacting the consumption/production pattern of each other. Agent-based modelling allows to mimic the behavior of human beings and simulate production, consumption and bidding processes, in which participants are modeled as adaptive agents with different strategies [14]. Agent-Based Models (ABMs) have been used to model the diffusion of energy efficient technologies through the society by the interaction of different agents [15,16]. ABMs are used to explore possible states of a system to understand plausible futures, trends, tendencies, and behaviors that can occur under specific circumstances [17].

Previous work on the use of ABMs for electricity grids, markets, and the injection of renewables have focused on the effect of prosumption and peer to peer supply and its effect on the grid management [18] and grid design strategies [19]. ABMs have also been used to predict price of energy trading in smart grids by the use of incomplete information by different agents to optimize their own utility [20]. Likewise, they have been employed as an e-laboratory to test different regulatory interventions before implementation [21]. Furthering the investigation on the profit RES-E producers, ABM has been used to study the optimum conditions for the wind power producers participating in a deregulated market with the inclusion of learning algorithms to optimize the bidding process [14]. Similarly, the technique has been employed to investigate the effect of storage possibilities in the form of electric vehicles on the profit of wind farms that engage in the electricity markets [22]. Based on the above-mentioned examples of application of ABMs for decision-making, technology diffusion, and market price calculation, the data for analysis were generated by an ABM that was developed specifically for this study.

1.1. Electricity Markets and Grid Balancing

Energy system flexibility is not a technological issue alone; it has a strong link to the energy markets as well [23]. Balancing the potential supply and demand of electricity at any given time ensures a reliable supply of electricity. Transmission System Operators (TSOs) are entrusted to carry out the necessary security checks and real-time operations of ensuring a smooth supply of electricity to the consumers [6]. To make this possible, the majority of electricity trade is conducted up to one day before delivery. Based on the time dimension, energy trade is divided into different markets in Europe. In this article, a Day Ahead Market (DAM) and an Imbalance Market (IM) are modeled based on the principles of the same markets in Belgium [24,25]. To ensure more transparent market pricing system, in both markets, buyers and sellers trade electricity following an energy exchange. For the DAM, the intersection of scheduled production and consumption profiles provide the market prices for each hour of the next day, as shown in Figure 1a. The RES-E technologies have the lowest marginal costs as compared to the other technologies and hence are the first ones in the order. The effect of RES pushes the supply curve to the right, and this is shown in Figure 1b.

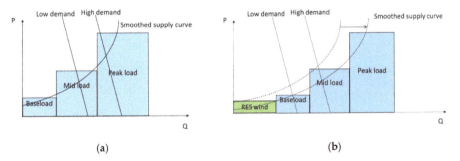

Figure 1. Theoretical merit order without (**a**) and with renewable energy from wind (**b**) (P = price of electricity, Q = installed capacity shown as ratio to the average system demand).

The potential forecasts for demand can be faulty and may still cause imbalances in real time, coupled with increased unpredictability due to increased injection of wind power resulting in higher demand for reserves [20]. IM or the balancing market represents the market where the trade of deviations from the scheduled market positions is dealt with [21]. A real-time balancing market is particularly useful for RES-E as they can provide higher forecast reliability closer to real time [6]. Due to the very fast response times required to balance this market and the connected security issues, this market is coordinated by the TSO [22]. Conventionally, TSOs contract minimum reserve from firm capacity, or power plants with technology that can be easily ramped up and down to balance the grid. Recently, regardless of the source technology, reserves are being contracted by the TSOs. Together, these reserves form the activation price ladder that is shown in Figure 2. The terminology, cheap, mid-priced, and expensive, refers to how much the TSO will have to pay for the reserves in case of grid imbalance.

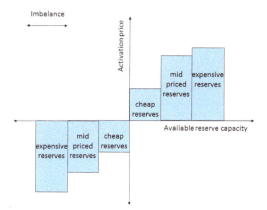

Figure 2. Bid ladder for activating reserves. It is positive when available reserve capacity is used for upward activation and negative when downward activation is required (based on [6]).

In order to ensure system security, TSOs procure balancing services from balancing service providers. Instead of balancing service providers, in this article, we deal with the market participants, called agents, who are the RES-E producers and industries as consumers and reserve providers. These agents are responsible for keeping their portfolio balanced for a given period of time. An agent's portfolio is defined by its nature. For the producers, the portfolio refers to the injection and also off-take if it has storage facilities; for the industries, it is the consumption profile, which can alter in both directions to provide the necessary response to grid imbalance.

Following the IM pricing mechanism in Belgium, in this article, we also modeled a one-price settlement mechanism for the IM. This represents the settlement side of the reserve market, where a price is quoted every quarter of an hour, which represents the marginal activation cost of the reserves.

1.2. Hypothesis Formulation

Feed-in tariffs have proven to be superior for wind power promotion in countries like Denmark, Germany, and Spain [26,27], as cited by [28], but such a system does not force the RES-E producers to operate cost efficiently [28]. Although the subsidies for RES-E producers are slowly being phased out, the question is if the subsidies are negatively affecting the unharnessed potential of DSR as a means to accommodate RES-E in the existing electricity network.

This is especially relevant for countries, like Belgium, where old and outdated nuclear or fossil fuel power plants are scheduled to be decommissioned. In the period of 2020–2025, 5000 MW of nuclear energy is scheduled to be phased-out when seven nuclear reactors will be shut down in Belgium [29]. If the phase-out is carried through, it is speculated that Belgium's carbon footprint will deteriorate, as the firm capacity will need to be replaced by fossil-based power plants. However, if Belgium replaces non-renewable power technologies with RES-E technologies, the effects on the grid balancing and market prices will be significant.

Currently, a feed-in tariff of 0.04 €/kWh is given to Belgian RES-E producers for every kWh of wind energy injected into the grid [30]—while the installed wind capacity accounts for 13.2% of the total installed power capacity [31]. Using Belgium's example, we assessed varying levels of feed-in tariffs (τ) (0.01, 0.02, 0.03 and 0.04 €/kWh) for their effect on the consumption of renewable energy from the grid. Likewise, the effect of increasing the installed capacity of wind farms (Δ_x) is tested to observe which of the two factors; τ or Δ_x, has a higher impact on increasing injection of wind energy in the grid. Although the example of Belgium is quoted here to design the experiments, our aim is to gain a principle mechanistic understanding in a virtual lab approach rather than analyze a specific case study.

The financial incentives for the RES-E producers are designed in a way to shift the additional cost to all ratepayers connected to the grid (commons)—hence, the more customers shift to responding to RE supply, the less the amount that is paid by the commons [32]. To mimic this behavior, industries are modeled to participate in the IM by providing reserves in the form of flexible demand, at three levels of reserve prices—cheap, mid-priced, and expensive. The energy intensive industries have been assessed for their high potential of DSR in the works of [11,33]. This affects the system in a way that the actions of RES-E producers and flexible consumers benefit the whole system by driving the price of electricity low. All consumers benefit from lower electricity prices and not just the providers of demand flexibility; the benefits of demand response can be considered to be truly societal in nature [32,34].

The assumptions explained above lead to the two hypotheses of the study; first, financial incentives coupled with high capacity of wind power production result in higher consumption from RES-E; second, these factors result in low electricity market prices.

The rest of the article is written to first present the model methodology following the ODD + D (Overview, Design concepts, Details + human Decision-making) protocol [35]. The next section gives the statistical analysis of the simulations and provides linear regression models that define the system outcomes based on the effect of feed-in tariffs and installed capacity of wind power. Results are followed by a discussion of the main findings of the article. In the last section, main conclusions are drawn based on the ABM to generate data for testing the hypotheses.

2. Methodology

This chapter first details the methodology behind the ABM that was prepared to run the simulations and then describes the statistical analysis that helped in testing the hypotheses by using the data generated by the model.

2.1. Developing the ABM

Netlogo (6.0.2, Northwestern University, Evanston, IL, USA) [36] was used for modelling the electricity grid for this paper. ODD + D protocol is followed to ensure comprehensiveness when reporting ABMs as it ensures that the description of the main theories and underlying assumptions in the model are clearly explained [35,37]. In this section, the parts of ODD + D that are included consist of Purpose; Entities, state variables and scales; Process overview and scheduling. The sections on Design concepts; Initialization; Input data; and sub-models are provided in Appendix A.

2.1.1. Purpose

The model has been designed for generating data to test the hypotheses that increased τ, increased Δ_x and demand flexibility from industries result in more inclusion of renewable power in the grid and lowered market prices.

2.1.2. Entities, State Variables and Scales

The electricity grid modeled in this paper consists of three main agent groups; the electricity producers that are the wind farms, the large electricity consumers that are the industries, and the Small and Medium sized Consumers (SMCs) that are the households and small businesses. All of the agents are connected to the grid, which is operated by a grid operator, who ensures that the grid frequency is kept stable by reducing the mismatch between the supply and demand to zero. This system needs an efficient information and communication technology support. However, the technical details of the smart grid are beyond the scope of this article.

The model runs with quarter hourly time steps over a period of one year. The electricity grid is modeled as an island (thus, imbalance is zero), where the connections to markets or production systems outside of the model do not exist. The system parameters and the state variables are provided in Table 1. The parameters and variables that are agent dependent are detailed in Appendix A (see Table A1).

Literature supports that fewer actors providing flexibility increases the likelihood of power they can exercise in defining the market price [38]. To avoid this, it was also assumed that the size or capacity of the actors does not limit their ability to participation in either of the two markets. The properties of the agents are further described in the section below.

a. **RES-E producers (2 groups)**

The large RES-E producers are modeled as onshore wind farms, with each turbine of an average capacity of 2 ± 0.4 MW and an average rotor diameter of 80 ± 20 m and a Levelized Cost Of Electricity (LCOE) of 0.053 €/kWh (for year 2017) [39]. LCOE is defined as the cost to produce 1 MWh of electricity with a given technology is the sum of the annualized investment costs, the fuel costs, the operational and management costs and the carbon costs [40].

The on-shore wind farms were selected over the offshore ones because their LCOE is comparable to the other technologies modeled in the ABM [39]. All RES-E producers can sell the produced electricity to the electricity markets. The profit of the RES-E producers is a function of subsidy, operating cost, and the market price in a particular moment. The market for selling electricity is chosen based on the difference between the nominated supply and actual supply. If the actual supply is less than or equal to the nominated supply, DAM price is used for profit calculation. However, if the actual supply is more than the nominated supply, the extra production is placed on the IM and the IM price is considered for profit calculation, if their provided reserves are engaged on IM. At the start of the model run, all RES-E producers are randomly assigned a production strategy, which divides them into two strategic groups:

1. Non-storing producers: RE producers who do not own storage but in cases of grid imbalance can curtail their production.
2. Storing producers: Storing RES-E producers who can store electricity when the actual supply exceeds nominated supply. They provide the stored electricity and the available storage capacity as reserves on the IM.

b. **Large industries (4 groups)**

The large consumers are grouped under the category of industries. All the industries are modeled to produce one unit of product per kWh of electricity consumed. The price of one unit of product is assumed to be 1€. Each industry has a smart metering system; hence, information of their own nominated and the actual consumption is available to all industries in real time. Each of the industries has a maximum capacity of 50% flexibility in their electricity consumption. However, they are divided into four groups, three provide reserves on the IM, while the fourth group does not. The bidding prices for each group are hypothesized and are based on the relative LCOE of other technologies that are included in the study, so that the bidding price of the most expensive reserve is not above the most expensive technology (modeled as an electrolyzer) and the price of the cheapest reserves is lower than the LCOE of wind (without subsidy). The groups are labelled as following based on their strategies:

- Group 0—non-flex: Industries that do not engage in the IM.
- Group 1—cheap reserves: industries that provide reserves at a symmetric price of 0.04 €/kWh.
- Group 2—mid-priced reserves: industries that provide reserves at a symmetric price of 0.08 €/kWh.
- Group 3—expensive reserves: industries that provide reserves at a symmetric price of 0.14 €/kWh.

c. **Small or medium sized consumers (SMCs) (2 groups)**

The households make up this agent group. They are defined by an average electricity consumption of 12 ± 1 kWh/day, which is the average consumption of a European household [41]. The consumption pattern of SMCs depends on the time of the day. Each agent in this group is charged with a bill at the end of the year for the amount of electricity that they consume. Half of the consumers also have

Photovoltaic (PV) panels and are hence termed prosumers. The electricity produced by prosumers is first used to meet own demand and the extra is placed on the grid. However, if there is no demand for this electricity, the grid operator can decide to cut the injection of electricity from prosumers. The prosumers do not receive the profit for injecting electricity in the grid because it is assumed that the cost of smart meters and the grid operational costs will balance the profit that the prosumers may gain. In the model, this electricity is placed by the TSO on the DAM with a price of 0.08 €/kWh, which is the LCOE of a PV [42]. The prosumers pay a fee for getting access to the grid. In Flanders (Belgium), it is an annual flat fee of 85 €, which is also used in this model to calculate the bill of the prosumers [43]. In the model, the SMCs fall into following two categories based on their strategies:

1. Prosumers: SMCs with PV panels,
2. Consumers: SMCs without PV panels.

All SMCs receive the bill at the end of the year, which is calculated by considering the annual average price of both electricity markets. In case of the prosumer, the self-consumption is billed as 0.

d. **Electricity markets**

There are two market environments modeled; DAM and IM. In the ABM, all technologies that participate in the market are ranked according to their LCOEs.

An inflexible base load (abbreviated as fixed-prod) is assumed to provide 20% of the average system consumption at an LCOE of 0.02 €/kWh, comparable to the cost of a hydro power plant in Europe [44]. 10% of the average system consumption is provided by the flexible or interruptible gas fired power plant (NG plant) at a cost of 0.04 €/kWh [40]. The renewable energy capacity from the RES-E producers (RES-wind) is modeled to match at least 25% and at maximum a 100% of the average demand of the system. Half of the SMCs are also modeled to own PV panels, the capacity of which as determined to meet the SMC's own average demand per annum. The electricity that is put on the grid by the SMCs is termed as RES-solar.

On the DAM, the consumers and producers nominate consumption and production capacity, respectively, for the next 24 h. The match between the supply and demand defines 24 values of the market price on the next day. This is done based on the merit order of cheaper to expensive technologies that are engaged to provide the supply. In case of limited supply and a DAM price higher than 0.1 €/kWh, it is assumed that a backup technology (R-tech) is used to provide the necessary electricity and ensures that the market price does not rise further and the system remains stable. The price of buying electricity from the backup technology is a constant 0.1 €/ kWh. Since consumption defines how much supply will be engaged and never the other way around, the price of DAM never drops below the price of the cheapest technology. It also ensures that the DAM price never rises above 0.1 €/kWh. The merit order of these technologies from the cheapest to the most expensive is shown in Figure 3.

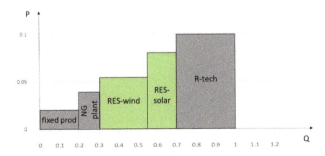

Figure 3. Merit order of the technologies that participate in Day Ahead Market (P = price of electricity, Q = installed capacity shown as ratio to the average system demand).

Increasing levels of RES-wind capacity and RES-solar are expected to stabilize the DAM price at a lower value. However, in the case of low demand, this increased production capacity may lead to a surge in the injection and would require to be settled in the IM. The IM is a quarter hourly market and hence operates to balance mismatch between supply and demand at a time scale of fifteen minutes. The default value for IM price is 0 €/kWh, unless the demand or supply deviate from their day ahead nominations, causing an imbalance. The former triggers a downward activation, which means that the reserves are requested to decrease consumption or an upward activation from the RES-E producers is required. The agents who engage in the IM are the industries who provide reserves and the RES-E producers. The other technologies in IM consist of a flexible Natural Gas (NG) fired power plant with a bid price of 0.04 €/kWh, and an electrolyzer with a symmetric bid price of 0.2 €/kWh. The merit order of these reserves is provided in Figure 4.

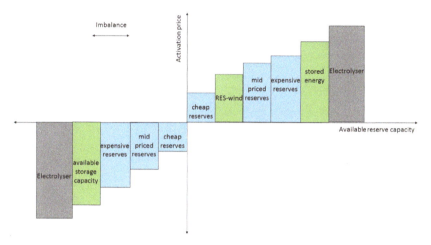

Figure 4. Bid ladder for reserves activation, without a feed-in tariff for wind farms.

The model includes a number of parameters for the agents, technologies, and the market environments that have been explained above. In addition, during the simulation runs, the flow of electricity and money between the agents is governed by different variables that again define the state of the agents, technologies, and the market environments. While Table 1 provides the information for the technologies and the market environment, the detailed information about the agents can be found in the annex (see Table A1).

Table 1. Parameters and state variables.

	Definition	Values	Unit
Parameters (Do Not Change during the Simulation Runs)			
C_{pv}	LCOE [1] of photovoltaic panels calculated over 20 years period [42].	0.088	€/kWh
C_{wind}	LCOE of wind turbines calculated over a time period of 20 years [42]	0.053	€/kWh
τ	feed-in tariffs given to RES-E [2] producers based on data from Belgium	0–0.04	€/kWh
Δ_x	total production capacity of wind farms as a ratio of average system consumption. x represents the ratio	0–100	%
wind	average wind velocity in Belgium [45]	4	m/s
C_{tech}	price of electricity bought and sold to the backup technology that can balance the grid imbalances and is engaged a day ahead of actual supply. The hypothetical value of 0.1 €/kWh is considered because this is higher than the LCOE of photovoltaic panels but still comparable to LCOE of biogas power plants [40]	0.1	€/kWh
Δ_{cheap}	sum of capacity provided by the cheap reserves		kWh
Δ_{medium}	sum of capacity provided by the mid-priced reserves		kWh
Δ_{expen}	sum of capacity provided by the expensive reserves		kWh
$\beta_{electro}$	symmetric bidding price of electrolyzer. Depending on the country the price may vary [46]	0.2	€/kWh
β_{wind}	bidding price of RES-E from wind farms	0.06	€/kWh
β_{store}	bidding price for the electricity provided or consumed by battery storage of wind farm owners	0.18	€/kWh
Δ_{inflex}	capacity of inflexible power production system	20% of average demand	kW
Δ_{tech}	capacity of the back-up system	∞	kW
C_{inflex}	LCOE of inflexible hydro power production system	0.02	€/kWh
Δ_{NG}	sum of capacity provided by the flexible natural gas plant that participates in DAM [3]	10% of average demand	kW
C_{NG}	LCOE of the flexible natural gas fired power plant [40]	0.04	€/kWh
State variables (may change in every time step)			
w_{pred}	predicted wind intensity at that quarter on the next day	0–1	range
s_{pred}	predicted solar irradiation at that quarter on the next day	0–1	range
$DAM.S_{pred}$	predicted and engaged supply to meet the demand on DAM		kWh
$DAM.D_{pred}$	predicted demand from the system on DAM		kWh
$RES.w_{pred}$	total predicted production from the wind farms		kWh
$RES.s_{pred}$	total predicted production from prosumers		kWh
$RES.w_{act}$	total production from the wind farms in real time		kWh
$DAM.S_{act}$	supply in real time before balancing		kWh
$DAM.D_{act}$	demand in real time before balancing		kWh
C_{DAM}	day ahead market price of electricity	−0.15–0.15	€/kWh
w_{act}	wind intensity in real-time	0–1	range
s_{act}	solar irradiation in real-time	0–1	range
$RES.s_{act}$	total production from the prosumers in real time		kWh
$RES.w_{IM}$	production from wind farms that has been made available to balance the grid at β_{wind}		kWh
$RES.w_{store}$	production from storing agents that has been made available to balance the grid at β_{store}		kWh
R_{wind}	ratio of the RES-wind-act that is needed for activation on IM		%
R_{tech}	capacity activated from the backup technology for balancing DAM		kWh
$C_{DAM.annum}$	annual DAM price. $\sum_{i=0}^{34656} C_{DAM}/34656$		
$C_{IM.annum}$	annual IM [4] price. $\sum_{i=0}^{34656} C_{IM}/34656$		
C_{IM}	imbalance market price	−0.2–0.2	€/kWh
$Q_{RE\%}$	percentage of the total yearly demand of the system met by RES-E	0–100	%

[1]: Levelized Cost of Electricity; [2]: Electricity from Renewable Energy Sources; [3]: Day Ahead Market; [4]: Imbalance Market.

For the data on wind velocity and solar irradiation, the database of Belgian Electricity Transmission System Operator, Elia was used [47]. The data on wind velocity and solar irradiation are not meant to depict the exact values but create a realistic pattern of wind speed and solar irradiation in a year for Belgium. More information on how these data were acquired and how the wind power and solar power are calculated is provided in the annex.

2.1.3. Process Overview and Scheduling

The sequence of actions for the model is depicted in Figure 5.

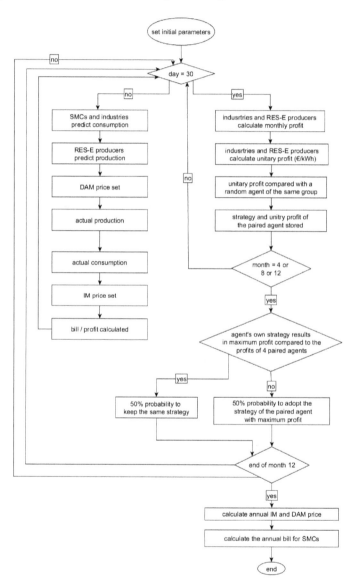

Figure 5. Process overview of the model.

After the model has been set up, the model is run in the following order:

1. Predicting consumption and production for the next day,
2. Setting a DAM price for each hour of the day,

3. Actual consumption and production in every quarter,
4. Calculating the system imbalance to decide to engage the IM,
5. Based on the imbalance, setting the IM price for every 15 min,
6. Updating the system variables,
7. Calculating profit,
8. Storing the unitary profit producers at the end of every month,
9. Storing the unitary bill of SMCs and industries at the end of every month,
10. Changing behavior based on the comparison of unitary bill and unitary profit with other agents in the past three months,
11. At the end of the year, calculate the bill for SMCs.

2.2. Statistical Analysis

The two main variables in this study that were varied to test their effect on the whole system are feed-in tariffs (τ), and the installed capacity of wind power as a ratio of the average demand of the whole system (Δ_x). Both variables are treated as continuous variables with ranges of 0 to 0.04 for τ and a range of 0 to 1.00 for Δ_x. Three response variables were observed in the analyses; $Q_{RE\%}$ (percentage of system demand met by RES-E), $C_{DAM.annum}$ (the annualized DAM price) and $C_{IM.annum}$ (the annualized IM price). The ABM was used to run 5000 simulations to generate data that were then fitted with linear regression models using the statistical program R [48]. All statistical tests were two sided and had a significance level of 0.05%.

3. Results

3.1. Effect on the RES-E Consumption

Figure 6 shows the mean RES-E consumption for all scenarios which is noted to increase sharply following the increase in Δ_x until the installed capacity reaches 35% after which the slope becomes less steep. To explain the effect of τ and Δ_x on $Q_{RE\%}$, the data were fitted with a linear regression model (Equation (1)).

$$\widehat{Q_{RE\%}} = 8.178 + 54.958(\Delta_x) - 0.185(\tau_{0.01}) + 0.173(\tau_{0.02}) + 1.063(\tau_{0.03}) + \\ 2.373(\tau_{0.04}) + 0.0806(\Delta_x.\tau_{0.01}) - 0.728(\Delta_x.\tau_{0.02}) - 0.476(\Delta_x.\tau_{0.03}) + \\ 11.333(\Delta_x.\tau_{0.04}). \quad (1)$$

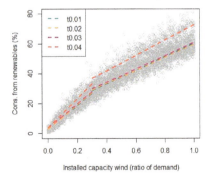

Figure 6. Linear regression line fitted to the observed values of consumption from renewable sources (percentage of total system consumption).

The linear model for $Q_{RE\%}$ explains 95% of the variations in the observed percentage of system consumption from renewable sources with a residual standard error of 4.16%. The curvature in the predictions for $Q_{RE\%}$ is not explained solely by the above linear equation. Hence, the data were divided into two sections with $\Delta_x < 35\%$ and $\Delta_x \geq 35\%$ for further explanation. This resulted in two regression models, which are depicted by the Equations (2) and (3). The regression model (Equation (2)) explains 88% of the variations in $Q_{RE\%}$, with a residual standard error of 3.14% (1740 degrees of freedom). While the second model (Equation (3)) explains 83% of the variation in $Q_{RE\%}$ with a residual standard error of 4.266% (3240 degrees of freedom). See Appendix B (Table A2) for the more detailed information on the parameter estimates for the regression models. The fitted trend line for each value of τ for each regression model is shown in Figure 6:

When $\Delta_x < 35\%$,

$$\widehat{Q_{RE\%}} = 3.315 + 77.813(\Delta_x) - 0.374(\tau_{0.01}) - 0.285(\tau_{0.02}) + 0.562(\tau_{0.03}) + \\ 0.424(\tau_{0.04}) + 1.846(\Delta_x.\tau_{0.01}) + 2.328(\Delta_x.\tau_{0.02}) + 2.710(\Delta_x.\tau_{0.03}) + 20.180(\Delta_x.\tau_{0.04}), \quad (2)$$

When $35\% \leq \Delta_x \leq 100\%$,

$$\widehat{Q_{RE\%}} = 15.701 + 44.560(\Delta_x) - 0.646(\tau_{0.01}) + 0.118(\tau_{0.02}) + 1.134(\tau_{0.03}) + \\ 5.742(\tau_{0.04}) + 0.670(\Delta_x.\tau_{0.01}) - 0.700(\Delta_x.\tau_{0.02}) - 0.618(\Delta_x.\tau_{0.03}) + 6.697(\Delta_x.\tau_{0.04}). \quad (3)$$

When the maximum Δ_x is less than 35%, the increase of every 10% in Δ_x in the absence of any feed-in tariffs will result in an increase of 7.7% in $Q_{RE\%}$. The regression lines (t0.01, t0.02, t0.03, and t0.04) show the effect of feed-in tariffs (Figure 6). When Δ_x is increased by 10%, it results in 3.4, 5.0, 6.5, and 9.1% increase in $Q_{RE\%}$, until Δ_x reaches 35%. Equation (3) shows a less steep slope in predictions for $Q_{RE\%}$ as Δ_x increases from 35% to 100%. It shows that, in the absence of feed-in tariffs when Δ_x increases by 10%, it results in an increase of 4.4% in $Q_{RE\%}$. In addition, the effect of feed-in tariffs at 0.01, 0.02, 0.03, and 0.04 €/kWh results in a respective increase of 4.5, 4.3, 4.3, and 5.1% in $Q_{RE\%}$ for every 10% increase in the value of Δ_x until it reaches 100%. This analysis shows that the increase in Δ_x is the main factor that affects the increase in $Q_{RE\%}$ as compared to increasing values of τ.

Conclusively, the statistical analysis shows that there is not enough evidence to reject that there is no significant effect of τ and the Δ_x on the consumption of renewable energy (p-value $< 2 \times 10^{-16}$). In fact, both factors result in increasing the consumption from RES-E, with the most rapid increase observed when feed-in tariffs for RES-E producers are provided at a value of 0.04 €/kWh while the installed capacity of wind power is between 0 and 35%.

3.2. Effect on the Market Prices

The two market prices dictate the profits of the industries and the producers and the bill for the SMCs in the system, hence the factors that affect the market prices influence all the agents in a direct or an indirect manner. The two graphs in Figure 7 show the effect of τ and Δ_x on the two market prices. For DAM, the four tariff levels show a significant effect as the Δ_x is increased. The four trend lines for each value of τ are shown in Figure 7a, while the linear model from where these trend lines are acquired is given in Equation (4). See Appendix B (Table A2) for the more detailed information on the parameter estimates for the regression model.

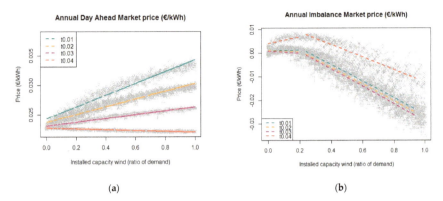

Figure 7. Annualized DAM (a) and IM (b) price observations from the simulations.

When the data observed for annual DAM prices were fitted in a linear regression model (Equation (4)), it showed significant effect of τ and Δ_x. The regression model for DAM prices explains 97% of the variation in the annualized DAM prices with a residual standard error of 0.0006169 (4990 degrees of freedom). See Appendix B (Table A2) for the more detailed information on the parameter estimates for the regression model. The regression model predicts that, under the sole effect of increasing Δ_x, the annualized DAM prices will increase by 0.01 €cents/kWh for every 10% of increase in Δ_x. From the four trend lines in Figure 7a, it is derived that, for 10% of increase in Δ_x and feed-in tariffs at 0.01, 0.02, and 0.03 €/kWh, a respective increase of 0.09, 0.06, and 0.03 €cents/kWh can be expected in the mean annualized DAM price—while a feed-in tariff of 0.04 €/kWh provided to the RES-E producers can result in a decrease of 0.0007 €/kWh in the mean annualized DAM price with every 10% of increase in Δ_x until it reaches 100%:

$$E[\widehat{C_{DAM.annum}}] = 0.002 + 0.001(\Delta_x) - 0.0006(\tau_{0.01}) - 0.001(\tau_{0.02}) - 0.001(\tau_{0.03}) - 0.0002(\tau_{0.04}) - 0.003(\Delta_x.\tau_{0.01}) - 0.006(\Delta_x.\tau_{0.02}) - 0.010(\Delta_x.\tau_{0.03}) - 0.013(\Delta_x.\tau_{0.04}). \quad (4)$$

The data for annualized IM prices shown in Figure 7b show an increase in the IM prices until Δ_x is above 25%, after which the data show a downward trend. Therefore, we divided the data into two parts and fitted separate regression models to them to explain the pattern that is followed by the IM prices. The linear regression model in Equation (5) explains the 72% of the variations in the IM prices when $\Delta_x < 25\%$, with a residual standard error of 0.001266 (1240 degrees of freedom). Equation (7) explains 87% of the variations in the IM prices when $25\% \leq \Delta_x \leq 100\%$, with a residual error of 0.003329 (3740 degrees of freedom). See Appendix B (Table A2) for the more detailed information on the parameter estimates for the regression models:

$$E[\widehat{C_{IM.annum}}] = 0.0062 - 0.029(\Delta_x) - 0.0004(\tau_{0.01}) - 0.0009(\tau_{0.02}) - 0.001(\tau_{0.03}) + 0.003(\tau_{0.04}) - 0.001(\Delta_x.\tau_{0.01}) - 0.002(\Delta_x.\tau_{0.02}) - 0.03(\Delta_x.\tau_{0.03}) - 0.009(\Delta_x.\tau_{0.04}). \quad (5)$$

The trend lines that are added to the graphs are indeed acquired from these main equations. It is visible in Figure 7b that t0.01, t0.02, and t0.03 have an almost equal slope, whereas t0.04 has a steeper slope in the first part of the graph and a smoother slope in the second part of the graph. Equation (6) shows that, in the absence of feed-in tariffs, with a 10% increase in Δ_x, the annualized IM prices will increase by 0.03 €cents/kWh. This is due to the fact that, when there is less wind power being produced, the RES-E producers cannot offer large volumes of power on DAM, resulting in deficit of supply. Hence, when IM prices also spike, RES-E producers (storing and non-storing) cannot offer much to balance the grid. This results in more expensive reserves being engaged on IM. In addition, when the feed-in tariff of 0.01 €/kWh is provided to the RES-E producers, it results in little effect on the position of RES-E producers in the bid ladder, and only results in increasing the IM prices by 0.004 €cents/kWh for every 10% increase in Δ_x.

For feed-in tariffs of 0.02 and 0.03 €/kWh, the RES-E producers move to a second spot on the merit order list for DAM. This leaves less reserves from RES-E producers being made available for IM. This shift of positions in the merit order causes more power being offered as supply (to compensate for the unpredictable nature of wind). This results in a decrease in IM prices by 0.033 and 0.044 €cents/kWh, respectively. Furthermore, when feed-in tariff of 0.04 €/kWh is provided to the RES-E producers, it moves their position to first in the DAM bid ladder. This results in more volumes being made available for DAM from all RES-E producers. This leaves almost no stored reserves available for the IM, which results in engaging more expensive reserves and ultimately increasing the IM prices.

When $\Delta_x < 25\%$,

$$E[\widehat{C_{IM.annum}}] = 0.001 + 0.0031(\Delta_x) - 0.0001(\tau_{0.01}) - 0.00005(\tau_{0.02}) - 0.0003(\tau_{0.03}) \\ + 0.0028(\tau_{0.04}) - 0.002(\Delta_x.\tau_{0.01}) - 0.006(\Delta_x.\tau_{0.02}) - 0.007(\Delta_x.\tau_{0.03}) + 0.011(\Delta_x.\tau_{0.04}). \quad (6)$$

When $25\% \leq \Delta_x \leq 100\%$,

$$E[\widehat{C_{IM.annum}}] = 0.009 - 0.034(\Delta_x) - 0.0007(\tau_{0.01}) - 0.001(\tau_{0.02}) - 0.001(\tau_{0.03}) \\ + 0.004(\tau_{0.04}) - 0.0005(\Delta_x.\tau_{0.01}) - 0.0007(\Delta_x.\tau_{0.02}) - 0.002(\Delta_x.\tau_{0.03}) + 0.008(\Delta_x.\tau_{0.04}). \quad (7)$$

This trend in IM price changes once Δ_x is increased above 25%. This results in decreasing the IM prices as Δ_x increases, with and without the provision of feed-in tariffs. In the absence of τ, every 10% increase in Δ_x results in a decrease of 0.03 €cents/kWh. It is simply an effect of extra volume of electricity being produced by the RES-E producers when there is no demand. The trend lines in Figure 7, derived from Equation (7), exhibit that, with every 10% increase in Δ_x until it reaches 100%, the IM price decreases by 0.034, 0.035, 0.036, and 0.026 €cents/kWh, respectively, when feed-in tariffs are 0.01, 0.02, 0.03, and 0.04 €/kWh. Other than the decrease in IM prices in relation to increasing Δ_x, it is also worth noting that the mean IM prices remain higher when a feed-in tariff of 0.04 €/kWh is provided to the RES-E producers. This is again an effect of the all electricity volumes being made available for DAM, leaving no predicted volumes for storage on the next day. This results in, firstly, too much supply (hence negative IM prices) and, secondly, no stored electricity reserves (hence more expensive reserves being engaged).

The statistical analyses presented above show that there is not enough evidence to reject the second hypothesis of the study and there is a significant effect of τ and the Δ_x on the two market prices (p-values $< 2 \times 10^{-16}$).

3.3. Effect on Different Agents

Graphs (a,b) in Figure 8 show the mean unitary profits for the two industry groups different feed-in tariffs and increasing Δ_x. It is evident that, with increasing Δ_x, the unitary profits of flexible industries, who engage in the IM, increase when τ is 0.04 €/kWh. For all other values of τ, the mean profits of flexible industries decrease with increasing Δ_x. This effect is owed to the modelling method of flexible industries, who always respect their nominated consumption pattern. This results in them paying the bill, which is heavily dictated by the DAM price. Thus, as the DAM price decreases, the profit of flexible industries increases. Although flexible industries respond to demand changes according to the imbalance on the grid, the IM bidding prices are not as high to compensate for the production losses. However, the unitary profit of the inflexible industries (which do not participate in IM and do not respect their nominated consumption) shows no variation as a response to increasing feed-in tariffs and installed capacity of wind power. The more selfish consumption of electricity results in a very stable profit for the inflexible industries. However, in reality, such deviations from nominated power can result in fines for large consumers.

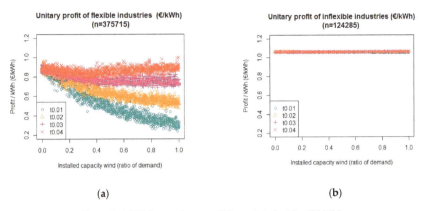

Figure 8. (a,b) Mean unitary profit for each industries (€/kWh).

The effects of the τ and Δ_x were also assessed for impact on the profits of the two producer groups separately. Figure 9a shows the mean unitary profits of storing RES-E producers, where the variation between the different simulations is very narrow and the effect of different feed-in tariffs does not appear to cause a pronounced variation in the profits. However, the general trend that can be observed from this figure is of decreasing profits as the installed capacity of wind increases. On the contrary, Figure 9b shows higher mean unitary profits of the non-storing agents. The most interesting conclusion from the graphs in Figure 9 is that the overall mean profit of non-storing agents is higher than the storing RES-E agents. In addition, increasing Δ_x negatively affects the profit of storing producers, while it increases the profit for non-storing agents when τ is 0.01 and 0.02 €/kWh but results in a decreasing profit as Δ_x increases for a value of 0.03 and 0.04 €/kWh for τ. The simple reason is the decreasing profits of storing and non-storing RES-E producer (only under τ of 0.02 and 0.03 €/kWh) is the extra volumes of wind power being made available on the grid, while the demand does not increase accordingly.

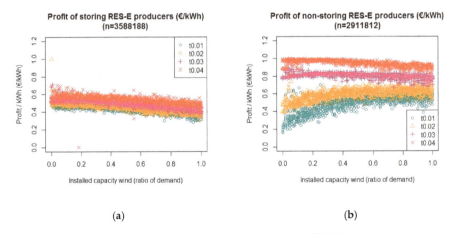

Figure 9. (a,b) Mean unitary profit of producers (€/kWh).

The numbers on top of Figure 9a,b show the number of storing and non-storing RES-E producers at the end of the simulation runs. It shows that the number of RES-E storing producers is almost double the number of RES-E non-storing producers. Due to the adaptation function, modeled in the ABM, it shows that more RES-E producers chose to have storage, as it would have prevailed as a more profitable strategy during the simulation runs. At the start of every simulation run, the number of RES-producers is modeled to be random with an equal chance of any RES-E producers appointed storage facilities. This effect could be a result of lower operating costs for the RES-E producers and hence a higher chance of being engaged on DAM (first position in the bid ladder) and IM (first position for non-stored electricity and fourth for the stored power).

Finally, the mean unitary bill for households with PV panels and without being in relation with increasing values of Δ_x is shown in Figure 10. Comparison of Figure 10a,b shows that the mean bill of SMCs follows the same pattern as the market prices. When the mean bill of consumers is separated according to the ownership of PV panels, it suggests that it is, in fact, not very profitable for households' own PV panels when the installed capacity of wind energy is above 50% of the average system demand, as compared to the households without PV panels. There are two factors that cause disparity between the bill of the prosumers and consumers; first, the amount of consumption of electricity from the grid, and, second, the effect of the prosumer tariff. The very limited variation in the bill of the prosumers is a result of their limited reliance on the grid to fulfill their needs, which results in almost no effect of the market prices on their unitary bill, as compared to the consumers who rely solely on the grid for the electricity supply.

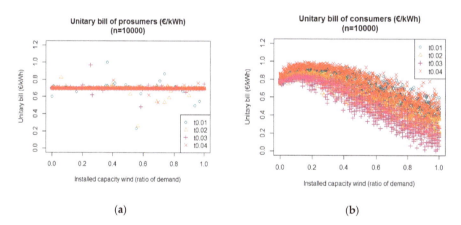

Figure 10. (a,b) Mean unitary bill (€/kWh) for each Small and Medium Sized Consumer group.

4. Discussion

Negative market prices for electricity are a rare phenomenon. In our results, the IM prices fall below zero with increasing values of Δ_x above 25%. In reality, the European energy grid allows the grid imbalances to be reduced from the different countries, while, in this model, the grid is modeled as a stand-alone system, hence negative values on IM are observed more frequently than in reality.

From the results, it is obvious that the two market prices are decoupled, where the DAM prices remain significantly higher than the IM prices. This is a result of how the markets were modeled, allowing for the wind farm owners to bid their extra capacity on the IM. The authors in [23] mentioned that, if capacity bids from RES-E are in use on the reserve market, the energy price on reserve markets may get lower than on the intra-day market, creating distorting incentives. It shows the ability of the presented ABM to depict the working of the electricity markets.

The decreasing market prices in the simulations as a result of the increasing installed capacity of wind energy have also been observed in Germany. The authors in [49] have shown that, on the German market, each additional GWh of RES-E fed to the grid has resulted in lowering the spot market price of electricity by $1.4–1.7/MWh. The authors in [50] found that the negative prices on the DAM and IM in Belgium, Germany, and France occur due to low consumption demand and high RE generation expectation; one of the reasons is the current support mechanisms for solar and wind power [6].

Conversely, it can be argued that decreasing the feed-in tariffs and increasing the installed capacity of wind energy may result in deteriorating the profit of the RES-E producers. This only stresses that, once the subsidies are taken away, there is a need for different rules for the flexible RES-E producers to support their participation in the market and increase the supply of RES-E.

Developments in the power electronic technologies have made the application of energy storage systems a possible solution for modern (flexible) power application [51,52]. It also has been shown that battery-based energy storage with several minutes of run time is optimal for stabilizing wind generation in weak grids [53]. However, these systems are still not economically viable for the wind farm producers, as shown in the low profits for the storing agents.

It needs to be mentioned that, since the average of the two market prices is considered for billing the SMCs, the bills do not reflect reality. In reality, the supplier would nominate the consumption on the market for the consumers under a contract and the consumers will be billed according to the mismatch from these nominations. The average bill for the SMCs exhibits an opposite trend to what was observed in Germany, where the electricity price increased by 30% from the year 2006 to 2012, while the average household income grew by 6% [54]. To improve the accuracy of the bill for the SMCs, it will be useful to include the service as well as the grid operation charges in the calculation of the bill.

In the simulation results, the very pronounced effect of feed-in tariffs for the RES-E producers on the market prices points to the need to include more power production technologies in the model, which will also reflect reality. One such technology could be dispatchable renewables, such as biomass. Authors in [55] suggested that, for a power system completely based on renewables, these technologies can be incentivized to increase flexibility. Whether it is more effective to incentivize wind farm owners so they can compete with other technologies or rather provide incentives to dispatchable renewables that can replace the fossil-fuel based systems could be another topic to use the presented ABM.

For businesses, the decision to provide flexibility as a reserve is complex and can result in major organizational and operational changes. In the model, the industries responded to supply changes regardless of the time of the day and neither did they consider any lead times; in reality, though, this is probably not the case. Although the simulations provide insightful results regarding industries' electrical flexibility as reserves, these results are not extended to other issues. For example, there are legal issues involved when industries plan to market negative tertiary reserve energy in small amounts because of tight storage restrictions [56]. Another reason to keep the industries from providing flexibility as demand response could lie in the relatively low energy price that they pay (as compared to other costs) and could be mitigated by policies opposite to the ones in practice that subsidize heavy industries [57]. Other incentives for energy intensive industries to reduce their energy costs lie in their ability to install combined heat and power plants. The authors in [58] assessed in detail the benefits for industries to engage in symbiotic relations and utilize waste (biomass) to fuel combined heat and power plants. One can argue in favor of such practices against consumption flexibility, especially if it does not incur changes in business as usual.

Finally, the complexity of a flexible electric grid poses a challenge to the diffusion process of flexibility [59]. Flexibility in consumption and production of power requires a longer time to be successful and completely diffused as an important component of the social aspect of the power system. It will require changes in human behavior and institutional setup; both domains with high inertia towards change [57]. One example of this phenomenon, termed response fatigue, occurs when the consumers tire of continuously responding to supply (and/or market price) signals. This behavior was reported in [60], with up to 98% of the residential consumers who participated in a demand response program. The results of the model point to higher need for flexibility and demand response from the consumers for the increased injection of RES-E in the grid. If the households are also to be included as active participants of demand response, there is a need to provide them with awareness and information on the energy markets, next to the provision of in-home display devices that will provide them with real-time information on their consumption and market prices [10].

5. Conclusions

The objective of this article was to model the two electricity markets (day ahead and imbalance market) by using Agent-based Model (ABM) and assess two hypotheses. The first hypothesis was to test the effect of increasing feed-in tariffs (τ) and installed capacity of wind energy (Δ_x) on increasing the consumption from renewables. The second hypothesis was to check the effect of the same factors on decreasing the two market prices. This objective was successfully met by using ABM to generate the data that were then fit into linear regression models to reach conclusions on the hypotheses.

The study concludes that, with increasing Δ_x by 10%, the consumption from RES-E increases by 7.8% in the absence of τ, until Δ_x reaches a maximum of 35%. At different levels of τ, the increasing consumption from RES-E increases differently. The most pronounced is when τ is set at the value of 0.04 €/kWh and the maximum Δ_x is 35%. For Δ_x higher than 35% and less than 100%, the increase in RES-E follows a less sharper increase and once again the sharpest increase is for $\tau = 0.04$ €/kWh, which under every 10% increase in Δ_x results in a 5.1% increase in RES-E consumption.

To test the hypothesis about the market prices, different regression models were fit to explain the Day Ahead Market (DAM) and Imbalance Market (IM) prices. DAM prices increase by 0.01 €cents/kWh for every 10% increase in Δ_x in the absence of τ. With increasing Δx when τ is provided at 0.01, 0.02 and 0.03 €/kWh, the increase in the DAM prices is less sharp. In addition, with every increase in the value of τ, the mean DAM price is lowered as compared to the previous value of τ. When the value of τ is 0.04 €/kWh, it results in decreasing DAM prices as Δ_x increases. The increasing values of τ enable RES-E producers to nominate more power on the DAM at lower marginal costs, thus lowering the overall DAM prices. At 0.04 €/kWh, the effect of τ is two-fold because, at this level, the storing RES-E producers can also nominate stored electricity on the DAM, while still being cost competitive. Hence, more electricity is nominated for DAM and electricity prices are lowered as a result.

The regression model to explain the trend observed in the IM prices had to be split into two further models. Briefly reported, the regression models show that, in the absence of τ, every 10% increase in Δ_x results in a decrease in IM price by 0.031 and 0.34 €cents/kWh when Δ_x is between 0 and 25% and between 25% and 100%, respectively. The models also showed that, until the maximum Δ_x is less than 25%, the IM prices increase for the values of τ at 0.01 and 0.04 €/kWh, but decrease for τ of 0.02 and 0.03 €/kWh. When Δ_x is between 25% to 100%, increasing the values of τ until 0.03 €/kWh result in lowering the mean IM price. However, at 0.04 €/kWh, the mean IM price is higher, showing the effect of no storage reserves being available on IM and more expensive reserves being engaged on the IM.

Conclusively, increasing values of τ and Δ_x increase the consumption of renewable energy and decreases the market prices; with the effect of Δ_x being more significant than the effect of τ. However, the effect of increasing values of both factors on the profit of storing RES-E producers is not positive, pointing to the need for customized rules and incentives to encourage their market participation and investment in storage facilities. The results support that, in the future, with more RES-E producers, different market rules may apply to the flexible RES-E and conventional generation [23].

Introducing flexibility in the power grid as a response of more renewable energy is a challenging task, as it requires institutional shift to a new way of production and consumption of electricity. Changes in consumer behavior will be crucial to this shift, which adds to the complexity of this inevitable undertaking. The approach of agent-based modelling can substantially contribute to the study of electricity production and consumption behavior, while contributing to a just distribution of costs and benefits between the different economic actors. It is worth mentioning that, though the technical details of the model for each agent can be refined to yield more insightful results, the presented ABM is capable of carrying out a detailed study of cost–benefit distribution between different agents in a grid solely fed by renewable power.

The results support that the RES-E agents do not have enough incentive to operate more efficiently when feed-in tariffs are being provided to them. There need to be other support mechanisms that promote investment in storage facilities for the RES-E producers. Market mechanisms that dictate fines for deviating from nominated power can further demotivate actors in the power generation business to switch to renewable energy technologies. The market mechanisms need to evolve to let more RES-E producers participate. Additionally, the demand side response will aid this transition. As more local balancing agents (aggregators) enter the power networks and virtual power plants are becoming a reality, smart metering would replace net metering systems. This will provide an opportunity to the consumers of all sizes to be flexible in response to production and market signals, ultimately resulting in a truly flexible grid. Depending on the specific markets and their respective mechanisms in different countries, it is up to the policy makers to incentivize the consumers to change, hence create a market pull for RES-E producers, and/or incentivize the RES-E producers to create a market push for change in the consumer behavior. Finally, although Belgian wind and solar profiles were used for the simulations, the observations from the model are transferrable to other countries where policy makers wish to incentivize renewable power.

Author Contributions: Conceptualization, A.S.M. and J.B.; methodology, A.S.M., J.B. and, S.L.; software, A.S.M. and S.L.; validation, J.B., S.L., and L.V.; formal analysis, A.S.M.; writing—original draft preparation, A.S.M.; writing—review and editing, J.B., S.L., L.V., and G.V.E.; supervision, G.V.E.

Funding: The research leading to these results has received funding from the European Union's Horizon 2020 research and innovation program under Grant No. 679386, EPOS project (Enhanced energy and resource Efficiency and Performance in process industry Operations via onsite and cross-sectorial Symbiosis). The sole responsibility of this publication lies with the authors. The European Union is not responsible for any use that may be made of the information contained herein.

Acknowledgments: This research has benefitted from a statistical consult with Ghent University FIRE (Fostering Innovative Research based on Evidence).

Conflicts of Interest: The authors declare no conflict of interest.

Appendix A. Methodology

Table A1. Variables and parameters for the different agents.

	Definition	Values	Unit
Small and medium sized consumers			
Agent properties (do not change during the simulation runs)			
α_{SMC}	consumption capacity of a household [41]	0.125	kWh
A_{PV}	capacity of a photovoltaic panel [41]	1–2	kWh
Agent Variables (may change in every time step)			
α_{pred}	predicted consumption for one quarter of an hour on the next day		
α_{act}	actual consumption in real time		
random.factor	a number generated every quarter of an hour to introduce randomness in the consumption profile of the consumers	0.01–0.05	
Q_{PV}	production from the photovoltaic panels in real time		
$\alpha_{self-cons}$	consumption from own PV panel (only for prosumers)		
Q_{SMC}	production from the PV-panels in real time that is planned for the $DAM.S_{pred}$		
bill	bill for the whole past year		€
$bill_{unit}$	per unit cost of electricity consumed in the past year		€/kWh
Industry			
Agent properties (do not change during the simulation runs)			
α_{ind}	average consumption of an industry	2000 (±400)	kWh
group	group number defining the strategy of the industry Group 0: bid-cap of 0 kW Group 1, 2, and 3: bid-cap of 50% of α_{ind}	0–3	

Table A1. Cont.

	Definition	Values	Unit
Agent variables (may change in every time step)			
α_{pred}	predicted consumption for one quarter of an hour on the next day		
α_{act}	actual consumption in real time		
α_{bid}	for group 0, $\alpha_{bid} = 0$ for group 1, $\alpha_{bid} = \Delta_{bid}\Delta R_{cheap}$ for group 2, $\alpha_{bid} = \Delta_{bid}\Delta R_{medium}$ for group 3, $\alpha_{bid} = \Delta_{bid}\Delta R_{expen}$		
α_{IM}	for group 0, $\alpha_{IM} = \alpha_{act} - \alpha_{pred}$ for group 1,2, and 3, $\alpha_{IM} = \alpha_{bid}$		
α_{tot}	total consumption in the past month		kWh
Δ_{bid}	bidding capacity (flexible demand)	50% of α_{ind}	kW
bill	bill for the past month		€
P	instantaneous profit in every time step		€
P_{unit}	unitary profit for the past month		€/kWh
RES-E Producers			
Agent properties (do not change during the simulation runs)			
Δ_{prod}	average production capacity of a wind farm	4000 (±100)	kW
$\Delta_{storage}$	average storage capacity	20% of Δ_{prod}	kW
C_{cur}	costs for curtailing [61]	0.022	€/kWh
C_{st}	LCOE [1] of battery storage [62]	0.176	€/kWh
strategy	strategy defining if the producer will have storage or not If 0, there is no storage facility If 1, there is storage facility	0 or 1	
Agent variables (may change in every time step)			
$\Delta_{req(D+1)}$	Required production per agent to meet the system demand		kWh
Q_{nom}	nominated power production for the next day		kWh
Q_{prod}	actual power production in real time		kWh
Q_{act}	part or all of the Q_{prod} made available for the system		kWh
Q_{curt}	curtailed power		kWh
$Q_{stored(t)}$	stored power in real time		kWh
Q_{DAM}	production sold at the DAM [2], always $\leq Q_{nom}$		kWh
Q_{bid}	production bid at the IM [3]		kWh
Q_{IM}	production sold at the IM If, $R_{wind} > 0$ $Q_{IM} = R_{wind} * Q_{bid}$		kWh
Q_{tot}	$Q_{DAM} + Q_{IM} + Q_{IM.st}$		kWh
Q_{sum}	total production traded in the markets in the past month		kWh
$Q_{IM.st}$	storage reserve engaged by IM. Value is positive when batteries are discharged, and negative when batteries are charged		kWh
P	instantaneous profit in every time step		€
P_{unit}	unitary profit for the past month		€/kWh

[1]: Levelized Cost of Electricity; [2]: Day Ahead Market; [3]: Imbalance Market.

Appendix A.1. Sub-Models

Appendix A.1.1. Prediction of Consumption and Production

The model process begins on day = 0 and tick = 0, which depicts the hour 00:00 of a day. For the first quarter of an hour (one time step), the industries and SMCs predict consumption for the same quarter on the next day. The prosumers from the SMCs also predict the production from the PV panels, as Q_{PV} depending on the capacity of their solar panels (Δ_{PV}). The producers calculate their production (Q_{prod}) based on the weather predictions for that quarter on the next day. For all RES-E producers, Q_{prod} is calculated as a product of their capacity (Δ_{prod}) and the predicted weather (w_{pred}).

Based on the strategy of the RES-E producer, the predicted production varies. For non-storing agents, it is equal to their Q_{prod}, while, for storing agents, $\Delta_{req(D+1)}$ and $Q_{pred.stored}$ define Q_{nom}, where $Q_{pred.stored}$ is the expected power production that will be stored, given that $Q_{pred.stored}$ does not exceed $\Delta_{storage}$. Hence, the Q_{nom} is based on Equations (A1) or (A3), and the value for $Q_{pred.stored(t+1)}$ is based on Equations (A2), (A4), or (A5). The conditions that define which equation is chosen for setting the values are explained below:

If $\Delta_{req(D+1)} \geq Q_{prod} + Q_{pred.stored(t)}$, then

$$Q_{nom} = Q_{prod} + Q_{pred.stored(t)}, \quad (A1)$$

$$Q_{pred.stored(t+1)} = 0. \quad (A2)$$

If $\Delta_{req(D+1)} < Q_{prod} + Q_{pred.stored(t)}$, then

$$Q_{nom} = \Delta_{req(D+1)}. \quad (A3)$$

If $\Delta_{storage} \geq Q_{prod} + Q_{pred.stored(t)} - Q_{nom}$

$$Q_{pred.stored(t+1)} = Q_{prod} + Q_{pred.stored(t)} - Q_{nom}. \quad (A4)$$

Otherwise,

$$Q_{pred.stored(t+1)} = \Delta_{storage}. \quad (A5)$$

Appendix A.1.2. Setting the Day Ahead Market Price

DAM price is calculated by a merit order economic dispatch procedure. First, the total predicted demand ($DAM.D_{pred}$) is calculated by summing the consumption ($\sum_{i=1}^{n.ind} \alpha_{pred} + \sum_{i=1}^{n.SMC} \alpha_{pred}$) and then matched with the available supply from different technologies arranged in order of increasing bid price.

The technology prices in ascending order are: C_{inflex}, C_{NG}, β_{wind}, C_{pv}, C_{tech}.

Once the supply volume is matched to the demand, the total predicted supply can be calculated as:

$$DAM.S_{pred} = \Delta_{inflex} + (R_{NG}\Delta\Delta_{NG}) + (R_{wind}\Delta RES.w_{act}) + (R_{solar}\Delta RES.s_{pred}) + R_{tech}, \quad (A6)$$

where

$$R_{tech} = DAM.D_{pred} - (\Delta_{inflex} + (R_{NG}\Delta\Delta_{NG}) + (R_{wind}\Delta RES.w_{act}) + (R_{solar}\Delta RES.s_{pred})). \quad (A7)$$

Since this process sets a price for every quarter, it is not representative of the DAM price. Hence, at the end of every four ticks (four quarters), the values of the last four DAM prices are averaged and one market price for the one whole hour is set. In this way on the next day, there are 24 DAM prices for each hour of the day.

Appendix A.1.3. Actual Consumption and Production

Once day 1 begins, the industries consume electricity according to the time of the day and the day of the week and their strategy. The SMCs consume electricity based on their respective profile and according to the time of the day, week of the month, and season.

For all SMCs, there consumption is a product of their predicted consumption (α_{pred}) and a random factor.

For consumers, α_{act} is the same as α_{cons}

For prosumers

If $\alpha_{cons} \geq Q_{PV}$

$$Q_{SMC} = 0, \quad (A8)$$

$$\alpha_{self-cons} = |Q_{PV} - \alpha_{cons}|, \quad (A9)$$

$$\alpha_{act} = \alpha_{cons} - Q_{PV}. \quad (A10)$$

If $\alpha_{cons} \leq Q_{PV}$

$$\alpha_{self-cons} = \alpha_{cons}, \quad (A11)$$

$$Q_{SMC} = Q_{PV} - \alpha_{self-cons}, \quad (A12)$$

$$\alpha_{act} = 0. \quad (A13)$$

The consumption from all SMCs and industries ($\sum_{i=1}^{n.SMC+n.ind} \alpha_{act}$) sets the value for $DAM.D_{act}$

The RES-E producers produce electricity according to the weather conditions, and their production is calculated based on their respective strategy.

For non-storing producers, they nominate production volumes first on the DAM, based on their knowledge of the expected consumption. In the model, this knowledge was substituted by using the total consumption demand of the system as an indicator for the expected demand. Which volumes will be offered on DAM and what will be offered to the IM are calculated as follows:

If $Q_{act} - Q_{nom} \geq 0$

$$Q_{DAM} = Q_{nom}, \quad (A14)$$

$$Q_{bid} = Q_{act} - Q_{DAM}. \quad (A15)$$

If $Q_{act} - Q_{nom} < 0$

$$Q_{DAM} = Q_{act}, \quad (A16)$$

$$Q_{bid} = 0 \quad (A17)$$

for storing producers

If $Q_{act} - Q_{nom} \geq 0$ and $\Delta_{storage} - Q_{stored(t-1)} \geq Q_{act} - Q_{nom}$,

$$Q_{DAM} = Q_{nom}, \quad (A18)$$

$$Q_{bid} = 0, \quad (A19)$$

$$Q_{stored(t)} = Q_{act} - Q_{nom} + Q_{stored(t-1)}. \quad (A20)$$

If $Q_{act} - Q_{nom} \geq 0$ and $\Delta_{storage} - Q_{stored(t-1)} < Q_{act} - Q_{nom}$,

$$Q_{DAM} = Q_{nom}, \quad (A21)$$

$$Q_{stored(t)} = \Delta_{storage}, \quad (A22)$$

$$Q_{bid} = Q_{stored(t)} + Q_{act} - Q_{DAM}. \quad (A23)$$

If $Q_{act} - Q_{nom} < 0$ and $Q_{stored(t-1)} \leq Q_{act} - Q_{nom}$,

$$Q_{DAM} = Q_{nom}, \quad (A24)$$

$$Q_{bid} = 0, \quad (A25)$$

$$Q_{stored(t)} = Q_{stored(t-1)} - (Q_{DAM} - Q_{act}). \quad (A26)$$

If $Q_{act} - Q_{nom} < 0$ and $Q_{stored(t-1)} > Q_{act} - Q_{nom}$

$$Q_{DAM} = Q_{act} + Q_{stored(t-1)}, \quad (A27)$$

$$Q_{stored(t)} = 0, \quad (A28)$$

$$Q_{bid} = 0. \quad (A29)$$

The Q_{bid} from all RES-E producers ($\sum_{i=1}^{n.prod} Q_{bid}$) provide the wind energy available for balancing the grid ($RES.w_{IM}$).

It has to be mentioned that the storing producers provide $Q_{stored(t)}$ to the grid balancing, the sum of which defines the whole stored electricity reserve ($RES.w_{store}$).

Whether that reserve, or part of it, is engaged, (Q_{IM-st}) will be declared in the following sub-model. Likewise, if the reserves are not engaged and the RES-E producers do not have the capacity to store the extra production or they do not own storage, then the extra production will be curtailed, setting the value for Q_{curt}.

The sum of production from all RES-E producers ($\sum_{i=1}^{n.prod} Q_{act}$) defines the value for $RES.w_{act}$ The sum of production from all prosumers ($\sum_{i=1}^{n.SMC} Q_{SMC}$) provides the value for $RES.s_{act}$.

At the end of this step, the supply from the technologies engaged on the previous day is calculated:

$$DAM.S_{act} = \Delta_{inflex} + (R_{NG} \cdot \Delta_{NG}) + RES.w_{act} + RES.s_{act}. \quad (A30)$$

Appendix A.1.4. Setting the Imbalance Market Price

Due to weather variations, there is a slight difference between the prediction and actual production, in addition, since the SMCs do not own smart meters, their actual consumption does not coincide with their predicted consumption at all times. Additionally, the inflexible industries (Group 0) also do not always respect the nominated demand. This leads to imbalances in the volumes of electricity being fed into the grid and the electricity that is taken-off, setting a non-zero value for IM_{imb} When $IM_{imb} \neq 0$, the extra demand ($IM.D_{act}$) is adjusted to meet the supply and supply ($IM.S_{act}$) is adjusted to meet the demand, which results in providing values for the following equations:

$$IM.D_{act} = DAM.D_{act} + \Delta_{cheap} \cdot R_{cheap} + \Delta_{medium} \cdot R_{medium} + \Delta_{expen} \cdot R_{expen} + \Delta_{store} \cdot R_{store} + Q_{elec}, \quad (A31)$$

$$IM.S_{act} = DAM.S_{act} + RES.w_{act} \cdot R_{wind} + RES.w_{store} \cdot R_{store} + Q_{elec}. \quad (A32)$$

If the value of IM_{imb} is positive, then the reserves on the right side of Figure A1 are activated, while, if the value is negative, then the reserves on the left side of the figure are activated. The price is set by the most expensive reserve that is engaged to balance the grid, in the ascending order of $\beta_{wind}, \beta_{cheap}, \beta_{medium}, \beta_{expen}, \beta_{store}, \beta_{electro}$.

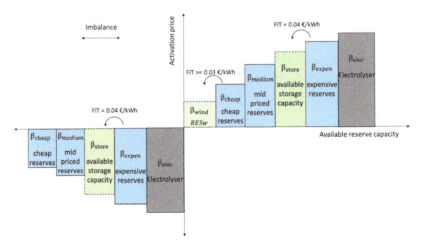

Figure A1. Bidding ladder for Imbalance Market.

However, in the presence of τ at the rate of 0.03 and 0.04 €/kWh, RES-E from wind and electricity from battery storage becomes cheaper and hence moves a step lower in the price ladder. At the end of this step, the reserves that were engaged are declared and each corresponding agent calculates its profit based on these values.

Appendix A.1.5. Calculating Profit for Industries and RES-E Producers

Producers' profit is calculated based on which market is used to trade electricity, the bidding price, subsidy level, and curtailed amount of electricity. If the metered volume is less than or equal to the nominated power, then DAM price is used for profit calculation. In the other case, the extra production is priced according to IM price only if it is engaged to balance the grid. If the surplus could not be balanced, then the profit is decreased as the cost for curtailing is considered in the equation. For producers with storage, the same procedure is followed for profit calculation, except for stored electrical energy that is used to balance the grid, also increases the costs because of the high LCOE of stored electricity.

For all RES-E producers:

If Q_{bid} is 0, then values of Q_{IM} and Q_{curt} are set to be 0 as well.

If R_{wind} and Q_{bid} are more than 0, then Q_{IM} is set as the product of Q_{bid} and R_{wind}. In addition, the value for Q_{curt} is then set at 0.

If R_{wind} is 0 but Q_{bid} is more than 0, then the value of Q_{IM} is set to 0 and the Q_{bid} is set as the value for Q_{curt}.

For storing agents:

If $R_{store} \neq 0$, the value for Q_{IM-st} is the product of $Q_{stored(t)}$ and R_{store}. What is left from stored electricity after assigning the Q_{IM-st} is the new value of stored electricity ($Q_{stored(t+1)}$).

The profit for the storing agents is calculated as

$$P_{prod} = Q_{DAM} \cdot C_{DAM} + Q_{IM} \cdot (\beta_{wind} - \tau) + |Q_{IM-st}| \cdot \beta_{store} - [Q_{tot} \cdot \{(C_{wind} - \tau) + (C_{cur} \cdot Q_{curt})\}]. \quad (A33)$$

The profit for the non-storing agents is calculated as

$$P_{prod} = Q_{DAM} \cdot C_{DAM} + Q_{IM} \cdot (\beta_{wind} - \tau) - [Q_{tot} \cdot \{(C_{wind} - \tau) + (C_{cur} \cdot Q_{curt})\}]. \quad (A34)$$

The total profit gets updated in every time step until, at the end of the month (P_{tot}), it is divided by the total production in the past month and the profit/kWh of electricity produced is obtained, P_{unit}.

The profit for the industries is the remainder of the profit from production of the industrial product and the electricity bill. The profit from the industrial product and electricity consumption is modeled at 1:1. The bill is calculated based on the consumption of electricity and which market the electricity is traded on.

For industries that do not engage in IM, if the consumption is lower than the nominated consumption, then DAM price is assigned as electricity cost; otherwise, the IM price is considered as cost. For industries, which engage in IM, the actual consumption is modeled to always match the nominated one. If the reserves are engaged on IM, then, depending on upward activation or downward activation, the consumption is recalculated. The profit is then calculated as follows:

For Group 0,

if actual consumption (α_{act}) is more than predicted consumption (α_{pred}), then the extra consumption is assigned as the consumption from IM (α_{IM}). Otherwise, the consumption from IM is set at 0.

The profit for Group 0 is calculated as

$$P = (\alpha_{DAM} + \alpha_{IM}) - \{(\alpha_{DAM} \cdot C_{DAM}) + (\alpha_{IM} \cdot C_{IM})\}. \quad (A35)$$

For Groups 1, 2, and 3, the consumption from IM is the product of their respective bidding capacity (Δ_{bid}) and the multiplicative factor (R_{cheap} or R_{medium} or R_{expen}). This multiplicative factor is calculated on a pro rata basis for all agents that provide reserves on the same price.

The profit for Groups 1, 2, and 3 is respectively calculated as follows:

$$P = (\alpha_{DAM} + \alpha_{IM}) + |\alpha_{IM} \cdot \beta_{cheap/medium/expen}| - \alpha_{DAM} \cdot C_{DAM}. \quad (A36)$$

The total profit gets updated in every time step until, at the end of the month, it is divided by the total consumption in the past month and the unitary profit (€/kWh) (P_{unit}) is obtained.

Appendix A.1.6. Updating the System Variables

In every time step, the predicted values of wind (w_{pred}) and solar irradiation (s_{pred}) are updated and set for the next quarter to be used for the prediction of consumption and production on the next day. In addition, the values for wind (w_{act}) and solar irradiation (s_{act}) in real time are set to be used for grid balancing and IM.

The value of DAM price (C_{DAM}) that was set on the day before is recalled from the memory and used for the quarter in real time. In addition, IM price (C_{IM}) for the past quarter is declared and stored for all agents to calculate their respective profit or bill. The value of the total system consumption is updated (Q_{system}); in addition, the variable for the total consumption from the renewables (Q_{RE}) is recalculated and stored.

Appendix A.1.7. Changing Strategies

At the end of the month after receiving their respective bills, each agent is randomly paired up with any other agent of the same group. They share the values of P_{unit} and strategy. In four months, the unitary profit (P_{unit}) of each agent is summed and averaged so it can be compared to the collected four values of P_{unit} from the paired agent.

After four months, the agent compares its own averaged profit against the four values collected from the randomly paired agents against its own averaged unitary profit over the past four months. If the agent has the highest profit as compared to the paired agents, it keeps its own strategy. However, if its own profit is not the highest, then there is a probability of 50% that it will adopt the strategy of the paired agent with the highest profit.

Appendix A.1.8. Calculating Bill for the SMCs

At the end of the year, in the last time step of the simulation, the bill for the SMCs is calculated based on the annually averaged value of C_{DAM} and C_{IM} and the total consumption in the year.

For the prosumers, self-consumption is not billed; however, a flat fee of 85 €/kW is charged for connection to the grid. This value is based on the prosumer fee that is charged in Flanders (Belgium) [43]:

$$\text{bill} = \sum_{i=0}^{34656} \alpha_{act} \cdot (C_{DAM.annum} + C_{IM.annum})/2 \quad (A37)$$

where 34,656 is the total number of quarters in a year, and α_{tot} is calculated as $\alpha_{tot} = \sum_{i=0}^{34656} \alpha_{act}$. The unitary bill (€/kWh) is calculated by dividing the total bill by the total consumption (bill/α_{tot}).

Appendix A.2. Design Concepts

1. Basic principles

The model is built on the hypothesis that subsidies given to producers of RE cause negative market prices and result in adoption of less flexible consumption practices by the consumers and a lack of incentive for RES-E producers to invest in storage and curtailment mechanisms.

The behavior of industries and producers is modeled to represent bounded rationality based on the availability of information about own profit. All the agents make decisions that maximize their own benefit. It is also assumed that all agents gather information once a month about the unitary profit

(€/kWh) from a randomly selected agent of their own group and, after three months, the agents make a decision with a probability of 50% to adopt the strategy that results in the maximum profit against the electricity produced or consumed.

The market prices included in this model only represent the energy content of the electricity that is traded. In reality, the physical electricity component of the consumers' bill is between 25–30% of the total bill, while 60–75% of the bill consists taxes, grid fees, transmission and distribution service charges, etc.

2. Emergence

A pattern is expected to emerge in the system due to the effect of adopting the strategies by the agents. For example, if most of the industries choose to provide cheap reserves on the IM, the whole system has a lower IM price. This will result in lowering the profit of the storing producers who may not get to be engaged in the IM; it will also lower the bill of the SMCs. In addition, it will decrease the costs for all industries in the system.

3. Adaptation

The RES-E producers adapt to the τ scheme and the market prices by adopting the more profitable strategy, to either buy storage, or only rely on curtailment whenever they produce more than the nominated power. The industries adapt to the effect of the strategy on their profit by choosing either to be part of the IM or not and what to price to bid for their reserves.

A sensitivity analysis was carried out to assess the effect of adaptation of the agents by using a Paired Samples Wilcoxon Test (non-parametric). The only variables that were tested for sensitivity to adaptation of agents; $Q_{RE\%}$ (percentage of system demand met by RES-E), $C_{DAM.annum}$ (the annualized DAM price), and $C_{IM.annum}$ (the annualized IM price). These are the same variables that are assessed for variation under the effect of τ and Δ_x. The results indicated that there is a significant difference in values of $Q_{RE\%}$ when the adaptation is turned on vs. when there is no adaptation (p-value 5.421×10^{-13}). The values of $C_{DAM.annum}$ and $C_{IM.annum}$ do not show any significant difference between the two sets of simulation results (p-values 0.1058 and 0.5518, respectively).

4. Objectives

The objective of producers and industries is to maximize their own benefit either by increasing the profit gained by selling electricity or by buying cheap electricity.

5. Learning

No individual or collective learning is included in the model.

6. Prediction

The producers use weather predictions to predict the power produced on the next day. Industries schedule their consumption for the next day based on time of the day.

7. Sensing

The producers and prosumers make use of the available weather information and predict their production. In case of τ, the producers calculate their profit by factoring them in. The industries and SMCs calculate their bill based on the market prices. When there is surplus (deficit) production, the agents respond by providing upward reserves on the IM.

8. Interaction

Direct interaction between every two agents of the same category takes place at the end of every month, when they share their unitary cost or profit with each other. Indirect interaction occurs between all agents in the grid due to their connectivity to the grid and the reliance of their profit on the market price that is calculated by pooling all the demand and production. Hence, the individual decisions of the agents not only affect their own profit or bill but also of all other agents connected to the grid.

9. Stochasticity

The interactions between the agents take place by random chance. At the end of every month, each agent is paired with another agent of the same group, and they exchange information about the unit cost of electricity consumed or produced.

The wind profile, ranging between 0 and 1, was generated by dividing the total consumption of wind power in Belgium by the population in the year 2018 and multiplying it with two random values generated around 4.0 m/s (the mean wind speed in Belgium) to introduce randomness in each quarter hour to depict the uncertainty of wind speed. Two values are generated because the producers are assumed to be located in two different locations. This assumption helps in causing extreme events in the simulations. The randomness factor is introduced for calculating both the prediction and actual production; hence, there is always a chance of slight difference between prediction and actual production.

The data for solar radiation are generated based on the time of the day and the season of the year, and a randomness factor is introduced to depict the unpredictability of weather, and, hence, there is always a chance of a slight difference between the predicted production and actual production by the prosumers. The consumption pattern of industries and SMCs is generated by taking into account the time of the day and the day of the week, whether it is a working day or a weekend. The consumption of SMCs also has randomness included in the actual production to include unpredictability of consumption by agents who have no access to information about their predictions and actual consumption.

10. Collectives

Collectives have been defined under the heading of entities, state variables, and scales.

11. bservation

All of the observations are collected for every quarter hour. When it is the observations that change every month or every three months, the values remain the same for every quarter up to the point that the agents change their strategy and the value changes. The observations collected from the model are:

1. Number of industries,
2. Number of RES-E producers,
3. Averaged unitary profit of RES-E producers,
4. Averaged unitary profit of industries,
5. Averaged unitary bill of consumers,
6. Averaged unitary bill of prosumers,
7. Annual DAM price,
8. Annual IM price,
9. Percentage of system consumption from renewables.

Appendix A.3. Initialization

The model is initialized by setting the total number of SMCs ($n.SMC$) at 4000. This creates two groups of agents that either have PV panels or not. All SMCs have an average consumption of 0.125 (±0.05) kWh. The total number of industries, $n.ind$ is calculated by dividing $n.SMC$ by 100. The average consumption (α_{ind}) of all industries is set as 2000 (±400) kWh. The industries are randomly distributed into four groups. The bidding capacities and respective prices for each group have already been described.

Now, the total required demand of the system, ($\Delta_{max.req}$) can be calculated by summing the average consumption of all the industries and the SMCs.

The level of τ is also selected from a drop-down lis with the options 0, 0.01, 0.02, 0.03, and 0.04 from the interface. In addition, from the interface, the percentage of total system demand (Δ_x) is selected from a slider with values between 0 and 100%. This provides the information to set the total number of RES-E producers by dividing the product of $\Delta_{max.req}$ and Δ_x by 500. The RES-E producers are randomly divided into groups. One group is assigned storage. The respective capacities and costs for each RES-E group have already been described.

For all RES-E producers, 500 MWh is the average production of a wind turbine considered in the model.

Then, the capacity of inflexible power production system is 20% of the $\Delta_{max.req}$. Finally, the capacity of the NG-plant is calculated as 10% of $\Delta_{max.req}$.

Appendix A.4. Input Data

For the data on wind speed, the statistics on wind power production were downloaded from the website of Belgian Electricity Transmission System Operator, Elia [47]. The data from year 2016 and 2018 were used to calculate the wind speed by using the formula, wind power (kW) = $1/2 C_p \rho A V^3$:

V = Wind speed, m/s,
C_p = 0.59 (theoretical maximum),
ρ = Air density, kg/m³,
A = Rotor swept area, m² or $\pi D^2/4$.

The data on wind speed are not meant to depict the exact values but create a realistic pattern of wind speed in a year for Belgium. The resulting value of wind speed (*wind*) is then used in every time step of the model. However, the value w is multiplied with a random variable with mean 4 m/s (average wind speed of Belgium), to introduce variation in the wind speeds. This value of w is then used to calculate the production volume of RES-E producers with the formula defined above. The formula used in the code is (3.14 × (rotor-dia)² × *wind*)/2. The value of rotor-dia has been defined as 80 (±20) m.

The data for solar radiation were also generated in the similar manner. The power production from PV panels was downloaded from Elia's website for the year 2018, and the solar radiation (H) was calculated for each quarter of the year by using the formula, solar power (kW) = $A \times r \times H \times PR$:

A = area of a solar panel (assumed to be 10 m² on average),
r = solar panel yield (assumed to be 40%),
Performance Ratio (PR) = 0.75 (default value),
H = average quarter hourly solar radiation (kW/m²).

The acquired value of solar irradiation (*solar*) is then loaded into the model for every quarter and solar power is calculated by multiplying this value with the capacity of PV panel of the prosumer. The PV capacity of each prosumer is set as 1 (±0.100) kW.

The consumption pattern of industries was generated to show the higher consumption during the weekdays and between the hours of 6:00 a.m. and 5:00 p.m., while a maximum consumption of 30% of average consumption was modeled for the night hours and weekends. For SMCs, the hours in the morning between 5:00 a.m. and 9:00 a.m. and hours in the late afternoon between 3:00 p.m. and 7:00 p.m. were modeled to have the highest consumption. Less to almost no consumption was modeled for early afternoon, later in the evening, and at night.

Appendix B. Results

Table A2. Parameter estimates for the regression models.

Equation (1)	95% Confidence Intervals	Standard Error	p-Values
Intercept	[7.6100895, 8.7469286]	0.28994	<2 × 10⁻¹⁶
(Δ_x)	[53.9763258, 55.9404355]	0.50093	<2 × 10⁻¹⁶
($\tau_{0.01}$)	[−0.9897179, 0.6180155]	0.41004	0.65039
($\tau_{0.02}$)	[−0.6306872, 0.9770462]	0.41004	0.67279
($\tau_{0.03}$)	[0.2593658, 1.8670992]	0.41004	0.00954
($\tau_{0.04}$)	[1.5699873, 3.1777207]	0.41004	7.5 × 10⁻⁹
($\Delta_x.\tau_{0.01}$)	[−1.3081767, 1.4694938]	0.70843	0.90936
($\Delta_x.\tau_{0.02}$)	[−2.1174333, 0.6602372]	0.70843	0.30378
($\Delta_x.\tau_{0.03}$)	[−1.8649325, 0.9127379]	0.70843	0.50159
($\Delta_x.\tau_{0.04}$)	[9.9443263, 12.7219968]	0.70843	<2 × 10⁻¹⁶

Table A2. Cont.

Equation (2)	95% Confidence Intervals	Standard Error	p-Values
Intercept	[2.7071620, 3.9960798]	0.3286	$<2 \times 10^{-16}$
(Δ_x)	[74.5869387, 81.0400927]	1.6451	$<2 \times 10^{-16}$
$(\tau_{0.01})$	[−1.2862439, 0.5365611]	0.4647	0.420
$(\tau_{0.02})$	[−1.1963856, 0.6264195]	0.4647	0.540
$(\tau_{0.03})$	[−0.348558, 1.4742464]	0.4647	0.226
$(\tau_{0.04})$	[−0.4867967, 1.3360083]	0.4647	0.361
$(\Delta_x.\tau_{0.01})$	[−2.7162018, 6.4099361]	2.3265	0.427
$(\Delta_x.\tau_{0.02})$	[−2.2348564, 6.8912815]	2.3265	0.317
$(\Delta_x.\tau_{0.03})$	[−1.8526038, 7.2735342]	2.3265	0.244
$(\Delta_x.\tau_{0.04})$	[15.6178810, 24.7440189]	2.3265	$<2 \times 10^{-16}$
Equation (3)	**95% Confidence Intervals**	**Standard Error**	**p-Values**
Intercept	[14.484822, 16.918209]	0.6205	$<2 \times 10^{-16}$
(Δ_x)	[42.828969, 46.291382]	0.8830	$<2 \times 10^{-16}$
$(\tau_{0.01})$	[−2.367283, 1.074046]	0.8776	0.461
$(\tau_{0.02})$	[−1.602670, 1.838659]	0.8776	0.893
$(\tau_{0.03})$	[−0.585964, 2.855365]	0.8776	0.196
$(\tau_{0.04})$	[4.022200, 7.463529]	0.8776	6.94×10^{-16}
$(\Delta_x.\tau_{0.01})$	[−1.777742, 3.118849]	1.2487	0.591
$(\Delta_x.\tau_{0.02})$	[−3.148456, 1.748135]	1.2487	0.575
$(\Delta_x.\tau_{0.03})$	[−3.067230, 1.829361]	1.2487	0.620
$(\Delta_x.\tau_{0.04})$	[4.248845, 9.145436]	1.2487	8.74×10^{-8}
Equation (4)	**95% Confidence Intervals**	**Standard Error**	**p-Values**
Intercept	[0.0249092567, 0.0250611015]	3.873×10^{-5}	$<2 \times 10^{-16}$
(Δ_x)	[0.0131371212, 0.0133994625]	6.691×10^{-5}	$<2 \times 10^{-16}$
$(\tau_{0.01})$	[−0.0007381475, −0.0005234065]	5.477×10^{-5}	$<2 \times 10^{-16}$
$(\tau_{0.02})$	[−0.0013410582, −0.0011263171]	5.477×10^{-5}	$<2 \times 10^{-16}$
$(\tau_{0.03})$	[−0.0020040095, −0.0017892684]	5.477×10^{-5}	$<2 \times 10^{-16}$
$(\tau_{0.04})$	[−0.0023555315, −0.0021407904]	5.47×10^{-5}	$<2 \times 10^{-16}$
$(\Delta_x.\tau_{0.01})$	[−0.0035230511, −0.0031520444]	9.462×10^{-5}	$<2 \times 10^{-16}$
$(\Delta_x.\tau_{0.02})$	[−0.0068965095, −0.0065255028]	9.462×10^{-5}	$<2 \times 10^{-16}$
$(\Delta_x.\tau_{0.03})$	[−0.0102137379, −0.0098427312]	9.462×10^{-5}	$<2 \times 10^{-16}$
$(\Delta_x.\tau_{0.04})$	[−0.0141593139, −0.0137883072]	9.462×10^{-5}	$<2 \times 10^{-16}$
Equation (5)	**95% Confidence Intervals**	**Standard Error**	**p-Values**
Intercept	[0.0249092567, 0.0250611015]	0.0002107	$<2 \times 10^{-16}$
(Δ_x)	[0.0131371212, 0.0133994625]	0.0003641	$<2 \times 10^{-16}$
$(\tau_{0.01})$	[−0.0007381475, −0.0005234065]	0.0002980	0.160095
$(\tau_{0.02})$	[−0.0013410582, −0.0011263171]	0.0002980	0.002045
$(\tau_{0.03})$	[−0.0020040095, −0.0017892684]	0.0002980	0.000215
$(\tau_{0.04})$	[−0.0023555315, −0.0021407904]	0.0002980	$<2 \times 10^{-16}$
$(\Delta_x.\tau_{0.01})$	[−0.0035230511, −0.0031520444]	0.0005149	0.049849
$(\Delta_x.\tau_{0.02})$	[−0.0068965095, −0.0065255028]	0.0005149	3.79×10^{-5}
$(\Delta_x.\tau_{0.03})$	[−0.0102137379, −0.0098427312]	0.0005149	1.88×10^{-11}
$(\Delta_x.\tau_{0.04})$	[−0.0141593139, −0.0137883072]	0.0005149	$<2 \times 10^{-16}$

Table A2. Cont.

Equation (6)	95% Confidence Intervals	Standard Error	p-Values
Intercept	[0.0009089505, 1.518687 × 10^{-3}]	1.554 × 10^{-4}	1.20 × 10^{-14}
(Δ_x)	[0.0009249548, 5.236665 × 10^{-3}]	1.099 × 10^{-3}	0.00513
($\tau_{0.01}$)	[−0.0005317846, 3.305135 × 10^{-4}]	2.198 × 10^{-4}	0.64709
($\tau_{0.02}$)	[−0.0004843669, 3.779311 × 10^{-4}]	2.198 × 10^{-4}	0.80870
($\tau_{0.03}$)	[−0.0007923893, 6.990876 × 10^{-5}]	2.198 × 10^{-4}	0.10048
($\tau_{0.04}$)	[0.0023973214, 3.259619 × 10^{-3}]	2.198 × 10^{-4}	<2 × 10^{-16}
($\Delta_x \cdot \tau_{0.01}$)	[−0.0056389054, 4.587736 × 10^{-4}]	1.554 × 10^{-3}	0.09583
($\Delta_x \cdot \tau_{0.02}$)	[−0.0094620968, −3.364418 × 10^{-3}]	1.554 × 10^{-3}	3.92 × 10^{-16}
($\Delta_x \cdot \tau_{0.03}$)	[−0.0105595729, −4.461894 × 10^{-43}]	1.554 × 10^{-3}	1.51 × 10^{-6}
($\Delta_x \cdot \tau_{0.04}$)	[0.0083587361, 1.445642 × 10^{-2}]	1.554 × 10^{-3}	3.84 × 10^{-13}

Equation (7)	95% Confidence Intervals	Standard Error	p-Values
Intercept	[0.009186941, 0.0106329549]	0.0003688	<2 × 10^{-16}
(Δ_x)	[−0.035489722, −0.0333098310]	0.0005559	<2 × 10^{-16}
($\tau_{0.01}$)	[−0.001799072, 0.0002459000]	0.0005215	0.136548
($\tau_{0.02}$)	[−0.002920207, −0.0008752344]	0.0005215	0.000278
($\tau_{0.03}$)	[−0.002860245, −0.0008152728]	0.0005215	0.000430
($\tau_{0.04}$)	[0.003440509, 0.0054854812]	0.0005215	<2 × 10^{-16}
($\Delta_x \cdot \tau_{0.01}$)	[−0.002047464, 0.0010353664]	0.0007862	0.519831
($\Delta_x \cdot \tau_{0.02}$)	[−0.002286895, 0.0007959363]	0.0007862	0.343084
($\Delta_x \cdot \tau_{0.03}$)	[−0.003969384, −0.0008865529]	0.0007862	0.002028
($\Delta_x \cdot \tau_{0.04}$)	[0.006221606, 0.0093044372]	0.0007862	<2 × 10^{-16}

References

1. European Commission. Renewable Energy Statistics—Eurostat Statistics Explained. Available online: https://ec.europa.eu/eurostat/statistics-explained/index.php/Renewable_energy_statistics (accessed on 3 June 2019).
2. European Commission. *Directive (EU) 2018/2001 of the European Parliament and of the Council of 11 December 2018 on the Promotion of the Use of Energy from Renewable Sources*; European Commission: Brussels, Belgium, 2018.
3. WindEurope.org. Wind Energy in Europe in 2018. Available online: https://windeurope.org/wp-content/uploads/files/about-wind/statistics/WindEurope-Annual-Statistics-2018.pdf (accessed on 16 May 2019).
4. Fanone, E.; Gamba, A.; Prokopczuk, M. The case of negative day-ahead electricity prices. *Energy Econ.* 2013, 35, 22–34. [CrossRef]
5. Brandstätt, C.; Brunekreeft, G.; Jahnke, K. How to deal with negative power price spikes?—Flexible voluntary curtailment agreements for large-scale integration of wind. *Energy Policy* 2011, 39, 3732–3740. [CrossRef]
6. De Vos, K. Negative Wholesale Electricity Prices in the German, French and Belgian Day-Ahead, Intra-Day and Real-Time Markets. *Electr. J.* 2015, 28, 36–50. [CrossRef]
7. Lund, P.D. Effects of energy policies on industry expansion in renewable energy. *Renew. Energy* 2009, 34, 53–64. [CrossRef]
8. Peak Gen Power. Available online: https://www.peakgen.com/ (accessed on 5 August 2019).
9. WindEurope.org. *Making Transition Work*; WindEurope: Brussels, Belgium, 2016.
10. Kim, J.-H.; Shcherbakova, A. Common failures of demand response. *Energy* 2011, 36, 873–880. [CrossRef]
11. Paulus, M.; Borggrefe, F. The potential of demand-side management in energy-intensive industries for electricity markets in Germany. *Appl. Energy* 2011, 88, 432–441. [CrossRef]
12. Qadrdan, M.; Cheng, M.; Wu, J.; Jenkins, N. Benefits of demand-side response in combined gas and electricity networks. *Appl. Energy* 2017, 192, 360–369. [CrossRef]
13. National Grid ESO. Power Responsive Steering Group by National Grid Electricity System Operator; and the Environmental Charity Sustainability First. In *Power Responsive: Demand Side Flexibility*; Annual Report; National Grid ESO: Gallows Hill, UK, 2018.

14. Li, G.; Shi, J. Agent-based modeling for trading wind power with uncertainty in the day-ahead wholesale electricity markets of single-sided auctions. *Appl. Energy* **2012**, *99*, 13–22. [CrossRef]
15. Sopha, B.M.; Klöckner, C.A.; Hertwich, E.G. Adoption and diffusion of heating systems in Norway: Coupling agent-based modeling with empirical research. *Environ. Innov. Soc. Transit.* **2013**, *8*, 42–61. [CrossRef]
16. Schramm, M.E.; Trainor, K.J.; Shanker, M.; Hu, M.Y. An agent-based diffusion model with consumer and brand agents. *Decis. Support Syst.* **2010**, *50*, 234–242. [CrossRef]
17. Van Dam, K.H.; Nikolic, I.; Lukszo, Z. (Eds.) *Agent-Based Modelling of Socio-Technical Systems*; Springer Science & Business Media: Berlin/Heidelberg, Germany, 2012; Volume 9.
18. Bellekom, S.; Arentsen, M.; van Gorkum, K. Prosumption and the distribution and supply of electricity. *Energy Sustain. Soc.* **2016**, *6*, 22. [CrossRef]
19. Fichera, A.; Pluchino, A.; Volpe, R. A multi-layer agent-based model for the analysis of energy distribution networks in urban areas. *Phys. A Stat. Mech. Appl.* **2018**, *508*, 710–725. [CrossRef]
20. Misra, S.; Bera, S.; Ojha, T.; Zhou, L. Entice: Agent-based energy trading with incomplete information in the smart grid. *J. Netw. Comput. Appl.* **2015**, *55*, 202–212. [CrossRef]
21. North, M.; Conzelmann, G.; Koritarov, V.; Macal, C.; Thimmapuram, P.; Veselka, T. *E-Laboratories: Agent-Based Modeling of Electricity Markets*; Argonne National Lab.: Lemont, IL, USA, 2002.
22. Vasirani, M.; Kota, R.; Cavalcante, R.L.G.; Ossowski, S.; Jennings, N.R. An Agent-Based Approach to Virtual Power Plants of Wind Power Generators and Electric Vehicles. *IEEE Trans. Smart Grid* **2013**, *4*, 1314–1322. [CrossRef]
23. Lund, P.D.; Lindgren, J.; Mikkola, J.; Salpakari, J. Review of energy system flexibility measures to enable high levels of variable renewable electricity. *Renew. Sustain. Energy Rev.* **2015**, *45*, 785–807. [CrossRef]
24. Elia. *The Day-Ahead Hub: A Platform at the Centre of ARPs Activities*; Elia: Brussels, Belgium, 2012.
25. Balancing Mechanism—Elia. Available online: https://www.elia.be/en/products-and-services/balance/balancing-mechanism (accessed on 6 August 2019).
26. Meyer, N.I. European schemes for promoting renewables in liberalised markets. *Energy Policy* **2003**, *31*, 665–676. [CrossRef]
27. Menanteau, P.; Finon, D.; Lamy, M.-L. Prices versus quantities: Choosing policies for promoting the development of renewable energy. *Energy Policy* **2003**, *31*, 799–812. [CrossRef]
28. Verhaegen, K.; Meeus, L.; Belmans, R. Towards an international tradable green certificate system—The challenging example of Belgium. *Renew. Sustain. Energy Rev.* **2009**, *13*, 208–215. [CrossRef]
29. World Nuclear News. Belgium Maintains Nuclear Phase-Out Policy. Available online: https://www.world-nuclear-news.org/Articles/Belgium-maintains-nuclear-phase-out-policy (accessed on 8 Novmber 2019).
30. Flemish Green Power Certificates (GSC)|Agency Innovation and Entrepreneurship. Available online: https://www.vlaio.be/nl/subsidies-financiering/subsidiedatabank/vlaamse-groenestroomcertificaten-gsc (accessed on 10 December 2018).
31. Generating Facilities. Available online: https://www.elia.be/en/grid-data/power-generation/generating-facilities (accessed on 8 November 2019).
32. Shum, K.L. Renewable energy deployment policy: A transition management perspective. *Renew. Sustain. Energy Rev.* **2017**, *73*, 1380–1388. [CrossRef]
33. Ashok, S.; Banerjee, R. Load-management applications for the industrial sector. *Appl. Energy* **2000**, *66*, 105–111. [CrossRef]
34. Baker, P. *Benefiting Customers while Compensating Suppliers: Getting Supplier Compensation Right*; The Regulatory Assistance Project (RAP): Brussels, Belgium, 2016.
35. Grimm, V.; Berger, U.; DeAngelis, D.L.; Polhill, J.G.; Giske, J.; Railsback, S.F. The ODD protocol: A review and first update. *Ecol. Model.* **2010**, *221*, 2760–2768. [CrossRef]
36. Wilensky, U. *Netlogo*; Northwestern University Evanston: Evanston, IL, USA, 1999.
37. Grimm, V.; Berger, U.; Bastiansen, F.; Eliassen, S.; Ginot, V.; Giske, J.; Goss-Custard, J.; Grand, T.; Heinz, S.K.; Huse, G.; et al. A standard protocol for describing individual-based and agent-based models. *Ecol. Model.* **2006**, *198*, 115–126. [CrossRef]
38. Borggrefe, F.; Neuhoff, K. *Balancing and Intraday Market Design: Options for Wind Integration*; DIW Discussion Papers; German Institute for Economic Research: Berlin, Germany, 2011.
39. IRENA. *Renewable Power Generation Costs in 2017*; International Renewable Energy Agency: Abu Dhabi, UAE, 2018; p. 160.

40. Kost, C.; Shammugam, S.; Jülch, V.; Nguyen, H.-T.; Schlegl, T. *Levelized Cost of Electricity—Renewable Energy Technologies*; Fraunhofer Institute for Solar Energy Systems ISE: Freiburg im Breisgau, Germany, 2013.
41. Mulder, G.; Six, D.; Claessens, B.; Broes, T.; Omar, N.; Mierlo, J.V. The dimensioning of PV-battery systems depending on the incentive and selling price conditions. *Appl. Energy* **2013**, *111*, 1126–1135. [CrossRef]
42. IRENA. *Renewable Energy Prospects: 2014*; International Renewable Energy Agency: Abu Dhabi, UAE, 2014.
43. Masson, G.; Neubourg, G. *PV Prosumer Guidelines Belgium*; Becquerel Institute: Brussels, Belgium, 2019; p. 8.
44. Alberici, S. *Subsidies and Costs of EU Energy (Annex 4–5)*; Ecofys: Berlin, Germany, 2014.
45. Government of Flanders Screen Flanders—Climate and Weather. Available online: https://www.screenflanders.be/en/film-commission/production-guide/facts-and-figures/climate-and-weather (accessed on 9 October 2019).
46. Team, F. The Potential Role of H2 Production in a Sustainable Future Power System. Available online: https://ec.europa.eu/jrc/en/publication/potential-role-h2-production-sustainable-future-power-system (accessed on 21 October 2019).
47. About Elia—Elia. Available online: http://www.elia.be/en/about-elia (accessed on 16 May 2019).
48. R Core Team. *R: A Language and Environment for Statistical Computing*; R Foundation for Statistical Computing: Vienna, Austria, 2013.
49. Cludius, J.; Hermann, H.; Matthes, F.C.; Graichen, V. The merit order effect of wind and photovoltaic electricity generation in Germany 2008–2016: Estimation and distributional implications. *Energy Econ.* **2014**, *44*, 302–313. [CrossRef]
50. De Vos, K.; Petoussis, A.G.; Driesen, J.; Belmans, R. Revision of reserve requirements following wind power integration in island power systems. *Renew. Energy* **2013**, *50*, 268–279. [CrossRef]
51. Kondoh, J.; Ishii, I.; Yamaguchi, H.; Murata, A.; Otani, K.; Sakuta, K.; Higuchi, N.; Sekine, S.; Kamimoto, M. Electrical energy storage systems for energy networks. *Energy Convers. Manag.* **2000**, *41*, 1863–1874. [CrossRef]
52. Zhao, H.; Wu, Q.; Hu, S.; Xu, H.; Rasmussen, C.N. Review of energy storage system for wind power integration support. *Appl. Energy* **2015**, *137*, 545–553. [CrossRef]
53. McDowall, J. Integrating energy storage with wind power in weak electricity grids. *J. Power Sources* **2006**, *162*, 959–964. [CrossRef]
54. Frondel, M.; Sommer, S.; Vance, C. The burden of Germany's energy transition: An empirical analysis of distributional effects. *Econ. Anal. Policy* **2015**, *45*, 89–99. [CrossRef]
55. Winkler, J.; Altmann, M. Market Designs for a Completely Renewable Power Sector. *Z. Energ.* **2012**, *36*, 77–92. [CrossRef]
56. Zwaenepoel, B.; Vansteenbrugge, J.; Vandoorn, T.L.; Van Eetvelde, G.; Vandevelde, L. Ancillary services for the electrical grid by waste heat. *Appl. Therm. Eng.* **2014**, *70*, 1156–1161. [CrossRef]
57. Verzijlbergh, R.A.; De Vries, L.J.; Dijkema, G.P.J.; Herder, P.M. Institutional challenges caused by the integration of renewable energy sources in the European electricity sector. *Renew. Sustain. Energy Rev.* **2017**, *75*, 660–667. [CrossRef]
58. Kikuchi, Y.; Kanematsu, Y.; Ugo, M.; Hamada, Y.; Okubo, T. Industrial Symbiosis Centered on a Regional Cogeneration Power Plant Utilizing Available Local Resources: A Case Study of Tanegashima. *J. Ind. Ecol.* **2016**, *20*, 276–288. [CrossRef]
59. Rogers, E.M. *Diffusion of Innovations*, 4th ed.; Simon and Schuster: New York, NY, USA, 2010; ISBN 978-1-4516-0247-0.
60. Larsen, J.K. Available online: https://studylib.net/doc/7736725/rocky-mountain-power-decision-summary-report-on-purpa-time (accessed on 8 November 2019).
61. Joos, M.; Staffell, I. Short-term integration costs of variable renewable energy: Wind curtailment and balancing in Britain and Germany. *Renew. Sustain. Energy Rev.* **2018**, *86*, 45–65. [CrossRef]
62. Wilson, M. Available online: https://www.lazard.com/media/450774/lazards-levelized-cost-of-storage-version-40-vfinal.pdf (accessed on 8 November 2019).

© 2019 by the authors. Licensee MDPI, Basel, Switzerland. This article is an open access article distributed under the terms and conditions of the Creative Commons Attribution (CC BY) license (http://creativecommons.org/licenses/by/4.0/).

Article

Analysis of Energy Storage Implementation on Dynamically Positioned Vessels

Aleksandar Cuculić [1,*], Dubravko Vučetić [1], Rene Prenc [2] and Jasmin Ćelić [1]

1 Faculty of Maritime Studies, University of Rijeka, Studentska 2, 51000 Rijeka, Croatia; vucetic@pfri.hr (D.V.); jcelic@pfri.hr (J.Ć.)
2 Faculty of Engineering, University of Rijeka, Vukovarska 58, 51000 Rijeka, Croatia; rprenc@riteh.hr
* Correspondence: cuculic@pfri.hr; Tel.: +385-(0)51-338-411

Received: 28 November 2018; Accepted: 30 January 2019; Published: 30 January 2019

Abstract: Blackout prevention on dynamically positioned vessels during closed bus bar operation, which allows more efficient and eco-friendly operation of main diesel generators, is the subject of numerous studies. Developed solutions rely mostly on the ability of propulsion frequency converters to limit the power flow from the grid to propulsion motors almost instantly, which reduces available torque until the power system is fully restored after failure. In this paper, a different approach is presented where large scale energy storage is used to take part of the load during the time interval from failure of one of the generators until the synchronization and loading of a stand-by generator. In order to analyze power system behavior during the worst case fault scenario and peak power situations, and to determine the required parameters of the energy storage system, a dynamic simulation model of a ship electrical power system is used. It is concluded that implementation of large scale energy storage can increase the stability and reliability of a vessel's electrical power system without the need for the reduction of propulsion power during a fault. Based on parameters obtained from simulations, existing energy storage systems were evaluated, and the possibility of their implementation in the maritime transportation sector was considered. Finally, an evaluation model of energy storage implementation cost-effectiveness was presented.

Keywords: energy storage; ship's electrical power system; dynamic positioning; blackout prevention; maritime transportation

1. Introduction

Dynamic positioning (DP) is used for the automatic control of a vessel's position when performing exploitation tasks such as underwater drilling, cable laying, building offshore constructions, etc. The movement of modern DP vessels is controlled by means of a complex system consisting of filters, observers, controllers, and propeller allocation systems. Many propulsion systems are diesel-electric, meaning that electrical energy is produced by synchronous generators driven by diesel-engines and the speed of electrical propulsion motors is controlled via static frequency converters.

With respect to power system redundancy requirements, DP vessels are divided into three classes: DP 1, DP 2, and DP 3. The power system on DP 1 class vessels does not need to be redundant. For DP 2 class vessels it must be possible to divide the system into two or more sections in such way that at least one section will remain operable after single fault. All requirements for DP 2 class vessels must be applied to DP 3 class vessels, but in addition to that every sub-system should be physically separated and located in different compartments [1].

When the vessel is in DP mode, electrical propulsion generally dominates the total power consumption and requires several diesel generators (DG) running in parallel in order to maintain the stability of the electrical power supply and thus the vessel's ability to keep its desired position.

Maximum efficiency and cost-effectiveness of the electrical power plant is achieved when DGs are running with optimal load (typically between 80% and 90% of the maximum rated power, P_r, for modern medium speed diesel engines). On the other hand, when DGs are running with an optimal load in closed bus bar configuration, the power system becomes more sensitive to step load increase caused by the sudden loss of one or more online generators, which may result in activation of appropriate protection circuits and very likely a partial or total blackout [2].

DP vessels are usually used in demanding and expensive off-shore projects, meaning that such blackouts may have negative, and sometimes even fatal, effects on the realized economic benefits (cutting the underwater cable or pipeline, abortion of drilling operation, etc.). Also, in specific cases (underwater drilling and off-shore oil exploitation) the risk of environmental incidents is significantly increased.

Current solutions for blackout prevention on DP vessels mainly rely on the ability of propulsion frequency converters to cut or reduce energy flow toward the propulsion motor almost instantly, allowing very fast load reduction (FLR) during a fault scenario. The frequency based load shedding (FBLS) method is taken from land based power grids and is activated when the frequency drops below a given set point [3,4]. The event based FLR (EB-FLR) algorithm activates load reduction after the power management system (PMS) receive the signal that one of the online generators has been disconnected from the grid [5]. In the fast phased back system (FPBS), frequency is monitored on every single propulsion unit which significantly reduces the time required for sending and processing information when a fault occurs [6]. The observer based fast load reduction (OB-FLR) algorithm detects the sudden disconnection of online generators by comparing electrical and mechanical torque. Available torque is calculated from available power that is determined by tracking the average acceleration of all online generators [7]. The advanced generator protection (AGP) system relies on parameters that are common to all electrical power systems where the main electrical sources (generator) are connected on the same bus bar. Individual parameters of every online generator are monitored and compared with parameters measured on the common bus bar in order to identify deviations from expected network behavior, and which can be manifested as serious faults in early warnings for potential system failures [8]. Dynamic load prediction (DLP) and dynamic load control (DLC) methods are based on future load prediction and direct communication with the generator control system and DP system in order to minimize sudden load changes by tolerating small changes in the vessel's position within the allowed tolerances [9].

The above-mentioned methods can significantly increase the availability of the vessel's electrical power plant, but they are still not able to predict and prevent the possible blackout situations caused by rapidly-developing faults on the main DGs, such as an engine governor fault, automatic voltage regulator (AVR) fault, the sudden trip of the engine, a short circuit, etc. Such faults will most certainly lead to the loss of one or more generator sets from the grid, which will instantly limit the available propulsion torque until the power is fully restored after the failure, which in extreme conditions may affect the vessel's position, or in some cases initiate blackout of the power system section under the fault. After the loss of one or more generator sets power can be fully restored after stand-by generator sets connect to the grid and take the required load, which should be done in a maximum of 45 s [10], but in practice this time rarely exceed 30 s.

One of the solutions for the stated problem, especially when used in combination with FLR methods, could be using large scale renewable energy storage (ES) during the short periods between the loss of one generator and the synchronization of stand-by generators to the grid, thus preserving the continuity of the electrical power supply. In addition to that, ES can also be used for covering short-term peak loads during operation in rough sea conditions, thus eliminating the need for the often unnecessary starting of stand-by generators.

The idea of ES implementation onboard marine vessels is not new. It has been the subject of research testing on board US Navy ships for many years, mainly related to amortization of peak power up to 250 kW, caused by the electric start and propulsion systems [11,12], and large short term pulsed loads caused by using electromagnetic weapons on future all-electric ships. For example, the flywheel based ES system for an electric gun system would require 800 MJ of stored energy with a total power of 40 MW. A schematic diagram of an electric navy ship power system with integrated ES can be found in [13] (p. 1). Based on the results of navy ship tests, it has been concluded that implementation of ES systems, primarily in the form of flywheels, super capacitors, and lithium-ion batteries, could also be possible on other types of ships in order to increase power plant reliability and lower the amount of greenhouse gas emissions [14,15].

In this work, the possibility of ES application on DP vessels is analyzed from the perspectives of power plant safety, reliability, and economics. The safety and reliability aspect is manifested through the availability of electrical energy (stored in ES) during the starting process of a stand-by generator, which allows continuity of DP operations and maintenance of the desired position. The economic aspect is mainly related to fuel and maintenance costs savings.

First, issues of blackout prevention and the advantages of operation with a closed bus bar are explained. After that, a simulation model of an electrical power system with ES is presented. Based on the simulation results an overview and evaluation of available ES devices is done. Finally, an evaluation model for ES implementation on DP vessels is presented.

2. Closed Bus Bar Operation and Blackout Prevention

Typical topology of a DP vessel electrical power system is shown in Figure 1. According to class requirements, in case of single fault, the DP vessel must be able to continue its operations without interruption until the remaining methods of holding position are sufficient to overcome external influences [16].

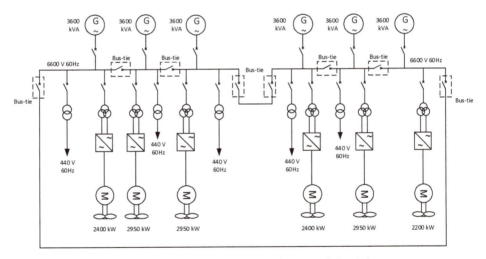

Figure 1. Typical topology of a dynamically positioned (DP) vessel electrical power system.

The easiest way to achieve such system integrity is to run the power plant as two (or more) separated systems with open bus-tie breakers [17]. That requires a larger number of generators on the grid than is strictly necessary, so they are running most of the time with a low load (typically 20% to 40% of rated power). This has a negative influence on the economic benefits due to higher fuel consumption, increased greenhouse gas emissions, and more accumulated running hours of diesel engines.

Although this practice is still very common, strict environmental rules and regulations, together with the increase of fuel oil prices, were sufficient incentive for finding an appropriate solution to reduce the risk of system failure during operation with closed bus bars and optimally loaded generators.

The most important challenges for closed bus bar operation are response time and the dynamics of the blackout prevention system, reliability and tolerance to governor and automatic voltage regulator (AVR) faults, power transients, and operation in extreme weather conditions [18,19].

The control algorithms of a vessel's power management system (PMS) must be able to distinguish short-term transients associated with daily operations and those associated with real faults, without compromising the integrity and security of the power plant. Depending on the current electrical consumption, PMS performs the automatic start and stop of DGs in order to prevent possible blackout situations, trying at the same time to ensure the optimal load on generators. In the event of a blackout, the PMS must automatically re-establish the electrical power supply for normal operation [20].

Class rules typically require DGs to start from stand-by, synchronize, and begin load sharing in a maximum time of 45 s [10]. This means that the PMS system has to anticipate possible load changes in advance, and start additional DGs before overloading the engines. During sudden and unexpected faults, primarily on diesel engines, it is practically impossible to prevent blackout situations without a sufficient power reserve on generators connected to the grid, which is ensured by limiting maximum DG load to a safe value, depending on the current conditions.

To determine safe DG power limits for closed bus bar operation it is assumed that all DGs have the same power ratings, operate in equal load mode, and are capable of taking 55% of the nominal power step load increase without activating under a frequency trip. Although it is not explicitly required by class level, it should be emphasized that generator sets on ships are usually allowed to take a maximum of 110% load during failure. Therefore, the safe DG load limit P_{DGmax} relative to DG rated power P_r during closed bus bar operation for different numbers of online generators N can be expressed as:

$$P_{DGmax} = \begin{cases} 0.55 P_r, & N = 2 \\ 0.73 P_r, & N = 3 \\ 0.82 P_r, & N = 4 \\ 0.88 P_r, & N = 5 \end{cases} \quad (1)$$

A specific fuel consumption curve for a typical medium speed diesel engine is shown in Figure 2. It shows how many grams of fuel are needed for production of 1 kWh of energy for different diesel engine loads which are expressed as a percentage of rated power. It can be seen that the lowest fuel consumption is when the diesel engine is loaded between 80% and 90% of its rated power.

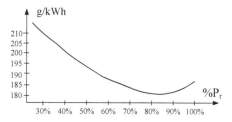

Figure 2. Specific fuel consumption of a medium speed diesel engine [21].

Figure 3 shows the electrical power consumption trend of a DP pipe laying vessel during a 27-day period that has been recorded by the authors. Sampling time is 1 second. Total load is scaled and presented as a percentage of a single generator rated power.

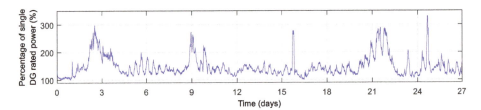

Figure 3. Electrical power consumption trend of DP vessel.

Based on data from Figure 3, DG utilization has been simulated for two different cases:

- Case A: the stand-by DG will start according conditions defined in (1),
- Case B: the stand-by DG will start if $P_{DGmax} \geq 0.9 P_r$.

The results of the simulation are presented in Figure 4. In case A, most of the time three DGs were online and a total of 1930 DG running hours were accumulated. In case B, the number of running hours was reduced to 1353, for a total reduction of 29.9%.

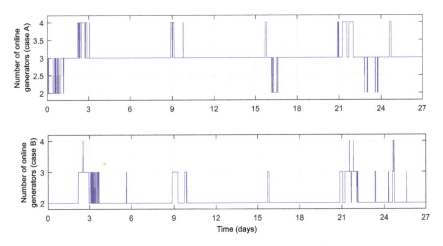

Figure 4. Simulation results of diesel generator (DG) utilization.

It is also interesting to compare DG utilization to specific fuel consumption. From Figure 5, it can be seen that most of the time DGs are running in the interval of 60% to 90% of diesel engine rated power, which corresponds to an area of low specific fuel consumption in Figure 2.

From the presented results, it can be concluded that a significant reduction of fuel and maintenance costs can be achieved when DGs are allowed to run with nominal loads and closed bus bar operation, but in order to prevent safety risks adequate blackout prevention methods must be implemented.

One of the solutions that may be used to achieve the aforementioned objectives is the implementation of large scale energy storage, which is analyzed in this work.

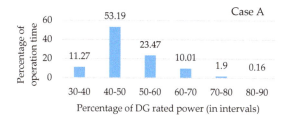

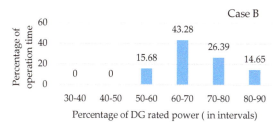

Figure 5. DG utilization in respect to fuel consumption.

3. Simulation Model of an Electrical Power System with ES

Since there is no reference DP vessel in service with a large scale ES system integrated in the electrical power plant, it is impossible to carry out any practical tests in line with the objectives of this work. For that reason, an appropriate simulation model for each system component that must be taken into account when evaluating the ES application was developed in Simulink.

A model of the DP vessel electrical power system with ES is shown in Figure 6. The aim of the presented model is to determine specific parameters required for technical analysis and selection of an appropriate ES device, such as required capacity, power and energy density, response time, speed of discharge, etc.

Therefore, ES is modeled as a DC voltage source connected via a bi-directional power converter with the possibility of active and reactive power control.

The diesel generator model consists of a synchronous generator block, a governor block, and a voltage regulator block. The standard fifth order model of a synchronous generator is used. It is assumed that all three phase voltages at generator terminals are equal and balanced, and only the fundamental harmonic is present in the air gap field (the influence of high order harmonics is neglected).

An equivalent circuit of a synchronous generator block in a dq reference frame is shown in Figure 7.

The electrical part of the model is based on the following voltage and flux s equations [22,23]:

$$\begin{bmatrix} v_{sd} \\ v_{sq} \\ v_{fd} \\ v_{kd} \\ v_{kq} \end{bmatrix} = \begin{bmatrix} R_s & 0 & 0 & 0 & 0 \\ 0 & R_s & 0 & 0 & 0 \\ 0 & 0 & R_{fd} & 0 & 0 \\ 0 & 0 & 0 & R_{kd} & 0 \\ 0 & 0 & 0 & 0 & R_{kq} \end{bmatrix} \begin{bmatrix} i_{sd} \\ i_{sq} \\ i_{fd} \\ i_{kd} \\ i_{kq} \end{bmatrix} + \begin{bmatrix} d\varphi_{sd}/dt \\ d\varphi_{sq}/dt \\ d\varphi_{fd}/dt \\ d\varphi_{kd}/dt \\ d\varphi_{kq}/dt \end{bmatrix} + \begin{bmatrix} -\omega_r \varphi_{sq} \\ -\omega_r \varphi_{sd} \\ 0 \\ 0 \\ 0 \end{bmatrix} \quad (2)$$

$$\begin{bmatrix} \varphi_{sd} \\ \varphi_{sq} \\ \varphi_{fd} \\ \varphi_{kd} \\ \varphi_{kq} \end{bmatrix} = \begin{bmatrix} L_d & 0 & L_{md} & L_{md} & 0 \\ 0 & L_q & 0 & 0 & L_{mq} \\ L_{md} & 0 & L_{fd} & L_{md} & 0 \\ L_{md} & 0 & L_{md} & L_{kd} & 0 \\ 0 & L_{mq} & 0 & 0 & L_{kq} \end{bmatrix} \begin{bmatrix} i_{sd} \\ i_{sq} \\ i_{fd} \\ i_{kd} \\ i_{kq} \end{bmatrix} \quad (3)$$

Variables in Equations (2) and (3) are defined as follows: v, voltage; i, current; φ, magnetic flux; L, inductance; R, resistance; and ω, angular velocity. Subscripts are: d, d axis; q, q axis; s, stator; r, rotor; f, field winding; k, damper winding; and m, mutual inductance.

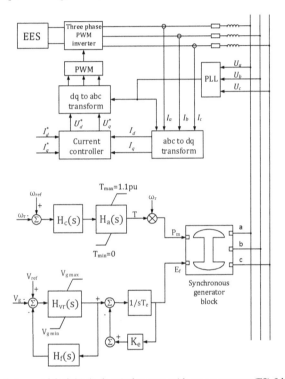

Figure 6. Simulation model of ship's electrical system with energy storage (ES) (block diagram).

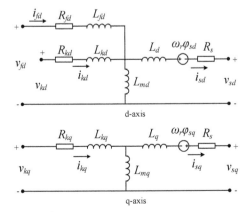

Figure 7. Equivalent circuit of synchronous generator block in a dq reference frame.

The equation of motion of a diesel generator rotor is [22]:

$$\frac{2J}{p}\frac{d\omega_r}{dt} = T_m - T_{em} - T_f \tag{4}$$

where T_m, T_{em}, and T_f are externally applied mechanical torque, electromagnetic torque developed by the diesel generator, and frictional torque in Nm, respectively, p is the generator pole number, ω_r is the rotor angular speed in rad/s, and J is the moment of inertia in kgm².

The generator speed reference value ω_{ref} is compared with the actual generator speed ω_r. The error signal is fed to the input of the controller modeled as a second order system with the transfer function:

$$H_c(s) = \frac{K_p(1+t_{3c}s)}{1+t_{1c}s+t_{1c}t_{2c}s^2}, \tag{5}$$

where K_p is gain and t_{1c}, t_{2c}, and t_{3c} are controller time constants. The actuator transfer function is:

$$H_a(s) = \frac{(1+t_{1a}s)}{S(1+t_{2a}s)+(1+t_{3a}s)}, \tag{6}$$

where t_{1a}, t_{2a}, and t_{3a} are actuator time constants [23].

The output of the actuator represents the prime mover mechanical torque which is limited to 110% of rated power, according the class requirements. Torque signal is multiplied by ω_r in order to get the required mechanic power P_m used in the synchronous generator model. Generator voltage V_g is compared with its reference value V_{ref} and the signal difference is the input of the voltage regulator with transfer function:

$$H_{vr}(s) = \frac{K_{vr}}{1+t_{vr}s}, \tag{7}$$

where K_{vr} is gain and t_{vr} is the voltage regulator time constant. In order to prevent oscillations of V_g, the following damping filter is used:

$$H_f(s) = \frac{K_f t_{3f} s^2 + K_f s}{t_{1f} t_{2f} s^2 + (t_{1f}+t_{2f})s + 1}, \tag{8}$$

K_f is gain and t_{1f}, t_{2f}, and t_{3f} are filters time constants. The exciter is a modeled PI controller with time constants t_e and gain K_e [24].

Active and reactive power in a rotating dq reference frame can be expressed as:

$$P = U_d I_d + U_q I_q, \tag{9}$$

$$Q = U_q I_d + U_d I_q, \tag{10}$$

where U_d and U_q are voltages at the point of common coupling (PCC) and I_d and I_q are inverter currents [25].

Phase locked loop (PLL) is used for synchronizing the inverter output voltage with the ship's electrical power grid [26]. The output of the current controller is:

$$U_d^* = K_I \int (I_d^* - I_d)dt + K_P \int (I_d^* - I_d) + U_d - \omega I_q \tag{11}$$

$$U_q^* = K_I \int (I_q^* - I_q)dt + K_P \int (I_q^* - I_q) + U_q - \omega I_d \tag{12}$$

where U^*_d, U^*_q, I^*_d, and I^*_q are d and q components of the inverter reference voltage and current.

The presented model can be applicable for any type of vessel, not only DP ones, because it allows parallel connection of DG and ES units in various topologies. The conditions for ES utilization can be set in PMS according the specific vessel requirements (e.g. blackout prevention, peak shaving, and maneuvering operation).

In a common bus bar configuration with m equally loaded DG units online, the step load increase ΔP_s on each remaining generator after one DG loss is:

$$\Delta P_s(m) = \frac{m}{(m-1)} \frac{P_{total}(m)}{m} \tag{13}$$

where $P_{total}(m)$ is the total instantaneous electrical consumption when m DGs are online (before fault). The maximum step load increase $\Delta P_{s\,max}$ is usually given by the diesel engine manufacturer or can be arbitrarily set in PMS. For stable operation of an electrical power plant it is required that $\Delta P_s \leq \Delta P_{smax}$ in all possible fault conditions, which affects the amount of required spinning reserve for safe operation and consequently the safe DG continuous load $P_{safe}(m)$. In order to run DG units at the desired (near optimum) load and taking into account that DG can supply 110% of rated power in an emergency situation, the minimum required ES output power P_{ES} for $P_{safe}(m) = P_{des}$ is:

$$P_{ES}(m) = \Delta P_s(m) - (1.1 P_r - P_{des}), \tag{14}$$

where P_{des} is the desired DG load set by operator.

It is realistic to assume that once the P_{ES} is determined for the worst case scenario, which according to (13) is one DG loss when m = 2, such ES can cover all expected load variation with respect to required power, including compensation of short term peak power demands. However, maximum ES utilization time depends only on its capacity which has to be determined by simulation for any scenario of interest.

Required ES capacity in the term of stored energy can be determined by integrating the power supplied by ES (P_{es}) over the time interval from the ES activation (t_1) to the end of the discharge process (t_2).

$$E_{stored} = \int_{t_1}^{t_2} P_{es}(t) dt \tag{15}$$

4. Model Parameters

Standard synchronous generator parameters that are usually available in generator data sheets and are used in the presented model are the main reactances X_d and X_q, generator leakage reactance X_l, transient reactances X_d' and X_q', subtransient reactances X_d'' and X_q'', stator resistance R_s, generator mechanical time constant T_m, time constants for subtransient state T_d'' and T_q'', and constant of inertia H. Equations which relate the standard parameters with variables in (2) and (3) can be found in [21] (pp. 302–304). Simulation parameter settings used in the proposed model are given in Table 1.

Table 1. Simulation parameters settings.

Synchronous Generator Parameter	
Rated power	3600 kVA
Line voltage	6600 V
Frequency	60 Hz
X_d	1.54 pu
X_d'	0.29 pu
X_d''	0.175 pu
X_q	1.04 pu
X_q''	0.175 pu
X_l	0.052 pu
T_d'	3.7 s
T_d''	0.05 s
T_q''	0.05 s
R_s	0.0036 pu
H	1.5 s

Table 1. *Cont.*

Speed Regulator Parameters	
Regulator gain K_p	12
Regulator time constants	$T_{1r} = 0.01$ s; $T_{2r} = 0.02$ s; $T_{3r} = 0.2$ s
Actuator time constants	$T_{1a} = 0.25$ s; $T_{2a} = 0.009$ s; $T_{3a} = 0.038$ s
Mechanical torque limits	$T_{min} = 0$; $T_{max} = 1.1$ pu
Voltage Regulator Parameters	
Voltage regulator gain K_a	400
Voltage regulator time constant	$T_{1m}(s) = 0.02$ s
Output voltage limits	$V_{g\ min} = 0$; $V_{g\ max} = 2.2$ pu
Damping filter gain K_{pf}	0.03
Damping filter time constant	$T_{1f} = 1$ s

5. Simulation and Results

In order to determine the characteristics of an ES system required for blackout prevention during closed bus bar operation, a time domain simulation was performed.

First, the sudden loss of one generator when two generators are online, each loaded with 85% of their nominal power, was simulated for electrical power systems without and with ES. After that, based on simulation results the required ES capacity was calculated for several diesel generators with different power ratings, covering the most common generator sizes installed on modern DP vessels. Finally, use of ES for peak shaving operation was simulated, using the recorded load profile of an actual DP vessel as a model input.

Electrical protections that may disconnect the generator breakers during the step load increase were set as follows:

- Under frequency protection was set to 90% of the rated frequency with a 5 s time delay.
- Over current protection was set to 120% of the rated current with a 20 s time delay.
- Under voltage protection was set to 70% of the rated voltage with a 2 s time delay.

It was assumed that the stand-by generator was connected to the network and ready for loading within 30 s, which was in accordance with the main DP class requirements. With respect to defined simulation scenarios, the effect of diesel engine turbo lag was ignored and it was assumed that diesel generators were able to take 55% of the rated power in one step. The upper diesel generator load limit was set to 110% of its rated power. Simulation results for the event of one generator loss, when the system was running without ES and with two 3.6 MVA generators online, equally loaded and operating with a 0.8 power factor, are shown in Figure 8.

At $t = 3$ s, generator 2 was suddenly disconnected from the grid causing the step load increase on generator 1 and its current rose above the over current protection limit. Maximum voltage undershoot was 13.5% of its nominal value.

Although the voltage remained above the under voltage protection limit, it failed to stabilize within ±3% of the nominal value within 1.5 s after the start of the transient, as required by class requirements [10]. The frequency continuously dropped and at $t = 10.66$ s the under frequency protection disconnected the generator breaker, causing a system blackout.

Results for the same scenario, but now with ES connected to the main bus bar via Pulse Width Modulated (PWM) inverter are shown in Figure 9.

After loss of one generator at $t = 3$ s, the ES instantly took the load, thus reducing the step load increase on the remaining generator. In order to minimize the amount of electrical energy required from ES, the load on the remaining generator was kept at 110% of the rated power until the stand-by generator was connected to grid. Voltage and frequency transients were significantly reduced with a maximum undershoot of 2.5% and 1.5% of the nominal value, respectively. It should be noted that even if the remaining generator was run with its maximum load, the ES could cover additional load demands up to a certain limit thus increasing the flexibility of the power system.

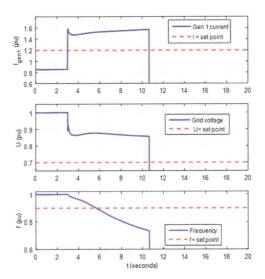

Figure 8. Simulation results for one DG loss without ES.

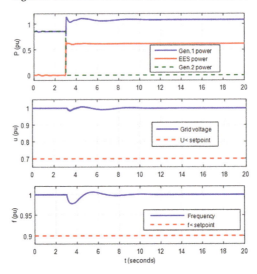

Figure 9. Simulation results for one DG loss with ES.

To determine the maximum required capacity of ES and its key characteristics for a given power system configuration, a worst case scenario must be considered:

- two DGs are running in parallel, each loaded with 95% of nominal power on the common bus,
- at $t = 10$ s, DG2 is disconnected from the grid due to a sudden failure,
- ES and DG1 instantly take the remaining load, provided that PMS limits the DG1 maximum load to 110% of the rated power and sends the start signal to stand-by DG3,
- DG3 is ready to take the load 30 s after starting with the rate of 0.05 P_r/s.

The simulation was performed for single generator power ratings of 2000 kVA, 2300 kVA, 2600 kVA, 3000 kVA, 3300 kVA, 3600 kVA, and 4000 kVA with a rated power factor of 0.8. These power ratings correspond to the most frequently used generator sizes on board average sized DP 2 and DP 3 class vessels. As example simulation scenario for a 3.6 MVA generator is shown in Figure 10, and the same scenario is repeated for other generators.

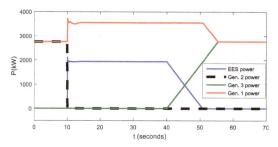

Figure 10. Simulation scenario for 3.6 MVA generator loss when two DGs are running in parallel, each loaded with 95% of nominal power.

Simulation results are shown in Table 2.

Table 2. Required ES capacity and power ratings for different DG sizes.

Generator Power (kVA)	Required ES Capacity (kWh)	Minimum Required ES Power (kW)
2000	12.44	1280
2300	14.31	1472
2600	16.18	1664
3000	18.67	1920
3300	20.53	2112
3600	22.42	2304
4000	24.89	2560

The typical load profile of a DP vessel is characterized by frequent short term load variations which are most often the result of the propulsion system response to stochastic external disturbances (i.e. wind, waves, current). Such power peaks can initiate unnecessary starting of stand-by DG and load shedding/limiting during peak duration. System behavior during a power peak is presented in Figure 11. Two DGs with rated power of 3600 MVA were connected to a common bus bar and operated in equal load mode. The PMS load limit for a single generator was set to 95% of P_r and the maximum power limit to 110% of P_r. The recorded power trend of an actual DP vessel for a duration of 400 s was used in simulation. At t = 122 s a power peak occurred, which caused the load increase on connected DG units above the PMS load limit and initiation of a third DG unit (point A). When load demand exceeded the DG power limit, total available power was limited (point B), which in some cases may affect the vessel's ability to keep the desired position. Approximately 30 s after the start request, the stand-by DG was connected to the grid and loaded (point C). Now all online DGs were running with lower than optimal load and consequently higher specific fuel consumption and exhaust gas emissions.

The same scenario, but now with implemented ES, is shown in Figure 12. It can be seen that single DG power was kept under the PMS load limit while the excess load was taken by ES (points A, B, and C). For this particular case, a total of 24.1 kWh of stored energy was consumed. Both online DGs were running near their optimal load and there was no need to start the third DG. It can be concluded that peak shaving with ES has a potential for significant reduction of fuel consumption and DG maintenance costs over longer exploitation periods, especially onboard vessels that operate in harsh environments with frequent propulsion load deviations.

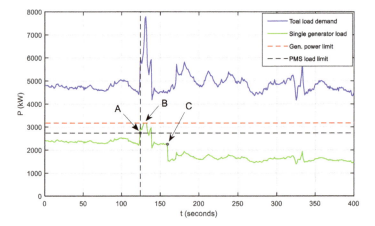

Figure 11. System behavior during a power peak.

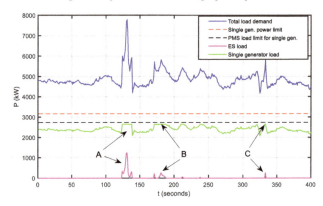

Figure 12. Power peak shaving with ES.

6. ES Utilization Scheme

A block diagram of an ES utilization scheme that can be implemented in a PMS system and that allows use of ES in combination with traditional protection methods is shown in Figure 13. It is assumed that ES is always connected to the grid. Energy flow can be in three modes: charging, discharging, and no power flow. The minimum amount of stored energy E_{min} required for proper function of ES is set according to its type and specifications. The proposed utilization scheme allows use of available spinning reserves for ES charging during periods with lower electrical consumption (i.e. during periods between peak shavings, or to compensate ES idle losses).

ES state of charge (SOC) is constantly monitored during the utilization phase in order to ensure that the amount of stored energy is within a safe operation region (which depends on the ES type and the manufacturer's recommendations), and also to control the charging process. Charging power and frequency depend on SOC and the available spinning reserve.

When ES is ready for use, total instantaneous electrical consumption is constantly monitored and compared with the safe limit (set in PMS). If total load exceeds the safe limit, ES is instantly connected to the grid and the PMS system checks the status of connected DG units. If all DG units are still online, ES is used for peak shaving. In case of DG unit loss, a stand-by unit is immediately started and ES is used until it is connected to the grid and loaded.

In order to ensure safe operation in all possible conditions, when ES is disconnected from the grid total consumption is again compared to the safe limit. If total load is still above the safe limit (meaning that the fault or power peak is still present and ES is fully discharged) then other standard protection methods must be used, otherwise normal operation is assumed.

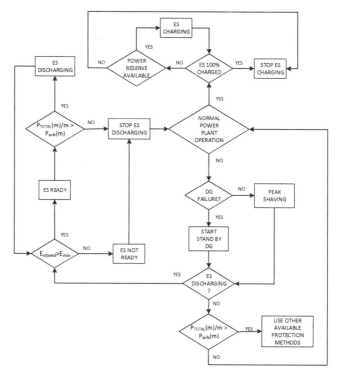

Figure 13. ES utilization scheme.

7. Overview of Available ES Technologies

Following the presented simulation results, specific requirements for ES are that it must have large specific power and a very fast, almost instantaneous response time to load changes. Specifically, in the considered case, about 85% of stored energy is consumed within the first 30 s after the ES has been connected to the grid. Furthermore the ES must be recharged as soon as possible to at least 90% of its full capacity after the discharging process.

Other important factors to consider are: rated power, charging time, efficient life cycle expressed through the number of complete charging and discharging cycles, efficiency, size and weight.

In this paper, only electrochemical batteries, flywheels, and super capacitors are considered and their key characteristics are summarized in Table 3 [27–31]. Other currently available alternatives would simply be too large and their implementation on board the ship would be technically impossible [32,33].

It can be seen that flywheels and super capacitors show a number of advantages over electrochemical batteries. Their advantages are clearly reflected in those parameters that are crucial for ES application onboard DP vessels. In addition to that, they are both faster and more efficient when absorbing energy from regenerative breaking comparing to electrochemical batteries [34]. Despite the unprecedented advantages, they also have shortcomings, above all a small energy density in kWh/kg, and consequently a larger size, and relatively large self-discharge losses. At the present moment, probably what super capacitors most lack is the ability to realize ES with the required capacities [34].

Table 3. Characteristics of considered ES technologies

Technology	Specific Power (W/kg)	Charge Time	Charge/Discharge Cycles	Efficiency (%)	Power Cost $/kW	Energy Cost $/kWh	Operation and Maintenance Costs $/kW per year
Lead Acid	700	Slow	≤1200	70–85	300–600	200–400	50
NiCd	700	Slow	≤5000	60–70	500–1500	800–1500	20
Li-Ion	2000	Slow	≤8000	90–97	1200–4000	600–2500	-
Super capacitors	10,000	Instant	>100,000	90–95	100–300	300–2000	6
Flywheel	5000	Very fast	>100,000	95–99	250–350	1000–5000	20

Small energy density is not as big a problem on ships as it is on land power grids where ES must deliver tens of megawatts over a longer time period (usually 15–20 min). As it can be seen from the simulation results, the required ES capacity for DP vessels is relatively small, averaging 20 kWh, which also reduces their size to somewhat acceptable values.

Excessive self-discharge losses are not such a problem on board DP vessels because both flywheels and super capacitors can be filled very quickly (super capacitors almost instantaneously, and flywheels in a maximum of about 10 s). In addition to that, DP vessels usually have a load profile which constantly alternates between periods with maximum generator load and those with a certain amount of reserve power which can be stored in ES.

At present time, among electrochemical batteries only lithium-ion ones have good enough characteristics and performances that they could be considered as potential ES, but there are still a number of critical safety issues. Namely, in the case of extreme loads, these batteries can discharge the liquid electrolyte through their ventilation openings and may cause ignition. To prevent this, it is necessary to use sophisticated protection methods that are integrated into the battery itself, which significantly increases installation costs.

Considering the availability and maturity of technology together with safety issues, it can be concluded that the flywheel is currently the only rational choice for large scale ES on board DP vessels. Flywheels that can store up to 25 kWh of energy with nominal power up to 400 kW are already available, meaning that several of such units connected in parallel can satisfy the required ES power and capacity [28,35].

Although ES systems based on super condensers and Li-ion batteries still do not meet all the criteria imposed by the specificities of DP vessels, they cannot be a priori rejected as inadequate solutions given the intense efforts invested in their research and development. Next generation of Li-ion batteries which should be available around 2025 will have much higher energy density due to use of NMC81 cathodes and less cobalt content [36], which should result in much smaller and cheaper ES battery packs. It is realistic to expect that the current shortcomings of these two technologies will be overcome in order to compete with the flywheel, or even outmatch it. In support of this, the US Navy is investing considerable resources in the development of Li-ion batteries [37], while super condensers are now being considered as a solution to compensate for peak load in hybrid ship propulsion systems [38].

8. Evaluation Model for ES Implementation on DP Vessels

Accurate data on fuel consumption and maintenance costs can be collected only after a longer period of system exploitation (typically a few years), before and after ES installation. Therefore, systematic recording and collection of exploitation data is of crucial importance for deciding on the installation of ES devices.

The evaluation model of ES implementation on DP vessels presented in this chapter is based on the knowledge of such data with the purpose of facilitating the calculation of ES implementation cost-effectiveness for ship owners and designers. The block diagram of ES implementation process (Figure 14) is divided in to eight phases.

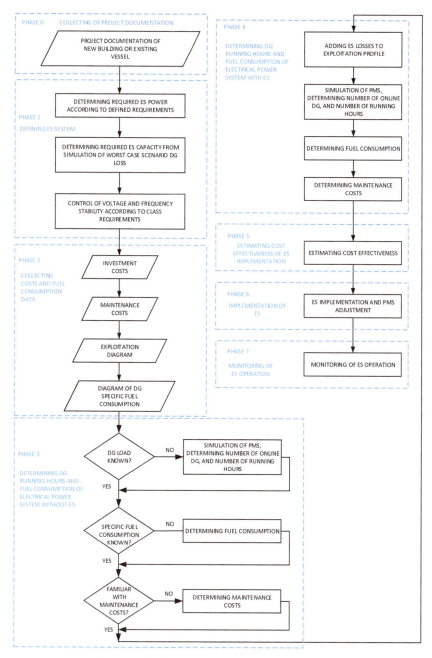

Figure 14. Block diagram of the ES implementation process.

After collecting project documentation of newly-built or existing vessels, the next step is defining the ES system with the main focus on determining its power and capacity for the worst case scenario that can be expected during its use. For this, it is necessary to develop a simulation model of the electrical power system of the considered vessel and perform appropriate simulations, as presented in

Chapters 3 and 4. It is of particular importance to conduct voltage and frequency stability control so that they comply with the class requirements. When the parameters of ES are determined, a suitable solution can be chosen based on the results of comparative analysis of ES systems that meet the requirements of the considered application (Chapter 5).

Once all available data of ES implementation and maintenance costs, as well DGs fuel consumption and maintenance costs, are collected, the estimation of ES cost-effectiveness can be done. In order to facilitate the calculation of fuel consumption from the electrical power consumption data, the DG specific fuel consumption curve (Figure 2) should be accurately approximated by the appropriate mathematical function.

First, it is necessary to determine the number of DG running hours and fuel consumption for the power system without ES. If an individual DG load is known, the calculation of running hours and fuel consumption is performed directly, and if only the total electrical consumption is known, it is necessary to first simulate the operation of the PMS system according to the defined load dependent start and stop tables, and based on the exploitation profile determine the number of DGs online and their individual loads.

In order to calculate the same data for the electrical power system with ES it is necessary to first add ES idle losses to the exploitation profile. From the PMS system simulation, now with the different conditions of starting and stopping DGs allowed by the use of ES, the required values can be determined. When fuel and maintenance costs for systems with and without ES are known, the cost-effectiveness of ES can be estimated. If installation appears to be viable, then the implementation and monitoring phase can begin.

9. Conclusions

In this paper, the possibility of large scale ES implementation on board DP vessels was analyzed. The main focus of this research was to perform analysis of the vessel's electrical power supply stability during a fault, with and without ES and to determine the required capacity and characteristics of ES. For the purpose of this analysis, a dynamic simulation model of the vessel electrical power system with ES was used. The simulation was performed for the worst case scenario that can theoretically happen during use with closed bus bars. For all simulation scenarios it was assumed that ES was able to replace one generator when it failed, until the stand-by generator was ready to take a load. In addition, system behavior during power peak and peak shaving with ES was simulated.

Simulation results have shown that implementation of ES can increase the stability and availability of the electrical power supply and enable the operation of diesel generators with optimal load when the system is running with a closed bus bar. Furthermore, simulation showed that ES is suitable for use on board DP vessels should have large specific power and an almost instantaneous response time to load changes. Given the current state of technology, the flywheel may be the best solution for implementing large scale ES on board DP vessels. Methodology used in this work can be used as a reference for the design of ship power systems with ES and evaluation of ES cost-effectiveness.

Author Contributions: This work has been done by A.C., D.V., R.P. and J.Ć. The manuscript was written by the first author—A.C.

Funding: This work has been financially supported by University of Rijeka under the Faculty of Maritime Studies projects.

Conflicts of Interest: The authors declare no conflict of interest.

References

1. International Marine Contractors Association (IMCA). *A Guide to DP Electrical Power and Control Systems*; M-206; IMCA: London, UK, 2010.

2. Settemsdal, S.O.; Haugan, E.; Aagesen, K.; Zahedi, B.; Drilling, S.A. New enhanced safety power plant solution for DP vessels operated in closed ring configuration. In Proceedings of the Dynamic Positioning Conference, Houston, TX, USA, 14–15 October 2014.
3. May, J.J.; Foss, H. Power Management System for the "Deepwater Horizon" a dynamically positioned all weather semisubmersible. In Proceedings of the Dynamic Positioning Conference, Houston, TX, USA, 17–18 October 2000.
4. Laghari, J.A.; Mokhlis, H.; Bakar, A.H.; Karimi, M.; Shahriari, A. An intelligent under frequency load shedding scheme for islanded distribution network. In Proceedings of the Power Engineering and Optimization Conference (PEDCO), Melaka, Malaysia, 6–7 June 2012; pp. 40–45.
5. Lauvdal, T.; Ådnanes, A.K. Power management system with fast acting load reduction for DP vessels. In Proceedings of the Dynamic Positioning Conference, Houston, TX, USA, 17–18 October 2000.
6. May, J.J. Improving engine utilization on DP drilling vessels. In Proceedings of the Dynamic Positioning Conference, Houston, TX, USA, 16–17 September 2003.
7. Radan, D. Integrated Control of Marine Electrical Power Systems. Ph.D. Thesis, Norwegian University of Science and Technology, Trondheim, Norway, 2008.
8. Cargill, S. A novel solution to common mode failures in DP Class 2 power plant. In Proceedings of the Dynamic Positioning Conference, Houston, TX, USA, 9–10 October 2007.
9. Mathiesen, E.; Realfsen, B.; Brievik, M. Methods for reducing frequency and voltage variations on DP vessels. In Proceedings of the Dynamic Positioning Conference, Houston, TX, USA, 9–10 October 2012.
10. Det Norske Veritas (DNV). *Offshore Stabdard DNV-OS-D201—Electrical Installations*; DNV GL: Oslo, Norway, 2011.
11. McGroarty, J.; Schmeller, J.; Hockney, R.; Polimeno, M. Flywheel energy storage system for electric start and an all-electric ship. In Proceedings of the IEEE Electric Ship Technologies Symposium, Philadelphia, PA, USA, 27 July 2005; pp. 400–406.
12. Holsonback, C.; Webb, T.; Kiehne, T.; Seepersad, C.C. System-level modeling and optimal design of an all-electric ship energy storage module. In Proceedings of the Electric Machines Technology Symposium, Philadelphia, PA, USA, 22–24 May 2006.
13. Domaschk, L.N.; Ouroua, A.; Hebner, R.E.; Bowlin, O.E.; Colson, W.B. Coordination of large pulsed loads on future electric ships. *IEEE Trans. Magn.* **2007**, *43*, 450–455. [CrossRef]
14. Tsekouras, G.J.; Kanellos, F.D. Optimal operation of ship electrical power system with energy storage system and photovoltaics: Analysis and application. *Trans. Power Syst.* **2013**, *8*, 145–155.
15. Kanellos, F.D. Optimal power management with GHG emissions limitation in all-electric ship power systems comprising energy storage systems. *Trans. Power Syst.* **2014**, *29*, 330–339. [CrossRef]
16. Det Norske Veritas (DNV). *Dynamic Positioning Vessel Design Philosophy Guidelines*; DNV GL: Oslo, Norway, 2012.
17. Garg, K.; Weingarth, L.; Shah, S. Dynamic positioning power plant system reliability and design. In Proceedings of the Petroleum and Chemical Industry Conference Europe Electrical and Instrumentation Applications, Rome, Italy, 7–9 June 2011; pp. 1–10.
18. Adnanes, A.K. Status and inventions in electrical power and thruster systems for drillships and semi-submersible rigs. In Proceedings of the Dynamic Positioning Conference, Houston, TX, USA, 28–30 September 2004.
19. Radan, D.; Johansen, T.A.; Sorensen, A.J.; Adnanes, A.K. Optimization of load dependent start tables in marine power management systems with blackout prevention. *Trans. Circuits Syst.* **2005**, *4*, 1861–1866.
20. Sørfon, I. Power Managemenet Control of Electrical Propulsion Systems. In Proceedings of the Dynamic Positioning Conference, Houston, TX, USA, 9–10 October 2012.
21. Wartsila 32 Product Guide. Available online: https://www.wartsila.com (accessed on 10 October 2018).
22. Ong, C.M. *Dynamic Simulation of Electric Machinery: Using MATLAB/SIMULINK*; Prentice Hall PTR: Upper Saddle River, NJ, USA, 1998.
23. Luo, L.; Gao, L.; Fu, H. The control and modeling of diesel generator set in electric propulsion ship. *Inf. Technol. Comput. Sci.* **2011**, *2*, 31–37. [CrossRef]
24. IEEE Power Engineering Society. *IEEE Recommended Practice for Excitation System Models for Power System Stability Studies*; IEEE Power Engineering Society: Piscataway, NJ, USA, 2005.

25. Khalifa, A.S. Control and Interfacing of Three Phase Grid Connected Photovoltaic Systems. Master's Thesis, University of Waterloo, Waterloo, ON, Canada, 2010.
26. Surprenant, M.; Hiskens, I.; Venkataramanan, G. Phase locked loop control of inverters in a microgrid. In Proceedings of the 2011 IEEE Energy Conversion Congress and Exposition, Phoenix, AZ, USA, 17–22 September 2011; pp. 667–672.
27. Chen, H.; Cong, T.N.; Yang, W.; Tan, C.; Li, Y.; Ding, Y. Progress in electrical energy storage system: A critical review. *Prog. Nat. Sci.* **2009**, *19*, 291–312. [CrossRef]
28. Fuchs, G.; Lunz, B.; Leuthold, M.; Sauer, D.U. *Technology Overview on Electricity Storage*; ISEA: Aachen, Germany, 2012.
29. Hadjipaschalis, I.; Poullikkas, A.; Efthimiou, V. Overview of current and future energy storage technologies for electric power applications. *Renew. Sustain. Energy Rev.* **2009**, *13*, 1513–1522. [CrossRef]
30. Nikolaidis, P.; Poullikkas, A. A comparative review of electrical energy storage systems for better sustainability. *J. Power Technol.* **2017**, *97*, 220–245.
31. Luo, X.; Wang, J.; Dooner, M.; Clarke, J. Overview of current development in electrical energy storage technologies and the application potential in power system operation. *Appl. Energy* **2015**, *137*, 511–536. [CrossRef]
32. Donaldson, A.J. Energy Storage—New technologies and new roles. In Proceedings of the Marine Engineer in the Electronic Age, Alexandria, VA, USA, 29–30 April 2002; pp. 237–245.
33. Hockney, R.; Polimeno, M.; Daffey, K. Flywheel Energy Storage Integration into a Naval Power System. In Proceedings of the Turbo Expo 2006: Power for Land, Sea, and Air, Barcelona, Spain, 8–11 May 2006; pp. 25–33.
34. Un-Noor, F.; Padmanaban, S.; Mihet-Popa, L.; Mollah, MN.; Hossain, E. A comprehensive study of key electric vehicle (EV) components, technologies, challenges, impacts, and future direction of development. *Energies* **2017**, *10*, 1217. [CrossRef]
35. Bolund, B.; Bernhoff, H.; Leijon, M. Flywheel energy and power storage systems. *Renew. Sustain. Energy Rev.* **2007**, *11*, 235–258. [CrossRef]
36. Mihet-Popa, L.; Saponara, S. Toward Green Vehicles Digitalization for the Next Generation of Connected and Electrified Transport Systems. *Energies* **2018**, *11*, 3124. [CrossRef]
37. Li-Ion Technology for Surface Ships Advanced Energy Storage for New Generation AES. Available online: http://alpha-energy.ru/D/0000009803/EU_Saft_LiIon_Mt_SurfaceShips_32027-2-0409_200904_en.pdf (accessed on 15 October 2018).
38. Chen, J.W.; Lindtjørn, J.O.; Wendt, F. *Hybrid Marine Electric Propulsion System*; ABB: Cary, NC, USA, 2012.

© 2019 by the authors. Licensee MDPI, Basel, Switzerland. This article is an open access article distributed under the terms and conditions of the Creative Commons Attribution (CC BY) license (http://creativecommons.org/licenses/by/4.0/).

Article

Building a Community of Users for Open Market Energy

Joao C. Ferreira [1,*] and Ana Lucia Martins [2]

1 ISTAR-IUL, Instituto Universitário de Lisboa (ISCTE-IUL), Lisboa 1649-026, Portugal
2 Business Research Unit (BRU-IUL), Instituto Universitário de Lisboa (ISCTE-IUL), Lisboa 1649-026, Portugal; almartins@iscte-iul.pt
* Correspondence: jcafa@iscte-iul.pt; Tel.: +351-210-464-277

Received: 20 July 2018; Accepted: 28 August 2018; Published: 4 September 2018

Abstract: Energy markets are based on energy transactions with a central control entity, where the players are companies. In this research work, we propose an IoT (Internet of Things) system for the accounting of energy flows, as well as a blockchain approach to overcome the need for a central control entity. This allows for the creation of local energy markets to handle distributed energy transactions without needing central control. In parallel, the system aggregates users into communities with target goals and creates new markets for players. These two approaches (blockchain and IoT) are brought together using a gamification approach, allowing for the creation and maintenance of a community for electricity market participation based on pre-defined goals. This community approach increases the number of market players and creates the possibility of traditional end users earning money through small coordinated efforts. We apply this approach to the aggregation of batteries from electrical vehicles so that they become a player in the spinning reserve market. It is also possible to apply this approach to local demand flexibility, associated with the demand response (DR) concept. DR is aggregated to allow greater flexibility in the regulation market based on an OpenADR approach that allows the turning on and off of predefined equipment to handle local microgeneration.

Keywords: blockchain; community; energy market; electric vehicle; Demand Response; gamification; microgeneration; renewable energy

---

1. Introduction

The energy market (production, control, and distribution) is changing from a centralized control system to a decentralized one with the introduction of new players. Information and Communication Technology (ICT) plays an essential role in this change [1]. This change comes under the topic of the smart grid, which targets the evolution of power grids towards more efficient, reliable, and environmentally sustainable systems. Adopting this approach, Distributed Energy Generation (DEG) based on renewable energy sources was introduced. The decrease in the price of solar panels and wind turbines allows the proliferation of this DEG in a microgeneration (MG) scenario. This situation is supported by new advances in the scope of the Internet of Things (IoT), with new communication devices and protocols, as well as smaller and cheaper sensors, allowing real-time measurement of distribution and transmission to a central IoT cloud platform [2].

In this context, peer-to-peer (P2P) models applied to financial transactions with associated security [3], nowadays called blockchain systems, allow the control of financial transactions without the presence of a central control entity. Blockchain can be applied to the smart grid [4]. These platforms can also benefit from collaboration systems that increase (and measure) users' participation in resorting to predefined goals, the so-called gamification platforms [5].

This new situation raises new research challenges, which we address in this work. In a first conceptual phase, we study the conditions and the potential of applying this new situation to energy markets. The primary outcome of this attempt is the creation of new conditions for small players (domestic consumers) to be part of the market, benefiting from reduced costs or receiving money. This can be applied to MG energy transactions, using the principle that the local energy produced is consumed locally and that associating blockchain with smart meters allows managing these transactions without a central control entity. This approach provides the opportunity to lower prices and increase market flexibility. An application example is the aggregation of electrical vehicles (EVs) as players in the energy market, as described in Section 5. This community creation approach for EVs can be applied to increase flexibility in consumption as a whole (rather than the usual individual behaviour), where a group of individuals is aggregated into a market player that is able to absorb or supply less energy according to predefined conditions. Figure 1 shows this approach where an aggregator can create communities (several local users working together) for electricity market participation based on the aggregation of users with a common predefined goal. Gamification manages users' behaviour towards the community goal, and blockchain allows secure financial transactions.

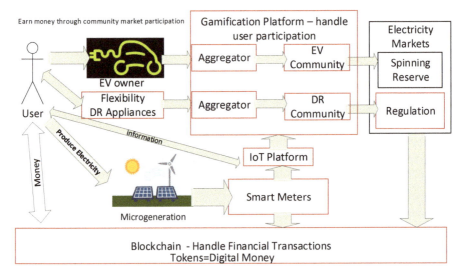

Figure 1. Outline of the main work goals to create electrical vehicle (EV) and demand response (DR) community market players and to decentralize financial transactions based on blockchain.

The electricity market is a system that allows energy transactions based on a bid approach. Bids and offers use traditional economic supply and demand principles to define the price. In Section 7, we propose a model based on historical data in which we check users' energy needs and current MG production is balanced against the whole energy available in the energy market (the price reflects this availability).

Other components of this electricity market are the so-called ancillary services [6]. These are supporting services to sustain the electricity distribution in a process in which production will always meet demand. These services are based on frequency control, spinning reserves, and operating reserves. These services, with the introduction of intermittent renewable energy, raise new challenges and new market players can be introduced. Currently, blockchain with gamification can be applied to create and maintain aggregated users in a community that can play a role in this business process. The present work is mainly focused on spinning reserves and regulation, which must be able to react very quickly to supply energy (minutes or seconds after demand occurs).

Spinning Reserves is the market concept related with the power capacity available in an unloaded form, normally used to overcome the failure of an operator [6]. This failure is defined as a short or long-term loss of electrical power in a specific area. As the probability of this occurrence is very low, it is interesting for EV owners to be part of a spinning reserve since there is little chance of them having their EV charge completely used but at the same time, they can receive money for participating in the market. This service is charged based on the time that the predefined power is available. For example, a 1 MW generator kept "spinning" and ready during a 24 h period would be sold as 1 MW-day, even though no energy was actually produced [7]. Based on this fact, and taking into account that EVs remain plugged in during most of the daytime [8,9], consumption patterns may change from case to case, but it is possible to forecast patterns using historical data analysed using a data mining approach [8,9]. As the possibility of taking an excessive amount of energy from an EV is low, the probability of reducing the EV's lifetime is minimized. Contracts for spinning reserves limit the number and duration of calls, with 20 calls per year and no more than 1 h on average per call [10]. Ancillary services account for 5–10% of the current electricity cost, with 80% of that cost going to regulation services [10]. Navegant Research [11] explained that energy storage solutions that can be connected to the grid and scheduled to deliver energy immediately when there is a disruption in distribution are beginning to play a more significant role in the Spinning Reserve (SR) market.

Regulation services are the actions that match energy production to demand. These can be divided into: (1) regulating up, where there is an increase in electricity output in response to the automatic generation control (AGC); and (2) regulating down, which is a decrease of electricity output to the AGC. Depending on the electricity market and the grid operator, regulation may overlap or be supplemented by slower adjustments, including "balancing service" (intra-hour and hourly) and/or "load following" [6]. Electricity users' flexible behaviour can also be aggregated into a community that can provide services in this regulation market, using Demand Response (DR) [6]. Individuals involved in this DR approach have already participated in the service, but, as in the former models, their actions were centrally coordinated, and users only benefited from low energy prices. If they are aggregated, and the processes are controlled locally, they can participate more closely in this market and additionally earn money as it is possible to provide regulation services. Due to the fact that the EV charging process requires a long period of time, EVs become an important element in this flexible process as it is possible to increase or decrease the charging power during the charging period.

Accordingly, we propose a software program, named Aggregator (see Section 4) that is responsible for collecting user data and aggregating this in a way that allows market participation. Based on these defined conditions it is the responsibility of central mechanics to turn off/on equipment based on the OpenADR protocol [7]. This community creation and manipulation can be successfully applied to a regulation market for DR aggregation flexibility, where the community is able to shift behaviour either to consume excess energy or to decrease consumption when availability is reduced. This approach can be applied in this DR community. Another community is the EV aggregation since EVs have batteries that can be used to store or deliver energy as requested by the control system.

This paper proposes two significant methods to allow an increase in users' participation in the electrical market using an integrated approach that combines reward gamification, the blockchain, and the IoT platform (see Figure 1):

(1) An MG transaction account in a decentralized regulated market based on blockchain and IoT platform implementation with associated smart meters;
(2) The creation of user communities (EV and DR) for participation in ancillary services markets. Gamification is applied to manage and give incentives for users' participation in community behaviour towards becoming a community market player. This approach allows EV owners and DR users to earn money, based on participation in the ancillary services market.

2. New Platforms: Blockchain, Gamification, and IoT

In this section, we give a description of new platforms that allow innovation in the energy market, also creating new study opportunities, such as blockchain, gamification, and IoT.

2.1. Blockchain

In this section, we examine how blockchain architecture can be used to distribute the aggregator's role across all devices on an MG network. It has been demonstrated that it is possible to integrate this architecture in a blockchain platform to control a simulated microgrid, addressing incentive issues while respecting operational constraints [12]. In recent years, there has been some academic research interest in using the distributed approach of blockchain technology to manage the complex system without centralized supervision [12].

Blockchains are platforms that support cryptocurrencies, such as Bitcoin [13]. They allow transactions without the traditional intervention of a third party (usually a bank), based on a shared list of blocks of transactions. These blocks are spread to all network nodes and hold all the transactions. New transactions are performed at the end of the chain and are connected to the previous block of transactions in a hash process, with the following advantages [12]:

- The users' community manages transactions and data;
- Resilience without a single point of failure due to their decentralized nature;
- Transparency and immutability—everything is public and can be seen by the community;
- Low transaction costs, because there are no third parties with commissions involved.

Blockchain can handle cyber-attacks, communication dropouts, and participants joining/departing the network. The associated smart contract supports monetary transactions in a transparent, conflict-free way while avoiding the services of a middleman. A smart contract is a set of predefined conditions for negotiation of the terms of an agreement, which is programmed to run autonomously.

When one considers that a contract is an individual agreement between two or more parties, this contract entails a specific transaction effort. A smart contract can be considered as a contract that is programmed in computer code. Two or more parties digitally agree upon individual rights, obligations, and possible outcomes.

A secure measurement environment should be addressed so that users will trust the measurements performed. For that, trusted computing using the Trusted Platform Module (TPM), Trusted Execution Environment (TEE), Secure Element (SE), or any similar component could be introduced in smart meters supported by a remote verification service. This approach allows both the users and the energy system to verify the software and hardware configurations of a smart meter to determine whether it is tampered with or not.

Our proposal includes IoT-based low-cost smart meters (see Section 4), where we account for energy transactions and where the blockchain allows distributed payments with virtual coins. Using this approach, the consumer receives energy directly from the producer(s) without using a central energy buffer, and a smart contract (a software program created based on predefined conditions) handles the process with predefined negotiated rules. The smart contract allows automatic transactions, checking if the requested amount of energy is currently available from one or more MG community producers. This smart contract also checks the price automatically, based on market prices and local MG availability. Contract negotiations can be automated and do not necessarily have to be performed manually by the involved entities. For example, the consumer or producer can predefine maximum prices to buy or minimum prices to sell, and the negotiations can then be carried out by the smart contract, which will seek to find an ideal compromise using a decision implementation process. The advantage of using smart contracts in the proposed context lies in the fact that they are immutable, and can be seen by every actor. Hence, when relying on a smart contract in negotiations, the parties have the guarantee that it will always perform as predefined. The first step is to define a price point agreement, and then the defined amount of money (digital money) is sent to a predefined address that works as an escrow account. After this process, the energy exchange takes place. An IoT approach controls the energy flow from both the producer's and the consumer's smart meter.

2.2. Gamification Platforms

Gamification is the strategy of interaction between people towards a pre-defined goal based on the offer of incentives that stimulate the public's engagement.

Gamification platforms use the same data-driven techniques used by game designers to motivate users' actions in the critical common goals scenario. These platforms measure users' efforts towards common goals, and incentivize users' participation with an associated reputation or digital currency. They reward commitment with recognition and visibility within the community [5,14].

We associated big data analytics with previously collected data to identify patterns and critical issues for a community goal—in this case, EV aggregated connected or flexible power, to identify critical periods. In EV aggregation, critical periods are associated with the daily hours when EVs are moving (mainly in the morning (from 7:00 a.m. to 10:00 a.m.) and the afternoon (from 5:00 p.m. to 8:00 p.m.)). In DR flexibility, these critical issues were identified from the current data analysis [12]. Thus, it is possible to identify the necessary efforts and to incentivize users with more points/tokens and increasing relevancy and visibility among peers. The community is maintained through users' high engagement levels over time, and also through compliant behaviour towards a pre-defined goal for performance improvement.

2.3. IoT Platforms

The excellent number of IoT platforms is a significant business issue that several companies are working on [15]. IoT platforms have the goal of receiving data from the IoT sensor, archiving them, and manipulating them towards a pre-defined knowledge extraction objective. Several data mining algorithms have already been implemented and are ready to use as a black box [15]. Also, there are reporting and visualization tools available which are ready to use. Gamification requires the identification of patterns and is performed once smart meter data is integrated into the IoT. In Section 4, we describe a locally-developed smart meter in a LoRa communication support system (version 1.0, Cyclope, Grenoble, France), which supports such theorization. Also, Node-Red approaches (flow-based programming for the Internet of Things) available in most IoT platforms allow for the identification of actions based on the sensor data received. This is used to perform OpenADR on/off commands over a pre-defined appliance using data decision criteria [7]. This data comes from the appliance-associated smart meters and external data reception (like renewable energy production) [7]. It would then be possible to implement a fast, centralized command center to manage the aggregator process for these two pre-defined communities. Nowadays, the most relevant (in terms of commercial use) IoT platforms in a market of more than 700 IoT platforms are [16]: (1) Amazon Web Services (AWS) from Amazon; (2) Microsoft Azure IoT; (3) Bluemix/Watson from IBM; (4) Oracle IoT; and (5) Kaa IoT. We chose IBM because of a partnership that was already in place, but all of the platforms perform similar functions in different environments.

3. Related Work

There is a growing research interest in smart grid decentralization processes. A blockchain is a new approach towards such unsupervised processes with technical support to manage distributed energy transactions [17]. A scalable solution for unsupervised control is presented in [18] where a communication infrastructure and protocol allows communication between all nodes to provide real-time consumption information and small scale validation. In [18], the authors discuss several issues of the current centralized system that require a central entity to control and manage payments at a single point of failure, whereas in [19] the security and privacy issues of blockchain approaches are discussed. Several startups are already paying attention to this new research output:

- Bankymoon [20] is a startup in South Africa that proposes the use of smart meters connected to a blockchain, allowing users to load Bitcoins to enable energy flow. This solution uses cryptocurrency only as a prepaid payment option.

- TransActive Grid [https://lo3energy.com] is developing one of the first blockchain based innovations aimed to revolutionize how energy can be generated, stored, purchased, sold, and used all at the local level.
- Solether [http://solether.mkvd.net] is an open software for energy management applied to renewable solar panels that use blockchain cryptocurrencies as payment.
- Slock.it is a blockchain-based approach that rents or sells anything directly without intermediaries. It is already used by several startups such as (1) BlockCharge, which proposes a smart plug to enable on-the-go charging of electric cars using cryptocurrency; (2) PriWatt [21] is a system to manage energy transactions; (3) NRGCoin [http://nrgcoin.org] a decentralized approach to support MG transactions [22]; (4) GridSingularity [https://gridsingularity.com], an energy finance market using a blockchain-based platform.

Examples of more advanced applications of blockchain technology are the SolarCoin [https://solarcoin.org/] and the GrünStromJeton [https://stromstunde.de] reward programs. SolarCoin is a global reward program for solar electricity generation with the goal to globally award solar energy producers with a digital currency in their name, where one coin represents one megawatt-hour (MWh) of solar electricity generated. In its technical implementation, SolarCoin describes its infrastructure as a lite version of Bitcoin that uses a script as a proof-of-work algorithm. GrunStromJeton, on the other hand, is a proposal to award customers with tokens that serve as an indicator of their sustainability behaviour determined by their CO_2 footprint.

Another example is the POWR—Pilot project, with decentralized energy management, using a Brooklyn Microgrid Pilot project, which connects 10 households in Brooklyn using a blockchain based microgrid [23]. The TenneT can also be highlighted, a European pilot project using decentralized, networked home energy storage systems and blockchain technology to stabilize the power grid.

Blockchain has allowed businesspeople to enter the electricity market to create proofs of concept, enabling anyone, anywhere to participate in and make money from the surge in solar generation globally. Economic benefits emerge from decentralized participation, with dynamic prices based on the fact that it is possible to perform transactions of small energy time units in real time and settled only on the basis of actual consumption. Both energy consumers and energy producers can act as prosumers.

It is then possible to conclude that the initial steps towards using blockchain technology to enable MG transactions in a distributed and dynamic way are already being pursued by several enterprises. In this work, we suggest consumption flexibility for MG prosumers in a locally defined community, based on an OpenADR (version 2.0, OpenADR Alliance, San Ramon, CA, USA) implementation over a blockchain.

4. Proposed Approach

Figure 2 shows the vision and the implementation proposal for the creation of two new flexible community market players: EV community and the DR community. This aggregation allows the reaction to perturbation in production and consumption based on predefined agreements supported by the aggregation performed to create the community. Also, this approach allows MG transactions without supervised control, based on a blockchain approach implementation. Participants, in this case, EV owners, consumers, or MG producers in the blockchain network, can come to a general agreement with predefined conditions and actions. Digital currency allows transactions and is the way to operationalise this smart contract, where Bitcoin and Ethereum are the best-known examples. The contract is recorded in the blockchain and executed by distributed nodes of the network, which eliminates the need for a trusted third party entity in the process [17]. As it is programmed, it will execute itself and will behave precisely as previously defined, allowing an automatic payment based on a BID. This approach also allows smart charging based on price, which is associated with energy availability.

This market scenario allows the use of Demand Response (DR), which is essential to the introduction of renewable sources, with prices based on the balance between production and demand, state-of-the-art technological approaches, normative regulation, as well as political, psycho-social, and cultural dimensions. These conditions need to be workable for all community members involved in the process.

A blockchain energy model can facilitate the creation and operation of communities. In our approach to MG, we assume a grid in a limited geographical area that shares the same energy distribution network, such as a local neighbourhood where the energy is produced and consumed locally, to build an energy community. A prosumer can either store the energy produced in local batteries or send it immediately to that local grid. Additionally, based on OpenADR [7], local neighbours or community members can increase or decrease consumption based on this energy MG availability. MG prosumers may produce, consume, and trade energy without any barriers using a blockchain (which provides a decentralization process) coupled with an IoT system to measure energy flows.

The smart meter described in this paragraph is the process that measures all energy transactions. A community control agent turns on/off equipment based on OpenADR. Complementary to trusted computing, we introduced an automated energy detection service from neighbour nodes to check the process of a node injecting energy into the grid. This would allow its neighbour nodes to detect the injected energy and validate it using a consensus solution like a mechanism to accumulate the measurements received for every expected energy transfer.

The currently proposed approach is based on the Steemit platform [https://steemit.com], which allows differentiating users' participation in the collective goal. The Steemit platform, launched in 2016, deploys a blogging and social networking website superimposed on the Steem blockchain database. The Steemit structure is based on a reputation system, whereby new accounts start with the endowment of a reputation. This approach, where the economic model can be decentralized, allows individual EV and MG owners to participate in the energy market and besides receiving a lower price for the energy can also earn money from the market. The associated gamification approach allows user participation towards a common goal, which is based on the application of game-design elements and game principles in non-game contexts. In a more structural way, the proposed system architecture, which is illustrated in Figure 2, is based on the following modules:

- V2G Smart System [24,25]: This is the system which controls EVs' connections to the power grid. It allows a smart charging process based on the energy needed for the owner's mobility process, available production, and network distribution limitations. Node-Red allows the giving of external commands to the developed charging system (charging on/off, increasing/decreasing charging power).
- IoT Platform with associated Smart meters: Data is stored in the IBM Watson (cloud version of 28.02.2018, IBM, Armonk, NY, USA), an IoT cloud platform, where data analytics algorithms and visualization tools are ready to use in Watson Analytics and Node-RED, which allows for the development, deployment, and scale server-side of JavaScript apps easily. Rules can be implemented in Node-RED to create automatic actions, such as sending an SMS or an email alert, or even commands (on/off) to appliances when consumption increases above a predefined value, with correlations with external data, like weather conditions, among others—making it necessary to add Node-RED as one of the services.
- OpenADR with a decision support system [7]: Predefined equipment, such as heating/cooling systems, the EV charging battery, and washing machines, among other equipment, have implemented an OpenADR that allows them to turn on/off based remotely on predefined criteria. Node-RED, with associated pre-defined flows, allows external OpenADR commands based on pre-defined conditions.
- Mobile apps [24] and related user profiles [26]: The development of user App was performed for Android. The app is the interface to the user (MG producer, EV owner, DR flexibility user) and is responsible for user registration, on the first access, and the further creation and maintenance of a user profile related with his electrical behaviour (EV type; time, date, and associated distance

traveled; equipment type; schedules for DR flexibility). Accordingly, this module will have the following functions/modules regarding the user: registration, communication interface, and profile. Also, an IoT dashboard was integrated to allow the user to visualize data (electricity consumption, MG production, transactions). Pre-defined templates allow easy visualization on a mobile App. An interface for Sttemit also allows a user to check their reputation (gamification) and missed goals, and check financial transactions.

- Aggregation process [9]: This module enables the community process that creates an interaction with the energy market. This module can be applied to EV aggregation or DR flexibility. Current and historical user data is manipulated using data mining (pattern identification) to generate consumption profiles of the users' community. Considering market energy bids and collected values, the users' community expresses its preferences (target market goals to be achieved, where identified patterns represent important decision criteria). A gamification approach is implemented to push users towards the definition of goals and measure their behaviour (profit division). This aggregator also looks for the user's geographical position in the distribution network—a community emerges from users who share a similar location [27] and interests towards energy market participation.
- Steemit platform: This module aims at measuring users' participation towards the community's common goal, and based on IoT data (smart meters), performs relevant financial transactions. All transactions between EVs and the power grid, MG, and DR actions are stored in an IoT cloud platform and are associated with financial transactions in Steemit. To ensure users' data privacy, data is stored without being directly related to the user.

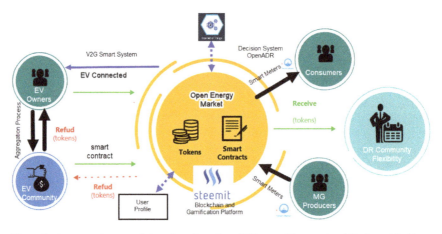

Figure 2. A proposed approach based on Steemit and Watson of International Business Machines Corporation (IBM) platforms.

5. IoT Implementation on a University Campus

The university at hand is a community of about 10,000 people (students, lecturers, and non-teaching staff), which has four buildings in a central area of Lisbon, with a total of 53,000 square meters of gross built area. The annual energy bill is about half a billion euros, corresponding to total energy of 4 GWh/year (81% electricity, 19% natural gas). As shown in Figure 3, a smart campus initiative was recently developed, where sensor data collected (electricity, temperature, humidity) was transmitted in real time to an IoT platform for analyses and saving actions were implemented [15]. These smart meters allow for the measurement of solar energy production, as well as the heating/cooling system, lights, and other configurable equipment.

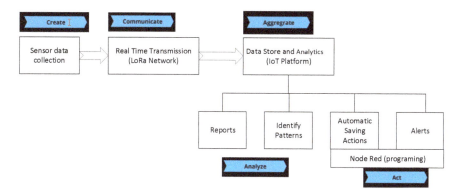

Figure 3. The main approach of the Smart Campus initiative.

In the context of the proposed system, we decided to measure electricity consumption and production to test a small MG energy exchange model. Due to the high number of sensors currently available in the market for each task, choice of the most suitable sensor was critical. The primary criterion for this decision process was smooth integration and data calibration. To measure electricity consumption, we chose the YHDC SCT013-000 current sensor (YHDC, Qinhuangdao, China), which is a current transformer (100 A: 50 mA) where its analogue output is received and processed by an Arduino with a Lora Module for wireless communication (see Figure 4).

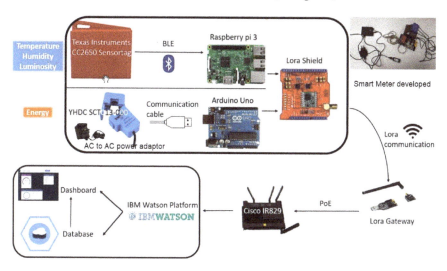

Figure 4. Smart meters for electricity measurement and a temperature/luminosity sensor with a Lora network, sending data to IBM Watson.

For the communication layer, we chose LoRa technology to provide wireless data communication inside the university campus, and a Cisco Lora network was installed to cover the entire campus. The choice of LoRa technology was based on its long-range coverage when compared to other available low-power wireless technologies, such as ZigBee and Bluetooth Low energy (BLE), and its low data rate requirements, as Lora data rates range from 0.3 kbps to 50 kbps. These sensors use low power networks like LoRaWAN to connect to the Lora Gateway. The Lora Gateway uses high-bandwidth networks like WiFi and Ethernet to connect to The Things Network using Cisco IR829 (Cisco Systems,

Inc., San Jose, CA, USA), which provides Power of Ethernet (PoE) to the Lora gateway, as well as an encryption connection (shown in Figure 4). From this IR829, data is sent to the IBM IoT platform for storage and to perform data analytics.

The Instituto Universitário de Lisboa (ISCTE-IUL) infrastructure is comprised of two Cisco Enterprise/Industry-class Gateways, installed in both indoor and outdoor environments, to accommodate diverse environments and support laboratory equipment, IT equipment, and other specific tools. Figure 3 shows images of the currently implemented solution, based on four layers: (1) a Lora Antenna, which runs the LoRaWAN protocol to communicate with the Lora gateways or sensors; (2) a Lora Gateway IoT Extension Module) (IMX), (Cisco Systems, Inc., San Jose, CA, USA)—the concentrator tunneling the LoRaWAN MAC frames between an endpoint and an IR829; (3) a Cisco IR829, which handles the LoRaWAN MAC traffic, performing endpoint and gateway management, LoRaWAN MAC layer security, and other functions; (4) an application management, Actility, which is a secure form of communication as all data are encrypted.

The Actility ThingPark Wireless™ platform (https://www.actility.com/products/) (version 5.0, Actility, Paris, France) enables connectivity with customers and allows devices to be used in multiple applications, such as smart cities, to promote sustainability. Cisco's Low-Power Wide-Area Network (LPWAN) equipment (Cisco Systems, Inc., San Jose, CA, USA), along with its Network Director management software, provides wireless connection between sensors, gateways, and the internet (or the customer's private network), while the Network Server Acuity ThingPark Operations Support System (OSS) ensures the correct routing of the data packages while allowing simple monitoring, supervision, and management of the network, from the sensors to the application.

The collected data is transmitted to the Arduino (version uno, nteraction Design Institute Ivrea (IDII) in Ivrea, Italy) and Raspberry PI gateways (version 3, Raspberry Pi Foundation, London, UK), and from them to a LoRa communication system using the implemented approach. For the connection of a Current Transform (CT) sensor to an Arduino to be effective, it is necessary to condition the output signal of the CT sensor to match the input requirements of the analogue inputs of the Arduino, i.e., a positive voltage between 0 V and the reference voltage, Analog-to-digital converters (ADC).

The sensor data is transferred through the LoRa network to the Steemit platform, where it is considered for an energy transaction account.

This solution allows real-time data to be obtained from various sources of information and is used in decision support tools. These can result in benefits and optimizations to the processes of continuous improvement of the services provided to the community, contributing to better knowledge of the campus community (in this case, ISCTE-IUL) dynamics and an increase in the quality of life.

6. Blockchain Applications

The following cases are examples of applications of this nature at the university campus:

Case 1—Classroom student footprint energy account in IBM blockchain

We measured all energy consumption, from the lighting, heating/cooling system, and power outlet every 15 min (this is a configurable parameter in our smart meters). It was possible to check student presence based on an identification card reading system connected to our academic management system. Every student could register their presence by inserting their magnetic card into the reader inside the classroom. Teachers used a similar card to open the door. Since we monitored electricity consumption, it was possible to create a transaction model that computed the energy consumption associated with each student in a blockchain. For example, a large classroom uses light, projecting devices, and a heating/cooling system, which consumes about 20 kW/h. In this case, the presence of 40 students equaled an individual consumption of about 500 W/h per student. Based on the student population in the monitoring classrooms (two), we tested blockchain transactions for a period of 3 months for a population of about 1000 students, with an average of 35 students per classroom transaction (see Figure 5). This energy consumption was transformed into a token at the blockchain, where we defined a token as a watt/hour of energy. Some students showed high transaction tokens due to the fact that they had more classes in that classroom, and in the same cohort, some students missed classes and therefore would show fewer tokens. It should be noted that we did not explore this energy consumption footprint, but the number of transactions performed. We had a classroom of about 100 students which generated 100 transactions in the blockchain every 15 min. Figure 6 shows the worst scenario observed, with data from the two classrooms generating 180 requests arriving simultaneously to the server. Machine CPU (IBM Watson IoT platform) went to 100% utilization as requests went up to 150. All transactions were performed in this period with these processes. We generated 350,000 transactions in total, with an average of 3500 per student.

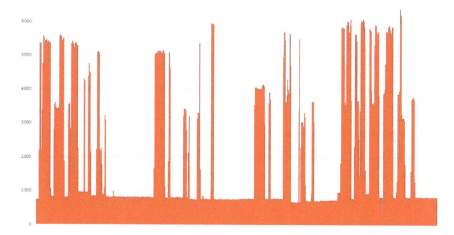

Figure 5. Average energy consumption per student in three classrooms, through the 3-month experiment, with y labelling the associated token; x is the student in a population of 1000.

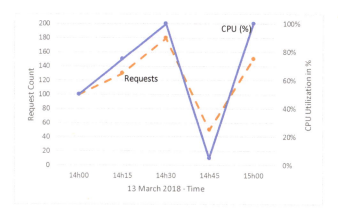

Figure 6. Worst-case transaction scenario, with IBM Internet of Things (IoT) central processing unit based on primary axis the numbers of the arrived transaction request (dashed line) and (CPU) utilization (solid line) on secondary axis.

Case 2—Microgeneration—Testing blockchain MG transaction model at our IoT Laboratory

We created a simulation environment using information from the real production of 16 solar panels, each producing about 250 W. We associated two panels (of 500 W each) in each classroom

(CR). Each CR represents a house and, based on classroom occupancy (occupied or not), we simulated electricity consumption. If the classroom (CR) was occupied, it had the capacity to consume—but if not, the MG went to the nearest CR. We assumed that lighting consumed 1.5 of the MG energy of each classroom (750 W). In this investigative scenario, we only accounted for MG transaction from CR-X to CR-Y, each trying to simulate a real case of MG energy transaction without a central control infrastructure. Excess production of MG went from one CR to the next, using the MG event and the CR occupancy. If CR1 was occupied, its light consumption took all its MG production, but if class lights were off, the energy went to the nearest CR. Based on this process, we tested the proposed approach with all transactions accounted for in the blockchain using 3 months' worth of data. Table 1 shows how our experiment expanded to 8 CRs, as well as the associated transactions in the blockchain. To simplify, we showed the kW consumption in the process as follows: In Table 1, the intersection between the second line in the fourth column shows CR1→CR2, which means that during this 3-month period, CR2 used 31 kW/h from CR1. This MG comes from solar panels 1 and 2, producing energy that was not used by CR1 because lights were off during that period, and CR2 was able to take that energy. The CR number represents the physical distance between the CRs as they were all located in the same hallway. Table 1 shows it is possible to account for these transactions in an implementation using the IoT blockchain from IBM. Although other blockchains could have been used, we chose IBM due to its fast development, since this approach was already integrated into IBM Watson. Values represent kW/h, but these are converted to tokens in the blockchain, considering time and the agreed prices. In this phase, static prices were applied, but it is possible to apply dynamic prices based on production offer.

Table 1. Microgeneration (MG) accounting processes in the blockchain.

		CR1	CR2	CR3	CR4	CR5	CR6	CR7	CR8
MG1/2→	CR1		31	14	6	1			
MG3/4→	CR2	24		39	11	2			
MG5/6→	CR3	8	22		26	12	3		
MG7/8→	CR4	1	7	19		23	12	3	2
MG9/10→	CR5		1	8	18		25	10	3
MG11/12→	CR6			2	7	15		23	14
MG13/14→	CR7				3	10	23		19
MG15/16→	CR8					3	12	28	

7. Gamification Process to Reduce Lighting Consumption

Here, we propose a public visualization of non-sustainable behaviour.

Figure 7 outlines a small example of data collected, where it is shown that the light was turned on at 4:15 p.m. This was done by the security personnel, and classes only started at 8:00 a.m. CRs had no windows, or these were small—and curtains prevented daylight from entering the room. Figure 7 shows that lights were on for most of the time, even during periods where no classes were taking place or no people were in the class. Our study showed there was an average waste of 100€ per year in each classroom due to the fact that lights were on even though classes were not being held or no people were present.

To overcome the problem of lights being left on even when rooms were not being used, a gamification approach was introduced, with light consumption being checked against luminosity. For example, if a class finished at 1:00 p.m. and the following one started at 6:00 p.m., the consumption during that time range was accounted for, which was around 5 kW/h. If the former class had 50 students, the system collected 100 W/h for each student, and 5 kW/h for the teacher. In this way, we made weekly and monthly announcements of the top ten most sustainable students (with the least energy accounted in the gamification platform) and the top ten least sustainable (with more electricity consumption in their account).

This approach provided a common behavioral example towards our sustainable goals for light consumption. This approach ran for three months and, based on the initial consumption levels (for the first month), led to savings, because the energy consumption patterns changed. It is also possible to identify more periods of all lights being turned off, such as that of March 13 at 12:15 p.m. We think we can go further with the saving behaviour, possibly reaching savings of more than 50%.

With this approach, it was possible to enable and motivate consumers to change their consumption levels and create more sustainable behaviour. The visualization board, in fact, creates a social comparison and serves to provide motivation towards reaching the pre-defined goal.

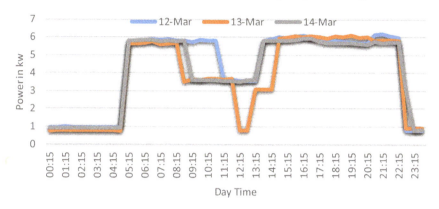

Figure 7. IoT data measured and represented. Example from the light consumption of a classroom.

8. EV Community and Associated Gamification

For the spinning reserve (SR) market, the EVs need to be aggregated to allow considerable energy stored in batteries. This load aggregation is more easily achieved during the night, as during the day, when the EVs are moving, availability is more difficult. Based on the EV driver's usage profile, created from a mobile APP that handles the EV charging process, it is possible to identify the availability pattern of each EV and the associated energy. It is then possible to associate the amount of energy available and the periods when that availability occurs based on historical data. EV owners define their participation in the spinning reserve market by providing information concerning the energy that they allow to give back to the system and when (hours). Based on this aggregation, a community profile is created. The market revenues are divided among the community considering the standard behaviour of each EV participant. A gamification process allows increasing EV participation to fulfil periods of time when most EVs are moving, and alerts allow setting targets for EV drivers to achieve. Figure 8 shows this gamification approach in a mobile APP (used as a user interface with the system), in which the system asks for collaboration to achieve a particular volume of energy that allows increased revenue and the EV driver can adjust their behaviour towards that goal. We use our V2G smart system, with LoRa communication and OpenADR interface. It is possible to collect charging data with this solution. Other market participation solutions can be tried out, but since the energy in the EV battery is a precious value and the charging/discharging process can damage battery lifetime, we propose that only the load available for the spinning reserve market is used. The daily distance travelled by each EV is not always the same, and therefore the level of energy stored in their batteries is not always the same throughout the day. The aggregator analyses historical data to identify deviations from the standard behaviour defined, such as:

- the time span each EV from a specific community is connected to the grid;
- the daily distance each EV travels;
- the State of charge (SOC) of each EV at each moment in time.

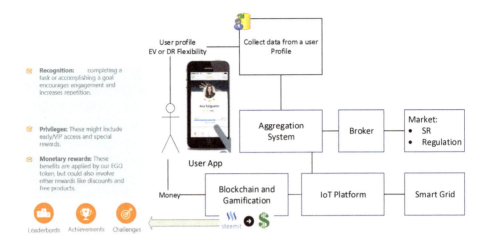

Figure 8. Gamification approach implemented towards EV spinning reserve market participation, as well as DR flexibility.

This data is analyzed from two perspectives: (1) individual data, and (2) collective community data. We propose the use of Naïve Bayes approach [8,9], where the probability of data being within defined parameters (with a predefined value, for example, 8am is represented as 8am plus or minus 5 min) is measured against other periods. In the scope of our proposed model, the following assumptions were used:

- Energy losses in the EV batteries are not considered as the losses at the charging stations that emerge due to conversion efficiency, or in the EV batteries, or due to transmission is minimal [25];
- The battery storage capacity of each EV is constant during the study period;
- Parking slots have significant capacity available, so there are no waiting times for charging (simplified approach);
- EVs are always connected to the grid where they are parked;
- The power of the charging stations and outlets is unlimited;
- When the number of EVs increases, new communities should emerge based on their geographical location for the physical electrical distribution networks;
- A user can belong to several communities, but during each connected period only belongs to one of them.

Different behaviour profile templates are available:

- EVs that are continually travelling, for example, taxis, and receive fast charging processes. These cannot be used by an aggregator;
- EVs that usually receive slow charging processes but at random locations, i.e., always travelling. These represent additional complexity for the aggregator to use because the behaviour cannot be predicted;
- EVs that are known to change charging location and time, but do different trip lengths. For this group, the charging level is variable;
- EVs for which the location of the charge station is known and usually doing the same trip.

The main idea is to promote a gamification approach, in which users are joined in communities based on a common goal. This effort is translated into tokens, which are then converted into digital currency. The aggregator identifies critical hours (periods of time when fewer EVs are connected) based on users' data.

Gamification handles this process where tokens are used to promote users' participation. The award of tokens is based on the periods of time when the EVs are plugged in, classified by their criticality level. This classification is developed based on: (1) the power offered by the electrical grid to the market, (2) the power made available by the community to be given back to the electrical grid, and (3) the criticality of the period of time (in our case, based on the criteria described above) for the goals of the community.

Users' misbehaviour (for instance, changes in the profile of their plugged-in time) are penalised with the loss of tokens. If that user *a priori* overcomes the failure by providing another user as a replacement, no penalty is applied. All these actions are available in the App; users need only to perform system interaction. If the misbehaviour is not reported in advance, the system heavily penalises the user and forwards the failure report so that an alternative solution can be found inside the community [9].

The gamification approach, illustrated in Figure 5, allows users' interaction and collaboration with the community goal. Users should try to fulfil the community offer, and disruption in predefined or expected user behaviour should be replaced by another community user with the incentive of tokens. The suggestions presented below aim to keep users informed, motivated, and willing to collaborate more frequently:

- Infrequent Changes of User's Plugging Time: users who cannot fulfil their plugged-in time commitment can find a replacement in the community to avoid penalties if an alert is provided in due time. When a user finds a replacement, the community goals remain unchanged.
- Area for Reporting Abuses or Faults: the app should have an area where users can report abuses, such as comments or wrong use of the System. The System Manager can penalise users for these abuses. This feature aims mainly aims to discourage users from performing misuses or faults.
- Token (Monetary) rewards to promote and recognize community behaviour towards market participation. These rewards are based on the token, which is digital money;
- Community Newsletter: this digital newsletter aims to keep the community informed and provide additional information concerning the EVs;
- Request: an area in the app for users to ask questions. This area can be used by the system manager to adjust the behaviour of the community;
- Users' Rankings: This aims to highlight the collaborators contributing most and is based on the tokens earned by each user. This is a feature of the gamification platform.

Our testing used data from seven V2G systems in the Nissan Leaf (five of them with 24 kW batteries and two with 30 kW). We extracted charging behaviour patterns, and gamification was tested with pre-defined behaviour checked against the real data collected. The V2G smart systems and LoRa protocols allowed for communication in most places. Our network has a range of 15 km, but other networks are also available.

If a user says that his car has been plugged in at 7:00 p.m. and it turns out not to be, the system will take tokens from him unless he sends a prior alert of this change and finds another user to replace him. The total power available in this small community is $5 \times 24 + 2 \times 30 = 180$ kW. Patterns show (Figure 9) that critical periods (with less aggregated power available) occur after mobility periods (no connection to the grid). It is relevant to check the gamification approach during these critical periods (8:00 a.m. to 10:00 a.m.) and (6:00 p.m. to 9:00 p.m.). We observed several changes in behaviour 15% of the time over 3 months' worth of data. Due to the small number of users in this pilot testing experiment, finding users to replace these changes was not always possible. Nonetheless, exceeding our expectations for such a small pilot, available power was always above 35 kW, and the system handled transactions based on a pre-defined value (introduced for market participation) with the associated division on blockchain with gamification inputs.

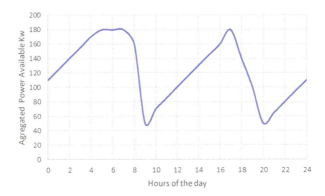

Figure 9. Aggregation data from the seven EV in an average daily distribution.

9. The flexibility of the Demand Response Community and Associated Gamification

The powerful global flexibility of the Demand Response (DR) approach has the goal of shifting demand from peak to off-peak hours. It is based on a two-way Internet Protocol (IP) communication connection between suppliers (offer) and consumers (demand). Grids can also quickly adapt to such transactions in order to allow the inclusion of other sources of renewable energy and lead to more ecological behavior from the users by reducing their consumption profile and, in parallel, increase their participation in the DR strategy. The proposed DR is grounded on demand management and on variables such as the price of the energy, the quantity of energy available and the forecasting of the level of production of renewable energy, which requires complex ways of signal handling and optimization. There are two perspectives for DR: (1) peak clipping when the total level of demand for electricity is unpredictable, and a financial incentive reduces the demand level in traditional peak periods; and (2) demand shifting, which consists of delaying or anticipating demand to off-peak periods.

In the electricity market, flexibility associated with DR can be defined as a consumption adjustment performed in a specified period of time to balance supply and demand at a given moment in time [27]. Individually, this behaviour will not have a market impact (will not be valued), but at an aggregated level it is possible to become an SR market player and profit from it. Our approach uses a predefined set of consumption templates from which users choose based on their equipment flexibility (type, power, and flexibility approach). The four templates considered are as follows [28]:

T1—Scheduled-Based Appliances (SBA)—This template is related to electrical appliances with flexible operation periods. Since there are household appliances that come within the scope of this template such as washing machines, drying machines, and dishwashers, users can pre-define their operation time frame based on their preferences and lifestyle.

T2—Range Temperature Based Appliances (RTBA)—This template is focused on appliances for which temperature can be regulated, such as refrigerators, heating systems, or air conditioners. In these situations, users can pre-define a temperature operation range or pre-accept a fully flexible range (deep learning data analysis can identify the main working temperature ranges, and the user can check if it is acceptable). This approach has already been applied in tensor flow [28], but the description is beyond the scope of this paper.

T3—Battery Assisted Smart Appliances (BASA)—This template relates to EVs. Their charging process can be conducted based on the availability of energy and on optimization of costs, e.g., based on the energy consumption of other electrical appliances that are connected to the same consumption node.

T4—Full Flexibility (FF) operation mode. Patterns extracted from historical data collected from smart sensors in flexible equipment allow users to check if the flexible approach is positive. For example, a user who chooses full flexibility for the heating system can check from historical data if he always has hot water in this approach and check if it is beneficial as if on one hand the full flexibility system leads to earning more from the system, on the other hand, the user may occasionally have cold water (although the probability is low, it makes sense to allow this to be based on the user's decision).

A Regional Aggregator (RA) (defined as an aggregator for a specific community) takes users' choice of the predefined templates to maximize the total power flexibility within the associated time period. Taking into account market goals, a gamification approach is applied to promote users' participation to achieve those goals. The RA manages the full set of electrical appliances at the same location with OpenADR interfaces based on user-defined profile and market operation needs. Based on regional capacity flexibility, this RA exchanges information with a central market operation, where the necessary actions towards the OpenADR command centre are defined. This command centre aims to share the excess production of renewable energy among the different RAs. This sharing is based on the loading and unloading capacity of each RA and, as previously discussed, this capacity varies throughout the day based on the user's definition of how the appliances will be used. The central RA also advises users on how to reduce their energy bills by producing suggestions to adjust appliance aggregation with OpenADR, expand flexibility periods, and manage heating/cooling systems based on the level of energy available in the market. The suggestions provided by the RA are registered in the local (home) energy management system. This system can be accessed by the user using a mobile or a web interface. Based on all the requests from the different users, the RA sends the aggregated demand level to the central system in the shape of a time function. As a first approach (others could be implemented), the central system suggestion is to share the renewable energy available among the several RAs based on their particular levels of demand. If the aggregated demand loads from all RAs is not enough to absorb all the excess energy produced, traditional reserves (such as batteries) should be used. If the production excess is lower than the power available in the flexible community a rationing approach between all RAs based on the priority of the templates (T1 to T4) should be implemented. Within each RA the energy should be distributed based on a similar approach, using the defined power profile. Examples of how to share this energy are already available in the literature [29]. In each household, the energy received also has to be distributed based on a pre-defined prioritization of the equipment template. If the level of demand is higher than the energy available, it is possible to turn off appliances according to the predefined sequence provided to the node-red flow.

Each input to turn on/off or increase/decrease power in the appliances originates a token transaction in the blockchain, and associated commands based on node-red actions using OpenADR appliance interfaces. Based on random events, we simulated a renewable production based on pre-defined rules with originating flexible behaviour. A small case study was performed in the IoT laboratory using data collected from the classrooms and information about class events and the number of persons in each class, where we simulated DR behaviour using blockchain and gamification. Data used came from the eight classrooms, the AVAC systems (T2 defined System), with the seven EV (T3 defined systems), and our IoT laboratory appliances (for T1 we used a power outlet and for T4 another power outlet where a local heating system is connected). The aggregated power was created based on the heating/cooling process and the EV charging process. Each AVAC in each classroom represents the DR flexibility of an individual (simulates a house with the power of 3 kW), and each EV represents one owner. Random events simulate changes in production with an on/off or increase/decrease in power consumption. The acceptance of this external command creates blockchain transactions associated with this flexible behaviour. Based on this approach, we created a process to account for flexible behaviour. We defined transaction time units of 5 min (a configurable parameter), and in future work will check the impact of different time units and improve the centralised coordination rule-based system towards the pre-defined collective market goal.

10. Current Status and Challenges

In Europe, smart meter real-time measurements and communications have only been implemented in large companies; in the small energy market, which includes domestic users, the large majority are not yet using IoT smart meters [4]. Overcoming this lack of flexibility requires OpenADR or similar approaches (which are still lacking standardization) with metering to implement DR at a residential level [30]. This situation with missing data sources for end users' consumption behaviour using specific equipment, for instance, the EV charging process, delays the application of data analysis. The unadapted current market status for the aggregation process of DR flexibility and EV is a fact [9,30]. Nevertheless, the smart grid vision of electricity markets requires open markets and demands flexible services. These markets work based on bids and have substantial requirements for minimum bidding volumes and bid duration. This situation has constraints that can be overcome through the use of powerful gamification platforms for users to develop joint efforts to achieve the market goal.

In summary, in the European Union, only a limited number of aggregators can be identified [31]. In many countries, the market rules for electricity do not favour the emergence of aggregators. Also, market rules are not yet similar in the different member countries, meaning a lack of coherence in the European Union. Therefore, policymakers should take a holistic approach to enhance community market participation, where DR flexibility and EV aggregated batteries could represent essential players as long as end users recognise the profits and benefits from this approach.

This aggregation, along with local MG, can be a solution to overcome network and supply constraint problems.

11. Conclusions and Future Work

Current technological developments allow prosumers to produce electrical energy in-house or in local green energy communities. However, the energy market is still dominated by big energy players. This means that, until now, the majority of prosumers only had access to the (energy) market by using standard bilateral agreements. This has profoundly impacted the expansion of MG as the economic advantages for the prosumers are limited. In this paper, we presented an energy model based on users to study the feasibility of implementing a solution for the micro-generation of in-house energy with the possibility of exchanging energy at a community level, leveraging on the disruptive potentialities of blockchain technologies. The proposed system is based on a blockchain platform with associated gamification and can manage decentralised MG transactions. It can also be applied to the EV spinning reserves market and DR flexibility. The advantages of this approach are diverse:

- It allows prosumers' true engagement in the energy market as they will be acting as enablers for the creation of energy communities;
- It enhances the transparency and trust of the energy market system;
- It guarantees a high level of security, integrity, and resilience (a consequence of the intrinsic nature of blockchains);
- It guarantees accountability while preserving privacy requirements;
- It promises new business opportunities that can emerge from the concept of the energy community.

To gather evidence of the viability of the described model, we have developed and tested the different substructures of the system, from its assembly and configuration of the different physical devices (solar panels, batteries, smart meters, IoT control devices) to the implementation of these substructures. Aggregation was simulated based on the local student population. The physical component of the system has some flexibility, and can be configured to work either autonomously or connected to a main grid. In terms of the functioning logic, the model proposed in our approach, and to the best of our knowledge, is the first release of the smart contract. Although at this point it is still at an embryonic level, we plan further developments for our model. We will continue this research aiming to assess the effectiveness of the model if used from a commercial perspective, i.e., assuring the interconnection with a real energy market platform. The system's business model deserves deeper analysis to be able to produce a final product that can be used in a real context. Furthermore, other essential factors that could have an impact on a prosumer-based energy model require further study, such as:

(a) Enhancing trust in the system by using enabled smart meters. Our LoRa network encrypted all sensor data in a secure environment;
(b) Increasing systems' measurement reliability by introducing a consensus mechanism on top of the proposed architecture;
(c) Extending the current implementation of the smart contract to include not only more complex subprocesses such as the ability of third parties to interact with coins, but also the ability to automatically control the transaction fees from each owner's account;
(d) Calculating and considering that there is energy loss during transfer, which is not under consideration at this point but should be considered in the implementation phase to allow further detail.

Another relevant research topic is to compute the most adjusted value of the tokens, but once the system is running these values can be improved.

Overall, considering the arguments used and our initial design, the deployment of a prosumer energy model is considered feasible. To facilitate its large-scale adoption in the single digital market, trust and cyber-security, in such a critical service, should be provided at the highest standard.

All work has applied to the LV (Low Voltage) market, but this can be applied to MV (Medium Voltage). To be able to cover the entire population, we conceptualize that several local blockchains will handle transactions regionally and an inter-regional blockchain will handle this in a global approach.

Author Contributions: Both authors contributed equally to the conceptualization and writing of the paper, and J.F. produced additional work on the development of the case studies and the implementation details.

Funding: This research was funded by Fundação para a Ciência e Tecnologia from ISTAR project UID/MULTI/4466/2016.

Conflicts of Interest: The authors declare no conflict of interest.

References

1. Miceli, R. Energy Management and Smart Grids. *Energies* **2013**, *6*, 2262–2290. [CrossRef]
2. Rawat, P.; Singh, K.D.; Chaouchi, H.; Bonnin, J.M. Wireless sensor networks: A survey on recent developments and potential synergies. *J. Supercomput.* **2014**, *68*, 1–48. [CrossRef]
3. Koshy, P.; Koshy, D.; McDaniel, P. An Analysis of Anonymity in Bitcoin Using P2P Network Traffic. In *Financial Cryptography and Data Security*; Springer: New York, NY, USA, 2014; pp. 469–485.
4. Rodríguez-Molina, J.; Martínez-Núñez, M.; Martínez, J.-F.; Pérez-Aguiar, W. Business Models in the Smart Grid: Challenges, Opportunities and Proposals for Prosumer Profitability. *Energies* **2014**, *7*, 6142–6171. [CrossRef]
5. Morschheuser, B.; Hamari, J.; Koivisto, J. Gamification in crowdsourcing: A review. In Proceedings of the 2016 49th Hawaii International Conference on System Sciences (HICSS), Koloa, HI, USA, 5–8 January 2016; pp. 4375–4384.
6. Kempton, W.; Tomić, J. Vehicle-to-grid power fundamentals: Calculating capacity and net revenue. *J. Power Sources* **2005**, *144*, 268–279. [CrossRef]
7. Ferreira, J.; Martins, H.; Barata, M.; Monteiro, V.; Afonso, J.L. OpenADR—Intelligent Electrical Energy Consumption towards Internet-of-Things. In *Proceedings of the Controlo 2016 12th Portuguese Conference on Automatic Control*; Garrido, P., Soares, F., Moreira, P.A., Eds.; Springer International Publishing: Cham, Switzerland, 2017; pp. 725–736.
8. Ferreira, J.; Afonso, J. Dynamic range prediction for an electric vehicle. In Proceedings of the Electric Vehicle Symposium and Exhibition (EVS27), Barcelona, Spain, 17–20 November 2013.
9. Ferreira, J.; Afonso, J. A conceptual V2G aggregation platform. In Proceedings of the EVS-25 25th World Battery, Hybrid and Fuel Cell Electric Vehicle Symposium & Exhibition, Shenzhen, China, 5–9 November 2010.

10. Shakeri, M.; Shayestegan, M.; Abunima, H.; Salim Reza, S.M.; Akhtaruzzaman, M.; Alamoud, A.R.M.; Sopian, K.; Amin, N. An intelligent system architecture in home energy management systems (HEMS) for efficient demand response in smart grid. *Energy Build.* **2017**, *138*, 154–164. [CrossRef]
11. *Market Data: Ancillary Service Markets for Energy Storage*; Navigant Consulting, Inc.: Chicago, IL, USA, 2017.
12. Fernández-Caramés, T.M.; Fraga-Lamas, P. A Review on the Use of Blockchain for the Internet of Things. *IEEE Access* **2018**. [CrossRef]
13. Crosby, M.; Pattanayak, P.; Verma, S.; Kalyanaraman, V. Blockchain technology: Beyond bitcoin. *Appl. Innov.* **2016**, *2*, 6–10.
14. Hansch, A.; Newman, C.; Schildhauer, T. *Fostering Engagement with Gamification: Review of Current Practices on Online Learning Platforms*; Elsevier: New York, NY, USA, 2015.
15. Ferreira, J.; Rato, V.; Filipe, P.P. ISCTE-IUL Campus of Things—IoT Approach Towards a Smart Campus. In Proceedings of the International Conference on Information System Modelling and ICT System Security (ICISMISS 2017), Kathmandu, Nepal, 27–28 October 2017.
16. Guth, J.; Breitenbücher, U.; Falkenthal, M.; Leymann, F.; Reinfurt, L. Comparison of IoT platform architectures: A field study based on a reference architecture. In Proceedings of the Cloudification of the Internet of Things (CIoT), Paris, France, 23–25 November 2016; pp. 1–6.
17. Münsing, E.; Mather, J.; Moura, S. Blockchains for decentralized optimization of energy resources in microgrid networks. In Proceedings of the 2017 IEEE Conference on Control Technology and Applications (CCTA), Kohala Coast, HI, USA, 27–30 August 2017; pp. 2164–2171.
18. Dorri, A.; Kanhere, S.S.; Jurdak, R. Blockchain in internet of things: Challenges and solutions. *arXiv* **2016**, arXiv:1608.05187.
19. Aitzhan, N.Z.; Svetinovic, D. Security and privacy in decentralized energy trading through multi-signatures, blockchain and anonymous messaging streams. *IEEE Trans. Dependable Secur. Comput.* **2016**. [CrossRef]
20. Bundock, R. Smart Meters Prepaid: Bankymoon Develops Bitcoin Solution. Available online: https://www.smart-energy.com/top-stories/smart-meters-payment-bankymoon-develops-bitcoin-solution/ (accessed on 25 August 2018).
21. Pop, C.; Cioara, T.; Antal, M.; Anghel, I.; Salomie, I.; Bertoncini, M. Blockchain based decentralized management of demand response programs in smart energy grids. *Sensors* **2018**, *18*, 162. [CrossRef] [PubMed]
22. Mihaylov, M.; Jurado, S.; Avellana, N.; van Moffaert, K.; de Abril, I.M.; Nowé, A. NRGcoin: Virtual currency for trading of renewable energy in smart grids. In Proceedings of the 2014 11th International Conference on the European Energy Market (EEM), Krakow, Poland, 28–30 May 2014; pp. 1–6.
23. Mengelkamp, E.; Gärttner, J.; Rock, K.; Kessler, S.; Orsini, L.; Weinhardt, C. Designing microgrid energy markets: A case study: The Brooklyn Microgrid. *Appl. Energy* **2018**, *210*, 870–880. [CrossRef]
24. Ferreira, J.; Monteiro, V.; Afonso, J.L. Vehicle-to-Anything Application (V2Anything App) for electric vehicles. *IEEE Trans. Ind. Inform.* **2014**. [CrossRef]
25. Monteiro, V.; Ferreira, J.C.; Pinto, G.; Pedrosa, D.; Afonso, J.L. iV2G charging platform. In Proceedings of the 13th International IEEE Conference on Intelligent Transportation Systems ITSC, Madeira, Portugal, 19–22 September 2010; pp. 409–414.
26. Ferreira, J.C.; Monteiro, V.; Afonso, J.L. Electric vehicle assistant based on driver profile. *Int. J. Electr. Hybrid Veh.* **2014**, *6*, 335–349. [CrossRef]
27. Ferreira, J. Simulation of Electrical Distributed Energy Resources for Electrical Vehicles Charging Process Strategy. In Proceedings of the 2010 Second Brazilian Workshop on Social Simulation, Sao Paulo, Brazil, 24–25 October 2010.
28. Ferreira, J.C.; Monteiro, V.; Pinto, J.G.; Martins, A.L.; Afonso, J.L. Decision Process to Manage Renewable Energy Production in Smart Grid Environment. BT—Highlights of Practical Applications of Cyber-Physical Multi-Agent Systems. In Proceedings of the International Conference on Practical Applications of Agents and Multi-Agent Systems, Porto, Portugal, 21–23 June 2017; pp. 299–306.

29. Samad, T.; Koch, E.; Stluka, P. Automated Demand Response for Smart Buildings and Microgrids: The State of the Practice and Research Challenges. *Proc. IEEE* **2016**. [CrossRef]
30. Eid, C.; Codani, P.; Perez, Y.; Reneses, J.; Hakvoort, R. Managing electric flexibility from Distributed Energy Resources: A review of incentives for market design. *Renew. Sustain. Energy Rev.* **2016**, *64*, 237–247. [CrossRef]
31. Eid, C.; Codani, P.; Chen, Y.; Perez, Y.; Hakvoort, R.A. Aggregation of demand side flexibility in a smart grid: A review for European market design. In Proceedings of the 2015 12th International Conference on the European Energy Market (EEM), Lisbon, Portugal, 19–22 May 2015; pp. 1–5.

© 2018 by the authors. Licensee MDPI, Basel, Switzerland. This article is an open access article distributed under the terms and conditions of the Creative Commons Attribution (CC BY) license (http://creativecommons.org/licenses/by/4.0/).

MDPI
St. Alban-Anlage 66
4052 Basel
Switzerland
Tel. +41 61 683 77 34
Fax +41 61 302 89 18
www.mdpi.com

Energies Editorial Office
E-mail: energies@mdpi.com
www.mdpi.com/journal/energies

CPSIA information can be obtained
at www.ICGtesting.com
Printed in the USA
BVHW022355180220
572581BV00034B/2339